NINETEENTH-CENTURY AMERICAN DRAMA:
A Finding Guide

by

Don L. Hixon

and

Don A. Hennessee

The Scarecrow Press, Inc.
Metuchen, N.J. & London
1977

Library of Congress Catalog Card No. 77-12057
ISBN 0-8108-1083-2

For

NELLIE AND ELBERT

CONTENTS

PREFACE

The plays indexed in this volume represent a cross-section of nineteenth-century drama presented on the American stage. Plays of great or slight dramatic consequence, as performed on the stage from San Francisco to New York and from New Orleans to Chicago; farces, tragedies, plays of social commentary, most evident in those dealing with temperance and the women's movement; plays written chiefly as literature with little or no thought given to public performance--all are represented. In addition, there are a large number of librettos and vocal scores to operas and operettas from Victor Herbert to Richard Wagner.

While the chief impetus for this volume was the necessity of providing a "finding guide" to the Readex Corporation's microprint collection of "American plays, 1831-1900," a portion of its *English and American plays of the nineteenth century,* the work should prove valuable to any library with a drama collection of the period, and to scholars working in nineteenth-century literature. In its collection, edited by the late George Freedley, formerly Curator of the Theatre Collection of the New York Public Library, and the late Allardyce Nicoll, formerly Professor of English Language and Literature at Birmingham University and Director of the Shakespeare Institute at Stratford-on-Avon, Readex has made every effort to assemble as exhaustive a collection as possible, intending eventually to include every play written during the nineteenth century, in printed and manuscript form, regardless of literary merit or form of dramatic presentation. With the deaths of Nicoll and Freedley, such strivings have not been fully realized, but there is no question that the Readex Corporation microprints represent one of the most significant repositories of the dramatic output of nineteenth-century America.

Provided here is a finding guide to the approximately 4,500 plays reproduced by Readex, including nearly 1,000 plays contained in eighty collections (volumes with three or more plays) and numerous "bound withs" (volumes containing two plays bound together); each of the plays in collections and "bound withs" have been analyzed individually. With the exception of such catalogues as those of the Library of Congress, the New York Public Library, and Brown University, for instance (refer to the "References" section for citations to these and other works mentioned in this volume), there appears to be no list of comparable comprehensiveness, and these compilations are often available financially only to the more affluent research libraries. For example, another source, *Dramatic compositions copyrighted in the United States, 1870-1916,* contains some 60,000 titles, but more than 20,000 were recorded but never received by the Library of Congress. Of the remaining 40,000, fewer than 14,000 titles, including duplication of titles issued by different publishers, were published prior to the 1900 cutoff date selected by Readex. None of the sources mentioned above also provides the capability of simultaneous access in one volume to these plays by author, title, series, subject, and ethnic/racial categories here made possible. While the most obvious purpose of this volume lies in its use as a finding guide to the plays contained in the Readex microprint collection, and in affording assistance to drama scholars working in the period, the volume should also be useful to those whose work lies outside the field of drama. It is hoped that the ethnic/racial appendix and the subject appendix will provide sufficient additional data to make this volume valuable to those doing research in the fields of sociology and ethnology. Drama was a dominant form of entertainment in the nineteenth century, and it is necessary only to read a few of these works to sense the potential they had for molding opinion. "Subliminal advertising" as a phrase was not to be invented until the present century, but some of these seemingly innocuous plays undoubtedly implanted messages of bias and prejudice, in many cases still unresolved today. Character exaggeration is often used in drama, but to the uninitiated, sitting in a small theatre, the characters seemed very real, and often left lasting impressions. Their study by those other than students of drama might open previously unexplored approaches to answering "why we are the way we are."

Despite Readex's title, "American plays, 1831-1900," coverage is not restricted to the works of American authors. Included are works of English and European origin which have been "Americanized" to the stage by an American editor, adaptor, arranger, or translator. It must be noted that the Readex microprints are supplied with printed headings at the top of each, and it is by these "entries" that the microprints must be arranged alphabetically. It is obvious that any given microprint, generally representing one play, may be filed in only one place, and therein lies the chief difficulty in maximum utilization of the set, and also one of the most significant assets of this volume. For instance, Readex has entered foreign works under the name of the American connected with the play, rather than under the name of the original author. For instance, Readex has entered an English adaptation of Goethe's *Die Fischerin* under Martha Ridgway Bannan, and the complete vocal score to Wagner's *Ring* under the American translator, Frederick Jameson. Occasionally, Readex appears to have gotten carried away in its efforts to enter plays under an American name at all costs. For example, the title page of an edition of *Merchant of Venice* reads: "as produced...by Edwin Booth. A new adaptation to the stage with notes, original and selected, and introductory articles by Henry L. Hinton." As long as Readex chose not to enter this play under Shakespeare, it is still curious that Booth was overlooked in favor of an entry under

Henry Hinton. A similar inconsistency is found in the works
which Readex has entered under Charles White. Many of these
are actually by other American authors and were "arranged" by
White. In many cases, the Library of Congress has entered these
works under the original authors, not under White. It cases
where Readex was unable to identify an American connected with a
particular work, it provided a title main entry, often leading
to still further complications. With different editions of
Hamlet entered variously under Edwin Booth, Walter Gay, George
Griffin, etc., and also under the title, but not under Shakespeare,
the problems arising from such fragmentation become obvious,
difficulties which in several instances led Readex to mistakenly
enter the same edition of the same play in two or three different
places. By providing cross references from the original author
to those entries selected by Readex, hopefully these inconsistencies
have been alleviated.

The bulk of this volume provides access to each play by the
main entry chosen by Readex, with cross references to this entry
from title, half title, and from other individuals connected
with the play (compilers, composers, librettists, and authors of
works on which American adaptations were based). In addition,
the first of the appendixes presents a series categorization,
"Appendix II" arranges the plays into various ethnic and racial
groups (Blacks in cast, Germans in cast, etc.), and "Appendix III"
provides a classified approach to the plays through a variety of
headings reflecting forms and subjects: minstrels, prompt-books,
music, temperance plays, United States--History--Revolution, etc.
The three appendices will be described in greater detail at the
beginning of each.

Each entry consists of the following components:

1. *Author*. The name used by Readex has been retained,
except where the Readex name has been discovered to be incomplete
or erroneous, in which case entry has been made here under the
complete and/or correct name, with appropriate cross references.
For the sake of comprehensiveness, references have been made also
from composers, even when the music itself has not been included,
as in the case with opera librettos.

2. *Author's birth and death dates* are those supplied by
Readex, unless standard bibliographic sources provide more
plausible dates. An effort was made to supply complete dates
where Readex's dates were either lacking or incomplete.

3. *Title*. Readex's title has been used except where
modification was required as a result of examination of the
photographed copy of the title page. Cross references have been
made from half titles. When given on the title page, a descriptive
phrase consisting of the type of play and the number of acts or
scenes has been added: a domestic farce in one act, a tragedy in
five acts, etc. In most cases, Readex has not supplied this
information. When the same title has been used by more than one

author, a single entry under title has been made with "see" and "see also" references to the several authors. In cases where it was not possible to identify the original titles of foreign works translated or adapted to the American stage, titles in English have been enclosed in brackets [ ]. For example, the title page of Augustin Daly's *Love in harness* indicates that the play was based on the French of Albin Valabrègue. Since it was not possible to identify precisely which play was used as the basis for Daly's work, the English title is enclosed in brackets under Valabrègue, with a reference to Daly.

4. *Imprint.* The place of publication has been given as found on the Readex card. The name of the publisher sometimes has been abbreviated in order to conserve space: Ames Publishing Company appears here as Ames. When the play was privately printed, or printed by a lesser-known firm, the name of the publisher or printer has been given in complete form: Hermann Bartsch, Job, Book and Music Typographer. The date of publication has been recorded as provided on the Readex card, except where such dates were discovered to be erroneous. In numerous cases, Readex has reproduced an edition of a play with a publication date after 1900. In such instances, indications of earlier copyright dates have been supplied when possible.

5. *Pagination* is that provided on the Readex card.

6. *Series.* In addition to those supplied by Readex, series found on examination of the play itself, or in checking other bibliographic sources, have been indicated. Series notations often appeared on the cover and not on the title page of the publication. Since many covers were lacking from the copies reproduced by Readex, or were not photographed, it is possible that some series statements unintentionally might have been omitted.

7. *Notes.* Where appropriate, notes are indicated in *italics* within brackets *[ ]*. The information may be general in nature, but frequently refers to the specific copy of the play reproduced by Readex.

It is very important to stress that each Readex card is supplied with a printed heading at the top, and it is by these "entries" that the microprints must be arranged alphabetically by the holding library, even when the Readex entry might appear inconsistent, incomplete, or even incorrect. It is for this reason that cross references in this volume lead the user of the microprint collection to the entry designated by Readex so that the desired plays may be retrieved.

The microprints used in the preparation of this volume are those housed in the Library of California State University, Long Beach, and gratitude must be extended to Lloyd Kramer, Associate Director of the Library, and to John Dorsey, Head, Humanities Reference Department, for their cooperation in making both the microprint collection and reader available for use outside the

Library. Sincere thanks must go also to the Acquisitions and
Catalog Departments of the University of California, Irvine,
Library, for providing released time during which to pursue
research related to portions of this volume.

In any compilation of this detail and complexity, involving
the development of a file consisting of over 18,000 references,
it seems that errors are inevitable, regardless of the care with
which the volume was prepared. The authors would be grateful
if errors were brought to their attention in order to help
insure future increased accuracy.

Don L. Hixon
Don A. Hennessee

Summer 1977

A., M. *see* Aldrich, Mildred

A., N. *[see also Nathan Appleton]*
A mysterious kiss. Boston: Fields, Osgood and Co., 1870. 56p. *[title page: translated from the French of Albéric Second and Jules Blerzy. "N. A." has been identified as Nathan Appleton, 1843-1906, q.v.]*

Aarbert *see* Marshall, William

Aar-u-ag-oos; or, An east Indian drug *see* Taylor, Malcom [sic, Malcolm] Stuart

Abarbanell, Jacob Ralph, 1852-1922.
All on account of a bracelet. A comedy in one act. Chicago: Dramatic Pub. Co., c1882. 11p. (Sergel's acting drama. no. 308) *[Ralph Royal, pseud. for Jacob Abarbanell, printed beneath Abarbanell's name on title page]*

A model pair. A comedy in one act. New York: De Witt, c1882. 12p. (De Witt's acting plays. no. 302) *[Ralph Royal, pseud. for Jacob Abarbanell, printed beneath Abarbanell's name on title page]*

My father's will. A comedy in one act. New York: S. French & Son, c1881. 16p. (French's parlor comedies. no. 9)

Under ma's thumb *see* Morter, E. J. and Abarbanell, Jacob Ralph.

The abbé de L'Épée *see* The lost heir; or, The abbé de L'Épée

The abbess of Jouarre *see* Delon, Georges and Rhodes, James F.

Abbie's experience *see* Bradley, Nellie H. Wine as a medicine; or, Abbie's experience

Abbott, Ernest Hamlin. Hamlet; or, The sport, the spook, and the spinster *see* Batchelder, Samuel Francis.

Abbott, Jacob, 1803-1879. Orkney, the peacemaker; or, The various ways of settling disputes. New York: Harper & Bros, 1857. 160p. (Harper's story books, vol. 10) [no. 30?, see note]
Contents: The lost ball.--The teasing brothers.--The wheelbarrow case.--All against the grain.--Playing cat and dog.--The kite paper. --Boasting.
[Although Readex assigns vol. 10 of Harper's story books to this title, there is no indication on the title page nor within the text to that effect. The Library of Congress has assigned this title as no. 30 of that series]

À Beckett, Gilbert Abbott,
1811-1856.
The man with the carpet bag
see Massey, Charles.
Massey's exhibition reciter

Abel's widow see Opal (pseud.)
The cloud of witnesses

An abject apology see Donaldson, Frank. Two comedies

Aborn, Edward.
A strawman. A farce in one
act. Boston: W. H. Baker,
c1895. 14p. (Baker's
edition of plays)

Abou Ben Adhem see Hunt,
Leigh. Abou Ben Adhem in
Massey, Charles. Massey's
exhibition reciter

Above the clouds see Baker,
George Melville

Absent-minded see Dumont,
Frank see also his The
amateur minstrel

The academy of stars see
Leavitt, Andrew J. and
Eagan, H. W.

Accelerate see Caldor,
M. T. Social charades

Acrisius, King of Argos see
Walker, Horace Eaton

Across the continent; or,
Scenes from New York life
and the Pacific Railroad
see McCloskey, James
Joseph

Actor and servant see
Cutler, F. L.

The actor and the singer; or,
Gaily the troubadour see
Griffin, George W. H.

The actor; or, A son of Thespis
see Nobles, Milton

The actors' scheme; or, How we
got our dinner see Walsh,
Joseph P.

Adams, Charles Frederick,
d.1918.
Rob, the hermit; or, The
black chapel of Maryland.
A romantic drama in four
acts. Concord, N.H.: n.pub.,
1876. 21p. [This and the
following were dramatized from
John Pendleton Kennedy's novel
entitled Rob of the bowl]

Rob, the hermit; or, The
black chapel of Maryland.
A romantic drama in four
acts. New York: H. Roorbach,
1879. 34p. (The acting drama.
no. 101)

Adams, Henry Austin, 1861-1931.
Napoleon. New York: J. Selwin
Tait & Sons, 1894. 224p.

Adams, Justin, 1862?-1937.
At the picket-line. A military drama of the Civil War
in five acts. Boston: W. H.
Baker, c1893. 39p. (Baker's
edition of plays)

Down east. A comedy drama in
four acts. Boston: W. H.
Baker, 1897. 41p. (Baker's
edition of plays)

The limit of the law. A drama
in five acts. Boston: W. H.
Baker, c1896. 40p. (Baker's
edition of plays) [Title page
lacking from copy reproduced
by Readex]

The rag-picker's child. A
drama in five acts. Boston:
W. H. Baker, c1895. 34p.
(Baker's edition of plays)

T'riss; or, Beyond the
Rockies. A drama of Western

life in four acts. Boston:
W. H. Baker, 1893. 34p.
(Baker's edition of plays)

Adams, Miss L. B.
Eva [bound with] A tragic
poem [from her: Plays and
poems of L. New York:
Delisser & Procter, 1859.
100p.] p.1-64 *[Readex
also enters this same title
under Catherine Swanwick]*

Adams, William Taylor, 1811-
1897 *see* Optic, Oliver
(pseud.)

Adam's fall *see* Heywood,
Delia A. Choice dialogues.
no. 1

Addis, J. B.
Vanity; or, A lord in Philadelphia *see* Vanity; or, A
lord in Philadelphia

Addison, Julia de Wolff Gibbs,
b.1866.
Blighted buds. A farce in
one act. Boston: W. H.
Baker, 1896. (Baker's
edition of plays)

Adelaïde. The romance of
Beethoven's life *see*
Howard, Edmond and Bispham,
David Scull

Adina; or, The elixir of love
see Weil, Oscar

Adler, George J., 1821-1868.
Iphigenia in Tauris. New
York: D. Appleton, 1850.
155p. *[Based on Goethe's
Iphigenie auf Tauris]*

Adorable Elizabeth *see*
Latour, Eugene

The adoration of the Magi
kings *see* Polding, Elizabeth. The dawn of redemption;

or, The adoration of the Magi
kings

Adrienne Lecouvreur. (From the
French of Scribe and Legouvé)
New York: Darcie & Corbyn,
1855. Bilingual text: French
and English. 79p. (Darcie &
Corbyn's edition of Mlle.
Rachel's plays)

Adrienne Lecouvreur. (From the
French of Scribe and Legouvré
[sic, Legouvé]) Adapted for
M. Ristori. The Italian
translation by Sig. Guilier.
New York: Baker & Godwin,
1866. Bilingual text: English
and Italian. 65p.

Adrienne Lecouvreur. (From the
French of Scribe and Legouvé)
New York: n.pub., 1880?
Bilingual text: English and
French. 64, 64p.

Adrienne Lecouvreur *see also*
Marlow, George *and* Schwab,
Frederick A.

Adrift *see* Babcock, Charles W.

Advent *see* Coxe, Arthur
Cleveland

Adventures of a Christmas Eve
see Thompson, William
Tappan. Major Jones courtship; or, Adventures of a
Christmas Eve

The adventures of little Red
Riding Hood *see* Hardman,
Richard

The adventuress; or, Lady
Evelyn's triumph *see*
Emerson, W. Burt

Advertising for a wife *see*
La Bree, Lawrence. Ebenezer
Venture; or, Advertising
for a wife

The advertising girls *see*
Sanford, Amelia

Advice to fools in pouring
water on a duck's back *see*
Steele, Silas Sexton *in his*
Collected works. Book of
plays.

Aeneas *see* Gildenhaus,
Charles *see also* Gildenhaus, Charles *in his* Plays

Aeschylus, 525-456 B.C.
Prometheus bound *see* More,
Paul Elmer. Prometheus bound

Aestheticism versus common
sense *see* Heywood, Delia
A. *in her* Choice dialogues.
no. 1

An affection of the heart *see*
Latour, Eugene

The afflicted family; or, A
doctor without a diploma
see Taylor, Malcolm Stuart

Afranius *see* Leavitt, John
McDowell

The African box; or, The magi-
cians troubles *see* White,
Charles

Africanus Bluebeard *see*
Dumont, Frank

After all *see* Monroe, Harriet
see also Monroe, Harriet
in her The passing show

After business hours *see*
Daly, Augustin

After taps *see* Baker, Rachel
E.

After ten years; or, The maniac
wife *see* Hollenbeck, Benjamin W.

After the circus *see* Chenoweth, Lawrence

After the matinée *see*
Howie, Hellen Morrison

After twenty years *see*
Booth, Helen *in* Dramatic
leaflets

Afterglow *see* Fuller, Henry
Blake *in his* Collected
works

An afternoon rehearsal *see*
Knapp, Lizzie Margaret

Against the American war *see*
Chatham, ? *in* Massey,
Charles. Massey's exhibition
reciter

Ahmed the cobbler; or, The
astrologer *see* Follen,
Eliza Lee Cabot. Home dramas
for young people

Aiken, George L., 1830-1876.
Uncle Tom's cabin; or, Life
among the lowly. New York:
Samuel French, 1858? 60p.
(French's standard drama.
no. 218) [217?] *[Based on
Harriet Beecher Stowe's
novel of the same title]*

Aikin, Miss *see* Barbauld,
Anna Letitia Aikin

Aikin, Anna Letitia *see*
Barbauld, Anna Letitia Aikin

Alabama *see* Thomas, Augustus

Aladdin; or, The wonderful
lamp. Boston: William V.
Spencer, 18-? 22p. (Spencer's
Boston theatre. no. 90)
[this is a prompt-book]

Aladdin; or, The wonderful
lamp. New York: O. Roorbach,
Jr., 1856. 22p. (The acting
drama. no. 18)

Aladdin; or, The wonderful
lamp *see* Shields, Sarah
Annie Frost

The Albany depot *see* Howells,
William Dean

The album *see* James, Henry

The alcalde of Zalamea *see*
Pierra, Adolfo. Nobility;
or, The alcalde of Zalamea

Alceste. Translated and arranged under the direction of
Theodore Thomas. Cincinnati:
John Church, c1877. Vocal
score. Bilingual text: English and German. 144p. *[Music
by Gluck]*

The alchemist's daughter *see*
Read, Thomas Buchanan

Alcibiades-Sheridan *see*
Townsend, Frederic *in his*
Spiritual visitors

Alcott, Louisa May, 1832-1888.
Comic tragedies. By ''Jo'' and
''Meg'' (pseud.) Boston:
Roberts Brothers, 1893. 317p.
  Contents: Norna; or, The
witch's curse.--The captive
of Castile; or, The Moorish
maiden's vow.--The Greek
slave.--Ion.--Bianca; an
operatic tragedy.--The unloved wife; or, Woman's faith.

Little men *see* Gould,
Elizabeth Lincoln. The little
men

Little women *see* Venable,
William Henry. Contentment
in his The school stage
see also Venable, William
Henry. Rigmarole *in his*
The school stage

Aldémah. The queens; being
passages from the lives of
Elizabeth, Queen of England,
and Mary, Queen of Scotland.

Chicago: F. J. Schulte,
1892. 205p.

Aldemon's daughter (Cassilda)
see Dorbesson, Fern

The alderman *see* Stephens,
Robert Neilson

Aldrich, Mildred, 1853-1928.
Nance Oldfield. By M. A.
Boston: Walter H. Baker,
1894. 22p. (Baker's edition
of plays) *[Charles Reade's
story Art: a dramatic tale,
earlier entitled Nance Oldfield, was based on Narcisse
Fournier's Tiridate]*

Aldrich, Thomas Bailey, 1836-
1907.
IV. Scene of Blanchette.
[From: The bells; a collection of chimes. By T. B. A.
New York: J. C. Derby, 1855.
144p.] p.131-143.

Mercedes. A drama in two acts
[From his: Mercedes, and
later lyrics. Boston: Houghton, Mifflin, 1884] p.7-56.

Pauline Pavlovna. [From:
The poems of Thomas Bailey
Aldrich. Boston and New
York: Houghton, Mifflin,
1897. (vol. 1, 204p.; vol.
2, 220p.)] vol. 2, p.99-109.

The set of turquoise. [From
his: The ballad of Babie
Bell and other poems. New
York: Rudd & Carleton, 1859.
117p.] p.85-112.

Aldrich, Thomas Bailey, The
household of *see* Bridges,
Robert *in his* Overheard
in Arcady

Aldridge, Ira, 1807-1867.
The black doctor. A romantic
drama in four acts. Adapted
to the English stage by Ira
Aldridge. London: John
Dicks, 188-?. 18p. (Dicks'

London acting edition of
standard English plays and
comic dramas. no. 460).

Alexander, Louis.
The reception of the months.
A Christmas play in one
scene. New York: Edgar S.
Werner, 1897. 24p.

Alexander, Sigmund Bowman.
King winter's carnival. New
York: Wehman Bros., c1894.
52p. *[Contains music by
Luigi Boccherini, Richard
Genée, and A. Gwyllyn Crown]*

Alexander, William, 1808-1875.
Ella; or, The Prince of Gilead's vow. [From his: The
poetical works...Philadel-
phia: J. B. Lippincott, 1847.
263p.] p.175-200.

Fall of Palmyra. [From his:
The poetical works...Phila-
delphia: J. B. Lippincott,
1847. 263p.] p.201-227.

Alfred *see* Barbauld, Anna
Letitia Aikin. Alfred *in*
Follen, Eliza Lee Cabot.
Home dramas for young people.

Alfred the king *see* Venable,
William Henry *in his* The
school stage

The Algerian *see* MacDonough,
Glen

Algernon (pseud.).
Torquato Tasso. (From the
German of Goethe) [From his:
Ideals and other poems.
Philadelphia: Henry Perkins,
1842. 102p.] p.80-102.
*[Based on Goethe's Torquato
Tasso]*

Algernon in London *see* Pullen, Elizabeth Jones

Alhalla; or, The lord of Tal-

ladega *see* Schoolcraft,
Henry Rowe

Ali Baba, Jr.; or, Morgiana
and the forty thieves *see*
Smith, Harry Bache

Ali Baba; or, Morgiana and the
forty thieves *see* Smith,
Harry Bache

Alice in Wonderland *see*
Harrison, Constance Cary

Aliso and Acne *see* Wickersham, James Alexander

Alive and kicking *see*
Williams, Barney

All a mistake *see* Parker,
Walter Coleman

All against the grain *see*
Abbott, Jacob *in his*
Orkney the peacemaker; or,
The various ways of settling
disputes

All for sweet charity *see*
Mathews, Frances Aymar

All in der family *see*
McDermott, J. J. and
Trumble

All is fair in love *see*
Denton, Clara Janetta Fort

All is fair in love and war
see Cahill, Frank *in*
Arnold, George? and Cahill,
Frank. Parlor theatricals;
or, Winter evening's entertainment

All on account of a bracelet
see Abarbanell, Jacob Ralph

All right *see* Barry, S. The
Dutchman's ghost; or, All
right

All that glitters is not gold *see* Shields, Sarah Annie Frost *in her* Parlor charades and proverbs

All the comforts of home *see* Gillette, William Hooker

Alladine and Palomides *see* Hovey, Richard *in his* The plays of Maurice Maeterlinck. Second series

Alladine and Palomides *see* Porter, Charlotte Endymion and Clarke, Helen Archibald

Allatoona *see* Kilpatrick, Hugh Judson and Moore, J. Owen

Allen, Ethan, 1832-1911. Washington; or, The Revolution. (In two parts. Each part, five acts.) London: F. T. Neely, c1894 and 1899. 500p.

Allen, John Henry, 1836-1890. The fruits of the wine cup. A drama in three acts. New York: Happy Hours Co., 18--. 28p. (The acting drama. no. 56)

The fruits of the wine cup. A drama in three acts. New York: Dick & Fitzgerald, 18--?. New edition. 28p.

Allen, Lucy. Débutantes in the culinary art; or, A frolic in the cooking class. New York: Roxbury, c1899. 23p. *[title page: Music arranged by Richard Thiele]*

Allender, George. Imbroglio. San Francisco: S. Carson, 1885. 186p.

Allingham, John Till, fl.1799-1810.

['Tis all a farce] *see* 'Tis all a farce

The weathercock *see* Dramatic leaflets

All's fair in love and war. A comedietta in three acts. New York: Harold Roorbach, c1877. 18p. (The amateur stage. no. 51)

All's well that ends well *see* Shields, Sarah Annie Frost *see also* White, Charles. The serenade

Allyn, Dave E. "In for it"; or, Uncle Tony's mistake. An Ethiopian farce in one act. Clyde, O.: Ames, 1893. 11p. (Ames' series of standard and minor drama. no. 319)

Midnight colic. A laughable sketch in one scene. Clyde, O.: Ames, 1888. 9p. (Ames' series of standard and minor drama. no. 256)

Alma Mater; or, The Georgetown Centennial *see* Finn, Sister Mary Paulina

Almost an elopement *see* McBride, H. Elliott *in his* Latest dialogues

Alotting the bride *see* Metcalfe, Irving. A game of chance; or, Alotting the bride

Alphange, Archbishop of Canterbury *see* Opal (pseud.) *in her* The cloud of witnesses

Alpine roses *see* Boyesen, Hjalmar Hjorth

Always too late *see* Denison, Thomas Stewart *in his*

Friday afternoon series of
dialogues

Am I one? *see* Phelps,
Lavinia Howe *in her*
Dramatic stories

Amateur and professional
acting *see* Massey, Charles
in his Massey's exhibition
reciter

The amateur minstrel *see*
Dumont, Frank

Amateur road agents *see*
Dumont, Frank. Jack Sheppard
and Joe Blueskin; or,
Amateur road agents

The amateur stage *see*
Mischievous Bob

An amateur triumph *see* Davis,
Paul P.

The Amazons *see* Woods,
Virna

The ambassador *see* Smith,
Harry Bache

Ambition *see* Carleton, Henry
Guy *see also* A collection
of temperance dialogues *see
also* White, Charles

"The ameer" *see* Ranken,
Frederic and La Shelle,
Kirke

America: a dramatic poem *see*
?Torrey, John or ?Torrey,
Mary C.

An American citizen *see*
Ryley, Madeleine Lucette

An American drama arranged in
four acts and entitled
Secret Service see
Gillette, William Hooker

American farmers *see*
Woodworth, Samuel. The
forest rose; or, American
farmers

The American forest girl
see Hemans, Felicia
Dorothea Browne *in*
Massey, Charles. Massey's
exhibition reciter

The American girl *see*
Donnelly, Henry Grattan

An American harem *see* Frank
Glynn's wife; or, An
American harem

American hearts *see* Mathews,
Frances Aymar

An American pasha *see*
Reynolds, William C.

An American wife. n.p.: n.pub.,
18--? Typescript. Prompt-
book. In four acts. Pag. by
acts. *[in the copy reproduced by Readex, this prompt
book has the names of
Geraldine Farrar and Lon
Chaney handwritten on the
page listing the cast. The
Goldwyn Motion Picture
Studios is indicated at
the beginning of Act II]*

Americans abroad *see* Fawcett,
Edgar *see also* Richardson,
Abbey Sage

Americans in England *see*
Paulding, James Kirke and
Paulding, William Irving.
The Bucktails; or, Americans
in England *in their*
Collected works. American
comedies

Americans in Paris: or, A game
of dominoes. A comedy in two
acts. As performed at Wallack's Theatre. New York:

S. French, c1858. 32p.
(French's standard drama.
no. 209) *[Note: Readex
also enters this same edition under author, William
Henry Hurlbert]*

Americans in Tripoli *see*
Jones, Joseph Stevens. The
usurper; or, Americans in
Tripoli

America's birthday party *see*
Bartlett, George *in his*
A dream of the centuries and
other entertainments for
parlor and hall

Ames, A. D., 1849-1887.
Driven to the wall; or,
True to the last. A play in
four acts. Clyde, O.: Ames,
1877? 34p. (Ames' series of
standard and minor drama.
no. 60)

The poacher's doom; or, The
murder of the Five Field's
Copse. A domestic drama.
By George Dibdin Pitt. Cur-
tailed and re-arranged by
A. D. Ames. Clyde, O.: Ames,
1873. 26p. (Ames' series of
standard and minor drama.
no. 18)

The spy of Atlanta. A grand
military allegory in six
acts. Clyde, O.: Ames, 1879.
29p. (Ames' series of standard and minor drama. no. 79)
[Joint author: C. G. Bartley]

Wrecked. A temperance drama
in two acts. Clyde, O.: Ames,
1877. 14p. (Ames' series of
standard and minor drama.
no. 58)

L'amico Fritz *see* Dole,
Nathan Haskell. Friend Fritz

Amina; or, The Shah's bride
see Brunswick, Herman

Among the breakers *see*
Baker, George Melville

Among the moonshiners; or,
A drunkard's legacy *see*
McFall, B. G.

Amor Patriae; or, The disruption and fall of these
states *see* Ganter, Franz S.

Amorita *see* Goldmark, George
and Rosenfeld, Sydney

Amory, Esmerie
The epistolary flirt. In four
exposures. Chicago: Way &
Williams, 1896. 100p.

The amours of Capt. Effingham
and the Lady Zarifa *see*
Whitley, Thomas W. The
Jesuit; or, The amours of
Capt. Effingham and the Lady
Zarifa

Amphion-Bellini *see* Townsend,
Frederic *in his* Spiritual
visitors

Amusement circle *see* Denison,
Thomas Stewart *in his* Friday afternoon series of
dialogues

Anarchy *see* MacKaye, James
Steele. Paul Kauvar; or,
Anarchy

The ancestors of King-Ki-Too
see Cook, Charles Emerson.
The Koreans; or, The ancestors of King-Ki-Too

And all about nothing *see*
Owens, Garrett W.

Anderson, Edward Lowell, 1842-
1916.
Nero, the parricide. An historical play in four acts.
Cincinnati: printed, not
published, 1870. 47p.

Anderson, Thomas F.
The trials of a country
editor. An original sketch.
Clyde, O.: Ames, 1889. 12p.
(Ames' series of standard
and minor drama. no. 263)

André, Richard.
Food for powder. A vaude-
ville. Chicago: Dramatic
Pub. Co., c1891. 24p. (American amateur drama)

A handsome cap. A comic
operetta in one act. Chicago:
Dramatic Pub. Co., c1891.
18p. (American amateur drama)
[Without the music]

Minette's birthday. A vaudeville in one act. Chicago:
Dramatic Pub. Co., c1890.
17p. (American amateur drama)

The new moon. (Music by I[si-
dore] De Solla.) Northampton:
Stanton and Son, Printers,
1891. 35p. Libretto.

The pigeons; or, The bonnie
lass of Brittany *see* Hardman, Richard

André *see* Lord, William
Wilberforce

Andrews, Fred G.
Hal Hazard; or, The federal
spy. A military drama in
four acts. Clyde, O.: Ames,
1883. 30p. (Ames' series of
standard and minor drama.
no. 117)

Love's labor not lost; or,
Cupid's pastimes. Clyde, O.:
Ames, c1886. 16p. (Ames'
series of standard and minor
drama. no. 174)

The mountebanks. A specialty
drama in four acts. Clyde,
O.: Ames, 1887. 21p. (Ames'
series of standard and minor
drama. no. 229)

The scarlet letter. A drama

in three acts. (From the
novel by Hawthorne.) Boston:
W. H. Baker, 1871. 24p.

Andrews, R. R.
Silverstone's wager. A
comedietta in one act.
Boston: Charles H. Spencer,
1870? 23p. (Spencer's
universal stage. no. 49)

Andromache. (From the French
of Racine.) New York: Darcie
& Corbyn, 1855. Bilingual
text: English and French.
36p. (Darcie & Corbyn's
edition of Mlle. Rachel's
plays) *[Based on Racine's
Andromaque]*

Andromache in captivity *see*
Bailey, William Entriken.
Dramatic poems

Andy Freckles, the mischievous
boy *see* Rawley, Bert C.

Angelo; or, The tyrant of
Padua. A drama of three
days. (From the French of
Hugo.) New York: Darcie and
Corbyn, 1855. Bilingual
text: French and English.
51p. (Darcie & Corbyn's
edition of Mlle. Rachel's
plays)

Angelo the tyrant of Padua
see Pray, Isaac Clarke

The angel's feast *see* Finn,
Sister Mary Paulina *in her*
Alma mater; or, The George-
town Centennial

The angel's meeting; or, Terra
Mariae. A brief allegorical
sketch for performance on
Maryland day *see* Finn,
Sister Mary Paulina *in her*
Alma mater; or, The George-
town Centennial

Anicet-Bourgeois, Auguste,
  1806-1871.
  Charlot *see* Planché,
  James Robinson. The follies
  of a night *in* The modern
  standard drama, vol. 6

  Le premier coup de canif
  see Kaler, James Otis.
  A case for divorce

Anicetus (pseud.) *see*
  Clark, William Adolphus

The animated portrait. An
  extravazanga in three acts.
  n.p., n.pub., n.d. 33p.

Anita's trial; or, Our girls
  in camp *see* Tiffany,
  Esther Brown

Anne Boleyn *see* Boker,
  George Henry

Anniversary meeting *see*
  Denison, Thomas Stewart
  in his Friday afternoon
  series of dialogues

Anois, Countess d' *see*
  Aulnoy, Marie Catherine
  Jumelle de Berneville,
  comtesse d'

Anspacher, Mrs. Louis Kauf-
  man *see* Kidder, Kathryn

An answer *see* Saltus,
  Francis Saltus. Dolce far
  niente [and] An answer

Anthon, Charles Edward,
  1797-1867.
  The son of the wilderness.
  New York: H. Ludwig, 1848.
  166p. *[Based on Münch-Bellinghausen's Der Sohn der
  Wildniss]*

Anti(Aunti)-Dote *see* Cahill,
  Frank *in* Arnold, George?
  and Cahill, Frank. Parlor
  theatricals; or, Winter

evening's entertainment

Antinoüs *see* Goodloe, Abbie
  Carter

Antipathies; or, The enthusi-
  asts by the ears *see*
  Paulding, James Kirke and
  Paulding, William Irving
  in their Collected works.
  American comedies

Antonio Melidori *see* Hayne,
  Paul Hamilton

Antonius *see* Heywood, Joseph
  Converse

Antony and Cleopatra *see*
  Sothern, Edward Hugh

Antony and Hero *see* Simon,
  Ferdinant Peter

Apajune, the water sprite *see*
  Rosenfeld, Sydney

The apartment *see* Mathews,
  Frances Aymar

Apollo's oracle *see* Tiffany,
  Esther Brown

The apostate *see* Shiel,
  Richard Lalor *in* The
  modern standard drama, vol. 8

Appeal on behalf of Greece *see*
  Lacey, ?. *in* Massey, Charles. Massey's exhibition
  reciter

Appearances are deceitful *see*
  Leland, Oliver Shepard. Blue
  and cherry; or, Appearances
  are deceitful

The apple of discord *see*
  Dugan, Caro Atherton *in her*
  Collected works

The apple of discord *see*
  Robinson, Charles. Ye gods

and goddesses; or, The apple
of discord

Apples *see* Steele, Silas
Sexton *in his* Collected
works. Book of plays

Appleton, Nathan, 1843-1906.
[see also A., N.]
Centennial movement, 1876.
A comedy in five acts. Bos-
ton: Lockwood, Brooks and
Co., 1877. 66p.
Reconciliation. (From the
French of Raimond Deslandes.)
London: T. H. Lacy, 1871.
59p.

The appointment *see* Denton,
Clara Janetta Fort *in her*
From tots to teens

Appomattox *see* Heller,
Robert Eugene

April fool *see* Denison,
Thomas Stewart *in his*
Friday afternoon series of
dialogues

April fools *see* Chapman,
W. F.

Arabella and Lionel *see*
Brewster, Emma E. *in her*
Parlor varieties

An Arabian night in the nineteenth century *see* Daly,
Augustin

Araminta Jenkins *see* Kavanaugh, Mrs. Russell *in her*
Original dramas, dialogues...

Archimedes-Fulton *see* Townsend, Frederic *in his*
Spiritual visitors

Ardent spirits and laughing
water *see* Walcot, Charles
Melton. Hiawatha; or, Ardent
spirits and laughing water

Argo and Irene *see* Monroe,
Jasper R.

Ariadne *see* Ellsworth,
Erastus Wolcott

Ariel and Caliban *see*
Cranch, Christopher Pearce

Aristides-Jay *see* Townsend,
Frederic *in his* Spiritual
visitors

Aristocracy *see* Howard,
Bronson

Ariston *see* Leavitt,
John McDowell

Aristophanes, 448?-380 B.C.
The wasps *see* Browne,
Irving. The suitors

Arizona *see* Thomas,
Augustus

Armada days *see* S., N. S.

Armand; or, The peer and the
peasant *see* Ritchie, Anna
Cora Ogden Mowatt

Armerine, the moonshiner *see*
Nelson, D. R.

Armstrong, L. M. C.
Gertrude Mason, M. D.; or,
The lady doctor. A farce in
one act for female characters only. New York: Fitzgerald, c1898. 14p.

Armstrong, Le Roy, 1854-1927.
An Indiana man. A comedy in
four acts. Chicago: T. S.
Denison, c1897. 48p.

Arnell, David Reeve.
Conrad and Stella. [From
his: Fruit of western life;
or, Blanche, and other
poems. New York: J. C.
Riker, 1847. 215p.] p.180-
200.

Arnold, Alexander Streeter,
b.1829.
In the nick of time. A serio-
comic drama in three acts.
Boston: Walter H. Baker,
c1892. 35p. (Baker's edition
of plays)

Arnold, George, 1834-1865.
*[supposed author; joint
author: Frank Cahill]*
Parlor theatricals; or,
Winter evening's entertain-
ment. New York: Dick &
Fitzgerald, c1859. 152p.
Contents: When the cat's
away the mice will play
(Arnold).--It never rains
but it pours (Cahill).--
Honor among thieves (Cahill).
--All is fair in love and
war (Cahill).--'Tis an ill
wind that blows nobody good
(Cahill).--There is no rose
without thorns (Arnold).--
Dramatic charades: Charade I,
Phan-Tom (Cahill).--Charade
II, Con-Test (Cahill).--
Charade III, Dram-At(t)ic
(Cahill).--Charade IV, Anti
(Aunti)-Dote (Cahill).--
Charade V, Friendship.--
Charade VI, Bandage.--Sweep-
stakes.--Pigtail.--Neighbor.
--Pastil.--Backgammon.--A
little misunderstanding.--
Orpheus and Eurydice.--Ir-
restibly impudent (Cahill).

Arnold, James Oliver.
Historical drama and tab-
leaux, *Uncle Tom's Freedom.*
Dayton, O.: n.pub., 1893.
36p.

Arnold, John.
Glycerine oil *see* White,
Charles

Gripsack *see* White, Charles

Obeying orders *see* White,
Charles

Arnold, Samuel James, 1774-

1852.
My aunt *see* My aunt

Arnold *see* Orton, Jason
Rockwood

Arnold and André *see* Calvert,
George Henry

Arnold; or, The treason of
West Point *see* Hubbell,
Horatio

Arnsworth, William Harrison,
1804-1888.
Rookwood *see* Bannister,
Nathaniel Harrington

Around the horn *see* Cutler,
F. L. Peleg and Peter; or,
Around the horn

Around the world in eighty
days. (From the story by
Jules Verne.) n.p.: 18-?
Prompt-book in Ms. 146p.

Aroused at last *see* Dallas,
Mary Kyle

Arrah de Baugh *see* Kinnaman,
C. F.

An arrant knave *see* MacKaye,
James Steele *in his* An
arrant knave & other plays

The arrival of Dickens *see*
Leavitt, Andrew J. and
Eagan, H. W.

L'Arronge, Adolf, 1838-1908.
[His wife's father] *see*
Morton, Martha. His wife's
father

Art and artifice *see* Dramatic
leaflets

Art and artifice *see* Steele,
Silas Sexton. The painter's
studio; or, Art and artifice
in his Collected works.
Book of plays

Arthur, Joseph, 1848-1906.
Blue jeans. New York, London: S. French, 1940. 125p.
[earlier copyright: 1888]

Arthur, Robert.
The Quakers. (From the German of Kotzebue). n.p.:
n.pub., n.d. p.9-29.
[author's possible dates: 1848?-1908]

Arthur, Timothy Shay, 1809-1885.
Ten nights in a bar-room
see Pratt, William W.

Three years in a man-trap
see Morton, Charles H.

Arthur Eustace; or, A mother's love see Todd, John W.

L'article 47; or, Breaking the ban see Williams, Henry Llewellyn

As by fire see McBride, H. Elliott

As you like it see Daly, Augustin see also Shakespeare, William. As you like it in The modern standard drama, vol. 9

Ascher, Anton, 1820-1884.
Scenes from Mary Stuart [bound with] Tit for tat.
By Roger (pseud.) Albany:
Weed, Parsons, 1880. 36p.
[the first work based on Schiller's Maria Stuart, the second from the German]

Asenjo y Barbieri, Francisco, 1823-1894.
Angelo, tiranno di Padova
see Pray, Isaac Clarke.
Angelo the tyrant of Padua

Robinson see Godoy, José Francisco. Robinson Crusoe

The assessor see Denison,

Thomas Stewart

Assisting Hezekiah see McBride, H. Elliott in his New dialogues

Aste, Ippolito d', 1810-1866.
Sansone see Howells, William Dean. Samson see also Samson

The astrologer see Ahmed the cobbler; or, The astrologer in Follen, Eliza Lee Cabot.
Home dramas for young people

At last see Vautrot, George S.

At Saint Judas's see Fuller, Henry Blake in his Collected works

At sunset see Schmall, Alice F. Zanetto [and] At sunset

At the barricade. An episode of the Commune of '71 see Sutherland, Evelyn Greenleaf Baker in her Collected works. Po' white trash and other one-act dramas

At the court of King Edwin see Leighton, William

At the court of King Winter see Hadley, Lizzie M.

At the fireside; or, Little bird blue see Polding, Elizabeth

At the foot of the rainbow see Block, Louis James in his Capriccios

At the goal see Monroe, Harriet in her The passing show

At the Grand Central see Mathews, Frances Aymar

At the picket-line see Adams, Justin

At the "Red Lion" *see* Booth,
Helen *in* Dramatic leaflets

Atalantis *see* Simms, William
Gilmore

Athaliah *see* Sumichrast,
Frederick Caesar John Martin
Samuel Roussy de

The atheist *see* Williams,
Espy William Hendricks

Athelwold *see* Troubetzkoy,
Amélie Rives Chanler

Athenia of Damascus *see*
Dawes, Rufus

Atherstone, Edwin, 1788-1872.
Last days of Herculaneum
see Massey, Charles.
Massey's exhibition reciter

Atherton, George.
A comedy of error; or, The
cousin and the maid. New
York: Roxbury, c1899. 16p.
*[title page lacking in
copy reproduced by Readex]*

A peaceful assault. New York:
Roxbury, c1899. 16p. *[title
page lacking in copy re-
produced by Readex]*

Atherton, Percy Lee, 1871-1944.
Hamlet; or, The sport, the
spook, and the spinster
see Batchelder, Samuel
Francis

Atout...coeur! *see* Hearts
are trumps; or, Atout...
coeur!

Atticum, Sal (pseud.)
Chums. A comedietta. New
York: S. French, c1899. 23p.
*[Sal Atticum is a pseud.
for Thomas Frost, q.v.]*

Attila. A lyric drama, in four
acts. The music by the cele-

brated G. Verdi. New York:
n.pub., 1850. 17p. Libretto.
*[Temistocle Solèra written
in as author]*

Attinelli, Joseph.
Matilda di Shabran and
Corradino; or, The triumph
of beauty. New York: J. M.
Elliott, 1834. 87p. *[Without
the music by Rossini. Based
on the libretto by Jacopo
Ferretti]*

The attorney. A drama in three
acts. Fall River: Monitor
Press, Henry Pratt, printer,
1849. 54p.

Auber, Daniel François Esprit,
1782-1871.
Fra Diavolo *see* Fra-Diavolo; or, The Inn of Terracina

Gustave III, ou Le bal masque
see Rattermann, Heinrich
Armin. Gustavus III; or, The
masked ball

Masaniello, ou la muette de
Portici *see* Masaniello
see also La muette; or, The
dumb girl of Portic

d'Aubigny (pseud.) *see*
Baudouin, Jean Marie

Audran, Edmond, 1842-1901.
Gillette de Narbonne *see*
Norcross, I. W. Gillette;
or, Count and Countess

La mascotte *see* Barker,
Theodore T. and Norcross,
I. W. The mascot *see also*
Elson, Louis Charles and
Norris, J. W. La mascotte

Les noces d'Olivette *see*
Olivette

Le serment d'amour *see*
Rosenfeld, Sydney. The
bridal trap

Augier, Guillaume Victor
Émile, 1820-1889.
Les Fourchambault *see*
Magnus, Julian and Bunner,
Henry Cuyler

Paul Forestier *see* Paul
Forrester

Augusta, Clara.
The matrimonial advertisement *see* Dramatic leaflets

Auld lang syne *see* Pocock,
Isaac. Rob Roy MacGregor;
or, Auld lang syne *in* The
modern standard drama, vol.
11

Auld Robin Gray *see* Taylor,
Malcolm Stuart

Aulnoy, Marie Catherine
Jumelle de Berneville, comtesse d', d.1705.
[The story of Fortunio, the
fortunate knight] *see* Fortunio and his seven gifted
servants

Aunt Dinah's pledge *see*
Seymour, Harry

Aunt Hepsaba's fright *see*
Mack, Robert Ellice. The
masquerade; or, Aunt Hep-
saba's fright

Aunt Jerusha's visit *see* Our
country aunt; or, Aunt
Jerusha's visit

Aunt Mehetible's scientific
experiment *see* Brewster,
Emma E. *see also* Brewster,
Emma E. *in her* Parlor
varieties

Aunt Susan Jones *see* McBride,
H. Elliott *in* Dramatic
leaflets

The aunt's legacy. A play for
little girls *see* Kavanaugh,

Mrs. Russell *in her* Original dramas, dialogues...

Austin, J. J.
The golden age to come; or,
The victory of faith, and
hope, and love. A sacred drama
written for the people. Boston: A. Tompkins, 1854. 124p.

Autodious (pseud.) *see* Osborn,
Laughton

An autograph letter *see*
Tiffany, Esther Brown

The avenger *see* Bird, Robert
Montgomery. Caridorf; or,
The avenger *in his* The
cowled lover and other plays
see also Koopman, Harry
Lyman. Orestes; or, The
avenger

The avenger of humble life
see Hill, Frederic Stanhope.
The shoemaker of Toulouse;
or, The avenger of humble
life

The avenger; or, The Moor of
Sicily. A melo-drama in three
acts. Boston: William V.
Spencer, 1859? 32p. *[Readex
has also entered and reproduced this title under Herbert Lee, q.v.]*

Awful girls; or, Big results
see Sertrew, Saul

An awful plot *see* Dumont,
Frank

An awkward squad *see* Baker,
Robert Melville

Ayer, Mrs. Harriet Hubbard,
1854-1903.
The widow. A comedy in three
acts. New York: De Witt,
c1877. 29p. (De Witt's acting
plays. no. 213) *[Based on La*

*veuve by Henri Meilhac and
Ludovic Halévy]*

Ayleenya the blameless   *see*
Fyles, Franklin

Aylmere; or, The bondman of
Kent and other poems   *see*
Conrad, Robert Taylor

Aymons, Xavier   *see*   Montépin,
Xavier Aymons, comte de,
1826-1902

Aytoun, William Edmondstone,
1813-1865.
The execution of Montrose
see Massey, Charles. Massey's exhibition reciter

Azára   *see*   Paine, John Knowles

Azlea   *see*   Victor, Frances A.

Azon, the invader of Eden; or,
Immortality snatched from
the Tree of life   *see*   Van
Waters, George

The Aztec god   *see*   Raymond,
George Lansing. The Aztecs
see also his   Collected works

The Aztecs   *see*   Raymond,
George Lansing   *see also*
Raymond, George Lansing.
The Aztec god   *in his*
Collected works

"B. B. & P."   *see*   Browne,
William Maynadier. A fool
for luck

Babcock, Charles W.
Adrift. A temperance drama
in three acts. Clyde, O.:
Ames, c1880. 23p. (Ames'
series of standard and minor
drama. no. 75)

Babcock, J. Frederick.
Floret; or, The poor girl.
A domestic drama in four
acts. Bangor: Samuel O.

Bailey, Printer, 1874. 62p.
*[Based on the tales by Pierce
Egan]*

The babes in the wood; or, The
ferocious uncle and the
avenging robins   *see*   Denison,
Thomas Stewart

Babie. A comedy in three acts.
(From the French of Émile de
Najac and Alfred Hennequin.)
Boston: W. H. Baker, c1880.
61p. (The Globe drama) *[Based
on Bébé by Najac and Henne-
quin]*

"The baby"   *see*   Osgood, Harry
O.

Baby coach parade   *see*   Tees,
Levin C.

The baby elephant   *see*   Stewart,
J. C.

A baby show at Skilletville   *see*
McBride, H. Elliott   *in his*
Latest dialogues

Bachelor girls' club   *see*
Denison, Thomas Stewart   *in
his*   Wide awake dialogues

Bachelor Hall   *see*   Baker,
Rachel E. and Baker, Robert
Melville

Bachelor maids   *see*   Tiffany,
Esther Brown

The bachelor's banquet; or, An
indigestible romance   *see*
Humphrey, Lewis D.

The bachelor's box   *see*
Williams, Henry Llewellyn

The bachelor's Christmas   *see*
Wilson, Ella Calista Handy

A bachelor's honeymoon   *see*
Stapleton, John

The bachelor's prize *see* Sertrew, Saul

A bachelor's romance *see* Morton, Martha

Back from Californy; or, Old clothes. An original Darky eccentricity. Chicago: T. S. Denison, 1895? 8p.

Backgammon *see* Arnold, George? and Cahill, Frank. Parlor theatricals; or, Winter evening's entertainment

A backward glance *see* Denton, Clara Janetta Fort *in her* From tots to teens

Bacon, Delia Salter, 1811-1859. The bride of Fort Edward, founded on an incident of the Revolution. New York: S. Colman, 1839. 174p.

Bacon, Francis, viscount St. Albans, 1561-1626. Robert, Earl of Sussex *see* Owen, Orville Ward

The bacteriologist *see* Ford, Daniel K.

Bad advice *see* Fuller, Horace Williams

A bad case *see* Bunner, Henry Cuyler and Magnus, Julian *see also* Matthews, Brander. Comedies for amateur acting

A bad job *see* McBride, H. Elliott

Bad whiskey *see* White, Charles

Badly mixed *see* Rawley, Bert C.

Badly sold *see* Coes, George H.

The bag of gold *see* Lucrezia; or, The bag of gold

Bagby versus Bagby *see* Leupp, Francis Ellington

Bailey, G.
Geneviève de Brabant. Opera bouffe in three acts. (From the French of Crémieux and Tréfeu.) New York: John A. Gray and Green, 1868. Bilingual text: English and French. 47p. Libretto.
[music by Jacques Offenbach; without the music]

Bailey, George W.
Diagram of a modern law suit; or, A satire on trial by jury. n.p., n.pub., c1891. 51p.

Bailey, John Jay, d.1873.
[see also Baily, Jno. Jay, as incorrectly entered by Readex]
Waldimar. A tragedy in five acts. New York: J. Van Norden, 1834. 124, 6p.
[prologue by Robert C. Sands, and epilogue by Theodore S. Fay; reviews from contemporary sources appear at the end of the play]

Bailey, William Entriken.
Dramatic poems. Philadelphia: the author, 1894. 117p.
   Contents: The sacrifice of Iphigenia (p.1-37).--Priam, King of Troy (p.38-68).--Andromache in captivity (p.69-91).--The daughters of Oedipus (p.92-117).
[on title page, author's surname spelled Baily]

Baily [sic, Bailey], Jno. Jay, d.1873. *[see also Bailey, John Jay]*
The way of life. A moral and allegorical fairy spectacle in ten scenes. St. Louis:

Missouri Democrat Book and
Job Office, c1867. 20p.
*[title page and copyright
note entered under surname
Bailey]*

Bajazet. A tragedy in five
acts. (From the French of
Racine.) New York: Darcie &
Corbyn, 1855. Bilingual
text: French and English.
38p.

Baker, Benjamin Archibald,
1818-1890.
A glance at New York. A
local drama in two acts.
New York: S. French, 189-?
32p. (French's standard
drama. The acting edition.
no. 216)

Baker, Delphine Paris.
Solon; or, The rebellion
of '61. A domestic and
political tragedy. Chicago:
S. P. Rounds, 1862. 74p.
*[title page gives author
as "Delphine"]*

Baker, George Augustus, 1849-
1910.
West Point. A comedy in
three acts. [From his: Mrs.
Hephaestus...together with
West Point. New York:
White, Stokes & Allen, 1887.
211p.] p.138-211.

Baker, George Melville, 1832-
1890.
Above the clouds. A drama in
two acts. Boston: G. M.
Baker, c1876. p.99-166.
(The amateur drama)

After taps *see* Baker,
Rachel E.

Among the breakers. A drama
in two acts. Boston: W. H.
Baker, c1889. p.107-170.
(Baker's edition of plays)

Better than gold. A drama

in four acts. Boston: W. H.
Baker, c1889. 58p. (Baker's
edition of plays)

Bonbons. A musical and dramatic entertainment. Boston:
Lee & Shepard, 1870. p.139-
189. (The amateur drama)
[without the music]

The Boston dip. A comedy in
one act. Boston: W. H. Baker,
c1876. p.215-240. (The amateur
drama)

Bread on the waters. A drama
in two acts. Boston: W. H.
Baker, c1889. p.221-290.
(Baker's edition of plays)

Capuletta; or, Romeo and
Juliet restored. An operatic
burlesque. Boston: W. H.
Baker, c1868. Prompt-book
with MS notes. p.79-105.
(The amateur drama)

The champion of her sex. A
farce in one act for female
characters. Boston: W. H.
Baker, 1920. p.109-131.
(Baker's edition of plays)
[earlier copyright: 1874]

A Christmas carol. [From his:
The exhibition drama...Boston
and New York: Lee and Shepard,
and Lee, Shepard & Dillingham,
c1874. 248p.] p.225-248. (The
amateur drama) *[title page:
"arranged as an entertainment
from Dickens' Christmas story]*

A close shave. A farce. Boston: C. H. Spencer, 1868.
19p. (The amateur drama)

Coals of fire. Boston: G. M.
Baker, c1876. p.63-77. (The
amateur drama)

Comrades. A drama in three
acts. Boston: W. H. Baker,
c1889. 52p. (Baker's edition
of plays)

Conjuration. A charade. Boston: G. M. Baker, c1872.
p.103-114.

Down by the sea. A drama in two acts. Boston: W. H. Baker, c1889. 61p. (Baker's edition of plays)

"A drop too much." A farce. Boston: W. H. Baker, 1894. p.142-161. (The amateur drama)

The duchess of Dublin. A farce. Boston: W. H. Baker, c1876. 34p. (The amateur drama)

Enlisted for the war; or, The home-guard. A drama in three acts. Boston: W. H. Baker, c1874. 81p. (The amateur drama)

Enlisted for the war; or, The home-guard. Boston: G. M. Baker, c1874. Presentation copy signed by the author. 81p.

The fairy of the fountain; or, Diamonds and toads. A musical play in two acts. Boston: W. H. Baker, c1906. 29p. (Baker's edition of plays) *[earlier copyright: 1878; taken from the fairy story, Diamonds and toads]*

The flower of the family. A comedy in three acts. Boston: W. H. Baker, c1893. 72p.

The flowing bowl. A drama in three acts. Boston: W. H. Baker, c1885. 66p. (The globe drama)

Forty minutes with a crank; or, The Seldarte craze. A farce. Boston: W. H. Baker, 1889. 29p. (The globe drama) *[a slightly-altered version of The Seldarte craze, 1887]*

Freedom of the press. A farce. Boston: W. H. Baker, c1894. p.162-183. (The amateur drama)

Gentlemen of the jury. A

farce in one act for male characters. [From his: The drawing-room stage. Boston: Lee and Shepard, 1873. 274p.] p.171-186.

The greatest plague in life. A farce for female characters only. Boston: W. H. Baker, c1894. p.114-127. (The amatuer drama)

A Grecian bend. A farce. Boston: W. H. Baker, c1898. p.73-92. (Baker's edition of plays)

Gustave the professor. A comedy in one act. (From the French.) Boston: W. H. Baker, c1888. 24p. (The globe drama) *[translation of C'est le professeur, by Gaston Maquis and Alfred Bertinot]*

Humors of the strike. A farce for male characters. Boston: W. H. Baker, c1896. p.209-220. (Baker's edition of plays)

The hypochondriac. Boston: Baker, 1872. p.17-26. (Baker's edition of plays)

Ignorance is bliss [and] A stitch in time saves nine. [From his: a Baker's dozen. Boston: Lee and Shepard, 1872. 137p.] p.49-53, 85-87.

The last loaf. A drama in two acts. Boston: W. H. Baker, c1898. 56p. (Baker's edition of plays)

Little brown jug. A drama in three acts. Boston: W. H. Baker, c1876. p.269-332. (Baker's edition of plays)

A little more cider. A farce. Boston: Lee & Shepard, 1870. p.241-262. (The amateur drama)

Love of a bonnet. Boston: G. M. Baker, c1868. p.113-123. (The amateur drama)

The man with the demijohn.
A farce. Boston: G. M.
Baker, c1876. p.128-139.

The merry Christmas of the
old woman who lived in a
shoe. Boston: W. H. Baker,
c1902. p.157-169. *[earlier
copyright: 1874]*

Mrs. Walthrop's bachelors.
A comedy in three acts.
Boston: W. H. Baker, 1878.
67p. (The globe drama)
*[translated and adapted
from the German of Julius
Roderich Benedix; joint
author: Willard Small]*

My brother's keeper. A drama
in three acts. Boston: W. H.
Baker, c1900. 67p. (Baker's
edition of plays) *[earlier
copyright: 1872]*

My uncle, the captain. A
farce. Boston: G. M. Baker,
1868. p.170-188. (The amateur drama)

A mysterious disappearance.
A farce. Boston: W. H. Baker,
c1904. p.71-97. (Baker's
edition of plays) *[earlier
copyright: 1876]*

Nevada; or, The lost mine.
A drama in three acts.
Boston: W. H. Baker, c1882.
55p. (Baker's edition of
plays)

Never say die. Boston: W. H.
Baker, 1893? p.85-106. (The
amateur drama)

New brooms sweep clean. A
farce. Boston: W. H. Baker,
c1898. p.263-281. (The
amateur drama)

Once on a time. [From his:
Amateur dramas. Boston:
Lee & Shepard, 1867. 252p.]
p.215-252.

One hundred years ago; or,
Our boys of 1776. A patriotic drama in two acts.

Boston: G. M. Baker, 1876.
54p. (The amateur drama.
no. 11)

Our folks. A play in three
acts. Boston: W. H. Baker,
1879. 78p. (Baker's edition
of plays) *[dramatized from
his Running to waste, the
story of a tomboy]*

Past redemption. A drama in
four acts. Boston: G. M.
Baker, c1875. 47p. (The globe
drama)

The peddler of Very Nice
[From his: Amateur dramas.
Boston: Lee & Shepard, 1867.
252p.] p.201-214. *[title
page: "burlesque of the trial-
scene in Merchant of Venice"]*

Poison. A farce. Boston: W. H.
Baker, c1882. 22p. *[title
page: "as performed by 'The
Hasty Pudding Club' of Harvard University."]*

A public benefactor. Boston:
G. M. Baker, c1872. Title
page lacking. p.27-37. (The
amateur drama)

Rebecca's triumph. A drama in
three acts for female characters. Boston: W. H. Baker,
c1879. 55p. (Baker's edition
of plays)

The red chignon. Boston: W. H.
Baker, c1893. p.89-100. (The
amateur drama)

The revolt of the bees. An
allegory for female characters. Boston: W. H. Baker,
c1874. p.69-84.

The rival poets. An interlude.
Boston: W. H. Baker, c1876.
p.195-200. (The amateur drama)

The runaways. Boston: W. H.
Baker, c1876. p.39-47. (The
amateur drama)

Santa Claus' frolics. A Christmas entertainment for little

folks. Boston: W. H. Baker, c1909. p.79-84. *[original copyright: 1872]*

The sculptor's triumph. A national allegory. Boston: W. H. Baker, c1876. p.184-194. (The amateur drama)

A sea of troubles. An original farce. Boston: W. H. Baker, c1894. p.91-113.

Seeing the elephant. [From his: The temperance drama... Boston: Lee and Shepard, 1874. 230p.] p.69-92.

The Seldarte craze. A farce. Boston: W. H. Baker, 1887. 32p. *[published in 1889 with slight changes under title, Forty minutes with a crank; or, The Seldarte craze]*

The seven ages. A tableaux entertainment. Boston: W. H. Baker, c1893. p.187-213. (The amateur drama)

Shall our mothers vote? Boston: W. H. Baker, 1904. p.169-187. *[earlier copyright: 1876]*

Snow-bound. A musical and dramatic entertainment. Boston: W. H. Baker, 1870. p.93-137. (The globe drama) *[without the music]*

"Stand by the flag." Chicago: Dramatic Pub. Co., c1866. p.49-61. (The amateur drama)

Sylvia's soldier. A comedy in two acts. Boston: G. M. Baker, c1866. 48p.

Sylvia's soldier. A comedy in two acts. Boston: W. H. Baker, c1893. 48p. (The amateur drama)

The tempter; or, The sailor's return. Boston: W. H. Baker, c1894. p.74-92. (Baker's edition of plays)

A tender attachment. A farce. Boston: W. H. Baker, c1900. p.85-106. (Baker's edition of plays) *[earlier copyright: 1872]*

Thief of time. Boston: W. H. Baker, 1876. p.7-15. (The amateur drama)

Thirty minutes for refreshments. A farce. Boston: W. H. Baker, c1898. 24p. (Baker's edition of plays)

A thorn among the roses. [From his: The exhibition drama... Boston and New York: Lee and Shepard and Lee, Shepard & Dillingham, 1874. 248p.] p.199-223. (The amateur drama)

Titania; or, The butterflies' carnival. A fairy extravaganza in two acts. Boston: W. H. Baker, c1907. 38p. *[earlier copyright: 1879]*

Too late for the train. A duologue. Boston: W. H. Baker, c1876. p.57-72. (The amateur drama)

The tournament of Idylcourt. An allegory. Boston: W. H. Baker, c1874. p.173-197.

Using the weed. Boston: W. H. Baker, c1900. p.101-111. (The amateur drama)

The visions of freedom. A national allegory. Boston: Baker, 1874. p.135-153. (The amateur drama)

Wanted, a male cook. A farce in one act. Boston: W. H. Baker, 1920. p.62-73. (Baker's edition of plays) *[original copyright date is 1920]*

The war of the roses. An allegory. Boston: W. H. Baker, c1870. p.205-218. (The amateur drama)

"We're all teetotalers." A farce. Boston: W. H. Baker,

c1866. p.128-141. (The
amateur drama)

Baker, George Pierce, 1866-
1935.
The revolving wedge see
Ware, Thornton M. and Baker,
George Pierce

Baker, Rachel E.
After taps. A drama in three
acts. Boston: W. H. Baker,
c1891. 45p. (Baker's edition
of plays) [cover: "From notes
and unfinished manuscript of
the late George M. Baker"]

Bachelor Hall. A comedy in
three acts. Boston: W. H.
Baker, 1898. 64p. (Baker's
edition of plays) [joint
author: Robert Melville
Baker]

The chaperon. A comedy in
three acts for female characters only. Boston: W. H.
Baker, c1891. 56p.

Her picture. A comedy in one
act. Boston: W. H. Baker,
c1894. 17p.

A king's daughter. A comedy
in three acts for female
characters only. Boston:
W. H. Baker, c1893. 59p.

Mr. Bob. A comedy in two
acts. Boston: W. H. Baker,
c1894. 39p. (Baker's edition
of plays)

Baker, Robert Melville, 1868-
1929.
An awkward squad. A sketch
in one scene. Boston: W. H.
Baker, c1899. 10p. (Baker's
edition of plays)

Bachelor Hall see Baker,
Rachel E. and Baker, Robert
Melville

Black magic. A burlesque
Negro sketch. Boston: W. H.
Baker, c1889. 13p.

For one night only. A comedy
in four acts. Boston: W. H.
Baker, c1899. 44p. [title
page: "translated from the
German"]

Baker, Theodore, 1851-1934.
Carmen. (From the French of
Meilhac and Halévy.) New
York: G. Schirmer, 1895.
Vocal score. Bilingual text:
English and French. 391p.
[music by George Bizet;
adapted from the novel by
Prosper Merimée, with libretto
by Henri Meilhac and Ludovic
Halévy]

Balatka, Hans, 1826-1899.
Peter the Great in Saardam;
or, The Czar and the carpen-
ter. (From the German of
Lortzing.) Chicago: Chicago
Musical Union, 1894. 16p.
Libretto. [the music is by
Lortzing; original German
title is Zar und Zimmermann,
which is based on Le bourg-
mestre de Sardam, by Anne
Honoré Joseph Duveyrier]

Balch, William Ralston, 1852-
1923.
Like Caesar's wife. Philadelphia?: n.pub., 1890? Typescript. Prompt-book. iii,
20, 16, 17 leaves.

Balfe, Michael William, 1808-
1870.
The Bohemian girl see Kellogg, Clara Louise

The Puritan's daughter see
The Puritan's daughter

The ballad of Babie Bell and
other poems see Aldrich,
Thomas Bailey. The set of
turquoise

Ballou, Maturin Murray, 1820-
1895.
Miralda; or, The justice of

BALM

Tacon. A drama in three acts.
Boston: W. V. Spencer, 1858.
29p. (Spencer's Boston
theatre. v.22, no.167 [i.e.,
169])

Balm of Gilead   *see*   Boltwood,
Edward

Balocchi, Luigi, 1766-1832.
Mosé in Egitto *see* Parker,
George S. Moses in Egypt
see also Ponte, Lorenzo da.
Moses in Egypt *see also*
Villarino, Jose J. Moses in
Egypt

Balzac, Honoré de, 1799-1850.
La bourse *see* Harris,
Theodore. The purse

[The oath] *see* Furber,
Pierce

Bamburgh, William Cushing.
Giacomo; a Venetian tale.
New York: privately printed
for the author, 1892. 19
leaves.

Bancroft, Frances Marsh.
Passe Rose *see* Paul, Anne
Marie

Bandage *see* Arnold, George?
and Cahill, Frank. Parlor
theatricals; or, Winter
evening's entertainment

Bangs, John Kendrick, 1862-
1922.
The bicyclers. New York:
Harper & Bros., c1896. 40p.

A chafing-dish party. New
York: Harper & Co., c1896.
46p.

A dramatic evening. [From
his: The bicyclers and three
other farces. New York:
Harper & Bros., 1896. 176p.]
p.41-84.

The fatal message. New York:
Harper & Bros., c1896. 41p.

Katharine. A travesty. New
York: n.pub., 1888. 127p.
[suggested by Shakespeare's
The taming of the shrew]

Mephistopheles. A profanation.
New York: Gilliss Brothers and
Turnure, Art Age Press, 1889.
97p. [suggested by Goethe's
Faust]

A proposal under difficulties.
[From his: The bicyclers and
three other farces. New York:
Harper & Bros., 1896. 176p.]
p.126-176.

The young folk's minstrels.
New York: Harper & Bros.,
c1897. 26p.

Banim, John, 1798-1842.
Damon and Pythias *see* Forrest, Edwin *see also* The
modern standard drama, vol. 5

The banker's daughter *see*
Howard, Bronson

The bankrupt *see* Boker, George
Henry. Glaucus & other plays

Bannan, Martha Ridgway.
The fisher maiden. A vaudeville written for the Court
at Weimar [and] The lover's
caprice. A pastoral play in
verse. (From the German of
Goethe.) Philadelphia: John
C. Yorston Pub. Co., 1899.
116p. [the first play suggested by Goethe's Die
Fischerin]

Bannister, Nathaniel Harrington,
1813-1847.
England's iron days. A tragedy
in five acts. New Orleans: W.
McKeon, 1837. 57p.

Gaulantis. A tragedy in five
acts. Cincinnati: Flash Ryder,
1836. 67p. [title page:
Gaulantus]

The gentleman of Lyons; or,

The marriage contract. A
play in five acts. New York:
Levison & Brother, 1838. 41p.

Putnam, the iron son of '76.
A national military drama in
three acts. Boston: W. V.
Spencer, 1859. 30p. (Spencer's Boston theatre. no.
156)

Rookwood. (From a book by
William Harrison Arnsworth.)
Philadelphia: 1849. Prompt-
book in Ms. In three acts.
(pag. by acts)

The three brothers; or,
Crime its own avenger. A
play in one act. Buffalo:
n.pub., 1840. 26p.

Banquet of Palacios see
Moore, Charles Leonard

Banville, Théodore Faullain
de, 1823-1891.
Socrate et sa femme see
Renauld, Charles. Socrates
and his wife

Barabbas see Mitchell, Silas
Weir

Barbara Freitchie [sic], the
Frederick girl! see Fitch,
Clyde

Barbauld, Anna Letitia Aikin,
1743-1825.
Alfred see Follen, Eliza
Lee Cabot. Home dramas for
young people

[Alfred the king] see
Venable, William Henry in
his The school stage

Master and slave see Follen, Eliza Lee Cabot. Home
dramas for young people

Barber, Jules, 1825-1901.
Faust see Kellogg, Clara
Louise

The barber of Seville. A comic
opera in three acts. New
York: Baker & Godwin, 1855.
38p. Libretto.

The barber of Seville. A comic
opera in two acts. New York:
John Douglas, 1847. Bilingual
text: English and Italian.
67p. Libretto. (Operatic
library no. 6) [music by
Gioacchino Rossini; without
the music]

The barber pards see Gibson,
Ad. H. Slick and Skinner; or,
The barber pards

Bardell vs. Pickwick see
Dialogues dramatized from
the works of Charles Dickens

Barham, Richard Harris, 1788-
1845 see Ingoldsby, Thomas

Barker, Benjamin Fordyce, 1818-
1891.
The rise in Harlem. New York:
Baker & Godwin, 1864. 67p.
[the title page gives no
author, and Readex has also
entered this same play under
title]

Barker, Theodore T.
Fatinitza. Boston: Oliver
Ditson, c1879. Vocal score.
Trilingual text: English,
German and Italian. 223p.
[title page: "...by Franz
von Suppé...translation and
adaptation of words to music
by Theo. T. Barker. Translation of dialogue by Sylvester
Baxter"; libretto by Richard
Genée; Readex also enters
the libretto to this work
under title]

The infanta's dolls. Boston:
Oliver Ditson, c1881. 72p.
Libretto. [music by Charles
Grisart; without the music;
original title: Les poupées
de l'infante]

The mascot. Boston: Oliver Ditson, c1881. Prompt-book, interleaved with Ms. notes. 68p. (paging irregular.) *[joint author: I. W. Norcross; music by Edmond Audran; without the music; original title: La mascotte]*

Barking up the wrong tree. A darkey sketch in one act and one scene. New York: Dick & Fitzgerald, 1886. 9p.

Barlow, Joel, 1754-1812. The Columbiad *see* Speed, Belle Lewis. Columbia

Barnard, Lady Anne Lindsay, 1750-1825. Auld Robin Gray *see* Taylor, Malcolm Stuart

Barnard, Charles, 1838-1920. The dreamland tree. A comedy with music, designed for an audience of young people of every age, from six to sixty. New York: T. T. De Vinnes, c1883. 38p. *[music by Frank A. Howson; without the music]*

He was never known to smile *see* Dramatic leaflets

Joe. A comedy of child life in two acts. Chicago: Dramatic Pub. Co., c1897. 22p.

Psyche, M.D. A comedy in one act. Boston: W. H. Baker, c1895. 14p. (Baker's edition of plays)

The silver dollar. A temperance monologue in one scene. New York: Edgar S. Werner, c1894. 8p.

The triple wedding. A drama in three acts. New York: Dick & Fitzgerald, c1887. 36p.

Barnes, Charlotte Mary Sanford, 1818-1863. The forest princess; or, Two centuries ago. An historical play in three parts. [From her: Plays, prose, and poetry. Philadelphia: E. H. Butler, 1848.] p.145-270.

Octavia Bragaldi; or, The confession. [From her: Plays, prose, and poetry. Philadelphia: E. H. Butler, 1848.] p.i-v, 6-118.

Barnes, James. The black barber; or, Humours of Pompey Suds' shaving saloon. A comic entertainment. London: F. Pitman, 1864? 16p.

The darkey breach of promise case. A nigger mock trial. New York: Fitzgerald Pub. Corp., c1898. 13p.

The darkey phrenologist. A nigger absurdity. New York: Dick & Fitzgerald, 190-? 11p.

Doctor Snowball. A negro farce in one act for three male characters. New York: Dick & Fitzgerald, c1897. 10p.

The Nigger night school. A farce in one act for six male characters. New York: Dick & Fitzgerald, c1896. 15p.

Barnes, William Henry Linow, 1836-1902. Solid silver. A play in five acts. San Francisco: Edward Basqui, 1871. 96p. *[Readex incorrectly spells author's name as William Henry Linou Barnes]*

Barnes, William Horatio. The drama of secession; or, Scenes from American history. Indianapolis: Merrill, 1862. 60p.

Barnet, Robert A., 1850-1933. "1492." Operatic extravaganza. Boston, New York, Chicago: White-Smith Music Pub. Co., c1892. Vocal score. 100p. *[Music by Carl Pflueger]*

Jack and the bean-stalk,
the strange adventures of.
A fairy extravaganza. Boston, New York, Chicago:
White-Smith Music Pub. Co.,
c1896. Vocal score. 118p.
[music by A. Baldwin Sloane]

Miladi and the musketeer.
A romantic extravaganza.
Boston, New York, Chicago:
White-Smith Music Pub. Co.,
c1900. 125p. [title page:
"music by Harry Lawson
Heartz [LC=Harts], with
additional numbers by
George Lowell Tracy, Edward
W. Corliss, D. K. Stevens
and R. G. Morse"]

"Prince pro-tem." Taunton,
Mass.: n.pub., 1893. Typescript. Prompt-book. Title
page lacking. 50 leaves.

Prince pro tem. Boston,
London: Miles & Thompson;
G. Ricordi, c1893. Vocal
score. 102p. [music by
Lewis Sabin Thompson]

Barnett, M. J.
Samson and Delilah. (From
the French of Lemaire.)
Boston: Oliver Ditson,
c1895. Bilingual text:
English and French. 26p.
Libretto. [music by Camille
Saint-Saëns; without the
music; based on Ferdinand
Lemaire's Samson et Dalila]

Barnett, Morris.
The serious family. A comedy
in three acts see The
modern standard drama,
vol. 10

Barney, Master.
Ambition see White, Charles

Bad whiskey see White,
Charles

The rehearsal; or, Barry's
old man see White, Charles

Barney the baron. A farce in
one act. New York: S. French,
187-? 16p.

Barney's courtship; or, Mollie
dear see Macarthy, Harry

Barnitz, Albert Trovillo
Siders, b.1833.
Duthmarno. A tragedy in five
acts [From his: The mystic
delvings. Cincinnati: A. Watson, 1857. 288p.] p.193-265.

Baron Rudolph see Howard,
Bronson

Barr, E. Nelson.
Broken links. A drama in five
acts. Clyde, O.: Ames, 1893.
23p. (Ames' series of standard
and minor drama. no. 321)

Clearing the mists. A drama
in three acts. Clyde, O.:
Ames, 1889. 21p. (Ames'
series of standard and minor
drama. no. 268) [joint author:
J. M. Hogan]

Barras, Charles M., 1826-1873.
The black crook. An original
magical and spectacular drama
in four acts. n.p.: n.pub.,
18-? Typescript. 66 leaves.

The modern saint. An original
comedy in three acts. Cincinnati: H. Watkin, 1857. 48p.

Barrie, James Mathew, bart.,
1860-1937.
The little minister see
Fraser, John Arthur

Peter Pan see Stewart,
Grant. A respectful burlesque
on Peter Pan

Barrie, James Mathew, The
household of see Bridges,
Robert in his Overheard
in Arcady

Barrière, Théodore, 1823-1877.
L'héritage de Monsieur Plu-

met *see* Fuller, Horace
William. Dear uncle!

La vie de Bohème *see*
Fitch, Clyde, Bohemia

Barring out the teacher *see*
Denison, Thomas *in his*
Wide awake dialogues

Barrington, George, 1755-1804.
Personal sketches *see*
Venable, William Henry.
Irish equivocation *in his*
The school stage

Barron, Elwyn Alfred, b.1855.
A mountain pink *see* Bates,
Morgan and Barron, Elwyn
Alfred. Realistic description of life among the
moonshiners of North Carolina

The Viking. Chicago: A. C.
McClurg, 1888. 141p.

Barry, S.
The Dutchman's ghost; or,
All right. An original farce
in one act. New York: S.
French, 187-? Prompt-book.
16p. (The minor drama. The
acting edition. no. 151)

The persecuted Dutchman; or,
The original John Schmidt.
A farce in one act. New
York: S. French, 1858? 15p.
(The minor drama. The acting
edition. no. 152)

The persecuted Dutchman; or,
The original John Schmidt.
A farce in one act. New
York: Dick & Fitzgerald,
189-? 17p.

Barry, Thomas.
The tempest. By William
Shakespeare. New York: S.
French, 18-? 44p. (French's
American drama. The acting
edition. no. 78)

Barry's old man *see* White,

Charles. The rehearsal; or,
Barry's old man

Barstow, Ellen M.
The mission of the fairies.
Portland: F. G. Rich, 1871.
29p.

Barthet, Armand, 1820-1874.
Le moineau de Lesbia *see*
The sparrow of Lesbia

Bartlett, George Bradford, 1832-
1896.
America's birthday party *see*
his A dream of the centuries
and other entertainments for
parlor and hall

A dream of the centuries and
other entertainments for parlor and hall. Boston: W. H.
Baker, c1889. 23 unnumbered
leaves. (Baker's novelties)
Contents: A dream of the
centuries (Elbridge Streeter
Brooks).--Mademoiselle's
Christmas gifts (Mary Graham).
--America's birthday party,
a centennial operetta (George
Bradford Bartlett).--Tell-
tale, a charade in three
scenes (G. B. Bartlett).--
Buoyant, a Dickens charade in
three scenes (Mrs. Lucia
Chase Bell).--Dotage, a
Dickens charade in three
scenes (Fannie M. Johnson).

Tell-tale *see his* A dream
of the centuries and other
entertainments for parlor
and hall

Bartley, C. G.
The spy of Atlanta *see*
Ames, A. D. and Bartley, C. G.

The bashful boy *see* Denison,
Thomas Stewart *in his* Friday
afternoon series of dialogues

The bashful suitor *see* Shettel, James W. and George,
Wadsworth M. A matchmaking
father; or, The bashful suitor

Basil (pseud.)
Love and money. A dramatic
sketch. New York: Pudney &
Russell, 1858. 39p. *[Basil
is a pseud. for Richard
Ashe King, 1839-1932]*

Bassett, Willard.
The mystic midgets' Lili-
putian carnival of nations
see Bertram, Eugene and
Bassett, Willard

The bat and the ball; or,
Negative evidence *see*
Chase, Frank Eugene

Batchelder, Samuel Francis,
1870-1927.
Hamlet; or, The sport, the
spook, and the spinster (By
G. B. Blake, J. A. Wilder,
S. F. Batchelder; music by
Percy Lee Atherton and
Ernest Hamlin Abbott). Bos-
ton: Miles & Thompson, c1893.
Vocal score. 84p. *[title
page: Musical score of the
'93 Hasty Pudding Play
(Harvard University)]*

Batchelor, W. H.
Ali Baba, jr.; or, Morgiana
and the forty thieves *see*
Smith, Harry Bache

Ali Baba; or, Morgiana and
the forty thieves *see*
Smith, Harry Bache

Bateman, Mrs. Sidney Frances
Cowell, 1823-1881.
Self. An original comedy in
three acts. New York: S.
French, c1856. 46p. (French's
standard drama. no. 163)

Bates, Arlo, 1850-1918.
A gentle jury. A farce in
one act. Boston: W. H.
Baker, c1897. 14p. (Baker's
edition of plays)

Bates, Ella Skinner.

The convention of the Muses.
A classical play for parlor
and school for nine females.
Boston: Baker, 1891. 8p.
(Baker's edition of plays)

Bates, Morgan.
Realistic description of life
among the moonshiners of North
Carolina. *A mountain pink*.
Milwaukee: Riverside Print.
Co., 18-? 24p. *[Note: the
actual play is not reproduced
on the Readex microprint, but
only background material,
synopses of the acts, and 11
illustrations. Joint author:
Elwyn Alfred Barron]*

The battery and the assault *see*
The demon phonograph; or, The
battery and the assault

The battle of Gettysburg *see*
The Union sergeant; or, The
battle of Gettysburg

The battle of King's Mountain
see Tayleure, Clifton W.
Horseshoe Robinson; or, The
battle of King's Mountain

The battle of Stillwater; or,
The maniac *see* Dawes, Rufus

Battle of the bulls and bears
of Wall Street; or, The comedy
of commerce and tragedy of
trade. n.p.: n.pub., c1882.
32p.

The battle of the comets *see*
Woodworth, Samuel. Shooting
stars; or, The battle of the
comets

The battle of the Thames *see*
Emmons, Richard. Tecumseh;
or, The battle of the Thames

The battle of Weldon railroad
see Osgood, L. W. The Union
spy; or, The battle of Weldon
railroad

The battlefield of Shiloh   *see*
Muscroft, Samuel J. The
drummer boy; or, The
battlefield of Shiloh

Baudouin, Jean Marie Théodore.
La pie voleuse   *see* Coale,
George B. Magpie and the
maid   *see also* The thieving
magpie

Baum, Louis F.
The maid of Arran. n.p.:
c1882. Typescript. 38 leaves.

Baum, Rosemary.
Love in a lighthouse. A
farce in one act. Boston:
W. H. Baker, c1896. 18p.
(Baker's edition of plays)

That box of cigarettes. A
farce in three acts. Boston:
W. H. Baker, c1892. 25p.
(Baker's edition of plays)

Bauman, E. Henri.
Everybody astonished. An
original farce in one act.
Clyde, O.: Ames, c1887. 6p.
(Ames' series of standard
and minor drama. no. 218)

Fun in a post office. A
farce in one act. Clyde, O.:
Ames, c1885. 9p. (Ames'
series of standard and
minor drama. no. 154)

Lauderbach's little surprise.
An original farce in one act.
Clyde, O.: Ames, 1887. 5p.
(Ames' series of standard
and minor drama. no. 228)

The patent washing machine;
or, The lover's dilemma.
An original farce in one
act. Clyde, O.: Ames, 1887.
7p. (Ames' series of standard and minor drama. no.
217)

Bausman, William.
Early California. A drama

in five acts. San Francisco:
n.pub., 1872. 42p. *[also
included are four pages of
tontemporary press reports]*

Baxter, Sylvester, 1850-1927.
Fatinitza   *see* Barker,
Theodore T. and Baxter,
Sylvester

Bayard, Jean François Alfred,
1798-1853.
La fille du régiment   *see*
The child of the regiment
see also The daughter of
the regiment   *see also* La
figlia del reggimento   *see
also* Seguin, Arthur Edward
Sheldon. Marie; or, The
daughter of the regiment

Un mari à la campagne (A
husband in the country)   *see*
Barnett, Morris. The serious
family *in* The modern
standard drama, vol. 10

Bayless, Bell.
Left in charge. A farce in
one act. Philadelphia: Penn
Pub. Co., 1912. 23p.
[earlier copyright: 1897]

Bayly, Thomas Haynes, 1797-1839.
Perfection; or, The maid of
Munster   *see* The modern
standard drama, vol. 4

Bayne, Peter, 1830-1896.
The days of Jezebel. An
historical drama. Boston:
Gould and Lincoln, 1872.
240p.

Be sure you're right, then
go ahead   *see* Murdoch,
Frank Hitchcock. Davy
Crockett; or, Be sure you're
right, then go ahead

Be truthful but courteous   *see*
Heywood, Delia A. *in her*
Choice dialogues. no. 1

Beach, Stanley Yale.
The widow Mullin's Christmas.
A Christmas entertainment
for children. Boston: W. H.
Baker, c1897. 34p. (Baker's
edition of plays) *[Joint
author: H. Arthur Powell]*

Beadle's...dialogues no. 2.
New York: M. J. Ivers, c1898.
95p.
Contents: The genius of
liberty (Dr. Le Grand).--
Cinderella; or, The little
glass slipper.--The society
for doing good, but saying
bad.--The golden rule (Dr.
Le Grand).--The gifts of
the fairy queen.--Taken in
and done for (Marie Thérèse
De Camp Kemble).--The country aunt's visit to the
city.--The two Romans.--
Trying the characters.--
The happy family.--The rainbow.--How to write "popular"
stories (adapted from Paulding's popular story "Madmen
all").--The new and the old.
--A sensation at last.--The
greenhorn.--The three men of
science.--The old lady's
will.--The little philosophers.--How to find an heir.
--The virtues.--A connubial
eclogue (John Godfrey Saxe).
--The public meeting.--The
English traveler.

Beale, Edmond D.
Kenilworth; or, Amy's aims
and Leicester's lesson *see*
McMichael, Clayton Fotterall

Beasley, Frederic Williamson,
1808-1878.
Henry Venola, the duellist.
Philadelphia: Herman Hooker,
1841. 64p.

Beatrice *see* Brayley,
Arthur Wellington

Beatrice; or, The false and the
true *see* Leland, Oliver
Shepard

Beaty, Thomas R.
Old Glory in Cuba. A drama in
four acts. Clyde, O.: Ames,
c1898. 30p. (Ames' series of
standard and minor drama.
no. 405)

Beau Brummel *see* Fitch, Clyde

Beaumont, Francis, 1584-1616.
The elder brother *see*
Beaumont, Francis and Fletcher,
John *in* The modern standard
drama, vol. 9

The maid's tragedy *see*
Knowles, James Sheridan. The
bridal *in* The modern standard drama, vol. 6

Beauty and the beast *see*
Kavanaugh, Mrs. Russell *in*
her Original dramas, dialogues...

The beauty of piety *see* Edgarton, Sarah Carter *in*
Dramatic leaflets

Because I love you *see* Fraser,
John Arthur

Because she loved him so *see*
Gillette, William Hooker

Beck, William L.
Beyond pardon; or, The
Countess of Lynn. A drama in
five acts. Clyde, O.: Ames,
1890. 52p. (Ames' series of
standard and minor drama.
no. 272) *[title page: "adapted*
from Bertha M. Clay's popular
novel of the same name." Clay
is a pseud. for Charlotte
Mary Brame]

Captured; or, The old maid's
triumph. A comedy in four
acts. Clyde, O.: Ames, 1888.

34p. (Ames' series of standard and minor drama. no.
248)

Becky Calico see Denison,
Thomas Stewart in his
Wide awake dialogues

Becky Sharp see Mitchell,
Langdon Elwyn

Beecher, Henry Ward, 1813-
1887.
Norwood see Daly, Augustin.
A legend of "Norwood"; or,
Village life in New England

Beethoven, Ludwig van, 1770-
1827.
Fidelio, oder die eheliche
Liebe see Fidelio; or,
Constancy rewarded

Before and after the war see
McClain, Billy

Before the execution see
McBride, H. Elliott in his
Latest dialogues

The beggar student see
Schwab, Emil

The beggar's opera see
Harrison, William

Behind a curtain. A monologue
see Harrison, Constance
Cary in her Short comedies
for amateur players

Beissier, Fernand, 1858-1936.
[A sudden shower] see
Daly, Augustin in his
Three preludes to the play

Belasco, David, 1859-1931.
La belle Russe. A duel in
four acts. New York: 1882.
Typescript, prompt-book
(paged by acts).

The cavalry ball. (Produced
as "The girl I left behind
me.") New York: Z. & L.

Rosenfield, 1893. Typescript.
In four acts (paged by acts).
[Joint author: Franklin Fyles]

The charity ball. A comedy
drama in four acts. New York:
American Play Co., n.d.
Typescript, prompt-book.
(pag. by act.) *[Joint author:
Henry Churchill De Mille]*

Governor Rodman's daughter
see De Mille, Henry Churchill and Belasco, David

The heart of Maryland. A
drama in four acts. n.p.:
n.pub., 1895. Typescript,
prompt-book. In four acts
(paged by acts.)

The heart of Maryland and
other plays. By G. Hughes
and G. Savage, editors.
Princeton: Princeton Univ.
Press, 1941. xii, 319p.
(America's lost plays. vol.
18)
Contents: La belle Russe
[earlier copyright: 1881].--
The stranglers of Paris
[earlier copyright: 1881].--
The girl I left behind me
*[joint author: Franklin
Fyles; earlier copyright:
1893]*.--The heart of Maryland *[earlier copyright:
1895]*.--Naughty Anthony
[earlier copyright: 1899].
*[Note: The stranglers of
Paris is an adaptation of
Adolphe Belot's Les étrangleurs de Paris]*

Hearts of oak; or, Chums see
Herne, James A. and Belasco,
David

The highest bidder. New York:
n.pub., 1887. Typescript,
prompt-book. 41, 35, 46
leaves. *[joint author: Edward
Hugh Sothern; title page:
"an original comedy...by
Maddison Morton and Robert
Reece]*

Lord Chumley. New York: 1888.

Typescript. In three acts (paged by acts.) *[joint author: Henry Churchill De Mille]*

Lord Chumley *see also* De Mille, Henry Churchill and Belasco, David

Madame Butterfly. A tragedy from Japan... from the story by John Luther Long. n.p.: n.pub., 1900. Typescript. Prompt-book. 26 leaves.

Marriage by moonlight; or, Hap-hazard *see* Herne, James A. and Belasco, David

May Blossom. A comedy in four acts. New York: S. French, c1883. 69p.

Men and women *see* De Mille, Henry Churchill and Belasco, David

Naughty Anthony. New York: 1900. Typescript, prompt-book. In three acts (paged by acts.)

Pawn ticket no. 210 *see* Greene, Clay Meredith and Belasco, David

The stranglers of Paris. New York: 19-? In seven acts (paged by acts.) *[cover: dramatization of Belot's famous novel, Les étrangleurs; title page lacking]*

Under the polar star. n.p.: n.pub., 1896. Typescript, prompt-book. 37, 41, 17 leaves. (Title page lacking) *[Joint author: Clay Meredith Greene]*

The wife. New York: 19-? Typescript. In four acts (paged by acts.) *[joint author: Henry Churchill De Mille; title page: re-written expressly for Mr. Charles Wyndhan (sic, Wyndham, whose real name*

was Charles Culverwell)]

Belden, N. H., b.1810. O'Neal, the great; or, Cogger na Caille [sic, Caillie] A drama in three acts. By N. H. Belden Clark (pseud.) New York: S. French, 1857. 40p. (French's standard drama. The acting edition. no. 331)

The pirate of the isles. A romantic drama in two acts. By N. H. Belden Clarke (pseud.) New York: S. French, 1870? 32p. (French's standard drama. The acting edition. no. 333)

Belinda Jane and Jonathan *see* McBride, H. Elliott. From Punkin Ridge; or, Belinda Jane and Jonathan

Belisarius. An opera in three acts. New York: New World Press, 18-? 24p. Libretto. *[music by Gaetano Donizetti; based on Salvatore Cammarano's Belisario; without the music]*

Belknap, Edwin Star. The better part. An original drama in one act. New York: 1891. Typescript, prompt-book. 20 leaves. *[joint author: Mason Carnes]*

Bell, Henry Glassford, 1803-1874. Mary Queen of Scots *see* Massey, Charles. Massey's exhibition reciter

Bell, Hillary. The social trust; or, The spider's web *see* Morris, Ramsay and Bell, Hillary

Bell, Lucia Chase. Buoyant *see* Bartlett, George Bradford. A dream of the centuries and other entertainments for parlor and hall

Bell, Robert, 1800-1867.
Temper. A comedy in three
acts *see* The modern
standard drama, vol. 7

La belle Hélène. Opera bouffe
in three acts. (From the
French of Meilhac and
Halévy.) (Music by Offen-
bach.) New York: John A.
Gray & Green, Printers,
1868. Bilingual text: French
and English. 40p. Libretto.

The belle of New York *see*
McLellan, Charles Morton
Stewart

La belle Russe *see* Belasco,
David *see also his* The
heart of Maryland and other
plays

The belles of Blackville *see*
Pelham, Nettie H.

The belle's stratagem *see*
Daly, Augustin

Bellini, Vincenzo, 1801-1835.
Norma *see* Fry, Joseph
Reese

   Il pirata *see* Ponte,
Lorenzo da. The pirate

   La sonnambula *see* The
somnambulist

The bells; a collection of
chimes *see* Aldrich,
Thomas Bailey. IV...

Bells in the kitchen. A negro
farce *see* Silsbee, Alice
M. and Horne, Mary Barnard
in their Jolly Joe's lady
minstrels

The bells of Bohemia *see*
Smith, Harry Bache

The bells; or, The Polish
Jew *see* Williams, Henry
Llewellyn

Belot, Adolphe, 1829-1890.
L'article 47 *see* Williams,
Henry Llewellyn. L'article
47; or, Breaking the ban

   Le drame de la Rue de la
Paix *see* Shapley, Rufus
Edmonds. Under the wheels

   Les étrangleurs de Paris *see*
Belasco, David. The stranglers
of Paris *see also his* The
heart of Maryland and other
plays

   Sapho *see* Ginty, Elizabeth
Beall. Sappho *see also*
Smith, Edgar McPhail and
Smith, Harry Bache. Sapolio

   The testament de César
Girodot *see* Walcot, Maria
Grace. The cup and the lip

Bel-Shar-Uzzar *see* Saltus,
Francis Saltus

Belshazzar *see* Blackall,
Christopher Rubey

Ben Israel; or, From under the
curse *see* Tullidge, Edward
Wheelock

Ben Jonson--Sam Johnson *see*
Townsend, Frederic *in his*
Spiritual visitors

The Benedicite *see* Opal
(pseud.) *in her* The cloud
of witnesses

Benedict, Frank Lee, 1834-1910.
The shadow worshiper. New
York: J. S. Redfield, 1857.
197p.
   Contents: The shadow worshiper.--Jessie Linden.--
True hearts.--Lady Ginevra.--
The hall of shadows.--The
poet's offering. *[note:
only the first is a play,
the others being poems which
might serve as monologues]*

Benedix, Julius Roderich, 1811-

1873.
Der Dritte *see* Rosenfeld,
Sydney。 Mabel's manoeuvre;
or, A third party

Die Eifersüchtigen *see*
Rosenfeld, Sydney. Married
bachelors; or, Pleasant
surprises

Die Hochzeitreise *see*
Sonneborn, Hilton Burnside.
The wedding trip

[Is lying easy?] *see* Wall,
Annie

Die Lügnerin *see* Sonneborn,
Hilton Burnside。 Who told
the lie?

[Mrs. Walthrop's bachelors]
see Baker, George Melville
and Small, Willard

Der Weiberfeind *see* Sonneborn, Hilton Burnside. The
woman hater

Bennett, John, 1865-1956.
Master Skylark *see* Lütkenhaus, Anna May Irwin

Bennett, W. L.
Katie's deception; or, The
troublesome kid. Farce in
one act. Clyde, O.: Ames,
1896. 9p. (Ames' series of
standard and minor drama.
no. 380)

Bennette, Wilson T.
Crawford's claim; or, Nugget
Nell, the pet of Poker Flat
see Cowley, E. J. and
Bennette, Wilson T.

Benson, William Henry。
Cousin Flavia. A domestic
drama of the present day in
three acts. Staunton:
Indicator Book and Job
Printing Establishment,
1875。 19p. [*Presumably a
shortened and revised version of his Three scenes in
the life of Lady Flavia*]

Frolicsome girls。 A comedy.
New York & London: G. P.
Putnam's Sons, 1884. 40p.
[*Presumably an enlarged and
revised version of his Three
scenes in the life of Lady
Flavia, also presented in
1875 in a shortened version
as Cousin Flavia*]

Three scenes in the life of
Lady Flavia. Baltimore:
Sherwood, 1866. Prompt-book。
32p.

Beresford benevolent society
see Brewster, Emma E. and
Scribner, Lizzie B.

Bergen, Helen Corinne, b.1868.
The Princess Adelaide. Washington: Neale, 1900. 30p.

Berger, William.
Paul Jones. A drama in five
acts. Philadelphia: T. K. &
P. G. Collins, 1839。 89p.
[*translated from Alexander
Dumas' Paul Jones*]

Bergerat, Émile, 1845-1923.
Plus que reine *see* Nirdlinger, Charles Frederick and
Meltzer, Charles Henry. More
than queen

Berlioz, Hector, 1803-1869.
La damnation de Faust *see*
La damnation de Faust *see
also* The damnation of
Faust

Der Freischütz *see* Der
Freischütz

Romeo et Juliette *see*
Cornell, John Henry. Romeo
and Juliet

Bernard, William Bayle, 1807-
1875.
The Kentuckian; or, A trip
to New York *see* Paulding,
James Kirke. The lion of the
West

Mesmerism *see* Massey,
Charles. Massey's exhibition
reciter
The nervous man and the man
of nerve. A farce in two
acts *see* The modern
standard drama, vol. 5

The passing cloud. A romantic drama in two acts *see*
The modern standard drama,
vol. 11

Bernard del Carpio *see*
Hemans, Mrs. Felicia
Dorothea Browne *in* Massey,
Charles. Massey's exhibition
reciter

Bernicat, Firmin, 1841-1883.
Fantine *see* Woolf,
Benjamin and Field, Roswell
Martin

Berquin *see* Crane, Elizabeth
Green

Bert, Frederick W., 1838-1916.
Snowflake and the seven
gnomes. A spectacular drama
in five acts. By Howard P.
Taylor and William W.
Randall. Revised by F. W.
Bert. n.p.: n.pub., c1880.
Typescript, prompt-book with
Ms. notes. 21, 20, 26, 23,
20 leaves.

Bertinot, Alfred.
C'est le professeur *see*
Baker, George Melville.
Gustave the professor

Bertram, Eugene, 1872-1941.
The mystic midget's Lili-
putian carnival of nations.
A juvenile fairy spectacle.
A cantata in two acts. New
York: Printed but not pub-
lished, c1895. 32p.
*[joint author: Willard
Bassett; music by J. D.
Smithdeal; without the music]*

Bertram *see* Simms, William
Gilmore

Bertram; or, The castle of St.
Aldobrand *see* Maturin,
Charles Robert *in* The
modern standard drama, vol. 7

Besant, Walter, 1836-1901.
The golden butterfly *see*
Griffith, Frank Carlos *see
also* A streak of luck

The best cure *see* Ingraham,
C. F.

"The best laid plans" *see*
Ford, Paul Leicester

The betrothal *see* Boker,
George Henry *see also*
Fox, H. K.

The betrothed; or, Love in
death *see* Sharswood,
William

Betsey Bobbett *see* Holley,
Marietta

Better late than never *see*
Cannon, Charles James. Collected works. Dramas

The better part *see* Belknap,
Edwin Star and Carnes, Mason

Better than gold *see* Baker,
George Melville

Between love and duty *see*
Rodebaugh, T. Wilson. Josh
Winchester; or, Between
love and duty

Between the acts *see* Griffith,
Benjamin Lease Crozer

Between two fires *see* Serrano,
Thomas K.

Between two foes *see* Heermans,
Forbes

Between two thorns *see*
Heermans, Forbes

Beware of tramps *see* Dumont,
Frank. Too little vagrants;
or, Beware of tramps

The bewitched closet *see*
Lambla, Hattie Lena

Beyond pardon; or, The Countess
of Lynn *see* Beck, William
L.

Beyond the grave *see* Clark,
John Franklin

Beyond the Rockies *see*
Adams, Justin. T'riss; or,
Beyond the Rockies

Bianca. An operatic tragedy
see Alcott, Louisa May
in her Comic tragedies

Bianca Capello *see* Osborn,
Laughton

Bianca Cappello *see* Kinney,
Elizabeth Clementine Dodge

Bianca Visconti *see* Willis,
Nathaniel Parker. Two ways
of dying for a husband

Bianca Visconti; or, The
heart overtasked *see*
Willis, Nathaniel Parker

Bickerstaff, Isaac, c1735-
c1812.
The hypocrite *see* Smith,
Solomon Franklin

The bicyclers *see* Bangs,
John Kendrick

Bidera, Emmanuele.
Gemma di Vergy *see* Révoil,
Bénédict Henry. Gemma of
Vergy

Bidwell, Jeanne Raymond.
Under protest. A comedy in

one act. (Adapted from the
Spanish.) Boston: W. H. Baker,
1896. 14p. (Baker's edition of
plays)

Bien, Herman Milton, 1831-1895.
Easter eve; or, The "New
Hagodoh Shel Pesach." A
metrical family-feast service,
consisting of a prologue and
one character poem; including
the old traditions, legends
and melodies, with supplement
illustration from Oppenheim's
celebrated painting, "The
Passover feast." Cincinnati:
Bloch Pub. and Print. Co.,
1886. 28p.

The feast of lights; or,
Chanukoh. Three character
poems and a grand tableau
finale. Vicksburg: Vicksburg
Print. and Pub. Co., 1885.
27p.

Purim. A series of character-
poems in four parts and tableaux. Cincinnati: Bloch Pub.
and Print. Co., 1889. Second
revised edition. 28p.

Samson and Delilah; or, Dagon
stoops to Sabaoth. A Biblio-
romantic tragedy in five
acts with a prelude. San
Francisco: Commercial Steam
Press, 1860. 79p.

The big banana *see* Sedgwick,
Alfred B.

The big bonanza *see* Daly,
Augustin

A big day in Bulger *see*
McBride, H. Elliott

Big mistake *see* White,
Charles

Big results *see* Sertrew,
Saul. Awful girls; or, Big
results

Bigelow, Walter S.
Dream camp; or, A modern
craze *see* Robinson,
Charles

Biglow papers *see* Massey,
Charles. Massey's exhibition
reciter

Bilhaud, Paul, 1854-1933.
La douche *see* Daly,
Augustin. A wet blanket *in
his* Three preludes to the
play

Ma bru *see* My daughter-
in-law

Bill Detrick; or, The mystery
of Oliver's Ferry *see*
Field, A. Newton

Bill Jepson's wife *see*
Meyers, Robert Cornelius V.
in Dramatic leaflets

The billet doux. A farce
comedy in one act and one
scene. New York: Dick &
Fitzgerald, c1886. 12p.
(Dick's American edition)

Bingham, Clifton, 1859-1913.
'Twas surely fate *see*
Schell, Stanley. An old
maid's conference

Bingham, Frank Lester.
Henry Granden; or, The
unknown heir. A drama in
three acts. Clyde, O.:
Ames, 1875? 25p. (Ames'
series of standard and
minor drama. no. 52)

The birch *see* Phelps,
Lavinia Howe *in her*
Dramatic stories

Bird, Robert Montgomery,
1806-1854.
The cowled lover and other
plays. Princeton: Princeton

Univ. Press, 1941. x, 221p.
(America's lost plays. vol.12)
Contents: The cowled lover.
--Caridorf; The avenger.--
News of the night; or, A trip
to Niagara.--'Twas all for the
best; or, 'Tis all a notion.

Nick of the woods *see* Medina,
Louisa H.

The Bird family and their friends
see Raynor, Verna M.

Bird's Island *see* Toler,
Sallie F.

Birth *see* Fitch, Clyde
The children. Three dialogues

The birth and death of the
prince *see* Block, Louis
James *in his* Capriccios

The birth of Galahad *see*
Hovey, Richard

The birthday cake *see* Tammie,
Carrie

Bishop Hooper *see* Opal (pseud.)
in her The cloud of witnesses

Bispham, David Scull, 1857-1921.
Adelaïde. The romance of
Beethoven's life *see* Howard,
Edmond and Bispham, David
Scull

Bisson, Alexandre Charles
Auguste, 1848-1912.
Feu Toupinel *see* Gillette,
William Hooker. Mr. Wilkin-
son's widow

Jalouse *see* Gillette,
William Hooker. Because she
loved him so

[The man from Mexico] *see*
Du Souchet, Henry A.

[No questions asked] *see*

Rosenfeld, Sydney and Bisson,
Alexandre Charles Auguste

Les surprises du divorce
see Daly, Augustin. The
lottery of love

Le veglione (Le bal masqué)
see Fitch, Clyde. The
masked ball

Un voyage d'agrément *see*
Chisnell, Newton. A pleasure
trip

A bit o' blarney *see* Murphy,
Fitzgerald

A bit of instruction. A little
comedy *see* Sutherland,
Evelyn Greenleaf Baker *in
her* Collected works. Po'
white trash and other one-
act dramas

A bitter dose *see* McBride,
H. Elliott

The bitter end *see* Welcker,
Adair *in his* Romer, King
of Norway and other dramas

Bitter-sweet *see* Holland,
Josiah Gilbert

Bixby, Frank L.
In the wilds of Tennessee.
Brooklyn: n.pub., 1898.
Prompt-book in Ms. 87p.

The little boss. A comedy
drama in four acts. Boston:
W. H. Baker, 1901. 44p.
(Baker's edition of plays)
[earlier copyright: 1900]

Bizet, Georges, 1838-1875.
Carmen *see* Baker,
Theodore

Björnson, Björnstjerne,
1832-1910.
En hanske *see* Sogård,
Peder Thyge Jesper. A glove

The black agate; or, Old foes
with new faces *see* Bowers,
Elizabeth

The black bachelor. Negro farce
in one act. Chicago: Dramatic
Pub. Co., c1898. 7p.

The black barber; or, Humours
of Pompey Suds' shaving
saloon *see* Barnes, James

Black blunders *see* Coes,
George H.

The black brigands *see* Dumont,
Frank

The black chap from Whitechapel
see Williams, Henry Llewellyn

The black chapel of Maryland
see Adams, Charles Frederick.
Rob, the hermit; or, The
black chapel of Maryland

The black chemist *see*
White, Charles

The black crook *see* Barras,
Charles M.

The black crook burlesque *see*
Griffin, George W. H.

A black diamond *see* Orne,
Martha Russell

The black doctor *see*
Aldridge, Ira

Black-ey'd William *see*
White, Charles

The black Forrest *see*
Williams, Henry Llewellyn

The black hussar. (From the
German of Wittmann and
Wohlmuth.) New York?: n.pub.,
188-? Title page lacking.

18p. Libretto. *[Based on Der Feldprediger by Hugo Wittmann and Alois Wohlmuth; music by Karl Millöcker; without the music]* see also Rosenfeld, Sydney

Black justice; or, Half an hour in a Kentucky court house. London and New York: S. French, 189-? 12p.

Black magic see Baker, Robert Melville

De black magician; or, The wonderful beaver see Williams, Henry Llewellyn

Black mail. An original negro comicality in one scene. London and New York: S. French, 18-? 14p. (French's acting edition. Late Lacy's)

The black Ole Bull see Leavitt, Andrew J. and Eagan, H. W.

A black sheep see Hoyt, Charles Hale

The black shoemaker see White, Charles

The black statue see White, Charles

The black statue (revised) see Sheddan, W. B. The joke on Squinim

A black trump see Risdon, Davis

Black vs. white; or, The nigger and the Yankee see Vautrot, George S.

Blackall, Christopher Rubey, 1830-1924. Belshazzar. Rochester: Democrat and Chronicle

Print., 1873. 8p. Title page lacking. *[music composed by James Austin Butterfield; without the music]*

Blackaller, Arthur. The printer and his devils see Moses, David and Blackaller, Arthur

The blackest tragedy of all; or, A peep behind the scenes see Leavitt, Andrew J. and Eagan, H. W.

Blackie, George. The excursion of 4th July, 1860. A heroic poem in nine cantos. By the poet laureate of the Blue Bird Club. Nashville: John T. S. Fall, 1860. 32p.

Blake, G. B. Hamlet; or, The sport, the spook, and the spinster see Batchelder, Samuel Francis

Blanchard, Amy Ella, 1856-1926. Hearts and clubs. A comedy in three acts. Philadelphia: Penn Pub. Co., 1913. 21p. *[earlier copyright: 1896]*

Blanche of Brandywine see Burnett, James Gilbert

Blanche of Devan; or, The death of Roderick Dhu see Steele, Silas Sexton *in his* Collected works. Book of plays

Blanche; or, The rival fairies see Corbyn, Wardle

Blanchette see Aldrich, Thomas Bailey. IV. Scene of Blanchette

Blandin, Isabella Margaret Elizabeth. From Gonzales to San Jacinto...A historical drama of the Texas revolution. Houston: Dealy & Baker, 1897. Title page lacking. 18p.

Blaney, Charles Edward, 1866?-
1944.
A run on the bank. A farcical comedy in three parts.
New York: n.p., 189-. Typescript. Prompt-book. 24,
21, 8 leaves.

Blanks and prizes *see* Smith,
Dexter

Blau, Édouard, 1836-1906.
Werther *see* Ginty, Elizabeth Bealle

Blaze, François Henri Joseph,
called Castil-Blaze, 1784-
1857.
La pie voleuse *see* Coale,
George B. Magpie and the
maid

Bleckley, Paul, 1859-
Thomas A'Becket. Atlanta:
Economical Book and Job
Printing House, 1873. 16p.

Blennerhassett; or, The irony
of fate *see* Pidgin,
Charles Felton

Blennerhassett's island *see*
Piatt, Donn *in his* Various
dramatic works

Blerzy, Jules.
[A mysterious kiss] *see*
A., N.

Blighted buds *see* Addison,
Julia de Wolff Gibbs

The blighted lily *see* Pilgrim, James. The female
highwayman; or, The blighted
lily

The blind *see* Hovey, Richard
in his The plays of Maurice
Maeterlinck [First series]

A blind attachment *see*
Tiffany, Esther Brown

Blind Eva *see* Phelps, Lavinia
Howe *in her* Dramatic stories

The blind girl of Castèl-Cuillè
see Morton, Marguerite W.

Blind Margaret *see* Thompson,
Caroline Eunice

The blind princess *see* Felix,
V. Rev. F.
The shepherdess of Lourdes;
or, The blind princess

Blinks and jinks *see* Leavitt,
Andrew J. and Eagan, H. W.

Bliss, Frank Chapman, fl.1872-
1888.
Lessons of life. A colloquial
poem. [From his: Queen Esther,
and other poems. Newark, N.J.:
F.C. Bliss, 1881. 209p.] p.
102-180.

Queen Esther. A tragic poem.
[From his: Queen Esther, and
other poems. Newark, N.J.:
F.C. Bliss, 1881. 209p.]
p.9-100.

Block, Louis James, 1851-1927.
Capriccios. New York: G.P.
Putnam's Sons, 1898. 130p.
Contents: The birth and
death of the prince.--On the
mountain top.--At the foot of
the rainbow.--Myriad-minded
man: an imaginary conversation.
--The day of days; A prothalamion.

Exile. A dramatic episode. By
Lewis [sic, Louis] J. Block.
St. Louis: G.I. Jones, 1880.
120p.

Blondel *see* Rice, George
Edward

Blood, Henry Ames, 1838-1901?
*[Blood also used pseud.
Raymond Eshobel, q.v.]*
How much I loved thee! New

York: C. M. Green, 1884.
153p.

Lord Timothy Dexter; or,
The greatest man in the
east. A comedy in five
acts. n.p.: n.pub., 1874.
43p.

The Spanish mission; or,
The member from Nevada.
A comedy in five acts.
n.p.: n.pub., c1874. 54p.

The blood-stained boot-jack;
or, The chambermaid's
revenge *see* Carter, John
Henton

Bloomer girls; or, Courtship
in the twentieth century
see Fraser, John Arthur

Blue and cherry; or, Appearances are deceitful *see*
Leland, Oliver Shepard

The blue and gray *see*
Vegiard, J. T. The Dutch
recruit; or, The blue and
gray

The blue and the grey *see*
Harrigan, Edward

Blue Beard *see* Follen, Eliza
Lee Cabot. Home dramas for
young people *see also*
Shields, Sarah Annie Frost

Blue devils *see* Colman,
George *in* The modern
standard drama, vol. 9

Blue jeans *see* Arthur,
Joseph

The blue-stocking *see*
Joseph, Delissa

Bluebeard. (From the French
of Meilhac and Halévy.) New
York: John A. Gray & Green,
1868. Bilingual text: English and French. 39p. Li-

bretto. *[Libretto of Barbe-
bleue, "opera bouffe in four
acts...music by J[acques]
Offenbach." Without the music]*
see also Motley, John Lothrop

Blum, Ernest, 1836-1905.
Rose Michel *see* MacKaye,
James Steele *see also*
MacKaye, James Steele *in his*
An arrant knave & other plays

Blumenthal, Oscar, 1852-1917.
[After business hours] *see*
Daly, Augustin

[Little Miss Million] *see*
Daly, Augustin

[A test case; or, Grass versus
granite] *see* Daly, Augustin

[When I come back]. n.p.:
n.pub., 1900. Typescript and
prompt-book. 41, 45, 38
leaves. (Pag. by act.)
*[joint author: Gustav Kadel-
burg; as of January 19, 1977,
Readex had not supplied Card
1 of this title]*

Blundering Bill *see* Hiland,
Frank E.

Boarding school *see* Leavitt,
Andrew J. and Eagan, H. W.

The boarding schools; or, Life
among the little folks *see*
Payne, John Howard

The boaster rebuked *see*
Denison, Thomas Stewart *in
his* Friday afternoon series
of dialogues

Boasting *see* Abbott, Jacob
in his Orkney the peacemaker;
or, The various ways of
settling disputes

Bob and his siter *see* Denton,
Clara Janetta Fort *in her*
When the lessons are over

Bobby Shaftoe *see* Bunner, Henry Cuyler *in his* Three operettas

Bobolino, the black bandit *see* Williams, Henry Llewellyn

Bocage, Henri, b.1835. Vie à deux *see* Daly, Augustin. Love in tandem

Boccaccio. (From the French of Wälzel and Genée.) Boston: O. Ditson, c1880. 37p. Libretto. *[title page: "Opera comique, in three acts, by Franz von Suppé." Without the music]*

Boccaccio; or, The prince of Palermo *see* Smith, Dexter

Boccherini, Luigi, 1743-1805. [King winter's carnival] *see* Alexander, Sigmund Bowman

The body snatchers *see* Leavitt, Andrew J.

Boero, Giuseppe, 1814-1884. La vocazione di San Luigi Gonzaga alla compagnia di Gesù *see* The vocation of St. Aloysius

The bogus injun *see* White, Charles

The bogus talking machine; or, The puzzled Dutchman *see* White, Charles

Bohemia *see* Fitch, Clyde

The Bohemian girl *see* Kellogg, Clara Louise

The Bohemians *see* Cowley, E. J.

Bohrmann, Heinrich, 1842-1908. Das Spitzentuch der Königin *see* Elson, Louis Charles.

The queen's lace handkerchief

Boieldieu, François Adrien, 1775-1834. La dame blanche *see* The white lady

Le petit chaperon rouge *see* F., W. F. The little red riding hood

Boker, George Henry, 1823-1890. Anne Boleyn. A tragedy. Philadelphia: A. Hart, 1850. 225p.

The betrothal. [From his: Plays and poems. Boston: Ticknor and Fields, 1857. Second edition. 2 vols.] vol. 2, p.1-122.

The betrothal. Philadelphia: Chestnut St. Theatre, 1871. Prompt-book, interleaved with Ms. notes. 122p.

Calaynos. A tragedy. Philadelphia: E. H. Butler, 1848. 218p.

Calaynos. A tragedy in five acts. London: G. H. Davidson, 1849. Prompt-book, interleaved with Ms. notes. 64p.

Francesca da Rimini. [From his: Plays and poems. Boston: Ticknor and Fields, 1857. Second edition. 2 vols.] vol. 1, p.347-474.

Francesca da Rimini. A tragedy in five acts. Chicago: Dramatic Pub. Co., 1901. 154p. (Greenroom edition of plays)

Glaucus & other plays. By Sculley Bradley, editor. Princeton: Princeton Univ. Press, 1940. xiv, 228p. (America's lost plays, vol. 3) Contents: The world a mask. --The bankrupt.--Glaucus.

Königsmark. [From his: Königsmark; or, The legend of the hounds, and other poems. Philadelphia: J. B. Lippincott, 1869. 244p.] p.7-156.

Leonor de Guzman. A tragedy.
[From his: Plays and poems.
Boston: Ticknor and Fields,
1857. Second edition. 2
vols.] vol. 1, p.235-345.

The podesta's daughter. A
dramatic sketch. [From his:
Plays and poems. Boston:
Ticknor and Fields, 1857.
Second edition. 2 vols.]
vol. 2, p.225-253.

The widow's marriage. [From
his: Plays and poems. Boston: Ticknor and Fields,
1857. Second edition, 2
vols.] vol. 2, p.123-221.

Bolts and bars *see* Shields,
Sarah Annie Frost

Boltwood, Edward, 1870-1924.
Balm of Gilead. A mixed
foursome in one act. New
York: De Witt Pub. House,
c1899. 18p. (De Witt's
acting plays. no. 412)

Bombastes furioso *see*
Rhodes, William Barnes *in*
Massey, Charles. Massey's
exhibition reciter

Bonbons *see* Baker, George
Melville

The bondmaid *see* Putnam,
Mary Trail Spence Lowell

The bondman. n.p.: n.pub.,
n.d. Typescript. 39, 34, 57,
40 leaves. (Paged by act.)

The bondman of Kent *see*
Conrad, Robert Taylor.
Aylmere; or, The bondman
of Kent

Bone squash *see* White,
Charles

The bonnie lass of Brittany

see Hardman, Richard. The
pigeons; or, The bonnie lass
of Brittany

The book of Esther *see*
Willner, Wolff

The bootblack *see* Denison,
Thomas Stewart *in his*
Wide awake dialogues *see
also* Phelps, Lavinia Howe
in her Dramatic stories

Booth, Edwin, 1833-1893.
The miscellaneous plays of
Edwin Booth. By William
Winter, editor. Philadelphia:
Penn Pub. Co., 1899. (vol. 3,
Supplement to Shakespearean
plays of...) 104, 96, 84,
57, 78p.
Contents: Richelieu *[by
Edward George Earle Lytton
Bulwer-Lytton].*--The fool's
revenge *[by Tom Taylor].*--
Brutus *[by John Howard Payne,
James Stark, and John Mc-
Cullough].*--Ruy Blas *[by
Victor Hugo].*--Don Caesar de
Bazan *[by Philippe François
Pinel Dumanois and Adolphe
Philippe Dennery].*

The Shakespearean plays of
Edwin Booth. By William
Winter, editor. Philadelphia:
Penn Pub. Co., 1899. vol. 1:
136, 104, 119, 104, 109p.;
vol. 2: 125, 72, 111, 71, 94,
50p.
Contents: vol. 1: Hamlet.--
Macbeth.--King Lear.--Julius
Caesar.--Merchant of Venice.
vol. 2: Othello.--Richard II.
--Richard III.--Henry VIII.
--Much ado about nothing.--
Katharine and Petruchio.

Booth, Helen.
After twenty years *see*
Dramatic leaflets

At the "Red Lion" *see*
Dramatic leaflets

An electric episode *see*
Dramatic leaflets

A fifty-dollar milliner's
bill *see* Dramatic
leaflets

Boothman, William.
His last scout. A military
drama in two acts. Chicago:
n.pub., c1887. 8p.

The border chief *see* Lawson,
James. Liddesdale; or, The
border chief

Border land *see* Townsend,
Charles

The border orphan *see*
O'Leary, James. Ellie Laura;
or, The border orphan

Bornier, Henri de, 1825-1901.
Le monde renversé *see*
Bunner, Henry Cuyler. A
courtship with variations
see also in Matthews,
Brander. Comedies for
amateur acting

A borrowed luncheon *see*
Griffith, Helen Sherman

A borrowed umbrella *see*
Tiffany, Esther Brown

Borrowing trouble *see*
Denison, Thomas Stewart

Boston and banditti *see*
Woodward, Matthew C. Ro-
sita; or, Boston and
banditti

The Boston dip *see* Baker,
George Melville

Boston in 1775 *see* Glover,
Stephen E. The cradle of
liberty; or, Boston in 1775

Botany Bay *see* Tees, Levin
C.

Both alike *see* Salmon, John.
Old and young; or, Both alike

Both sides of good society *see*
Mathews, Cornelius. False
pretences; or, Both sides of
good society

Both sides of the counter *see*
Mathews, Frances Aymar

Bothwell *see* De Peyster, John
Watts

The bottle imp. A dramatic spectacle in two acts [From R. B.
Peake's play of the same
title] Philadelphia: Frederick
Turner, 184-? 35p. *[The title
page incorrectly gives author
as Richard Brinsley Peake;
this should read Robert Brinsley Peake]*

The bottom of the sea *see*
Jackson, N. Hart

Boucicault, Dion, 1820-1890.
The Corsican brothers *see*
Griffin, George W. H. Corsican
twins

London assurance *see* The
modern standard drama, vol. 4

Old heads and young hearts
see The modern standard
drama, vol. 8

The poor of New York *see*
Williams, Frederick. The
streets of New York

Rip Van Winkle *see* Jefferson,
Joseph and Boucicault, Dion

Bouffer and breeze *see* Mansfield, Richard

Bouilly, Jean Nicholas, 1763-
1842.
L'abbé de L'Épée *see* The
lost heir; or, The abbé de
L'Épée

Léonore, ou l'amour conjugal

see Fidelio; or, Constancy
rewarded

The bould boy of the mountain
see Pilgrim, James. Shandy
Maguire; or, The bould boy
of the mountain

Bounce *see* White, Charles
One, two, three

Bound by an oath *see* Hildreth, David W.

The boundary line *see*
Steele, Silas Sexton. Two
families in one room; or,
The boundary line *in his*
Collected works. Book of
plays

Bouquet *see* Woodward, John A.

Bowers, E.
The man about town. A negro
farce in one act. Boston:
W. H. Baker, 1894. 10p.
(Baker's darkey plays)

Bowers, Elizabeth.
The black agate; or, Old foes
with new faces. A play in
five acts. Philadelphia:
(for the author) U.S. Steam-
Power Book and Job Printing,
1859. *[From Charles Kingsley's novel, Hypatia]*

Bowler, Rev. G.
The try company *see* A
collection of temperance
dialogues

Box and Cox *see* Christy,
Edwin Byron

A box of monkeys *see* Furniss,
Grace Livingston

Boxer, James.
Sacred dramas. Boston: Lee
and Shepard, 1875. 174p.
Contents: Naaman, the
Syrian.--Finding of Moses.--
Jephthah's daughter.

The boy and the purse *see*
Steele, Silas Sexton. The
Yankee tar's return; or, The
boy and the purse *in his*
Collected works. Book of plays

The boy martyrs of Sept. 12, 1814
see Tayleure, Clifton W.

Boy who was a coward *see*
Denison, Thomas Stewart *in
his* Wide awake dialogues

Boyesen, Hjalmar Hjorth, 1848-
1895.
Alpine roses. A romantic play
in two acts. New York: Printed
privately for...M. H. Mallory,
1883. 56p. *[music by Frank A.
Howson; without the music]*

The boys of Kilkenny *see*
Walsh, Townsend

A boy's rehearsal *see* McBride,
H. Elliott

Bozzaris *see* Deering, Nathaniel

Brachvogel, Albert Emil, 1824-
1878.
Narciss *see* Schönberg, James.
Narcisse the vagrant

Bradbury, Louise A.
Game of dominoes. A comedy in
one act. Boston: Walter H.
Baker, 1885. 28p. *[from the
French of Louis-Émile Dubry]*

Bradbury, Sophia Louise Appleton.
The pirate. A serio-comic opera
in three acts. Cambridge:
Printed for the author by Welch,
Bigelow, 1865. 55p. *[title page:
"the music partly original, but
chiefly...from Mozart, Rossini,
Donizetti, Verdi, etc., and
from old English ballads";
without the music]*

Braddon, Mary Elizabeth, 1837-
1915.

Marjorie Daw. A domestic comedietta in two acts. New York: Dramatic Pub. Co., c1885. 13p. (De Witt's acting plays. no. 338) *[title page: prepared for the American stage by Henry Llewellyn Williams]*

Bradley, A. F.
The bridal wine cup *see* Dramatic leaflets

The premature proposal *see* Dramatic leaflets

Bradley, Nellie H.
The first glass; or, The power of woman's influence [and] The young teetotaler; or, Saved at last. Rockland, Maine: Z. Pope Vose, 1868. p.1-19, 20-25. (New temperance dialogues)

Marry no man if he drinks; or, Laura's plan, and how it succeeded. Rockland, Maine: Z. Pope Vose, 1868. 24p. (New temperance dialogues) *see also* A collection of temperance dialogues

Reclaimed; or, The danger of moderate drinking. Rockland, Maine: Z. Pope Vose, 1868. 23p. (New temperance dialogues)

The stumbling block; or, Why a deacon gave up his wine. Rockland, Maine: Z. Pope Vose, 1871. 33p. (New temperance dialogues)

A temperance picnic with the old woman who lived in a shoe. New York: National Temperance Society and Publication House, 1888. 45p. *[contains music, but with no indication of its composer]*

Wine as a medicine; or, Abbie's experience. Rockland,

Maine: Z. Pope Vose, 1873. 22p. (New temperance dialogues)

Brady, William A., 1863-1950.
Lights of London. [From a play by George R. Sims] n.p.: n.pub., 1895. Prompt-book in Ms. 26, 14, 6, 26, 12, 19 leaves. (Paged by act)

The wages of sin. By Frank Harvey. n.p.: n.pub., 18-? Prompt-book in Ms. 38, 42, 44, 37, 15, 3 leaves. (Paged by act)

Braeme, Charlotte Mary *see* Brame, Charlotte Mary

Brame, Charlotte Mary, 1836-1884.
Beyond pardon; or, The Countess of Lynn *see* Beck, William L. *[Charlotte Mary Brame is the real name of Bertha M. Clay]*

Brangonar *see* Calvert, George Henry

Brann, William Cowper, 1855-1898.
That American woman. [In: Brann the playwright with... By E. G. Fletcher and J. L. Hart, editors. Austin: Univ. of Texas, 1941. 68p.] 68p.

Brantley *see* Lynd, William John

Brass buttons *see* Luce, Grace A.

A brass monkey *see* Hoyt, Charles Hale

Brave little Mary *see* Denton, Clara Janetta Fort *in her* From tots to teens

A brave man *see* Campbell, Bartley Theodore

Brayley, Arthur Wellington,
1863-1919.
Beatrice. By ?. Boston: N.
Wilson, 1892. 67 unnumbered
pages.

The brazen drum; or, The Yankee
in Poland see Steele, Silas
Sexton

Brazzà-Savorgnan, Cora Ann
Slocomb, Contesa di, 1862-?.
A literary farce. By The
Countess di Brazzà (Cora
Slocomb). Boston: Arena Pub.
Co., 1896. 36p.

A breach of promise. An original burletta in three acts.
New Haven: Tuttle, Morehouse
& Taylor, 1876. 22p. [title
page: "written and arranged
for the Yale Thanksgiving
Jubilee, by a member of '77"]

Bread on the waters see
Baker, George Melville see
also McBride, H. Elliott
in his New dialogues

Breaking his bonds see
Dale, Horace C.

Breaking the ban see
Williams, Henry Llewellyn.
L'article 47; or, Breaking
the ban

Breaking up the exhibition
see McBride, H. Elliott
in his New dialogues

Breck, Joseph.
West Point; or, A tale of
treason. An historical drama,
in three acts. Baltimore:
Bull & Tuttle, 1840. 22p.
[title page: "dramatised
from Ingraham's Romance of
American history...with a
prologue by John H. Hewitt
...epilogue by R. Horace
Pratt."]

A breezy call see Townsend,
Charles

Breezy Point see Locke,
Belle Marshall

Bremer, Fredrika, 1801-1865.
Trälinnan see Putnam, Mary
Trail Spence Lowell. The
bondmaid

Brewster, Emma E.
Aunt Mehetible's scientific
experiment. A farce in one
act for female characters
only. Boston: W. H. Baker,
1901 (copyright 1880). 11p.
(Baker's edition of plays)

Beresford benevolent society.
A farce in one act. Boston:
W. H. Baker, 1906. 22p.
(Baker's edition of plays)
[joint author: Lizzie B.
Scribner; earlier copyright:
1885]

A dog that will fetch will
carry. A farce in two scenes
for female characters only.
Boston: W. H. Baker, 1901
(copyright 1880). 37p.
(Baker's edition of plays)

The Christmas box. [From:
Christmas entertainments for
school and home...by Jay
Kaye. Boston: W. H. Baker,
c1887. 104p.] p.37-56.

Eliza's bona-fide offer. A
farce in one act for female
characters only. Boston:
W. H. Baker, 1901 (copyright
1880). 12p. (Baker's edition
of plays)

How the colonel proposed. A
farce in three scenes. Boston:
W. H. Baker, 1901 (copyright
1880). 19p. (Baker's edition
of plays)

Parlor varieties. Plays,
pantomimes and charades.
Boston: Lee and Shepard,

c1880. 261p.
Contents: My sister's husband.--The Christmas box.--The free ward.--Jane's legacy.--Aunt Mehetible's scientific experiment.--A pretty piece of property.--Poor Peter.--The Don's stratagem.--How the colonel proposed.--Elizabeth Carisbrooke with a "P".--Eliza's bona-fide offer.--Zerubbabel's second wife.--A dog that will fetch will carry.--Charade: Holidays.--Charade: Cent-any-all-Centennial.--Pantomime: Arabella and Lionel.--A bunch of buttercups.

Zerubbabel's second wife. A farce in one act. Boston: Walter H. Baker, 1880. 15p. (Baker's edition of plays)

Brian *see* MacSwiney, Paul

Brian O'Linn. A farce in two acts. New York: S. French, 187-? 16p. (French's American drama. The acting edition. no. 16) *[Readex also enters this title under Samuel D. Johnson, q.v.]*

The bridal *see* Knowles, James Sheridan *in* The modern standard drama, vol. 6

The bridal of the borders *see* The rose of Ettrick Vale; or, The bridal of the borders

The bridal trap *see* Rosenfeld, Sydney

The bridal wine cup *see* Bradley, A. F. *in* Dramatic leaflets

The bride-elect *see* Sousa, John Philip

A bride in a barrack room *see* Steele, Silas Sexton. The soldier's wife; or, A bride in a barrack room *in his* Collected works. Book of plays.

The bride of Fort Edward *see* Bacon, Delia Salter

Bride roses *see* Howells, William Dean

Bridegroom *see* Shields, Sarah Annie Frost *in her* Parlor charades and proverbs

Bridgeman, John Vipon, 1819-1889.
Puritan's daughter *see* Puritan's daughter

Bridges, Robert, 1858-1941.
Overheard in Arcady. New York: Charles Scribner's Sons, 1894. 133p.
Contents: The household of W. D. Howells.--The household of Henry James.--The household of Thomas Bailey Aldrich.--The household of Frank R. Stockton.--The household of Richard Harding Davis.--The household of F. Marion Crawford.--The household of Rudyard Kipling.--The household of George Meredith.--The household of Robert Louis Stevenson.--The household of James M. Barrie.--The home of romance.--A little dinner in Arcady.

Bridget Branagan's troubles; or, The masquerade ball *see* Haskett, Emmett

Brier, Warren Judson, 1850-1929.
Jedediah Judkins, J. P. A drama in four acts. Chicago: T. S. Denison, c1888. 62p. (Alta series)

A soldier of fortune. A
modern comedy-drama in five
acts. Chicago: T. S. Denison,
c1909. 50p. (Amateur series)
[earlier copyright: 1881]

Les brigands. Opera buffe in
three acts. (From the French
of Meilhac and Halévy.)
(Music by Offenbach.) New
York: Metropolitan Job
Printing and Engraving
Establishment, 1870. Bi-
lingual text: French and
English. 64, 5p. Libretto.
*[Libretto of Les brigands
by Ludovic Halévy and Henri
Meilhac, with music by
Jacques Offenbach]*

Brigham Young; or, The prophet's last love *see*
McKinley, Henry J.

The bright and dark sides of
girl-life in India *see*
Phillips, Ida Orissa

Bright Bohemia *see* Nobles,
Milton. Interviews; or,
Bright Bohemia

Brincklé, J. G.
The Electra of Sophocles.
Philadelphia: John Campbell,
1873. 92p.

Bringing back the sunshine
see Phelps, Lavinia Howe
in her Dramatic stories

Brinton, Daniel Garrison,
1837-1899.
Maria Candelaria. An historical drama from American
aboriginal life. Philadelphia: D. McKay, 1897. xxix,
98p.

Bristow, George Frederick,
1825-1898.
Rip Van Winkle *see* Shannon,
J. W. *see also* Wainwright,

John Howard

The British slave; or, Seven
years of a soldier's life
see Howe, J. Burdette

Broad, John Astor.
Columbia *see* Estabrook,
Jonas E.

Broadhurst, George Howells,
1866-1952.
The red knight. A comedy in
four acts. n.p.: n.pub.,
n.d. Typescript. In four
acts (paged by acts.)

What happened to Jones. An
original farce in three acts.
New York: S. French, c1910.
107p. (French's standard
library edition)

Why Smith left home. An
original farce in three acts.
New York: S. French, c1912.
112p. (French's standard
library edition)

The wrong Mister Wright. An
original comedy in three
acts. New York: S. French,
c1918. 93p. (French's standard library edition)

Broken bonds *see* Hiland,
Frank E.

Broken fetters *see* Townsend,
Charles

The broken home *see* Wilkins,
W. Henri. Three glasses a
day; or, The broken home

Broken links *see* Barr, E.
Nelson

Broken promises *see* Cook,
S. N.

Broken trust *see* Winslow,
Catherine Mary Reignolds

Brokmeyer, Henry Conrad, 1826-

1906.
A foggy night at Newport.
St. Louis, Mo.: Printed by
W. E. Foote, 1860. 39p.
*[Readex also enters this
play under title]*

Brontë, Charlotte, 1816-1855.
Jane Eyre *see* Venable,
William Henry. The little
dependent *in his* The
school stage

Brooke, Van Dyke。
The quicksands of Gotham.
A drama in prologue and
three acts. Boston: W. H。
Baker, 1899。43p. (Baker's
edition of plays)

Brooks, Byron Alden, 1845-1911.
King Saul. A tragedy. New
York: Nelson & Phillips,
1876. 144p.

Brooks, Charles Timothy, 1813-
1883.
Faust. Boston: Ticknor and
Fields, 1856. 234p. *[trans-
lated from the German of
Goethe]*

William Tell. A drama in
five acts. (From the German
of Schiller.) Providence:
B. Cranston, 1838. 120p.
*[based on Schiller's Wil-
helm Tell]*

Brooks, E. S. *see* Brooks,
Elbridge Streeter

Brooks, Edward, b.1868?.
Mary Stuart. (From the
German of Schiller.) Phila-
delphia: David McKay, c1898。
165p。*[based on Schiller's
Maria Stuart]*

Brooks, Elbridge Streeter,
1846-1902.
David the son of Jesse; or,
The peasant, the princess
and the prophet. A sacred

operetta in two parts...music
by E. C. Phelps. Brooklyn:
E。C. Phelps, c1883. 35p.
*[music by Ellsworth C. Phelps;
without the music]*

A dream of the centuries *see*
Bartlett, George Bradford. A
dream of the centuries and
other entertainments for
parlor and hall

Brooks, F. M.
Mitsu-yu-nissi; or, The Japa-
nese wedding *see* Scudder,
Vida Dutton and Brooks, F. M.

Brother against brother *see*
Moore, Bernard Francis

Brothers in name *see* Milner,
Frances S.

The brothers of Padua *see*
Steele, Silas Sexton. The
well of death; or, The
brothers of Padua *in his*
Collected works. Book of
plays

Broughall, George.
The tearful and tragical tale
of the tricky troubadour; or,
The truant tracked. A four
act burlesque in grand opera.
Winnipeg: Off. of the Manitoba
Free Press, 1886。34p. *[title
page: music from Verdi's
opera, "Il Trovatore." Without
the music]*

Brown, Abbie Farwell, d.1927.
Quits. A comedy in one act.
Boston: W. H. Baker, 1896.
21p. (Baker's edition of
plays)

Brown, Charles Hovey.
Elfins and mermaids; or, The
red rock wave cruiser. A
serio-comic opera and nautical
burlesque...in two acts. New
York: A. S. Seer's Engraving
and Printing Establishment,

1881. 42p. Libretto.
[music by the author; with-
out the music. This work
also appears under title,
The red rock wave]

Moses. Boston: Gorham Press,
Richard G. Badger, 1902. 69p.

The red rock wave. Albany:
Argus, 1880. 20p. Libretto.
[music by the author; with-
out the music. This work
also appears under title,
Elfins and mermaids; or,
The red rock wave cruiser]

Brown, David Paul, 1795-1872.
The prophet of St. Paul's.
A play in five acts. Philadelphia: Carey & Hart, 1836.
50p.

Brown, J. H.
Katrina's little game. A
Dutch act with songs and a
dance. New York: R. M.
De Witt, c1876. 8p. (De
Witt's Ethiopian and comic
drama. no. 103)

Brown, J. S.
A southern rose. A military
drama. Clyde, O.: Ames,
c1899. 25p. (Ames' series
of standard and minor drama.
no. 409)

Brown, John Henry.
Julian. [From his: Poems,
lyrical and dramatic.
Ottawa: J. Durie & Sons,
1892. 204p.] p.55-64.

A mad philosopher. [From
his: Poems, lyrical and
dramatic. Ottawa: J. Durie
& Sons, 1892. 204p.] p.103-
204.

Brown, Marsden.
A modern proposal. Duologue
in one act. Chicago: Dramatic
Pub. Co., c1897. 11p. (American amateur drama)

Brown, S. J.
In the enemy's camp; or,
Stolen despatches. A drama
in three acts. Boston: W. H.
Baker, c1889. 33p. (Baker's
edition of plays)

A brown paper parcel *see*
W., J. M. *see also* Williams,
Marie Josephine

Browne, Frances Elizabeth.
Ruth. [From her: Ruth: a
sacred drama and original
lyrical poems. New York:
Wynkoop & Hallenbeck, 1871]
p.4-30.

Browne, Irving, 1835-1899.
Doctor Polyanthus; or, Where
there's a will there's a way.
A farce in two acts. Troy,
New York: Troy Book Printing
House, 18-? 53p.

Our best society. Being an
adaptation of the Potiphar
Papers in four acts. Troy,
New York: Privately printed,
1868. 50p. *[an adaptation of*
the Potiphar papers, by
George William Curtis]

The suitors. New York: G. P.
Putnam and Sons, 1871. 79p.
[title page: translated...
from the French of Racine.
author's preface: constructed
from Wasps of Aristophanes]

Browne, M. C.
The landlord's revenge; or,
Uncle Tom up to date. A farce
in two scenes. Clyde, O.:
Ames, 1894. 9p. (Ames' series
of standard and minor drama.
no. 328)

Browne, W. Gault.
Ripples. A farce in one act.
Clyde, O.: Ames, 1886. 8p.
(Ames' series of standard
and minor drama. no. 180)

Browne, William Maynadier.
A fool for luck. A comedy in
two acts. Boston: W. H.
Baker, c1889. 28p. (Baker's
edition of plays) [the
original title of this play
was "B. B. & P."]

Red or white? A decision in
one act. Boston: Walter H.
Baker, 1893. 10p. (Baker's
edition of plays)

The trustee. A play in four
acts. Boston: W. H. Baker,
c1891. 38p. (Baker's edition
of plays)

Brownson, Orestes Augustus,
1803-1876.
Simpson. A comic dramina.
Dubuque: n.pub., n.d. 32p.

The Bruce see Opal (pseud.)
in her The cloud of wit-
nesses

Bruised and cured see White,
Charles

Brunnhofer, Will H.
Our hotel; or, Rats, the
bell boy. A farce in one
act. Clyde, O.: Ames,
c1894. 14p. (Ames' series
of standard and minor drama.
no. 340)

Brunswick, Herman.
Amina; or, The Shah's bride.
An original Persian comic
opera in two acts...composed
by Frederick Wink. Phila-
delphia: n.pub., c1890. 32p.
[without the music]

Brutus see Payne, John
Howard in Booth, Edwin.
The miscellaneous plays of
Edwin Booth

Brutus; or, The fall of Tarquin see Payne, John
Howard in The modern
standard drama, vol. 8

Bryant, Daniel, 1833-1875.
The live injin; or, Jim Crow
see White, Charles

The buccaneer of the Gulf see
Pilgrim, James. Yankee Jack;
or, The buccaneer of the Gulf

Bucer see Opal (pseud.) in her
The cloud of witnesses

Buckstone, John Baldwin, 1802-
1879.
The drunkard's story see
Massey, Charles. Massey's
exhibition reciter

Leap year; or, The ladies'
privilege. A comedy in three
acts see The modern standard
drama, vol. 11

The queen of a day see The
queen of a day

The rough diamond see Dramatic leaflets

The Bucktails; or, Americans in
England see Paulding, James
Kirke and Paulding, William
Irving in their Collected
works. American comedies

Buddha see Hartmann, Sadakichi

Budworth, James, 1831-1875.
The first night see White,
Charles

Buel, David Hillhouse, 1862-1923.
Penikeese; or, Cuisine and
cupid. An entirely original
comic opera in two acts...
music by Thos. G. Shepard.
New York: Wm. A. Pond, c1882.
36p. [without the music]

Bürstenbinder, Elisabeth, 1838-
1918.
Vineta see Mayo, Frank and
Wilson, John G. Nordeck

Buffington, George E. C.
A game of chess. A powerfully

mis-constructed comic
operatic spectacular bur-
lesque extravaganza in four
acts. Providence: Providence
Press, 1875. 17p.

Bullock, Cynthia, b.1821.
Dialogue. Poet and musician.
[From her: Washington and
other poems. New York:
Published for the author
[by] Reid & Cunningham,
1847. 108p.] p.71-73.

The bumblebee see Phelps,
Lavinia Howe in her
Dramatic stories

Bumble's courtship see
Dialogues dramatized from
the works of Charles Dickens

Bunce, Oliver Bell, 1828-1890.
Fate; or, The prophecy. A
tragedy. New York: For
private circulation, 1856.
74p.

Love in '76. Comedietta in
two acts. New York: S.
French, 18-? 22p. (The
minor drama. no. 111)

A bunch of buttercups see
Brewster, Emma E. in her
Parlor varities

A bunch of keys; or, The hotel
see Hoyt, Charles Hale and
Edouin, Winnie

A bunch of roses see Davis,
Mary Evelyn Moore see also
Felter, Will D.

Bunn, Alfred, 1796?-1860.
The Bohemian girl see
Kellogg, Clara Louise

Bunner, Henry Cuyler, 1855-
1896 [see also Oakes, A. H.
(pseud.)]
A bad case. An original
comedy in one act. Boston:

W. H. Baker, c1879. 22p.
(Baker's edition of plays)
[joint author: Julian Magnus]
see also Magnus, Julian and
Bunner, Henry Cuyler in
Matthews, Brander. Comedies
for amateur acting

A courtship with variations.
Comedy in one act for one
male and one female. New York:
Edgar S. Werner, c1879. 36p.
[based on Le monde renverse,
by Henri de Bornier] see
also Matthews, Brander.
Comedies for amateur acting

Les Fourchambault see
Magnus, Julian and Bunner,
Henry Cuyler

The seven conversations of
dear Jones and Baby Van
Rensselaer see Matthews,
Brander and Bunner, Henry
Cuyler

The seven old ladies of
Lavender Town. New York and
London: Harper & Brothers,
c1879. 37p. Libretto.
[music by Oscar Weil; without
the music]

Three operettas. New York:
Harper & Brothers, 1897.
163p. Vocal score.
Contents: The three little
kittens of the land of Pie.--
The seven old ladies of
Lavender Town.--Bobby Shaftoe.
[music by Oscar Weil]

The buntling ball see Fawcett,
Edgar

Buoyant see Bell, Lucia Chase
in Bartlett, George Bradford.
A dream of the centuries and
other entertainments for
parlor and hall

Burani, Urbain Rocoux, called
Paul, 1845-1901.
Fantine see Woolf, Benjamin
Edward and Field, Roswell
Martin

Le roi malgré lui *see*
Goodwin, John Cheever. The
merry monarch

Burdette, Thomas *see* Howe,
J. Burdette

The burglar alarm *see*
Griffith, Helen Sherman

Burglar to slow music *see*
Thomas, F. J. Commercial
infidelity; or, Burglar
to slow music

Burglars *see* Julian, Robert

Burgwyn, Collison Pierrepont
Edwards, 1852-1915.
The lost diamond. Richmond,
Va.: J. W. Randolph, 1894.
23p.

Buried treasure; or, The
Connecticut buccaneers *see*
Greene, R. F.

Burke, Charles, 1822-1854.
Rip Van Winkle; a legend of
the Catskills. A romantic
drama in two acts. (Adapted
from Washington Irving's
Sketch Book.) New York:
S. French, 186-? 27p.
(French's standard drama.
Acting edition. no. 174)

Burke, James.
Shannon boys; or, Mount
Shannon. A romantic Irish
drama in three acts. Chi-
cago: Dramatic Pub. Co.,
c1895. 27p. (Sergel's
acting drama. no. 402)

Burkhardt, Charles B.
Der Freischütz. (From the
German of Kind.) New York:
Wynkoop, Hollenbeck &
Thomas, c1856. Bilingual
text: English and German.
16, 4p. Libretto. *[libretto
of Der Freyschütz by Fried-*

*rich Kind; music by Karl Maria
Friedrich Ernst von Weber.
Without the music]*

Burleigh, George S.
The conqueror conquered *see*
Dramatic leaflets

Burleigh, William Henry, 1812-
1871.
Dramatic sketch. [From his:
Poems. Philadelphia: J. Miller
M'Kim, 1841. 248p.] p.187-194.

Burlesque circus *see* White,
Charles. Hippotheatron; or,
Burlesque circus

Burnand, Francis Cowley, 1836-
1917.
B. B. *see* Williams, Henry
Llewellyn. The black chap
from Whitechapel

Cox and Box *see* Christy,
Edwin Byron

Sullivan the slugger *see*
Sullivan the slugger

Villikins and his Dinah *see*
Griffin, Caroline Stearns.
Villikins and his Diniah *see
also* White, Charles. Vilikens
and Dinah

Burnett, Frances Hodgson, 1849-
1924.
Editha's burglar *see* Thomas,
Augustus and Smith, Edgar
McPhail

Esmeralda. A comedy drama in
four acts founded on the
story of the same name. New
York and London: S. French,
c1881-1909. 59p. *[joint
author: William Hooker
Gillette]*

Esmeralda. New York: Madison
Square Theatre, 1881. 124p.
*[joint author: William Hooker
Gillette]*

Little Lord Fauntleroy. A

drama in three acts founded
on the story of the same
name. New York: S. French,
1889. 60p. (French's international copyrighted
edition of the works of the
best authors. no. 42)

Burnett, James Gilbert.
Blanche of Brandywine. An
American patriotic spec-
tacle. New York: S. French,
1858. Prompt-book. 73p.
(French's standard drama.
The acting edition. no. 206)

Burr and Hamilton see Dowd,
Jerome

Burton, Mrs. Henry S.
Don Quixote de la Mancha.
(From Cervantes' novel.)
San Francisco: J. H. Car-
many, 1876. 63p.

Burton, James.
In the wrong clothes. A
farce in one act. Clyde,
O.: Ames, 1842? 16p.
(Ames' series of standard
and minor drama. no. 95)

Busch, William, b.1836.
The dawn of liberty; or,
Cadunt regum coranae; vicit
libertas. An original drama,
serio-comical in three
acts. By Prometheus (pseud.)
Chicago: Co-operative
Print., 1869. 48p.

The maid of the lighthouse.
A drama in three acts. n.p.:
n.pub., 1879. Title page
lacking. 36p.

Sorosis; or, The onward
march to freedom. A drama
in four acts. Chicago: S. S.
Jones, 1868. 47p.

Tell tale eyes; or, Daisy
and Don. A drama in four
acts. n.p.: n.pub., c1879.
37p.

That guilty pair; or, A
paroxysm of passion. A
comedietta in one act. St.
Louis: n.pub., c1894.
8 unnumbered leaves.

Bushby (pseud.)
A night in Buenos Ayres.
A new drama in five acts.
Washington, D.C.: A. L.
Settle, 1854. 46p.

But once a year see Denton,
Clara Janetta Fort. When
the lessons are over

Butterfield, James Austin,
1837-1891.
Belshazzar see Blackall,
Christopher Rubey

The butterflies see Carleton,
Henry Guy

The butterflies' carnival see
Baker, George Melville.
Titania; or, The butterflies'
carnival

Butternut's bride see Tees,
Levin C. She would be a
widow; or, Butternut's bride

Buxton, Ida M.
Carnival of days. Clyde, O.:
Ames, 1888. 10p. (Ames'
series of standard and
minor drama. no. 250) [cover
title: Festival of days]

Cousin John's album. Clyde,
O.: Ames, 1888. 7p. (Ames'
series of standard and
minor drama. no. 260)

Festival of days see her
Carnival of days

How she has her own way. An
interlude in one scene.
Clyde, O.: Ames, 18-? 5p.
(Ames' series of standard
and minor drama. no. 50)

Matrimonial bliss. A scene
from real life. Clyde, O.:

Ames, 1884. 6p. (Ames'
series of standard and
minor drama. no. 139)

On to victory. Temperance
cantata. Clyde, O.: Ames,
c1887. 13p. (Ames' series
of standard and minor drama.
no. 215)

Our awful aunt. A comic
drama in two acts. Clyde,
O.: Ames, c1885. 12p.
(Ames' series of standard
and minor drama. no. 146)

A sewing circle of the
period. An original farce
in one act. Clyde, O.:
Ames, c1884. 7p. (Ames'
series of standard and
minor drama. no. 138)

Taking the census. Original
farce in one act. Clyde,
O.: Ames, 1883. 6p. (Ames'
series of standard and
minor drama. no. 137)

Tit for tat. An original
sketch in one scene. Clyde,
O.: Ames, c1884. 8p.
(Ames' series of standard
and minor drama. no. 142)

Why they joined the Rebeccas. An original farce in
one act. Clyde, O.: Ames,
c1885. 5p. (Ames' series
of standard and minor
drama. no. 155)

Buzzell, Arthur L.
Captain Dick; or, Our war
correspondent. An original
comedy drama in three acts.
New York: Dick & Fitz-
gerald, 1899. 38p.

By force of impulse see
Vogt, Harry V.

By force of love; or, Wedded
and parted see Goddard,
Edward

By special desire. A drawing-
room monologue. Chicago:
Dramatic Pub. Co., 189-? 5p.

By telephone see Hageman,
Maurice

Byars, William Vincent, b.1857.
Tannhäuser. A mystery in two
parts. St. Louis: C. W. Alban,
1895? 106p. [this work bears
no relationship to Wagner's
opera, Tannhäuser]

Byers, Samuel Hawkins Marshall,
1838-1933.
Pocohontas. A melo-drama in
five acts. n.p.: n.pub.,
1875. 91p.

Byington, Alice.
"Cranford" dames. A play in
five scenes for female
characters. New York: Dick &
Fitzgerald, c1900. 25p.
[adapted from the novel
Cranford, by Elizabeth
Cleghorn Stevenson Gaskell]

Byrne, Charles Alfred, 1848-
1909.
Gabriella. A lyric drama in
one act. London: Robert Cocks,
c1893. Vocal score. Bilingual
text: English and Italian.
103p. [Italian libretto by
Fulvio Fulgonio; music by
Emilio Pizzi; joint author:
Mowbray Marras]

Pearl of Pekin; or, The
dashing tar outwitted by his
wife. A tragic comic opera
in three acts...music by
Lecocq; some original numbers
by G. A. Kerker. New York:
Rice and Dixey, 1888. 48p.
Libretto. [adaptation of
Fleur-de-thé by Henri Chivot
and Alfred Duru; music by
Alexandre Charles Lecocq;
without the music]

Pélléas and Mélisande.
(From the German of Maurice
Maeterlinck.) Boston: Poet-
Lore, 1894. (vol. 4, nos.
8 and 9.) p.413-452.

Byron, George Gordon Noël
Byron, 6th baron, 1788-1824.
Werner *see* The modern
standard drama, vol. 9

Darkness *see* Massey,
Charles. Massey's exhibition
reciter

C., D. T. *see* Calhoun,
D. T.

C. A. P. & Co. *see* The
Xlanties; or, Forty thieves

Cadbury, Richard Tapper *see*
Comfort, Richard (pseud.)

Cadunt regum coranae; vicit
libertas *see* Busch,
William. The dawn of
liberty; or, Cadunt regum
coranae; vicit libertas

Caesar *see* Peterson, Henry

Cagliostro. Play in three
acts. n.p.: n.pub., n.d.
Typescript. Prompt-book.
27, 13, 29, 10, 14 leaves.
see also Doyle, Edward

Cahill, Frank.
All is fair in love and war
see Arnold, George? and
Cahill, Frank. Parlor
theatricals; or, Winter
evening's entertainment

Aunti(Aunty)-Dote *see*
Arnold, George? and Cahill,
Frank. Parlor theatricals;
or, Winter evening's entertainment

Con-Test *see* Arnold,
George? and Cahill, Frank.
Parlor theatricals; or,
Winter evening's entertain-
ment

Dram-at(t)ic *see* Arnold,
George? and Cahill, Frank.
Parlor theatricals; or,
Winter evening's entertain-
ment

Honor among thieves *see*
Arnold, George? and Cahill,
Frank. Parlor theatricals;
or, Winter evening's entertainment

Irrestibly impudent *see*
Arnold, George? and Cahill,
Frank. Parlor theatricals;
or, Winter evening's entertainment

It never rains but it pours
see Arnold, George? and
Cahill, Frank. Parlor
theatricals; or, Winter
evening's entertainment

Parlor theatricals; or,
Winter evening's entertainment *see* Arnold, George?
and Cahill, Frank

Phan-Tom *see* Arnold,
George? and Cahill, Frank.
Parlor theatricals; or,
Winter evening's entertain-
ment

'Tis an ill wind that blows
nobody good *see* Arnold,
George? and Cahill, Frank.
Parlor theatricals; or,
Winter evening's entertain-
ment

Caigniez, Louis Charles, 1762-
1842.
La pie voleuse *see* Coale,
George B. Magpie and the
maid *see also* The thieving
magpie

Caillavet, Gaston Armand de,
1869-1915.
Monsieur de la Palisse *see*
Smith, Harry Bache. The
ambassador

Cain, ancient and modern *see*

Murray, Ellen *in* Dramatic
leaflets

Caius Gracchus *see* McCord,
Louisa Susannah Cheves

Caius Marius *see* Simms,
William Gilmore *see also*
Smith, Richard Penn

The cake walk *see* Dumont,
Frank

Calaynos *see* Boker, George
Henry

Calcaterra, G.
Lucrezia Borgia. A grand
opera in four acts. (From
the Italian of Romani.)
New Orleans: Printed at the
office of the Picayune,
1843. 24p. Libretto. *[title
page: poetry by Romani,
music by Donizetti, translated into English by G.
Calcaterra. Based on Victor
Hugo's Lucrèce Borgia;
without the music]*

Caldcleugh, William George.
Pan, the wood-god. [From
his: The branch...and other
poems. Philadelphia: James
Challen & Sons, 1862. 96p.]
p.31-38.

Calderón *see* Calhoun, D. T.

Calderón de la Barca, Pedro,
1600-1681.
El alcalde de Zalamea *see*
Pierra, Adolfo. Nobility;
or, The alcalde of Zalamea

El pintor de su deshonra
see Payne, John Howard.
The Spanish husband; or,
First and last love

Caldor, M. T.
Social charades. Boston:
Lee and Shepard, 1873. 169p.
Contents: College Ned.--

Diamonds and toads.--Accele-
rate.--Curiosity.--Parsimony.
--Conjuration.--The pilgrim's
choice.--Cinderella.--Elocu-
tion.

Calhoun, D. T. (pseud.)
Calderón. [From: Madrona,
etc. By D. T. C. San Francisco: Francis & Valentine,
1876] 43, 152p. *[D. T. Calhoun is a pseud. for Daniel
Thomas Callaghan, 1846-1916]*

Call, S. C.
The ugly aunt; or, Falsehood
and truth. (From a Norwegian
tale by J. G. Saxe.) Boston:
n.pub., 1880. 14p. *[from a
tale by John Godfrey Saxe]*

Call at number 1-7 *see*
Triplet, James

Callaghan, Daniel Thomas *see*
Calhoun, D. T. (pseud.)

Callahan, Charles Edward, 1845-
1917.
White sulphur; or, A day at
the springs. An American
comedy in four acts. Cincinnati: for the author, 1875.
37p.

Called away *see* Quinn,
Richard

Calmstorm, the reformer *see*
Mathews, Cornelius

Calsabigi, Ranieri de', 1715-
1795.
Orfeo ed Euridice *see*
Raymond, Fanny Malone. Orpheus

Calvary *see* Osborn, Laughton

Calvert, George Henry, 1803-
1889.
Arnold and André. An historical drama. Boston: Little,

Brown and Co., 1864. 95p.

Brangonar. A tragedy. Boston: Lee and Shepard, c1883. 110p.

Comedies. Boston: Phillips, Sampson & Co., 1856. 125p.
Contents: The will and the way.--Like unto like.

Count Julian. A tragedy. Baltimore: N. Hickman, 1840. 69p.

Don Carlos. (From the German of Frederick Schiller.) Baltimore: William & Joseph Neal, 1834. 223p.

The maid of Orleans. An historical tragedy. New York: G. P. Putnam's Sons, 1874. 134p.

Mirabeau. An historical drama. Boston: Lee and Shepard, c1883. 103p.

The camera obscura *see* Denison, Thomas Stewart *in his* Wide awake dialogues

Camille *see* La dame aux camélias *see also* Griffin, George W. H.

Camille; or, The fate of a coquette *see* Olwine, Wayne

Camillus; or, The self-exiled patriot *see* Phillips, Jonas B.

Cammarano, Salvatore, 1801-1852.
Belisario *see* Belisarius

Lucia di Lammermoor *see* Lucia di Lammermoor *see also* Lucie of Lammermoor *see also* Lucy of Lammermoor

Saffo *see* Sappho

Camoletti, Luigi, 1804-1880.
Suor Teresa; o, Elisabetta Soarez *see* Pray, Isaac

Clarke. Sor Teresa; or, Isabella Suarez

Campbell, Amelia Pringle.
The great house; or, Varities of American life. New York: Edward O. Jenkins, 1882. 56p. (title page lacking)

Campbell, Bartley Theodore, 1843-1888.
A brave man. Oxford, N. C.: n.pub., 1882. Prompt-book in Ms. In five acts (paged by acts.) Title page lacking.

Fate. n.p.: n.pub., 1872. Prompt-book in Ms. 113p. Title page lacking.

Little sunshine. Play in five acts. London and New York: S. French, 18--. 54p. (Lacy's acting edition. vol. 110)

My partner. A play in four acts. New York: n.pub., 1879? 66p.

My partner. A play in four acts. New York?: n.pub., c1880. Typescript. Prompt-book. 66 leaves.

Siberia. A picturesque romantic drama of Russian life in six acts. New York: H. C. Kennedy, 1911. 129p. *[1911 is the copyright renewal date; the original copyright date did not appear in the publication itself]*

The white slave. n.p.: n.pub., n.d. Typescript. In six acts. (Paged by act.)

The white slave and other plays. Princeton: Princeton Univ. Press, 1941. lxxxi, 248p. (America's lost plays, vol. 19)
Contents: The Virginian.--My partner.--The galley slave.--Fairfax.--The white slave.

Campbell, Lorne J.
King Darnley. An historical
tragedy. Madison, Wisc.:
n.pub., 1895. 51p.

Campbell, Marian D.
A Chinese dummy. A farce in
one act for female characters
only. Boston: W. H. Baker,
c1899. 17p. (Baker's edition
of plays)
An open secret. A farce in
two acts. Boston: W. H.
Baker, c1898. 16p.
Sunbonnets. A farce-comedy
in two acts. Boston: W. H.
Baker, 1900. 39p. (Baker's
edition of plays)

Campbell, Thomas, 1777-1844.
The wizard's warning; or,
The warrior's faith see
Steele, Silas Sexton. Col-
lected works. Book of plays

Campbell, William Wilfred,
1858?-1918.
Collected works. Poetical
tragedies. Toronto: William
Briggs, 1908. 319p.
Contents: Mordred.--Daulac.
--Morning.--Hildebrand.
[Readex gives Campbell's
birthdate as 1838?, but
Library of Congress indicates
dates as given above]

Canada's welcome see Dixon,
Frederick Augustus

The candid critic see
Sargent, Epes

Candy-pulling see Phelps,
Lavinia Howe in her
Dramatic stories

Cannon, Charles James, 1800-
1860.
Collected works. Dramas.
New York: E. Dunnigan [sic,
Dunigan] and Bro., 1857.
355p.

Contents: The sculptor's
daughter.--Dolores.--Better
late than never.--The oath
of office.

The compact. A mask. [From
his: Poems, dramatic and
miscellaneous. New York:
Edward Dunigan and Bro.,
1851. 208p.] p.63-89.
The oath of office. A tragedy.
New York: William Taylor,
1854. 91p.
Rizzio. [From his: Poems,
dramatic and miscellaneous.
New York: Edward Dunigan and
Bro., 1851. 208p.] p.1-61.

Canonicus see Hamilton,
Alexander

Cantell, Lilia Mackay.
Jephthah's daughter. A
Biblical dance drama in
three scenes. n.p.: n.pub.,
18-? Typescript. Prompt-
book, interleaved with Ms.
notes. 8, 10, 7 leaves.

Capendu, Ernest, 1826-1868.
L'héritage de Monsieur Plumet
see Fuller, Horace William.
Dear uncle!

The capitol see Thomas,
Augustus

Capriccios see Block, Louis
James

Caprice; or, A woman's heart
see Leland, Oliver Shepart

Captain Dick; or, Our war
correspondent see Buzzell,
Arthur L.

Captain Jack; or, The Irish
outlaw see Moore, Bernard
Francis

Captain John Smith see Opal
(pseud.) in her The cloud
of witnesses

Captain Kidd; or, A peerless
peeress and a haughty pirate
see Morrison, George Austin

Captain Kyd; or, The wizard of
the sea see Jones, Joseph
Stevens

Captain Lettarblair see
Merington, Marguerite

Captain Mary Miller see
Robinson, Harriet Jane Hanson

Capt. Racket see Townsend,
Charles

Captain Swell see Hiland,
Frank E.

Captain Walrus; or, The game
of three see Laidlaw,
Alexander Hamilton

The captain's wager see
Townsend, Charles

The captive of Castile; or,
The Moorish maiden's vow
see Alcott, Louisa May
in her Comic tragedies

Captured; or, The old maid's
triumph see Beck, William
L.

Capuletta; or, Romeo and
Juliet restored see Baker,
George Melville

Capus, Alfred, 1858-1922.
Les maris de Léontine see
The husbands of Leontine

Card, Evelyn G. Whiting.
A confidence game. A comedy
in two acts. Boston: Walter
H. Baker, 1900. 26p. (Baker's
edition of plays) *[originally
produced under the title,
Vacation days]*

The Cardinal see Robinson,
Fayette

Careless, George Edward Percy,
b.1839.
Ben Israel; or, From under
the curse see Tullidge,
Edward Wheelock

Careless cupid see Hiland,
Frank E.

Careo, Zella.
The hidden treasures; or,
Martha's triumph. A drama in
a prologue and four acts.
Clyde, O.: Ames, 1883. 15p.
(Ames' series of standard and
minor drama. no. 141) *[even
though Readex gives a publi-
cation date of 1883, New York
Public Library gives 1888]*

Caridorf; or, The avenger see
Bird, Robert Montgomery in
his The cowled lover and
other plays

Carleton, Henry Guy, 1856-1910.
Ambition. A comedy in three
acts. New York: n.pub., 1895.
Typescript. 60, 71, 53 leaves.

The butterflies. A comedy in
three acts. New York: n.pub.,
1894? Typescript. Prompt-book
with Ms. notes. 58, 66, 61
leaves.

The butterflies. A comedy in
three acts. New York and
London: S. French, 1908.
107p. (French's international
copyrighted edition of the
works of the best authors.
no. 141)

A gilded fool. New York:
n.pub., 189-? Typescript,
prompt-book. (paged by acts.)

Lem Kettle. In four acts.
New York: n.pub., 1894. Title
page lacking. Typescript.
40, 44, 22, 37 leaves.

The lion's mouth. A drama in
four acts. New York: n.pub.,
1892. Typescript. Prompt-book
with Ms. notes. 57, 31, 16,
24 leaves.

Memnon. A tragedy in five acts. Chicago: printed, not published, 1881. 171p.

Victor Durand. A drama in four acts. New York: W. L. Onyans, 1884. Typescript. 28, 18, 23, 18 leaves.

More sinned against than sinning. An original Irish drama in prologue and three acts. Chicago: Dramatic Pub. Co., c1883. 26p. (American acting drama)

Carlos, Frank (pseud.) see Griffith, Frank Carlos

Carlotta see Roskoten, Robert

Carmen see Baker, Theodore

Carmichael, Montgomery, 1857-1922.
Rosmersholm. A play in four acts. (From the Norwegian of Ibsen.) Boston: Walter H. Baker, c1890. 108p.

Carmouche, Pierre François Adolphe, 1797-1868.
La lune de miel see Harrison, Constance Cary. A Russian honeymoon

Carnes, Mason.
The better part see Belknap, Edwin Star and Carnes, Mason

Carnival of days see Buxton, Ida M.

A carnival of sports see Minster, Verend (pseud.)?

Carnival; or, Mardi Gras in New Orleans see Reynartz, Dorothy

The carpenter and his apprentice; or, The secret order of the Confrierie see Jones, Joseph Stephens in Steele,

Silas Sexton. Collected works. Book of plays

The carpenter of Rouen; or, The massacre of St. Bartholomew see Jones, Joseph Stevens

The carpet-bagger in New Orleans see Meriwether, Elizabeth Avery. The Ku Klux Klan; or, The carpet-bagger in New Orleans

Carré, Albert, 1852-1938.
Le veglione (Le bal masque) see Fitch, Clyde. The masked ball

Carré, Fabrice, 1855-1921.
Ma bru see My daughter-in-law

Carré, Michel, 1819-1872.
Faust see Kellogg, Clara Louise

Faust et Marguerite see Faust and Marguerite

Carrington, Kate.
Aschenbrode see Morse, Woolson. Cinderella at school

Carroll, Lewis (pseud.) see Dodgson, Charles Lutwidge

Carroll, Philip H. see Lewis, Richard Henry (pseud.)

Carter, Alfred G. W., 1819-1885.
Ring rule and ring ruin. New York: n.pub., c1875. Reading edition. 34p. Title page lacking.

Carter, Alice P.
The fairy steeplecrown. A play for children in one scene. Boston: W. H. Baker, c1887. 24p.

Carter, John Henton, 1832-1910.
The blood-stained bootjack; or, The chambermaid's

revenge. [From his: The log
of Commodore Rollingpin, his
adventures afloat and ashore.
New York: G. W. Carleton,
1874.] p.248-258. *[Commodore
Rollingpin was a pseud. used
by Carter]*

Carter, St. Leger Landon, 1785-
1851.
Debate on the crow bill.
[From his: Nugae, by Nugator;
or, Pieces in prose and
verse. Baltimore: Woods and
Crane, 1844. 215p.] p.72-75.

Carter, William.
Port wine vs. jealousy *see*
White, Charles

Carthage *see* Saltus, Francis
Saltus

Case, Laura U.
May court in Greenwood *see*
Dramatic leaflets

The veiled priestess *see*
Dramatic leaflets

A case for divorce *see* Kaler,
James Otis

A case of jealousy *see* Wood,
J. M. G.

The case of Smythe vs. Smith
see Dumont, Frank

A case of suspension *see*
Wilson, Louise Latham

The casino girl *see* Smith,
Harry Bache

Cassilda *see* Dorbesson,
Fern. Aldemon's daughter
(Cassilda)

Cassius' whistle *see* Meyers,
Robert Cornelius V. *in*
Dramatic leaflets

Cast upon the world *see*
Perine, Charles E.

Castil-Blaze, François Henri
Joseph *see* Blaze, François
Henri Joseph, called Castil-
Blaze

Casting a boomerang *see* Daly,
Augustin. 7-20-8; or,
Casting a boomerang

Castle, Harriet Davenport,
b.1843.
The courting of Mother Goose.
An entertainment. Chicago:
Dramatic Pub. Co., n.d. 27p.

The castle of Cataldo *see*
Midnight banquet; or, The
castle of Cataldo

The castle of St. Aldobrand
see Maturin, Charles Robert.
Bertram; or, The castle of
St. Aldobrand *in* The
modern standard drama, vol. 7

Catharina the Second. A tragedy
in five acts. (From the German of Lindner.) New York:
Fanny Janaushek, 18-?. Bilingual text: German and
English. 43p.

"Catherine" *see* Smith,
Edgar McPhail

Catnip tea *see* Phelps,
Lavinia Howe *in her*
Dramatic stories

The catspaw *see* Jerrold,
Douglas William *in* The
modern standard drama,
vol. 11

Caught at last *see* Nomad
(pseud.)

Caught in his own trap *see*
Hildreth, David W. The
granger; or, Caught in his
own trap

Caught in the act *see* Chisnell, Newton

Caught napping *see* Lewis,
Abbie Goodwin

Caughy, Charles M.
Love and jealousy. An historical drama of the days of
the Stuart Insurrection of
1745. Baltimore: John Murphy,
1873. 68p.

A cause for divorce *see* Ros-
setti, Joseph. Household
affairs; or, A cause for
divorce

Cavalleria rusticana *see*
Day, Willard Gibson

The cavalry ball *see* Belasco,
David and Fyles, Franklin

Caverly, Robert Boodey, 1806-
1887.
Chochorua in the mountains.
An historical drama. Boston:
The author, 1885. p.251-301.
(Drama no. 5...Battle of
the bush)

King Philip. An historical
drama. Boston: The author,
1884. p.127-190. (Drama
no. 3...Battle of the bush)

The last night of a nation.
An historical drama. Boston:
The author, 1884. p.31-57.
(Drama no. 1...Battle of
the bush)

Miantonimo. An historical
drama. Boston: The author,
1884. p.61-124. (Drama no.
2...Battle of the bush)

The regicides. An historical
drama. Boston: The author,
1884. p.193-247. (Drama no.
4...Battle of the bush)

Cazaurah, Augustus R., 1820-
1889.
A celebrated case. A drama
in prologue and four acts.
(From the French of D'Ennery
and Cormon.) New York: S.

French, n.d. 69p. (French's
standard drama. The acting
edition. no. 442) *[based on
Une cause célèbre by Adolphe
Dennery and Eugène Cormon,
pseud. of Pierre Piestre.
Readex also enters this play
under title (see below)]*
The man of success. A play
in five acts. New York: 18-?.
Typescript. (From the French
of Octave Feuillet.) 82p.

Cecil the seer *see* Raymond,
George Lansing Cecil *in his*
Collected works

A celebrated case. New York and
London: S. French, 18-?. 69p.
*[Readex also enters this play
under Cazauran (see above)]*

Cent-any-all.--Centennial *see*
Brewster, Emma E. *in*
Parlor varieties

Centaurine *see* Gerardy, D.

Centennial movement, 1876 *see*
Appleton, Nathan

Centlivre, Susanna, 1667?-1723.
The wonder! A woman keeps a
secret *see* Daly, Augustin

Ceres *see* Crumpton, M. Nataline

Cergrinn, H. H.
Vela of Alava. Paris: Firmin-
Dido, 1896. Limited ed. 52p.

Cervantes Saavedra, Miguel de,
1547-1616.
Don Quijote de la Mancha *see*
Burton, Mrs. Henry S. Don
Quixote de la Mancha *see also*
Smith, Harry Bache. Don
Quixote

Chabrier, Emmanuel, 1841-1894.
Le roi malgré lui *see* Goodwin, John Cheever. The merry

monarch, song words of...

Chadwick, J. M.
Joseph in bondage *see*
Staples, H. A.

A chafing-dish party *see*
Bangs, John Kendrick

Challenge dance. n.p.: n.pub.,
n.d. 10p. Title page lacking.
(French's acting edition.
Late Lacy's. no. 43) *[Readex
also enters this same edition
under the author, Henry
Llewellyn Williams]*

The chambermaid's revenge
see Carter, John Henton.
The blood-stained bootjack;
or, The chambermaid's
revenge

Chamisso, Adelbert von, 1781-
1838.
Faust *see* Phillips, Henry

Champagne and oysters; or, One
lie leads to another *see*
Runnion, James B.

Champignol despite himself.
(From the French of Feydeau
and Desvallières.) New York:
Rosenfield Typewriting,
1892. Typescript. 46, 77,
36 leaves. *[based on Champignol malgré lui, by
Georges Léon Jules Marie
Feydeau and Maurice Des-
vallières]*

The champion of her sex *see*
Baker, George Melville

A champion, though no fighter
see Venable, William Henry
in his The school stage

Chandler, A. N.
Crimp's trip to the Centen-
nial. A negro farce. Clyde,
O.: Ames, 1877. 10p. (Ames'

series of standard and minor
drama. no. 190)

Chandler, Bessie, b.1856.
The pearl of Ohio *see*
Drake, Frank C. Rosberry
Shrub, sec.

Chaney, Mrs. George L.
William Henry. Boston: James
R. Osgood, 1875. 74p. *[title
page: "dramatized from Mrs.
A. M. Diaz's books 'William
Henry letters, from Crooked
Pond School,' and 'William
Henry and his friends.'"]*

A change of base *see* Curtis,
Ariana Randolph Wormeley

A change of color *see* Denton,
Clara Janetta Fort

The changing scales *see*
Moates, William Gurney

Channing, William Ellery, 1780-
1842.
John Brown and the heroes of
Harper's Ferry. Boston:
Cupples, Upham, 1886. 143p.
*[Readex incorrectly assigns
Channing's birth date as
1782]*

Chanukoh *see* Bien, Herman
Milton. The feast of lights;
or, Chanukoh

The chaperon *see* Baker,
Rachel E.

The chaperons (3rd part of a
trilogy) *see* Grant, Robert
in his The little tin god-
on-wheels; or, Society in
our modern Athens

Chapman, John Jay, 1862-1933.
The two philosophers. A
quaint sad comedy. Boston:
J. G. Cupples, 1892. 37p.

Chapman, W. F.
   April fools. A farce in one
   act for three male characters. New York: Dick & Fitzgerald, c1890. 16p.

   Over the garden fence. A
   farce in one act. Chicago:
   Dramatic Pub. Co., c1901.
   16p. (Sergel's acting drama.
   no. 470)

   Wanted: a confidential
   clerk. A farce in one act.
   New York: Fitzgerald Pub.
   Corp., c1887. 23p.

   Won by strategy. A capital
   farce in one act and one
   scene. New York: Dick &
   Fitzgerald, c1886. 21p.
   (Dick's American edition)

A character play see Heywood, Delia A. in her
   Choice dialogues no. 1

Charade in two syllables and
   three scenes see Follen,
   Eliza Lee Cabot. Home dramas
   for young people

The charge of the hash brigade
   see Skelly, Joseph P.

Charicles see Quincy, Josiah
   Phillips

The charity ball see Belasco,
   David and De Mille, Henry
   Churchill

Charity begins at home see
   Shields, Sarah Annie Frost
   in her Parlor charades and
   proverbs

Charlecote; or, The trial of
   William Shakespeare see
   Thacher, John Boyd

Charles II; or, The merry
   monarch see Payne, John
   Howard in The modern
   standard drama, vol. 3

Charles the Twelfth see
   Planché, James Robinson in
   The modern standard drama,
   vol. 6

Charles O'Malley's aunt see
   Williams, Henry Llewellyn

Charles Rovellini see Rocchietti, Joseph

Chas. Wengleigh, the Duke see
   Tillson, Jesse Paxon in his
   Collected works

Charlie's Christmas dream see
   Gutterson, John H.

Charlotte Corday see Morey,
   Amos C.

A charming conversationalist
   see Mathews, Frances Aymar

The charms of music see
   Laidlaw, Alexander Hamilton

Chase, Frank Eugene, 1857-1920.
   The bat and the ball; or,
   Negative evidence. A farce
   in one act. Boston: W. H.
   Baker, c1889. 20p. (Baker's
   edition of plays)

   The great umbrella case.
   A mock trial. Boston: W. H.
   Baker, c1883. 36p. (Baker's
   edition of plays)

   In the trenches. A drama of
   the Cuban war in three acts.
   By Abel Seaman (pseud.)
   Boston: W. H. Baker, 1898.
   37p. (Baker's edition of
   plays)

   A personal matter. A comedy
   in one act. Boston: G. M.
   Baker, 1880. 22p. (The
   Globe drama)

   A ready-made suit; or, A
   mock trial. Boston: W. H.
   Baker, 1913. 41p. (Baker's
   edition of plays) [earlier
   copyright: 1885]

Santa Claus the first. A
Christmas entertainment.
Boston: Walter H. Baker,
c1880. 23p. (Baker's edition
of plays)

Chase, George B.
Haunted by a shadow; or,
Hunted down. A drama in
four acts. Clyde, O.: Ames,
1890. 23p. (Ames' series of
standard and minor drama.
no. 283)

Pen Hapgood; or, The Yankee
schoolmaster. Clyde, O.:
Ames, 1890. 34p. (Ames'
series of standard and minor
drama. no. 278) *[based on
the story Cudjo's cave, by
John Townsend Trowbridge]*

Simple Silas; or, The detective from Plunketsville. A
drama in three acts. Clyde,
O.: Ames, 1890. 24p. (Ames'
series of standard and minor
drama. no. 275)

Chase, Lucien Bonaparte, 1817-
1864.
The young man about town.
A comedy in three acts. New
York: n.pub., 1854. 42p.

Chatham, ?.
Against the American war
see Massey, Charles. Massey's exhibition reciter

Chatrian, Alexandre, 1826-1890.
L'ami Fritz *see* Dole,
Nathan Haskell. Friend Fritz

Le juif polonais *see*
Williams, Henry Llewellyn.
The bells; or, The Polish
Jew

Chatterton *see* Lacy, Ernest

A cheerful liar *see* Fraser,
John Arthur

Cheney, John Vance, 1848-1922.

Queen Helen. [From his:
Queen Helen, and other poems.
Chicago: Way & Williams,
1895] p.1-52.

Cheney, Lon, 1883-1930 *see*
An American wife

Chenoweth, Lawrence.
After the circus. Farce in
one act. Clyde, O.: Ames,
c1900. 17p. (Ames' series
of standard and minor drama.
no. 422)

Cherrytree, Herr (pseud.).
More truth than poetry. [From
his: Prose and poetry. New
York: John B. Alden, 1889.
88p.] p. 27-30. *[Herr Cherrytree is the pseud. for
Edward T. Kirschbaum]*

The renegade [and] More
truth than poetry. [From:
Cherries from a young tree.
n.p.: n.pub., 1888. 36p.]
p.6-10.

Chézy, Wilhelmine Christiane
von Klencke von, 1783-1856.
Euryanthe *see* Schwab,
Frederick A.

A Chicago lady *see* Relief

Chihuahua *see* Miller,
Chester Gore

The child of Babylon *see*
Joseph and his brethren, the
Hebrew son; or, The child
of Babylon

The child of the camp *see*
Willard, Charles O. Little
Goldie; or, The child of the
camp

The child of the regiment...
the music composed by Donizetti. New York: Sheridan
Corbyn, 1853. Bilingual text:
English and Italian. 45p.

[music by Gaetano Donizetti;
libretto by Jules Henri Vernoy de Saint-Georges and
Jean François Alfred Bayard]
see also The daughter of
the regiment see also La
figlia del reggimento

The children see Fitch,
Clyde

Childs, Nathaniel.
Robinsonade. (Music by A.
Darr.) Boston: Oliver Ditson, c1880. Prompt-book
with Ms. notes. 22p. [music
by Alphons Darr; without
the music]

Chilpéric. Opera-bouffe in
three acts and four tableaux.
(From the French of Hervé.)
New York: n.pub., 1869.
Bilingual text: English and
French. 38p. Libretto.
[Hervé is the professional
name of Florimond Ronge,
who wrote both words and
music]

Chinese damsel see Venable,
William Henry in his The
school stage

A Chinese dummy see Campbell,
Marian D.

A Chinese wedding see
Wilson, Bertha M.

Chipman, Adelbert Z.
The little wife. A comedy
drama in four acts. Clyde,
O.: Ames, c1900. 39p. (Ames'
series of standard and
minor drama. no. 417)

Ruben Rube; or, My invalid
aunt. Farce in one act.
Clyde, O.: Ames, c1900. 15p.
(Ames' series of standard
and minor drama. no. 416)

Chiqui see MacKaye, James

Steele. An arrant knave in
his An arrant knave & other
plays

Chisnell, Newton.
Caught in the act. A comedy...
adapted from the French.
Clyde, O.: Ames, 1888. 37p.
(Ames' series of standard and
minor drama. no. 257)

The cigarette. A comedy in
one act. Clyde, O.: Ames,
1884. 17p. (Ames' series of
standard and minor drama.
no. 131)

A pleasure trip. (From the
French of E. Gondinet and
A. Bisson.) Clyde, O.: Ames,
1885. 45p. (Ames' series of
standard and minor drama.
no. 168) [based on Un voyage
d'agrément, by Edmond Gondinet and Alexandre Charles
Auguste Bisson]

The three hats. A farce-
comedy in two acts. Clyde,
O.: Ames, c1892. 35p. (Ames'
series of standard and minor
drama. no. 306)

A thrilling item. An original
farce in one act. Clyde, O.:
Ames, 18-?. 17p. (Ames'
series of standard and minor
drama. no. 123)

Chittenden, Ezra Porter, 1851-
1917.
The pleroma. A poem of the
Christ. In two books of seven
cantos each, written in semi-
dramatic form. New York and
London: G. P. Putnam's Sons,
1890. xv, 347p.

Chivers, Thomas Holley, 1809-
1858.
The sons of Usna: tragi-
apotheosis, in five acts.
Philadelphia: C. Sherman &
Sons, 1858. 92p.

Chivot, Henri, 1830-1897.
Fleur-de-lis *see* Goodwin,
John Cheever

Fleur-de-thé *see* Byrne,
Charles Alfred. Pearl of
Pekin; or, The dashing tar
outwitted by his wife

Gillette de Narbonne *see*
Norcross, N. W. Gillette;
or, Count and countess

La mascotte *see* Elson,
Louis Charles and Norris,
J. W.

Les noces d'Olivette *see*
Olivette

Chocorua in the mountains *see*
Caverly, Robert Boodey

The choice *see* Packard,
Hannah James

Choice dialogues. no. 1 *see*
Heywood, Delia A.

Choosing a trade *see* A collection of temperance
dialogues

Chops *see* Shackell, G.

Chosroes the second *see*
Opal (pseud.) *in her* The
cloud of witnesses

Christ *see* Hartmann, Sadakichi

Christ is born. A mystery.
Baltimore: Loyola College,
1879. 82p.

Christian slave *see* Stowe,
Harriet Elizabeth Beecher
in Follen, Eliza Lee Cabot.
Home dramas for young people

Christie, Albany James, 1817-
1891.
The martyrdom of St. Cecily.
A drama in three acts. New

York: D. & J. Sadlier, 1876.
36p.

Christmas *see* Wilson,
Olivia W. *in her* The luck
of the golden pumpkin

A Christmas address *see*
Phelps, Lavinia Howe *in her*
Dramatic stories

The Christmas box *see*
Brewster, Emma E. *see also*
in her Parlor varieties

Christmas boxes *see* Davis,
Mary Evelyn Moore

A Christmas carol *see*
Baker, George Melville *see*
also Satterlee, Clarence

Christmas charades, etc. *see*
Steele, Silas Sexton *in his*
Collected works. Book of
plays

Christmas dramatic plays *see*
Schwalm, Francis

A Christmas eve adventure *see*
Keatinge, Ella *in her*
Short plays for children

Christmas Eve in the South;
or, Uncle Caleb's home *see*
Collyer, Dan

The Christmas fairies; or,
Shakespeare's dream *see*
Hartmann, Theodore

A Christmas masque of Saint
Roch *see* Davis, Mary
Evelyn Moore

The Christmas ship *see*
Pelham, Nettie H.

The Christmas tragedy *see*
Hartmann, Theodore. The
Christmas fairies; or,
Shakespeare's dream

Christopher Columbus. A drama
in four acts. By F. G.
Notre Dame: "Ave Maria"
Press, 18-?. New edition,
revised. 39p. *[title page:*
translated from the Italian
by F. G.] see also Hartnedy, M. M. A.

Christopher junior *see* Ryley,
Madeleine Lucette

Christus *see* Longfellow,
Henry Wadsworth

Christy, Edwin Byron, 1838-
1866.
Box and Cox. In one act.
Africanized expressly for
George Christy. New York:
Happy Hours Co., 188-?.
21p. (The Ethiopian drama.
no. 2) *[based on Sir*
Francis Cowley's Cox and
Box]

Christy, George.
The Fenian spy; or, John
Bull in America *see* Grif-
fin, George W. H. and
Christy, George

The chronothanatoletron; or,
Old times made new. An
entertainment for female
characters. Boston: W. H.
Baker, c1889. 23p.

Chrysostom-Channing *see*
Townsend, Frederic *in his*
Spiritual visitors

Chums *see* Atticum, Sal *see*
also Harris, Francis
Augustine *see also* Herne,
James A. and Belasco, David.
Hearts of oak; or, Chums

Churchill, Winston, 1871-1947.
Richard Carvel *see* Rose,
Edward Everett

The Church's triumph *see*

Finn, Sister Mary Paulina
in her Alma mater; or,
The Georgetown Centennial

Cibber, Colley, 1671-1757.
The non-juror *see* Smith,
Solomon Franklin. The
hypocrite

Richard III *see* Shakespeare,
William *in* The modern
standard drama, vol. 2

She wou'd and she wou'd not;
or, The kind imposter *see*
Daly, Augustin *see also*
Waldauer, Augustus. The
female cavalier

Cicely's cavalier *see* Dix,
Beulah Marie

The Cid of Seville *see*
Osborn, Laughton *in his*
Ugo da Este

La cigale *see* Delafield,
John H.

The cigarette *see* Chisnell,
Newton

A cigarette from Java *see*
Sullivan, Thomas Russell

Cinderella *see* Caldor, M. T.
in his Social charades *see*
also Dugan, Caro Atherton
in her Collected works
see also Field, Henrietta
Dexter and Field, Roswell
Martin. Collected works *see*
also Henley, Anne and
Schell, Stanley *see also*
Ludlow, Fitz-Hugh

Cinderella. Opera in three
acts. Boston: n.pub., 18--.
Prompt-book. In Ms. 23, 9,
15 leaves. *[without the*
music]

Cinderella. Under the auspices
of the auxiliary society of

the N. O. A. A. Newark,
N. J.: Stephen Hollbrook,
1876. 24p.

Cinderella at school *see*
Morse, Woolson

Cinderella; or, Pride punished
see Corner, Julia *in*
Venable, William Henry. The
school stage

Cinderella; or, The fairy
and little glass slipper.
New York: S. French, 1858?
35p. (French's standard
drama. no. 164) *[music by
Gioacchino Rossini; without
the music]*

Cinderella; or, The fairy
and little glass slipper.
An opera in three acts...
music by Rossini. Boston:
J. H. Eastburn's Press,
1855. 39p. Libretto.
[without the music]

Cinderella, or the glass
slipper. Simplified from
the original *see* Kava-
naugh, Mrs. Russell *in her*
Original dramas, dialogues

Cinderella; or, The little
glass slipper *in* Beadle's
dialogues no. 2

Cinderella; or, The silver
slipper *see* Hubner,
Charles William

The circumlocution office
see Dialogues dramatized
from the works of Charles
Dickens *[from Dickens'
Little Dorrit]*

Circumstances alter cases *see*
Hoppin, William Jones *see
also* Sedgwick, Alfred B.

Circumstantial evidence *see*
Green, John B. *see also*

Morris, Felix James

Civil death (La morte civile.)
A drama in five acts. (From
the Italian of Giacometti.)
New York: George F. Nesbitt,
1873. Bilingual text:
English and Italian. 99p.

Claim ninety-six *see* Ward,
Lew

The clandestine marriage *see*
Colman, George *in* The
modern standard drama, vol. 5

Clapp, William Warland, 1826-
1891.
La Fiammina. (Founded upon a
play by Mario Uchard.) Boston: W. V. Spencer, 1857.
35p. (Spencer's Boston
theatre [vol. 20] no. 160)

My husband's mirror. A
domestic comedietta in one
act. New York: S. French,
1857? 14p. (French's minor
drama. The acting edition.
no. 201)

Clappé, Arthur A.
Canada's welcome *see*
Dixon, Frederick Augustus

Clarence *see* Snider, Denton
Jaques

Claribel *see* Malone, Walter

Clarissa's first party *see*
Hardman, Richard

Clark, John Franklin.
Beyond the grave. New York:
American News Co., 1889. 34p.

Clark, N. H. Belden *see*
Belden, N. H.

Clark, William Adolphus, 1825-
1906.
Gen. Grant; or, The star of
union and liberty. A play in

three acts. By Anicetus
(pseud.) New York: S. French,
1868. 46p. (French's standard
drama. The acting edition.
no. 351)

Clarke, Helen Archibald,
1860-1926.
Alladine and Palomides *see*
Porter, Charlotte Endymion
and Clarke, Helen Archibald

The seven princesses *see*
Porter, Charlotte Endymion
and Clarke, Helen Archibald

The sightless *see* Porter,
Charlotte Endymion and
Clarke, Helen Archibald

Clarke, Hugh Archibald,
1839-1927.
Harold. (From the German of
von Wildenbruch.) Philadelphia: Poet-Lore, 1891. (vol.
3, nos. 8 and 9) p.393-488.

Clarke, Joseph Ignatius
Constantine, 1846-1925.
The first violin. (From the
novel by Jessie Fothergill.)
New York: n.pub., 1898.
Typescript, prompt-book. In
five acts (paged by acts.)
*[joint author: Merridan
Phelps]*

Luck. A comedy in three
acts. New York: DeLacy &
Willson, 1877. 46p.

Robert Emmet. A tragedy of
Irish history. New York:
G. P. Putnam's Sons, 1888.
vii, 134p.

Clarke, N. H. Belden (pseud.)
see Belden, N. H.

Class day *see* Harris,
Francis Augustine

A class-day conspiracy *see*
Tassin, Algernon De Vivier

Claudy, Frank, 1844-1919.
Faust. The first part. (From

the German of Goethe.)
Washington, D. C.: Wm. H.
Morrison, 1886. 182p.

Clay, Bertha M. (pseud.) *see*
Brame, Charlotte Mary

Clayton, Estelle.
The Viking. Comic opera in
two acts. (Music by E. I.
Darling and E. R. Steiner.)
New York: Springer and
Welty, c1893. First limited
edition. 46p. Libretto.

Clearing the mists *see* Barr,
E. Nelson and Hogan, J. I.

Clemens, Samuel Langhorne,
1835-1910.
Pudd'nhead Wilson *see*
Mayo, Frank

Clement, E. H.
Sir Harry Vane *see* Sir
Harry Vane

Cleveland, E. E.
Our family umbrella. Farce
in two acts. Clyde, O.: Ames,
1896. 22p. (Ames' series of
standard and minor drama.
no. 381)

Cleveland's reception party
see Williams, George W.

Cliffe, Clifton.
A wife by advertisement. An
entirely new and original
farce. Chicago: Dramatic
Pub. Co., c1884. 7p.
(American acting drama)

Clifton, Mary A. Delano.
Schnapps. A farce in one
act. Clyde, O.: Ames, n.d.
6p. (Ames' series of standard
and minor drama. no. 48)

Der two subprises. A farce
in one act. Clyde, O.: Ames,
n.d. 7p. (Ames' series of
standard and minor drama.
no. 49)

The wrong box. An Ethiopian farce in one act. Clyde, O.: Ames, n.d. 6p. (Ames' series of standard and minor drama. no. 47) *[title page: In the wrong box]*

A close shave *see* Baker, George Melville

The closing of the "Eagle" *see* McBride, H. Elliott

The cloud of witnesses *see* Opal (pseud.)

Clouds *see* Silver, W. A.

A cloudy day *see* Griffith, Benjamin Lease Crozer

Clover farm *see* Patten, Gilbert

The club friend; or, A fashionable physician *see* Rosenfeld, Sydney

Coale, George B.
The drop of water. A comedy in one act. Chicago and New York: Dramatic Pub. Co., c1884. 12p. (Sergel's acting drama) *[based on Le goutte d'eau by Jacques Clary Jean Normand]*

Magpie and the maid. An opera in three acts. By G. B. C. (From the French of M. Castil-Blaze.)(Music by Rossini) Baltimore: E. J. Coale, 1831. Bilingual text: French and English. 131p. Libretto. *[based on Castil-Blaze's La pie voleuse; first performed under the title La gazza ladra, with libretto by Giovanni Gherardini and based on the story by Louis Charles Caigniez and Jean Marie Baudouin]*

On his devoted head. A domes-

tic scene. Chicago: Dramatic Pub. Co., c1885. 8p. (Sergel's acting drama. no. 836) *[translated from Un crane sous une tempete, by Abraham Dreyfus]*

Coalheaver's revenge *see* White, Charles

Coals of fire *see* Baker, George Melville

Cobb, Charles E.
The heroes of '76. A dramatic cantata of the Revolution in three parts. Boston: Oliver Ditson, c1877. 146p. Vocal score and libretto. *[music by J. E. Trowbridge; pp.41-42, 107-108, and 145-146 lacking from copy reproduced by Readex]*

Cobb, Josephine H.
The Oxford affair. A comedy in three acts. Philadelphia: Penn Pub. Co., 1911. 31p. (Dramatic library, vol. 1, no. 109) *[joint author: Jennie E. Paine; earlier copyright: 1896]*

Cobb, Mary L.
Poetical dramas for home and school. Boston: Lee and Shepard, 1873. 189p.
Contents: Lady of the lake, arranged from Walter Scott.--The Spanish gypsy, arranged from George Eliot.--Peace or war.--Coming of spring.--Home.--Mars and Venus.--The sirens and muses.--The rolling year.--Moses in the bullrushes (Hannah More.)--Feast of tabernacles (Rev. Henry Ware.)--The coming of the Messiah (Rev. S. H. Winkley.)--Deborah and Barak.--Queen Vashti.

The cobbler *see* Denison, Thomas Stewart

The cobbler and the king *see*
Smith, Harry Bache. Jupiter;
or, The cobbler and the king

Cobwebs *see* Goodrich, Elizabeth P.

Codman, Henry.
The Roman martyrs. A tragedy
in three acts. Providence:
Sidney S. Rider, 1879. 83p.

Coes, George H., 1828-1897.
Badly sold. A negro act in
two scenes. Boston: W. H.
Baker, 1893. 10p. (Baker's
darkey plays)

Black blunders. An Ethiopian
farce in two scenes. Boston:
W. H. Baker, 1893. 13p.
(Baker's darkey plays)

Everyday occurences. A finale to the "first part" of
a negro minstrel entertainment. Boston: W. H. Baker,
1893. 6p. (Baker's darkey
plays)

The faith cure. A farce in
one act. Boston: W. H.
Baker, 1895. 15p. (Baker's
darkey plays)

A finished education. A
finale for the "first part"
of a negro minstrel entertainment. Boston: W. H.
Baker, 1893. 6p. (Baker's
darkey plays)

Here she goes and there she
goes. An Ethiopian farce in
two scenes. Boston: W. H.
Baker, c1893. 12p. (The
vaudeville stage)

The intelligence office.
A negro act in one scene.
Boston: W. H. Baker, 1894.
10p. (Baker's darkey plays)

Mistaken identity. An Ethiopian farce in one scene.
Boston: W. H. Baker, 1893.
8p.

Mrs. Didymus' party. A negro
sketch in one scene. Boston:
W. H. Baker, 1893. 12p.
(The vaudeville stage)

Music vs. elocution. A negro
sketch in one scene. Boston:
W. H. Baker, 1902? 8p.
[earlier copyright: 1893]

Oh, well, it's no use. An
original negro sketch in one
scene. Boston: W. H. Baker,
1894. 10p. (Baker's darkey
plays)

The old parson. A "first part
finish" for a negro minstrel
entertainment. Boston: W. H.
Baker, c1893. 6p.

Our colored conductors. An
original Ethiopian sketch in
two scenes. Boston: W. H.
Baker, c1893. 9p.

A perplexing predicament. A
negro act in one scene.
Boston: W. H. Baker, 1895.
8p. (Baker's edition of
plays)

The police court. An Ethiopian act in one scene. Boston: W. H. Baker, 1895. 5p.
(Baker's darkey plays)

Scenes in a sanctum. An
Ethiopian farce in one act.
Boston: W. H. Baker, 1895.
9p. (Baker's darkey plays)

Sublime and ridiculous. A
negro act. Boston: W. H.
Baker, 1893. 10p. (Baker's
darkey plays)

That dorg; or, The old toll
house mystery. A black tragedy
in two scenes. Boston: W. H.
Baker, 1895. 8p. (Baker's
darkey plays)

The three o'clock train; or,
The haunted house. A negro
act in one scene. Boston:
W. H. Baker, c1894. 7p.

Tricks upon travellers. A

negro act in one scene.
Boston: W. H. Baker, 1894.
5p. (Baker's darkey plays)

Cogger na Caille [sic, Caillie]
see Belden, N. H. O'Neal,
the great; or, Cogger na
Caille

Coglan, Charles Francis, 1848-
1899.
La partie de piquet *see*
Hollenius, Laurence John.
A game of cards

A coincidence *see* Shettel,
James and George, Wadsworth
M.

Colburn, Carrie W.
His last chance; or, The
little joker. A comedy in
three acts. Boston: W. H.
Baker, c1895. 63p. (Baker's
edition of plays)

Colcleugh, Emma Shaw *see*
Colclough, Emma Shaw

Colclough, Emma Shaw.
An object lesson in history.
An historical exercise for
school exhibitions. New York
and Chicago: E. L. Kellogg,
1896. 24p. Title page lacking. *[although the Readex
entry agrees with the title
page, it is probable that
this was written by Emma
Shaw Colclough, 1847-1940]*

Colcraft, Henry Rowe *see*
Schoolcraft, Henry Rowe

Cold-water cross *see* Dramatic leaflets

Coleman, Mrs. Wilmot Bouton.
Maud Stanley; or, Life scenes
and life lessons. An original
domestic drama in five acts.
New York: n.pub., 1874.
xxxvi, 241 leaves. Prompt-

book in Ms. *[adapted from
Elvira L. Mills' novel,
Maud Stanley]*

A collection of temperance dialogues. By S. T. Hammond,
compiler. Ottawa: S. T.
Hammond, 1869. 112p.
Contents: Marry no man if
he drinks; or, Laura's plan
and how it succeeded (Nellie
E. Bradley.)--Starting in
life.--Ambition.--The ills
of dram-drinking.--Choosing
a trade.--The schoolmaster
abroad.--Moderation; or, I
can take it or leave it
alone (Thomas Ritchie.)--
Debates of conscience with a
distiller, a wholesale
dealer and a retailer.--The
drunkard's daughter (Julia E.
Loomis McConaughy.)--White
lies.--The trial of alcohol.
--A plea for the pledge.--
The try company (G. Bowler.)
--My mother's gold ring.--
The virtues.--The old lady's
will.

College Ned *see* Caldor, M. T.
Social charades

Collins, Wilkie, 1824-1889.
Man and wife *see* Daly,
Augustin *see also* Webber,
Harry A.

A new Magdalen *see* Field,
A. Newton

Collyer, Dan, 1853-1918.
Christmas Eve in the South;
or, Uncle Caleb's home. An
Ethiopian farce in one act
and five scenes. New York:
Dramatic Pub. Co., c1882.
8p. (De Witt's Ethiopian
and comic drama. no. 148)

The milliner's shop. An
Ethiopian sketch in one scene.
New York: De Witt, c1882. 7p.
(De Witt's Ethiopian and

comic drama. no. 147)

Colman, George, 1732-1794.
The clandestine marriage
see The modern standard
drama, vol. 5

The jealous wife *see* The
modern standard drama,
vol. 4

Colman, George, 1762-1836.
Blue devils *see* The
modern standard drama,
vol. 9

The forty thieves *see* The
forty thieves

The heir at law *see* The
modern standard drama,
vol. 12

The iron chest *see* The
modern standard drama,
vol. 6

[Love and madness; or, The
recluse of the mountain]
see Steele, Silas Sexton
in his Collected works.
Book of plays

The mountaineers *see* The
modern standard drama,
vol. 8

The poor gentleman *see*
The modern standard drama,
vol. 3

Sylvester Daggerwood *see*
Massey, Charles. Massey's
exhibition reciter

Who wants a guinea? *see*
Wright, J. B. Jonathan in
England

Colman, Julia, 1828-1909.
No king in America. A pa-
triotic temperance program
in three parts. New York:
National Temperance Society
and Publications House,
1888. 31p.

A colonel's mishap *see*

Pinkopki, Phillip

A colonial girl *see* Hill,
Grace Livingston and Richardson, Abbey Sage

Colored senators *see* Richards,
Bert

A colored witness *see* Venable,
William Henry *in his* The
school stage

Columbia *see* Estabrook, Jones
E. *see also* Speed, Belle
Lewis

Columbia and Mr. "They Say"
see Denton, Clara Janetta
Fort. When the lessons are
over

Columbia and the boys *see*
Denton, Clara Janetta Fort.
When the lessons are over

Columbia, the gem of the ocean
see Winters, Elizabeth

Columbus *see* Peterson, Henry
see also Raymond, George
Lansing. Columbus the dis-
coverer *see also* Raymond,
George Lansing *in his*
Collected works

Columbus and Isabella *see*
Harden, John J.

Columbus; or, A hero of the
new world *see* Preston,
Daniel S.

Columbus the discoverer *see*
Raymond, George Lansing *see*
also his Collected works
see also Warren, Walter

Columbus, the great discoverer
of America. A drama in five
acts. By an Ursuline. New
York: Benziger Bros., 1892.
55p.

The combat with a dragon *see*
Cox, Ethel Louise

A comedie Royall. Being a
forgotten episode of Elizabeth's day *see* Sutherland,
Evelyn Greenleaf Baker *in
her* Collected works. Po'
white trash and other one-
act dramas

Comedies for amateur acting
see Matthews, Brander

Comedies for children *see*
Merriman, Effie Woodward

The comedy of canonization.
New York: Pott and Amery,
1868. 91p.

The comedy of commerce and
tragedy of trade *see*
Battle of the bulls and
bears; or, The comedy of
commerce and tragedy of
trade

A comedy of error; or, The
cousin and the maid *see*
Atherton, George

The comedy of errors. By
William Shak[e]speare.
Boston: William V. Spencer,
1856. 52p. (Spencer's
Boston theatre. no. 34)

Comfort, Richard.
Nero, a tragedy. Philadelphia: n.pub., 1880. 94p.

The comic drama *see* Williams,
Henry Llewellyn. Bobolino,
the black bandit

Comic tragedies *see* Alcott,
Louisa May

The coming man *see* White,
Charles

The coming man; or, Fifty

years hence *see* Varrie,
Vida

Coming of spring *see* Cobb,
Mary L. Poetical dramas for
home and school

The coming of the Messiah *see*
Winkley, Rev. S. H. *in*
Cobb, Mary L. Poetical
dramas for home and school

The coming woman *see* Curtis,
Ariana Randolph Wormeley. The
spirit of seventy-six; or,
The coming woman

Commelin, Anna Olcott.
Hymettus. [From her: Of such
is the kingdom and other
poems. New York: Fowler &
Wells, 1894. 110p.] p.87-
110.

The commercial drummer *see*
Jessop, George Henry. Sam'l
of Posen; or, The commercial
drummer *see also* Melrose,
Thorn

Commercial infidelity; or,
Burglar to slow music *see*
Thomas, F. J.

Commodus *see* Wallace, Lewis

The compact *see* Cannon,
Charles James

Comrades *see* Baker, George
Melville

Comstock, William.
Rum; or, The first glass.
A drama in three acts. New
York: R. M. De Witt, c1875.
31p. (De Witt's acting
plays. no. 194) *see also*
Smith, W. H. The drunkard;
or, The fallen saved

Con O'Ragen's secret *see*
Moore, Bernard Francis. The

haunted hill; or, Con O'-
Ragen's secret

The Confederate spy *see*
Stedman, W. Elsworth

"Confederates" *see* Woodville, Henry

The confession *see* Barnes,
Charlotte Mary Sanford.
Octavia Bragaldi; or, The
confession

A confidence game *see* Card,
Evelyn G. Whiting

The confidential clerk *see*
Stedman, W. Elsworth

Congdon, James Bunker, 1802-
1880.
Quaker quiddities; or,
Friends in council. Boston:
Crosby, Nichols, Lee, 1860.
48p.

Congreve, William, 1670-1729.
Love for love *see* Wallack,
James William

A conjugal lesson *see*
Danvers, H. *in* Steele,
Silas Sexton. Collected
works. Book of plays.

Conjuration *see* Baker,
George Melville *see also*
Caldor. M. T. *in his*
Social charades

Conn; or, Love's victory *see*
Powell, L. S. and Frank,
J. C.

The Connecticut buccaneers
see Greene, R. F. Buried
treasure; or, The Connec-
ticut buccaneers

Connecticut courtship *see*
Conway, H. J. Our Jemimy;
or, Connecticut courtship

Connell, George Stanislaus.
The old patroon and other
plays. New York: William H.
Young, 1899. 103p.
Contents: The old patroon.
--A trilogy in miniature.--
My youngster's love affair.--
The guardian angel.--The mild
monomaniac.

Connelly, James Henderson,
1840-1903.
A drama. In three acts. n.p.:
n.pub., 189-? Prompt-book in
Ms. 74 leaves.

A connubial eclogue *see* Saxe,
John Godfrey *in* Beadle's...
dialogues no. 2

The conqueror conquered *see*
Burleigh, George S. *in*
Dramatic leaflets

The conquerors and conquered;
or, The Spanish and Aztec
races *see* Cuevas, José de
Jesús. The heart and the
sword; or, The conquerors
and conquered; or, The
Spanish and Aztec races

Conrad, Robert Taylor, 1810-
1858.
Aylmere; or, The bondman of
Kent. [From his: Aylmere, or,
The bondman of Kent; and
other poems. Philadelphia:
E. H. Butler, 1852] 6p.,
p.13-165, 287-308.

Jack Cade, the captain of the
commons. A tragedy in four
acts. London: T. H. Lacy,
1869? 65p. (Lacy's acting
edition of plays. vol. 83)
*[since the title given at
the head of the list of
characters reads Jack Cade,
the bondsman of Kent, this
would appear to be a shortened version of Conrad's
Aylmere; or, The bondman of
Kent]*

Conrad and Stella *see*
Arnell, David Reeve

Conrad; or, The hand of a
friend *see* Dumont, Frank

A considerable courtship *see*
Smith, Bessie Blair

The conspiracy *see* Lytton,
Edward George Earle Lytton
Bulwer-Lytton. Richelieu;
or, The conspiracy *in*
Booth, Edwin. The miscel-
laneous plays of Edwin
Booth *see also his*
Richelieu; or, The conspir-
acy *in* The modern standard
drama. vol. 1

The conspirators and lovers
see Landis, Simon Mohler.
The social war of 1900; or,
The conspirators and lovers

The conspirators of Thompson
Street *see* White, Charles.
Julius the snoozer; or, The
conspirators of Thompson
Street

Constancy rewarded *see*
Fidelio; or, Constancy
rewarded

Contentment *see* Venable,
William Henry *in his* The
school stage

Con-Test *see* Cahill, Frank
in Arnold, George? and
Cahill, Frank. Parlor
theatricals; or, Winter
evening's entertainment

A convention of papas *see*
Denison, Thomas Stewart

The convention of the Muses
see Bates, Ella Skinner

The convert *see* Poyas,
Catharine Gendron

Conway, H. J., 1800-1860.
The battle of Stillwater;
or, The maniac *see* Dawes,
Rufus? [or] Conway, H. J.?

Dred. A tale of the great
Dismal Swamp. New York: J. W.
Amerman, 1856. 48p. *[title
page: "founded on the novel
of the same title by H. B.
Stowe"]*

Hiram Hireout; or, Followed
by fortune. A farce in one
act. New York: Samuel French,
1868? 21p. (The minor drama.
The acting edition. no. 170)

Our Jemimy; or, Connecticut
courtship. A farce in one
act. New York: Samuel French,
1856? 25p. (French's American
drama. The acting edition.
no. 78)

The talisman; or, The fairy's
favor. A grand fairy spectacle. n.p.: n.pub., 18-?
152p. Prompt-book in Ms.

Cook, Charles Emerson, 1869-
1941.
The Koreans; or, The ancestors of King-Ki-Too. A comic
opera in three acts. Boston:
B. F. Wood Music Co., c1898.
Vocal score. x, 151p. *[music
by Lucius Hosmer; this play
also appears under the title,
The walking delegate]*

The tie that binds *see*
Wells, David Dwight and
Cook, Charles Emerson

The walking delegate. Boston:
Oliver Ditson, c1897. 42p.
Libretto. *[music by Lucius
Hosmer; contains no music;
this play also appears under
the title, The Koreans; or,
The ancestors of King-Ki-Too]*

Cook, Eliza, 1818-1889.
The mourners *see* Massey,
Charles. Massey's exhibition
reciter

Cook, S.
Uncle Ethan. A farce in one
act. Clyde, O.: Ames, 1892.
10p. (Ames' series of standard and minor drama. no.
312)

Cook, S. N.
Broken promises. A temperance drama in five acts.
New York: Happy Hours,
c1879. 41p.

Out in the streets. A temperance play in three acts.
New York: Dick & Fitzgerald,
18-? 22p.

Uncle Jack; or, Testing
hearts. A comedietta in one
act. New York: Dick & Fitzgerald, 18-? 26p.

The wanderer's return. A
drama in four acts. New
York: Dick & Fitzgerald,
1879. 54p. *[founded on
Tennyson's Enoch Arden]*

Cook, Sherwin Lawrence.
A valet's mistake. A comedy
in two acts. Clyde, O.:
Ames, c1894. 15p. (Ames'
series of standard and
minor drama. no. 329)

The cool collegians *see*
Fales, Willard Henry

Coolidge, Henry Dingley,
1858-1922.
Dead reckoning. A farce.
Boston: W. H. Baker, 1895.
17p. (Baker's edition of
plays)

Coon, Hilton.
Under the American flag.
A Spanish American drama
in four acts. Clyde, O.:
Ames, 1898. 39p. (Ames'
series of standard and
minor drama. no. 415)

The widow from the West;

or, The late Mr. Early. A
farce comedy in three acts.
Boston: W. H. Baker, 1898.
26p. (Baker's edition of
plays)

Cooper, James Fenimore, 1789-
1851.
The last of the Mohicans *see*
The last of the Mohicans

Lionel Lincoln; or, The
leaguer of Boston *see* Glover,
Stephen E. The cradle of
liberty; or, Boston in 1775

The wept of wish-ton-wish
see The wept of wish-ton-
wish

The Coopers *see* White,
Charles

Copcutt, Francis.
Edith. A play in five acts.
New York: John A. Gray, 1857.
83p.

Coppée, François, 1842-1908.
Le passant *see* Renauld,
Charles. The wanderer *see
also* Schmall, Alice F.
Zanetto

Rivales *see* Reynolds, S. S.
Nelly's rival

Copperfield's proposal *see*
Dialogues dramatized from the
works of Charles Dickens

The coquette *see* Josselyn,
Robert *see also* Morris,
Thomas Hollingsworth. Mariana;
or, The coquette

Corbyn, Wardle.
Blanche; or, The rival
fairies. New York: Wardle
Corbyn, 1856. 12p. Scenario.
*[title page: "invented and
composed by M. Robert"]*

Corelli, Marie (pseud.) *see*
Mackay, Mary

Corinna-Lady Jane Grey *see*
Townsend, Frederic *in his*
Spiritual visitors

Coriolanus. By William Shakespeare. As performed by
Tommaso Salvini...New York:
J. J. Little, 1885. 43p.

Coriolanus; or, The Roman
matron *see* Ludlow, Noah
Miller

Corliss, Edward Warren, 1872-
1916.
Miladi and the musketeer
see Barnet, Robert A.

Cormon, Eugène (pseud.) *see*
Piestre, Pierre Étienne

Corneille, Pierre, 1606-1684.
Horace *see* Horace

Polyeucte, martyr; tragédie
chrétienne *see* Polyeuctes,
the martyr

Cornell, John Henry, 1828-1894.
Romeo and Juliet. (From the
French of Deschamps.) New
York: John J. Caulon, 1884?
4p. Libretto. *[title page:*
"Dramatic symphony...composed
from the tragedy of Shake-
speare by Hector Berlioz";
without the music]

Corner, Julia, 1798-1875.
Cinderella; or, Pride punished *see* Venable, William
Henry. The school stage

The corner lot chorus *see*
Furniss, Grace Livingston

Cornish, O. W.
Foiled; or, A struggle for
life and liberty. A drama in
four acts. Chicago: Dramatic
Pub. Co., c1871. 41p. (Ser-

gel's acting drama. no. 102)

Coronaro, Gaetano, 1852-1908.
[At sunset] *see* Schmall,
Alice F. Zanetto [and] At
sunset

The coronation of the rose *see*
Crosby, Frances Jane. The
flower queen; or, The coronation of the rose

A coroner's inquisition *see*
Hall, Abraham Oakey

The corsair's doom *see*
Williams, Charles. Gonsalvo;
or, The corsair's doom

The Corsican brothers *see*
Grangé, Eugène and Montépin,
Xavier Aymons, comte de *in*
The modern standard drama,
vol. 12

Corsican twins. An Ethiopian
burlesque on The Corsican
brothers. London and New
York: S. French, 188-? 8p.
see also Griffin, George
W. H.

Cortez, the conqueror *see*
Thomas, Lewis Foulk

Corwin, C. J.
The man-hater. Sedalia, Mo.:
Sedalia Democrat, c1880.
Title page lacking. 20p.

Corwin, Jane Hudson, 1809-1881.
A dialogue between Mr. Native
and Mrs. Foreigner, on
literary subjects. [From her:
The harp of home...Cincinnati:
Moore, Wilstach, Keys, 1858.
382p.] .p.15-32.

Cosmos *see* Moore, A. S.

Costley, Rosa Fairfax.
Fantasma *see* Fantasma

Côté, Marie.
The witch of bramble hollow.
A drama in four acts. New
York: William H. Young,
1899. 62p.

The Council of Constance see
The Jewess

Counsel for the plaintiff see
Hurd, St. Clair

Count and countess see Norcross, J. W. Gillette; or,
Count and countess

Count Julian see Calvert,
George Henry

A counterfeit presentment see
Howells, William Dean

The counterplot see Fowle,
William Bentley in his
Parlor dramas

The Countess Gucki see Daly,
Augustin

The Countess of Lynn see
Beck, William L. Beyond
pardon; or, The Countess
of Lynn

The country aunt's visit to
the city see Beadle's
dialogues no. 2

The country cousin; or, The
rough diamond see Steele,
Silas Sexton in his
Collected works. Book of
plays

Country cousins see Fowle,
William Bentley in his
Parlor dramas

The country girl see Daly,
Augustin

Country justice see Denison,
Thomas Stewart

A country kid see Scoville,
Nesbit Stone

A country romance see Emerson, W. D.

The country school see Orne,
Martha Russell

The coup d'état. A drama in
five acts. New York: F.
Widdows, 1858. 21p.

Coupon bonds see Trowbridge,
John Townsend

Courcy, Charles de, b.1836.
Vie à deux see Daly,
Augustin. Love in tandem

The courier see Mathews,
Frances Aymar

The court of James the third
see White, James. Feudal
times; or, The court of
James the third in The
modern standard drama,
vol. 6

The court of Prussia see
Gayler, Charles. The love of
a prince; or, The court of
Prussia

The courting of Mother Goose
see Castle, Harriet
Davenport

Courting the wrong lass see
In quod; or, Courting the
wrong lass

Courtright, William, b.1848.
The motor bellows. A comedy
in one act and one scene.
New York: De Witt, c1877.
6p. (De Witt's Ethiopian
and comic drama. no. 117)

Private boarding. An original
comedy in one act and one
scene. New York: C. T. De
Witt, c1877. 6p.

Zacharias' funeral. An
original farce in one act
and one scene. New York:
C. T. De Witt, c1877. 5p.
(De Witt's Ethiopian and
comic drama. no. 116)

Courtship in the twentieth
century *see* Fraser, John
Arthur. Bloomer girls; or,
Courtship in the twentieth
century

The courtship of the deacon
see McFall, B. G. Miss
Topsy Turvy; or, The courtship of the deacon

Courtship under difficulties
see Dramatic leaflets

A courtship with variations
see Bunner, Henry Cuyler
see also Matthews, Brander.
Comedies for amateur acting

The cousin and the maid *see*
Atherton, George. A comedy
of error; or, The cousin and
the maid

Cousin Faithful *see* Lippmann,
Julie Mathilde

Cousin Fannie *see* Mack,
Robert Ellice

Cousin Flavia *see* Benson,
William Henry

Cousin Frank *see* Mathews,
Frances Aymar

Cousin Joe's visit *see*
Leavitt, Andrew J. and
Eagan, H. W.

Cousin John's album *see*
Buxton, Ida M.

Cousin Josiah *see* Cutler,
F. L.

The cousins; or, The dying

requisition *see* Logan,
Thomas B.

The cow that kicked Chicago
see McBride, H. Elliott

Cowan, Frank, 1844-1905.
The three-fold love. A comedy
in five acts. Greensburg,
Pa.: "Herald" Job Off., 1866.
65p.

The cowboy and the lady *see*
Fitch, Clyde

The cowled lover *see* Bird,
Robert Montgomery *in his*
The cowled lover and other
plays

Cowley, E. J.
The Bohemians. A comedy in
3 acts. Boston: W. H. Baker,
c1898. Title page missing.
43p. (Baker's edition of
plays)

Crawford's claim; or, Nugget
Nell, the pet of Poker Flat.
A drama in prologue and three
acts. New York: Dick and
Fitzgerald, c1890. 46p.
[joint author: Wilson T.
Bennette]

Cowley, Hanna Parkhouse, 1743-
1809.
The belle's stratagem *see*
Daly, Augustin

Cox, Eleanor Rogers, 1867-1931.
A duel at dawn. A one act
tragedy [bound with] A
millionaire's trials. A
comedy. New York: P. J.
Kenedy, Excelsior Pub. House,
1894. 45p. (Kenedy's new
series of plays)

Cox, Ethel Louise.
The combat with a dragon.
[From her: Poems, lyric and
dramatic. Boston: Richard G.
Badger, The Gorham Press,

1904. 195p.] p.177-195.

Coxe, Arthur Cleveland, 1818-1896.
Advent. A mystery. New York: J. S. Taylor, 1837. 132p.
Saul. A mystery. New York: D. Appleton, 1845. 297p.

Coyle, Susan Edmond.
Passe Rose *see* Paul, Anne Marie

Coyne, Joseph Stirling, 1803-1868.
The vicar of Wakefield *see* The modern standard drama, vol. 11

The cradle of liberty; or, Boston in 1775 *see* Glover, Stephen E.

Cranch, Christopher Pearse, 1813-1892.
Ariel and Caliban. [From his: Ariel and Caliban with other poems. Boston and New York: Houghton, Mifflin, 1887. 232p.] p.1-19.

Satan: a libretto. Boston: Roberts Bros., 1874. 36p. *[pref.: "I call this poem a libretto because...the verses may suggest or accompany ...music"]*

Crane, Eleanor Maud.
"Just for fun." An up-to-date society comedy in three acts. New York: Dick & Fitzgerald, c1899. 52p.

The lost New Year. A play in two scenes for children. New York: Dick & Fitzgerald, c1897. 23p.

Crane, Elizabeth Green.
Berquin. A drama in five acts. New York: Charles Scribner's Sons, 1897. vi, 110p.

"Cranford" dames *see* Byington, Alice

Crary, J. E.
The Irish squire of Squash Ridge. A farce in two scenes. Clyde, O.: Ames, 1892. 8p. (Ames' series of standard and minor drama. no. 308)

Jacob Shlaff's mistake. A farce in one act. Clyde, O.: Ames, 1892. 13p. (Ames' series of standard and minor drama. no. 305)

Johanes Blatz's mistake; or, The two elopements. A farce comedy in two acts. Clyde, O.: Ames, 1893. 15p. (Ames' series of standard and minor drama. no. 323)

The old Wayside Inn. A drama in five acts. Clyde, O.: Ames, 1894. 30p. (Ames' series of standard and minor drama. no. 331)

Olivet; or, A rare Teutonic specimen. A farce in one act. Clyde, O.: Ames, 1894. 15p. (Ames' series of standard and minor drama. no. 334)

Crawford, Francis Marion, 1854-1909.
In the palace of the king *see* Kester, Paul *see also* Stoddard, Lorimer

Crawford, Francis Marion, The household of *see* Bridges, Robert *in his* Overheard in Arcady

Crawford's claim; or, Nugget Nell, the pet of Poker Flat *see* Cowley, E. J. and Bennette, Wilson T.

A crazy idea *see* Hageman, Maurice

A crazy lot! *see* Rawley, Bert C.

Creagh, Henry.
The sorrows of Satan. New
York: Barney's Copying
Office, 1898. Typescript.
Prompt-book with Ms. notes.
33, 27, 20 leaves. *[based
on The sorrows of Satan; or,
The strange experience of
one Geoffrey Tempest,
millionaire, by Mary Mackay
(pseud. Marie Corelli)]*

The creation *see* Opal
(pseud.) The creation *in
her* The cloud of witnesses

The creator *see* Vogelsang,
G.

Cremation *see* White, Charles

Crémieux, Hector Jonathan,
1828-1892.
Geneviève de Brabant *see*
Bailey, G.

Orphée aux enfers *see*
Orpheus and Eurydice

Crime its own avenger *see*
Bannister, Nathaniel Har-
rington. The three brothers;
or, Crime its own avenger

Crimp's trip to the Centennial
see Chandler, A. N.

Crippen, Thomas George.
Joseph in Egypt. A Biblical
drama in five acts. By C. J.
Hanssen, editor. New York:
Roxbury Pub. Co., 18-? 28p.

The critic *see* The modern
standard drama. vol. 8

The critique of the vision of
Rubeta *see* Osborn, Laughton

The crock of gold; or, The
toiler's trials *see* Steele,
Silas Sexton

Crockett, Ingram.
The Inca's daughter. [From
his: Beneath blue skies and
gray. New York: R. H. Russell, c1898. 108p.] p.89-93.

Cromwell *see* Hamilton,
Alexander

Cromwell: an historical play
see Wiley, Sara King

Cronkhite, Henry McLean,
b.1834.
Reymond. A drama of the
American Revolution. New
York: G. P. Putnam's Sons,
1886. 101p.

Crosby, Frances Jane, 1820-1915.
The flower queen; or, The
coronation of the rose. A
cantata in two parts. New
York: Mason Bros., 1852.
15p. Libretto. *[music composed by George F. Root;
without the music]*

The flower queen; or, The
coronation of the rose.
(Music by George F. Root.)
Buffalo: George C. Rexford,
18-? 24p. Libretto.

Crosby, Frank.
Teacher wanted *see* Dramatic
leaflets

The cross of honor *see*
Rideal, Charles Frederick and
Winter, C. Gordon

Cross purposes. A comedietta in
one act. New York: Happy
Hours Co., c1879. 14p. (The
acting drama. no. 120) *see
also* O'Brien, Constance

Crossy, John Stewart *see*
Stewart, J. C. (pseud.)

The crowded hotel; or, The
tricky nig *see* Hall, J.
Griffin

Crowding the season *see*
Hardy, Edward Trueblood

Crown, A. Gwyllyn.
King winter's carnival *see*
Alexander, Sigmund Bowman

Crown jewels *see* Wuttke,
Hermann

Crowning the queen of vegetables *see* Lewis, E. A.
and Lewis, C. M. Mother
earth and her vegetable
daughter's [sic]; or,
Crowning the queen of
vegetables

A cruel hoax *see* Heywood,
Delia A. *in her* Choice
dialogues. no. 1

Cruel to be kind *see* Vezin,
Hermann

Crumpton, M. Nataline, 1857-
1911.
Ceres. A mythological play
for parlor and school in
three acts. Boston: Walter
H. Baker, c1890. 17p.
Libretto. (Baker's edition
of plays)

Pandora. A classical play
for parlor and school in
three acts. Boston: Walter
H. Baker, c1890. 11p.
(Baker's edition of plays)

Theseus. A play for parlor
and school in five acts.
Boston: Walter H. Baker,
1902. 29p. Libretto. (Baker's
edition of plays) *[earlier
copyright: 1892]*

The crusaders *see* Murray,
Ellen *in* Dramatic leaflets

A crushed mother-in-law *see*
File, Franklin

The crystal slipper; or,
Prince Prettywitz and little

Cinderella *see* Smith, Harry
Bache and Thompson, Alfred

The Cuban patriots *see*
Pierra, Adolfo

The Cuban spy *see* Dumont,
Frank

The Cucumber Hill debating
club *see* McBride, H.
Elliott *in his* New dialogues

Cuevas, José de Jesús, 1842-
1901.
The heart and sword; or, The
conquerors and conquered; or,
The Spanish and Aztec races.
Mexico: n.pub., 1879. 24p.

Cuff's luck *see* Cutler, F. L.

Cuisine and cupid *see* Buel,
David Hillhouse. Penikeese;
or, Cuisine and cupid

Cummings, G. D.
The history of Geronimo's
summer campaign in 1885.
n.p.: n.pub., 1890. 73p.

Cunningham, H.
The golden goose. Boston:
Walter H. Baker, c1890. 24p.
*[title page: "dramatized from
'Gammer Grethel.'" Gammer
Grethel was Frau Katherina
Viehmannin, a German peasant
woman whose stories were
immortalized by the Brothers
Grimm; this particular tale
was originally published
under the title Die goldene
Ganz]*

Cunningham, Mrs. P. C. *see*
Cunningham, Virginia Juhan

Cunningham, Virginia Juhan,
1834-1874.
Madelaine, the bell of Faubourg. Boston: W. V. Spencer,
1856. Prompt-book, interleaved
with Ms. notes. 40p. *[in the*

biography published at the
beginning of the play, the
author's name is given as
Mrs. P. C. Cunningham]

The maid of Florence; or, A
woman's vengeance. A pseudo-
historical tragedy in five
acts. Charleston: S. S.
Miller, 1839. 92p. *[Readex*
enters a different edition
of this play under title]

The cup and the lip *see*
Walcot, Maria Grace

A cup of coffee *see* Reynartz, Dorothy

A cup of tea from 1773 *see*
Wheeler, Esther Gracie
Lawrence

The cup of youth *see*
Mitchell, Silas Weir

Cupid and cupidity *see*
Drey, Sylvan

Cupid in shirt sleeves *see*
Scott, W. Atkins

Cupid on wheels *see* Wyeth,
Albert Lang

Cupid's capers *see* Richards,
Bert

Cupid's eye-glass *see*
Picton, Thomas

Cupid's frolics *see* Dumont,
Frank *see also his* The
amateur minstrel

Cupid's little game. A Newport
drama in three acts [bound
with] A doctor in spite of
himself. (By H. G. W.)(Not)
by Molière. Providence:
E. L. Freeman, 1881. 64p.
[the somewhat awkward
punctuation given above has
been transcribed from the

title page]

Cupid's pastimes *see* Andrews,
Fred G. Love's labor not
lost; or, Cupid's pastimes

A cure for a bad appetite *see*
The temperance school dialogues

A cure for dumbness *see*
Wood, C. A. F. The Irish
broom-maker; or, A cure for
dumbness

A cure for the "Blues" *see*
Steele, Silas Sexton. The
hypochrondriac; or, A cure
for the "Blues" *in his*
Collected works. Book of
plays

A cure for the heartache *see*
Morton, Thomas *in* The
modern standard drama,
vol. 2

The cure of love *see* Paulding,
James Kirke and Paulding,
William Irving. Madmen all;
or, The cure of love *in*
their Collected works.
American comedies

The cure of souls *see* Fuller,
Henry Blake *in his* Collected works

Curiosity *see* Caldor, M. T.
in his Social charades

Currie, William H.
Facts and fancies *see*
Tooth, William

The curse *see* Jones, R.?
Wacousta; or, The curse

The curse of drink *see*
McCloskey, James Joseph. The
fatal glass; or, The curse
of drink

The curtain lifted; or, The
Order of the Sons of Mars
see Hiland, Frank E.

Curtis, Ariana Randolph
Wormeley, 1833-1922.
A change of base. [From
her: The spirit of seventy-
six; or, The coming woman...
followed by A change of base
and Doctor Mondschein. Boston: Little, Brown, 1868.]
p.75-110. *[Readex gives a*
birth date of 1835, while
the Library of Congress and
other bibliographical
sources give 1833. Similarly,
Readex spells Curtis' first
name Arriana, while other
sources give Ariana]

Doctor Mondschein; or, The
violent remedy. [From her:
The spirit of seventy-six;
or, The coming woman...
followed by A change of base
and Doctor Mondschein. Boston: Little, Brown, 1868.]
p.111-141.

The spirit of seventy-six;
or, The coming woman. [From
her: The spirit of seventy-
six; or, The coming woman...
followed by A change of
base and Doctor Mondschein.
Boston: Little, Brown, 1868.]
p.3-73.

Curtis, Austice.
One question *see* One
question

Curtis, George William, 1824-
1892.
The Potiphar papers *see*
Browne, Irving. Our best
society

Curtis, Herbert Pelham.
Lying will out. A comedy
in four acts. Boston: W. H.
Baker, c1880. 35p.

None so deaf as those who

won't hear. A comedietta in
one act. Boston: G. M. Baker,
1880. 22p.

Uncle Robert; or, Love's
labor saved. A comedy in
three acts. Boston: W. H.
Baker, c1861. 34p. (Baker's
edition of plays)

Curzon, Sarah Anne, 1833-1898.
Laura Secord, the heroine of
1812. [From her: Laura
Secord...and other poems.
Toronto: C. Blackett Robinson,
1887. 215p.] p.1-66.

The sweet girl graduate. A
comedy in four acts. [From
her: Laura Secord...and
other poems. Toronto: C.
Blackett Robinson, 1887.
215p.] p.122-137.

Cusack, Sister Mary Frances
Clare, 1830-1899.
Tim Carty's trial; or,
Whistling at landlords. A
play for the times. New York:
S. Mearns, 1886. 57p. *[Readex*
uses the masculine form
"Francis," which is the form
given on the title page, but
other bibliographical sources
give "Frances."]

Cushing, Eliza Lanesford
Foster, b.1794.
Esther. [From her: Esther, a
sacred drama: with Judith,
a poem. Boston: Joseph Dowe,
1840. 118p.] p.1-103.

Cushing, Harry H.
The lost child *see* Dramatic
leaflets

Cutler, F. L.
Actor and servant. A Dutch
farce in one act. Clyde, O.:
Ames, 1884. 7p. (Ames' series
of standard and minor drama.
no. 132)

Cousin Josiah. A musical
sketch in one scene. Clyde,
O.: Ames, 1891. 5p. (Ames'
series of standard and
minor drama. no. 287)

Cuff's luck. Ethiopian
sketch in one scene. Clyde,
O.: Ames, 1883. p.11-14.
(Ames' series of standard
and minor drama. no. 145)

The Dutch prize fighter.
A Dutch farce in one act.
Clyde, O.: Ames, 1886. 6p.
(Ames' series of standard
and minor drama. no. 188)

Hans, the Dutch J. P. A
Dutch farce in one act.
Clyde, O.: Ames, 1878. 7p.
(Ames' series of standard
and minor drama. no. 66)

Joe, the waif; or, The pet
of the camp. A comedy drama
in six acts. Clyde, O.: Ames,
c1898. 39p. (Ames' series of
standard and minor drama.
no. 402)

Kitty and Patsy; or, The
same thing over again. An
Irish musical sketch in one
scene. Clyde, O.: Ames,
1897. 6p. (Ames' series of
standard and minor drama.
no. 389)

Lodgings for two. A farce
in one act. Clyde, O.:
Ames, 1880. 6p. (Ames'
series of standard and
minor drama. no. 106)

Lost!; or, The fruits of the
glass. A temperance drama
in three acts. Clyde, O.:
Ames, 1882. 10p. (Ames'
series of standard and
minor drama. no. 104)

The mashers mashed. A farce
in two acts. Clyde, O.: Ames,
1891. 10p. (Ames' series of
standard and minor drama.
no. 285)

The musical darkey. A farce
in one act. Clyde, O.: Ames,
1884. 7p. (Ames' series of
standard and minor drama.
no. 128)

Old Pompey. An Ethiopian
sketch in one scene. Clyde,
O.: Ames, 1883. p.21-23.
(Ames' series of standard and
minor drama. no. 150)

Peleg and Peter; or, Around
the Horn. A farce-comedy in
four acts. Clyde, O.: Ames,
1892. 23p. (Ames' series of
standard and minor drama.
no. 301)

Pomp's pranks. Ethiopian
farce in one act. Clyde, O.:
Ames, c1884. 7p. (Ames'
series of standard and minor
drama. no. 134)

A scale with sharps and flats.
An operatic and musical
comedy in one act. Clyde, O.:
Ames, c1888. 15p. (Ames'
series of standard and minor
drama. no. 239)

Seeing Bosting. A farce in
one act. Clyde, O.: Ames,
1884. 6p. (Ames' series of
standard and minor drama.
no. 133)

The sham professor. A farce
in one act. Clyde, O.: Ames,
1879. 6p. (Ames' series of
standard and minor drama.
no. 68)

Struck by lightning. A farce
in one act. Clyde, O.: Ames,
c1887. 8p. (Ames' series of
standard and minor drama.
no. 241)

That boy Sam. An Ethiopian
farce in one act. Clyde, O.:
Ames, 1878. 6p. (Ames' series
of standard and minor drama.
no. 64)

$2,000 reward; or, Done on

both sides. A change act
comedy in one act. Clyde,
O.: Ames, 1887. 15p. (Ames'
series of standard and
minor drama. no. 240)

Wanted a husband. A Dutch
sketch in one scene. Clyde,
O.: Ames, c1883. 8p. (Ames'
series of standard and
minor drama. no. 151)

Cutter, Rollin.
Pistols for two. A come-
dietta in one act. Phila-
delphia: Penn Pub. Co.,
1908. 17p. *[earlier copyright: 1897]*

Cuttyback's thunder; or,
Frank Wilde [sic, Wylde]
see Matthews, Brander

A cyclone for a cent *see*
Phelps, Pauline

The cynic *see* Miles, George
Henry. Mary's birthday; or,
The cynic

Cyrano de Bergerac *see*
Renauld, Charles *see also*
Smith, Harry Bache

The Czar and the carpenter
see Balatka, Hans. Peter
the Great in Saardam; or,
The Czar and the carpenter

Czibulka, Alphons, 1842-1894.
Pfingsten in Florenz *see*
Goldmark, George and Rosen-
feld, Sydney. Amorita

D., F. A.
Maiden Mona the mermaid.
A fairy play for fairy
people. Toronto: Belford
Bros., 1877. 42p.

D., F. I. (pseud.) *see*
Duncan, Florence I.

Dagon stoops to Sabaoth *see*
Bien, Herman Milton. Sam-

son and Delilah; or, Dagon
stoops to Sabaoth

Daguerreotypes; or, The picture
gallery *see* White, Charles

Dailey, W. B.
Saratoga. A dramatic romance
of the revolution. [From his:
Saratoga...and other historical romances of American
history. Corning: Thomas
Messenger, 1848. 96p.] p.1-48.

Daisy and Don *see* Busch,
William. Tell tale eyes; or,
Daisy and Don

Daisy Garland's fortune *see*
Davis, Edwin Abraham

Daisy Miller *see* James, Henry

Daland, William Clinton, d.1921.
The song of songs. Alfred
Center, N. Y.: American
Sabbath Tract Society Steam
Print., 1888. Second edition.
50p.

The song of songs. Leonards-
ville, N. Y.: For the author,
1887. 24p.

Dale, Horace C.
Breaking his bonds. A comedy-
drama in four acts. New York:
Dick & Fitzgerald, c1894. 34p.

The deacon. An original comedy
drama in five acts. New York:
Dick & Fitzgerald, c1892. 50p.

The deacon's tribulations. An
original comedy-drama in four
acts. New York: Dick & Fitzgerald, c1897. 32p. Title
page mutilated.

Imogene; or, The witch's
secret. An original realistic
drama in four acts. New York:
Dick & Fitzgerald, 1892. 42p.

Josiah's courtship. A farce
comedy drama in four acts.
New York: Dick & Fitzgerald,

1896. 37p.

Strife. An original comedy
drama in four acts. New
York: Fitzgerald Pub. Corp.,
c1890. 72p. (Roorbach's
American edition of acting
plays. no. 49)

A white lie. An original
comedy drama in four acts.
New York: H. Roorbach,
c1899. 44p.

Dallas, Mary Kyle, 1830-1897.
Aroused at last. A comedy
in one act. Chicago:
Dramatic Pub. Co., c1892.
22p. (Sergel's acting
drama. no. 440)

Our Aunt Robertina. A
comedietta in one act.
Boston: W. H. Baker, 1902.
12p. (Baker's edition of
plays) *[earlier copyright:
1891]*

Daly, Augustin, 1838-1899.
After business hours. Comedy
in four acts. (From the
German of Dr. Oscar Blu-
menthal.) New York: Privately printed for the
author as Ms. only, 1886.
67p.

An Arabian night in the
nineteenth century. A
comedy in four acts. (From
the German of G. von Moser.)
New York: Printed as manuscript only, for the author,
1884. 84p.

As you like it. (From
Shakespeare.) [With fac-
simile reprint of the
edition of 1623] New York:
Privately printed for Mr.
Daly, 1890. 88p. p.185-207.

The belle's stratagem.
(Condensed from Mrs. Hannah
Parkhouse Cowley's comedy.)
New York: Printed from the
prompt-book of Daly's Theatre,
1892. 41p.

The big bonanza. A comedy of
our time in five acts. New
York: Printed from Ms. only
for the author, 1884. 77p.
*[title page: "from the German
of von Moser"]*

The Countess Gucki. A comedy
in three acts. (From the
German of Franz von Schoenthan.) New York: Privately
printed for the author, c1895.
85p.

The country girl. A comedy in
three acts. (Altered and
adapted by David Garrick,
from "The Country Wife," by
William Wycherly and arranged
for presentation by Augustin
Daly.) New York: Printed as
played at Daly's Theatre,
1884. 47p.

Denise. (From the French of
Alexandre Dumas the younger.)
New York: n.pub., 1885. Typescript, parts-book. 8 parts
(pag. by parts.)

Divorce. New York?: 187-?.
Sides for twenty-four parts.

Divorce. A play of the period
in five acts. New York: For
the author, 1884. 93p.

Divorce. [From: America's
lost plays, vol. 20. Princeton, N. J.: Princeton Univ.
Press, 1942] p.73-161.

Dollars and sense; or, The
heedless ones. A comedy of
today in three acts. New
York: Printed, as manuscript
only, for the author, 1885.
71p.

A flash of lightning. A drama
of life in our day in five
acts. New York: Printed as
Ms. only, for the author,
1885. 72p.

"Frou Frou." A comedy of powerful human interest in five acts. New York: S. French, c1870. 59p. (French's standard drama. no. 359) [based on the French of Meilhac and Halévy]

The great unknown. A comedy in three acts. (From the German of Schoenthan and Kadelburg.) New York: Printed for the author as Ms., 1890. 64p.

Griffith Gaunt; or, Jealousy. A drama in five acts. New York: W. C. Wemyss, 1868. 45p. (Wemyss' acting drama. no. 3)

Hazardous ground. An original adaptation in four acts. (Adaptation of "Nos bons villageois" by Victorien Sardou.) New York: W. C. Wemyss, 1868. 46p. (Wemyss' acting drama. no. 4)

Horizon. An original drama of contemporaneous society and of American frontier perils in five acts and seven tableaux. New York: Printed, as manuscript only, for the author, 1885. 67p.

The hunchback. A comedy in five acts. By Sheridan Knowles. New York: for Augustin Daly, 1893. 71p.

The inconstant; or, The way to win him. (From a comedy by George Farquhar.) New York: Privately printed for Mr. Daly, 1889. 57p. [title page: "...an original epilogue by William Winter"]

An international match. A comedy in four acts. (From the German of Franz von Schoenthan.) New York: Privately printed for the author, 1890. 63p.

The last word. A comedy in

four acts. (From the German of Franz von Schoenthan.) New York: The author, 1891. Prompt-book with Ms. notes. 71p.

Leah: the forsaken. A play in five acts. (From the "Deborah" of Mosenthal.) New York: Printed for the author, 1863. 33 leaves.

Leah, the forsaken. London: S. French, 1872. 44p. (French's acting edition)

A legend of "Norwood"; or, Village life in New England. An original dramatic comedy of American life in four acts. New York: For the author, 1867. 79p. [based on Norwood by Henry Ward Beecher]

Lemons. (From the German of Julius Rosen.) New York: Privately printed for Augustin Daly, 1877. 61p.

Little Miss Million. A comedy in four acts. (From the German of Blumenthal.) New York: Printed as Ms., for the author only, 1893. 78p.

The lottery of love. An eccentric comedy in three acts. (From the French of Bisson and Mars.) New York: Privately printed for the author, 1889. 64p.

Love in harness. A comedy in three acts. (From the French of Albin Valabrègue.) New York: Privately printed for the author as Ms. only, 1887. 63p.

Love in tandem. A comedy in three acts. (From the French of Bocage and de Courcy.) New York: Printed as Ms. for the author, 1892. 84p. [based on Vie à deux by Pierre-François Tousey Bocage and Charles de Courcy]

Love on crutches. A comedy in three acts. (From the German of Stobitzer.) New York: Printed as Ms. only, for the author, 1885. Prompt-book. 66p.

Love's labour's lost. (From Shakespeare.) New York: J. W. Morrissey, 1874. 53p.

Love's labor [sic] lost. (From the play by William Shakespere [sic]) New York: Privately printed for Mr. Daly, 1891. 64p.

Madelaine Morel. A play in four acts. (From the German of Mosenthal.) New York: Printed as Ms. only, for the author, 1884. 67p.

Man and wife. (From: America's lost plays. vol. 20. Princeton, N. J.: Princeton Univ. Press, 1942) p.1-72. *[based on a novel by Wilkie Collins. It is interesting to note that Collins tried to prevent Daly from performing this unauthorized version of his play; see Wilkie Collins and Charles Reade, by Morris L. Parrish (New York: Burt Franklin, 1968, reprint of 1940 ed.), p.83]*

The merchant of Venice. (From Shakespeare.) New York?: Privately printed, 1896. 69p.

The merry wives of Windsor. (From Shakespeare.) New York: Trow's Printing & Bookbinding Co., 1886. 71p.

The merry wives of Windsor ...a facsimile...together with a reprint of the prompt-copy...By William Shakespeare. New York: n.pub., printed for Mr. Daly, 1886. xi, xi, 72p.

A midsummer night's dream.

By William Shakespere [sic]) New York: For Mr. Daly, 1888. 75p.

Monsieur Alphonse. A play in three acts. (From the French of Alexandre Dumas.) New York: For the author, 1886. 60p.

Much ado about nothing. (From Shakespeare.) London: Privately printed for the author, 1897. Prompt-book. 80p.

Nancy and company. An eccentric piece in four acts. (From the German of Rosen.) New York: Printed as manuscript for the author, 1886. 63p. *[based on Halbe Dichter, by Julius Rosen]*

Needles and pins. A comedy of the present in four acts. (From the German of Rosen.) New York: Printed as manuscript only, for the author, 1884. 77p. *[based on Starke Mitteln, by Julius Rosen]*

A night off; or, A page from Balzac. A comedy in four acts. (From the German of the Schoenthan Brothers.) New York: Printed as Ms. only, for the author, 1885. 75p.

Our English friend. A comedy in four acts. New York: Printed as manuscript only, for the author, 1884. 78p. *[an adaptation of Reif-reiflingen, by Gustav von Moser]*

The passing regiment. A comedy of the day in five acts. (From the German of G. von Moser and Franz von Schoenthau [sic, Schoenthan]) New York: Printed, as manuscript only, for the author, 1884. 79p.

Pique. A play of to-day in five acts. New York: Printed as Ms. only, for the author, 1884. 97p.

The railroad of love. A comedy in four acts. (From the German of Schoenthan and Kadelburg.) New York: Printed for the author, 1887. 72p.

The recruiting officer. (Re-arranged and adapted from the comedy by George Farquhar.) New York: Trow's Printing & Bookbinding Co., 1885. 62p.

Rehearsing a tragedy. A conceit in one act. (Altered and adapted from "The Critic" by Richard Brinsley Sheridan.) New York: Privately printed for Mr. Daly, 1889. 32p.

The school for scandal. A comedy in five acts. (Re-arranged from the play by Richard Brinsley Sheridan.) New York: S. French & Son, c1874. Prompt-book. 72p.

7-20-8; or, Casting a boomerang. A comedy of today in four acts. (From the German of Schoenthan.) New York: Printed as Ms. only, for the author, 1884. 73p.

She wou'd and she wou'd not. (Rearranged and adapted from a comedy by Colley Cibber.) New York: Printed for Daly's Theatre, 1886. 68p. *[based on She wou'd and she wou'd not; or, The kind imposter, by Colley Cibber, which was based in part on John Leanerd's Counterfeits]*

A sister's sacrifice. New York: Werner, 18-? p.183-186. (Werner's readings and recitations. no. 4)

Taming a butterfly. (From Sardou's "La papillonne.") New York: Printed for the authors, 1864. 43 leaves. *[joint author: Frank Wood]*

Taming of the shrew. A comedy by William Shakspere [sic] New York: Privately printed for Mr. Daly, 1887. Centenary edition. 75p.

Taming of the shrew. By William Shakspere [sic] New York: Privately printed, 1887. 69p.

The tempest. By William Shakspere [sic] New York: Douglas Taylor, 1897. 51p.

A test case; or, Grass versus granite. A comedy in four acts. (From the German of Blumenthal and Kadelburg.) New York: Printed as Ms. only for the author, 1893. 76p.

[Three preludes to the play] New York: Douglas Taylor, n.d. 63p.
  Contents: Love's young dream. Translated from the French.--A wet blanket. From the French of Bilhaud and Lévy.--A sudden shower. From the French of Beissier.

Twelfth night; or, What you will. (From Shakespeare.) New York: Privately printed for Augustin Daly, 1893. 70p.

The two gentlemen of Verona. By William Shakespeare. New York: n.pub., 1895. Presentation copy signed by the author. 57p.

Under the gaslight. A totally original and picturesque drama of life and love in these times in five acts. New York?: n.pub., 18-? Prompt-book. 93p.

Under the gaslight. A totally original and picturesque drama of life and love in these times in five acts. New York: W. C. Wemyss, 1867. 47p. (Wemyss' acting drama)

The wonder! a woman keeps a secret. (Arranged from the comedy by Mrs. Susannah Centlivre.) New York: Privately printed for Mr. Daly, 1893. 61p.

La dame aux camélias. (Camille) A play in five acts. (From the French of A. Dumas, the younger.) New York: F. Rullman, c1880. Bilingual text: French and English. 45p.

The damnation de Faust. Dramatic legend in four parts. (Songs by Bayard Taylor.) New York: n.pub., 1880. 16p. *[based on La damnation de Faust by Gérard de Nerval and Almire Gandonnière, originally derived from Goethe's Faust; without the music by Berlioz]*

The damnation of Faust. By Dr. Leopold Damrosch, editor. (From the French of Berlioz.) New York: G. Schirmer, c1880. New and revised edition. Vocal score. Bilingual text: English and German. 236p.

Damon and Pythias *see* Banim, John *in* The modern standard drama, vol. 5 *see also* Forrest, Edwin *see also* White, Charles

Damrosch, Leopold, 1832-1885. The damnation of Faust *see* The damnation of Faust

Damrosch, Walter Johannes, 1862-1950. The scarlet letter *see* Lathrop, George Parsons

Dana, Eliza A. Fuller. Iona. An Indian tragedy. [From her: Gathered leaves. Cambridge: Private edition, H. O. Houghton, Printer, 1864] 160p.

The dance of death *see* Lazarus, Emma

Dancing attendance *see* Williams, Henry Llewellyn

The dancing Dutchman *see* Kavanaugh, Mrs. Russell *in* her Original dramas, dialogues

Dancing mad. An Ethiopian eccentricity in one scene. New York: Happy Hours, c1875. 6p. (The Ethiopian drama. no. 109)

The dandy prince *see* Phelps, Lavinia Howe *in her* Dramatic stories

The danger of moderate drinking *see* Bradley, Nellie H. Reclaimed; or, The danger of moderate drinking

The danger signal *see* Denison, Thomas Stewart

Daniel Rochat *see* Prichard, Joseph Vila

Daniel v. Dishcloth *see* Stevens, ? *in* Massey, Charles. Massey's exhibition reciter

The Danites in the Sierras *see* Miller, Joaquin

Danvers, H. A conjugal lesson *in* Steele, Silas Sexton. Collected works. Book of plays

Daphne; or, The pipes of Arcadia *see* Merington, Marguerite

Da Ponte, Lorenzo *see* Ponte, Lorenzo da *[Readex enters Da Ponte's works under Ponte, contrary to Library of Congress practice]*

Darcy, Fred.
The devil's mine. A sensa-
tional drama in four acts.
New York: n.pub., 1890.
Typescript, prompt-book.
Sides for eleven parts.

D'Arcy, James J.
Dark before dawn. A drama...
for male characters only.
Notre Dame, Ind.: Ave Maria
n.d. 30p.

D'Arcy of the guards; or, The
fortunes of war see
Shipman, Louis Evan

Dark before dawn see
D'Arcy, James J.

Dark deeds. A sensational
play in three acts. New York:
Happy Hours, 1876. 11p.
(Parlor plays for home performance. no. 10)

A dark noight's business see
McDermott, J. J. and Trumble

A dark romance from the "Rail-
way library" see Williams,
Henry Llewellyn. Fetter
Lane to Gravesend; or, A
dark romance from the
"Railway library"

The dark tragedian see
Townsend, Charles

Darkest Russia see Donnelly,
Henry Grattan

The darkey breach of promise
case see Barnes, James

The darkey phrenologist see
Barnes, James

The darkey sleep-walker; or,
Ill-treated ill somnambulo
see Williams, Henry
Llewellyn

The darkey tragedian. An
Ethiopian sketch in one
scene. New York: Dick &
Fitzgerald, c1874. 7p.
[this play is identical with
the play of the same title
by Charles Townsend, q.v.]

The darkey wood dealer see
Townsend, Charles

The darkey's stratagem see
White, Charles

Darkness see Byron, George
Gordon in Massey, Charles.
Massey's exhibition reciter

The darktown bicycle club
scandal see Horne, Mary
Barnard

Darley, Francis T. S.
Fortunio and his seven gifted
servants see Fortunio and
his seven gifted servants

Darling, Edward I., b.1863.
The Viking see Clayton,
Estelle

Darnley, James Henry.
Facing the music. An original
farcical comedy in three
acts. New York: S. French,
c1905. 71p. (French's international copyrighted edition
of the works of the best
authors. no. 81)

Darr, Alphons, 1811-1866.
Robinsonade see Childs,
Nathaniel

Dar's de money see Williams?,
Henry Llewellyn

The dashing tar outwitted by
his wife see Byrne, Charles
Alfred. Pearl of Pekin; or,
The dashing tar outwitted by
his wife

Daudet, Alphonse, 1840-1897.
Sapho *see* Fitch, Clyde.
Sappho *see also* Ginty,
Elizabeth Beall. Sappho
see also Smith, Edgar
McPhail and Smith, Harry
Bache. Sapolio

A daughter of Athens *see*
Grice, Louis May

The daughter of the regiment.
A grand opera in two acts.
(From the English of Fitzball.) Boston: J. H. Eastburn's, 1855. 38p. Libretto.
[based on the libretto by
Jules Henri Vernoy de Saint-
Georges and Jean François
Alfred Bayard, with music
by Gaetano Donizetti;
without the music] *see also*
The child of the regiment
see also La figlia del
reggimento *see also* Seguin,
Arthur Edward Sheldon. Marie;
or, The daughter of the
regiment

The daughters of Oedipus *see*
Bailey, William Entriken.
Dramatic poems

Daulac *see* Campbell, William
Wilfred. Collected works.
Poetical tragedies

Daveau, Illion.
The plague of my life. A
farce in one act. New York:
Wheat & Cornett, c1875.
p.20-28. (New York Drama
vol. 1, no. 6)

Davenport, Fanny Lily Gypsy,
1850-1898.
Olivia. Vicar of Wakefield.
(Adapted from the play by
W. G. Wills.) New York:
n.pub., 1878. Prompt-book
in Ms. 209p. (Pag. irreg.)
[based on William Gorman
Wills' Olivia, and on
Oliver Goldsmith's The vicar

of Wakefield]

La Tosca. n.p.: n.pub., 1888.
Title page lacking. Prompt-
book in Ms. 115 irregularly
paginated leaves. *[based*
on the play of the same name
by Victorien Sardou]

David and Abigail *see* Lampman,
Archibald

David and Uriah. A drama in
five acts. Philadelphia:
The author, 1835. 34p.

David Garrick *see* Sullivan

David Harum *see* Hitchcock,
James Ripley Wellman and
Hitchcock, Martha Wolcott
Hall

David Laroque *see* Johns,
George Sibley

David the son of Jesse; or,
The peasant, the princess
and the prophet *see*
Brooks, Elbridge Streeter

Davidson, Belle L.
A visit from Mother Goose.
New York: E. L. Kellogg,
c1896. 12p.

Davidson, Gustav.
Melmoth, the wanderer. A
melo-dramatic romance in three
acts founded on the popular
novel of that name. Baltimore:
J. Robinson, 1831. 41p. *[joint*
author: Joseph Koven; based on
Melmoth the wanderer, by
Charles Robert Maturin]

Davidson, Robert, 1808-1876.
Elijah. [From his: Elijah,
a sacred drama, and other
poems. New York: Charles
Scribner, 1860] p.7-101.

Davies, Dotie, 1859-1938.
'Twas surely fate *see*

Schell, Stanley. An old maid's conference *[Dotie Davies is the real name of Hope Temple]*

Davis, Edwin Abraham. Daisy Garland's fortune. A sensational comedy drama in five acts. Clyde, O.: Ames, 1894. 23p. (Ames' series of standard and minor drama. no. 343)

Davis, Mary Evelyn Moore, 1852-1909. A bunch of roses. A romantic comedy. New York: E. S. Werner, c1899. 24p.

Christmas boxes. New York: Edgar S. Werner, c1907. Title page lacking. p.92-131. *[earlier copyright: 1899]*

A Christmas masque of Saint Roch. [From her: A Christmas masque, Père Dagobert and Throwing the wanga. Chicago: A. C. McClurg, 1896] p.1-5, 9-34, 57-58.

A dress rehearsal. New York: Edgar S. Werner, c1907. Title page lacking. p.134-202. *[earlier copyright: 1899]*

The new system. New York: [Edgar] S. Werner, c1907. Title page lacking. p.205-257. *[earlier copyright: 1899]*

Queen Anne cottages. Romantic comedy. New York: Edgar S. Werner, c1907. Title page lacking. p.26-47. *[earlier copyright: 1899]*

Davis, Paul P. An amateur triumph. A comedietta in one act. Philadelphia: Penn Pub. Co., 1915. *[earlier copyright: 1895]*

Davis, Richard Harding, 1864-1916.

The boy orator of Zepata City *see his* The orator of Zepata City

Her first appearance *see* Hilliard, Robert Cochrane. The littlest girl

The orator of Zepata City. Chicago: Dramatic Pub. Co., c1900. 12p. (Sergel's acting drama. no. 411) *[based on the author's story entitled The boy orator of Zepata City]*

Davis, Richard Harding, The household of *see* Bridges, Robert *in his* Overheard in Arcady

Davison, E. Mora, d.1948. The New Englanders. A comedy of the Revolution in three acts. New York: For private circulation, Collins & Brother, 1882. 55p.

Davy Crockett; or, Be sure you're right, then go ahead *see* Murdoch, Frank Hitchcock

Dawes, Rufus, 1803-1859. Athenia of Damascus. A tragedy. New York: S. Colman, 1839. 118p. (Colman's dramatic library)

Athenia of Damascus. A tragedy. [From his: Geraldine, Athenia of Damascus and miscellaneous poems. New York: Samuel Colman, 1839. 343p.] p.113-201. (American dramatic library. vol. 1)

The battle of Stillwater; or, The maniac. n.p.: n.pub., 1840? In Ms. In three acts (pag. by acts.) *[see below]*

The battle of Stillwater; or, The maniac. [From: Metamora and other plays. By E. R. Page, editor. Princeton: Princeton Univ. Press, 1941.

(America's lost plays, vol.
14) 399p.] p.107-142 *[while
authorship is uncertain,
this play has been attributed to Rufus Dawes and to
H. J. Conway]*

The dawn of ethics   *see*
Fawcett, Edgar

The dawn of liberty; or, Cadunt
regum coranae; vicit libertas
see Busch, William

The dawn of redemption; or, The
adoration of the Magi kings
see Polding, Elizabeth

Dawson, J. H.
Lights and shadows of the
great rebellion; or, The
hospital nurse of Tennessee.
A grand military drama of
the Great Rebellion in four
acts and five tableaux.
Clyde, O.: Ames, c1885. 39p.
(Ames' series of standard and
minor drama. no. 194) *[joint
author: B. G. Whittemore]*

Day, Richard Edwin, b.1852.
Mneme and Elpis. [From his:
Lines in the sand. Syracuse,
New York: John T. Roberts,
1878. 110p.] p.88-94.

Thor. A drama representative
of human history. Syracuse,
New York: J. T. Roberts,
1880. 37p.

Day, Willard Gibson.
Cavalleria rusticana. Philadelphia: n.pub., 1890. Bilingual text: English and
Italian. 8, 8p. Libretto.
*[music composed by Pietro
Mascagni, with libretto by
Giovanni Targioni-Tozzetti
and Guido Menasci, founded
on the story of the same
name by Giovanni Verga;
without the music]*

The lovely Galatea. Mytholo-

gic comic opera. By Franz von
Suppé. Boston: Oliver Ditson,
c1884. Vocal score. 91p.
*[libretto by Leonhard von
Kohlenegg]*

The day after the wedding *see*
Kemble, Marie Thérèse De Camp
in The modern standard drama,
vol. 5

The day and the night *see*
Woolf, Benjamin Edward. Manola; or, The day and the
night

A day at the springs *see*
Callahan, Charles E. White
sulphur; or, A day at the
springs

The day before the wedding *see*
Meyers, Robert Cornelius V.
in Dramatic leaflets

A day in a doctor's office *see*
Hoefler, Henry A.

The day of days; a prothalamion
see Block, Louis James *in
his* Capriccios

A day with the National Guard
see Ingraham, Jean. The raw
recruit; or, A day with the
National Guard

The days of Jezebel *see*
Bayne, Peter

The days of the know nothings.
A farce, with a peep at the
secrets of the order. By one
who doesn't know much. Key-
port, N. J.: Henry Morford-
Standard Office, 1854. 44p.

Dazey, Charles Turner, 1855-
1938.
In old Kentucky. New York:
n.pub., 1893. Typescript.
Prompt-book. Title page
lacking. 3, 26, 21, 21, 12
leaves.

The deacon *see* Dale, Horace
C.

Deacon Jones' wife's ghost
see Rawley, Bert C.

The deacon's tribulations *see*
Dale, Horace C.

A dead heat. A comedy in one
act for female characters.
Boston: Walter H. Baker,
c1896. 13p. (Baker's edition
of plays) *[New York Public
Library attributes this play
to Maurice de Feraudy]*

The dead-and-alive *see*
Fuller, Henry *in his*
Collected works

Dead reckoning *see* Coolidge,
Henry Dingley

Dead Sea fruit *see* Rose,
Con., Jr.

The dead witness *see* Ward,
Lew. Gyp, the heiress; or,
The dead witness

Deaf as a post *see* Leavitt,
Andrew J. and Eagan, H. W.

Deaf in a horn. n.p.: n.pub.,
n.d. 7p. (French's acting
edition. Late Lacy's)
*[Readex also enters this
same play under Henry
Llewellyn Williams]*

Deaf--in a horn *see* Williams,
Henry Llewellyn

The deamons of the glass *see*
Optic, Oliver *in* Dramatic
leaflets

Dean, Frank J.
Joe Ruggles; or, The girl
miner. A comedy-drama in
four acts. Chicago: Dramatic
Pub. Co., c1895. 29p. (Ser-

gel's acting drama. no. 404)

Dear Uncle! *see* Fuller,
Horace William

Death *see* Fitch, Clyde *in
his* The children. Three
dialogues

The death letter *see* Tilden,
Len Ellsworth. The finger of
fate; or, The death letter

The death of Capt. Nathan Hale
see Trumbell, David

The death of Cleopatra *see*
Simms, William Gilmore

The death of Novalis *see*
Opal (pseud.) *in her* The
cloud of witnesses

The death of Roderick Dhu *see*
Steele, Silas Sexton. Blanche
of Devan; or, The death of
Roderick Dhu *in his* Collected works. Book of plays

The death of the discoverer
see Steell, Willis

The death of Tintagiles *see*
Hovey, Richard *in his* The
plays of Maurice Maeterlinck.
Second series

A debate in Squigginsville *see*
McBride, H. Elliott *in his*
Latest dialogues

Debate on the crow bill *see*
Carter, St. Leger Landon

Debates of conscience with a
distiller, a wholesale dealer,
and a retailer *see* A collection of temperance dialogues

The debating society *see*
Denison, Thomas Stewart *in
his* Friday afternoon series
of dialogues

Debenham, L.
Grannie's picture. New York:
S. French, c1899. 8p.
(Children's plays. no. 18)

Deborah. (From the German of
Mosenthal.) New York:
Wynkoop & Hollenbeck, 18-?
Title page lacking. Bilingual
text: English and German. 37p.

Deborah *see* Mitchell, Langdon
Elwyn

Deborah and Barak *see* Cobb,
Mary L. Poetical dramas for
home and school

Débutantes in the culinary art;
or, A frolic in the cooking
class *see* Allen, Lucy

Deception *see* Townsend,
Charles

The decision of the court *see*
Matthews, Brander

Declined with thanks *see*
Williams, Henry Llewellyn

Decourcelle, Pierre Henri
Adrien, 1821-1892.
Je dine chez ma mère *see*
McLachlan, Charles. I dine
with my mother

The decree of divorce *see*
Sedgwick, Alfred B.

Deeds of darkness *see*
McCarthy, Harry

Deering, Nathaniel, 1791-1881.
Bozzaris. A tragedy in five
acts. Portland: J. S. Bailey,
1851. 66p.

The "Deestrick Skule" of fifty
years ago *see* Jaquith,
Mrs. M. H.

The defender. New York: 187-?

Prompt-book in Ms. 46 leaves.

Defending the flag; or, The
message boy *see* Downing,
Laura Case

DeKoven, Reginald, 1859-1920.
The Algerian *see* MacDonough,
Glen

The casino girl *see* Smith,
Harry Bache

Don Quixote *see* Smith,
Harry Bache

The fencing master *see*
Smith, Harry Bache

Foxy Quiller *see* Smith,
Harry Bache

The highwayman *see* Smith,
Harry Bache

The Knickerbockers *see*
Smith, Harry Bache

Maid Marian *see* Smith,
Harry Bache

The mandarin *see* Smith,
Harry Bache

Rob Roy *see* Smith, Harry
Bache

Rob Roy; or, The thistle and
the rose *see* Smith, Harry
Bache

Robin Hood *see* Smith, Harry
Bache

The three dragoons *see*
Smith, Harry Bache

The tzigane *see* Smith,
Harry Bache

Delacour, Alfred Charlemagne
Lartigue, known as, 1817-1883.
La cagnotte *see* Fuller,
Horace Williams. A red letter
day

Le procès Veauradieux *see*
Kaler, James Otis. A case for
divorce *see also* Prichard,
Joseph Vila. My mother-in-
law; or, A divorce wanted

Delafield, John H.
La cigale. A comedy in three
acts. (From the French of
Meilhac and Halévy.) New York:
Happy Hours, 1879. viii, 72p.

Foresight; or, My daughter's
dowry. A comedy in two acts.
(From the French of Legouvé.)
New York: Happy Hours, c1879.
28p. (The acting drama. 135)

The last drop. A temperance
drama in one act. New York:
Happy Hours, c1876. 15p. (The
amateur stage. no. 46)

De Lange, Louis.
Pousse cafe see Smith, Edgar
McPhail and De Lange, Louis

Delano, Alonzo, 1806-1874.
A live woman in the mines; or,
Pike county ahead! A local
play in two acts. By "Old
Block" (pseud.) New York: S.
French, c1857. 36p. (The minor
drama. The acting edition.
no. 130)

Delanoy, Mary Frances Hanford.
The outcast's daughter. A
drama in four acts. By Marion
Eddy (pseud.) Chicago: Drama-
tic Pub. Co., c1899. 32p.
(Sergel's acting drama)

De Lara; or, The Moorish bride
see Hentz, Caroline Lee
Whiting

De La Ramée, Marie Louise,
1839-1908.
Under two flags see
Mitchell, A.

Delavigne, Germain, 1790-1868.
Masaniello, ou la muette de
Portici see Masaniello see
also La muette; or, The dumb
girl of Portic

The delegate see Ledoux,
Albert Reid

De Lesdernier, Emily Pierpont.

Heloise. A drama of the pas-
sions in four acts. [From her:
Voices of life. Paris: E.
Brière, 1862. 101p.] p.63-101.

A delicate question see
Fraser, John Arthur

Delilah see Moore, Eugene

Delon, Georges.
The abbess of Jouarre. (From
the French of Ernest Renan.)
New York: G. W. Dillingham,
1888. 131p. [joint author:
James F. Rhodes; based on
Renan's L'abbesse de Jouarre]

Delphine (pseud.) see Baker,
Delphine Paris

Dem good ole times; or, Sixteen
thousand years ago see
Williams, Henry Llewellyn

Dement, Richmond Sheffield.
Napoleon. Chicago: Knight,
Leonard, 1893. 183p.

Napoleon and Josephine. A
tragedy in a prologue and
five acts. Author's edition.
Chicago: Legal News, 1876.
154p.

Demetria see Hillhouse,
James Abraham

The "demi-monde" see Leslie,
Miriam Folline Squier

DeMille, Beatrice M., d.1923.
The greatest thing in the world
see Ford, Harriet and DeMille,
Beatrice M.

De Mille, Henry Churchill.
The charity ball see
Belasco, David and De Mille,
Henry Churchill

Governor Rodman's daughter.
A drama of our times in four
acts. New York: A. S. Knowl-
ton, n.d. Typescript, prompt-

book. Act III lacking.
(paged by acts.) *[joint
author: David Belasco]*

John Delmer's daughters. A
comedy in three acts. New
York: n.pub., c1883. Prompt-
book. 66p.

Lord Chumley. New York: L.
Rosenfield, 1888? Typescript,
prompt-book. In three acts.
Pagination by acts. *[joint
author: David Belasco]* see
also Belasco, David and
De Mille, Henry Churchill

The lost paradise. (From
the German of Ludwig Fulda.)
New York: S. French, c1897.
94p.

The lost paradise. Drama in
three acts. (From the German
of Ludwig Fulda.) New York:
Goldmark and Conried, c1897.
77p.

Men and women. A drama of
our times in four acts. New
York: n.pub., 1890. Type-
script, prompt-book. (pag.
by acts.) *[joint author:
David Belasco]*

The wife *see* Belasco,
David and De Mille, Henry
Churchill

Democracy in 1689 *see* Smith,
Elizabeth Oakes Prince. Old
New York; or, Democracy in
1689

The demon phonograph; or, The
battery and the assault.
Negro farce in one act.
Chicago: Dramatic Pub. Co.,
c1898. 7p. (The darkey and
comic drama)

Denier, John.
Humpty Dumpty. A pantomime
in prologue and one act.
By George L. Fox. Arranged
by John Denier. Chicago:
Dramatic Pub. Co., 18-? 22p.

*[The original shorter version
of this play by George
Washington Lafayette Fox is
entered by Readex under
that author]*

Denier, Tony.
Rooms to let without board
see Griffin, George W. H.
and Denier, Tony

Denise *see* Daly, Augustin

Denison, Thomas Stewart, 1848-
1911.
The assessor. Chicago: T. S.
Denison, c1878. p.145-149.

The babes in the wood; or,
The ferocious uncle and the
avenging robins. A domestic
tragedy in one act. Chicago:
T. S. Denison, 188-? 8p.

Borrowing trouble. A farce.
Chicago: T. S. Denison, c1878.
p.173-182.

The cobbler. A monologue of
humor and pathos. Chicago:
T. S. Denison, c1895. 8p.

A convention of papas, suggested by the convention of
mothers. A farce. Chicago:
T. S. Denison, c1897. 17p.
(Amateur series)

Country justice. Chicago:
T. S. Denison, c1878. p.165-
170.

The danger signal. A drama
in two acts. Chicago: T. S.
Denison, c1883. 42p.

A dude in a cyclone. A farce.
Chicago: T. S. Denison, c1895.
12p. (Amateur series)

A family strike. A farce.
Chicago: T. S. Denison, c1877.
p.97-106.

A first-class hotel. A farce.
Chicago: T. S. Denison, c1895.
14p. (Amateur series)

Friday afternoon series of

dialogues. A collection of
original dialogues suitable
for boys and girls in school
entertainments. Chicago:
T. S. Denison, c1879, 1907.
159p.
   Contents: A domestic wanted.
--The secretary.--Getting up
a picnic.--The ghost in the
kitchen.--Temptation resisted.
--The boaster rebuked.--The
tea party.--The bashful boy.
--The May queen.--The anniversary meeting.--The runaways.--The quack.--The debating society.--The amusement circle.--The patent
right agent.--The society for
the suppression of gossip.--
A lawsuit.--The lost opportunities.--An April fool.--
Always too late.--Scandinavia.
--Grateful.--Scintillate.--
Intensity.--Stockade.--A
parlor entertainment. By H.
Elliott McBride.--Lessons
in cookery.--The traveler.--
Taking the census.--The paper
don't say.

The great doughnut corporation. A farce. Chicago: T. S.
Denison, c1903. 19p. (Amateur
series)

The great pumpkin case of
Guff vs. Muff. A farcical
trial. Chicago: T. S. Denison,
c1903. 20p. (Amateur series)

Hans von Smash. A farce.
Chicago: T. S. Denison,
c1878. p.49-59.

Hard cider. A temperance
drama. Chicago: T. S. Denison,
c1880. 8p.

Initiating a granger. A farce.
Chicago: T. S. Denison, c1877.
p.43-51.

The Irish linen peddler. A
farce. Chicago: T. S. Denison,
c1879. 17p.

Is the editor in? A farce.

Chicago: T. S. Denison, c1879.
11p.

It's all in the pay-streak.
A comedy. Chicago: T. S.
Denison, c1895. 42p. (Alta
series)

The Kansas immigrants; or,
The great exodus. A farce.
Chicago: T. S. Denison, c1879.
12p.

Louva, the pauper. A drama.
Chicago: T. S. Denison, c1878.
36p. (The Star drama. no.
1363)

Madame Princeton's temple of
beauty. A farce. Chicago:
T. S. Denison, c1895. 14p.
(Amateur series)

The new woman. A comedy of
A. D. 1950 in three acts.
Chicago: T. S. Denison, c1895.
31p. (Amateur series)

Odds with the enemy. A drama
in five acts. Chicago: T. S.
Denison, c1876. 40p.

Only cold tea. A temperance
farce. Chicago: T. S. Denison,
c1895. 14p.

An only daughter. A drama in
three acts. Chicago: T. S.
Denison, c1879. 24p.

Our country. A historical and
spectacular representation in
three parts. Chicago: T. S.
Denison, 1878. p.63-75.

Patsy O'Wang. An Irish farce
with a Chinese mix-up. Chicago:
T. S. Denison, c1895. 29p.
(Amateur series)

Pets of society. A farce.
Chicago: T. S. Denison, c1880.
15p. (Amateur series. no. 408)

The pull back. Chicago: T. S.
Denison, c1878. p.39-46.

Rejected; or, The tribulations
of authorship. A farce. Chicago: T. S. Denison, c1895.
26p. (Amateur series)

The school-ma'am. A comedy. in four acts. Chicago: T. S. Denison, c1879. 39p.

Seth Greenback. A drama in four acts. Chicago: T. S. Denison, c1877. p.55-77.

The sparkling cup. A temperance drama in five acts. Chicago: T. S. Denison, c1877. p.109-141.

Too much of a good thing. A comedietta. Chicago: T. S. Denison, c1880. 25p. (Amateur series)

Topp's twins. A farce-comedy in four acts. Chicago: T. S. Denison, c1895. 72p. (Alta series)

Two ghosts in white. A farce. Chicago: T. S. Denison, c1878. p.153-162.

Under the laurels. A drama in five acts. Chicago: T. S. Denison, c1881. 41p. (The Star drama)

Wanted: a correspondent. A farce in two acts. Chicago: T. S. Denison, c1877. p.79-95.

Wide awake dialogues. Chicago: T. S. Denison, c1903. 125p.
Contents: Barring out the teacher.--Bachelor girl's club.--Becky Calico.--The bootblack.--Boy who was a coward.--The camera obscura. --The durbar.--Fred's visit to town.--Going to California.--The gold brick.--The gossipers.--Got a new suit. --The lady novelist.--Lemonade stand.--Monkey and Madstone.--New boy in school. --Old photograph album.-- Playing married.--The seance. --Sea serpent vs. mermaid.-- Sitting up for husbands to come home.--Slow beau and

fast beau.--Stolen pocketbook.--Stolen sweets.-- Stolen watermelons.--Trying the new teacher.--What bird would you be?--When I am a woman.

Wide enough for two. A farce. Chicago: T. S. Denison, c1883. 20p. (Amateur series)

Dennery, Adolphe Philippe, 1811-1899.
Une cause célèbre *see* Cazauran, Augustus R. A celebrated case

Les deux orphelines *see* Jackson, N. Hart. The two orphans *see also* Stevenson, Kate Claxton Cone. Two orphans *see also* The two orphans

Don Caesar de Bazan *see* Dumanoir, Philippe François Pineal and Dennery, Adolphe Philippe *in* Booth, Edwin. The miscellaneous plays of Edwin Booth *see also* Dumanoir, Philippe François Pinel and Dennery, Adolphe Philippe *in* The modern standard drama, vol. 2

The dentist's clerk; or, Pulling teeth by steam *see* Von Culin, Everett

Denton, Clara Janetta Fort.
All is fair in love. A drama in three scenes. Boston: W. H. Baker, 1897. 19p. (Baker's edition of plays)

A change of color. A drama in one act. Boston: W. H. Baker, 1897. 12p. (Baker's edition of plays)

From tots to teens. A book of original dialogues for boys and girls. Some merry times for young folks. Chicago: T. S. Denison,

c1897. 125p.
    Contents: Part first. Dia-
logues for older boys and
girls: Appointment.--A backward glance.--The four
judges.--The four photo-
graphs.--The ghost in the
closet.--The lost letter.--
The lost opportunity.--In
nonsense land.--Parliamen-
tary law.--Professor's
present.--The rebellion.--
A rebuff.--What is a gentleman?--Writing a book. Part
second. Dialogues for the
wee ones: Brave little
Mary.--In the morning.--The
invitation.--Leaflets and
ladybugs.--Some noted
characters.--A terrible
threat.--What they will do.
Part third. Dialogues for
special occasions: Keep the
holidays.--New Christmas.--
Primary class (Washington's
birthday.)--That other
fourth.

The man who went to Europe.
A comedy in one act. Boston:
J. W. Baker, 1897. 12p.
(Baker's edition of plays)

Surprised. A comedy in one
act. Philadelphia: Penn Pub.
Co., 1908. 11p. *[earlier
copyright: 1892]*

To meet Mr. Thompson. A farce
in one act for female
characters. Boston: Walter
H. Baker, c1890. 9p.
(Baker's edition of plays)

"W. H." A farce in one act.
Boston: Walter H. Baker,
1897. 14p. (Baker's edition
of plays)

When the lessons are over.
Dialogues, exercises and
drills for the primary
classes. Chicago: T. S.
Denison, c1891. 114p.
    Contents: Bob and his
sister.--But once a year.--

Columbia and the Boys.--
Columbia and Mr. "They Say."
--Drills. Parasol.--Drills.
Hats.--Drills. Handerchiefs.
--Gay Christmas ball.--Going
to the corner.--The gold
spinner.--"In memoriam."--
Joe's way of doing chores.--
Lazy or not.--Lesson from
the sunflowers.--Like a
nettle.--Making an orator.--
A medley.--Message to the
children.--Nuts to crack.
No. 1.--Nuts to crack. No. 2.
--The obedient servants.--
The pine tree's choice.--
A peace maker.--The school
bell.--School is out.--Served
him right.--Something to be
thankful for.--The laughing
family.--The weed and the
boy.--When I'm a woman.--
While the joy goes on.

De Peyster, John Watts, 1821-
1907.
    Bothwell (James Hepbum,
fourth earl of Bothwell,
third husband of Mary, Queen
of Scots.) An historical
drama. New York: C. H.
Ludwig, 1884. 96, 48p.

A night with Charles XII of
Sweden; or, A soldier's
wife's fidelity. n.p.: n.pub.,
185-? Title page lacking. 12p.

De Roberval *see* Duvar, John
Hunter *see also* Hunter-
Duvar, John *[note: Readex
enters this play under both
forms of the author's name]*

Désaugiers, Marc Antoine
Madeleine, 1772-1827.
    L'hôtel garni; ou La leçon
singulière *see* Smith,
Richard Penn. Quite perfect

Deschamps, Émile, 1791-1871.
    Les Huguenots *see* Kellogg,
Clara Louise

Romeo et Juliette *see*
Cornell, John Henry. Romeo
and Juliet

Deseret deserted; or, The last
days of Brigham Young. Being
a strictly business trans-
action in four acts and
several deeds, involving
both prophet and loss. New
York: S. French, 1858. 28p.
(French's standard drama.
The acting edition. no. 208)

The deserters *see* Leavitt,
Andrew J. and Eagan, H. W.

Deslandes, Raimond, 1828-1890.
Reconciliation *see* Appleton, Nathan *[Dictionnaire
de biographie française,
vol. 10, p.1418 (1965) gives
Deslandes' birth date as
1825 and spells his Christian
name Raymond; the dates and
form of name given above are
those supplied by Readex]*

De Solla, Isidore.
The new moon *see* André,
Richard

A desperate encounter *see*
Meyers, Robert Cornelius V.
in Dramatic leaflets

A desperate situation *see*
Dumont, Frank *see also his*
The amateur minstrel

Dessalines: a dramatic tale
see Easton, William Edgar

Desvaillières, Maurice,
1857-1926.
Champignol malgré lui *see*
Champignol despite himself

The detective from Plunketsville *see* Chase, George B.
Simple Silas; or, The
detective from Plunketsville

A detective in petticoats *see*
Enebuske, Sarah Folsom

The devil in America *see*
Lacon (pseud.)

A devil of a scrape; or, Who
paid for the supper *see*
Kaler, James Otis

The devil's dance *see* Meriwether, Elizabeth Avery

The devil's mine *see* Darcy,
Fred

Dewey, the hero of Manila *see*
Fraser, John Arthur

Dey, F. Marmaduke, 1861-1922.
H. M. S. Plum (his mollified
sugar plum.) A musical sketch
in one act. Clyde, O.: Ames,
1883. 8p. (Ames' series of
standard and minor drama.
no. 120) *["nearly all the
airs...are the same as in
H. M. S. Pinafore."]*

Passions. An original comedy
in four acts. Clyde, O.:
Ames, 1881. 24p. (Ames'
series of standard and
minor drama. no. 114)

Dey, Frederick Van Rensselaer
see Dey, F. Marmaduke
*[note: Mr. Dey used at least
seven other pseudonyms!]*

Diagram of a modern law suit
see Bailey, George W.

A dialogue *see* Duer, Caroline
and Miller, Alice Duer.
Overheard in a conservatory
[and] A dialogue

Dialogue. Poet and musician *see*
Bullock, Cynthia

A dialogue between Mr. Native
and Mrs. Foreigner, on lite-

rary subjects *see* Corwin,
Jane Hudson

Dialogues dramatized from the
works of Charles Dickens.
Chicago: T. S. Denison,
18-? 96p.
Contents: Copperfield's
proposal [David Copperfield].
--The Prentice knights [Bar-
naby Rudge].--Spenlow &
Jorkins [David Copperfield].
--The refreshmenting room at
Mugby [Mugby Junction].--
Return of Sol Gills [Domby &
Son].--Mr. Pecksniff [Martin
Chuzzlewit].--The friendly
move [Our mutual friend].--
Squeer's school [Nicholas
Nickleby].--Mrs. Gamp's tea
[Martin Chuzzlewit].--
Bumble's courtship [Oliver
Twist].--The circumlocution
office [Little Dorrit].--
Bardell vs. Pickwick [Pick-
wick Papers].--Mr. Micawber
[David Copperfield]

The diamond king *see* Hamilton, George H. Sunlight;
or, The diamond king

Diamonds and hearts *see*
Merriman, Effie Woodward

Diamonds and toads *see*
Baker, George Melville. The
fairy of the fountain; or,
Diamonds and toads *see also*
Caldor, M. T. *in his* Social
charades *see also* Valentine, Laura Jewry *in*
Venable, William Henry. The
school stage

Diaz, Abby Morton, 1821-1904.
William Henry letters, from
Crooked Pond School, and
William Henry and his
friends *see* Chaney, Mrs.
George L. William Henry

Dick Crowninshield, the assassin and Zachary Taylor, the

soldier *see* Wright, Henry
Clarke

Dickens, Charles, 1812-1870.
Barnaby Rudge *see* The
Prentice knights *in* Dialogues dramatized from the
works of Charles Dickens

A Christmas carol *see*
Baker, George Melville *see*
also Satterlee, Clarence

Cricket on the hearth *see*
Johnson, Fannie M. Dotage
in Bartlett, George Bradford. A dream of the centuries and other entertainments
for parlor and hall

David Copperfield *see*
Copperfield's proposal *in*
Dialogues dramatized from
the works of Charles Dickens
see also Mr. Micawber *in*
Dialogues dramatized from
the works of Charles Dickens
see also Spenlow & Jorkins
in Dialogues dramatized from
the works of Charles Dickens

Domby & Son *see* Return of
Sol Gills *in* Dialogues
dramatized from the works
of Charles Dickens

Great expectations *see*
Tees, Levin C. Botany Bay

Little Dorrit *see* The
circumlocution office *in*
Dialogues dramatized from the
works of Charles Dickens

Martin Chuzzlewit *see* Mr.
Pecksniff *in* Dialogues
dramatized from the works
of Charles Dickens *see also*
Mrs. Gamp's tea *see also*
Mrs. Gamp's tea *in* Dialogues dramatized from the
works of Charles Dickens

Mugby Junction *see* The
refreshmenting room *in*
Dialogues dramatized from
the works of Charles Dickens

Nicholas Nickelby (scenes)
see Bell, Lucis Chase.
Buoyant *in* Bartlett,
George Bradford. A dream of
the centuries and other
entertainments for parlor
and hall *see* Squeer's
school *in* Dialogues
dramatized from the works
of Charles Dickens

Oliver Twist *see* Bumble's
courtship *in* Dialogues
dramatized from the works
of Charles Dickens

Our mutual friend *see*
The friendly move *in*
Dialogues dramatized from
the works of Charles Dickens

Pickwick Papers *see*
Bardell vs. Pickwick *in*
Dialogues dramatized from
the works of Charles Dickens
see also Sam Weller's visit

Dickinson, Eva Lyle.
A Thanksgiving lesson *see*
Schell, Stanley. A real
Thanksgiving [and] A Thanks-
giving lesson

Did you ever see a ghost? *see*
Meyers, Robert Cornelius V.
in Dramatic leaflets

Dido *see* Miller, Frank Justus

Dillaye, Ina.
Ramona. A play in five acts.
Syracuse, New York: F. LeC.
Dillaye, c1887. 40p. *["adap-
ted from Helen Hunt Jackson's
novel..."]*

Dinner at six *see* Tubbs,
Arthur Lewis

Dinsmore, William.
His chris cross mark. "The
man of mark." An original
comic opera in three acts.
New York: n.pub., c1879. 53p.
*[music by Mortimer Wiske;
without the music]*

Diogenes-Rabelais *see* Townsend, Frederic *in his*
Spiritual visitors

Diplomacy. A comedietta in one
act. (From the French of
Gustave Droz.) New York:
Happy Hours, c1879. 17p.
(The acting drama. no. 116)

Diplomates *see* Williams,
Henry Llewellyn

The discarded daughter *see*
Pirsson, Joseph P.

Disengaged *see* James, Henry.
Tenants

Disinherited *see* Kimball,
George M.

The disinherited son *see*
Williams, Charles. The
elopement; or, The disin-
herited son

The disruption and fall of
these states *see* Ganter,
Franz S. Amor Patriae; or,
The disruption and fall of
these states

The district school at Blueberry Corners *see* Parsons,
Laura Matilda Stephenson

The divine tragedy *see*
Longfellow, Henry Wadsworth
see also his Christus

Divorce *see* Daly, Augustin
see also Fitch, Clyde *in
his* The children. Three
dialogues

A divorce wanted *see* Prichard,
Joseph Vila. My mother-in-
law; or, A divorce wanted

Dix, Beulah Marie, b.1876.
Cicely's cavalier. A comedy
in one act. Boston: W. H.
Baker, 1897. 19p. (Baker's
edition of plays)

Dixon, Frederick Augustus,
1843-1919.
Canada's welcome. Ottawa:
McLean, Roger & Co., 1879.
19p. Libretto. *[music composed by Arthur A. Clappé;
without the music]*

Djakh and Djill *see* Woolf,
Benjamin Edward

Do not trifle with edge tools
see Shields, Sarah Annie
Frost *in her* Parlor
charades and proverbs

The doctor *see* Townsend,
Charles

Dr. Baxter's servants *see*
Lindon, Patrick C.

Dr. Bluff in Russia; or, The
Emperor Nicholas and the
American Doctor *see*
Gayarré, Charles Étienne
Arthur

Doctor Cure-All. A comedy in
two acts. n.p.: n.pub.,
189-? 21p. Title page
lacking.

A doctor in spite of himself
see Cupid's little game
[bound with] A doctor in
spite of himself

Dr. Jekyll and Mr. Hyde; or,
A mis-spent life *see*
Forepaugh, Luella and Fish,
George F.

Dr. Kearny. n.p.: n.pub., 18-.
Title page lacking. Type-
script. Prompt-book. 32
leaves (numb. irreg.)

Dr. McBeatem *see* Hiland,
Frank E.

Doctor Mondschein; or, The
violent remedy *see* Curtis,
Ariana Randolph Wormeley

The doctor of Alcantara *see*
Woolf, Benjamin Edward

Doctor Polyanthus; or, Where
there's a will there's a
way *see* Browne, Irving

Doctor Snowball *see* Barnes,
James

A doctor without a diploma *see*
Taylor, Malcolm Stuart. The
afflicted family; or, A
doctor without a diploma

The doctor's assistant *see*
Wyke, Byam

Documentary evidence *see*
Whalen, E. C.

Dodging the police; or, Enforcing the Sunday law *see*
Dumont, Frank

Dodgson, Charles Lutwidge,
1832-1898.
Alice's adventures in Wonderland *see* Harrison, Constance
Cary. Alice in Wonderland

A dog that will fetch will
carry *see* Brewster, Emma E.
see also her Parlor varieties

Dolce far niente *see* Saltus,
Francis Saltus

Dole, Nathan Haskell, 1852-1935.
Friend Fritz. L'amico Fritz.
Lyrical comedy in three acts,
by P. Suardon (pseud.) Music
by Pietro Mascagni. New York:
G. Schirmer, c1891. Vocal
score. Bilingual text: English
and Italian. 184p. *[P. Suardon
is a pseud. for Émile Erckmann
and Alexandre Chatrian]*

Dollars and cents *see* Hollenius, Laurence John

Dollars and sense; or, The heedless ones *see* Daly, Augustin

Dolly's doctor *see* Dulcken, Henry William *in* Venable, William Henry. The school stage

Dolores *see* Cannon, Charles James. Collected works. Dramas

Domestic *see* Shields, Sarah Annie Frost *in her* Parlor charades and proverbs

Domestic accomplishments *see* Dunne, Norah. Mrs. Plodding's nieces; or, Domestic accomplishments

A domestic wanted *see* Denison, Thomas Stewart *in his* Friday afternoon series of dialogues

Dominic You *see* Ogden, Octavius Nash

Don Caesar de Bazan *see* Dumanoir, Philippe François Pineal and Dennery, Adolphe Philippe *in* Booth, Edwin. The miscellaneous plays of Edwin Booth *see also in* The modern standard drama, vol. 2

Don Carlos *see* Calvert, George Henry

Don Giovanni. (Music by Mozart.) New York: S. French, 18-? Bilingual text: Italian and English. 65p. Libretto. (The operatic library. no. 29) *[libretto by Lorenzo Da Ponte; without the music]*

Il Don Giovanni. New York: Snowden, 1850. Bilingual text: English and Italian. 95p. Libretto. *[music by Mozart; libretto by Lorenzo Da Ponte; without the music]*

Don Giovanni *see also* Sher-

wood, W.

Don Juan *see* Mansfield, Richard

Don Quixote de la Mancha *see* Burton, Mrs. Henry S.

Don Seiglemon. Four acts *see* Tillson, Jesse Paxon *in his* Collected works

Donaldson, Frank, d.1906. Two comedies: An ill wind [and] An abject apology. Boston: Cupples, Upham & Co., 1887. 79p.

The donation party; or, Thanksgiving Eve at the parsonage *see* Orne, Martha Russell

Done on both sides *see* Cutler, F. L.. $2,000 reward; or, Done on both sides

Donizetti, Gaetano, 1797-1848. Belisario *see* Belisarius

L'elisir d'amore *see* The elixir of love *see also* The love-spell *see also* Weil, Oscar. Adina; or, The elixir of love

La favorita *see* La favorita *see also* The favorite *see also* Révoil, Bénèdict Henry. La favorite. (The king's mistress)

La fille du régiment *see* The child of the regiment *see also* The daughter of the regiment *see also* La figlia del reggimento *see also* Seguin, Arthur Edward Sheldon. Marie; or, The daughter of the regiment

Il furioso all'isola di San Domingo *see* The maniac at the island of St. Domingo

Gemmy di Vergy *see* Révoil, Bénèdict Henry

Linda di Chamounix *see*
Linda of Chamouni

Lucia di Lammermoor *see*
Lucia di Lammermoor *see also*
Lucie of Lammermoor *see also*
Lucy of Lammermoor

Lucrezia Borgia *see* Calcaterra, G. *see also* Lucretia
Borgia

Parisina *see* Parisina

Donnell, Florence T.
A revolutionary marriage.
Drama in five acts. New
York: William R. Jenkins,
1890. 82p.

Donnelly, Henry Grattan, 1850-
1941.
The American girl. A comedy
drama of two continents.
n.p.: n.pub., 1900? Type-
script. 18, 20, 5, 11, 6,
13 leaves.

Darkest Russia. n.p.: n.pub.,
189-? Typescript. In four
acts (pag. by acts.)

Donoho, Thomas Seaton.
Oliver Cromwell. A tragedy
in five acts. Washington,
D.C.: W. H. Moore, 1860.
72p.

Don Quixote *see* Smith,
Harry Bache

The Don's stratagem *see*
Brewster, Emma E. *in her*
Parlor varieties

Don't forget your opera-
glasses *see* Woolf,
Benjamin Edward

Don't get weary; or, Johnny,
you've been a bad boy.
Musical sketch in one act.
Chicago: Dramatic Pub. Co.,
c1885. p.9-12. (The darkey
and comic drama) *[music composed by J. M. Turner] see*

also Gentlemen's coon
parade...and Don't get
weary; or, Johnny, you've
been a bad boy

Don't marry a drunkard to
reform him *see* McBride,
H. Elliott

Don't tell her husband *see*
Thomas, Augustus

Dorbesson, Fern, d.1960.
Aldemon's daughter (Cassilda.)
Tragedy in prose in four acts.
New York: T. A. Wright, 1890.
43p. *[Library of Congress
gives the form of the author's
name as Fernand D'Orbesson]*

Dot mad tog *see* McDermott,
J. J. and Trumble

Dot madrimonial adverdisement
see McDermott, J. J. and
Trumble

Dot quied lotgings *see*
McDermott, J. J. and Trumble

Dot, the miner's daughter; or,
One glass of wine *see*
Elwyn, Lizzie May

Dotage *see* Johnson, Fannie M.
in Bartlett, George Bradford. A dream of the centuries
and other entertainments for
parlor and hall

The double deceit; or, The
husband-lovers *see* Osborn,
Laughton *in his* The silver
head, The double deceit;
comedies

A double deception *see* Tubbs,
Arthur Lewis

A double election *see* Whalen,
E. C.

The double ghost *see* Fowle,
William Bentley *in his*
Parlor dramas

A double life; or, Where
there's a will there's a
way *see* Mackay, Frank
Findley

A double shuffle *see*
Hanlon, Henry Oldham

The double triumph *see*
O'Reilly, Augustine J.

Douglass, John J.
My new curate. Louisville,
Ky.: Brother Benjamin, n.d.
Fourth edition. 64p.

Wooing under difficulties.
A farce in one act. New
York: Dick & Fitzgerald,
1870. 14p.

Dow, James M.
The widower's trials. A
sketch from real life in two
acts. Clyde, O.: Ames, 1864.
9p. (Ames' series of standard
and minor drama. no. 135)

Dowd, Jerome.
Burr and Hamilton. A New
York tragedy in five acts.
New York: Geo. W. Wheat,
1884. 34p.

Down by the sea *see* Baker,
George Melville

Down east *see* Adams, Justin

Down in Dixie *see* Marble,
Scott *see also* Townsend,
Charles

Down the Black Cañon; or, The
silent witness *see* Heermans, Forbes

Downing, Laura Case, 1843-1914.
Defending the flag; or, The
message boy. Military drama
in five acts. Clyde, O.:
Ames, 1894. 34p. (Ames'
series of standard and minor
drama. no. 342)

Doyle, Arthur Conan, 1859-1930.
Sherlock Holmes *see*
Gillette, William Hooker and
Doyle, Arthur Conan

Doyle, Edward, b.1854.
Cagliostro. A dramatic poem
in five acts. New York: The
author, c1882. 131p.

Doyle, Edwin Adams, 1867-1941.
Phocion: a dramatic poem.
1897. [From his: Phocion...
and other poems. Winchester,
O.: The author, 1910. 214p.]
p.1-72.

The draft *see* White, Charles

Drake, Frank C.
Rosberry Shrub, sec. A
comedy in one act and two
scenes. New York: S. French,
c1899. 19p. (French's standard drama) *[the idea for
this play came from Bessie
Chandler's short story, The
pearl of Ohio]*

A drama. [From: The univercoelum
and spiritual philosopher. New
York: Published by an association, 1848. vol. 1.] vol. 1,
p.318-319, 334-335.

A drama *see* Connelly, James
Henderson

A drama of ambition *see*
Meyers, Benjamin F. *in his*
Collected works

The drama of deceit. A satire
in verse on the Rev. Henry
Ward Beecher. Worcester and
Clinton, Mass.: The Independent Tract Society, 1875.
12p. Title page lacking.

The drama of earth *see* Kidder,
Jerome

The drama of secession; or,

Scenes from American history *see* Barnes, William Horatio

Dram-At(t)ic *see* Cahill, Frank *in* Arnold, George? and Cahill, Frank. Parlor theatricals; or, Winter evening's entertainment

A dramatic evening *see* Bangs, John Kendrick

Dramatic fragments *see* Smith, Richard Penn *see also* Van Winkle, Edgar Simeon

Dramatic leaflets. Comprising original and selected plays. Philadelphia: P. Garrett, c1877. 1 vol. in 20 parts. (pag. irreg.)
    Contents: Practical jokes (Robert C. V. Meyers.)--Art and artifice.--The ugliest of seven (adapted from the German by Miss G. M. Towsend.)--Scene from The rivals (R. B. Sheridan.)--The day before the wedding (Robert C. V. Meyers.)--Balcony scene from Romeo and Juliet (Shakespeare.)--Where's my hat (Robert C. V. Meyers.)--The student and his neighbors (N. A. Woodward.)--Cain, ancient and modern (Ellen Murray.)--The queen of beauty.--A queer fit.--Trusty and true.--A frightened lodger.--Bill Jepson's wife (Robert C. V. Meyers.)--An electric episode (Helen Booth.)--Vanity vanquished (H. Elliott McBride.)--The long lost nephew (Robert C. V. Meyers.)--Ghost scene from Hamlet (Shakespeare.)--The conqueror conquered (George S. Burleigh.)--Cold-water cross.--The deamons of the glass (Oliver Optic.)--The veiled priestess (Laura U. Case.)--Saved.--Two lives (Geo. M. Vickers.)--Cassius' whistle (Robert C. V. Meyers.)--The matrimonial advertisement (Clara Augusta.)--Teacher wanted (Frank Crosby.)--The unwelcome guest (M. Elliott McBride.)--Did you ever see a ghost? (Robert C. V. Meyers.)--Courtship under difficulties.--Falstaff's boasting (Shakespeare.)--The trees of the Bible (M. B. C. Slade.)--Licensed snakes: temperance dialogue (Ellen Murray.)--Fighting the rum-fiend (Julia M. Thayer.)--Pepita, the gipsy girl of Andalusia.--A fifty-dollar milliner's bill (Helen Booth.)--The infernal machine (H. Elliott McBride.)--The crusaders (Ellen Murray.)--The premature proposal (A. F. Bradley.)--After twenty years (Helen Booth.)--He was never known to smile (Charles Barnard.)--The bridal wine cup (A. F. Bradley.)--May court in Greenwood (Laura U. Case.)--A soft black overcoat with a velvet collar (Robert C. V. Meyers.)--The rough diamond (Buckstone.)--Esau and Jacob (Ellen Murray.)--The beauty of piety (S. C. Edgarton.)--Heavenly foundations (Orrie M. Gaylord.)--Signing the pledge.--Lessons from Scripture flowers (M. B. C. Slade.)--Fourth act of The merchant of Venice (Shakespeare.)--Quarrel scene from School for scandal (R. B. Sheridan.)--Under an umbrella (Robert C. V. Meyers.)--The top landing (Robert C. V. Meyers.)--The lost child (Harry H. Cushing.)--At the Red Lion (Helen Booth.)--The weathercock (J. T. Allingham.)--Aunt Susan Jones

(H. Elliott McBride.)--A
desperate encounter (Robert
C. V. Meyers.)

Dramatic sketch *see* Burleigh,
William Henry

Dramatic stories *see* Phelps,
Lavinia Howe

A drawing-room car. A petite
comedy in one act. (From
the French of Verconsin.)
New York: De Witt, c1876.
12p. (De Witt's acting
plays. no. 201? or 204?
[number illegible])

Dream camp; or, A modern
craze *see* Robinson, Charles

The dream of Eugene Aram *see*
Hood, Thomas *in* Massey,
Charles. Massey's exhibition
reciter

A dream of fair women and
brave men *see* Gaddess,
Mary L.

Dream of realms beyond us
see Welcker, Adair *in his*
Romer, King of Norway and
other dramas

A dream of the centuries *see*
Brooks, E. S. *in* Bartlett,
George Bradford. A dream of
the centuries and other
entertainments for parlor
and hall

Dreaming by moonlight *see*
Savage, John

The dreamland tree *see*
Barnard, Charles

Dred; a tale of the great
Dismal Swamp *see* Conway,
H. J.

A dress rehearsal *see* Davis,
Mary Evelyn Moore

Drey, Sylvan.
Cupid and cupidity. A comedy
in three acts. London and
New York: T. H. French,
n.d. 52p. (French's standard
drama. The acting edition.
no. 421)

Woman's rights. A comedy.
Baltimore: Cushings & Bailey,
1884. 45p.

Dreyfus, Abraham, 1847-1926.
Un crane sous une tempete
see Coale, George B. On
his devoted head

[The silent system] *see*
Matthews, Brander

Drifting apart *see* Herne,
James A. *in his* The early
plays...

Drifting apart; or, Mary,
the fisherman's child *see*
Herne, James A. (2 editions)

Driven from home; or, A
father's curse *see* Dunn,
Herb H.

Driven to the wall; or, True
to the last *see* Ames, A. D.

Drogheda (pseud.) *see*
Moore, A. S.

The drop of water *see* Coale,
George B.

"A drop too much" *see* Baker,
George Melville

Droz, Gustave, 1832-1895.
[Diplomacy] *see* Diplomacy

Un pacquet de lettres *see*
The registered letter

The drummer boy; or, The battlefield of Shiloh *see* Muscroft, Samuel J.

The drunkard; or, The fallen
saved *see* Smith, William
Henry *see also in* The

modern standard drama,
vol. 11

The drunkard's daughter *see*
McConaughy, Julia E. Loomis
in A collection of temperance dialogues

The drunkard's family *see*
Merriman, Effie Woodward
see also in her Comedies
for children

The drunkard's home. A temperance drama in two acts. New
York: Harold Roorbach, 18-?
42p. (The acting drama.
no. 63)

A drunkard's legacy *see*
McFall, B. G. Among the
moonshiners; or, A drunkard's
legacy

The drunkard's story *see*
Buckstone, John Baldwin
in Massey, Charles.
Massey's exhibition reciter

The drunkard's warning *see*
Taylor, C. W.

Dubreuil, Ernest, 1833-1886.
Fantine *see* Woolf, Benja-
min Edward and Field,
Roswell Martin

Dubry, Louis Émile.
[Game of dominos] *see*
Bradbury, Louise A.

The duchess of Dublin *see*
Baker, George Melville

A dude in a cyclone *see*
Denison, Thomas Stewart

A duel at dawn *see* Cox,
Eleanor Rogers

A duel to the death *see*
Meyers, Robert Cornelius V.

The duenna *see* Sheridan,
Richard Brinsley Butler *in*
The modern standard drama,
vol. 7

Duer, Caroline, 1865-1956.
Overheard in a conservatory
[and] A dialogue. [From
their: Poems. New York:
George H. Richmond, 1896.
62p.] p.27-30, 42-44. *[joint
author: Alice Duer Miller]*

Duet for the breakfast table
see Halpine, Charles Graham

Dugan, Caro Atherton.
Collected works. The king's
jester and other short plays
for small stages. Boston and
New York: Houghton, Mifflin,
1899. 364p. *[note: all except
Cinderella and Pandora con-
tain music]*
Contents: The king's jester.
--Cinderella.--The gypsy girl
of Hungary.--The queen's
coffer.--The sleeping beauty.
--Pandora.--The gift of
Aphrodite.--Nino's revenge.--
The apple of discord.--
Undine.--The flight of the
sun goddess.

Duganne, Augustine Joseph
Hickey, 1823-1884.
Woman's vows and Mason's
oaths. New York: Dramatic
Pub. Co., c1874. 76p.

The duke for a day *see*
Mickle, Isaac. The old North
Tower; or, The duke for a day

Dulcken, Henry William.
Rhyme and reason *see his*
Dolly's doctor *in* Venable,
William Henry. The school
stage *see also his* Master
Goat, the tailor *in* Venable,
William Henry. The school
stage

Dumanoir, Philippe François
Pinel.
Don Caesar de Bazan *see*
Booth, Edwin. The miscel-
laneous plays of Edwin
Booth *see also* The
modern standard drama,
vol. 2

Le sergent Frédéric *see*
Gayler, Charles. The love
of a prince; or, The court
of Prussia

Dumanois, M. M. *see* Dumanoir,
Philippe François Pinel

Dumas, Alexandre, 1802-1870.
Le comte de Monte-Cristo
see O'Neill, James. "Monte
Cristo"

Les frères corses *see*
Grangé, Eugène and Montépin,
Xavier Aymons, comte de.
The Corsican brothers *in*
The modern standard drama,
vol. 12 *see also* Griffin,
George W. H. Corsican twins

L'invitation à la valse *see*
Hoppin, William Jones. Circumstances alter cases

Kean; ou, désordre et génie
see Jessop, George Henry
and St. Maur, J. Edmund
Kean; or, The life of an
actor

Mademoiselle de Belle-Isle
see Gabrielle de Belle-Isle
see also Mademoiselle de
Belle-Isle

Mattien *see* Hanshew,
Thomas W. Will-o'-the-wisp;
or, The shot in the dark

Paul Jones *see* Berger,
William

Pauline *see* Pauline

Les trois mosquetaires *see*
Mayo, Frank and Wilson,
John G. The royal guard
see also Smith, Edgar

McPhail. "The three musketeers"

Dumas, Alexandre, 1824-1895.
La dame aux camélias *see*
Griffin, George W. H.
Camille *see also* Olwine,
Wayne. Camille; or, The fate
of a coquette *see also* La
dame aux camélias

Le demi-monde *see* Leslie,
Miriam Folline Squier. The
"demi-monde"

Denise *see* Daly, Augustin

L'étrangère *see* The
foreigner

Monsieur Alphonse *see*
Daly, Augustin

DuMaurier, George Louis Pal-
mella Busson, 1834-1896.
Trilby *see* Herbert, Joseph
W. "Thrilby" *see also*
Smith, Edgar McPhail

Dumb Andy *see* Edgeworth,
Maria *in* Follen, Eliza Lee
Cabot. Home dramas for young
people

The dumb girl of Portic *see*
La muette; or, The dumb girl
of Portic

Dumont, Frank, 1848-1919.
Absent minded. A genteel
farce in one act. Chicago:
Dramatic Pub. Co., c1881.
8p. (The comic drama)

Africanus Bluebeard. A musical Ethiopian burlesque in
one scene. New York: De Witt,
c1876. 14p. (De Witt's
Ethiopian and comic drama.
no. 107)

The amateur minstrel. New
York: Weyman Bros., 180-?
114p. [*cover title: Wehman's
burnt cork; or, The amateur
minstrel*]

*[note: the section of "gags,"
"stump speeches," "comic
recitations," and "conun-
drums" have not been analyzed, as they vary in length
from one paragraph to not
more than 1-1/2 pages. One
section, entitled "finales,"
includes the following:*
  Queer, quaint and quizzical questions.--A visit to
the zoological gardens.--
The race track.
*The other section analyzed
is entitled "Ethiopian
dramas," and includes the
following:]*
  The mid-night train.--
Cupid's frolics.--A desperate situation.--Happy Uncle
Rufus.--The wonderful telephone.--Absent-minded.--
Pete and the peddler.--
Stupid servant.

An awful plot. A comic
Ethiopian farce in one
scene. Chicago: Dramatic
Pub. Co., c1880. 8p.

The black brigands. New
York: De Witt, c1884. 6p.

The cake walk. A farce in
one scene. Chicago: Dramatic
Pub. Co., c1897. 8p. (The
darkey and comic drama)

The case of Smythe vs.
Smith. A mock trial court
scene in one act. Phila-
delphia: Penn Pub. Co.,
1915. 22p. *[earlier copyright: 1899]*

Conrad; or, The hand of a
friend. A drama in three
acts. Chicago: Dramatic
Pub. Co., 1897. 39p. (Sergel's acting drama. no. 508)

The Cuban spy. A comedy
drama in four acts. Philadelphia: Penn Pub. Co.,
1915. 58p. *[earlier copyright: 1898]*

Cupid's frolics. A sketch in
one scene. New York: De Witt,
c1881. 5p.

A desperate situation. A
farce in one scene. New York:
De Witt, c1881. 7p. (De Witt's
Ethiopian and comic drama.
no. 139)

Dodging the police; or, Enforcing the Sunday law. A
whimsical farce in one act.
Chicago: Dramatic Pub. Co.,
c1889. 7p. (The darkey and
comic drama)

Election day. An Ethiopian
farce in two scenes. New
York: De Witt, c1880. 6p.

False colors. A black sketch
in two scenes. Chicago:
Dramatic Pub. Co., c1897. 9p.
(The darkey and comic drama)

Gambrinus, king of lager
beer. A diabolical, musical,
comical and non-sensical
Ethiopian burlesque. Music
arranged...by A. B. Sedg-
wick. New York: Dramatic
Pub. Co., c1876. 19p. (De
Witt's Ethiopian and comic
drama. no. 106)

Get-rich-quick society; or,
One hundred for thirty.
Chicago: Dramatic Pub. Co.,
c1898. 7p. (The darkey and
comic drama)

The girl from Klondike; or,
Wide awake Nell. A comedy-
drama in three acts. Chicago:
Dramatic Pub. Co., c1898.
26p. (American acting drama)

A girl of the century. A
comedy in one act. Phila-
delphia: Penn Pub. Co.,
1897. 13p. (Keystone edition
of popular plays)

Happy Uncle Rufus. A musical
sketch in one scene. Chicago
and New York: Dramatic Pub.
Co., c1888. 7p. (The comic
drama. no. 142)

Helen's funny babies. An Ethiopian burlesque in one scene. New York: De Witt, c1878. 6p.

How to get a divorce. A farce in one act. Chicago: Dramatic Pub. Co., c1897. 9p. (The darkey and comic drama)

Jack Sheppard and Joe Blue-skin; or, Amateur road agents. Melo-dramatic burlesque in one act. Chicago: Dramatic Pub. Co., c1897. 10p. (The darkey and comic drama)

The lady barber. Sketch in one scene. Chicago: Dramatic Pub. Co., c1897. 9p. (The comic drama. no. 169)

Little Miss Nobody. A comedy-drama in three acts. Philadelphia: Penn Pub. Co., 1916. 46p. [earlier copyright: 1897]

Love in all corners. A farce in one act. Chicago: Dramatic Pub. Co., c1898. 8p. (The darkey and comic drama)

The lunatic. A negro sketch in one scene. Chicago: Dramatic Pub. Co., c1876. 6p. (The comic drama. no. 90)

Making a hit. An Ethiopian farce in two scenes. New York: De Witt, c1876. 7p. (De Witt's Ethiopian and comic drama. no. 109)

The midnight intruder. An Ethiopian farce. Chicago: Dramatic Pub. Co., c1876. 8p.

My wife's visitors. A comic drama in one scene. New York: De Witt, c1879. 8p. (De Witt's Ethiopian and comic drama. no. 119)

The new woman's husband. A

satire in one scene. Philadelphia: Penn Pub. Co., 1912. 8p. [earlier copyright: 1897]

The noble savage. A comic Ethiopian farce in one scene. New York: De Witt, c1880. 9p. (De Witt's Ethiopian and comic drama. no. 132)

Norah's good-bye. A musical Irish sketch in one scene. Chicago: Dramatic Pub. Co., c1884. 6p. (The darkey and comic drama)

One night in a medical college. Chicago: Dramatic Pub. Co., c1877. 9p. (The comic drama. no. 114)

Other people's troubles. An eccentricity in one scene. Chicago: Dramatic Pub. Co., c1897. 10p. (The comic drama. no. 171)

The painter's apprentice. An Ethiopian farce in one scene. New York: De Witt, c1876. 8p. (De Witt's Ethiopian and comic drama. no. 51)

Pleasant companions. An Ethiopian sketch in one scene. New York: De Witt, c1880. 7p. (De Witt's Ethiopian and comic drama. no. 135)

The polar bear. An Ethiopian farce in one scene. New York: De Witt, c1876. 8p. (De Witt's Ethiopian and comic drama. no. 92)

The rival barber shops. An Ethiopian farce in one scene. Chicago: Dramatic Pub. Co., c1880. 7p. (The comic drama)

Scenes in front of a clothing store. A farce in one scene. New York: De Witt, c1889. 6p. (De Witt's Ethiopian and comic drama. no. 160)

The scout of the Philippines.

A military comedy drama in three acts. Philadelphia: Penn Pub. Co., 1913. 40p. *[earlier copyright: 1899]*

The serenade party; or, The miser's troubles. A black sketch in one act. Chicago: Dramatic Pub. Co., c1897. 9p. (The darkey and comic drama)

Society acting. Farce in one act. Chicago: Dramatic Pub. Co., c1898. 10p. (The darkey and comic drama)

The sulphur bath. A farce in one scene. New York: De Witt, c1884. 5p. (De Witt's Ethiopian and comic drama. no. 154)

Too little vagrants; or, Beware of tramps. A farce in one act. Chicago: Dramatic Pub. Co., c1897. 8p. (The comic drama. no. 193)

The two awfuls. A negro sketch. Chicago and New York: Dramatic Pub. Co., c1876. 5p.

The undertaker's daughter. Original farce in one act. Chicago: Dramatic Pub. Co., 19-? 11p. (The darkey and comic drama)

Unexpected visitors. A farce. Chicago: Dramatic Pub. Co., c1898. 6p. (The darkey and comic drama)

Unlimited cheek; or, The sewing machine agents. A comic Ethiopian farce in one scene. New York: De Witt, c1880. 6p. (De Witt's Ethiopian and comic drama. no. 134)

Vinegar bitters *see* White, Charles

What shall I take? An Ethiopian farce in one act. New York: De Witt, c1876. 9p.

(De Witt's Ethiopian and comic drama. no. 93)

Who's the actor? An Ethiopian farce. Chicago: Dramatic Pub. Co., c1876. 8p. (The darkey and comic drama)

Whose baby is it? An Ethiopian sketch in one scene. Chicago: Dramatic Pub. Co., c1880. 6p. (The darkey and comic drama)

The wonderful telephone. A black sketch in one scene. New York: De Witt, 188-? 6p. (De Witt's Ethiopian and comic drama. no. 143)

The yellow kid who lives in Hogan's Alley. New York: Dramatic Pub. Co., 1897. 9p. Title page lacking. (De Witt's Ethiopian and comic drama. no. 164)

Duncan, Florence I.
Ye last sweet thing in corners. Being ye faithful drama of ye artists' vendetta. By F. I. D. Philadelphia: Duncan & Hall, c1880. 66p.

Dunn, Herb H.
Driven from home; or, A father's curse. A domestic drama in four acts. Clyde, O.: Ames, 1885. 15p. (Ames' series of standard and minor drama. no. 152)

Dunne, Norah.
Miss tom boy. A comedy in one act. Chicago and New York: Dramatic Pub. Co., c1899. 15p. (Sergel's acting drama. no. 539)

Mrs. Plodding's nieces; or, Domestic accomplishments. A comedy in one act for young ladies. Chicago and New York: Dramatic Pub. Co., c1899. 22p. (Sergel's acting drama. no. 453)

The durbar *see* Denison,
Thomas Stewart *in his*
Wide awake dialogues

Durfee, Job, 1790-1847.
The school of Queen Mab.
[From his: Complete works...
Edited by his son. Provi-
dence: Gladding and Proud,
1849. 523p.] p.179-196.

Durivarge, Oliver Everett.
The fellow that looks like
me *see* White, Charles

The lady of the Lions. A
burlesque in one act. By
O. E. Durivage. New York
and London: S. French, 1857?
16p. (French's minor drama.
no. 228)

The stage-struck Yankee. A
farce in one act. New York:
S. French, 186-? 16p.
(French's minor drama. The
acting edition. no. 215)

The stage-struck Yankee. A
farce in one act. Chicago:
Dramatic Pub. Co., 189-?
New edition, revised and
improved. 19p. (Sergel's
acting drama. no. 460)

Duru, Alfred, 1829-1889.
Fleur-de-lis *see* Goodwin,
John Cheever

Fleur-de-thé *see* Byrne,
Charles Alfred. Pearl of
Pekin; or, The dashing tar
outwitted by his wife

Gillette de Narbonne *see*
Norcross, J. W. Gillette;
or, Count and countess

La mascotte *see* Elson,
Louis Charles and Norris,
J. W.

Les noces d'Olivette *see*
Olivette

Du Souchet, Henry A., b.1852.
The man from Mexico. A

farcical comedy in three acts.
(From the French of Genedinet
[sic, Gondinet] and Bisson.)
New York: S. French, c1897.
107p. (French's standard
library edition)

My friend from India. A farcical comedy in three acts. New
York: S. French, c1894. 95p.

Dusk of the Gods *see* Jameson,
Frederick

Dutch justice *see* White,
Charles

The Dutch prize fighter *see*
Cutler, F. L.

The Dutch recruit; or, The blue
and gray *see* Vegiard, J. T.

Dutchey vs. Nigger *see* Luster,
James O.

A Dutchman in Ireland. A comic
sketch. Chicago: Dramatic
Pub. Co., 18-? 8p. (The
darkey and comic drama)

The Dutchman's ghost *see*
White, Charles

The Dutchman's ghost; or, All
right *see* Barry, S.

The Dutchman's picnic *see*
Haskett, Emmett

Duthmarno *see* Barnitz, Albert
Trovillo Siders

Duty and safety of emancipation
see Neal, John

Duval, Alexandre Vincent Pineux,
1767-1842.
La jeunesse de Henry V *see*
Payne, John Howard. Charles
II; or, The Merry monarch
in The modern standard
drama, vol. 3

Duval, Georges, 1847-1919.
  Le coup de fouet *see* The
  lash of the whip

Duvar, John Hunter, 1830-1899.
  De Roberval. [From his: De
  Roberval...the emigration...
  the triumph of constancy.
  Saint John, N. B.: J. & A.
  McMillan, 1888. 192p.]*[only
  De Roberval is reproduced on
  this microprint. Readex also
  enters this title under
  Hunter-Duvar, which is the
  form of the name used by the
  Library of Congress]*

Duveyrier, Anne Honoré Joseph,
  1787-1865 [pseud.: Mélesville]
  Le bourgmestre de Sardam
  see Balatka, Hans. Peter
  the Great in Saardam; or,
  The Czar and the carpenter

  La lune de miel *see*
  Harrison, Constance Cary.
  A Russian honeymoon

  Sullivan *see* Sullivan

  Zampa *see* Zampa; or, The
  marble bride

The dwarf *see* Rees, James

Dyer, Elizabeth.
  A tangled skein, in three
  knots. Providence: J. A. &
  R. A. Reid, 1881. 31p.

The dying requisition *see*
  Logan, Thomas B. The cousins;
  or; The dying requisition

Dying to keep him; or, Tortesa
  the usurer *see* Willis,
  Nathaniel Parker. Two ways
  of dying for a husband

Dying to lose him; or, Bianca
  Visconti *see* Willis,
  Nathaniel Parker. Two ways
  of dying for a husband
  *[Readex has reproduced this
  play also under the title,*

  *Bianca Visconti; or, The
  heart overtasked]*

E., A. *see* Trumbull, Annie
  Eliot

E. C. B. Susan Jane; or, A
  sailor's life on the raging
  main *see* Hart, George G.

Eagan, H. W., b.1841.
  The academy of stars *see*
  Leavitt, Andrew J. and Eagan,
  H. W.

  The arrival of Dickens *see*
  Leavitt, Andrew J. and Eagan,
  H. W.

  The black Ole Bull *see*
  Leavitt, Andrew J. and Eagan,
  H. W.

  The blackest tragedy of all;
  or, A peep behind the scenes
  see Leavitt, Andrew J. and
  Eagan, H. W.

  Blinks and jinks *see*
  Leavitt, Andrew J. and Eagan,
  H. W.

  Boarding school *see* Leavitt,
  Andrew J. and Eagan, H. W.

  Cousin Joe's visit *see*
  Leavitt, Andrew J. and Eagan,
  H. W.

  Deaf as a post *see* Leavitt,
  Andrew J. and Eagan, H. W.

  The deserters *see* Leavitt,
  Andrew J. and Eagan, H. W.

  The intelligence office *see*
  Leavitt, Andrew J. and Eagan,
  H. W.

  Jeemes the poet *see* Leavitt,
  Andrew J. and Eagan, H. W.

  The lucky number *see*
  Leavitt, Andrew J. and Eagan,
  H. W.

  No tator; or, Man-fish *see*
  Leavitt, Andrew J. and Eagan,
  H. W.

Rip Van Winkle *see* Leavitt, Andrew J. and Eagan, H. W.

Ten days in the Tombs *see* Leavitt, Andrew J. and Eagan, H. W.

That wife of mine *see* Leavitt, Andrew J. and Eagan, H. W.

A trip to Paris *see* Leavitt, Andrew J. and Eagan, H. W.

The two Pompeys *see* Leavitt, Andrew J. and Eagan, H. W.

The upper ten thousand *see* Leavitt, Andrew J. and Eagan, H. W.

Who stole the chicken? *see* Leavitt, Andrew J. and Eagan, H. W.

Early California *see* Bausman, William

Early vows *see* Townsend, Charles

Earning a living *see* McCracken, J. L. H.

An east Indian drug *see* Taylor, Malcom [sic, Malcolm] Stuart. Aar-u-ag-oos; or, An east Indian drug

Easter eve; or, The "New Hagodoh Shel Pesach" *see* Bien, Herman Milton

Easton, William Edgar, b.1861. Dessalines: a dramatic tale...Galveston, Texas: J. W. Burson, 1893. 138p.

Ebenezer Venture; or, Advertising for a wife *see* La Bree, Lawrence

Eberhart, B. F.

Home rule. A charade in two scenes. Clyde, O.: Ames, 1896. p.10-15. (Ames' series of standard and minor drama. no. 377)

Yacob's hotel experience. A farce in one set. Clyde, O.: Ames, 1896. p.1-9. (Ames' series of standard and minor drama. no. 377)

Ebony flats and black sharps *see* Goode, George W.

The echo *see* The railroad explosion [and] The echo

Echoes from Bethlehem *see* Finn, Francis James

Echols, Walter Jarrell. The general manager; or, A shot from the kitchen range. A musical farce-comedy in three acts. Clyde, O.: Ames, 1892. 24p. (Ames' series of standard and minor drama. no. 304)

An economical boomerang *see* Neall, Walter H.

Eddy, Jerome H. The village postmaster *see* Ives, Alice Emma and Eddy, Jerome H.

Eddy, Marion (pseud.) *see* Delanoy, Mary Frances Hanford

Edgarton, Sarah Carter, 1819-1848. The beauty of piety *see* Dramatic leaflets

Edgcome, John. The last coat. A comedy in one act. Chicago: Dramatic Pub. Co., c1899. 17p. (Sergel's acting drama. no. 560)

A web of lies; or, Fibs and

foibles. A comedy in one
act. Chicago: Dramatic Pub.
Co., c1899. 18p. (Sergel's
acting drama. no. 565)

Edged tools see Matthews,
Brander

Edgeworth, Maria, 1767-1849.
Dumb Andy see Follen,
Eliza Lee Cabot. Home
dramas for young people

The grinding organ see
Follen, Eliza Lee Cabot.
Home dramas for young
people

Lazy Lawrence; or, Industry
and idleness contrasted
see Venable, William
Henry in his The school
stage

Old Poz see Follen, Eliza
Lee Cabot. Home dramas for
young people

Tarlton see Venable,
William Henry. Tarleton
in his The school stage
["Tarleton" is the title
used by Venable, although
Edgeworth's work is pro-
perly entitled, "Tarlton"]

Edith see Copcutt, Francis

Editha's burgler see
Thomas, Augustus and Smith,
Edgar McPhail

An editor who wanted office
see Monroe, Jasper R.

The editor's troubles see
Harrigan, Edward

Edmund Kean; or, The life of
an actor see Jessop,
George Henry and St. Maur, J.

Edouin, Winnie.
A bunch of keys; or, The
hotel see Hoyt, Charles

Hale and Edouin, Winnie

Edwards, Julian, 1855-1910.
Jupiter; or, The cobbler and
the king see Smith, Harry
Bache

The Princess Chic see
La Shelle, Kirke

Effervescing see Seitz,
B. Frank

Egan, Pierce, 1772-1849.
[Tales] see Babcock, J.
Frederick. Floret; or, The
poor girl

Life in London see Tom
and Jerry; or, Life in
London

The Egyptian princess see
Rosse, Jeanie Quinton

Eh? What did you say? see
Toler, Mrs. H. M.

Eh? What is it? see Stewart,
J. C.

Eichberg, Julius, 1824-1893.
The doctor of Alcantara see
Woolf, Benjamin Edward

The two cadis. A comic opera
in one act. Boston: Oliver
Ditson, c1868. Vocal score.
108p.

The elder brother see Beaumont, Francis and Fletcher,
John in The modern
standard drama, vol. 9

Eldyle see Magnus, Maurice

Ele, Rona.
Woman's lefts. A drama in
three acts. Philadelphia and
Boston: Geo. Maclean, 18-?
16p.

Election day see Dumont,
Frank

The Electra of Sophocles *see*
Brincklé, J. G.

An electric episode *see* Booth,
Helen *in* Dramatic leaflets

Electric light *see* Hazelton,
William B. and Spencer,
Edward

Electric love *see* Morris,
Felix James

The elephant of Siam and the
fire fiend *see* Gallot,
John

An elephant on ice. An Ethiopian interlude in one scene.
New York: Dick & Fitzgerald,
c1875. 6p.

The elevator *see* Howells,
William Dean

The elf-king; or, Wealth and
poverty *see* Lehmann, M.

Elfins and mermaids; or, The
red rock wave cruiser *see*
Brown, Charles Hovey

Elfrida *see* Rishell, Dyson

Elijah *see* Davidson, Robert

Eliot, Annie (pseud.) *see*
Trumbull, Annie Eliot

Eliot, George, 1819-1880
[real name: Mary Ann Evans]
The Spanish gypsy *see* Cobb,
Mary L. Poetical dramas for
home and school

The elixir of love. A comic
opera in two acts. New York:
John Douglas, 1848. Bilingual
text: English and Italian.
59p. (The operatic library.
no. 24) *[music by Gaetano
Donizetti to the libretto
L'elisir d'amore by Felice
Romani]* see also Weil,

Oscar. Adina; or, The elixir
of love

Eliza and Claudio; or, Love
protected by friendship *see*
Ponte, Lorenzo da

Elizabeth Carisbrooke with a
"P" *see* Brewster, Emma E.
in her Parlor varieties

Elizabeth of England *see*
Tullidge, Edward Wheelock

Eliza's bona-fide offer *see*
Brewster, Emma E. *see also
her* Parlor varieties

Ella; or, The Prince of
Gilead's vow *see* Alexander,
William

Ellet, Elizabeth Fries Lummis,
1818-1877.
Euphemio of Messina. New York:
Monson Bancroft, 1834. 62p.
*[translated from the Italian
of Silvio Pellico]*

Teresa Contarini. A tragedy
in five acts. [From her:
Poems, translated and
original. Philadelphia:
Key & Biddle, 1835] p.137-229.

Ellie Laura; or, The border
orphan *see* O'Leary, James

Elliott, Everett.
Santa Claus' daughter. A
musical Christmas burlesque
in two acts. Clyde, O.: Ames,
c1892. 17p. (Ames' series of
standard and minor drama.
no. 309) *[joint author:
F. W. Hardcastle]*

Elliott, William, 1788-1863.
Fiesco. A tragedy. New York:
The author, 1850. 64p.
*[founded on Le conjuration
du comte Jean-Louis de
Fiesque, by Cardinal Jean
François de Retz]*

Ellsworth, Erastus Wolcott,
1822-1902.
Ariadne. [From his: Poems.
Hartford: F. A. Brown, 1855.
272p.] p.18-57.

Elocution see Caldor, M. T.
in his Social charades

The elopement see Kavanaugh,
Mrs. Russell in her
Original dramas, dialogues
see also Stewart, J. C.

The elopement; or, Love and
duty see Morris, Robert

The elopement; or, The disinherited son see Williams,
Charles

Elshemus, Louis Michael, 1864-
1941.
Om. Mammom. [From his: Om.
Mammom. A spirit song. New
York: Eastman Lewis, 1897.
126p.] p.7-109.

Elson, Louis Charles, 1848-1920.
La mascotte. Comic opera in
three acts. (From the French
of Audran.) Boston: White,
Smith, c1881. 71p. Libretto.
[music by Edmond Audran with
libretto by Henri Chivot and
Alfred Duru; without music;
joint author: J. W. Norris]

The merry war. Opera in
three acts. Boston, Chicago:
White, Smith, c1882. Vocal
score. 206p. [music by
Johann Strauss on libretto
entitled Der lustige Krieg
by Richard Genée and Camillo
Wälzel]

Nanon. Opera comique in three
acts. (From the French of
Genée.) Boston, Chicago:
White, Smith, c1885. 58p.
Libretto. [music by Richard
Genée on libretto by Camillo
Wälzel, based on M. E. G.
Théaulon de Lambert's Nanon,
Ninon et Maintenon]

The queen's lace handkerchief.
Opera in three acts. Boston,
Chicago: White, Smith, c1882.
Vocal score. 197p. [music by
Johann Strauss on libretto
entitled Das Spitzentuch der
Königin by Richard Genée and
Heinrich Bohrmann]

Elwyn, Lizzie May.
Dot, the miner's daughter;
or, One glass of wine. A
drama in four acts. Clyde, O.:
Ames, c1888. 36p. (Ames' series
of standard and minor drama.
no. 254)

Millie, the quadroon; or, Out
of bondage. A drama in five
acts. Clyde, O.: Ames, c1888.
36p. (Ames' series of standard
and minor drama. no. 251)

Murder will out. A farce in
one act for six female characters. New York: Fitzgerald
Pub. Corp., c1890. 14p.

Rachel, the fire waif. A drama
in four acts. Clyde, O.: Ames,
1900. 29p. (Ames' series of
standard and minor drama.
no. 420)

Sweetbrier; or, The flower
girl of New York. A drama in
six acts. Clyde, O.: Ames,
1899. 31p. (Ames' series of
standard and minor drama.
no. 266)

Switched off. A temperance
farce in one act. Clyde, O.:
Ames, 1899. 16p. (Ames'
series of standard and minor
drama. no. 413)

Emerson, M. Burt see Emerson,
W. Burt

Emerson, W. Burt.
The adventuress; or, Lady
Evelyn's triumph. A drama in
four acts. Clyde, O.: Ames,
c1893. 23p. (Ames' series of
standard and minor drama.
no. 318)

The musical captain; or, The
fall of Vicksburg. A drama
of the late rebellion in
four acts. Clyde, O.: Ames,
1890. 14p. (Ames' series of
standard and minor drama.
no. 277)

Snow ball, a colored valet.
Farce in one act. Clyde, O.:
Ames, 1895. 9p. (Ames'
series of standard and minor
drama. no. 358) [Readex
enters this title under
M. Burt Emerson, instead of
W. Burt Emerson, because of
a printing error on the
title page]

Emerson, W. D.
A country romance. A pathetic episode in one act.
Chicago: Dramatic Pub. Co.,
c1899. 10p. (Sergel's acting
drama. no. 434) [the title
page of William D. Emerson's
An unknown rival (see below)
indicates that the same
author wrote A country
romance, which Readex has
entered under W. D. Emerson]

Emerson, William D.
A country romance see
Emerson, W. D.

The unknown rival. A comedy
in one act. Chicago: Dramatic
Pub. Co., c1899. 9p. (American acting drama) [the title
page gives the title as
An unknown rival]

Emerson, William R.
Putkins, Heir to--Castles in
the air. Boston: G. M. Baker,
c1871. 16p.

Emery, E.
The gypsy's secret. Peoria,
Ill.: Transcript Company,
1879. 51p.

The emigrant's daughter see
Tilden, Len Ellsworth

Emmett, Daniel Decatur, 1815-
1904.
Hard times see White,
Charles

Emmons, Richard, b.1788.
Tecumseh; or, The battle of
the Thames. A national drama
in five acts. Philadelphia:
n.pub., 1836. 36p.

Emotional insanity see Piatt,
Donn in his Various dramatic
works

The Emperor Nicholas and the
American doctor see Gayarré,
Charles Étienne Arthur. Dr.
Bluff in Russia; or, The
Emperor Nicholas and the
American doctor

En voyage see Mathews,
Frances Aymar

The enchanted clogs see
Mumbo Jum; or, The enchanted
clogs

The end of the way see
Sutherland, Evelyn Greenleaf
Baker in her Collected
works. Po' white trash and
other one-act dramas

Endicott see Longfellow,
Henry Wadsworth. The New
England tragedies

Enebuske, Sarah Folsom.
A detective in petticoats.
A comedy in three acts for
female characters only.
Boston: W. H. Baker, c1900.
32p. (Baker's edition of
plays)

Enéleh, H. B.
One year. A comedy-drama in
four acts. Chicago: Dramatic
Pub. Co., c1884. 20p. (Sergel's acting drama. no. 319)
[H. B. Enéleh is a pseud.
for Helen Herzog]

Tempest tossed. An original drama in four acts. New York: De Witt, c1885. 26p. (De Witt's acting plays. no. 337)

An enemy to the king *see* Stephens, Robert Neilson

Enforcing the Sunday law *see* Dumont, Frank. Dodging the police; or, Enforcing the Sunday law

An engaged girl *see* Hyde, Elizabeth A.

An engaging position *see* Macbrayne, Lewis E.

Engländer, Ludwig, 1853-1914. The bells of Bohemia *see* Smith, Harry Bache

The casino girl *see* Smith, Harry Bache

The little corporal *see* Smith, Harry Bache

The rounders *see* Smith, Harry Bache

England's iron days *see* Bannister, Nathaniel Harrington

Engle, Walter K. "Medica." A farce in one set. New York: Dick & Fitzgerald, c1892. 15p.

English, Thomas Dunn, 1819-1902. The Mormons; or, Life at Salt Lake City. A drama in three acts. New York: S. French, 1858. 43p. (French's standard drama. The acting edition. no. 205)

English, William B. Rosina Meadows *see* Saunders, Charles Henry

The English traveler *see* Beadle's dialogues no. 2

Enlisted for the war; or, The home-guard *see* Baker, George Melville

D'Ennery, Adolphe Philippe *see* Dennery, Adolphe Philippe

The enthusiasts by the ears *see* Paulding, James Kirke and Paulding, William Irving. Antipathies; or, The enthusiasts by the ears *in their* Collected works. American comedies

Ephraim's Breite *see* Harned, Mary

The epistolary flirt *see* Amory, Esmerie

An equal chance. A sketch in one act. Boston: W. H. Baker, n.d. 10p. (Baker's edition of plays)

Erckmann, Émile, 1822-1899. L'ami Fritz *see* Dole, Nathan Haskell. Friend Fritz

Le Juif polonais *see* Williams, Henry Llewellyn. The bells; or, The Polish Jew

"Erin go bragh"; or, The mountain rebel *see* Moore, Bernard Francis

Erminia; a tale of Florence *see* Read, Harriette Fanning *in her* Dramatic poems

Ernani. n.p.: n.pub., 18-? Bilingual text: English and Italian. 63p. Libretto. *[music by Giuseppe Verdi on a libretto by Francesco Maria Piave]*

Ernest *see* Harding, Edward John

Ernest Maltravers *see* Medina, Louisa H.

Esau and Jacob *see* Murry,
Ellen *in* Dramatic leaflets

Eshobel, Raymond.
How much I loved thee!
Washington, D. C.: The
author, c1884. 153p. *[Raymond
Eshobel is a pseud. for Henry
Ames Blood, q.v.]*

Esmeralda *see* Burnette,
Frances Hodgson and Gillette,
William Hooker

Estabrook, Jones E.
Columbia. A patriotic cantata. Worcester: West & Lee
Game and Printing Co., 1874.
12p. Libretto. *[music by
John Astor Broad; without
the music]*

Esther *see* Cushing, Eliza
Lanesford Foster *see also*
Mendes, Henry Pereira *see
also* Moses, Anna Jonas

Estranged *see* Sedgwick,
Alfred B.

Eugene Aram *see* Williams,
Espy William Hendricks

Euphemio of Messina *see*
Elliot, Elizabeth Fries
Lummis

Euripides, 480B.C.?-406B.C.
Medea *see* Patterson, John.
The Medea of Euripides

Euryanthe *see* Schwab,
Frederick A.

Eustis, Fred J.
The crystal slipper; or,
Prince Prettywitz and little
Cinderella *see* Smith,
Harry Bache and Thompson,
Alfred

Eva *see* Adams, Miss L. B.
see also Swanwick, Cathe-
rina

Evadue; or, The statue *see*
Sheil, Richard Lalor *in*
The modern standard drama,
vol. 7

Evans, Mary Ann *see* Eliot,
George (pseud.)

Eveleen Wilson, the flower of
Erin *see* Pilgrim, James

Evelyn Gray; or, The victims
of our western Turks *see*
Stern, H. I.

Evening dress *see* Howells,
William Dean

The evening party *see* The
temperance school dialogues

Everett, Alexander Hill, 1790-
1847.
The Grecian gossips [bound
with] The exile's lament
[and] scenes from Goethe's
Faust. [From his: Critical
and miscellaneous essays...
Boston: James Munroe, 1845.
563p.] p.484-514.

Everybody astonished *see*
Bauman, E. Henri

Every-day life. By C. W. S.
New York: S. French, c1858.
40p. (French's standard
drama)

Everyday occurences *see*
Coes, George H.

The evil eye *see* Phillips,
Jonas B.

Excelsior; or, The heir
apparent *see* Lookup,
Alexander (pseud.?)

Excise trials *see* White,
Charles

Ex-Confederate officer *see*
The tyrant of New Orleans

The excursion of 4th July,
1860 *see* Blackie, George

The execution of Montrose
see Aytoun, William
Edmondstone *in* Massey,
Charles. Massey's exhibition
reciter

"Exerbition"; or, The deestrick
skule of fifty years ago
see Jaquith, Mrs. M. H.

Exile *see* Block, Louis James

The exile's lament *see*
Everett, Alexander Hill
in his The Grecian gossips

Experience the best teacher
see The kidnapped clergyman; or, Experience the
best teacher

Eyes and no eyes *see* The
temperance school dialogues

Ez-Zahra *see* Gailey, Florence
Louise

F., W. F.
The little red riding hood.
A fairy opera in three acts.
(From the French of Théaulon.)
Baltimore: E. J. Coale, 1831.
Bilingual text: French and
English. 131p. *[cover: Le
petit chaperon rouge...
musique de M. Boieldieu]*

Facing the music *see* Darnley,
James Henry *see also*
Hanlon, Henry Oldham

Facts and fancies *see* Tooth,
William

The facts in the case *see*
Lippmann, Julie Mathilde

The fag's revolt *see* Venable,
William Henry *in his* The
school stage

Faint heart never won fair lady
see Planché, James Robinson
in The modern standard drama,
vol. 6 *see also* Shields,
Sarah Annie Frost *in her*
Parlor charades and proverbs

The fair truant *see* Ward,
Thomas

Fairfax *see* Campbell, Bartley
Theodore *in his* The white
slave and other plays

Fairly taken in *see* Kemble,
Marie Thérèse De Camp *in*
Steele, Silas Sexton. Collec-
ted works. Book of plays

Fairman, James, 1826-1904.
The voice of the sea. A comedy
in three acts. n.p.: printed
for the author, c1882. 103p.

The fairy and the little glass
slipper *see* Cinderella;
or, The fairy and the little
glass slipper

Fairy favor *see* Thaxter,
Adam Wallace. The grotto
nymph; or, Fairy favor

The fairy grotto *see* Stratton,
George William

The fairy of the fountain; or,
Diamonds and toads *see*
Baker, George Melville

The fairy of the tunnel *see*
Ward, Lew. My pard; or, The
fairy of the tunnel

The fairy steeplecrown *see*
Carter, Alice P.

The fairy's favor *see* Conway,
H. J. The talisman; or, The
fairy's favor

Faith *see* Lart, John

The faith cure *see* Coes, George H.

Faithful unto death *see* Hanshew, Thomas W. Oath bound; or, Faithful unto death

Fales, Willard Henry. The cool collegians. A comedy in two acts. By Miles Medic (pseud.) Boston: W. H. Baker, c1883. 31p. (The Globe drama)

The fall of Ahriman *see* Ormusd's triumph; or, The fall of Ahriman

The fall of Ingalls *see* Ware, Eugene Fitch. The Kansas bandit; or, The fall of Ingalls

Fall of Palmyra *see* Alexander, William

The fall of Tarquin *see* Payne, John Howard. Brutus; or, The fall of Tarquin *in* The modern standard drama, vol. 8

The fall of the Alamo *see* Nona, Francis

The fall of Vicksburg *see* Emerson, W. Burt. The musical captain; or, The fall of Vicksburg

A fallen idol *see* Griffith, Helen Sherman

The fallen saved *see* Smith, William Henry. The drunkard; or, The fallen saved *see also in* The modern standard drama, vol. 11

The false and the true *see* Leland, Oliver Shepard. Beatrice; or, The false and the true

False colors *see* Dumont, Frank

The false friend *see* Fawcett, Edgar *see also* Vautrot, George S.

A false note *see* Gibbs, Julia De Witt

False pretenses; or, Both sides of good society *see* Mathews, Cornelius

False pretentions *see* Fuller, Horace Williams

The false prophet *see* Knox, John Armoy and Snyder, Charles McCoy

Falsehood *see* Shields, Sarah Annie Frost *in her* Parlor charades and proverbs

Falsehood and truth *see* Call, S. C. The ugly aunt; or, Falsehood and truth

Falsely accused *see* Lawrence, F. N. Lanty's luck; or, Falsely accused

Falstaff's boasting *see* Shakespeare, William. Henry IV *in* Dramatic leaflets

A family affair *see* Townsend, Charles

The family cure *see* Frank, J. C. Homeopathy; or, The family cure

Family discipline *see* Zediker, N.

A family strike *see* Denison, Thomas Stewart

Fanchon, the cricket *see* Waldauer, Augustus

Fanning, Brosse.

Police court *see* White,
Charles. Dutch justice

Fantasma. A fairy tale in five
parts. [From: Fantasma and
other poems. Kansas City,
Mo.: Ramsey, Millett &
Hudson, 1879. 318p.] p.5-142.
*[although Readex enters this
play under title, the author
is Rosa Fairfax Costley]*

Fantine *see* Woolf, Benjamin
Edward and Field, Roswell
Martin

Farmer Larkin's boarders *see*
Osborn, Merit

Farnie, Henry Brougham, 1836-
1889.
Olivette *see* Olivette

Farquhar, George, 1677?-1707.
The inconstant; or, The way
to win him *see* Daly,
Augustin

The recruiting officer *see*
Daly, Augustin

Farrar, Geraldine, 1882-1967
see An American wife

Farrell, John Rupert.
The haunted hat. Farce in
one act. Clyde, O.: Ames,
1898. 7p. (Ames' series of
standard and minor drama.
no. 398)

Hearts of gold. A drama in
four acts. Clyde, O.: Ames,
1896. (Ames' series of
standard and minor drama.
no. 374)

Fashion; or, Life in New York
see Ritchie, Anna Cora Ogden
Mowatt *see also her* Plays

A fashionable physician *see*
Rosenfeld, Sydney. The club
of friends; or, A fashionable
physician

Fashions and follies of Washington life *see* Preuss, Henry
Clay

Fast, Edward Gustavus.
The gentleman of the color;
or, Washington reconstructed.
A burlesque in three acts.
By Ben Horst (pseud.) Baltimore: John J. Webb, 1874.
48p.

Fast men of olden time. A
musical comedy in three acts.
(From Moncrieff's Rochester;
or, King Charles the Second's
merry days.) Boston: Boston
Museum, 1860. Prompt-book,
interleaved with Ms. notes.
64p.

The fatal glass; or, The curse
of drink *see* McCloskey,
James Joseph

The fatal message *see* Bangs,
John Kendrick

Fate *see* Campbell, Bartley
Theodore

The fate of a coquette *see*
Olwine, Wayne. Camille; or,
The fate of a coquette

Fate; or, The prophecy *see*
Bunce, Oliver Bell

Father Junipero Serra *see*
Miller, Chester Gore

Father Nile-Father Mississippi
see Townsend, Frederic *in
his* Spiritual visitors

A father's curse *see* Dunn,
Herb H. Driven from home;
or, A father's curse

A father's will *see* Martin,
W. H. Servants vs. master;
or, A father's will

Fatinitza. A comic opera in

three acts. (From the German of von Suppé.) New York: A. S. Seer, Theatrical Printer, 1879. 40p. Libretto. *[music by Franz von Suppé on libretto by Richard Genée; Readex enters the vocal score of this work under Barker, Theodore T. and Baxter, Sylvester]*

Faucet, Edwin *see* Fawcett, Edgar

Faugh-a-Ballagh; or, The wearing of the green *see* Moore, Bernard Francis

Faust *see* Brooks, Charles Timothy *see also* Grau, Maurice *see also* Kellogg, Clara Louise *see also* Phillips, Henry *see also* Taylor, Bayard

Faust. The first part *see* Claudy, Frank

Faust (scenes from) *see* Everett, Alexander Hill *in his* The Grecian gossips

Faust and Marguerite. A romantic spectacular drama. In three acts. Adapted from the French and German. New York and London: Samuel French, 18-? 36p. (French's standard drama. The acting edition. no. 279) *[based on Faust et Marguerite by Michel Carré, which was founded on Goethe]*

Faust's death *see* Moelling, Carl Erdwin

La favorita (The favorite). A lyrical drama in four acts. (Music by Donizetti.) New York: M. Douglas, 18-? Bilingual text: English and Italian. 53p. Libretto. (The operatic library. no. 1) *[the title page indicates this title as no. 16 in the series The operatic library, whereas a list of the series found on the page previous to the title page notes that this is actually no. 1, which is correct, and the title page is in error. Music by Gaetano Donizetti on libretto by Alphonse Royer, Jean Nicolas Gustave von Nieuwenhuysen and Augustin Scribe; without the music]*

The favorite. A lyrical drama in four acts. New York: Snowden's Job Printing Establishment, 1851. Bilingual text: English and Italian. 59p. Libretto. *[music by Gaetano Donizetti on libretto by Alphonse Royer, Jean Nicolas Gustave von Nieuwenhuysen and Augustin Scribe; without the music]*

La favorite (The king's mistress) *see* Révoil, Bénédict Henry

Fawcett, Edgar, 1847-1904. Americans abroad. A comedy of international contrasts. n.p.: n.pub., 1881. Typescript. 24, 25, 24, 28 leaves (numb. irreg.)

The buntling ball. A Graeco-American play; being a poetical satire on New York society. New York: Funk & Wagnalls, 1884. 154p.

The dawn of ethics. [From his: Voices and visions. London: Eveleigh Nash, 1903. 197p.] p.77-79.

The false friend. A drama in four acts and a prologue. n.p.: n.pub., 1880. In Ms. 19, 32, 25, 36, 21 leaves. *see also* Wright, N. M. Fielding manor

How a queen loved. [From
his: Songs of doubt and
dream. New York, London,
Toronto: Funk & Wagnalls,
1891. 311p.] p.152-171.

The icicle, [From his: Songs
of doubt and dream. New York,
London, Toronto: Funk &
Wagnalls, 1891. 311p.] p.
270-308.

An idyl of the slums. [From
his: Voices and visions.
London: Eveleigh Nash,
1903. 197p.] p.45-47.

In the year ten thousand.
[From his: Songs of doubt
and dream. New York, London,
Toronto: Funk & Wagnalls,
1891. 311p.] p.51-60.

The new King Arthur. An
opera without music. New
York: Funk & Wagnalls, 1885.
164p.

Fay, Theodore Sedgwick, 1807-
1898.
Waldimar *see* Bailey,
John J.

Fazio; or, The Italian wife
see Milman, Henry Hart *in*
The modern standard drama,
vol. 1

Fear of scandal *see* St.
Clair, Clarence

Feast *see* Griffin, George
W. H.

The feast of lights; or,
Chanukoh *see* Bien,
Herman Milton

The feast of tabernacles *see*
Ware, Henry *in* Cobb,
Mary L. Poetical dramas
for home and school

Fechter, Charles.
Monte Cristo *see* O'Neill,
James

The federal spy *see* Andrews,
Fred G. Hal Hazard; or,
The federal spy

Felch, William Farrand, 1855-
1930.
The pet of Parsons' ranch.
A comedy-drama in five acts.
Chicago: T. S. Denison,
1886. 33p. (Amateur series)

Shadow castle. A comedy-
drama in four acts. Chicago:
T. S. Denison, c1888. 61p.

Felix, V. Rev. F., d.1924.
Pontia: the daughter of
Pilate. Drama in four acts.
Baltimore: J. Murphy, 1899.
52p.

The shepherdess of Lourdes;
or, The blind princess. A
drama in five acts. Baltimore: J. Murphy, 1899. 66p.

The fellow that looks like me
see White, Charles

Felter, Will D.
A bunch of roses. A burlesque
musical entertainment. New
York: Dick & Fitzgerald,
c1898. 23p. Libretto.

Over the garden wall. A
musical burlesque in one act.
New York: Dick & Fitzgerald,
c1897. 21p.

The Sweet family. A burlesque
musical entertainment. New
York: Dick & Fitzgerald,
c1892. 20p.

The widow's proposals. A
farce in one act. New York:
Dick & Fitzgerald, c1894.
11p.

Felts, William B.
Hernarne. n.p.: for the
author, 1890. 288p.

The female cavalier *see*
Waldauer, Augustus

The female highwayman; or,
The blighted lily *see*
Pilgrim, James

The fencing master *see*
Smith, Harry Bache

The Fenian spy; or, John Bull
in America *see* Griffin,
George W. H. and Christy,
George

Feraudy, Maurice de, b.1859.
A dead heat *see* A dead
heat

Ferguson, of Troy *see*
Moore, Bernard Francis

Fernanda; or, Forgive and
forget *see* Williams,
Henry Llewellyn

Fernande *see* Schönberg,
James

The ferocious uncle and the
avenging robins *see*
Denison, Thomas Stewart.
The babes in the wood; or,
The ferocious uncle and
the avenging robins

Ferretti, Jacopo, 1784-1852.
La cenerentola *see*
Cinderella; or, The fairy
and little glass slipper

Il furioso all' isola di
San Domingo *see* The
maniac at the Island of
St. Domingo

Matilda di Shabran *see*
Attinelli, Joseph

Ferrier, Paul, 1843-1920.
Le roman d'une pupille
see Oakes, A. H. A
teacher taught *see also*
in Matthews, Brander.
Comedies for amateur
acting

Fessenden, Helen May Trott.
Troublesome children; or,

The unexpected voyage of
Jack and Pen. A play for
children. Pittsfield, Mass.:
J. A. Maxim, 1892. 46p.
*[dramatized from Troublesome
children, their ups and
downs, by William Wilberforce
Newton]*

Festival of days *see* Buxton,
Ida M. Carnival of days

Fetter Lane to Gravesend; or,
A dark romance from the
"Railway library" *see*
Williams, Henry Llewellyn

Feudal times; or, The court of
James the Third *see* White,
James *in* The modern
standard drama, vol. 6

Feuillet, Octave, 1821-1890.
Le clef d'or *see* Goodrich,
Frank Boott and Warden,
Frank L. Romance after
marriage; or, The maiden wife

[The man of success] *see*
Cazauran, Augustus R.

Le sphinx *see* Schwab,
Frederick A.

Feydeau, Ernest Aimé, 1821-1873.
La dame de chez Maxim *see*
The lady at Maxim's [or, The
girl from Maxim's]

Feydeau, Georges Léon Jules
Marie, 1862-1921.
Champignol malgré lui *see*
Champignol despite himself

Preté [sic] moi ta femme
see Townsend, Charles. A
family affair

Fezandié, Eugène.
Let love but hold the key
see Morette, Edgar

La Fiammina *see* Clapp,
William Warland

Fibs and foibles *see* Edgcome,

John. A web of lies; or,
Fibs and foibles

Fidelio; or, Constancy
rewarded. An opera in three
acts. New York: H. Kimber,
1839. 30p. Libretto. *[music
by Ludwig van Beethoven,
libretto on Joseph Sonn-
leithner's Fidelio, oder
die eheliche Liebe, which
was founded on Léonore, ou
l'amour conjugal, by Jean
Nicolas Bouilly]*

Field, A. Newton.
Bill Detrick; or, The
mystery of Oliver's Ferry.
A melo-drama in three acts.
Clyde, O.: Ames, 1883. 11p.
(Ames' series of standard
and minor drama. no. 113)

The new Magdalen. A drama
in a prologue and three
acts. Clyde, O.: Ames,
c1882. 37p. (Ames' series
of standard and minor
drama. no. 112) *[based
on Wilkie Collins' story
of the same name]*

Other people's children.
An Ethiopian farce in one
act. Clyde, O.: Ames, 1880.
7p. (Ames' series of
standard and minor drama.
no. 109)

The pop-corn man. An
Ethiopian farce in one act.
Clyde, O.: Ames, c1880. 7p.
(Ames' series of standard
and minor drama. no. 118)

Reverses. A domestic drama
in five acts. Clyde, O.:
Ames, 1882. 26p. (Ames'
series of standard and
minor drama. no. 110)

School. An Ethiopian farce
in one act. Clyde, O.:
Ames, 1880. 7p. (Ames'
series of standard and
minor drama. no. 107)

Those awful boys. An
Ethiopian farce in one act.
Clyde, O.: Ames, 1880. 7p.
(Ames' series of standard
and minor drama. no. 108)

Twain's dodging. An Ethiopian
farce in one act. Clyde, O.:
Ames, 1880. 7p. (Ames' series
of standard and minor drama.
no. 4)

The Yankee duelist. An
original farce. Clyde, O.:
Ames, 1882. 9p. (Ames' series
of standard and minor drama.
no. 111)

Field, Annie Adams, 1834-1915.
Orpheus. A masque. Boston and
New York: Houghton, Mifflin,
1900. 41p.

Pandora. A festival play.
[From her: Under the olive
tree. Boston: Houghton,
Mifflin, 1881. 317p.] p.197-
275.

Sophocles [and] The return
of Persephone [From her:
Under the olive tree. Boston:
Houghton, Mifflin, 1881.
317p.] p.25-34, 139-185.

Field, Henrietta Dexter.
Collected works. The muses
up-to-date. Chicago: Way
and Williams, 1897. xi, 3,
278p. *[joint author: Roswell
Martin Field]*
    Contents: The muses up-to-
date. A mythological liberty
in two acts with a prologue.
--Cinderella. A fairy comedy
in three acts.--Trouble in
the garden. A horticultural
episode in three acts with
living pictures.--The modern
Cinderella. An exploded fairy
tale in three brief acts.--
The wooing of Penelope. An
incident of depravity in
five acts.--A lesson from
fairy land. A tribute to

early convictions in three
acts and an intermezzo.

Field, Joseph M., 1810-1856.
Job and his children. A
domestic drama in two acts.
[From: Metamora and other
plays. By E. R. Page,
editor. Princeton: Princeton Univ. Press, 1941.
399p.] p.235-259. (America's
lost plays, vol. 14)

Field, Roswell Martin.
Collected works *see*
Field, Henrietta Dexter and
Field, Roswell Martin

Fantine *see* Woolf,
Benjamin Edward and Field,
Roswell Martin

The muses up-to-date *see*
Field, Henrietta Dexter
and Field, Roswell Martin

Fielding manor *see* Wright,
M. L.

Fiesco *see* Elliott, William

The Fifth Ave. Hotel *see*
Harrigan, Edward. Porter's
troubles; or, The Fifth
Ave. Hotel

The fifth wheel *see*
Williams, Henry Llewellyn

A fifty-dollar milliner's
bill *see* Booth, Helen
in Dramatic leaflets

Fifty years hence *see*
Varrie, Vida. The coming
man; or, Fifty years hence

A fighting chance; or, For
the blue or the gray *see*
Shoemaker, Dora Adèle

Fighting for the union *see*
Griffin, George W. H.

Fighting the rum-fiend *see*

Thayer, Julia M. *in* Dramatic leaflets

The fighting troubadour *see*
Gunter, Archibald Clavering

La figlia del reggimento. A
romantic opera in two acts.
New York and London: Samuel
French, 188-? Bilingual
text: English and Italian.
23p. Libretto. *[music by
Gaetano Donizetti, libretto
by Jules Henri Vernoy de
Saint-Georges and Jean
François Alfred Bayard;
without the music] see also*
The child of the regiment
see also The daughter of
the regiment

File, Franklin.
A crushed mother-in-law. New
York: Sun Office, c1878.
Galley proof. 12 unnumbered
sheets.

A loyal lover. New York:
n.pub., c1878. Galley proofs.
11 sheets.

Proof positive. New York:
S. W. Green, 1879. 40p.

Supremacy. A drama in four
acts. Boston: Mills, Knight,
1881. 57p. *[joint author:
Edward P. Call]*

Three days. New York: Sun
Office, c1876. Galley proof.
11 unnumbered sheets.

Finding of Moses *see* Boxer,
James *in his* Sacred dramas

The finger of fate; or, The
death letter *see* Tilden,
Len Ellsworth

A finished coquette *see*
Mathews, Frances Aymar

A finished education *see*
Coes, George H.

Finn, Francis James, 1859-
1928.
Echoes from Bethlehem. A
Christmas "miracle." St.
Louis, Mo.: B. Herder,
1912. Third editon. 24p.
[earlier copyright: 1897]

Finn, Sister Mary Paulina,
b.1842.
Alma mater; or, The George-
town Centennial and other
dramas. By M. S. Pine
(pseud.) Washington, D.C.:
For Georgetown Visitation
Convent, 1913. 253p.
Contents: Alma mater; or,
The Georgetown Centennial.
--Hermine.--Heart of gold,
true and tried.--The Church's
triumph.--The Angel's feast.
--The star of Bethlehem.--
The Angel's meeting; or,
Terra Mariae.--A Georgetown
reunion and what became of it

Finnegan and Flanagan *see*
Parker, Walter Coleman

Finnigan's fortune *see*
Townsend, Charles

The fireman *see* Johnson,
Samuel D.

First aid to the injured
see Sutphen, William
Gilbert Van Tassel

First and last *see* The
temperance school dialogues

First and last love *see*
Payne, John Howard. The
Spanish husband; or, First
and last love

The first born *see* Powers,
Francis

A first class hotel *see*
Denison, Thomas Stewart

The first glass *see* Com-

stock, William. Rum; or, The
first glass

The first glass; or, The power
of woman's influence *see*
Bradley, Nellie H.

The first kiss *see* Hageman,
Maurice

First love *see* Hollenius,
Laurence John

The first night *see* White,
Charles

The first violin *see* Clarke,
Joseph Ignatius Constantine
and Phelps, Merridan

Fish, George F.
Dr. Jekyll and Mr. Hyde; or,
A mis-spent life *see*
Forepaugh, Luella and Fish,
George F.

Fisher, Abraham Lincoln.
Little trump; or, A Rocky
Mountain diamond. A drama in
three acts. Boston: W. H.
Baker, c1900. 50p. (Baker's
edition of plays)

A manager's trials. A farce
in one act. New York: Fitzgerald Pub. Corp., 1894. 16p.

The marquis. A comedy in one
act. Philadelphia: Penn Pub.
Co., 1912. 21p. *[earlier
copyright: 1897]*

The fisher maiden *see*
Bannan, Martha Ridgway

A fisherman's luck *see*
Getchell, Wendell P. *see
also* White, Charles

Fiske, Minnie Maddern Davey,
1865-1932.
The rose. A comedy in one
act. n.p.: n.pub., 1892?
Typescript. 21 leaves.

Fitch, Anna Mariska.
Items. A Washington society
play in five acts. New York:
P. F. McBreen, c1874. Contains Ms. notes. 52p.

Fitch, Clyde, 1865-1909.
Barbara Freitchie [sic],
the Frederick girl! New
York: Kauser, 1899? Type-
script, prompt-book. In
four acts (pagination by
acts)

Barbara Frietchie [sic],
the Frederick girl. New
York: Life Pub. Co., 1900.
128p.

Beau Brummel. New York:
Rosenfield Typewriting Co.,
1890? Typescript, prompt-
book. In four acts (paged
by acts) *[Readex enters
this title under William
Clyde Fitch, which would
separate in filing order
this title from the
author's other works,
which Readex enters under
Clyde Fitch]*

Beau Brummel. A play in
four acts. New York: J.
Lane, 1908. 142p.

Bohemia. A play in a pro-
logue and four acts. New
York: Rosenfield, 1895?
Typescript. In a prologue
and four acts (pagination
by acts) *[cover: the author
is indebted to...Henri
Murger and Théodore Barrière
for most of the material
made use of in this play]*

The children. Three dia-
logues: I. Divorce. II.
Birth. III. Death [From
his: The smart set.
Chicago and New York:
Herbert S. Stone, 1897.
201p.] p.63-82. *[these
could be performed as
three separate plays]*

The cowboy and the lady.
New York: n.pub., 1899.
Typescript, prompt-book.
Sides for nineteen parts.
*[this complete play would
require five microprints,
but as of February 1977,
Readex had not supplied
cards 2-3. Readex enters
this title under William
Clyde Fitch, which would
separate in filing order
this title from the author's
other works, which Readex
enters under Clyde Fitch]*

Frederic Lemaitre. A comedy
in one act. n.p.: n.pub.,
c1890. Typescript. Prompt-
book. 18 leaves. *[Readex
enters this title under
William Clyde Fitch, which
would separate in filing
order this title from the
author's other works, which
Readex enters under Clyde
Fitch]*

The gamblers. [From his:
The smart set. Chicago and
New York: Herbert S. Stone,
1897. 201p.] p.185-201.

The masked ball. (From the
French of Bisson and Carré.)
n.p.: n.pub., 1892. Type-
script. Prompt-book. 59 pag.
irreg., 69, 54 leaves (paged
by act) *[this complete play
would require four micro-
prints, but as of February
1977, Readex had not supplied
cards 1-2. Based on Le
veglione (Le bal masqué) by
Alexandre Bisson and Albert
Carré]*

The moth and the flame. New
York: Alice Kauser, c1908.
60p.

Nathan Hale. In four acts.
New York: R. H. Russell,
1899. 100p.

Pamela's prodigy. A lively

comedy. New York: G. M.
Allen, 1893. 107p.

Sappho. (From the novel by
Alphonse Daudet.) n.p.:
n.pub., 1900? Typescript,
prompt-book. In four acts
(pag. by acts) *[act 4 of
Readex copy mutilated]*

Fitch, William Clyde *see*
Fitch, Clyde

Fitzball, Edward, 1792-1873.
The daughter of the regi-
ment *see* The daughter
of the regiment

Fitzwilliam, Edward Francis,
1824-1857.
The queen of a day *see*
The queen of a day

Five centuries *see*
Guernsey, Alice M.

The five hour law; or, Scenes
in Athens *see* Ford,
Alfred

Five o'clock tea *see*
Howells, William Dean

Flagg, -----.
Scotland *see* Massey,
Charles. Massey's exhibi-
tion reciter

Flaherty, Bernard, 1823-1876
see Williams, Barney

A flash of lightning; a drama
of life in our day *see*
Daly, Augustin

Flavia *see* Welcker, Adair
see also his Romer, King
of Norway and other dramas

Flers, Robert de la Motte-
Ango, marquis de, 1872-1927.
Monsieur de la Palisse *see*
Smith, Harry Bache. The
ambassador

Fletcher, John, 1579-1625.
The elder brother *see*
Beaumont, Francis and
Fletcher, John *in* The
modern standard drama,
vol. 9
The maid's tragedy *see*
Knowles, James Sheridan *in*
The modern standard drama,
vol. 6

Fleur-de-lis *see* Goodwin,
John Cheever

Flewellyn, Julia Collitan,
b.1850.
It is the law. A drama in
five acts. Lockport?, N. Y.:
n.pub., 1896? 43p.

The flight of the sun goddess
see Dugan, Caro Atherton
in her Collected works

Flirtation and what comes of
it *see* Goodrich, Frank
Boott

Flirtation cured *see* Lester,
Francis

Flockton, C. P.
Hagar and Ishmael. New York:
Van Fleet Printer, c1898.
54p.

Flora; or, The gipsy's frolic
see Ward, Thomas

Flora; or, The lover's ordeal.
An operetta in two acts.
Huntington: Long Islander
Print, 1857. 7 leaves.
[without the music]

Flora's festival. A cantata in
three parts. n.p.: n.pub.,
1854. 16p. Libretto.

Floret; or, The poor girl *see*
Babcock, J. Frederick

Florio, Caryl (pseud.) *see*
Robjohn, William James

The flower girl of New York
    see Elwyn, Lizzie May.
    Sweetbrier; or, The flower
    girl of New York

The flower of the family see
    Baker, George Melville

The flower queen; or, The
    coronation of the rose see
    Crosby, Frances Jane

The flowing bowl see
    Baker, George Melville

Floyd, William Ralph, 1832-
    1880.
    Handy Andy. New York: S.
    French, 186-? 29p. (French's
    standard drama. The acting
    edition. no. 332) *[adapted
    from Samuel Lover's novel
    of the same name]*

The flying Dutchman see
    Neumann, Louis see also
    Robjohn, William James

The flying islands of the
    night see Riley, James
    Whitcomb

The flying wedge see
    Furniss, Grace Livingston

A foggy night at Newport.
    St. Louis, Mo.: Wm. E.
    Foote's Premium Job Office,
    1860. 39p. *[Readex also
    enters this play under
    Henry Conrad Brokmeyer]*

Foiled; or, A struggle for
    life and liberty see
    Cornish, O. W.

Follen, Eliza Lee Cabot,
    1787-1860.
    Home dramas for young
    people. Compiled by E. L.
    Follen. Boston: J. Monroe,
    1859. 441p.
        Contents: Mrs. Pecks'
    pudding (Mrs. Follen.)--

The olive merchants of Bag-
    dat.--Alfred (Miss Aikin
    [Anna Letitia Aikin Barbauld]).
    The sword.--Ahmed the cobbler;
    or, The astrologer.--Old Poz
    (Miss Edgeworth.)--Much coin,
    much care (Mrs. Jameson).--
    The little gleamer.--The
    sleeper awakened (Mrs. Pulsky.)
    --Dumb Andy (Miss Edgeworth.)
    --The grinding organ (Miss
    Edgeworth.)--Christian slave
    (extracts)(Mrs. H. B. Stowe.)
    --Honesty is the best policy.
    --Parkington (charade)(Mrs.
    Follen et al.)--Blue Beard
    (charade)--Charade in two
    syllables and three scenes.--
    Patriot (charade)--Historical
    acting charades.--Master and
    slave (Miss Aikin.)

Mrs. Peck's pudding see her
    Home dramas for young people

The follies of a night see
    Planché, James Robinson in
    The modern standard drama,
    vol. 6

Followed by fortune see
    Conway, H. J. Hiram Hireout;
    or, Followed by fortune

Food for powder see André,
    Richard

A fool and his money see
    Lippmann, Julie Mathilde

A fool for luck see Browne,
    William Maynadier

The fool from Boston see
    Willard, Charles O. Stubs;
    or, The fool from Boston

Fooling with the wrong man
    see Richards, Bert

A foolish investment see
    Morse, Mabel

The fool's revenge see
    Taylor, Tom in Booth,

Edwin. The miscellaneous
plays of Edwin Booth

For a very little boy *see*
Denton, Clara Janetta Fort.
From tots to teens

For myself alone. A drama in
three acts. By Marius
(pseud.) New York: De Witt,
c1884. 20p. (De Witt's
acting plays. no. 322)

For old love's sake *see*
Woodhull, Mary G.

For one night only *see*
Baker, Robert Melville

For the blue or the gray *see*
Shoemaker, Dora Adèle.
A fighting chance; or, For
the blue or the gray

For the red, white and blue
see Fraser, John Arthur.
Santiago; or, For the red,
white and blue

Forced to the war; or, The
subrunners of '63-4 *see*
Hildreth, David W.

Ford, Alfred.
The five hour law; or,
Scenes in Athens. [From
his: Scenes and sonnets.
New York: Tappen Bowne,
c1872] p.21-31.

Jael and Sisera. [From his:
Scenes and sonnets. New
York: Tappen Bowne, c1872]
p.1-14.

Ford, Daniel K.
The bacteriologist. An
original comedy in five
acts. St. Paul: Samuel
Carman Printing Co., 1897.
94p.

My friend Isaac. An original
comedietta in one act.
Boston: J. Wilson & Son,
c1859. 35p. Prompt-book.

Ford, Harriet, 1868-1949.
The greatest thing in the
world. A play in four acts.
London: Mrs. Marshall's
Typewriting Office, 1899.
Typescript. 18, 16, 16, 12
leaves. *[joint author:
Beatrice M. De Mille]*

Ford, Paul Leicester, 1865-1902.
The best laid plans. As
enacted in two social cups
of tea, two social jokes, and
one social agony. New York?:
n.pub., 1889. 27p.

Janice Meredith *see* Rose,
Edward Everett and Ford,
Paul Leicester

Man proposes. In several
declarations and one act.
[From his: Tattle-tales of
Cupid. New York: Dodd, Mead,
1898. 264p.] p.197-264.

The foreigner. (From the
French of Dumas.) New York:
Chickering & Sons, 18-? Title
page lacking. 173p. *[based
on L'étrangère by Alexandre
Dumas, the younger]*

Forepaugh, Luella.
Dr. Jekyll and Mr. Hyde; or,
A mis-spent life. A drama in
four acts. New York and
London: S. French, c1897.
40p. (French's international
copyrighted edition of the
works of the best authors.
no. 15) *[joint author: George
F. Fish; adapted and arranged
from Robert Louis Stevenson's
novel]*

The forerunners *see* Robins,
Mary Ellis

Foresight; or, My daughter's
dowry *see* Delafield,
John H.

The forest princess; or, Two
centuries ago *see* Barnes,
Charlotte Mary Sanford

The forest rose; or, American farmers *see* Woodworth, Samuel

The forgers *see* White, John Blake

Forget-me-nots *see* Griffith, Benjamin Lease Crozer

Forgive and forget *see* Williams, Henry Llewellyn. Fernanda; or, Forgive and forget

Forgiven *see* Greene, Clay Meredith

The forgotten friend *see* Griffin, Gerald. Gisippus; or, The forgotten friend *in* The modern standard drama, vol. 9

Forrest, Edwin, 1806-1872. Damon and Pythias. New York: W. A. Moore & C. S. Bernard, c1860. 57p. *[based on John Banim's work of the same name]*

King Lear. A tragedy in five acts. By William Shakespeare. As played by Edwin Forrest at Niblo's Garden...New York: W. A. Moore & C. S. Bernard, 1860? 69p.

Othello. By William Shakespeare. New York: W. A. Moore & C. S. Bernard, c1860. 72p.

Forrest, Harry. Marie Antoinette: Queen of France. An historical drama in five acts with a prologue. (From the Italian of Giacometti.) London: Thomas Hailes Lacy, 1868? 72p. (Lacy's acting edition. vol. 83)

Fortune and men's eyes *see* Peabody, Josephine Preston

The fortune hunters; or, Lost and found. Comedy in two acts. New York: Roxbury Pub. Co., c1899. 21p. (The wizard series)

The fortune-teller *see* Schlesinger, Olga Steiner *see also* Smith, Harry Bache

The fortune teller of Lynn *see* Jones, Joseph Stevens. Moll Pitcher; or, The fortune teller of Lynn

The fortunes of war *see* Shipman, Louis Evan. D'Arcy of the guards; or, The fortunes of war

Fortunio and his seven gifted servants. An operatic extravaganza in four scenes. (From the English of Planché.) New York and Philadelphia: J. M. Stoddart, c1883. 40p. *[music composed by Francis T. S. Darley; without the music; founded on the nursery tale by Countess D'Anois, whose real name was Marie Catherine Jumelle de Berneville, comtesse d'Aulnoy]*

Forty minutes with a crank; or, The Seldarte craze *see* Baker, George Melville

The forty-niners. A drama of the gold mines *see* Hanshew, Thomas W.

'49; Forty-nine. An idyl drama of the Sierras *see* Miller, Joaquin

Forty thieves. A grand melodramatic romance in two acts. New York: S. French, 185-? Prompt-book. 26p. (French's American drama. The acting edition. no. 117) *[music by Michael Kelly; without the music; New York Public*

Library notes that this
play is "variously ascribed
to Sheridan, George Colman,
the younger, and others"]
see also The Xlanties; or,
Forty thieves

Foster, Joseph C.
The seven dwarfs; or, Harlequin in the world of
wonders. A gorgeous spec-
tacular pantomime. New
York: n.pub., c1869. 13p.

Fothergill, F.
Race for a wife. A farce in
one act. Chicago: Dramatic
Pub. Co., c1898. 14p.
(Sergel's acting drama.
no. 487)

Fothergill, Jessie, 1851-1891.
The first violin see
Clarke, Joseph Ignatius
Constantine and Phelps,
Merridan

The foundling; or, Yankee
fidelity see McLellan,
Rufus Charles

The fountain of youth. n.p.:
n.pub., n.d. 88p. (title
page lacking)

Four a.m. see Townsend,
Charles

The four judges see Denton,
Clara Janetta Fort in
her From tots to teens

The four-leaved clover see
Horne, Mary Barnard

The four-leaved shamrock see
Hamilton, C. J.

The four photographs see
Denton, Clara Janetta Fort
in her From tots to teens

Les Fourchambault see Magnus,
Julian and Bunner, Henry
Cuyler

Fournier, Narcisse, 1803-1880.
Tiridate see Aldrich,
Mildred. Nance Oldfield

"1492" see Barnet, Robert A.

Fowle, William Bentley, 1795-
1865.
Parlor dramas. Boston: Morris
Cotton, 1857. 312p.
Contents: Woman's rights.--
Country cousins.--The will.--
The fugitive slave.--The
pendant.--Love at sight.--
William Tell.--The counter-
plot.--The well of St. Keyne.
--The oddity.--The tables
turned.--The double ghost.--
The tea party.--The tear.--
The Jesuit in America.

Fowler, Egbert Willard, d.1901?
A matrimonial advertisement.
A comedietta in one act.
Boston: W. H. Baker, 1893.
9p. (Baker's edition of
plays)

Our Jim. A comedy in four
acts. Boston: Walter H.
Baker, c1897. 44p. (Baker's
edition of plays)

An unexpected legacy. A
comedietta in one act.
Boston: W. H. Baker, 1894.
11p. (Baker's edition of
plays)

Fox, George Washington Lafayette, 1825-1877.
Humpty Dumpty. An original
burlesque. New York: n.pub.,
1868. 10p. [Readex has
entered another version of
this play under John Denier]

Jack and Gill went up the
hill. The new, original,
dazzling, and gorgeous comic
pantomime. New York: n.pub.,
1866. 10p.

Fox, H. K.
The betrothal. An opera in
three acts. Philadelphia:

Geo. S. Harris, 1869. 16p.
Libretto. *[music by John E.
Kochersperger; without the
music]*

Foxy Quiller *see* Smith,
Harry Bache

Fra-Diavolo; or, The Inn of
Terracina. A comic opera in
three acts. (From the
English of M. R. Lacy.)
New York: S. French, 1854.
45p. Libretto. *[music by
Daniel François Esprit
Auber on libretto by
Michael Lacy and Augustin
Scribe]*

France and Algeria *see*
Wallack, Lester. The
veteran; or, France and
Algeria

Francesca da Rimini *see*
Boker, George Henry

Francesco Carrara *see*
Manning, Kathryn

Francis Drake *see* Mitchell,
Silas Weir

Il franco arciero *see* Der
Freischütz

François Villon *see*
Mitchell, Silas Weir

Frank, J. C.
Conn; or, Love's victory
see Powell, L. S. and
Frank, J. C.

Homeopathy; or, The family
cure. A farce in one act.
Chicago: T. S. Denison,
c1884. 15p. (Amateur series)

Frank Glynn's wife; or, An
American harem. A comedietta
in one act. Chicago: Dramatic Pub. Co., c1897. 14p.
(Sergel's acting drama. no.
461)

Frank Wilde [sic Wylde] *see*
Matthews, Brander. Cuttyback's
thunder; or, Frank Wilde
[sic Wylde] *see also* Frank
Wylde

Frank Wylde *see* Matthews,
Brander *in his* Comedies
for amateur acting *see also*
Frank Wilde

Franklin, Sidney.
A question of honor. A dramatic sketch in one act.
Philadelphia: Penn Pub. Co.,
1899. 19p. (Dramatic library.
vol. 1, no. 188)

Fraser, John Arthur.
Because I love you. A drama
in four acts. Chicago:
Dramatic Pub. Co., c1899.
60p. (Sergel's acting drama.
no. 447)

Bloomer girls; or, Courtship
in the twentieth century.
A satirical comedy in one
act. Chicago: Dramatic Pub.
Co., c1896. 23, 14p. (pag.
irreg.) (American amateur
drama)

A cheerful liar. Farcical
comedy in three acts. By
J. A. Fraser, Jr. Chicago:
Dramatic Pub. Co., c1896.
56p. (Sergel's acting drama.
no. 415)

A delicate question. An
original comedy drama in
four acts. By J. A. Fraser,
Jr. Chicago: Dramatic Pub.
Co., c1896. Author's edition.
64p. (American amateur drama)

Dewey, the hero of Manila.
Great naval battle in four
acts. Chicago: n.pub., c1897.
Typescript. Prompt-book with
Ms. notes. 73 leaves.

The little minister. (From
J. M. Barrie's play of the
same title.) Chicago:
Dramatic Author's Exchange,

c1900. Typescript. Prompt-
book with Ms. notes. 15,
22, 21, 23 leaves.

The merry cobbler. An
original comedy drama in
four acts. Chicago:
Dramatic Pub. Co., c1895.
48p. (Sergel's acting
drama. no. 362)

A modern Ananias. A comedy
in three acts. By J. A.
Fraser, Jr. Chicago:
Dramatic Pub. Co., 1895.
Author's edition. 66p.
(Sergel's acting drama.
no. 361)

A noble outcast. Drama in
four acts. Chicago:
Dramatic Pub. Co., c1896.
45p. (American acting
drama)

Our starry banner. An
original patriotic drama
in five acts. Chicago:
Dramatic Pub. Co., c1897.
50p. (Sergel's acting
drama. no. 517)

Santiago; or, For the red,
white and blue. A war drama
in four acts. Chicago:
Dramatic Pub. Co., c1898.
58p. (Sergel's acting drama.
no. 314)

The showman's ward. A comedy
in three acts. Chicago:
Dramatic Pub. Co., c1896.
49p. (American amateur
drama)

'Twixt love and money. A
comedy drama in four acts.
Chicago: Dramatic Pub. Co.,
c1896. 68p. (American
acting drama)

A woman's honor. Drama in
four acts. Chicago:
Dramatic Pub. Co., c1899.
53p. (Sergel's acting
drama. no. 431)

The fraud of the dry goods

boxes *see* The Tipperary
warbler; or, The fraud of the
dry goods boxes

Freaks and follies. A farce in
one act. [From Alexander's
Modern Acting Drama...Phila-
delphia: Carey & Hart, Hogan
& Thompson, and W. Marshall,
1835. vol. 2. 277p.] p.175-
203.

Frederic Lemaitre *see* Fitch,
Clyde

Fred's visit to town *see*
Denison, Thomas Stewart *in
his* Wide awake dialogues

A free knowledge-ist; or, Too
much for one head *see*
Smith, S. Jennie

The free ward *see* Brewster,
Emma E. *in her* Parlor
varieties

Freedom of the press *see*
Baker, George Melville

Freeman, Mary Eleanor Wilkins,
1852-1930.
Giles Corey, yeoman. By Mary
E. Wilkins. New York: Harper
& Bros., 1893. 108p. (Harper's
black and white series)

The Freeman mill strike *see*
Rawley, Bert C.

Der Freischütz (Il franco
arciero.) A lyric drama in
three acts. New York: Snowden,
1850. Bilingual text: English
and Italian. 57p. Libretto.
*[title page: "music by Weber
...with recitatives, by
Hector Berlioz"; without the
music; libretto by Friedrich
Kind]* see also Burkhardt,
Charles B.

French, Arthur W.
Gipsy queen (The Tyrolean

Queen revised.) Operetta in
two acts. Boston: O. Ditson,
c1890. Vocal score. 83p.
*[music by Charles F. Hanson
(actually Carl Fredrik
Hanson); this is a revised
and abridged edition of The
Tyrolean queen]*

Tyrolean queen. Operetta in
four acts. Boston: Oliver
Ditson, c1879. Vocal score.
150p. *[music by Charles F.
Hanson (actually Carl
Fredrik Hanson)]*

The Frenchman and his pupil
see Sedgwick, Alfred B.
Tootle, tootle, too; or,
The Frenchman and his pupil

Der Freyschutz *see* Macy,
James Cartwright

Friars, Austin.
Loved and lost. A drama in
one act. Chicago: Dramatic
Pub. Co., c1884. 8p. (De
Witt's acting plays. no. 332)
(American acting drama)

Number two. A lively farce
in one act. New York: De
Witt, c1884. 9p. (De Witt's
acting plays. no. 327)

Friday afternoon at Deestrick
No. 4 *see* Richards, Bert.
The spellin' skewl; or,
Friday afternoon at Dee-
strick No. 4

Friday afternoon series of
dialogues *see* Denison,
Thomas Stewart

Fridthjof and Ingerborg *see*
Hanson, Carl Fredrik

Friend Fritz *see* Dole,
Nathan Haskell

The friendly move *see*
Dialogues dramatized from

the works of Charles Dickens

Friends in council *see*
Congdon, James Bunker. Quaker
quiddities; or, Friends in
council

Friendship *see* Arnold, George?
and Cahill, Frank. Parlor
theatricals; or, Winter
evening's entertainment

A frightened beau *see* McBride,
H. Elliott *in his* Latest
dialogues

A frightened lodger *see*
Dramatic leaflets

Fröhlich, Herr (pseud.)
The old Catholics at Cologne.
A sketch in three scenes.
New York: James A. McGee,
1873. 155p.

A frog he would a wooing go
see Miller, Charles T.
Frog opera with pollywog
chorus

Frog opera with pollywog chorus
see Miller, Charles T.

The frogs of Windham *see*
Leavitt, Nason W.

A frolic in the cooking class
see Allen, Lucy. Débutantes
in the culinary art; or, A
frolic in the cooking class

Frolicsome girls *see* Benson,
William Henry

From affluence to poverty *see*
McBride, H. Elliott. Stepping
down; or, From affluence to
poverty *in his* Latest
dialogues

From Gonzales to San Jacinto
see Blandin, Isabella
Margaret Elizabeth

From Punkin Ridge; or, Belinda
Jane and Jonathan *see*
McBride, H. Elliott

From Sire to Son; or, The hour
and the man *see* Nobles,
Milton

From Sumter to Appomattox *see*
Whalen, E. C.

From the curse of coquetry
see Hartshorne, Henry

From tots to teens *see*
Denton, Clara Janetta Fort

From under the curse *see*
Tullidge, Edward Wheelock.
Ben Israel; or, From under
the curse

Frost, S. A. (pseud.) *see*
Shields, Sarah Annie Frost

Frost, Thomas *[see also
Atticum, Sal (pseud.)]*
Hesitation. A comedietta in
one act. New York: De Witt,
c1893. 16p. (De Witt's
acting plays. no. 397)

Frothingham, Ellen, 1835-1902.
Nathan the wise. (From the
German of Lessing.) New
York: Leypoldt and Holt,
1868. Second edition, revi-
sed. xxiii, 1, 259p.

Sappho. A tragedy in five
acts. (From the German of
Grillparzer.) Boston:
Roberts Bros., 1876. 136p.

Frou frou. (From the French
of Meilhac and Halévy.)
New York: Chickering and
Sons, 1881. Bilingual text:
English and French. 142p.
*[this is the Sarah Bernhardt
version]* *see also* Daly,
Augustin *see also* Schwab,
Frederick A.

The fruit of his folly *see*
Tubbs, Arthur Lewis

The fruits of the glass *see*
Cutler, F. L. Lost!; or,
The fruits of the glass

The fruits of the wine cup *see*
Allen, John Henry

Fry, Emma Viola Sheridan *see*
Sheridan-Fry, Emma

Fry, Horace B.
Little Italy. A tragedy in
one act. New York: R. H.
Russell, 1902. 50p.

Fry, Joseph Reese, 1811-1865.
Leonora. A lyrical drama in
three acts. [The first
American opera written and
produced in America.] Words
by J. R. Fry; music by
William Henry Fry. New York:
E. Ferrett, 1846. 429p.

Norma. A lyrical tragedy in
three acts. (From the Italian
of Romani.) Philadelphia:
John H. Gibson, 1841. 33p.
Libretto *[music by Vincenzo
Bellini on a libretto by
Felice Romani; without the
music]*

Notre-Dame of Paris. A
lyrical drama in four acts.
Philadelphia: King & Baird,
1864. 30p. *[cover: The subjects from Victor Hugo's novel
of the same name. Music by
William Henry Fry; without
the music]*

Fry, William Henry, 1815-1864.
Leonora *see* Fry, Joseph
Reese

Notre-Dame of Paris *see*
Fry, Joseph Reese

The fugitive fortune *see* Van
Harlingen, Katherine. An

original widow's pension;
or, The fugitive fortune

The fugitive slave *see*
Fowle, William Bentley
in his Parlor dramas

The fugitives. [From Star of
Emancipation. Boston: John
Putnam, 1841. 105p.] p.37-68.

Fulda, Ludwig, 1862-1939.
Das verlorene Paradies *see*
De Mille, Henry Churchill.
The lost paradise

Fulgonio, Fulvio.
Gabriella *see* Byrne,
Charles Alfred and Marras,
Mowbray

Fuller, Frances A. (pseud.)
see Victor, Frances A.

Fuller, Henry Blake, 1857-1929.
Collected works. The puppet-
booth. Twelve plays. New
York: Century, 1896. 212p.
Contents: The cure of
souls.--On the whirlwind.--
The love of love.--After-
glow.--The ship comes in.--
At Saint Judas's.--The light
that always is.--The dead-
and-alive.--Northern lights.
--The story-spinner.--The
stranger within the gates.--
In such a night.

Fuller, Horace Williams, 1844-
1901.
Bad advice. A comedy in
three acts. (From the French.)
Chicago: Dramatic Pub. Co.,
c1888. 35p. (American acting
drama) [based on Petits
oiseaux by Eugène Marin
Labiche]

Dear Uncle! A comedy in four
acts. (From the French of
"L'héritage de M. Plumet"
by Théodore Barrière.) New
York: Dramatic Pub. Co.,

c1890. 42p. (De Witt's acting
plays. no. 353) [based on
L'héritage de Monsieur Plumet
by Théodore Barrière and
Ernest Capendu]

False pretentions. (From
the French.) Chicago:
Dramatic Pub. Co., c1887.
35p. (Sergel's acting drama.
no. 346) [adapted from La
poudre au yeux by Eugène
Marin Labiche and Édouard
Martin]

A red letter day. A farcical
comedy in four acts. New
York: De Witt, c1888. 32p.
(De Witt's acting plays.
no. 349) [adapted from La
cagnotte by Eugène Marin
Labiche and Alfred Charlemagne Delacour]

Fulton, Harry Clifford.
Jean Valjean; or, The shadow
of the law. (From the French
of Hugo's Les misérables.)
Davenport, Iowa: Glass &
Axtmon, Printers and Binders,
1886. 65p.

Fun in a cooper's shop *see*
Wilton, M. J.

Fun in a grocery store *see*
Gordinier, Charles A. Tim
Flannigan; or, Fun in a
grocery store

Fun in a post office *see*
Bauman, E. Henri

Fun in a school-room *see*
Shelland, Harry E.

Furber, Pierce.
The oath. (From a tale by
Balzac.) Wayne, Pa.: n.d.
Typescript. 36p.

Furlong, John Ryan, b.1855.
Tried and true. A drama in
three acts. New York: Dick &
Fitzgerald, c1890. 43p.

Furman, Alfred Antoine, b.1856.
Philip of Pokanoket. An
Indian drama. New York:
Stettiner, Lambert, 1894.
136p.

Furness, Horace Howard, 1865-
1930.
Nobody's money. Comedy in
three acts. Cambridge:
W. H. Wheeler, 1886. 48p.

Furniss, Grace Livingston,
1864-1938.
A box of monkeys. A parlor
farce in two acts. (Reprinted
from "Harper's Bazaar,"
December 21, 1889.) Boston:
W. H. Baker, 1890. 31p.
(Baker's edition of plays)

The corner lot chorus.
A farce in one act for
female characters only.
Boston: Baker, c1891. 19p.
(Baker's edition of plays)

The flying wedge. A football
farce in one act. Boston:
W. H. Baker, c1896. 15p.
(Baker's edition of plays)

The flying wedge. Boston:
W. H. Baker, 1896. Seymour's
prompt-book, interleaved,
with Ms. notes. 15p.

The Jack trust. New York:
Harper & Sons, c1891. 63p.

Robert of Sicily. A romantic
drama in four acts. New York:
n.pub., 1900. Typescript.
32, 25, 21, 17 leaves (numb.
irreg.) *["suggested by the
leading incident in Long-
fellow's...'King Robert of
Sicily'"]*

Second floor, Spoopendyke.
A farce in two acts. Boston:
W. H. Baker, c1889. 27p.
(Baker's edition of plays)

Tulu. New York: Harper &
Bros., c1891. 97p.

The veneered savage. New
York: Harper & Bros., c1891.
35p.

Furst, William, 1852-1917.
Electric light *see* Hazelton,
William B. and Spencer,
Edward

Fleur-de-lis *see* Goodwin,
John Cheever

Fyles, Franklin, 1847-1911.
Ayleenya the blameless. New
York: n.pub., 1900? Typescript,
prompt-book. 53p.

The cavalry ball ("The girl I
left behind me") *see* Belasco,
David and Fyles, Franklin

The girl I left behind me
see Belasco, David and
Fyles, Franklin *in* Belasco,
David. The heart of Maryland
and other plays

G., B. C.
La muette; or, The dumb girl
of Portic *see* La muette;
or, The dumb girl of Portic

G., F.
Christopher Columbus *see*
Christopher Columbus

Gabriel, Charles Hutchinson,
1856-1932.
The merry milkmaids. An
amateur operetta in two parts.
Cincinnati, New York: Fillmore
Bros., c1891. Vocal score.
128p. *[both words and music
are by C. H. Gabriel]*

Gabriella *see* Byrne, Charles
Alfred and Marras, Mowbray

Gabriella de Belle Isle. A play
in five acts. (From the French
of Dumas.) New York: Wheat &
Cornett, c1880. p.1-23. (New
York Drama. vol. 5, no. 56)

Gaddess, Mary L.
A dream of fair women and
brave men. Tableaux vivante
for any number of males and
females. New York: Edgar S.
Werner, c1891. 16p.

The Ivy Queen. A cantata
for any number of girls.
Boston: Walter H. Baker,
c1891. 14p. (Baker's edition
of plays)

Gailey, Florence Louise.
Ez-Zahra. A tragedy of the
tenth century. Detroit:
n.pub., 1898. Typescript.
Prompt-book with Ms. notes.
104 unnumbered leaves.

Gaily the troubadour *see*
Griffin, George W. H. The
actor and the singer; or,
Gaily the troubadour

Galatea of the toy-shop *see*
Sutherland, Evelyn Greenleaf
Baker *in her* Collected
works. Po' white trash and
other one-act dramas

The galley slave *see* Campbell, Bartley Theodore
in his The white slave
and other plays

Gallot, John.
The elephant of Siam, and
the fire fiend. A magnifi-
cent eastern drama in three
acts. Philadelphia: W.
Turner, 1831. 67p.

Gallus Jake. An Ethiopian
comicality in one scene.
New York: Dick & Fitzgerald,
c1874. 7p.

The gamblers *see* Fitch,
Clyde

Gambrinus, king of lager beer
see Dumont, Frank

A game for two *see* Wilstach,
Paul

A game of billiards *see*
McDermott, J. J. and Trumble

A game of cards *see* Hollenius,
Laurence John

A game of chance; or, Alotting
the bride *see* Metcalfe,
Irving

A game of chess *see* Buffington, George E. C. *see also*
Meyers, Robert Cornelius V.

A game of dominoes *see*
Americans in Paris; or, A
game of dominoes *see also*
Bradbury, Louise A. *see also*
Hurlbert, William Henry.
Americans in Paris; or, A
game of dominoes

A game of nuts *see* Phelps,
Lavinia Howe *in her*
Dramatic stories

The game of three *see* Laidlaw,
Alexander Hamilton. Captain
Walrus; or, The game of three

The gamester *see* Moore,
Edward *in* The modern
standard drama, vol. 2

Gandéra, Félix, b.1885.
Atout...coeur! *see* Hearts
are trumps; or, Atout...
coeur!

Gandonnière, Almire, b.1814.
La damnation de Faust *see*
La damnation de Faust [and]
The damnation of Faust

Ganter, Franz S., fl.1871-1873.
Amor Patriae; or, The disruption and fall of these
states. A tragedy in five
acts. St. Louis: George Knapp,
1860. 103p.

García y Santisteban, Rafael,
1829-1893.
Robinson *see* Godoy, José
Francisco. Robinson Crusoe

Gardener, Helen Hamilton
Chenoweth, 1853-1924.
An unofficial patriot *see*
Herne, James A. The Reverend
Griffith Davenport *in his*
The early plays...

Garland, Hamlin, 1860-1940.
Under the wheel. A modern
play in six scenes. Boston:
Barta Press, 1890. 26 unnumbered leaves.

A garland to Sylvia *see*
McKaye, Percy

Garnier, John Hutchinson,
c1810-1898.
Prince Pedro: a tragedy.
Toronto: Belford Bros.,
1877. 158p.

Garrick, David, 1717-1779.
The country girl *see*
Daly, Augustin

Garrick and the tailor *see*
Massey, Charles. Massey's
exhibition reciter

The garroters *see* Howells,
William Dean

Gaskell, Elizabeth Cleghorn
Stevenson, 1810-1865.
Cranford *see* Byington,
Alice. "Cranford" dames
see also Horne, Mary
Barnard. The ladies of
Cranford

Gasparone *see* Rosenfeld,
Sydney

Gaulantis *see* Bannister,
Nathaniel Harrington

Gaunt, Percy, 1852?-1896.
A trip to Chinatown; or, An

idyl of San Francisco *see*
Hoyt, Charles Hale

Gay, John, 1685-1732.
The beggar's opera *see*
Harrison, William

Gay, Walter.
Hamlet. A tragedy in three
acts. New York: S. French,
18-? 47p. *[title page: ...by
William Shakespeare. Adapted
and condensed by Walter Gay]*

A gay Christmas ball *see*
Denton, Clara Janetta Fort.
When the lessons are over

Gayarré, Charles Étienne Arthur,
1805-1895.
Dr. Bluff in Russia; or, The
Emperor Nicholas and the
American doctor. A comedy in
two acts. New Orleans: Bronze
Pen Print., 1865. 49p.

The school for politics. A
dramatic novel. New York: D.
Appleton, 1854. 158p.

Gayler, Charles, 1820-1892.
The love of a prince; or, The
court of Prussia. A drama in
three acts. New York: S.
French, c1857. 45p. (French's
standard drama. no. 168)
*[adapted from Le sergent
Frédéric by Louis Émile
Vanderburch and Philippe
François Pinel Dumanoir]*

The son of the night. A drama
in three days and a prologue.
New York: S. French, c1857.
42p. (French's standard
drama. no. 169)

Gaylord, Orrie M.
Heavenly foundations *see*
Dramatic leaflets

Geewhilekins *see* Tillson,
Jesse Paxon *in his*
Collected works

Gemma of Vergy *see* Révoil,
Bénèdict Henry

Genée, Richard, 1823-1895.
Apajune der Wassermann *see*
Rosenfeld, Sydney. Apajune,
the water sprite

Boccaccio *see* Boccaccio
see also Smith, Dexter.
Boccaccio; or, The Prince
of Palermo

Fatinitza *see* Barker,
Theodore T. and Baxter,
Sylvester *see also*
Fatinitza

Gasparone *see* Rosenfeld,
Sydney

[King winter's carnival]
see Alexander, Sigmund
Bowman

Der lustige Krieg *see*
Elson, Louis Charles. The
merry war *see also*
Norcross, I. W. The merry
war

Nanon *see* Elson, Louis
Charles

Pfingsten in Florenz *see*
Goldmark, George and Rosenfeld, Sydney. Amorita

Das Spitzentuch der Königin
see Elson, Louis Charles.
The queen's lace handker-
chief

Genée, Rudolf, 1824-1914.
Der Bettelstudent *see*
Schwab, Emil. The beggar
student

Gen. Grant; or, The star of
union and liberty *see*
Clark, William Adolphus

The general manager; or, A
shot from the kitchen
range *see* Echols, Walter
Jarrell

Geneviève de Brabant *see*
Bailey, G.

The genius of liberty *see*
Le Grand, Dr. *in* Beadle's
dialogues no. 2

Gentil de Chavagnac, Michel
Joseph, 1769-1846.
L'hôtel garni; ou La leçon
singulière *see* Smith,
Richard Penn. Quite correct

A gentle jury *see* Bates, Arlo

A gentleman from Idaho *see*
Griffith, Frank Carlos

A gentleman from Ireland *see*
O'Brien, Fitz-James

The gentleman of Lyons; or, The
marriage contract *see*
Bannister, Nathaniel Harrington

The gentleman of the color; or,
Washington reconstructed *see*
Fast, Edward Gustavus

Gentlemen coons' [sic, coon's]
parade. Musical sketch in one
act. Chicago: Dramatic Pub.
Co., c1885. 8p. (The darkey
and comic drama) *[music by
W. S. Mullaly and words by
George Thatcher]*

Gentlemen coon's parade...and
Don't get weary; or, Johnny,
you've been a bad boy. New
York: De Witt, c1885. 12p.
(De Witt's Ethiopian and
comic drama. no. 157) *[the
music to Don't get weary...
is by John M. Turner]*

Gentlemen of the jury *see*
Baker, George Melville

George, Wadsworth M.
A coincidence *see* Shettel,
James and George, Wadsworth M.

A matchmaking father; or,
The bashful suitor *see*
Shettel, James W. and
George, Wadsworth M.

Nanka's leap year venture;
or, How she settled her
bills *see* Shettel, James
W. and George, Wadsworth M.

Pomp Green's snakes *see*
Shettel, James W. and
George, Wadsworth M.

George Barnwell *see* Lillo,
George *in* The modern
standard drama, vol. 11

The Georgetown Centennial *see*
Finn, Sister Mary Paulina.
Alma mater; or, The George-
town Centennial

A Georgetown reunion and what
came of it *see* Finn,
Sister Mary Paulina *in her*
Alma mater; or, The Georgetown Centennial

Gérard de Nerval, Gérard
Labrunie, known as, 1808-
1855.
La damnation de Faust *see*
La damnation de Faust [and]
The damnation of Faust *see*
also The damnation of Faust

Gerardy, D.
Centaurine. A drama in five
acts. New York: C. L. Jones,
1869. Prompt-book. 82p.
(pag. irreg.) Libretto.
[title page: "music com-
posed by Mr. Millard"]

The German baron *see*
Spangler, W. H. New Years
in New York; or, The German
baron

The German emigrant; or, Love
and sourkrout *see* White,
Charles

The German volunteer *see*

Saphar, Will D.

Gertie's vindication *see*
Pierce, G. H.

Gertrude Mason, M. D.; or, The
lady doctor *see* Armstrong,
L. M. C.

Gertrude Wheeler, M. D. *see*
Parker, Harry

Getchell, Wendell P.
A fisherman's luck. A comedy-
drama in four acts. Boston:
W. H. Baker, c1893. 47p.
(Baker's edition of plays)

Get-rich-quick society; or,
One hundred for thirty *see*
Dumont, Frank

Gettin' de bag to hold; or,
The United States mail *see*
White, Charles

Getting square on the call boy
see White, Charles

Getting up a picnic *see*
Denison, Thomas Stewart *in*
his Friday afternoon series
of dialogues

Gettysburg *see* McKee, W. J.

Gherardini, Giovanni, 1778-1861.
La gazza ladra *see* Coale,
George B. Magpie and the maid
see also The thieving magpie

The ghost *see* White, Charles

The ghost in the boarding school
see Schlesinger, Olga Steiner

The ghost in the closet *see*
Denton, Clara Janetta Fort
in her From tots to teens

The ghost in the kitchen *see*
Denison, Thomas Stewart *in*
his Friday afternoon series
of dialogues

The ghost of an idea *see*
Sanford, Amelia

Ghost of Rosalys *see* Moore,
Charles Leonard

Giacometti, Paolo, 1816-1882.
Maria Antonietta *see*
Forrest, Harry. Marie Antoi-
nette: Queen of France *see*
also Pray, Isaac Clarke.
Marie Antoinette

La morte civile *see* Civil
death *see also* The outlaw

Giacomo; a Venetian tale *see*
Bamburgh, William Cushing

Gibbs, Julia De Witt.
A false note. A comedy in
one act. Boston: Walter H.
Baker, c1888. 23p. (Baker's
edition of plays)

Under a spell. A comedy in
one act. Boston: Walter H.
Baker, 1888. 24p. *[trans-
lated from the French of
Eugène Marin Labiche and
Alphonse Jolly (pseud. for
Alphonse Leveaux)]*

Gibson, Ad. H.
The lick skillet wedding.
An original sketch in one
act. Clyde, O.: Ames, 1884.
6p. (Ames' series of standard and minor drama. no.
127)

Slick and Skinner; or, The
barber pards. An original
sketch in one act. Clyde,
O.: Ames, 1889. 9p. (Ames'
series of standard and
minor drama. no. 270)

A Texan mother-in-law. A
farce in one act. Clyde, O.:
Ames, 1885. 8p. (Ames' series
of standard and minor drama.
no. 166)

The gift of Aphrodite *see*

Dugan, Caro Atherton *in her*
Collected works

The gifts of the fairy queen
see Beadle's dialogues no. 2

Gilbert, Clayton H.
Rescued. An original temper-
ance drama in two acts.
Clyde, O.: Ames, 1874. 17p.
(Ames' series of standard
and minor drama. no. 51)

Gilbert, John.
Ali Baba; or, Morgiana and
the forty thieves *see*
Smith, Harry Bache

Gilbert, Sir William Schwenck,
1836-1911.
H. M. S. Pinafore *see*
Dey, F. Marmaduke. H. M. S.
Plum *see also* Moss, Alfred
Charles *see also* Wilkins,
W. Henri. S. H. A. M. Pina-
fore

A gilded brick *see* Holcomb,
Willard

A gilded youth *see* Townsend,
Charles

Gildehaus, Charles, 1856-1909.
Aeneas. A drama. St. Louis:
A. Unger, 1884. 54p.

Plays. St. Louis: J. L. Bo-
land Book and Stationery Co.,
1888. 258p.
Contents: Sibyl.--Telemachus.
--Aeneas.

Giles Corey of the Salem farms
see Longfellow, Henry
Wadsworth *in his* Christus

Giles Corey, yeoman *see*
Freeman, Mary Eleanor Wilkins

Gill, William.
My sweetheart *see* Maeder,
Frederick George and Gill,
William

Gillette, William Hooker,
1853-1937.
All the comforts of home.
A comedy in four acts. New
York?: 1890? Typescript,
prompt-book.

All the comforts of home.
A comedy in four acts. New
York, London: S. French,
c1897, 1924. 123p.

An American drama arranged
in four acts and entitled
Secret Service. A romance
of the Southern confederacy.
New York: S. French, c1898.
183p. (French's standard
library edition) *[Readex
also enters this same
play under the title Secret
Service; the two editions
are identical]*

Because she loved him so.
(From the French play,
"Jalouse.") n.p.: n.d. Typescript. 58p. Title page
lacking. *[based on Jalouse
by Alexandre Charles Auguste
Bisson and Adolphe Leclerc]*

Esmeralda *see* Burnett,
Frances Hodgson and Gillette,
William Hooker

Held by the enemy. New York:
188-? Typescript, prompt-
book. In five acts. (paged
by acts)

A legal wreck. n.p.: n.d.
Typescript. In four acts.
(pag. by acts)

Mr. Wilkinson's widows.
(From the French.) n.p.:
189-? Typescript, prompt-
book. In three acts. (pag.
by acts) *[cover: "...on the
basis of the French comedy
'Feu Toupinel' in combination with a few little ideas
of his own." Feu Toupinel
was written by Alexandre
Charles Auguste Bisson]*

Secret Service. New York,

London: S. French, c1898.
183p. *[Readex also enters
this same play under the
title An American drama
arranged in four acts and
entitled Secret Service;
the two editions are iden-
tical]*

Sherlock Holmes. A drama in
four acts. New York: Z. and
L. Rosenfield, 1900. Typescript, prompt-book. *[joint
author: Arthur Conan Doyle]*

Too much Johnson. The three-
act farcical comedy. New
York, London: S. French,
c1912. 129p. *[based on Le
plantation Thomasin by
Maurice Ordonneau]*

Gillette; or, Count and countess
see Norcross, J. W.

Gilman, Caroline Howard, 1794-
1888.
Isadore [From her: Tales and
ballads. Boston: William
Crosby, 1839. 190p.] p.90-94.

Ginevra *see* Rogers, Samuel
in Massey, Charles. Massey's
exhibition reciter

Ginty, Elizabeth Beall.
Sappho. A play in five acts.
(From the French of Daudet
and Belot.) New York: F.
Rullman, c1895. Bilingual
text: English and French.
41p.

Werther. A lyric opera in
four acts and five tableaux.
(From the French of Blau,
et al.) New York: F. Rullman,
c1894. 25p. Libretto.
*[based on Werther by Édouard
Blau, Paul Milliet, and
Georges Hartmann, originally
founded on Goethe's Die Leiden
des jungen Werthers, with
music by Jules Massenet;
without the music]*

Giordano *see* Lawson, James

Giorgione, the painter of
Venice *see* Walker,
Alfred

Giovanna of Naples *see*
Watson, Henry C.

The gipsey's prophecy *see*
Terry, Daniel. Guy Manne-
ring; or, The gipsey's
prophecy *in* The modern
standard drama, vol. 10

Gipsy queen (The Tyrolean
Queen revised) *see*
French, Arthur W.

The gipsy's frolic *see*
Ward, Thomas. Flora; or,
The gipsy's frolic

Giradin, Delphine Gay de,
"Mme. Émile de Giradin,"
1804-1855.
Le joie fait peur *see*
Sunshine follows rain

Lady Tartuffe *see* Lady
Tartuffe

The girl from Klondike; or,
Wide awake Nell *see*
Dumont, Frank

The girl from Maxim's *see*
The lady at Maxim's [; or,
The girl from Maxim's]

The girl from midway *see*
Moore, Bernard Francis

The girl from up there *see*
McLellan, Charles Morton
Stewart

"The girl I left behind me"
see Belasco, David and
Fyles, Franklin. The
cavalry ball. (Produced as
"The girl I left behind
me") *see also* Belasco,
David and Fyles, Franklin

in Belasco, David. The heart
of Maryland and other plays

The girl miner *see* Dean,
Frank J. Joe Ruggles; or,
The girl miner

A girl of the century *see*
Dumont, Frank

Girl wanted *see* Stephens,
Robert Neilson

A girls' debate *see* McBride,
H. Elliott *in his* Latest
dialogues

Gisippus; or, The forgotten
friend *see* Griffin, Gerald
in The modern standard
drama, vol. 9

Il giuramento; or, The oath.
A melo-dramatic opera in
three acts. (From the Italian
of Gaetano Rossi.) New York:
John Douglas, 1848. Bilingual
text: Italian and English.
47p. Libretto. (The operatic
library. no. 21) *[music by
Saverio Mercadante; without
the music]*

The gladiator. New York: Z. and
L. Rosenfield, 18-? Typescript,
prompt-book. 3, 17, 17, 15,
10, 15 leaves. (Pag. by act.)

Gladney, R. S. (supposed author)
The devil in America *see*
Lacon (pseud.)

A glance at New York *see*
Baker, Benjamin Archibald

A glass of double X *see*
The temperance school dialogues

Glaucus *see* Boker, George
Henry. Glaucus & other plays

Glengall, Richard Butler, Earl

of, 1794-1858.
The Irish tutor *see* Massey,
Charles. Massey's exhibition
reciter

Glenn, M. L.
Vice versa. A farce in one
act. Clyde, O.: Ames, 1887.
7p. (Ames' series of standard
and minor drama. no. 216)

Gloria Victis *see* Norton,
Morilla Maria

A glove *see* Sogård, Peder
Thyge Jesper

Glover, Howard, 1819-1875.
Palomita; or, The veiled
songstress. An operetta in
one act. New York: J. L.
Peters, c1875. Vocal score.
60p.

Glover, Stephen E., 1812-1870.
The cradle of liberty; or,
Boston in 1775. (Adapted
from Cooper's "Lionel Lin-
coln; or, The leaguer of
Boston.") Boston: William V.
Spencer, 1857? 39p.

Gluck, Christoph Willibald,
1714-1787.
Alceste *see* Alceste

Iphigénie en Tauride *see*
Tiffany, Esther Brown.
Apollo's oracle

Orfeo ed Euridice *see*
Raymond, Fanny Malone.
Orpheus

Glycerine oil *see* White,
Charles

Go and get tight *see*
Williams, Henry Llewellyn

Goddard, Edward.
By force of love; or, Wedded
and parted. A domestic
drama in five acts. Clyde,
O.: Ames, 1895. 25p. (Ames'

series of standard and minor
drama. no. 350)

Godoy, José Francisco, 1851-
1931.
Robinson Crusoe. An opera
bouffe in three acts. (From
the Spanish of Don Rafael
García Santisteban.) San
Francisco: B. F. Sterrett,
1875. 28p. Libretto. *[music
by Francisco Asenjo Barbieri;
without the music]*

Godwin, William, 1756-1836.
Caleb Williams; or, Things as
they are *see* Colman, George.
The iron chest *in* The
modern standard drama, vol. 6

Görlitz, Karl, 1830-1890.
Eine volkommense Frau *see*
Rosenfeld, Sydney. Her only
fault

Goethe, Johann Wolfgang von,
1749-1832.
Faust *see* Bangs, John
Kendrick. Mephistopheles
see also Brooks, Charles
Timothy *see also* Claudy,
Frank *see also* La damnation
de Faust *see also* The
damnation of Faust *see also*
Faust and Marguerite *see
also* Grau, Maurice *see also*
Kellogg, Clara Louise *see
also* Taylor, Bayard

Faust (scenes from) *see*
Everett, Alexander Hill *in
his* The Grecian gossips

Die Fischerin *see* Bannan,
Martha Ridgway. The fisher
maiden [and] The lover's
caprice

Iphigenie auf Tauris *see*
Adler, George J. Iphigenia
in Tauris

Die Laune des Verliebten *see*
Bannan, Martha Ridgway. The
lover's caprice *in her* The
fisher maiden [and] The
lover's caprice

Die Leiden des jungen
Werthers *see* Ginty,
Elizabeth Beall. Werther

Torquato Tasso *see*
Algernon (pseud.)

Going for the cup; or, Old
Mrs. Williams' dance *see*
White, Charles

Going to California *see*
Denison, Thomas Stewart
in his Wide awake dialogues

Going to the corner *see*
Denton, Clara Janetta Fort.
When the lessons are over

The gold brick *see* Denison,
Thomas Stewart *in his*
Wide awake dialogues

The gold bug *see* Hagarty,
W. H.

A gold mine *see* Matthews,
Brander and Jessop, George
Henry

The gold snuff-box *see*
Phelps, Lavinia Howe *in
her* Dramatic stories

The gold spinner *see* Denton,
Clara Janetta Fort. When
the lessons are over

Golden, William Echard
Michael, 1865-1930.
Hearts. A comedy in one act.
New York and London: T. H.
and S. French, c1892. 20p.
(Lacy's acting edition.
vol. 134)

The golden age to come; or,
The victory of faith, and
hope, and love *see* Austin,
J. J.

The golden butterfly *see*
Griffith, Frank Carlos

The golden cup *see* McLellan,
Charles Morton Stewart. The
girl from up there

The Golden Eagle; or, The
privateer of '76 *see* Howe,
J. Burdette

The golden goose *see* Cunningham, H.

The golden gulch *see* Townsend,
Charles

The golden horseshoe *see*
McCarty, William Page

The golden legend *see* Longfellow, Henry Wadsworth
in his Christus

The golden rule *see* Le Grand,
Dr. *in* Beadle's dialogues...
no. 2

A golden wedding *see* Phelps,
Lavinia Howe *in her*
Dramatic stories

Goldmark, George.
Amorita. Opera comique in
three acts. (From the French
of Genée and Riegen.) New
York: Hermann Bartsch, 1885.
17p. Libretto. *[music by
Alphons Czibulka; without
the music; joint author:
Sydney Rosenfeld; Amorita is
the English version of the
authors' Pfingsten in Flo-
renz]*

Goldschmidt, William, b.1841.
Hadassah; or, The Persian
queen. Operetta in three
acts. n.p.: n.pub., c1891.
35p. Libretto. *[music by
Sigmund Sabel; without the
music]*

Goldsmith, Oliver, 1728-1774.
She stoops to conquer *see*
The modern standard drama,
vol. 10 *see also* She

stoops to conquer

The vicar of Wakefield *see*
Coyne, Joseph Stirling *in*
The modern standard drama,
vol. 11 *see also* Davenport,
Fanny Lily Gypsy. Olivia。
Vicar of Wakefield

Gondinet, Pierre Edmond Julien,
1828-1888.
[The man from Mexico] *see*
Du Souchet, Henry A.

Un voyage d'agrément *see*
Chisnell, Newton. A pleasure
trip

Gonsalvo; or, The corsair's
doom *see* Williams, Charles

Good actions mend bad actions
see Venable, William Henry
in his The school stage

"A good fellow" *see* Walcot,
Charles Melton

Good night, Schatz *see*
Hepner, Adolf

Good night's rest *see* White,
Charles

The good St. Nicholas *see*
Hidden treasure; or, The
good St. Nicholas *see*
also Warren, Nathan Boughton. Hidden treasure; or,
The good St. Nicholas

Goode, George W.
Ebony flats and black sharps.
A nonsensical black-face
melange in one act and
various situations. Boston:
W. H. Baker, c1897. 12p.

Goodfellow, Mrs. E. J. H.
Vice versa. A comedy in
three acts. Philadelphia:
Penn Pub. Co., 1912. p.83-
103. *[earlier copyright:*
1892]

Young Dr. Devine. A comedietta
in two scenes. Philadelphia:
Penn Pub. Co., 1916. 12p.

Goodloe, Abbie Carter, b.1867.
Antinoüs. A tragedy. Philadelphia: J. B. Lippincott,
1891. 139p.

Goodrich, Elizabeth P。
Cobwebs. A juvenile operetta
in three acts. Boston: Lee &
Shepard, c1879. Libretto and
vocal score. 47p.

Goodrich, Frank Boott, 1826-1894.
Flirtation, and what comes of
it. A comedy in five acts.
New York: Rudd and Carleton,
1861. 92p.

Romance after marriage; or,
The maiden wife. (From the
romance "La clef d'or.")
New York: S. French, 1870?
28p. (French's standard
drama. The acting edition.
no. 187) *[joint author:*
Frank L. Warden; based on
La clef d'or by Octave
Feuillet]

Goodwin, John Cheever, 1850-
1912.
Fleur-de-lis, songs, words
of。..Comic opera...in three
acts. (From the French of
Chivot and Duru.) (Music by
William Furst.) New York:
T. B. Harms, c1895. 43p.
Libretto.

Madam Piper *see* Morse,
Woolson

The merry monarch, song
words of...A comic opera in
three acts. New York: T. B.
Harms, 1890. 32p. Libretto.
[music by Emmanuel Chabrier
and Woolson Morse to libretto
originally entitled Le roi
malgré lui by Émile Najac
and Urbain Rocoux Burani]

$34.21. A farce in one act.
Boston: J. E. Farwell, 1872.
24p.

Wang, song words of. Operatic burletta in two acts.
New York: T. B. Harms,
c1891. 32p. Libretto.
[music by Woolson Morse;
without the music]

Gordinier, Charles A.
Tim Flannigan; or, Fun in
a grocery store. A farce
in one act. Clyde, O.: Ames,
1891. 7p. (Ames' series of
standard and minor drama.
no. 292)

Gorman, Richard.
Half a day off. An original
farce in one act and three
scenes. By Dick Gorman.
New York: Nash Typewriting,
18-. Typescript, prompt-
book. 35 leaves.

The gossipers *see* Denison,
Thomas Stewart *in his*
Wide awake dialouges

Got a new suit *see* Denison,
Thomas Stewart *in his*
Wide awake dialogues

Gotthold, J. Newton.
The vow of the Ornani. A
drama in three acts. Clyde,
O.: Ames and Holgate, c1870.
26p. (Ames and Holgate's
series of standard and minor
drama. no. 7)

When women weep. A comedietta in one act. Clyde, O.:
Ames and Holgate, 1891. Title
page lacking. 20p. (Ames and
Holgate's series of standard
and minor drama. no. 5)

Gould, Edward Sherman, 1808-
1885.
The very age! A comedy in
five acts. New York: D.
Appleton, 1859. 153p.

Gould, Elizabeth Lincoln, d.1914.
The "Little men." A two-act
play. (From L. M. Alcott's
story of the same title.)
Philadelphia: Curtis Pub. Co.,
1900. 103p.

Gounod, Charles François, 1818-
1893.
Faust *see* Kellogg, Clara
Louise

The governess. A comedy in one
act. Boston: W. H. Baker,
c1889. 11p. (Baker's edition
of plays)

Government despatches *see*
White, Charles. The lost will

Governor Rodman's daughter *see*
De Mille, Henry Churchill and
Belasco, David

Gracie and Genaro *see*
McMechan, Robert I.

Graham, Mary.
Mademoiselle's Christmas gifts
see Bartlett, George Bradford.
A dream of the centuries and
other entertainments for
parlor and hall

Grammatical difficulties *see*
Heywood, Delia A. *in her*
Choice dialogues. no. 1

The grand baby show. An entertainment for little folks.
By the Sisters of Mercy.
Boston: Walter H. Baker,
c1896. 8p. (Baker's novelties)
[cover: Sisters of Mercy,
Meriden, Conn.]

The grand duchess of Gerolstein.
A comic opera in three acts.
(From the French of Meilhac
and Halévy.) New York: John A.
Gray & Green, 1867. Bilingual
text: English and French. 45p.
Libretto. *[music by Jacques*
Offenbach; without the music]

Grand historical spectacular
[sic, spectacle] masterpiece
America *see* Kiralfy, Imre

Grand national allegory and
tableaux *see* Hager, J. M.

The granddaughter of the
Caesars; or, The hag of the
earth and syren of the
waters *see* Lookup, Alexander (pseud.?)

Grandfather Whitehead *see*
Lemon, Mark *in* The modern
standard drama, vol. 2

Grandjean, Moritz Anton, 1821-
1885.
Das hohe C *see* Rosenfeld,
Sydney. High C

Rote Haare *see* Rosenfeld,
Sydney. The hair apparent;
or, The treacherous wig

Grandmother Hildebrand's
legacy; or, Mae Blossoms
reward *see* Lamson, C. A.

Grandpa *see* Smith, S. Decatur

Grangé, Eugène, 1812?-1887.
Le frères corses *see*
Griffin, George W. H. Corsican twins

The Corsican brothers *see*
The modern standard drama,
vol. 12

The granger; or, Caught in his
own trap *see* Hildreth,
David W.

Grannie's picture *see*
Debenham, L.

Grans, Heinrich, 1822-1893.
Adrienne Lecouvreur *see*
Marlow, George

Grant, James, 1822-1887.
Frank Hilton; or, The queen's
own *see* Wallack, Lester.

The veteran; or, France and
Algeria

Grant, John B.
The mystic isle; or, The laws
of average *see* Rosenfeld,
Sydney

Grant, Robert, 1852-1940.
The lambs. A tragedy. Boston:
J. R. Osgood, 1883. 61p.

The little tin gods-on-wheels;
or, Society in our modern
Athens. A trilogy... [Bound
with: Oxygen! A Mount Desert
pastoral] Cambridge, Mass.:
C. W. Sever, 1879. Second
edition. 32p. *[cover: From
the "Harvard Lampoon"]*
Contents: The little tin
god-on-wheels; or, Society
in our modern Athens [which
consists of:] The wallflowers.
--The little tin gods-on-
wheels.--The chaperons.--[and]
Oxygen! A Mount Desert pastoral.

Grass versus granite *see* Daly,
Augustin. A test case; or,
Grass versus granite

Grateful *see* Denison, Thomas
Stewart *in his* Friday
afternoon series of dialogues

Grau, Maurice, 1849-1907.
Faust. A tragedy in three acts.
(From the German of Goethe.)
New York: Saxton, Torrey,
"Season" Press, 1870? Bilingual text: English and German.
52p.

The grave digger's revenge *see*
The lost "spade"; or, The
grave digger's revenge

Gray, Henry David, b.1873.
Hannibal. A tragedy in five
acts. Auburn, N. Y.: Privately
printed, c1893. 77p.

Gray, William W.
Nobody's Moke. An original
farce in one act. Clyde, O.:
Ames, 1888. 9p. (Ames' series
of standard and minor drama.
no. 259)

The gray tigers of Smithville;
or, He would and he wouldn't
see Roth, Edward, ed.

The great arrival *see*
Griffin, George W. H.

The great catastrophe *see*
Locke, Belle Marshall

Great cry and little wool.
[From Memorabilia sophomorum
edita et publicata àtyrone
classe...Princeton: Oppidum
Principis, 1859. 48p.] p.33-
36.

The great doughnut corporation
see Denison, Thomas Stewart

The great exodus *see* Denison,
Thomas Stewart. The Kansas
immigrants; or, The great
exodus

The great Hindoo secret *see*
Prichard, Joseph Vila

The great house; or, Varieties
of American life *see*
Campbell, Amelia Pringle

The great libel case *see*
Shelland, Harry E.

The great moral dime show *see*
Horne, Mary Barnard. The last
of the Peak sisters; or, The
great moral dime show

The great pumpkin case of Guff
vs. Muff *see* Denison,
Thomas Stewart

The great rebellion. Buffalo,
N. Y.: Matthews & Warren,

c1865. 32p. Libretto. *see*
also Ward, Cyrenus Osborne

A great success *see* Winkle,
William

The great train robbery *see*
Marble, Scott

The great umbrella case *see*
Chase, Frank Eugene

The great unknown *see* Daly,
Augustin

The greatest man in the east
see Blood, Henry Ames. Lord
Timothy Dexter; or, The
greatest man in the east

The greatest plague in life
see Baker, George Melville

The greatest thing in the
world *see* Ford, Harriet
and De Mille, Beatrice M.

A Grecian bend *see* Baker,
George Melville

The Grecian gossips *see*
Everett, Alexander Hill

The Greek slave *see* Alcott,
Louisa May *in her* Comic
tragedies

Green, Anna Katharine (after-
wards Mrs. Charles Rohlfs),
1846-1935.
Risifi's daughter. A drama.
New York: G. P. Putnam's
Sons, 1887. 109p.

Green, John B.
Circumstantial evidence. An
original comedietta in one
act. Troy, N. Y.: Marshall
Infirmary Press, 1874. 25p.

The Green Mountain boy *see*
Jones, Joseph Stevens

Green-room rivals *see*
Trumbull, Annie Eliot

Greene, Clay Meredith, 1850-
1933.
Forgiven. n.p.: 188-. Typescript. 49p.

The new south. n.p.: n.pub.,
1893. Typescript. Prompt-
book with Ms. notes. 29, 22,
23, 19 leaves. (Title page
lacking) *[joint author:
Joseph Rhode Grismer]*

Pawn ticket no. 210. n.p.:
189? In Ms. 98p. *[joint
author: David Belasco]*

Under the polar star *see*
Belasco, David and Greene,
Clay Meredith

Greene, Henry Copley, b.1871.
Théophile. A miracle play.
Boston: Small, Mayard, 1898.
32p.

Greene, R. F.
Buried treasure; or, The
Connecticut buccaneers. A
farce in one act. Chicago:
Dramatic Pub. Co., c1898.
14p. (Sergel's acting drama.
no. 407)

The greenhorn *see* Beadle's
dialogues...no. 2

Greenly, William Jay, b.1805.
The three drunkards [bound
with] Ira Perkins. New
Albany, Indiana: n.pub.,
1858. 70p.
Contents: The three drunk-
ards.--Husbands don't stay
long.--John Allen and Ira
Perkins (Wm. J. Greenly.)--
The pen and the press (Wm.
J. Greenly.)

Greenough, James Bradstreet,
1833-1901.
Queen of hearts. A dramatic
fantasia. Boston: Ginn Heath,

1885. 46p. (Diversions for
students. no. 1)

The rose and the ring. (Adapt-
ed from Thackeray's "Christmas
Pantomime.") Cambridge: C. W.
Sever, 1880. 43p.

Greenwood, Frederick L.
Our daughters. A society
comedy in four acts. Clyde,
O.: Ames, c1883. 44p. (Ames'
series of standard and minor
drama. no. 126) *[cover: From
the German]*

Gregg, Helen A.
The little vagrants. An
operetta in two acts. New
York: Edgar S. Werner, 1898.
28p. Libretto.

Gretna Green; or, Matrimony in
Scotland. A popular petit
comedy in two acts. Philadelphia: Turner & Son, 1833?
20p. (Turner's acting stage)

Grice, Louis May, b.1868.
A daughter of Athens. A
tragedy in five acts. [From
his: A daughter in Athens...
and miscellaneous poems.
Baltimore: Crisson-D'Vere,
1892. 116p.] p.1-74.

Griffin, Caroline Stearns,
b.1868.
Villikins and his Diniah...
and Hallowe'en fun. New
York; A. S. Barnes, c1906.
16p. *[earlier copyright: 1900;
this play is based on Sir
Francis Cowley Burnand's
Villikins and his Dinah;
another edition is entered
under Charles White, Vilikens
and Dinah]*

Griffin, George W. H., 1829-1879.
The actor and the singer; or,
Gaily the troubadour. New
York: Dick & Fitzgerald,
187-? 8p.

The black crook burlesque.
London: S. French, 1881?
8p. (French's acting edition.
no. 83)

Camille. An Ethiopian interlude. New York: Happy Hours,
186-? 8p. (The Ethiopian
drama. no. 40) *[based on*
Alexandre Dumas' La dame
aux camélias]

Corsican twins. An Ethiopian
burlesque on the "Corsican
brothers." New York: Happy
Hours, 1874. 8p. (The
Ethiopian drama. no. 50)
[this burlesque may be based
on either of the following:
Alexandre Dumas' Le frères
corses, which was made into
a play of the same title by
Eugène Grangé and Xavier
Aymon, comte de Montépin,
(translated into English by
Charles Webb), or the
adaptation of Dumas' work
made by Dion Boucicault]

Feast. An Ethiopian burles-
que opera. New York: S.
French, 1864? 8p. (The
Ethiopian drama. no. 36)

The Fenian spy; or, John
Bulls [sic, Bull] in America.
New York: Happy Hours, 1873?
8p. (The Ethiopian drama.
no. 37) *[joint author:*
George Christy]

Fighting for the union. An
Ethiopian farce. New York:
Happy Hours, 188-? 8p.

The great arrival. Professor
Cheatum from Humbug. An
Ethiopian scene. New York:
Dick & Fitzgerald, 186-? 7p.

Hamlet the dainty. New York:
Happy Hours, 188-? 8p. (The
Ethiopian drama. no. 49)
[cover: an Ethiopian bur-
lesque on Shakespeare's
Hamlet]

Hunk's wedding day. An Ethiopian burlesque in one scene.
New York: Happy Hours, 1874.
8p. (The Ethiopian drama.
no. 78)

The hypochondriac. An Ethiopian farce in one act and two
scenes. New York: Happy Hours,
1860? 8p. (The Ethiopian
drama. no. 33)

Jack's the lad. An Ethiopian
drama. New York: Happy Hours,
187-? 8p. (The Ethiopian
drama. no. 38)

Les misérables. An Ethiopian
farce in one act and one
scene. New York: Happy Hours,
186-? 8p. (The Ethiopian
drama. no. 26) *[based on*
Victor Hugo's Les misérables]

New Year's calls. New York:
Happy Hours, 187-? 10p.

No cure, no pay. An original
Ethiopian farce in one act.
New York: Fitzgerald Pub.
Corp., 18-? 8p.

Nobody's son. An Ethiopian
act. New York: Happy Hours,
187-? 8p.

Othello. A burlesque. New
York: Happy Hours, 188-? 8p.
(The Ethiopian drama. no. 39)
[based on Shakespeare's play
of the same title]

Quarrelsome servants. An
Ethiopian interlude. London:
S. French, 1860? 8p. (French's
acting edition. no. 27)

Rooms to let without board.
An Ethiopian farce. New York:
Dick & Fitzgerald, 18-? 8p.
[joint author: Tony Denier;
this farce also includes one
character in the makeup of a
"Brazilian monkey"]

Rose Dale. An Ethiopian burlesque. (From Lester Wallack's

"Rosedale.") New York: Happy
Hours, 189-? 8p. (Title page
mutilated)

Shylock. A burlesque. New
York: S. French, 1876? 8p.
(The Ethiopian drama. no.
44) *[based on Shakespeare's
Merchant of Venice]*

Sports on a lark. An Ethiopian interlude. London and
New York: S. French, 1881?
8p.

The ticket-taker; or, The
masquerade ball. A popular
Ethiopian farce. London:
S. French, 186-? 8p. (French's
acting edition. no. 65)

The troublesome servant. An
Ethiopian interlude. New
York: Dick & Fitzgerald,
187-? 8p.

An unhappy pair. An Ethiopian farce in one scene.
London: S. French, 187-?
10p. (French's acting
edition. no. 50)

William Tell. An Ethiopian
interlude. As performed by
Griffin & Christy's Min-
strels. New York: Happy
Hours, 18-? 8p. (The
Ethiopian drama. no. 34)
*[based on Schiller's Wil-
helm Tell]*

Griffin, Gerald, 1803-1840.
Gisippus; or, The forgotten
friend *see* The modern
standard drama, vol. 9

Griffith, Benjamin Lease
Crozer, 1869-1900.
Between the acts. A comedy
in three acts. Philadelphia:
Penn Pub. Co., 1903. 49p.
(Keystone edition of popular
plays) *[earlier copyright:
1892]*

A cloudy day. A farce in one
act. Philadelphia: Penn Pub.

Co., 1917. *[earlier copyright:
1894]*

Forget-me-nots. A curtain
raiser. [From his: School and
parlor comedies. Philadelphia:
Penn Pub. Co., 1910. 49, 10,
12, 11, 7, 62p. (pag. by play)]
10p. *[earlier copyright: 1894]*

A mistake in identity. A
sketch. Chicago: T. S. Denison,
c1894. 8p. (Amateur series)

Not at home. A sketch. Chicago:
T. S. Denison, c1894. 9p.
(Amateur series)

Pro tem. A comedy in three acts.
[From his: School and parlor
comedies. Philadelphia: Penn
Pub. Co., 1910. 49, 10, 12,
11, 7, 62p. (pag. by play)]
62p. *[earlier copyright: 1894]*

A rival by request. A comedy
in three acts. Boston: W. H.
Baker, c1896. 63p. (Baker's
edition of plays)

Wanted--a valet. An original
Ethiopian sketch. [From his:
School and parlor comedies.
Philadelphia: Penn Pub. Co.,
1910. 49, 10, 12, 11, 7, 62p.
(pag. by play)] 11p. *[earlier
copyright: 1894]*

Griffith, Frank Carlos, 1851-1939.
A gentleman from Idaho. A drama
in prologue and three acts.
Boston: Walter H. Baker, c1889.
25 unnumbered leaves. *[This
appeared earlier in a longer
and altered version under the
title The golden butterfly]*

The golden butterfly. A drama
in prologue and four acts. By
Frank Carlos (pseud.) Boston:
Walter H. Baker, c1886. 67p.
*[dramatized from the novel of
the same name by Walter Besant
and James Rice; this appeared
later in a shorter version
under the title A gentleman
from Idaho]*

Griffith, Helen Sherman,
b.1873.
A borrowed luncheon. A
farce. Chicago: T. S.
Denison, c1899. 16p.

The burglar alarm. A comedietta in one act. Phila-
delphia: Penn Pub. Co.,
1899. 17p. (Dramatic library.
vol. 1, no. 180)

A fallen idol. A farce in
one act. Philadelphia:
Penn Pub. Co., 1911. 16p.
[earlier copyright: 1900]

Griffith, William, 1876-1936.
Trialogues. Kansas City,
Mo.: Hudson-Kimberly Pub.
Co., 1897. 65p.

Griffith Gaunt; or, Jealousy
see Daly, Augustin

Grillparzer, Franz, 1791-1872.
Medea *see* Medea

Sappho *see* Frothingham,
Ellen

Grimm, Edward.
The king's judges. An
original comedy in four
acts. San Francisco: James
H. Barry, 1892. 45p.

Grimm, Jacob Ludwig Karl,
1785-1863.
Die goldene Gans *see*
Cunningham, H. The golden
goose

Schneewittchen *see* Little
Snow-White and the seven
dwarfs

Grimm, Wilhelm Karl, 1786-
1859.
Die goldene Gans *see*
Cunningham, H. The golden
goose

Schneewittchen *see* Little
Snow-White and the seven
dwarfs

The grinding organ *see* Edgeworth, Maria *in* Follen,
Eliza Lee Cabot. Home dramas
for young people

Grinnell, Charles Edward, 1841-
1916.
Jurgium Geminorum; or, Rumpus
Romali Remique. A tragedy in
five acts. Cambridge?: n.pub.,
1862. 15p.

Grinnell, V. B.
The heroic Dutchman of seventy-
six. A comedy in five acts.
Clyde, O.: Ames, c1880. 26p.
(Ames' series of standard and
minor drama. no. 207)

Gripsack *see* White, Charles

Grisart, Charles Jean Baptiste,
1837-1904.
Les poupées de l'infante *see*
Barker, Theodore T. The
infanta's dolls

Griselda *see* Prentiss,
Elizabeth Payson

Grismer, Joseph Rhode, 1849-
1922.
The new south *see* Greene,
Clay Meredith and Grismer,
Joseph Rhode

Way down east *see* Parker,
Lottie Blair

Grit as well as manners *see*
Venable, William Henry *in*
his The school stage

Gross, Samuel Eberly, 1843-
1913.
The merchant prince of Cornville. A comedy in five acts.
Chicago: Rand, McNally,
c1896. 168p.

Grossi, Tommaso, 1791-1853.
I Lombardi alla prima
crociata *see* The Lombards
at the first crusade

The grotto nymph; or, Fairy
favor *see* Thaxter, Adam
Wallace

Grover, J. Holmes.
That rascal Pat. A farce in
one act. Philadelphia: Penn
Pub. Co., 1901. 21p. *[earlier
copyright: 1890]*

Grover, Leonard, b.1836?.
Our boarding house. [From:
America's lost plays. vol. 4.
Princeton, N. J.: Princeton
Univ. Press, 1940] p.191-231.
[earlier copyright: 1876]

Grover the First. A drama in
three acts. San Francisco:
Cubery, 189-? 36p.

Grub Mudge and Co. *see*
Hirst, Lucas

The guardian angel *see*
Connell, George Stanislaus
in his The old patroon and
other plays

Guatemozin *see* MacDonald,
Malcolm

Guepner, Willard.
Locked in a dress-maker's
room; or, Mr. Holiday's
flirtation. A farce in one
act. Clyde, O.: Ames, 1892.
7p. (Ames' series of standard
and minor drama. no. 302)

Guernsey, Alice M., 1850-1924.
Five centuries. A centennial
drama in five acts. Boston:
New England Pub. Co., 1876.
41p.

The guests of Brazil; or, The
martyrdom of Frederick *see*
Huntington, Gurdon

Gützkow, Karl Ferdinand, 1811-
1878.
Uriel Acosta *see* Hovey,
Richard and Jones, François

Stewart *see also* Uriel
Acosta

Guide to the stage; or, Unappreciated talent *see*
White, Charles

A guilded fool *see* Carleton,
Henry Guy

Guiney, Louise Imogen, 1861-1920.
The martyrs' idyl. [From her:
The martyrs' idyl and shorter
poems. Boston and New York:
Houghton, Mifflin, 1899. 81p.]
p.1-30.

Gulliver and the Lilliputians
up to date *see* Horne, Mary
Barnard

Gulzara; or, The Persian slave
see Ritchie, Anna Cora Ogden
Mowatt

Gunter, Archibald Clavering,
1847-1907.
The fighting troubadour. A
romantic drama in four acts.
n.p.: n.d. Typescript, prompt-
book. In four acts (pag. by
acts)

The fighting troubadour.
n.p.: n.pub., 1899. 111p.

Mr. Barnes of New York. n.p.:
n.pub., 188-? In Ms. 66p.

Prince Karl. A farce comedy
in four acts. New York: J.
Neill, 1886. Typescript,
prompt-book. 40, 28, 40, 26
leaves.

Prince Karl. New York?: J.
Neill, 1886. Typescript. In
four acts (pag. by acts)
Title page lacking.

Gustave the professor *see*
Baker, George Melville

Gustavus III; or, The masked
ball *see* Rattermann, Heinrich Armin

Gutterson, John H.
Charlie's Christmas dream.
[From: Christmas entertainments for home and school...
by Jay Kaye. Boston: W. H.
Baker, c1887. 104p.] p.100-
104.

Guttle and Gulpit *see* Tally
Rhand (pseud.)

Guy Fawkes; or, A match for a
king *see* Massey, Charles.
Massey's exhibition reciter

Guy Mannering; or, The gipsey's
prophecy *see* Terry, Daniel
in The modern standard
drama, vol. 10

Guyet, J. A.
Jeanne l'orpheline *see*
Jane the orphan

Gyp the heiress; or, The dead
witness *see* Ward, Lew

The gypsy girl of Hungary *see*
Dugan, Caro Atherton *in her*
Collected works

The gypsy's secret *see*
Emery, E.

H. M. S. Pinafore; oder, Das
maedle und ihr sailor Kerl
see Moss, Alfred Charles

H. M. S. Plum *see* Dey, F.
Marmaduke

Hadassah; or, The Persian
queen *see* Goldschmidt,
William

Hadley, Lizzie M.
At the court of King Winter.
A Christmas play for schools.
New York: E. L. Kellogg,
c1896. 14p.

Hadley *see* Norcross, Frederick Walter

The hag of the earth and syren
of the waters *see* Lookup,
Alexander (pseud.?) The
granddaughter of the Caesars;
or, The hag of the earth and
syren of the waters

Hagar and Ishmael *see* Flockton,
C. P.

Hagarty, W. H.
The gold bug. A melodrama in
five acts. (A dramatization
of Poe's story.) n.p.: n.pub.,
c1896. Typescript, prompt-
book. 15, 17, 17 leaves (numb.
irreg.)

Hageman, Maurice.
By telephone. Chicago: Dramatic Pub. Co., c1897. 13p.
(Sergel's acting drama. no.
486)

A crazy idea. A comedy in four
acts. (From the German of Carl
Laufs.) Chicago: Dramatic
Pub. Co., c1897. 48p. (Sergel's acting drama. no. 413)
*[based on Laufs' Ein toller
Einfal]*

The first kiss. A comedy in
one act. Chicago: Dramatic
Pub. Co., c1897. 16p. (Sergel's
acting drama. no. 421)

Hector. A farce in one act.
Chicago: Dramatic Pub. Co.,
c1897. 23p. (Sergel's acting
drama. no. 483)

I'll remain single. A monologue for a gentleman. Chicago:
Dramatic Pub. Co., c1898. 10p.

Mrs. Mulcahy. A comedy in one
act. Chicago: Dramatic Pub.
Co., c1899. 21p. (Sergel's
acting drama. no. 499)

Professor Robinson. A comedy
in one act. Chicago: Dramatic
Pub. Co., c1899. 18p. (American acting drama)

Sowing wild oats; or, Uncle
John's private secretary.
Comedy in four acts. Chi-
cago: Dramatic Pub. Co.,
c1899. 82p. (Sergel's
acting drama. no. 445)
[translation of Gustav von
Moser's Der Bibliothekar]

To rent. Comedietta in one
act. Chicago: Dramatic Pub.
Co., c1898. 10p. (American
acting drama)

Two veterans. Farce in one
act. Chicago: Dramatic Pub.
Co., c1899. 12p. (American
acting drama)

What became of Parker. A
farce-comedy in four acts.
Chicago: Dramatic Pub. Co.,
c1898. 72p. (Sergel's acting
drama. no. 443)

Hager, J. M.
Grand national allegory and
tableaux. Buffalo, N. Y.:
Matthews & Warren, Stereo-
typers & Printers, c1865.
32p. Title page lacking.

Haid, P. Leo, 1849-1924.
Major John André. An historical drama in five acts.
Baltimore: J. Murphy, 1876.
68p.

The hair apparant; or, The
treacherous wig see
Rosenfeld, Sydney

Hal Hazard; or, The federal
spy see Andrews, Fred G.

Hale, Sarah Josepha Buell,
1788-1879.
The judge. A drama of
American life. [From:
Godey's magazine and Lady's
book. vol. 42. Philadelphia:
n.pub., 1851] p.21-26, 87-93,
154-160, 237-245, 298-301.

Halévy, Jacques François Fro-

mental Élie, 1799-1862.
[The maid of honor] see
Weil, Oscar

Les mousquetaires de la reine
see Révoil, Bénèdict Henry.
The queen's musketeers

La reine de Chypre see
Révoil, Bénèdict Henry. The
queen of Cyprus

Le Val d'Andorre see The
valley of Andorre

Halévy, Ludovic, 1834-1908.
Barbe-bleue see Bluebeard

La belle Hélène see La
belle Hélène

Les brigands see Les
brigands

Carmen see Baker, Theodore.
Carmen

La cigale see Delafield,
John H.

Frou Frou see Daly, Augustin see also Frou Frou
see also Schwab, Frederick A.

Le grande duchesse de Gerolstein see The grand
duchess of Gerolstein

Orphée aux enfers see
Orpheus and Eurydice

Le petit duc see Williams,
Frederick and Sullivan,
Thomas Russell. The little
duke

Le petit hôtel see Williams,
Henry Llewellyn. The bachelor's box

La veuve see Ayer, Harriet
Hubbard. The widow

Half a day off see Gorman,
Richard

Half an hour in a Kentucky court
house see Black justice; or,
Half an hour in a Kentucky
court house

Hall, Abraham Oakey, 1826-1898.
A coroner's inquisition. A
farce in one act. New York:
S. French, 1857. 19p. (The
minor drama. no. 117)

Hall, J. Griffin.
The bogus talking machine;
or, The puzzled Dutchman
see White, Charles

The crowded hotel; or, The
tricky nig. A comedy sketch
in one scene. Chicago:
Dramatic Pub. Co., c1882.
12p. (The comic drama. no.
144) (De Witt's Ethiopian
and comic drama. no. 144)

Hall, John Lesslie, 1856-1928.
Judas. A drama in five acts.
Williamsburg, Va.: Henley T.
Jones, 1894. 87p.

Hall, Louisa Jane Park, 1802-
1892.
Miriam. A dramatic poem.
Boston: Hilliard, Gray,
1837. 124p.

Miriam. A dramatic poem.
Boston: H. P. Nichols, 1838.
Second edition revised.
x, 122p.

Miriam. [A revised edition,
p.115-131 contains a "Dramatic Fragment."] [From her:
Miriam and Joanna of Naples,
with other pieces in verse
and poetry. Boston: W. Crosby & H. P. Nichols, 1850]
p.1-131.

The hall of shadows see
Benedict, Frank Lee in his
The shadow worshiper

Hallabahoola, the medicine
man; or, The squirtgun
treatment see Richards,
Bert

Hallowe'en see Leahy,
William Augustine. The

wedding feast...with a prologue. Hallowe'en

Hallowe'en fun see Griffin,
Caroline Stearns. Villikins
and his Diniah...and Hallowe'en
fun

Halm, Friedrich (pseud.) see
Münch-Bellinghausen, Eligius
Franz Joseph, Freiherr von

Halpine, Charles Graham, 1829-
1868.
Duet for the breakfast table.
[From his: Lyrics. By the
letter. H. New York: J. C.
Derby, 1854. 228p.] p.151-154.

Some talk about poets. [From
his: Lyrics. By the letter.
H. New York: J. C. Derby,
1854. 228p.] p.160-162.

Haman and Mordecai see Levy,
Clifton Harby

Hamilton, Alexander, 1815-1907.
Canonicus. A tragedy in five
acts. [From his: Dramas and
poems. New York: Dick &
Fitzgerald, c1887] p.7-54.

Cromwell. A tragedy in five
acts. New York: Dick &
Fitzgerald, c1868. 124p.

Thomas a'Becket. A tragedy in
five acts. New York: Dick &
Fitzgerald, c1863. 106p.

Hamilton, C. J.
The four-leaved shamrock. A
comedy in three acts.
Chicago: Dramatic Pub. Co.,
188-? 26p. (Sergel's acting
drama. no. 532)

Hamilton, George H.
Hotel Healthy. Farce in one
act. Clyde, O.: Ames, 1896.
13p. (Ames' series of standard
and minor drama. no. 366)

Sunlight; or, The diamond

king. A Western drama in
four acts. Clyde, O.: Ames,
1896. 29p. (Ames' series
of standard and minor drama.
no. 372)

Hamilton, John R.
Marion; or, The reclaimed.
A play in three acts. Cincinnati: H. W. Derby, 1857.
56p.

Hamlet. By William Shakespeare.
New York: n.pub., 1882. 119p.
see also Gay, Walter *see
also* Hinton, Henry L. Shakespeare's Hamlet *see also*
Rush, James *see also* Shakespeare, William *in* Booth,
Edwin. The Shakespearean
plays of Edwin Booth *see also*
Shakespeare, William *in* The
modern standard drama, vol. 3

Hamlet (Ghost scene)
Shakespeare, William
Dramatic leaflets

Hamlet; or, The sport, the
spook, and the spinster *see*
Batchelder, Samuel Francis

Hamlet, Prince of Denmark. By
William Shakespeare. Boston:
Ticknor, Reed and Fields,
1852. 59p. *[preface: "The
following bagatelle being a
version of the Play of Hamlet, was made by the writer
for the purpose of amusing
himself, while he was convalescent after an illness;
and he submits this as an
apology for his levity";
Readex also enters this same
play under the author,
George Edward Rice]* see
also Rice, George Edward.
An old play in a new garb.
Hamlet, Prince of Denmark

Hamlet revamped *see* Soule,
Charles Carroll

Hamlet the dainty *see* Griffin,
George W. H.

Hamlet's brides *see* Sterling,
Sara Hawkins [bound with]
Taylor, M. M. The Shakespeare
wooing--a play of shreds and
patches

Hamley, Sir Edward Bruce,
1824-1893.
Lady Lee's widowhood *see*
Wallack, Lester. Rosedale

Hammond, S. T., comp.
A collection of temperance
dialogues *see* A collection
of temperance dialogues

The hand of a friend *see*
Dumont, Frank. Conrad; or,
The hand of a friend

Handicapped; or, A racing
romance *see* Toler, Sallie F.

Handkerchief drill *see* Denton,
Clara Janetta Fort. When the
lessons are over

A handsome cap *see* André,
Richard

Handsome Jack *see* Howe, J.
Burdette

Handy Andy. A negro farce in
one act. Chicago: T. S.
Denison, 18-? 9p. *see also*
Floyd, William Ralph

Hanlon, Henry Oldham.
A double shuffle. A come-
dietta in one act. Boston:
W. H. Baker, 1891. 16p.
(Baker's edition of plays)

Facing the music. A come-
dietta in one act. Boston:
Walter H. Baker, c1894. 15p.
(Baker's edition of plays)

A picked-up dinner. A farce

in one act. Boston: W. H.
Baker, c1892. 11p. (Baker's
edition of plays) *[Readex
gives a presumably incorrect
publication date of 1889]*

Hannibal *see* Gray, Henry
David

Hans Brummel's cafe *see*
Ingraham, C. F.

Hans, the Dutch J. P. *see*
Cutler, F. L.

Hans von Smash *see* Denison,
Thomas Stewart

Hanshew, Thomas W., 1857-1914.
The 'forty-niners. A drama
of the gold mines. Drama-
tized from his own story of
the same title. Philadelphia:
n.pub., 1906. p.235-276.

Oath bound; or, Faithful
unto death. A domestic
drama in three acts. Clyde,
O.: Ames, 18-? 20p. (Ames'
series of standard and
minor drama. no. 196)

Will-o'-the-wisp; or, The
shot in the dark. A comedy
drama in three acts. (From
the French of Dumas' novel
"Mattien" [sic, Mattieu])
Clyde, O.: Ames, 1884. 24p.
(Ames' series of standard
and minor drama. no. 121)

Hanson, Carl Fredrik, b.1849.
Fridthjof and Ingerborg.
Opera in three acts. Wor-
cester: C. F. Hanson &
Sons, c1898. Vocal score.
Bilingual text: English and
Swedish. 138p. *[dramatized
from Esaias Tegner's Fridth-
jof's Saga by Anna Cornjelm
Wallberg]*

Gipsy queen *see* French,
Arthur W.

Tyrolien queen *see* French,
Arthur W.

Hanson, Charles F. *see*
Hanson, Carl Fredrik

Hanssen, C. J.
The queen of Sheba. A Biblical
drama in three acts for young
ladies. Chicago: Dramatic Pub.
Co., 1899? 24p. (Sergel's
acting drama. no. 457)

Hap-hazard *see* Herne, James A.
and Belasco, David. Marriage
by moonlight; or, Hap-hazard

The happy couple *see* White,
Charles

A happy day *see* Williams,
Henry Llewellyn

The happy family *see* Beadle's
dialogues no. 2

Happy Uncle Rufus *see* Dumont,
Frank *see also his* The
amateur minstrel

A happy woman *see* McBride,
H. Elliott *in his* New
dialogues

A hard case *see* Picton,
Thomas

Hard cider *see* Denison,
Thomas Stewart

Hard of hearing *see* Schlesinger, Olga Steiner

Hard times *see* White, Charles

Hardcastle, F. W.
Santa Claus' daughter *see*
Elliott, Everett and Hard-
castle, F. W.

Harden, John J.
Columbus and Isabella. An
historical drama. Part
second. Chicago: John J.
Harden, c1891. 91p.

Harding, Edward John, b.1851.
Ernest [From his: Cothurus

and lyre. New York: The
Author's Pub. Co., 1878.
126p.] p.9-89.

Hardman, Richard.
The adventures of little
Red Riding Hood. An operetta
in four acts for the young.
New York: Joseph F. Wagner,
c1899. 49p. Libretto and
vocal score.

Clarissa's first party. A
musical comedietta for
young ladies. New York:
Roxbury Pub. Co., c1899.
Title page lacking. 19p.

The pigeons; or, The bonnie
lass of Brittany. An operetta
for the amateur stage and
the drawing room. New York:
Roxbury Pub. Co., c1899. 18p.
Libretto and vocal score.
[the words by R. André]

Hardy, Arthur Sherburne,
1847-1930.
Passe Rose *see* Paul, Anne
Marie

Hardy, Edward Trueblood.
Crowding the season. A
comedy in three acts. New
York: S. French, 1870. 32p.
(French's minor drama.
no. 317)

Widow Freeheart; or, The
woman haters. A comedy in
five acts. New York: S.
French, n.d. Prompt-book.
(French's standard drama.
no. 358)

Harlequin in the world of
wonders *see* Foster,
Joseph C. The seven dwarfs;
or, Harlequin in the world
of wonders

Harlequin old bogey; or, The
imps of the school and the
secret of the old oak chest
see Tracy, J. Perkins

The harlequin travellers *see*
The touchstone of truth; or,
The harlequin travellers

A harmonious family *see*
Polding, Elizabeth

Harned, Mary.
Ephraim's Breite. A drama in
five acts. (From the German
of Carl Hauptmann.) Boston:
Poet-Lore, 1900. vol. 12,
no. 4. p.465-536.

Johannes. (From the German of
Hermann Sudermann.) Boston:
Poet-Lore, 1899. vol. 11,
no. 2. p.161-236. *[joint
author: W. H. Harned]*

Morituri: Teias. (From the
German of Hermann Sudermann.)
Boston: Poet-Lore, 1897. vol.
9, no. 3. p.330-352. *[trans-
lation of Sudermann's Morituri: Teja]*

The sunken bell. A drama in
five acts. (From the German
of Gerhard Hauptmann.) Boston:
Poet-Lore, 1898. vol. 10, no.
2. p.161-234. *[translation of
Hauptmann's Die versunkene
Glocke]*

Harned, W. H.
Johannes *see* Harned, Mary
and Harned, W. H.

Harold *see* Clarke, Hugh
Archibald

Harolde, the envoye of Artois
see Neafie, John Andrew
Jackson

Harrigan, Edward, 1845-1911.
The blue and the grey. A
dramatic sketch in two scenes.
New York: n.pub., 1875. 12p.

The editor's troubles. A
farce in one scene. Chicago:
Dramatic Pub. Co., 1875. 7p.
(The comic drama. no. 67)

Porter's troubles; or, The Fifth Ave. Hotel. An amusing sketch in one scene. New York: De Witt, 1875. 6p. (De Witt's Ethiopian and comic drama. no. 65)

Harris, Francis Augustine, 1845-1911.
Chums. A farce in one act. By the author of Class Day. Boston: Walter H. Baker, c1890. 22p.

Class day. A farce in one act. Boston: Walter H. Baker, c1877. 23p. (Baker's edition of plays)

A majority of one; or, Love and mushrooms. A farce in one act. Boston: W. G. Baker, 1892. 23p. (Baker's edition of plays) [title page: "from the German"]

Harris, Theodore.
The purse. A comedy in two acts. (From the French of Balzac.) Chicago: Dramatic Pub. Co., 1887. 31p.

Harrison, Mrs. Burton *see* Harrison, Constance Cary

Harrison, Constance Cary, 1843-1920.
Alice in Wonderland. A play for children in three acts. By Mrs. Burton Harrison. Chicago: Dramatic Pub. Co., c1890. 35p. [based on Lewis Carroll's Alice's adventures in Wonderland]

A Russian honeymoon. A comedy in three acts. By Mrs. Burton Harrison. (From the French of Scribe.) New York: De Witt, 1890. 68p. (De Witt's acting plays. no. 359) [based on La lune de Miel by Augustin Scribe, Pierre Carmouche, and Anne Honoré Joseph Duveyrier (pseud. Mélesville)]

Short comedies for amateur players. By Mrs. Burton Harrison. New York: De Witt, 1889. 116p. ["English versions of French originals"]
Contents: The mouse-trap.--Weeping wives.--Behind a curtain.--Tea at four o'clock.--Two strings to her bow.

Two strings to her bow. A comedy in two acts. By Mrs. Burton Harrison. New York: De Witt, c1892. 36p. (De Witt's acting plays. no. 376)

Harrison, Gabriel, 1818-1902.
The scarlet letter. A romantic drama in four acts. (From the novel by Hawthorne.) Brooklyn: Harry M. Gardner, Jr., 1876. 50p.

Harrison, William, 1813-1868.
The beggar's opera. Boston: Eastburn's Press, 1854. 36p. Libretto. [Cover: By John Gay. Title page: Without the music, compiled and arranged, and the overture composed, by John Christopher Pepusch. Preface: Revised by Mr. Harrison and the objectionable dialogue expunged]

The marriage of Georgette. Boston: J. H. Eastburn's Press, 1855. 25p. Libretto. [music by Victor Massé; without the music]

Hart, Daniel L., b.1868.
The parish priest. A domestic drama in three acts. Wilkes Barre, Pa.: 1900. Typescript. In three acts (pag. by acts)

Hart, George G.
E. C. B. Susan Jane; or, A sailor's life on the raging main. An original poetical effusion in one act. Chicago: Dramatic Pub. Co., c1879. 23p. Libretto. (Sergel's acting drama. no. 283)

Hart, Robert.
A slippery day *see* White,
Charles

Harte, Bret, 1836-1902.
The judgment of Bolinas
Plain *see* Harte, Bret
and Pemberton, Thomas Edgar.
Sue

Sue. A play in three acts.
(Adapted from Bret Harte's
story "The judgment of
Bolinas Plain.") London:
Greening, 1902. xi, 168p.
*[joint author: Thomas Edgar
Pemberton]*

Two men of Sandy Bar. A drama
in four acts. Boston: Houghton, Mifflin, 1882. 151p.

Hartmann, Georges, d.1900.
Werther *see* Ginty,
Elizabeth Beall

Hartmann, Sadakichi, 1867-1944.
Buddha. A drama in twelve
scenes. New York: Author's
edition, 1897. 45p.

Christ. A dramatic poem in
three acts. n.p.: n.pub.,
1893. Author's edition. 81p.

A tragedy in a New York flat.
A dramatic episode in two
scenes. New York: The author,
1896. 11p.

Hartmann, Theodore.
The Christmas fairies; or,
Shakespeare's dream [bound
with: The Christmas tragedy]
[From his: Charity Green;
or, The varieties of love.
New York: J. W. Norton,
1859. 601p.] p.386-440.

The Christmas tragedy *see his*
The Christmas fairies; or,
Shakespeare's dream

Hartnedy, M. M. A.
Christopher Columbus. A
drama in three acts. By V.

Rev. M. M. A. Hartnedy.
Steubenville, Ohio: Columbus
Club, c1892. 51p. *["The
Catholic American play of
the year"]*

Harts, Harry Lawson *see*
Heartz, Harry Lawson

Hartshorne, Henry, 1823-1897.
From the curse of coquetry.
[From his: Summer songs. By
H. H. M. Philadelphia:
Ashmead & Evans, 1865. 108p.]
p.70-78.

Harvard Lampoon *see* Grant,
Robert. The little tin gods-
on-wheels; or, Society in
our modern Athens

Harvard University. Hasty
Pudding Club *see* Baker,
George Melville. Poison
see also Batchelder, Samuel
Francis. Hamlet; or, The
sport, the spook, and the
spinster

The harvest storm. A domestic
drama in one act. New York:
Fitzgerald Pub. Co., 188-?
p.50-65. (The amateur stage)

Harvey, Frank.
The wages of sin *see* Brady,
William A.

Hash! *see* Wilkins, W. Henry

Haskett, Emmett.
Bridget Branagans' [sic,
Branagan's] trouble's [sic];
or, The masquerade ball. An
Irish farce in one act. Clyde,
O.: Ames, 1895. 11p. (Ames'
series of standard and minor
drama. no. 352)

The Dutchman's picnic. A
farce in one act. Clyde, O.:
Ames, 1896. 8p. (Ames' series
of standard and minor drama.
no. 379)

Jake and Snow. A musical
sketch in one act. Clyde,
O.: Ames, 1895. 6p. (Ames'
series of standard and
minor drama. no. 361)

The wonderful telephone.
A farce in one act. Clyde,
O.: Ames, 1890. 7p. (Ames'
series of standard and
minor drama. no. 7)

Hasty Pudding Club *see*
Harvard University. Hasty
Pudding Club

Hat drill *see* Denton, Clara
Janetta Fort. When the
lessons are over

Haughwout, L. May.
The princess. (From
Tennyson's poem of the
same title.) New York:
Edgar S. Werner, 1890 &
1914. 52p. (Werner's plays)

Haunted by a shadow; or,
Hunted down *see* Chase,
George B.

The haunted dell *see*
Roberts, T. W. Waldeck;
or, The haunted dell

The haunted hat *see*
Farrell, John Rupert

Haunted house. An Ethiopian
act. New York: Dick &
Fitzgerald, 189-? 8p.
see also Coes, George H.
The three o'clock train;
or, The haunted house

The haunted mill; or, Con
O'Ragen's secret *see*
Moore, Bernard Francis

Hauptmann, Carl Ferdinand
Maximilian, 1858-1921.
Ephraims Breite *see*
Harned, Mary

Hauptmann, Gerhard, 1862-1946.
Die versunkene Glocke *see*
Harned, Mary. The sunken bell
see also Meltzer, Charles
Henry. The sunken bell

Hawthorne, Nathaniel, 1804-1864.
The scarlet letter *see*
Andrews, George H. *see also*
Harrison, Gabriel *see also*
Lathrop, George Parsons *see*
also Najac, Émile de and
Landers, Jean Margaret *see*
also Peck, Elizabeth Weller
see also Smith, James Edgar.
The scarlet stigma

Hay, Henry Hanby, 1849-1940.
The student prince [From his:
Created gold and other poems.
Philadelphia: A. Edward
Newton, 1893. 143p.] p.123-
143.

Hayes, Maude Blanche.
The royal revenge. A romantic
drama in five acts. n.p.:
n.pub., c1898. Typescript.
18, 20, 15, 24, 26 leaves.

The haymakers *see* Root,
George Frederick

Hayne, Paul Hamilton, 1830-1886.
Antonio Melidori [bound with]
Allan Herbert [and] Dramatic
fragments (from The conspira-
tor) [From his: Avolio...
Boston: Ticknor and Fields,
1860. 244p.] p.185-219.

Hazard, Eleanor.
An old plantation night. A
representation of life "in
de quarters." New York:
Dick & Fitzgerald, c1890.
44p. *[joint author:*
Elizabeth Hazard]

Hazard, Elizabeth, 1799-1882.
An old plantation night *see*
Hazard, Eleanor and Hazard,
Elizabeth

Hazardous ground *see* Daly,
Augustin

Hazel Adams *see* Jordon,
Clifton E.

Hazel Kirke *see* MacKaye,
James Steele

Hazelton, George Cochrane,
1868-1921.
Mistress Nell. A merry play
in four acts. [From: Monte
Christo [sic]...and other
plays. By J. B. Russak,
editor. Princeton: Princeton
Univ. Press, 1941. (America's
lost plays, vol. 16) 360p.]
p.129-196. *[earlier copyright: 1900]*

Hazelton, William B.
Electric light. An American
comic opera in three acts.
(Music by W. W. Furst.)
Baltimore: Sun Book and Job
Printing Office, 1879. 42p.
Libretto. *[joint author:
Edward Spencer]*

He was a very jonteel man for
all dat *see* Massey,
Charles. Massey's exhibition
reciter

He was never known to smile
see Barnard, Charles *in*
Dramatic leaflets

He would and he wouldn't *see*
Roth, Edward, ed. The gray
tigers of Smithville; or,
He would and he wouldn't

Head, Edward Francis.
Poltroonius. A tragic farce
in one act. Boston: A.
Williams, 1856. 31p.

Head, M. T.
The lonely pollywog of the
mill-pond. A sanguinary
drama in three scenes. New
York: Happy Hours, 1875.

6p. (The variety stage)

The headsman *see* R., H.

Health vs. riches *see*
Kavanaugh, Mrs. Russell
in her Original dramas,
dialogues...

The heart and sword; or, The
conquerors and conquered;
or, The Spanish and Aztec
races *see* Cuevas, José
de Jesús

The heart broken lover; or,
A tale of a tragical life
see Lookup, Thomas

The heart of a hero *see*
Tubbs, Arthur Lewis

The heart of David, the psalmist-king *see* Heaton,
Augustus George

Heart of gold, true and tried.
A colonial drama in five
acts *see* Finn, Sister
Mary Paulina *in her* Alma
mater; or, The Georgetown
Centennial

The heart of her husband *see*
Kidder, Kathryn

The heart of Maryland *see*
Belasco, David *in his*
The heart of Maryland and
other plays

The heart of Maryland and
other plays *see* Belasco,
David

The heart of Mid-Lothian *see*
Pilgrim, James. Jeanie
Deans; or, The heart of
Mid-Lothian

The heart overtasked *see*
Willis, Nathaniel Parker.
Bianca Visconti; or, The
heart overtasked

The hearthstone; or, My colleen *see* Herne, James A.

The heartless brother *see* Lookup, Thomas. A mad match; or, The heartless brother

A heartrending affair *see* Locke, Belle Marshall

Hearts *see* Golden, William Echard Michael

Hearts and clubs *see* Blanchard, Amy Ella

Hearts and diamonds *see* Runnion, James B.

Hearts are trumps; or, Atout... coeur! Comedy in three acts. (From the French of Gandera.) New York: Rosenfield, 189-. Typescript, prompt-book with Ms. notes. 39, 64, 39 leaves.

Hearts of gold *see* Farrell, John Rupert

Hearts of men *see* McIntyre, John Thomas

Hearts of oak; or, Chums *see* Herne, James A. and Belasco, David

The heart's ordeal *see* Whitney, Thomas Richard. Love; or, The heart's ordeal

The heart's sacrifice *see* Osborn, Laughton *in his* The last Mandeville

Heartz, Harry Lawson, b.1869. Miladi and the musketter *see* Barnet, Robert A.

Heath, James Ewell. Whigs and Democrats; or, Love of no politics. A comedy in three acts. Rich-mond: T. White, 1839. 80p.

Heaton, Augustus George, 1844-1930. The heart of David, the psalmist-king. Washington, D. C.: Neale, 1900. 389p. *[Augustus George Heaton changed his name to Augustus Goodyear Heaton, and it is this latter form which is used by Library of Congress]*

Heaton, Augustus Goodyear *see* Heaton, Augustus George

Heavenly foundations *see* Gaylord, Orrie M. *in* Dramatic leaflets

A heavy shower *see* McBride, H. Elliott *in his* New dialogues

The Hebrew son; or, The child of Babylon *see* Joseph and his brethren, the Hebrew son; or, The child of Babylon

Hector *see* Hageman, Maurice

The heedless ones *see* Daly, Augustin. Dollars and sense; or, The heedless ones

Heermans, Forbes, 1856-1928. Between two foes. An original war drama in four acts. Philadelphia: Penn Pub. Co., 1910. 79p. *[this is a later edition of the author's On both sides; earlier copyright: 1898]*

Between two thorns. An original scene on a stair-case. New York: De Witt, 1892. 15p. (De Witt's acting plays. no. 378)

Down the Black Cañon; or, The silent witness. A drama of the Rocky Mountains in four acts. Chicago: Dramatic Pub. Co., c1890. 40p. (Sergel's acting drama. no. 357)

In the fire-light. An original episode in one act. Chicago: Dramatic Pub. Co., c1892. 14p. (Sergel's acting drama. no. 380)

Love by induction. An original comedy in one act. New York: De Witt, c1892. 31p. (De Witt's acting plays. no. 377)

Love's warrant. A farce in one act. Chicago: Dramatic Pub. Co., c1892. 32p. (Sergel's acting drama. no. 381)

An old vagabond. A pathetic comedy in one act. Syracuse, N. Y.: n.pub., 189-? Typescript, prompt-book, with Ms. notes. 55 leaves.

On both sides. An original drama of the Civil War in four acts. n.p.: n.pub., 1898. Typescript. 163 leaves. *[this is an earlier edition of the author's Between two foes]*

Two negatives make an affirmative. A photographic comedy in one act. Chicago: Dramatic Pub. Co., c1888. 28p. (Sergel's acting drama. no. 379)

The heir apparent *see* Lookup, Alexander (pseud.?) Excelsior; or, The heir apparent

The heir at law *see* Colman, George *in* The modern standard drama, vol. 12

Held by the enemy *see* Gillette, William Hooker

Hélène de la Seiglière. Comedy in four acts. (From the French of Sandeau.) New York: F. Rullman, at the Theatre Ticket Office, c1888. Bilin-

gual text: English and French. 54p. *[based on the work of Jules Sandeau; title page gives Helena de la Seiglière]*

Helen's funny babies *see* Dumont, Frank

Heller, Robley Eugene. Appomattox. A drama relating to the Civil War...in four acts. Abingdon, Ill.: Enterprise-Herald Press, 1899. 78p.

Helm, Charles E. Muolo, the monkey; or, The missing link. A farce in one act. New York: Happy Hours, c1879. 13p.

Heloise, a drama of the passions *see* De Lesdernier, Emily Pierpont

Hemans, Felicia Dorothea Browne, 1793-1835. The American forest girl *see* Massey, Charles. Massey's exhibition reciter

Bernard del Carpio *see* Massey, Charles. Massey's exhibition reciter

Hemmed in *see* Stewart, J. C.

Hendrick, Welland. Pocahontas. A burlesque opera in two acts. Chicago: T. S. Denison, c1886. 19p. Libretto. (Amateur series) (Denison's acting plays. Amateur series)

Henermans, Herman. The "Hope." A play in four acts. New York: Z. and L. Rosenfield Typewriting, 189-. Typescript. Promptbook. 38, 32, 23, 27 leaves.

Henley, Anne. Cinderella. Illustrated play

in four scenes for children.
New York: Edgar S. Werner,
c1913. 21p. *[joint author:*
Stanley Schell; earlier
copyright: 1895]

Mayanni. A play for children.
New York: Edgar S. Werner,
18-? 8p.

Hennequin, Alfred, 1846-1914.
Bébé *see* Babie

Le procès Veauradieux *see*
Kaler, James Otis. A case
for divorce

Hennequin, Maurice, 1863-1926.
Le coup de fouet *see* The
lash of the whip

The Henrietta *see* Howard,
Bronson

Henry, Patrick, 1736-1799.
In favor of the American
war *see* Massey, Charles.
Massey's exhibition reciter

Henry, Richard (pseud.) *[also*
Richard-Henry (pseud.)]
A happy day *see* Williams,
Henry Llewellyn

Henry, Sarepta Myrendal Irish,
1839-1900.
Victoria; or, The triumph of
virtue. [From her: Victoria
with other poems. Cincinnati:
Poe & Hitchcock, 1865. 186p.]
p.1-140.

Henry IV of Germany. A tragedy
in five acts. New York:
Osborn & Buckingham, 1835.
85p. *[Readex also enters*
this play under Thomas J. F.
Kelly]

Henry the Fifth *see* Perine,
Charles E.

Henry VIII *see* Shakespeare,
William *in* Booth, Edwin.

The Shakespearean plays of
Edwin Booth

Henry Dandolo-Peter Stuyvesant
see Townsend, Frederic *in*
his Spiritual visitors

Henry Granden; or, The unknown
heir *see* Bingham, Frank
Lester

Henry Venola, the duellist *see*
Beasley, Frederic Williamson

Hentz, Caroline Lee Whiting,
1800-1856.
De Lara; or, The Moorish
bride. A tragedy in five
acts. Tuscaloosa, Ala.:
Woodruff and Olcott, 1843.
79p.

Hepburn, I. P.
Julian. Baltimore: Bull &
Tuttle, 1843. 59p. *[Readex*
uses the initials "H. P."]

Hepner, Adolf, b.1846.
Good night, Schatz! Realistic
joke and earnest in one act.
St. Louis: St. Louis News
Co., 1894. 47p.

Her only fault *see* Rosenfeld,
Sydney

Her picture *see* Baker,
Rachel E.

Her trump card *see* Stafford,
J. Benson

Herbert, Bernard.
A lesson in elegance; or, The
true art of pleasing. A
comedy in one act. New York:
Dick & Fitzgerald, c1887. 20p.

Second sight; or, Your fortune for a dollar. A farcical
comedy in one act. New York:
H. Roorbach, 1887? 34p.
(Roorbach's American edition
of acting plays. no. 47)

Herbert, Joseph W., 1863-1923.
"Thrilby." A musical bur-
lesque in three acts. New
York: Rosenfield Typewriting,
1895. Typescript, prompt-
book. 35, 29 leaves. Libretto.
*[based on Du Maurier's novel
Trilby; music by Charles
Pürner; without the music]*

Herbert, Victor, 1859-1924.
"The ameer" *see* Ranken,
Frederic and La Shelle,
Kirke

Cyrano de Bergerac *see*
Smith, Harry Bache

The fortune teller *see*
Smith, Harry Bache

The idol's eye *see* Smith,
Harry Bache

The serenade *see* Smith,
Harry Bache

The singing girl *see*
Smith, Harry Bache

The viceroy *see* Smith,
Harry Bache

The wizard of the Nile *see*
Smith, Harry Bache

Herder *see* Opal (pseud.)
in her The cloud of
witnesses

Here she goes and there she
goes *see* Coes, George H.

Heredity *see* Matthews,
Brander. Too much Smith;
or, Heredity *see also*
Penn, Arthur *in* Matthews,
Brander. Comedies for
amateur acting

Heresy and planets *see*
Kastelic, George Anton.
Thirty hours for three
thousand years; or, Heresy
and planets

Herford, Oliver, 1863-1935.

Two out of time. [From his:
Overheard in a garden. New
York: Charles Scribner's
Sons, c1900. 104p.] p.69-84.

Hermine *see* Finn, Sister
Mary Paulina *in her* Alma
mater; or, The Georgetown
Centennial

Hermione *see* Meyers, Benjamin
F. *in his* Collected works

Hernarne *see* Felts, William B.

Herne, James A., 1839-1901.
Drifting apart; or, Mary, the
fisherman's child. n.p.:
n.pub., c1888. Typescript.
19, 12, 21, 6, 4 leaves.
(pag. by act) *[Rice gives
Herne's birth date as Feb. 1,
1840]*

The early plays of James A.
Herne. By Arthur Hobson
Quinn, editor. Princeton:
Princeton Univ. Press, 1940.
(America's lost plays. vol.
7) x, 106p.
  Contents: Within an inch
of his life.--The Minute Men
of 1774-1775.--Drifting
apart.--The Reverend Griffith
Davenport.

The hearthstone; or, My
colleen. An Irish comedy drama
in four acts. n.p.: n.pub.,
1892? Typescript. 25, 20, 17,
11 leaves.

Hearts of oak; or, Chums.
An original American play in
five acts and six tableaux.
New York: Rosenfield, c1879.
Typescript. 19, 12, 23, 13,
15, 8 leaves. *[joint author:
David Belasco]*

Marriage by moonlight; or,
Hap-hazard. A powerfully
romantic play in five tableaux. n.p.: n.pub., c1879.
25, 22, 17, 17 leaves (pag.

by act.) Typescript. Act II
lacking. *[joint author:
David Belasco; adapted from
Watts Phillips' Camilla's
husband]*

Sag Harbor. A comedy in four
acts. New York: Stannard
Mears, 1899? Typescript.
33, 35, 28, 27 leaves.

Shore Acres. n.p.: n.pub.,
1893? Typescript, prompt-
book. With Ms. notes. 26,
29, 8, 25 leaves.

A hero of the new world *see*
Preston, Daniel S. Columbus;
or, A hero of the new world

Herod *see* Iliowizi, Henry

Herod and Mariamne *see*
Trobetzkoy, Amélie Rives
Chanler

Herodias *see* Heywood,
Joseph Converse

The heroes of '76 *see* Cobb,
Charles E.

The heroic Dutchman of seventy-
six *see* Grinnell, V. B.

Hérold, Louis Joseph Ferdinand,
1791-1833.
Zampa *see* Zampa; or, The
marble bride

Herrick, Ada Elizabeth.
Passe Rose *see* Paul, Anne
Marie

Hervé, Florimond Ronge, 1825-
1892.
Chilpéric *see* Chilpéric

L'oeuil crevé *see* The
pierced eye

Hervey, Alfreton.
Only a flirtation. [From:
The New York Drama. New
York: Wheat & Cornett,

1878. vol. 4, no. 47] p.345-
348.

Hervilly, Ernest d', 1839-1911.
Silence dans le rangs! *see*
Silence in the ranks

Herzog, Helen *see* Enéleh, H. B.

Heseltine, William.
The last of the Plantagenets
see Keteltas, Caroline M.

Hesitation *see* Frost, Thomas

Hesper; an American drama *see*
Thayer, William Roscoe

Hewitt, John Hill, 1801-1890.
Jephtha. Baltimore: Bull and
Tuttle, 1845. 11p. Libretto.

West Point; or, A tale of
treason (prologue) *see*
Breck, Joseph

The heyden *see* Shields, Sarah
Annie Frost *in her* Parlor
charades and proverbs

Heywood, Delia A.
Choice dialogues. No. 1. By
Polly Ann Pritchard [Delia A.
Heywood.] Chicago: A. Flana-
gan, c1896. 104p.
  Contents: Aestheticism ver-
sus common sense.--Adam's
fall.--An object lesson.--
A reunion.--A tea party.--
A character play.--A cruel
hoax.--A shrewd guess.--Be
truthful but courteous.--
Grammatical difficulties.--
How the grown folks minded.--
How the fun resulted.--Hos-
pitality on the frontier.--
Insect (a charade.)--Keeping
up appearances.--Kindness
softens even savage hearts.--
Labor is honorable.--Little
pitchers.--Mrs. Peabody's
boarder.--Pseudo (a charade.)
--Perils of moderate drinking.--Quizzing a quack.--

Search for a wardrobe.--
Sickly sentimentalism.--The
professor is interrupted.--
Trials of a country editor.

Heywood, Joseph Converse,
d.1900.
Antonius. A dramatic poem.
New York: Hurd and Hough-
ton, 1867. 272p.

Herodias. A dramatic poem.
New York: Hurd and Hough-
ton, 1867. 251p. *[this is
identical with Heywood's
Salome, the daughter of
Herodias (1862)]*

Il nano Italiano. By Il
Seignior Maestro Infelice
Trovatore (pseud.) *[attri-
buted to Heywood]* New York:
William L. Jones, 1862. 28p.
*[cover title: Il nano
Italiano: a most musical,
most melancholy, most
lamentably laughable, very
fasionably unintelligible
lyric tragedy in five acts]*

Salome. A dramatic poem.
New York: Hurd and Houghton,
1867. 222p.

Salome, the daughter of
Herodias. A dramatic poem.
New York: Putnam, 1862.
251p. *[reissued in 1867
under the title Herodias.
A dramatic poem]*

Sforza. A tragedy with
incidental music for the
last act. London: Kegan
Paul, Trench, 1883. 124p.

The Hiartville Shakespeare
club *see* Locke, Belle
Marshall

Hiawatha; or, Ardent spirits
and laughing water *see*
Walcot, Charles Melton

Hick'ry Farm *see* Stern,
Edwin M.

The hidden hand *see* Jones,
Robert

Hidden treasure; or, The good
St. Nicholas. An operetta
for Twelfth Night. [Preface
by N. B. W.] New York: Wm.
A. Pond, c1881. 85p. Libretto
and vocal score. *[N. B. W.
signifies Nathan Boughton
Warren, and a non-musical
version of this title is
entered under Warren]*

The hidden treasures; or,
Martha's triumph *see*
Careo, Zella

Hide and seek; or, Love in all
corners *see* Steele, Silas
Sexton *in his* Collected
works. Book of plays

Higgins, Richard T. *see*
Rickey, Sam (pseud.)

High C *see* Rosenfeld, Sydney

High Jack, the heeler *see*
White, Charles

High life in New-Orleans *see*
Local hits; or, High life
in New-Orleans

The higher education *see*
Williams, Francis Howard

The highest bidder *see*
Belasco, David and Sothern,
Edward Hugh

Highest price for old clothes;
or, The tailor's strike. An
original darkey eccentricity
in one scene. New York:
Harold Roorbach, 189-? 8p.
(Roorbach's acting drama)

The highland treason *see*
Holland, Elihu Goodwin

The highwayman *see* Smith,
Harry Bache

Hiland, Frank E.
Blundering Bill. A farce in
two scenes. Boston: W. H.
Baker, c1899. 16p. (Baker's
edition of plays)

Broken bonds. A drama in
four acts. Boston: W. H.
Baker, 1897. 37p. (Baker's
edition of plays)

Captain Swell. A negro farce
in two scenes. Boston: W. H.
Baker, c1896. 8p. (Baker's
edition of plays)

Careless Cupid. A negro
farce in one act. Boston:
W. H. Baker, 1896. 12p.
(Baker's Darkey plays)

The curtain lifted; or, The
Order of the Sons of Mars.
A burlesque initiation
ceremony. Chicago: Dramatic
Pub. Co., c1896. 20p.

McBeatem. A farce in one
act. Boston: W. H. Baker,
c1899. 11p. (Baker's edition
of plays)

The lady lawyer. A farce in
two scenes. Boston: W. H.
Baker, 1897. 12p. (Baker's
edition of plays)

The old country store. An
entertainment...being a
description of what happened
in General Jackson's time.
Boston: W. H. Baker, c1895.
27p. (Baker's edition of
plays)

Rooney's restaurant. A farce
in one act. Boston: W. H.
Baker, c1896. 10p. (Baker's
edition of plays)

A town meeting. An enter-
tainment. Boston: Walter H.
Baker, c1895. 20p. (Baker's
edition of plays)

Who caught the count? A
farce in one act. Boston:
W. H. Baker, 1899. 13p.
(Baker's edition of plays)

Hildebrand. An historical
tragedy *see* Campbell,
William Wilfred. Collected
works. Poetical tragedies
see also Lucas, Daniel
Bedinger *in his* Collected
works

Hildreth, David W.
Bound by an oath. A domestic
drama in four acts and a
prologue. By David Hill
(pseud.) Boston: W. H. Baker,
c1890. 80p. (Baker's edition
of plays)

Forced to the war; or, The
subrunners of '63-4. A drama
in four acts. By David Hill
(pseud.) Boston: Walter H.
Baker, c1886. 76p. (Baker's
edition of plays)

The granger; or, Caught in
his own trap. A comedy. By
David Hill (pseud.) Boston:
W. H. Baker, c1890. 63p.
(Baker's edition of plays)

Joining the Tinpanites; or,
Paddy McFling's experience.
A mock initiation in three
parts. By David Hill (pseud.)
Boston: W. H. Baker, c1891.
In three parts: Part 1, 22p.
Part 2, 20p. Part 3, 20p.
(Baker's novelties)

Lone Tree mine. A Rocky
Mountain drama in five acts.
By David Hill (pseud.) Philadelphia: Penn Pub. Co., 1913.
68p. *[earlier copyright:
1899]*

Out of his sphere. A drama in
three acts. By David Hill
(pseud.) Boston: W. H. Baker,
c1889. 35p. (Baker's edition
of plays)

Placer gold; or, How Uncle
Nathan lost his farm. A New
England drama in three acts.
By David Hill (pseud.) Bos-
ton: W. H. Baker, c1890. 84p.
(Baker's edition of plays)

The volunteers; or, The pride
of Company G. A war drama in
three acts. By David Hill
(pseud.) Boston: Walter H.
Baker, 1897. 52p. (Baker's
edition of plays)

Hill, David (pseud.) *see*
Hildreth, David W.

Hill, Frederic Stanhope, 1805-
1852.
The shoemaker of Toulouse;
or, The avenger of humble
life. A drama in four acts.
New York: S. French & Son,
1852? 48p. (French's standard
drama. The acting edition.
no. 253)

The six degrees of crime; or,
Wine, women, gambling, theft,
murder and the scaffold. A
melodrama in six parts.
Boston: W. V. Spencer, 1855.
50p. (The Boston theatre,
no. 1)

Hill, Grace Livingston, 1865-
1947.
A colonial girl. Comedy in
three acts. By Grace Livingston and Abbey Sage Richardson. n.p.: n.pub., 189-.
Typescript, prompt-book. 49,
42, 57 leaves. *[joint author:
Abbey Sage Richardson]*

Hillhouse, James Abraham, 1789-
1841.
Demetria. Tragedy in five
acts [From his: Dramas, dis-
courses, and other pieces.
Boston: C. C. Little & J.
Brown, 1839. vol. 1] p.1-85.

Hilliard, Robert Cochrane,
1857-1927.
The littlest girl. A play in
one act. (Dramatized from
Richard Harding Davis's
story, "Her first appear-
ance.") Chicago: Dramatic
Pub. Co., c1898. 10p. (Ameri-

can acting drama)

Hinton, Henry L., 1840-1913.
King Richard III. By William
Shakespeare. New York: Hurd
and Houghton, c1868. 98p.
(Booth's series of acting
plays. no. 2)

The merchant of Venice. New
York: C. A. Alvord, 1867. 46p.

Romeo and Juliet. By William
Shakespeare. New York: Hurd
and Houghton, c1868. 88p.
(Booth's series of acting
plays. no. 5)

Shakespeare's...Hamlet. As
produced by Edwin Booth. New
York, London: S. French,
c1866. 40p. (Booth's series
of acting plays. no. 1)

Shakespeare's...Macbeth. As
produced by Edwin Booth. New
York: Hinton, 1868. 80p.

Shakespeare's...Othello the
Moor of Venice. New York:
Hurd and Houghton, 1869. 96p.
(Booth's series of acting
plays. no. 3)

Hippotheatron; or, Burlesque
circus *see* White, Charles

Hiram Hireout; or, Followed by
fortune *see* Conway, H. J.

Hirst, Lucas.
Grub Mudge and Co. A comedy
in one act. Philadelphia:
Stokes and Brother, 1853.
Second edition, revised and
corrected. 36p.

His chris cross mark. "The man
of mark" *see* Dinsmore,
William

His excellency the governor
see Marshall, Robert

His father's son *see* Howie,
Hellen Morrison

His hat and cane. A comedy in
one act. By members of the
Bellevue Dramatic Club of
Newport. Boston: Walter H.
Baker, 1902. 26p. (Baker's
edition of plays) *[based
on Vladimir Sollogub's Sa
canne et son chapeau]*

His heroine *see* Holbrook,
Margaret Louise

His last chance; or, The
little joker *see* Colburn,
Carrie W.

His last scout *see* Boothman,
William

His partner's wife *see*
Landis, Leonard Lincoln.
The playwright [bound with
"His partner's wife"]

His wife's father *see* Morton,
Martha

Historical acting charades
see Follen, Eliza Lee Cabot.
Home dramas for young people

Historical and biographical
notes illustrative of the
tragedy of Tecumseh *see*
Jones, George. Tecumseh
and the prophet of the west

Historical cantata. (By pupils
of the Collegiate Department,
Packer Collegiate Institute.)
n.p.: n.pub., 1859. 31p.

Historical drama and tableaux,
Uncle Tom's Freedom see
Arnold, James Oliver

The history of Geronimo's
summer campaign in 1885
see Cummings, G. D.

Hitchcock, James Ripley
Wellman, 1857-1918.
David Harum. New York: Rosen-
field Typewriting, c1898.

Typescript, prompt-book. 50,
53, 37 leaves. *[joint author:
Martha Colcott Hall Hitchcock; based on the novel of
the same name by Edward
Noyes Westcott]*

Hitchcock, Martha Wolcott
Hall, d.1903.
David Harum *see* Hitchcock,
James Ripley Wellman and
Hitchcock, Martha Wolcott
Hall

Hockenbery, Frank.
Prof. Blacks' phunnygraph;
or, Talking machine. A
colored burlesque on the
phonograph. Chicago: T. S.
Denison, c1886. 7p. (The
Ethiopian drama)

Hoefler, Henry A.
A day in the doctor's office.
A farce in one act. Clyde,
O.: Ames, 1893. 11p. (Ames'
series of standard and minor
drama. no. 324)

Hoffmann, Henry.
Harlequin old bogey; or, The
imps of the school and the
secret of the old oak chest
see Tracy, J. Perkins

Hogan, J. M.
Clearing the mists *see* Barr,
E. Nelson and Hogan, J. M.

Holbrook, Amelia Weed.
Jack, the commodore's grandson. New York: Nash Type-
writing, c1893. Typescript,
prompt-book. 29, 32, 54, 23
leaves.

Holbrook, Margaret Louise.
His heroine. A farce in one
act. Philadelphia: Penn Pub.
Co., 1911. 14p. *[earlier
copyright: 1894]*

Holcomb, Willard.
A gilded brick. A comedy in

one act. Philadelphia: Penn
Pub. Co., 1913. 16p. [earlier
copyright: 1898]

Holcroft, Thomas, 1745-1809.
The man of ten thousand see
The man of ten thousand

The road to ruin see The
modern standard drama, vol. 7

A hole in the ground see
Hoyt, Charles Hale

The hole in the wall see
The secret; or, The hole
in the wall

Holidays see Brewster, Emma
E. in her Parlor varieties

Holland, Elihu Goodwin, 1817-
1878.
The highland treason. A
drama in five acts [From
his: Essays: and a drama in
five acts. Boston: Phillips,
Sampson, 1852. 400p.] p.341-
400.

Holland, Josiah Gilbert, 1819-
1881.
Bitter-sweet. New York:
Charles Scribner's Sons,
1890. 202p.

Hollenbeck, Benjamin W., b.
1850.
After ten years; or, The
maniac wife. An original
romantic drama in three acts.
Clyde, O.: Ames, c1885. 35p.
(Ames' series of standard and
minor drama. no. 164)

Zion. A drama in a prologue
and four acts. Clyde, O.:
Ames, 1886. 38p. (Ames'
series of standard and minor
drama. no. 192)

Hollenius, Laurence John.
Dollars and cents. An original American comedy in three
acts. New York: Nelson Row,
1869. 47p.

Dollars and cents. New York:
R. M. De Witt, c1867. Second
revised editon. 40p.

Dollars and cents. New York:
De Witt, c1867. Fifth revised
edition. 41p.

First love. A comedy in one
act. (From the French of
Scribe.) New York: R. M.
De Witt, 1873. 16p. [based
on Scribe's Les premières
amours; ou, Les souvenirs
d'enfance]

A game of cards. Comedietta
in one act. Chicago: Dramatic
Pub. Co., c1875. 16p. (Sergel's acting drama. no. 192)
[based on Charles Francis
Coglan's La partie de piquet]

Maria and Magdalena. A play
in four acts. New York: R. M.
De Witt, 1874. 44p. [title
page: Adapted for the American
stage from the German original
of Paul Lindau]

Holley, Marietta, 1836-1926.
Betsey Bobbett. New York:
W. J. Allen, Book and Job
Printer, 1899. 40p. [cover:
"Scenes drawn from the book
My Opinions and Betsey Bob-
bett's by Josiah Allen's
wife"; Josiah Allen's wife
is the pseud. used by Mar-
ietta Holley]

Hollister, Gideon Hiram, 1817-
1881.
Thomas à Becket. A tragedy
[From his: Thomas à Becket:
a tragedy, and other poems.
Boston: W. V. Spencer, 1866]
p.1-108.

Holmes, Oliver Wendell, 1809-
1894.
Scene from unpublished play
[From: The Evergreen. New
York: J. Winchester, 1840.
vol. 1. 692p.] p.127-128.
[head of title, p.127: The
Red Seal--scenes from...]

The Holy Graal and other fragments *see* Hovey, Richard

A holy terror *see* Wenlandt, Oliver

Home *see* Cobb, Mary L. Poetical dramas for home and school *see also* Hovey, Richard *in his* The plays of Maurice Maeterlinck. Second series

A home by two brides *see* Mitchell, T. Berry

The home-guard *see* Baker, George Melville. Enlisted for the war; or, The home-guard

Home jewels *see* Wallace, John J. Little Ruby; or, Home jewels

The home-made bonnet *see* Waters, Roland

The home of romance *see* Bridges, Robert *in his* Overheard in Arcady

Home rule *see* Eberhart, B. F.

Home, sweet home *see* Seymour, Charles W.

Homeopathy; or, The family cure *see* Frank, J. C.

Honesty is the best policy *see* Follen, Eliza Lee Cabot. Home dramas for young people *see also* House, Rupert. Honesty wins [or, Honesty is the best policy]

Honesty is the best policy; or, True to the core *see* Maguire, John

Honesty wins [or, Honesty is the best policy] *see* House, Rupert

The honey-moon *see* Tobin, John *in* The modern standard drama, vol. 1

A honeymoon eclipse *see* Taylor, Malcolm Stuart

The honeymoon; fourth quarter *see* Mathews, Frances Aymar

Honor among thieves *see* Cahill, Frank *in* Arnold, George? and Cahill, Frank. Parlor theatricals; or, Winter evening's entertainment

Hood, Thomas, 1835-1874. The dream of Eugene Aram *see* Massey, Charles. Massey's exhibition reciter

The little vulgar boy *see* Massey, Charles. Massey's exhibition reciter

Hook, Theodore Edward, 1788-1841. Doubts and fears *see* Smith, Richard Penn. Quite correct

The hop of fashion *see* White, Charles

Hope, Kate. Our utopia. An aesthetic comedietta in two acts. New York: Roorbach, 1882. 18p. (The acting drama. no. 174)

The "Hope" *see* Henermans, Herman

Hopkins, Joseph R. (attributed author) Lucrezia; or, The bag of gold *see* Lucrezia; or, The bag of gold

Hopkins, Rufus Clement, b.1816. Losada [From his: Roses and

thistles. San Francisco:
William Doxey, 1894. 480p.]
p.129-158.

Malinche [From his: Roses
and thistles. San Francisco:
William Doxey, 1894. 480p.]
p.31-77.

Hoppin, William Jones, 1813-
1895.
Circumstances alter cases.
A comedietta in one act.
(From L'invitation à la
valse of Alexandre Dumas.)
New York: S. French, 186-?.
24p. (French's minor drama.
The acting edition. no. 294)

The lady of the bed-chamber.
A farce in one act. New York:
S. French, 1858. 17p.
(The minor drama. The acting
edition. no. 166)

Horace. (From the French of
Corneille.) New York:
Darcie & Corbyn, 1855. Bi-
lingual text: English and
French. 28p.

Horizon see Daly, Augustin

Horn, Charles Edward, 1786-
1849.
The maid of Saxony; or,
Who's the traitor? see
Morris, George Pope

Horne, Mary Barnard, b.1845.
The darktown bicycle club
scandal. A colored sketch
in one act for lady min-
strels. Boston: W. H. Baker,
c1897. 16p.

The four-leaved clover. An
operetta in three acts.
Boston, New York, Chicago:
White-Smith Music Pub. Co.,
1890. 64p. Libretto and
vocal score.

Gulliver and the Lilliputians
up to date. An entertainment
in one act. Boston: Walter

H. Baker, 1903. 13p. *[earlier
copyright: 1896]*

Jolly Joe's lady minstrels
see Silsbee, Alice M. and
Horne, Mary Barnard

The ladies of Cranford. A
sketch of English village
life 50 years ago in three
acts. Boston: Walter H.
Baker, c1899. (Baker's edition
of plays) *[based on Elizabeth
Cleghorn Gaskell's Cranford]*

The last of the Peak sisters;
or, The great moral dime show.
An entertainment in one scene.
Boston: W. H. Baker, c1892.
17p. (Baker's novelties)

The other fellow. A comedy in
three acts. Boston: Walter H.
Baker, 1904. 144p. *[earlier
copyright: 1903]*

The Peak sisters. An enter-
tainment. Boston: Walter H.
Baker, c1887. 20p. Libretto.
(Baker's novelties)

Plantation bitters. A colored
fantasy in two acts for male
characters only. Boston:
W. H. Baker, c1892. 29p.

Prof. Baxter's great invention. An unclassified entertainment in one act. Boston:
Walter H. Baker, c1891. 24p.
(Baker's edition of plays)

A singing school of ye olden
time. Boston: Walter H. Baker,
c1894. 23p. (Baker's edition
of plays)

Hornett, Stephen Francis.
In the way; or, Over the
cliff. A drama in five acts.
Pittsburgh: Barr and Myers,
c1874. 20p.

Hornung, Ernest William, 1866-
1921.
Raffles *see* Smith, Edgar
McPhail. "Waffles"

Horseshoe Robinson; or, The
battle of King's Mountain
see Tayleure, Clifton W.

Horst, Ben (pseud.) *see*
Fast, Edward Gustavus

Hosmer, Lucius, 1870-1935.
The Koreans; or, The
ancestors of King-Ki-Too
see Cook, Charles Emerson

The walking delegate *see*
Cook, Charles Emerson

The hospital nurse of Tennessee *see* Dawson, J. H.
and Whittemore, B. G. Lights
and shadows of the great
rebellion; or, The hospital
nurse of Tennessee

Hospitality on the frontier
see Heywood, Delia A.
in her Choice dialogues.
no. 1

Hotchkiss, Zort P.
Saved. Richmond, Ind.:
Telegram Steam Printing Co.,
1874. 38p.

The hotel *see* Hoyt, Charles
Hale and Edouin, Winnie.
A bunch of keys; or, The
hotel

Hotel Healthy *see* Hamilton,
George H.

The hour and the man *see*
Nobles, Milton. From sire
to son; or, The hour and
the man

House, Edward Howard, 1836-
1901.
Larcher's victories. Comedy
in three acts. n.p.: n.pub.,
186-? Prompt-book. 15 un-
numbered leaves.

Honesty wins [or, Honesty is
the best policy] A comedy in
four acts for male characters

only. Chicago and New York:
Dramatic Pub. Co., c1899.
20p. (Sergel's acting drama.
no. 465)

The house on the avenue; or,
The little mischief-makers
see Rover, Winnie

The house that Jack built *see*
Steele, Silas Sexton *in his*
Collected works. Book of
plays

Household affairs; or, A cause
for divorce *see* Rosetti,
Joseph

The household of F. Marion
Crawford *see* Bridges,
Robert *in his* Overheard
in Arcady

The household of Frank J.
Stockton *see* Bridges,
Robert *in his* Overheard in
Arcady

The household of George
Meredith *see* Bridges,
Robert *in his* Overheard
in Arcady

The household of Henry James
see Bridges, Robert *in
his* Overheard in Arcady

The household of James M.
Barrie *see* Bridges, Robert
in his Overheard in Arcady

The household of Richard
Harding Davis *see* Bridges,
Robert *in his* Overheard
in Arcady

The household of Robert Louis
Stevenson *see* Bridges,
Robert *in his* Overheard
in Arcady

The household of Rudyard
Kipling *see* Bridges,
Robert *in his* Overheard in
Arcady

The household of Thomas Bailey
Aldrich *see* Bridges,
Robert *in his* Overheard
in Arcady

The household of William Dean
Howells *see* Bridges,
Robert *in his* Overheard
in Arcady

The household tragedy *see*
Mitchell, Thomas

Houston, Harry.
Sea drift. A melodrama in
four acts with prologue.
Chicago: T. S. Denison,
c1890. 42p. (Star series)

Hovey, Richard, 1864-1900.
The birth of Galahad [From
his: Launcelot and Guenevere:
a poem in dramas. vol. 3.
Boston: Small, Maynard,
1898. 124p.] p.1-80.

The Holy Graal and other
fragments [From his: Launcelot and Guenevere: a poem in
dramas. vol. 5. New York:
Duffield, 1907. 128p.]
p.1-99.

The marriage of Guenevere
[From his: Launcelot and
Guenevere: a poem in dramas.
vol. 2. Boston: Small, Maynard, 1898. 179p.] p.3-79.

The plays of Maurice Maeter-
linck [First series] Chicago:
Stone and Kimball, 1895.
Limited edition. 369p.
Contents: Princess Maleine
[La princesse Maleine].--
The intruder [L'intruse].--
The blind [Les aveugles].--
The seven princesses [Les
sept princesses]

The plays of Maurice Maeterlinck. Second series. Chicago: Stone and Kimball,
1896. xv, 1, 235p.
Contents: Alladine and

Palomides [Alladine et Palo-
mides].--Pélléas and Mélisande [Pélléas et Mélisande].
--Home [Intérieur].--The
death of Tintagiles [La mort
de Tintagiles]

The quest of Merlin [From
his: Launcelot and Guenevere:
a poem in dramas. vol. 1.
Boston: Small, Maynard, 1898.
80p.]

Taliesin [From his: Launcelot
and Guenevere: a poem in
dramas. vol. 4. Boston: Small,
Maynard, 1900. 58p.]

Uriel Acosta. Drama in four
acts. (From the German of
Karl Gützkow.) Boston: Poet-
Lore, 1895. vol. 7, nos.
1-7. p.6-18, 83-96, 140-149,
198-203, 263-270, 333-349.
[joint author: François
Stewart Jones]

How a queen loved *see* Fawcett,
Edgar

How much I loved thee! *see*
Blood, Henry Ames *see also*
Eshobel, Raymond

How she has her own way *see*
Buxton, Ida M.

How she settled her bills *see*
Shettel, James W. and George,
Wadsworth M. Nanka's leap
year venture; or, How she
settled her bills

How Sister Paxley got her child
baptized *see* Shaw, J. S. R.

How the colonel proposed *see*
Brewster, Emma E. *see also*
her Parlor varieties

How the fun resulted *see*
Heywood, Delia A. *in her*
Choice dialogues. no. 1

How the grown folks minded *see*

Heywood, Delia A. *in her* Choice dialogues. no. 1

How to find an heir *see* Beadle's...dialogues no. 2

How to get a divorce *see* Dumont, Frank

How to get below par *see* The temperance school dialogues

How to get rid of them *see* The widow's maid and the bachelor's man; or, How to get rid of them

How to make one's fortune *see* The parasite; or, How to make one's fortune

How to pay the rent *see* Wilton, M. J.

How to write "popular" stories *see* Beadle's...dialogues no. 2

How Uncle Nathan lost his farm *see* Hildreth, David W. Placer gold; or, How Uncle Nathan lost his farm

How we got our dinner *see* Walsh, Joseph P. The actors' scheme; or, How we got our dinner

Howard, Bronson, 1842-1908. Aristocracy. A comedy in four acts. n.p.: n.pub., c1898. Prompt-book. 74p.

The banker's daughter. A drama in five acts and six tableaux. (Also produced under the titles "Lilian's last love" and "The old love and the new.") [From: America's lost plays. Princeton, N. J.: Princeton Univ. Press, 1941. vol. 10] p.81-137. *[earlier copyright: 1879]*

Baron Rudolph. A drama in four acts. [From: America's lost plays. vol. 10. Princeton, N. J.: Princeton Univ. Press, 1941] p.139-192. *[earlier copyright: 1881]*

The Henrietta. A comedy in four acts. (Original title: "The millionaire.") New York: n.pub., 1887. Typescript, prompt-book. Sides for twelve parts.

The Henrietta. A comedy in four acts. New York: S. French, c1901. 82p. (French's acting edition of plays. vol. 157)

Hurricanes. A comic drama in three acts. [From: America's lost plays. vol. 10. Princeton, N. J.: Princeton Univ. Press, 1941] p.1-56. *[earlier copyright: 1878]*

Old love-letters. A comedy in one act. Prompt-book in Ms. n.d. 22 leaves.

Old love letters. A comedy in one act. [From: America's lost plays. vol. 10. Princeton, N. J.: Princeton Univ. Press, 1941] p.57-80. *[earlier copyright: 1878]*

One of our girls. A comedy in four acts. [From: America's lost plays. vol. 10. Princeton, N. J.: Princeton Univ. Press, 1941] p.237-297. *[earlier copyright: 1897]*

Saratoga; or, Pistols for seven. A comic drama in five acts. New York, London: S. French, c1898. 68p. (French's standard drama. The acting edition. no. 369)

Shenandoah. A military comedy in four acts. New York: S. French, c1897. 71p.

Young Mrs. Winthrop. A play in four acts. New York: Madison Square Theatre, 1882. Prompt-book. 47p.

Young Mrs. Winthrop. New York: Madison Square Theatre, 1882. 47p.

Howard, Edmond.
Adelaïde. The romance of Beethoven's life. (From the German of Müller.) New York: n.pub., 1897. 6 unnumbered leaves. *[joint author: David Scull; based on Adelaïde by Hugo Müller]*

Howard, George H.
Tyrrel. A tragedy in five acts. Baltimore: Charles Harvey, 1874. 61p.

Howe, C. E. B.
Signing the Declaration of Independence; or, Scenes in Congress, July 4th, 1776. A national sketch in one act. New York, London: S. French, c1887. 14p. (French's minor drama. no. 299)

Howe, J. Burdette, 1828-1908.
The British slave; or, Seven years of a soldier's life. An original drama in four acts. Boston: W. V. Spencer, 1856. 43p. (Spencer's Boston theatre. no. 106) *[Readex uses the form J. Burdett Howe, which the Library of Congress corrects to Burdette; Howe's actual name is Thomas Burdette]*

The Golden Eagle; or, The privateer of '76. A national drama in three acts and a prologue. New York: S. French, c1857. 37p. (French's standard drama. no. 171)

Handsome Jack. A melo-drama in three acts. London, New York: S. French, 186-? 36p. (French's acting edition. Late Lacy's. no. 698)

Handsome Jack. A melo-drama in three acts. London and New York: S. French, 18-.

36p. (Lacy's acting edition. vol. 114)

Scarlet Dick; the King's highwayman [or, The road and the riders] An original drama in four acts. London and New York: S. French, 18-. 44p. (Lacy's acting edition. vol. 114)

The woman of the world; or, A peep at the vices and virtues of country and city life. An entirely original drama in four acts. New York: Happy Hours, 1858? 36p. (The acting drama. no. 100)

Howe, Julia Ward, 1819-1910.
The world's own. Boston: Ticknor & Fields, 1857. 141p.

Howell, S.
A marriage for revenge. A drama in five acts. New Orleans: Office of the Picayune, 1874. 34p.

Howells, William Dean, 1837-1920.
The Albany depot. A farce. New York: Harper & Brothers, 1892. 68p. (Harper's black and white series)

Bride roses. Boston: Houghton, Mifflin, 1900. 48p.

A counterfeit presentment. Boston: J. R. Osgood, 1877. 155p.

The elevator. A farce in three acts. Boston: J. R. Osgood, 1885. 84p.

Evening dress. A farce. New York: Harper & Brothers, 1893. 59p. (Harper's black and white series)

Five o'clock tea. [From his: The mouse-trap and other farces. New York: Harper & Brothers, c1889] p.57-97.

The garroters. New York:

Harper & Brothers, 1886.
90p.

An Indian giver. A comedy in
one act. Boston: Houghton,
Mifflin, 1900. 99p.

A letter of introduction.
New York: Harper & Brothers,
c1892. 61p. (Harper's black
and white series)

A likely story [From his:
The mouse-trap and other
farces. New York: Harper &
Brothers, c1889] p.139-184.

The mother and the father.
New York and London: Harper
& Brothers, 1909. 54p.
[earlier copyright: 1900]

The mouse-trap [From his:
The mouse-trap and other
farces. New York: Harper &
Brothers, c1889] p.99-137.

Out of the question. A
comedy. Boston: J. R. Osgood,
1877. 183p.

The parlor car. A farce in
one act. Boston: Houghton,
Mifflin, 1883. 74p.

A previous engagement. A
comedy. New York: Harper &
Brothers, 1897. 65p.

The register. A farce.
Boston: J. R. Osgood, 1884.
91p.

Room forty-five. A farce in
one act. Boston: Houghton,
Mifflin, 1900. 61p.

Samson. A tragedy in four
acts. (From the Italian of
D'Aste.) New York: D. Koppel,
1889. Bilingual text: English
and Italian. 51p.

A sea-change; or, Love's
stowaway. A lyricated farce
in two acts and an epilogue.
Boston: Ticknor, 1888. 151p.

The sleeping car. A farce.
Boston: Ticknor, c1883. 74p.

The smoking car. A farce in
one act. Boston: Houghton,
Mifflin, 1900. 70p.

The unexpected guests. A
farce. New York: Harper &
Brothers, 1893. 54p. (Harper's
black and white series)

Howells, William Dean, The
household of *see* Bridges,
Robert *in his* Overheard
in Arcady

Howie, Hellen Morrison.
After the matinée. A comedy
in one act. Philadelphia:
Penn Pub. Co., 1899. 19p.
(Dramatic library, vol. 1,
no. 185)

His father's son. A farce
comedy in one act. Phila-
delphia: Penn Pub. Co.,
1900. 20p.

The reformer reformed. A
comedy sketch. Philadelphia:
Penn Pub. Co., 1899. 11p.
(Dramatic library, vol. 1,
no. 187)

Howson, Frank A.
Alpine roses *see* Boyesen,
Hjalmar Hjorth

The dreamland tree *see*
Barnard, Charles

Hoyt, Charles Hale, 1860-1900.
A black sheep. A dramatic
composition with original
lyrics in three acts. New
York: n.pub., c1896. Typescript, prompt-book. 39,
43, 20 leaves.

A brass monkey. n.p.: n.pub.,
18-? Title page lacking.
Prompt-book with Ms. notes.
81 leaves (pag. irreg.)

A bunch of keys; or, The
hotel. A comedy in three
acts. n.p.: n.pub., c1883.
Prompt-book in Ms. 172 leaves.
[joint author: Winnie Edouin]

A bunch of keys; or, The hotel [From: America's lost plays. vol. 9. Princeton, N. J.: Princeton Univ. Press, 1940] p.3-51.

A hole in the ground. n.p.: n.pub., 1887. Title page lacking. Typescript, prompt-book with Ms. notes. 53, 49, 40 leaves (pag. by act.)(Pag. irreg.)

The maid and the moonshiner. (Music by Edward Solomon.) New York: P. F. McBreen, n.d. 24p. (p.5-6 lacking)

A midnight bell. An original comedy in four acts. n.p.: n.pub., c1883. Typescript, prompt-book. 27, 17, 21, 10 leaves (pag. by act)

A midnight bell [From: America's lost plays. vol. 9. Princeton, N. J.: Princeton Univ. Press, 1940] p.55-103.

A milk white flag. New York: n.pub., 1894? Typescript, prompt-book. 49, 37, 19 leaves (pag. by act)

A milk white flag [From: America's lost plays. vol. 9. Princeton, N. J.: Princeton Univ. Press, 1940] p.195-240.

A parlor match. n.p.: n.pub., 1884? Typescript, prompt-book. 27, 26, 27 leaves (pag. by act) (pag. irreg.)

A rag baby. N.B. Please don't expect a wax doll with real hair and eyes that open and shut. A dramatic composition in three acts, descriptive of life in a drug store and post office. Boston: n.pub., 1884. Title page lacking. Prompt-book. 99, 163, 89p.

A temperance town [From: America's lost plays. vol. 9. Princeton, N. J.: Princeton Univ. Press, 1940] p.153-191.

A temperance town. Boston: Mrs. Jas. S. Smith, copyist, 1893? Title page lacking. Typescript, prompt-book with Ms. notes. 32, 28, 23, 24 leaves (pag. by act) (pag. irreg.) *[in reality, this is an anti-temperance drama]*

A Texas steer. Musical farce comedy in four acts. n.p.: n.pub., 18-? Title page lacking. Typescript, prompt-book with Ms. notes. 15, 30, 21, 16 leaves (pag. irreg.) *[without the music; this appears to be a lengthened version of his Texas steer; or, Money makes the mare go]*

Texas steer; or, Money makes the mare go. n.p.: n.pub., 18-? Typescript, prompt-book with Ms. notes. 3, 31 leaves (numb. irreg.) *[this appears to be a shortened version of his A Texas steer]*

A tin soldier. New York: C. L. Goodwin, Typewriter, 1885. Title page lacking. Typescript, prompt-book. 1-3, 28, 27, 21 leaves (pag. irreg.)

A trip to Chinatown. n.p.: n.pub., 18-? Typescript, prompt-book with Ms. notes. 2nd Vs. 27, 29, 17 leaves (pag. by act) *[without the music]*

A trip to Chinatown [From: America's lost plays. vol. 9. Princeton, N. J.: Princeton Univ. Press, 1940] p.107-148. *[title page: A trip to China-town; or, An idyl of San Francisco]*

A trip to Chinatown; or, An idyl of San Francisco, with songs. n.p.: n.pub., 18-? 14, 19, 12, 15 leaves (pag. by act) *[music by Percy Gaunt; included is the famous "The Bowery"]*

Hubbard, Harvey, d.1862.
Ixion [From his: Ixion and
other poems. Boston: Ticknor,
Reed, and Fields, 1852. 165p.]
p.1-19.

Hubbell, Horatio.
Arnold; or, The treason of
West Point. A tragedy in
five acts. Philadelphia:
H. Young, 1847. 75p.

Hubert, Charles, b.1794.
Les deux pensions *see*
Payne, John Howard. The
boarding schools; or, Life
among the little folks

Hubner, Charles William, 1835-
1929.
Cinderella; or, The silver
slipper. Lyrical drama in
four acts. Atlanta: Dodson &
Scott, 1879. 24p.

Hughes, Louise Marie.
Love's stratagem. A comedy.
Philadelphia: Penn Pub. Co.,
1896. 10p. (Keystone edition
of popular plays) (Dramatic
library, vol. 1, no. 43)

Hughes, Thomas, 1822-1896.
School days at Rugby *see*
Venable, William Henry. The
fag's revolt *in his* The
school stage. *[Hughes' work
is known also under the title
Tom Brown's school days]*

Hugo, Victor Marie, comte,
1813-1869.
Angelo, tirano de Pâdue *see*
Angelo; or, The tyrant of
Padua *see also* Pray, Isaac
Clarke. Angelo the tyrant
of Padua

Lucrèce Borgia *see* Calcaterra, G. Lucrezia Borgia
see also Lucretia Borgia

Les misérables *see* Fulton,
Harry Clifford. Jean Valjean;
or, The shadow of the law

see also Griffin, George
W. H.

Notre Dame de Paris *see*
Fry, Joseph Reese. Notre-Dame
of Paris

Ruy Blas *see* Booth, Edwin.
The miscellaneous plays of
Edwin Booth

The Huguenot daughters; or,
Reasons for adherence to
the faith *see* Poyas,
Catharine Gendron

The Huguenots *see* Kellogg,
Clara Louise

Humbert, Albert, 1835-1886.
Fantine *see* Woolf, Benjamin
Edward and Field, Roswell
Martin

The humor of the court room;
or, Jones vs. Johnson, a
lawful comedy *see* Lindsley,
Philip

Humors of the strike *see*
Baker, George Melville

Humours of Pompey Suds' shaving
saloon *see* Barnes, James.
The black barber; or, Humours
of Pompey Suds' shaving saloon

Humphrey, Lewis D.
A bachelor's banquet; or, An
indigestible romance. A farce
in one act. Boston: W. H.
Baker, c1899. 28p. (Baker's
edition of plays) *[produced
originally under the title
An indigestible romance]*

Humpty Dumpty *see* Denier,
John *see also* Fox, George
Washington Lafayette

The hunchback *see* Daly,
Augustin *see also* Knowles,
James Sheridan *in* The
modern standard drama,
vol. 2

Hunk's wedding day *see*
Griffin, George W. H.

Hunt, Arzalea.
The lost dog. A comic dia-
logue. Lebanon, O.: March
Bros., 189-? 9p.

The menagerie in the school-
room. Darrowville, O.: School
Pub. Co., 1895. 14p.

A wedding notice. Lebanon,
O.: March Bros., 189-? 8p.

The wood fairies. An Arbor
Day entertainment. New York:
Harold Roorbach, 1895. 17p.

Hunt, Leigh, 1784-1859.
Abou Ben Adhem *see* Massey,
Charles. Massey's exhibition
reciter

Hunt, Violet, 1866-1942.
The maiden's progress. A
novel in dialogue. New York:
Harper & Bros., 1894. 252p.

Hunted down *see* Chase, George
B. Haunted by a shadow; or,
Hunted down

Hunter, Wesley J.
Strawberry shortcake. Ethio-
pian farce in one scene.
Clyde, O.: Ames, 1887. 5p.
(Ames' series of standard
and minor drama. no. 238)

The hunter of Monadnoc. A
romantic drama in three acts.
Dedham: n.pub., 1834. 35p.
(p.13-24 lacking.)

Hunter-Duvar, John, 1830-1899.
De Roberval [From his: De
Roberval...also...and the
triumph of constancy. Saint
John, N. B.: J. & A. McMillan,
1888. 12, 192p.] 12p., p.1-
149. *[Readex also enters this
title under Duvar, John Hunter; Library of Congress
uses Hunter-Duvar, John]*

Huntington, Gurdon, 1818-1875.
The guests of Brazil; or,
The martyrdom of Frederick.
A tragedy [From his: The
shadowy land, and other poems,
including The guests of
Brazil. New York: J. Miller,
1861] p.409-506.

Hurd, St. Clair.
Counsel for the plaintiff. A
comedy in two acts. Boston:
W. H. Baker, c1891. 27p.
(Baker's edition of plays)

Hurlburt, Elisha P. (supposed
author)
The model house *see* The
model house

The pattern man *see* The
pattern man

Hurlburt, William Henry, 1827-
1895.
Americans in Paris; or, A
game of dominoes. A comedy in
two acts. New York: S. French,
c1858. 32p. (French's standard
drama. The acting edition. no.
209) *[Readex also enters this
same edition under title]*

Hurly burly *see* Smith, Harry
Bache and Smith, Edgar McPhail

Hurricanes *see* Howard, Bronson

The husband *see* Williams,
Espy William Hendricks

The husband-lovers *see* Osborn,
Laughton. The double deceit;
or, The husband-lovers *in his*
The silver head, The double
deceit; comedies

Husbands and wives. A comedy in
two acts [From: Alexander's
modern acting drama...Phila-
delphia: Carey & Hart, Hogan
& Thompson, and W. Marshall,
1835. vol. 2. 277p.] p.229-
277.

Husbands don't stay long *see*
Greenly, William Jay *in his*
The three drunkards

The husbands of Leontine.
Comedy in three acts. (From
the French of Capus.) New
York: n.pub., 1900? Type-
script. 54, 60, 43 leaves.

A husband's sacrifice *see*
St. Mark; or, A husband's
sacrifice *in* Wilkins,
John H. Signor Marc

Huse, Carolyn Evans.
Under the greenwood tree.
A Christmas operetta in one
act. New York: Edgar S.
Werner, c1895. 16p. Libretto.

The hustler. n.p.: n.pub.,
1896. Typescript, prompt-
book. 26, 27, 13 leaves.

Hyde, Elizabeth A.
An engaged girl. A comedy.
Chicago: T. S. Denison,
c1899. 18p. (Amateur series)

Hymettus *see* Commelin,
Anna Olcott

Hypnotizing a landlord *see*
Tees, Levin C.

The hypochondriac *see* Baker,
George Melville *see also*
Griffin, George W. H.

The hypochondriac; or, A cure
for the "blues" *see* Steele,
Silas Sexton *in his* Collected works. Book of plays

The hypocrite *see* Smith,
Solomon Franklin

I can take it or leave it alone
see Ritchie, Thomas. Moderation; or, I can take it or
leave it alone *in* A collection of temperance dialogues

I dine with my mother *see*
McLachlan, Charles

I love your wife *see*
Sedgwick, Alfred B.

"I shall write the major" *see*
Rosenfeld, Sydney

Ibsen, Henrik, 1828-1906.
Rosmersholm *see* Carmichael,
Montgomery

The icicle *see* Fawcett,
Edgar

The idiot boy *see* Pray, Isaac
Clarke

The idol's eye *see* Smith,
Harry Bache

The Idumean *see* Leavitt, John
McDowell

An idyl of San Francisco *see*
Hoyt, Charles Hale. A trip to
Chinatown; or, An idyl of
San Francisco

An idyl of the slums *see*
Fawcett, Edgar

Ignorance is bliss *see*
Baker, George Melville

Iliowizi, Henry, 1850-1911.
Herod. A historical tragedy
in five acts. Minneapolis,
Minn.: Printed at the Tribune
Book Rooms, 1884. 80p.

Isaac's blessing. n.p.: n.pub.,
1888? 14p.

Joseph. A dramatic represen-
tation in seven tableaux.
Minneapolis, Minn.: Tribune
Job Printing, 1885. 46p.

Saul. A tragedy in five acts.
Philadelphia: Anvil Print.
Co., 1894. 84p.

I'll remain single *see* Hageman,
Maurice

I'll stay awhile   *see*
McBride, H. Elliott

Ill-treated ill somnambulo
see Williams, Henry
Llewellyn. The darkey
sleep-walker; or, Ill-
treated ill somnambulo

An ill wind   *see*   Donaldson,
Frank. Two comedies

The ills of dram-drinking
see A collection of temperance dialogues

Imaginary possessions *see*
Venable, William Henry *in*
his The school stage

Imbroglio *see* Allender,
George

The immortal *see* Nack, James

Immortality snatched from the
Tree of life *see* Van Waters,
George. Azon, the invader of
Eden; or, Immortality snatched
from the Tree of life

Imogene; or, The witch's secret
see Dale, Horace C.

The imposter *see* Myles,
George B. The winning hand;
or, The imposter *see also*
Tartuffe; or, The imposter

The imps of the school and the
secret of the old oak chest
see Tracy, J. Perkins.
Harlequin old bogey; or,
The imps of the school and
the secret of the old oak
chest

Impulse *see* Rowe, Bolton

In a spider's web *see*
Kinnaman, C. F.

In and out *see* White, Charles

In and out of place *see*
Johnson, Samuel D.

In Aunt Chloe's cabin. A negro-
comedy sketch in one act *see*
Sutherland, Evelyn Greenleaf
Baker *in her* In office
hours and other sketches for
vaudeville or private acting

In far Bohemia *see* Sutherland,
Evelyn Greenleaf Baker *in*
her Collected works. Po'
white trash and other one-act
dramas

In favor of the American war
see Henry, Patrick *in*
Massey, Charles. Massey's
exhibition reciter

"In for it"; or, Uncle Tony's
mistake *see* Allyn, Dave E.

In Klondike *see* Merriman,
Effie Woodward

In Klondyke *see* Merriman,
Effie Woodward *in her*
Comedies for children

"In memoriam" *see* Denton,
Clara Janetta Fort. When the
lessons are over

In nonsense land *see* Denton,
Clara Janetta Fort *in her*
From tots to teens

In office hours. A comedy
sketch in one act *see*
Sutherland, Evelyn Greenleaf
Baker *in her* In office
hours and other sketches for
vaudeville or private acting

In office hours and other
sketches for vaudeville or
private acting *see* Sutherland, Evelyn Greenleaf Baker

In old Kentucky *see* Dazey,
Charles Turner

In quod; or, Courting the
wrong lass. A comedy in two
acts. n.p.: n.pub., n.d.
32p.

In spite of all *see* MacKaye,
James Steele *see also his*
An arrant knave & other
plays

In such a night *see* Fuller,
Henry Blake *in his* Collected works

In the dark *see* Sutphen,
William Gilbert Van Tassel

In the enemy's camp; or,
Stolen despatches *see*
Brown, S. J.

In the fire-light *see*
Heermans, Forbes

In the forest *see* Rosetti,
Joseph

In the god's shadow *see*
Major, George MacDonald

In the morning *see* Denton,
Clara Janetta Fort *in her*
From tots to teens

In the nick of time *see*
Arnold, Alexander Streeter

In the palace of the king
see Kester, Paul *see also*
Stoddard, Lorimer

In the season *see* Mitchell,
Langdon Elwyn

In the toils *see* McIntyre,
John Thomas

In the trenches *see* Chase,
Frank Eugene

In the way; or, Over the cliff
see Hornett, Stephen
Francis

In the wilds of Tennessee *see*
Bixby, Frank L.

In the wrong box *see* Clifton,
Mary A. Delano. The wrong box

In the wrong clothes *see*
Burton, James

In the year ten thousand *see*
Fawcett, Edgar

The Inca's daughter *see*
Crockett, Ingram

Inconstant *see* Shields, Sarah
Annie Frost *in her* Parlor
charades and proverbs

The inconstant; or, The way to
win him *see* Daly, Augustin

An Indian giver *see* Howells,
William Dean

An Indiana man *see* Armstrong,
Le Roy

An Indiana romance *see*
Nugent, John Charles

An indigestible romance *see*
Humphrey, Lewis D. A bachelor's banquet; or, An indigestible romance

The industrious moth; or, The
perplexity of Monsieur Victor
see Knapp, A. Melvin

Inez *see* Malone, Walter

The infanta's dolls *see*
Barker, Theodore T.

The infernal machine *see*
McBride, H. Elliott *in*
Dramatic leaflets *see also*
his Latest dialogues

Ingersoll, Charles, 1805-1882.
Women rule. A comedy in five
acts. Philadelphia: Collins,
1868. 126p.

Ingersoll, Charles Jared,
1782-1862.
Julian. A tragedy in five
acts. Philadelphia: Carey &
Lea, 1831. 87p.

Ingoldsby, Thomas.
Look at the clock *see*
Massey, Charles. Massey's
exhibition reciter.
[*Ingoldsby's real name is*
Richard Harris Barham]

Ingomar, the barbarian. A
play in five acts. (From
the German of Bellinghausen.)
New York: George F.
Nesbitt, 1873. Bilingual text: English
and Italian. 93p. [*title*
page: "by F. Halm." Friedrich
Halm is the pseud. used by
Eligius Franz Joseph, Frei-
herr von Münch-Bellinghausen.
Based on Der Sohn der Wild-
niss by Münch-Bellinghausen;
the Italian title is Il fi-
glio delle selve]

Ingomar the barbarian. (From
the German of Münch-Bellinghausen.) New York: Seer's
Printing Establishment,
1880. Bilingual text: English and Italian. 93p. [*see*
notes above] *see also*
Lovell, Maria Anne Lacy *in*
The modern standard drama,
vol. 12 *see also* Sothern,
Edward Hugh and Marlowe,
Julia

Ingraham, C. F.
The best cure. An Ethiopian
farce in one act. Clyde, O.:
Ames, 1888. 9p. (Ames'
series of standard and minor
drama. no. 253)

Hans Brummel's cafe. An
original farce in one act.
Clyde, O.: Ames, 1889. 6p.
(Ames' series of standard
and minor drama. no. 271)

Jimmie Jones; or, Our hopeful
son. A farce in one act.
Clyde, O.: Ames, 1892. 7p.
(Ames' series of standard
and minor drama. no. 299)

Ingraham, Jean.
The raw recruits; or, A day
with the National Guard. A
military comedy drama in two
acts. Clyde, O.: Ames, 1893.
10p. (Ames' series of standard and minor drama. no. 322)

Ingraham, Joseph Holt, 1809-
1860.
Captain Kyd; or, The wizard
of the sea *see* Jones,
Joseph Stevens

West Point; or, A tale of
treason *see* Breck, Joseph

Initiating a granger *see*
Denison, Thomas Stewart

The Inn of Terracina *see*
Fra-Diavolo; or, The Inn of
Terracina

Innisfail; or, The wanderer's
dream *see* Quinn, Richard

Insect (a charade) *see*
Heywood, Delia A. *in her*
Choice dialogues. no. 1

Instincts of childhood *see*
Neal, John

The insurance agent *see*
Miller, Harry S.

The insurrection *see*
Ricord, Elizabeth Stryker

The insurrection at Harper's
Ferry *see* Swayze, Mrs.
J. C. Ossawattomie Brown;
or, The insurrection at
Harper's Ferry

The intelligence office *see*
Coes, George H. *see also*

Leavitt, Andrew J. and
Eagan, H. W.

Intensity *see* Denison,
Thomas Stewart *in his*
Friday afternoon series of
dialogues

An international match *see*
Daly, Augustin

Interviews; or, Bright Bohemia
see Nobles, Milton

Into the world *see* Waller,
Daniel Wilmarth

An introductory speech *see*
McBride, H. Elliott *in his*
Latest dialogues

The intruder *see* Hovey,
Richard *in his* The plays
of Maurice Maeterlinck
[First series]

The invisible hand *see*
Sadlier, Mary Anne Madden

The invitation *see* Denton,
Clara Janetta Fort *in her*
From tots to teens

Ion *see* Alcott, Louisa May
in her Comic tragedies
see also Talfourd, Thomas
Noon *in* The modern standard drama, vol. 1

Iona: an Indian tragedy *see*
Dana, Eliza A. Fuller

Iphigenia in Tauris *see*
Adler, George J.

Ireland and America; or,
Scenes in both *see* Pil-
grim, James

The Irish agent *see* Moore,
Bernard Francis

Irish assurance and Yankee
modesty *see* Pilgrim, James

The Irish broom-maker; or, A
cure for dumbness *see*
Wood, C. A. F.

Irish equivocation *see*
Venable, William Henry
in his The school stage

Irish inspiration *see* Walsh,
John

The Irish linen peddler *see*
Denison, Thomas Stewart

The Irish lion *see* Stewart,
Silas Sexton *in his* Collected
works. Book of plays

The Irish outlaw *see* Moore,
Bernard Francis. Captain Jack;
or, The Irish outlaw

The Irish squire of Squash Ridge
see Crary, J. E.

The Irish tutor *see* Glengall,
Richard Butler, Earl of
Massey, Charles. Massey's
exhibition reciter

The Irish valet *see* Venable,
William Henry *in his* The
school stage

An Irishman's maneuver *see*
Mack, Robert Ellice *see also*
Mike Donovan's courtship

The iron chest *see* Colman,
George, 1782-1836 *in* The
modern standard drama, vol. 6

The iron hand *see* Townsend,
Charles

The iron master *see* Prichard,
Joseph Vila

Ironquill (pseud.) *see*
Ware, Eugene Fitch

The irony of fate *see* Pidgin,
Charles Felton. Blennerhassett;
or, The irony of fate

Irresistibly impudent *see*
Cahill, Frank *in* Arnold,
George? and Cahill, Frank.
Parlor theatricals; or,
Winter evening's entertain-
ment

Irving, Washington, 1783-1859.
Rip Van Winkle *see* Burke,
Charles *see also* Jefferson,
Joseph and Boucicault, Dion
see also Rauch, Edward H.
Pennsylvania Dutch Rip Van
Winkle *see also* Shannon,
J. W. *see also* Wainwright,
John Howard

Is it too dear? New York:
J. H. and C. M. Goodsell,
1869. 15p. *[translated from
the French of Francisque
Sarcey's Est-ce trop cher?;
F. Sarcey is the pseud. of
Satané Bimet]*

Is lying easy? *see* Wall,
Annie

Is the editor in? *see*
Denison, Thomas Stewart

Isaac; A type of redeemer *see*
Sands, Robert Charles

Isaac's blessing *see* Iliowizi, Henry

Isabella Orsini *see* Williams,
Henry Llewellyn

Isabella Suarez *see* Pray,
Isaac Clarke. Sor Teresa;
or, Isabella Suarez

Isadore *see* Gilman, Caroline
Howard

Isham, Frederic Stewart, 1866-
1922.
The toy shop. A drama for
children. London and New
York: T. H. French, c1891.
12p. (Lacy's acting edition.

vol. 134) *[joint author:
Edward Winfield Weitzel]*

Isoleri, Antonio.
Religion and fatherland; or,
The martyrs of Corea. Phila-
delphia: Press of D. J.
Gallagher, 1887. 53p.

It is never too late to mend
see Reynartz, Dorothy

It is no use to cry over spilt
milk *see* Shields, Sarah
Annie Frost *in her* Parlor
charades and proverbs

It is the law *see* Flewellyn,
Julia Collitan

It never rains but it pours
see Cahill, Frank *in*
Arnold, George? and Cahill,
Frank. Parlor theatricals;
or, Winter evening's entertainment

It passes by *see* Monroe,
Harriet *in her* The passing
show

The Italian bride *see* Levy,
Samuel Yates

The Italian wife *see* Milman,
Henry Hart. Fazio; or, The
Italian wife *in* The modern
standard drama, vol. 1

Italiener, Heinrich.
Der Rattenfänger von Hameln
see Williams, Frederick.
The rat-charmer of Hamelin

Items *see* Fitch, Anna Mariska

It's all in the pay-streak *see*
Denison, Thomas Stewart

Itzel, Adam, 1864-1893.
The tar and the tartar *see*
Smith, Harry Bache

Ives, Alice Emma, d.1930.
The village postmaster. A
domestic drama in four acts.
New York and London: S.
French, c1894. 93p. (French's
standard library edition)
*[joint author: Jerome H.
Eddy]*

The Ivy Queen *see* Gaddess,
Mary L.

Ixion *see* Hubbard, Harvey

J., A. F. *see* Jenks, Almet F.

J., M. E. *see* Jenks, M. E.

J. S. of Dale (pseud.) *see*
Stinson, J. Frederic Jessup

Jack and Gill went up the hill
see Fox, George Washington
Lafayette

Jack and the bean-stalk, the
strange adventures of *see*
Barnet, Robert A.

Jack Cade, the bondsman of
Kent *see* Conrad, Robert
Taylor

Jack Cade, the captain of the
commons *see* Conrad,
Robert Taylor

Jack Sheppard and Joe Blueskin;
or, Amateur road agents *see*
Dumont, Frank

Jack, the commodore's grandson
see Holbrook, Amelia Weed

The Jack trust *see* Furniss,
Grace Livingston

Jack's the lad *see* Griffin,
George W. H.

Jackson, Helen Maria Fiske
Hunt, 1831-1885.
Ramona *see* Dillaye, Ina

Jackson, John Jasper.
A political pull. A comedietta
in one act. Boston: Walter H.
Baker, 1900. 20p.

Jackson, N. Hart.
The bottom of the sea. A
grand spectacular drama in
five acts and a tableaux.
n.p.: n.pub., 1877. Prompt-
book. 31, 20, 27, 32 leaves
(pag. by act.)

The two orphans. A play in
six acts. (From the French of
Adolphe Philippe Dennery and
Eugène Cormon.) New York?:
Printed not published, 187-?
70p. *[based on Les deux
orphelines, by Dennery and
Pierre Étienne Piestre
(pseud. Eugène Cormon.)
Readex has reproduced the
same edition of this play
under three different
entries: N. Hart Jackson,
Kate Claxton Cone Stevenson,
and The two orphans (title
entry)]*

Jacob Busby. Four acts *see*
Tillson, Jesse Paxon *in his*
Collected works

Jacob Shlaff's mistake *see*
Crary, J. E.

Jael and Sisera *see* Ford,
Alfred

Jaëll, Alfred, 1832-1882.
La fille du régiment *see*
Seguin, Arthur Edward
Sheldon. Marie; or, The
daughter of the regiment

The jail bird *see* Townsend,
Charles

Jaimson, George.
The Revolutionary soldier.
A farce in one act. Boston:
William V. Spencer, 1850.
22p. (Spencer's Boston

Theatre. no. 205) [title
page: The Revolutionary
soldiers; or, The old
seventy-sixer]

Jake and Snow see Haskett,
Emmett

James, Charles, d.1901.
Joan of Arc. Washington,
D. C.: Neale, 1899. xii,
64p.

James, Henry (1811-1882), The
household of see Bridges,
Robert in his Overheard
in Arcady

James, Henry, 1843-1916.
The album. In three acts
[From his: Theatricals.
Second series. The album.
The reprobate. New York:
Harper & Bros., 1895]
p.i-xiv, 1-191.

Daisy Miller. A comedy in
three acts. Boston: J. R.
Osgood, 1883. 189p.

Disengaged. In three acts
[From his: Theatricals. Two
comedies. Tenants. Disengaged. London: Osgood, McIl-
vaine, 1894] p.i-iv, 145-
325. see also his Tenants

The reprobate. In three acts
[From his: Theatricals.
Second series. The album.
The reprobate. New York:
Harper & Bros., 1895]
p.i-xiv, 193-416.

Tenants. In three acts
[From his: Theatricals. Two
comedies. Tenants. Disengaged. New York: Harper & Bros.,
1894. 325p.] p.1-13, 4-143.

Jameson, Mrs.
Much coin, much care see
Follen, Eliza Lee Cabot.
Home dramas for young people

Jameson, Frederick, 1839-1916.

Dusk of the gods. New York:
G. Schirmer, 1900. Vocal
score. Bilingual text:
English and German. 340p.
[the vocal score of Wagner's
Die Gotterdämmerung]

The mastersingers of Nuremberg. New York: G. Schirmer,
1903. Vocal score. Bilingual
text: English and German.
569p. [the vocal score of
Wagner's Die Meistersinger
von Nürnberg]

The Rhinegold. New York:
G. Schirmer, c1899. Vocal
score. Bilingual text:
English and German. 221p.
[the vocal score of Wagner's
Das Rheingold]

Siegfried. New York: G.
Schirmer, 1900. Vocal score.
Bilingual text: English and
German. 337p. [the vocal
score of Wagner's Siegfried]

The Valkyrie. New York: G.
Schirmer, c1899. Vocal score.
Bilingual text: English and
German. 305p. [the vocal
score of Wagner's Die Walküre]

Jamieson, Guy Arthur, b.1867.
Prof. James' experience
teaching a country school.
A comedy in three acts.
Clyde, O.: Ames, 1889. 15p.
(Ames' series of standard
and minor drama. no. 264)

Jane Shore see Rowe,
Nicholas in The modern
standard drama, vol. 12

Jane the orphan. By Th. Xr. K.
(From the French of Guyet.)
St. Louis: P. Fox, 1878. 58p.
[Readex gives the author,
incorrectly, as Xr. Th. K.;
based on J. A. Guyet's
Jeanne l'orpheline]

Jane's legacy see Brewster,
Emma E. in her Parlor
varieties

Janet, the flower girl *see*
Mullen, Nicholas

Janice Meredith *see* Rose,
Edward Everett and Ford,
Paul Leicester

The Japanese girl (O Hanu San)
see Rosse, Jeanie Quinton

The Japanese wedding *see*
Scudder, Vida Dutton and
Brooks, F. M. Mitsu-yu-
nissi; or, The Japanese
wedding

Jaquith, Mrs. M. H.
The "Deestrick Skule" of
fifty years ago. Chicago:
Dramatic Pub. Co., c1888.
37p.

"Exerbition"; or, The
Deestrick Skule of fifty
years ago. (Sequel to "The
Deestrick Skule.") Chicago:
Dramatic Pub. Co., c1890.
50p.

Ma Dusenberry and her gearls.
Chicago: Dramatic Pub. Co.,
c1896. 12p.

Parson Poor's donation party.
Burlesque entertainment in
two scenes. Chicago: Dramatic Pub. Co., c1896. p.31-
49. (Sergel's acting drama.
no. 441)

Jarosy, Rudolf.
Im Schneegestöber *see*
Morse, Mabel. A warm
reception

Jasmin, Jacques, 1798-1864.
L'aveugle de Castel-Culier
see Morton, Marguerite W.
The blind girl of Castèl-
Cuillè *see also* Thompson,
Caroline Eunice. Blind
Margaret

The jealous husband *see*
Kobbé, Gustav *see also his*

Plays for amateurs *see also*
White, Charles

The jealous wife *see* Colman,
George *in* The modern
standard drama, vol. 4

Jealousy *see* Daly, Augustin.
Griffith Gaunt; or, Jealousy

Jean Valjean; or, The shadow
of the law *see* Fulton,
Harry Clifford

Jeanie Deans; or, The heart of
Mid-Lothian *see* Pilgrim,
James

Jedediah Judkins, J. P. *see*
Brier, Warren Judson

Jeemes the poet *see* Leavitt,
Andrew J. and Eagan, H. W.

Jefferson, Joseph, 1829-1905.
Rip Van Winkle. As played by
Joseph Jefferson. New York:
Dodd, Mead, 1895. 199p.
*[joint author: Dion Bouci-
cault; based on Washington
Irving's Rip Van Winkle]*

The rivals. (By R. B.
Sheridan.) n.p.: n.pub.,
18-? Typescript, prompt-
book with Ms. notes. 7, 20,
41, 33 leaves. (Title page
lacking)

Jeffries, L. Q.
Tim M'Quain's bother. Elk
Point, D. T.: W. M. K. Cain,
1875. 17p.

Jenks, Almet F.
Robinson Crusoe. An operetta
in two acts. Words by A. F. J.
Music by M. E. J. Brooklyn:
n.pub., 1883. Title page
lacking. 38p. Libretto.
[without the music]

Jenks, M. E.
Robinson Crusoe *see* Jenks,
Almet F.

Jephtha *see* Hewitt, John Hill

Jephthah's daughter *see*
Boxer, James *in his* Sacred
dramas *see also* Cantell,
Lilia Mackay

Jerrold, Douglas William,
1803-1857.
The catspaw *see* The
modern standard drama, vol.
11

The rent-day *see* The
modern standard drama, vol. 4

Jervey, Caroline Howard *see*
Jervey, Mrs. Lewis

Jervey, Mrs. Lewis.
The lost children. A musical
entertainment in five acts.
Boston: H. Spencer, c1870.
30p. Libretto. (Plays for
children. no. 1) *[Mrs. Lewis
Jervey actually is Caroline
Howard Jervey]*

Jessie Linden *see* Benedict,
Frank Lee *in his* The
shadow worshiper

Jessop, George Henry, d.1915.
Edmund Kean; or, The life
of an actor. By Alexandre
Dumas. The English adaptation
of G. H. Jessop and J. St.
Maur...Washington?: n.pub.,
1881. 24p. *[based on Dumas'
Kean; ou, Désordre et génie]*

A gold mine *see* Matthews,
Brander and Jessop, George
Henry

On probation *see* Matthews,
Brander and Jessop, George
Henry

Sam'l of Posen; or, The last
commercial drummer. A comedy-
drama in three acts. [From:
America's lost plays. vol. 4.
Princeton, N. J.: Princeton
Univ. Press, 1940] p.149-185.
[earlier copyright: 1880]

Shamus O'Brien. A romantic
comic opera in two acts.
London and New York: Boosey,
c1896. Vocal score. 183p.
*[based on the poem Le Fanu
by Joseph Sheridan; music
by Charles Villers Stanford]*

The Jesuit in America. A drama
in three acts *see* Fowle,
William Bentley *in his*
Parlor dramas

The Jesuit; or, The amours of
Capt. Effingham and the Lady
Zarifa *see* Whitley, Thomas
W.

The Jewess. A romantic drama
in three acts. (Adapted from
Moncrieff's The Jewess.)
Boston: Boston Museum, 1858.
Prompt-book, interleaved with
Ms. notes. 54p. (Duncombe's
edition) *[title page: The
Jewess; or, The Council of
Constance]*

The Jewish captives *see*
Leavitt, John McDowell

Jim Crow *see* White, Charles.
The live injin; or, Jim Crow

Jimmie Jones; or, Our hopeful
son *see* Ingraham, C. F.

Jimmy the newsboy *see* Parker,
Walter Coleman

"Jo" (pseud.) *see* Alcott,
Louisa May. Comic tragedies

Joan of Arc. A tragedy in five
acts. (From the French of
Soumet.) New York: Darcie &
Corbyn, 1855. Bilingual text:
French and English. 36p.
*[based on the French of
Alexandre Soumet] see also*
James, Charles *see also*
Opal (pseud.) *in her* The
cloud of witnesses

Job and his children   *see*
Field, Joseph M.

Joe, a comedy of child life
see Barnard, Charles

Joe Ruggles; or, The girl
miner *see* Dean, Frank J.

Joe Simpson's double *see*
Reid, Charles S.

Joe, the waif; or, The pet
of the camp *see* Cutler,
F. L.

Joe's way of doing chores *see*
Denton, Clara Janetta Fort
in her When the lessons are
over

Johanes Blatz's mistake; or,
The two elopments *see*
Crary, J. E.

Johannes *see* Harned, Mary
and Harned, W. H.

John Allen and Ira Perkins
see Greenly, William Jay
in his The three drunks

John Brown and the heroes of
Harper's Ferry *see*
Channing, William Ellery

John Bull in America *see*
Griffin, George W. H. and
Christy, George. The Fenian
spy; or, John Bulls [sic,
Bull] in America

John Delmer's daughters *see*
De Mille, Henry Churchill

John Endicott *see* Longfellow,
Henry Wadsworth *in his*
Christus

John Park and Dr. Dott's
doings *see* Lesaulnier,
Louis

John Smith-Sydney Smith *see*
Townsend, Frederic *in his*
Spiritual visitors

John the almoner *see* Opal
(pseud.) *in her* The cloud
of witnesses

Johnny, you've been a bad boy
see Don't get weary; or,
Johnny, you've been a bad
boy *see also* Gentlemen
coon's parade...and Don't
get weary; or, Johnny, you've
been a bad boy

Johns, George Sibley, b.1857.
David Laroque. Domestic
drama in four acts. St. Louis:
n.pub., c1897. 28p.

Johnson, Edwin, b.1836.
The mouth of gold. A series
of dramatic sketches illustrating the life and times
of Chrysostom. New York:
A. S. Barnes, 1873. 109p.

Johnson, Fannie M.
Dotage *see* Bartlett, George
Bradford. A dream of the
centuries and other entertainments for parlor and hall

Johnson, Samuel D., 1813-1863.
Brian O'Linn. A farce in two
acts. New York: S. French,
18-? 16p. (French's American
drama. Acting edition. no.
63) *[Readex also enters this
play under title]*

The fireman. A drama in three
acts. New York: S. French,
1856. 36p. (French's standard
drama. no. 263)

In and out of place. A burletta in one act. New York:
S. French, 1856. Prompt-
book. 13p. (The minor drama.
no. 107)

Our gal. A farce in one act.
New York: S. French, c1856.
9p. (The minor drama. no. 78)

The Shaker lovers. A drama
in one act. New York: S.
French, 1857? 10p. (French's
minor drama. no. 255)

Joining the Tinpanites; or,
Paddy McFling's experience
see Hildreth, David W.

The joke on Squinim see
Sheddan, W. B.

Jolly, Alphonse (pseud.)
[Under a spell] see
Gibbs, Julia De Witt [Jolly
is a pseud. for Alphonse
Leveaux]

Jolly Joe's lady minstrels
see Silsbee, Alice M. and
Horne, Mary Barnard

The jolly millers see White,
Charles

The jolly tramp see Rawley,
Bert C. Our summer boarder's
[sic]; or, The jolly tramp

Jonathan in England see
Wright, J. B.

Jones, François Stewart.
Uriel Acosta see Hovey,
Richard and Jones, François
Stewart

Jones, George, 1810-1879.
The evil eye see Phillips,
Jonas B.

Tecumseh and the prophet of
the west. An historical
Israel-Indian tragedy in
five acts [From his: Tecumseh
...with a life of General
Harrison...and the first
oration...London: Longman,
Brown, Green & Longmans,
1844. 242p.] p.1-113. [the
"first oration upon the life
...of Shakespeare" noted in
Readex's main entry (above)
is not reproduced on the

Readex microprint, but "Historical and biographical
notes illustrative of the
tragedy of Tecumseh," which
Readex does not mention in
its main entry, has been
reproduced]

Jones, Gertrude Manly.
Miss Matilda's school. A
comic operetta for boys and
girls. Boston: W. H. Baker,
c1892. 12p. (Baker's edition
of plays)

Jones, Henry Arthur, 1851-1929.
Harmony see The organist

Jones, Joseph Stevens, 1811-
1877.
Captain Kyd; or, The wizard
of the sea. A drama in four
acts. Boston: W. V. Spencer,
18--. Prompt-book. 44p.
(Spencer's Boston theatre.
no. 6) [based on Joseph Holt
Ingraham's work of the same
title]

The carpenter and his apprentice; or, The secret order of
the Confrierie see his
Carpenter of Rouen (scene)
in Steele, Silas Sexton.
Collected works. Book of plays

The carpenter of Rouen; or,
The massacre of St. Bartholomew. A romantic drama in four
parts. New York: S. French,
18--? Prompt-book. 32p.
(French's American drama.
Acting edition. no. 35)

The Green Mountain boy. A
comedy in two acts. New York:
S. French, 1860. 29p.
(French's minor drama. The
acting edition. no. 278)

Moll Pitcher; or, The fortune
teller of Lynn. A drama in
four acts. New York: S.
French, (pref. 1855.) 64p.
(French's standard drama.
no. 232)

The people's lawyer. A comedy
in two acts. Boston: William
V. Spencer, 1856. Prompt-
book. 36p. (Spencer's Boston
theatre. New series. no. 32)
*[also published under the
title Solon Shingle]*

The silver spoon. A character
sketch in four parts. (Revised and reconstructed.)
Boston: W. H. Baker, 1911.
65p. (The William Warren
edition of standard plays)
*[the introduction to this
play gives Jones' birth date
as 1809; the first performance date is 1852, based on
the preface to Jones' Usur-
per]*

Solon Shingle; or, The
people's lawyer. A comedy
in two acts. Boston: W. H.
Baker, 1890. 32p. (Baker's
edition of plays) *[also
published under the title
The people's lawyer]*

The surgeon of Paris. An
historical drama in four
acts. Boston: W. V. Spencer,
1856. 41p. (Spencer's Boston
theatre, no. 36)

The surgeon of Paris; or,
The massacre of St. Bar-
tholomew. An historical
drama in four acts. London:
Dicks, 1886. 18p.

The usurper; or, Americans
in Tripoli. Boston: n.pub.,
1842. Prompt-book in Ms.
67p.

The usurper; or, The Americans in Tripoli [From:
Metamora and other plays.
By E. R. Page, editor.
Princeton, N. J.: Princeton
Univ. Press, 1941. 399p.]
p.143-174. (America's lost
plays. vol. 14) *[earlier
copyright: 1835? or 1841,
according to the preface]*

Jones, Major (pseud.) *see*
Thompson, William Tappan

Jones, R.?
Wacousta; or, The curse.
A romantic military drama in
four acts. n.p.: n.pub.,
1851. Prompt-book in Ms.
29, 19, 5, 18 leaves. *[based
on John Richardson's Wacousta;
a tale of the Pontiac conspiracy, later revised under
the title Wacousta; or, The
prophecy]*

Jones, Robert.
The hidden hand. A drama in
five acts. (From Mrs. Emma D.
E. N. Southworth's novel of
the same name.) Boston:
W. H. Baker, c1889. 45p.
(Baker's edition of plays)

Jones vs. Johnson *see*
Lindsley, Philip. The humor
of the court room; or, Jones
vs. Johnson

Jordon, Clifton E.
Hazel Adams. A drama in three
acts. Clyde, O.: Ames, c1897.
28p. (Ames' edition of plays.
no. 386)

Joseph, Delissa.
The blue-stocking. A comedietta in one act. Chicago:
Dramatic Pub. Co., c1884.
6p. (Sergel's acting drama.
no. 532)

Joseph *see* Iliowizi, Henry

Joseph and his brethren, the
Hebrew son; or, Child of
Babylon. New York: n.pub.,
1860. Prompt-book in Ms.
In three acts plus sides for
two parts (pag. by act.)

Joseph in bondage *see* Staples,
H. A.

Joseph in Egypt *see* Crippen,
Thomas George

Josephine *see* Nash, Joseph

Josh Winchester; or, Between
love and duty *see* Rode-
baugh, T. Wilson

Joshua Blodgett, from Blodgett's Holler *see* McFall,
B. G.

Josiah Allen's wife (pseud.)
see Holley, Marietta

Josiah's courtship *see*
Dale, Horace C.

Josselyn, Robert, 1810-1884.
The coquette. A domestic
drama in five acts. Austin,
Texas: The author, 1878. 54p.

Jouy, Victor Joseph Étienne,
1764-1846.
Mosé in Egitto *see* Parker,
George S. Moses in Egypt
see also Ponte, Lorenzo
da. Moses in Egypt *see*
also Villarino, Jose J.
Moses in Egypt

Juan Ponce de Leon and Barto-
lomé de las casas *see*
Larremore, Wilbur

Judas *see* Hall, John Lesslie

Judas Maccabaeus *see* Mendes,
Henry Pereira

Judd, Sylvester, 1813-1853.
Philo: an evangelist. Boston:
Phillips, Sampson, 1850.
244p.

The judge *see* Hale, Sarah
Josepha Buell

A judge by proxy *see* Moore,
Bernard Francis

Julian, Robert.
Burglars. A comedy sketch in
one scene. Chicago: Dramatic
Pub. Co., c1896. 9p. (Sergel's acting drama. no. 446)

Will you marry me? A farce in
one act. Chicago: Dramatic
Pub. Co., c1896. 12p. (Sergel's acting drama. no. 450)

Julian *see* Brown, John Henry
see also Hepburn, I. P. *see*
also Ingersoll, Charles
Jared

Julietta Gordini, the miser's
daughter *see* Pray, Isaac
Clarke

Julius Caesar *see* Shakespeare,
William *in* Booth, Edwin.
The Shakespearean plays of
Edwin Booth *see also*
Shakespeare, William *in*
The modern standard drama,
vol. 11 *see also* Shake-
speare's...Julius Caesar
see also Willard, Edward

Julius Caesar-Zachary Taylor
see Townsend, Frederic *in*
his Spiritual visitors

Julius the snoozer; or, The
conspirators of Thompson
Street *see* White, Charles

Jumbo-Jum! An original farce
in one act. New York, London:
S. French, 185-? 16p.
(French's minor drama. The
acting edition. no. 243)

Jupiter; or, The cobbler and
the king *see* Smith, Harry
Bache

Jurgium Geminorum; or, Rumpus
Romali Remique *see* Grinnell,
Charles Edward

"Just for fun" *see* Crane,
Eleanor Maud

The justice of Tacon *see*
Ballou, Maturin Murray.
Miralda; or, The justice
of Tacon

K., Th. Xr. *see* Jane the orphan

Kadelburg, Gustav, 1851-1925.
[The great unknown] *see* Daly, Augustin
[The railroad of love] *see* Daly, Augustin
[A test case; or, Grass versus granite] *see* Daly, Augustin
[When I come back] *see* Blumenthal, Oscar and Kadelburg, Gustav

Kaler, James Otis, 1848-1912.
A case for divorce. As told by the maiden lady across the way. Chicago and New York: Dramatic Pub. Co., c1877. 49p. *[based on Le procès Veauradieux by Alfred Charlemagne Lartigue Delacour and Alfred Hennequin and on Le premier coup de canif by Auguste Anicet-Bourgeois]*
A devil of a scrape; or, Who paid for the supper. Providence, R. I.: n.pub., 1878. Prompt-book interleaved. 34p.

The Kansas bandit; or, The fall of Ingalls *see* Ware, Eugene Fitch

The Kansas immigrants; or, The great exodus *see* Denison, Thomas Stewart

Karr, Jean-Alphonse, 1808-1890.
[The betrothed; or, Love in death] *see* Sharswood, William

Kastelic, George Anton.
Thirty hours for three thousand years; or, Heresy and planets. Comedy-drama in five acts. New York:

n.pub., c1892. 47p.

Kate McDonald *see* Lucas, Daniel Bedinger *in his* Collected works

Kate's infatuation *see* Shields, Lottie

Katharine *see* Bangs, John Kendrick

Katharine and Petruchio *see* Shakespeare, William *in* Booth, Edwin. The Shakespearean plays of Edwin Booth

Kathleen Mavourneen; or, St. Patrick's Eve. A domestic Irish drama in four acts. New York, London: S. French, 187-? 32p. (French's standard drama. no. 352)

Kathleen O'Neil *see* Roberts, T. W.

Kathleen O'Neil; or, A picture of feudal times in Ireland *see* Pepper, George

Kathleen's honor *see* White, George

Katie's deception; or, The troublesome kid *see* Bennett, W. L.

Katrina's little game *see* Brown, J. H.

Katty O'Sheal *see* Pilgrim, James

Kavanaugh, Mrs. Russell.
Original dramas, dialogues... Louisville, Ky.: John P. Morton, 1884. 252p.
Contents: The wreath of virtue.--Cinderella, or the glass slipper.--Beauty and the beast.--The tattler.--The aunt's legacy.--Pre-

position vs. proposition.--
The mechanic's daughter (for
mixed schools.)--The mechanic's daughter (for girls
alone.)--The spelling lesson.
--The pea-green glazed
cambric.--The elopement.--
Mrs. Vatican Smythe's party.
--The perfection of beauty.
--The old man's pocket-book.
--Araminta Jenkins.--The
dancing Dutchman.--The Relief
Aid Sewing Society, or Mrs.
Jones's vow.--Health vs.
riches.--The minister's
guests.--Marrying a fortune.
[the "Declamations," "May-
Queen Celebration," "American Oratory," and "Tableaux
vivans" have not been
individually analyzed]

Keatinge, Ella.
The legend of the Christmas
tree. A play for children
in three acts. Chicago and
New York: Dramatic Pub. Co.,
c1899. 12p.

The nightingale and the lark.
Chicago: Dramatic Pub. Co.,
c1899. 9p.

The old trunk in the garret.
A play for children in two
acts. By Ella Keatings [sic]
Chicago and New York: Dramatic Pub. Co., c1899. 7p.

Short plays for children...
New York: Roxbury Pub. Co.,
c1899. 16p.
Contents: The little
magician.--The sick doll.--
The nightingale and the lark.
--A Christmas eve adventure.

A white lie. A comedy in
two acts. Chicago and New
York: Dramatic Pub. Co.,
c1899. 12p. (Sergel's acting
drama. no. 455)

Keatings, Ella see Keatinge,
Ella

Kedney, John Steinfort, 1819-
1911.
Love and astronomy [From:
Catawba River, and other
poems. By John Steinfort
Kidney [sic] New York: Baker
and Scribner, 1847. 119p.]
p.32-38.

Keep the holidays see Denton,
Clara Janetta Fort in her
From tots to teens

Keeping the cold out see
The temperance school dialogues

Keeping up appearances see
Heywood, Delia A. in her
Choice dialogues. no. 1

Kelley, Edgar Stillman, 1857-
1944.
The tragedy of Macbeth. San
Francisco: C. A. Murdock,
1885. viii, 78p. [title
page: The tragedy of Macbeth
by William Shakespeare with
original music by Edgar S.
Kelley]

Kellogg, Clara Louise, 1842-
1916.
The Bohemian girl. Opera in
three acts. By A. Bunn.
Revised and adapted by Miss
Clara Louise Kellogg. Baltimore: Sun Printing Establishment, 1874. 39p. Libretto.
[music by Michael William
Balfe; without the music]

Faust. Grand opera in a
prologue and four acts.
Baltimore: Sun Printing
Establishment, 1874. 33
leaves. [music by Charles-
François Gounod; libretto
by Jules Barbier and Michel
Carré; originally based on
Goethe's Faust]

The Huguenots. Grand opera
in five acts by Meyerbeer.

(From the French of Scribe
and Deschamps.) Baltimore:
Sun Printing Establishment,
c1875. 35p. Libretto.
[without the music]

The star of the north. Opera
in three acts by G. Meyerbeer. Baltimore: Sun Printing
Establishment, c1876. 48p.
Libretto. *[based on L'étoile
du nord by Augustin Eugène
Scribe]*

Kellogg, E.
Sparticus to the gladiators
at Capua *see* Massey,
Charles. Massey's exhibition
reciter

Kelly, Michael, 1764?-1826.
The forty thieves *see*
Forty thieves

Kelly, Thomas J. F.
Henry IV of Germany. A
tragedy in five acts. New
York: Osborn & Buckingham,
1835. 85p. *[Readex also
enters this play under
title]*

Kemble, Mrs. Charles *see*
Kemble, Marie Thérèse De
Camp

Kemble, John Philip, 1751-1832.
Hamlet *see* Shakespeare,
William *in* The modern
standard drama, vol. 3

Kemble, Marie Thérèse De Camp,
1774-1838.
The day after the wedding
see The modern standard
drama, vol. 5

Fairly taken in *see*
Steele, Silas Sexton. Collected works. Book of plays

Taken in and done for *see*
Beadle's...dialogues no. 2

Kenilworth; or, Amy's aims and

Leicester's lesson *see*
McMichael, Clayton Fotterall

Kennedy, John Pendleton, 1795-
1870.
Rob of the bowl *see* Adams,
Charles Frederick. Rob, the
hermit; or, The black chapel
of Maryland

Kenney, James, 1780-1849.
Sweethearts and wives *see*
The modern standard drama,
vol. 10

The Kentuckian; or, A trip to
New York *see* Paulding,
James Kirke. The lion of
the West

Kerker, Gustave Adolph, 1857-
1923.
The belle of New York *see*
McLellan, Charles Morton
Stewart

Fleur-de-thé *see* Byrne,
Charles Alfred. Pearl of
Pekin; or, The dashing tar
outwitted by his wife

The girl from up there *see*
McLellan, Charles Morton
Stewart

The kernel of corn *see*
Phelps, Lavinia Howe *in her*
Dramatic stories

The Kerry Gow *see* Silver,
W. A.

Kesiah and the scout *see*
Woodward, T. Trask. The
veteran of 1812; or, Kesiah
and the scout

Kester, Paul, 1870-1933.
In the palace of the king.
n.p.: n.pub., 1900? Type-
script, prompt-book. In five
acts. *[based on In the palace
of the king by Francis Marion
Crawford; though there is
much similarity, this is a*

different play from that of
the same title by Lorimer
Stoddard]

Keteltas, Caroline M.
The last of the Plantagenets.
A tragic drama in three acts.
New York: R. Craighead, 1844.
56p. [based on the novel of
the same title by William
Heseltine]

Kettell, Samuel, 1800-1855.
The two moschetoes. A medley
[From his: Yankee notions...
By Timo. Titterwell, Esq.
(pseud.) Boston: Otis
Broaders, 1838. 255p.]
p.242-255.

A kettle of fish. A farcical
comedy in three acts. (From
the German of Schönthan.)
Boston: W. H. Baker, c1890.
53p. (Baker's edition of
plays) [based on Franz von
Schönthan's Der Schwaben-
streich]

Keyes, Frederick J.
A life poem [From his: A life
poem and other poems. Boston:
Phillips, Sampson, 1855.
118p.] p.11-94.

Kidder, Jerome.
The drama of earth. New York:
A. Ranney, 1857. 360p.

Kidder, Kathryn (supposed
author)
The heart of her husband.
A domestic drama in three
acts and two scenes. New
York?: n.pub., 187-? Typescript, prompt-book with Ms.
notes. 40, 62, 21 leaves.

The kidnapped clergyman; or,
Experience the best teacher.
Boston: Dow & Jackson, 1839.
123p.

Kidney, John Steinfort see
Kedney, John Steinfort

Killing time. A farce in one
act. Clyde, O.: Ames, 1880?
9p. (Ames' series of standard
and minor drama. no. 82)
[title page: "From the French"]

Killing two birds with one stone
see Shields, Sarah Annie Frost
in her Parlor charades and
proverbs

Kilpatrick, Hugh Judson, 1836-
1881.
Allatoona. An historical and
military drama in five acts.
New York: S. French, c1875.
48p. (French's standard drama.
no. 376) [joint author: J.
Owen Moore]

Kimball, George M., b.1866.
Disinherited. n.p.: n.pub.,
189-? Prompt-book in Ms.
111p. Title page lacking.
[imperfect copy: all pages
after p.111 lacking]

Kimball, Hannah Parker, b.1861.
Merlin revivified and the
hermit. Boston: Poet-Lore,
1900. (vol. 12, no. 4) p.537-
540.

Victory [From her: Victory
and other verses. Boston:
Copeland and Day, 1897. 76p.]
p.1-12.

Kim-Ka; or, The misfortunes of
Ventilator see Ravel,
Jerome

Kind, Friedrich, 1768-1843.
Der Freischütz see Burk-
hardt, Charles B. see also
Der Freischütz see also
Macy, James Cartwright

Kindness softens even savage
hearts see Heywood, Delia
A. in her Choice dialogues.
no. 1

King, Richard Ashe see
Basil (pseud.)

King Alfred *see* Van Rensselaer, Henry and Stanton,
William J.

King Darnley *see* Campbell,
Lorne J.

King Friedrich Wilhelm First.
The story of the youth of
Frederick the Great. n.p.:
n.pub., 18-. Typescript,
prompt-book with Ms. notes.
37, 10, 17, 18, 26, 13
leaves.

King Henry IV, Part I *see*
Shakespeare, William *in*
The modern standard drama,
vol. 10

King Henry V *see* Mansfield,
Richard

King Henry VIII *see* Shakespeare, William *in* The
modern standard drama, vol.
10

King John *see* Shakespeare,
William *in* The modern
standard drama, vol. 5

King Lear *see* Forrest, Edwin
see also Mayo, Frank *see
also* Shakespeare, William
in The Shakespearean plays
of Edwin Booth *see also*
Shakespeare, William *in*
The modern standard drama,
vol. 9 *see also* Shake-
speare's...King Lear *see
also* Sothern, Edward Hugh

The King of Angelo *see*
Louisville Literary Brass
Band

The king of the beavers *see*
Scribble, Sam (pseud.)

The king of the commons *see*
White, James *in* The
modern standard drama, vol. 4

King Philip *see* Caverly,
Robert Boodey

King Richard III *see* Hinton,
Henry L. *see also* Mansfield,
Richard

King Saul *see* Brooks, Byron
Alden

King winter's carnival *see*
Alexander, Sigmund Bowman

A king's daughter *see* Baker,
Rachel E.

The king's jester *see* Dugan,
Caro Atherton *in her*
Collected works

The king's judges *see* Grimm,
Edward

A king's love *see* Piatt, Donn
in his Various dramatic
works

The king's mistress *see*
Révoil, Bénèdict Henry. La
favorite (The king's mistress)

The king's stratagem; or, The
pearl of Poland *see* Lewis,
Estelle Anna Blanche Robinson

Kingsley, Charles, 1819-1875.
Hypatia *see* Bowers, Eliza-
beth. The black agate; or,
Old foes with new faces

Kinnaman, C. F.
Arrah de Baugh. A drama in
five acts. Clyde, O.: Ames,
18-? 28p. (Ames' series of
standard and minor drama.
no. 43)

In a spider's web. Musical
farce comedy in three acts.
By Mr. and Mrs. Kinnaman.
Clyde, O.: Ames, c1900. 33p.
(Ames' series of standard and
minor drama. no. 421) *[with-
out the music]*

Kinnaman, Mrs. C. F.
In a spider's web *see*
Kinnaman, C. F.

Kinney, Elizabeth Clementine
Dodge, 1810-1889.
Bianca Cappello. A tragedy.
New York: Hurd and Houghton,
1873. 146p.

Kipling, Rudyard, 1865-1936.
The household of Rudyard
Kipling *see* Bridges,
Robert *in his* Overheard
in Arcady

Kiralfy, Imre, 1845-1919.
Grand historical spectacular
[sic, spectacle] masterpiece
America. In four acts and
seventeen scenes. Chicago:
I. Kiralfy, c1893. 36p.
[music by Angelo Venanzi;
words of songs written by
F. Rossi; without the music]

Kirschbaum, Edward T. *see*
Cherrytree, Herr (pseud.)

A kiss in the dark *see*
Steele, Silas Sexton *in his*
Collected works. Book of
plays

Kissing the wrong girl *see*
Parker, Walter Coleman

Kitchel, Mrs. Francis W.
The wager. A comedy dia-
logue. New York: Edgar S.
Werner, 1894. 8p.

The kite paper *see* Abbott,
Jacob *in his* Orkney the
peacemaker; or, The various
ways of settling disputes

Kittie's wedding cake *see*
Zediker, N.

Kitty *see* Young, Margaret

Kitty and Patsy; or, The same
thing over again *see*

Cutler, F. L.

Knapp, A. Melvin.
The industrious moth; or, The
perplexity of Monsieur Victor.
A comedy in three acts. New
York: For private circulation,
1871. 39p. *[title page: "From*
the French"]

Mardoche. A drama in five acts.
New York: For private circula-
tion, 1871. 48p. *[based on*
Mardoche by Alfred de Musset]

Knapp, Lizzie Margaret.
An afternoon rehearsal. A
comedy in one act for female
characters only. Boston:
Walter H. Baker, c1892. 14p.
(Baker's edition of plays)

The knave of hearts *see*
Lee, Albert

Knaves and fools *see* Schindler,
Anthony J.

The Knickerbockers *see* Smith,
Harry Bache

A knight of the quill *see*
Mathews, Frances Aymar

Knighthood *see* Shields, Sarah
Annie Frost *in her* Parlor
charades and proverbs

The knights of the cross. A
sacred drama in three acts.
By a Franciscan Brother.
New York: P. O'Shea, 1876. 36p.

Knortz, Karl, 1841-1918.
[Little snow white. A melo-
drama] *see* Venable, William
Henry. The school stage

Knowles, James Sheridan, 1784-
1862.
The bridal *see* The modern
standard drama, vol. 6

The hunchback *see* Daly,
Augustin *see also* The

modern standard drama, vol. 2

Love *see* The modern
standard drama, vol. 9

The love-chase *see* The
modern standard drama, vol. 3

Virginius *see* McCullough,
John *see also* The modern
standard drama, vol. 4

The wife *see* The modern
standard drama, vol. 1

William Tell *see* The
modern standard drama, vol. 5

Knox, John Armoy, 1851-1906.
The false prophet. A comic
opera in three acts. (Music
by Robert Stoepel.) New
York: n.pub., c1887. 58p.
Libretto. *[joint author:*
Charles McCoy Snyder; music
by Robert August Stoepel;
without the music]

Kobbé, Gustav, 1857-1918.
The jealous husband. A farce
in one act. New York: Dick &
Fitzgerald, c1892. 17p.

Loving yet hating. A comedy
in two acts. New York: Dick &
Fitzgerald, c1892. 28p.

The memory of a song. A
comedy in two acts. New York:
Dick & Fitzgerald, c1892.
19p.

Plays for amateurs. New York:
Harold Roorbach, c1892. 102p.
Contents: Wanted--a nurse.
--Two belles to a beau; or,
The leap-year proposal.--
The jealous husband.--The
memory of a song.--Loving
yet hating.

Two belles to a beau; or,
The leap-year proposal. A
society burlesque in one
act. New York: Dick & Fitzgerald, c1892. 14p.

Wanted--a nurse. A farce in

one act. New York: Dick &
Fitzgerald, c1892. p.6-21.

Kochersperger, John E.
The betrothal *see* Fox,
H. K.

Königsmark *see* Boker, George
Henry

Kohn von Kohlenegg, Leonhard,
1834-1875.
Die schöne Galathea *see*
Day, Willard Gibson. The
lovely Galatea

Koopman, Harry Lyman, 1860-1937.
Orestes; or, The avenger
[From his: Orestes, a dramatic
sketch, and other poems.
Buffalo, N. Y.: Moulton, Wen-
borne, 1888] p.7-27.

Woman's will. A love-play in
five acts [From his: Woman's
will...with other poems.
Buffalo, N. Y.: Moulton,
Wenborne, 1888. 63p.] p.1-60.

The Koreans; or, The ancestors
of King-Ki-Too *see* Cook,
Charles Emerson

Kotzebue, August Friedrich
Ferdinand von, 1761-1819.
Menschenhass und Reue *see*
his The stranger *in* The
modern standard drama, vol. 2

Die Quäker *see* Arthur,
Robert. The Quakers

Die Spanier in Peru *see*
Sheridan, Richard Brinsley
Butler. Pizarro *in* The
modern standard drama, vol. 3

Der Taubstumme *see* The lost
heir; or, The abbé de L'Épée

Koven, Joseph.
Melmoth, the wanderer *see*
Davidson, Gustav and Koven,
Joseph

Koven, Reginald De *see*
DeKoven, Reginald

The Ku Klux Klan; or, The
carpet-bagger in New Orleans
see Meriwether, Elizabeth
Avery

L., T. *see* Olivette

An L. A. W. rest *see* Scott,
W. Atkins

La Beaumelle, Laurent Angliviel de, 1726-1773.
Le peintre de son deshonneur
see Payne, John Howard. The
Spanish husband; or, First
and last love

Labiche, Eugène Marin, 1815-
1888.
Le baron de Fourchevif *see*
Gibbs, Julia De Witt. Under
a spell

La cagnotte *see* Fuller,
Horace Williams. A red
letter day

Les deux timides *see*
Magnus, Julian. A trumped
suit *see also in* Matthews,
Brander. Comedies for amateur acting

Les petits oiseaux *see*
Fuller, Horace Williams.
Bad advice

La poudre aux yeux *see*
Fuller, Horace Williams.
False pretentions

Labor is honorable *see*
Heywood, Delia A. *in*
Choice dialogues. no. 1

La Bree, Lawrence.
Ebenezer Venture; or, Adver-
tising for a wife. A farce
in one act. New York: S.
French, 1841? Prompt-book.
18p. (The minor drama.
The acting edition. no. 174)
[Readex incorrectly gives

*the series number as 74; 174
actually is correct]*

Labrunie, Gérard *see* Gérard
de Nerval (pseud.)

Lacey, -----
Appeal on behalf of Greece
see Massey, Charles. Massey's
exhibition reciter

Lachaume, Aimé, b.1871.
Die versunkene Glocke *see*
Meltzer, Charles Henry. The
sunken bell

Lacon (pseud.)
The devil in America. A
dramatic satire. Philadelphia:
J. B. Lippincott, 1860. 225p.
*[The Library of Congress
notes that R. S. Gladney is
the supposed author of this
title because of an advertisement appearing on the
final page: "Aberdeen (Miss)
female college" signed, Rev.
R. S. Gladney, M. A."]*

Lacy, Ernest, 1863-1916.
Chatteron [From his: Plays
and sonnets. Philadelphia:
Sherman, 1900. 237p.] p.1-7,
2-28. *[the majority of biographical sources consulted
give 1916 as Lacy's year of
death, whereas Readex uses
1915]*

Rinaldo, the doctor of
Florence [From his: Plays and
sonnets. Philadelphia: Sherman, 1900. 237p.] p.1-6,
30-174.

Lacy, Maria *see* Lovell,
Mrs. G. W.

Lacy, Michael Rophino, 1795-
1867.
Fra Diavolo *see* Fra-Diavolo;
or, The Inn of Terracina

The two friends *see* The
modern standard drama, vol. 12

The ladies of Cranford. A
sketch of English village
life 50 years ago *see*
Horne, Mary Barnard

The ladies' privilege *see*
Buckstone, John Baldwin.
Leap year; or, The ladies'
privilege *in* The modern
standard drama, vol. 11

The lady at Maxim's [; or, The
girl from Maxim's] (From the
French of Feydeau.) New York?:
n.pub., 1899? Typescript. 65,
51, 45 leaves.

The lady barber *see* Dumont,
Frank

The lady doctor *see* Armstrong,
L. M. C. Gertrude Mason; or,
The lady doctor

Lady Evelyn's triumph *see*
Emerson, W. Burt. The adventuress; or, Lady Evelyn's
triumph

The lady from Philadelphia *see*
Sherman, Helen Hoyt

Lady Ginevra *see* Benedict,
Frank Lee *in his* The shadow
worshiper

The lady lawyer *see* Hiland,
Frank E.

The lady novelist *see* Denison,
Thomas Stewart *in his* Wide
awake dialogues

The lady of Lyons; or, Love and
pride *see* Lytton, Edward
George Earle Lytton Bulwer-
Lytton *in* The modern
standard drama, vol. 1

The lady of the bed-chamber *see*
Hoppin, William Jones

Lady of the lake *see* Scott,

Sir Walter *in* Cobb, Mary
L. Poetical dramas for home
and school *see also*
Thomson, Mortimer Neal

The lady of the Lions *see*
Durivage, Oliver Everett

The lady or the tiger? *see*
Rosenfeld, Sydney

Lady Tartuffe. A prose comedy
in five acts. (From the
French of Girardin.) New
York: Darcie & Corbyn, 1855.
Bilingual text: French and
English. 84p.

A lady's note *see* Meyers,
Robert Cornelius V.

"Lafayette;" or, "The maid
and the marquis" *see*
Morrison, George Austin

Laidlaw, Alexander Hamilton,
1869-1908.
Captain Walrus; or, The game
of three. A play in one act.
New York and London: S.
French, c1907. 20p. (French's
international copyrighted...
edition of the works of the
best authors. no. 121)

The charms of music. Farce
in one act and one scene.
New York: S. French, c1891.
20p. (French's minor drama.
The acting edition. no. 358)

Laidlaw, F. Allan.
True! An entirely new and
original play. New York:
De Witt, c1884. 12p. (De
Witt's acting plays. no. 325)
*[The U. S. Copyright Office's
Dramatic compositions copyrighted in the United States,
1870-1916 gives the author
of this play as T. Allan
Laidlaw, whereas Readex and
the National Union Catalog
use F. Allan Laidlaw]*

Laila *see* Stratton, George
William

Lambla, Hattie Lena.
The bewitched closet. A
dramatic sketch in one act.
Clyde, O.: Ames, 18-? 6p.
(Ames' series of standard and
minor drama. no. 38)
Obedience; or, Too mindful by
far. A comedietta in one act.
Clyde, O.: Ames, 1872? 6p.
(Ames' series of standard and
minor drama. no. 44)
That mysterious bundle. A
farce in one set. Clyde, O.:
Ames, 1872? 7p. (Ames' series
of standard and minor drama.
no. 40)

The lambs *see* Grant, Robert

La Motte Fouqué, Friedrich
Heinrich Karl, 1777-1843.
Undine *see* Undine; or, The
spirit of the waters

Lampman, Archibald, 1861-1899.
David and Abigail. A poem in
dialogue [From: The poems of
...By Duncan Campbell Scott,
editor. Toronto: George N.
Morang, 1900. 473p.] p.357-
407.

The lampoon *see* Sargent,
Epes

Lamson, C. A.
Grandmother Hildebrand's
legacy; or, Mae Blossom's
reward. A drama in five acts.
Clyde, O.: Ames, 1892. 25p.
(Ames' series of standard
and minor drama. no. 300)

Lancaster, Charles Sears.
Advice to husbands *see*
Sedgwick, Alfred B. Estranged

Landers, Jean Margaret.
The scarlet letter *see*
Najac, Émile de and Landers,

Jean Margaret

Landis, Leonard Lincoln, b.1870.
The playwright [bound with]
His partner's wife. By Leonard
Landes [sic] New York: Cham-
ber's Print., 1900. 91p.

Landis, Simon Mohler, fl.1857-
1888.
The social war of 1900; or,
The conspirators and lovers.
A thrilling "prophetic"
drama in five acts. Philadelphia: Printed by the
author, c1873. 47p.

The landlord's revenge; or,
Uncle Tom up to date *see*
Browne, M. C.

Landor, Walter Savage, 1775-1864.
Citation of William Shakespeare *see* Thacher, John
Boyd. Charlecote; or, The
trial of William Shakespeare

Lanty's luck; or, Falsely
accused *see* Lawrence, F. N.

Lapoint, William W.
Loyal hearts. A patriotic
melo-drama. Founded on the
American and Spanish War of
1898...By the author of the
Two nephews. Randolph, Vt.:
Buck Printing Co., 1900. 92p.

Larcher's victories *see*
House, Edward

"The Larks" *see* The Shakespeare water-cure. By "The
Larks"

Larremore, Wilbur, 1855-1918.
Juan Ponce de Leon and Barto-
lomé de las Casas [From his:
Mother Carey's chickens. New
York: Cassell, c1888. 90p.]
p.63-73.

Lart, John.
Faith. An original play in

three acts. New York: John
M. Burnet's Sons, 1883. 71
numbered leaves.

The lash of the whip. A play
in three acts. (From the
French of Hennequin.) New
York: Z. and L. Rosenfield,
1900. Typescript, prompt-
book with Ms. notes. 50,
70, 43 leaves. *[based on
the French of Maurice
Hennequin and Georges Duval]*

La Shelle, Kirke, 1862-1905.
"The ameer" *see* Ranken,
Frederic and La Shelle,
Kirke

The Princess Chic. Opera
comique in three acts. New
York, Chicago: M. Witmark,
1900. Vocal score. 239p.
[music by Julian Edwards]

The last coat *see* Edgcome,
John

The last days of Brigham Young
see Deseret deserted; or,
The last days of Brigham
Young

Last days of Herculaneum *see*
Atherstone, Edwin *in*
Massey, Charles. Massey's
exhibition reciter

The last days of Pompeii *see*
Medina, Louisa H.

The last drop *see* Delafield,
John H.

The last loaf *see* Baker,
George Melville

The last Mandeville *see*
Osborn, Laughton

The last night of a nation
see Caverly, Robert Boodey

The last of the Mohicans. An

Indian drama in four acts.
(From the novel by James
Fenimore Cooper.) n.p.:
1849? Prompt-book in Ms.
107p. *see also* Stewart,
J. C.

The last of the Peak sisters;
or, The great moral dime
show *see* Horne, Mary
Barnard

The last of the Plantagenets
see Keteltas, Caroline M.

Ye last sweet thing in corners.
Being ye faithful drama of
ye artists' vendetta *see*
Duncan, Florence I.

The last witness *see* Taylor,
W. A. and M'Kee, W. J.

The last word *see* Daly,
Augustin

The late Mr. Early *see* Coon,
Hilton. The widow from the
West; or, The late Mr. Early

Latest dialogues *see* McBride,
H. Elliott

Lathrop, George Parsons, 1851-
1898.
The scarlet letter. A dramatic composition. New York:
Transatlantic Pub. Co., 1896.
52p. Libretto. *[based on
Nathaniel Hawthorne's Scarlet
letter; music by Walter
Damrosch; without the music]*

Yaddo: an autumn masque.
n.p.: printed privately,
1897. 26p.

Latour, Eugene.
Adorable Elizabeth. A comedy
in one act. New York: Roxbury
Pub. Co., c1899. 25p. (Wizard
series)

An affection of the heart. A

comedy in two acts. New York: Roxbury Pub. House, 1899. 17p. (The wizard series)

A meeting of the young ladies club. A comedy in one act. Chicago and New York: Dramatic Pub. Co., c1899. 15p. (Sergel's acting drama. no. 548)

Tricks of trade; or, An obstinate Romeo. A farce comedy in one act. New York: Roxbury Pub. Co., 1899. 19p. (The wizard series)

Latour, H. J.
    True wealth. A drama in four scenes. New York: National Temperance Society and Publications House, 1889. 15p.

Latour de Saint-Ybars, Isidore Latour, called, 1810-1891.
    Virginie *see* Virginia

Lauderbach's little surprise *see* Bauman, E. Henri

Laufs, Carl, 1858-1900.
    Ein toller Einfal *see* Hageman, Maurice. A crazy idea

Laugh when you can *see* Murdoch, James Edward

The laughing family *see* Denton, Clara Janetta Fort. When the lessons are over

Laughing gas *see* White, Charles

Laura Secord, the heroine of 1812 *see* Curzon, Sarah Anne

Laura's plan and how it succeeded *see* Bradley, Nellie

H. Marry no man if he drinks; or, Laura's plan and how it succeeded *see also in her* A collection of temperance dialogues

Lavedan, Henri Léon Émile, 1859-1940.
    Catherine *see* Smith, Edgar McPhail

The law allows it *see* Sedgwick, Alfred B.

Lawford, L. E.
    Mrs. Baxter's baby. A farce in one act. New York: Dick & Fitzgerald, n.d. 13p.

Lawn-tennis *see* Woolf, Benjamin Edward. Djakh and Djill

Lawrence, F. N.
    Lanty's luck; or, Falsely accused. A drama of Irish life in three acts. Boston: Baker, c1897. 30p. (Baker's edition of plays)

The laws of average *see* Rosenfield, Sydney. The mystic isle; or, The laws of average

Lawson, James, 1799-1880.
    Giordano. A tragedy. New York: E. B. Clayton, 1832. 102p.

    Liddesdale; or, The border chief. A tragedy. New York: Printed, not published, Tinson, printer, 1861. 114p.

    The maiden's oath. A domestic drama. Yonkers: n.pub., 1877. p.193-312.

Lawsuit *see* Denison, Thomas Stewart *in his* Friday afternoon series of dialogues

The lawyer, doctor, soldier and actor; or, Many minds in a minute *see* Steele, Silas Sexton *in his* Collected works. Book of plays

Layman, Frederick O.
Maximilian I. A conflict between the old world and the new. Tragedy in four acts. San Francisco: Printed as a manuscript, 1886. 108p.

Lazarus, Emma, 1849-1887.
The dance of death. An historical tragedy in five acts [From her: Songs of a Semite: The dance of death, and other poems. New York: Office of "The American Hebrew," 1882] p.5-48.

Orpheus [From her: Admetus and other poems. New York: Hurd and Houghton, 1871. 229p.] p.25-59.

Prologue for the theatre [From her: Admetus and other poems. New York: Hurd and Houghton, 1871. 229p.] p.201-209.

Scene from Faust [From her: Admetus and other poems. New York: Hurd and Houghton, 1871. 229p.] p.210-229.

The Spagnoletto. A play in five acts [From her: The poems of Emma Lazarus. Boston and New York: Houghton, Mifflin, 1889. vol. 1, 342p.; vol. 2, 257p.] vol.1, p.222-342. *[earlier copyright: 1876]*

Lazy Lawrence *see* Venable, William Henry *in his* The school stage

Lazy or not *see* Denton, Clara Janetta Fort. When the lessons are over

A leaf from the life of Maria

Jane *see* Wilson, Bertha M. The show at Wilkins' Hall; or, A leaf from the life of Maria Jane

Leaflets and ladybugs *see* Denton, Clara Janetta *in her* From tots to teens

Leah: the forsaken *see* Daly, Augustin

Leahy, William Augustine, 1867-1941.
The siege of Syracuse. A poetical drama in five acts. Boston: D. Lothrop, 1889. 105p.

The wedding feast. A tragic comedy in three acts with a prologue, Hallowe'en. Boston: n.pub., c1896. Prompt-book with Ms. notes. 47p.

Leanerd, John, fl.1679.
Counterfeits *see* Daly, Augustin. She wou'd and she wou'd not

Leap year *see* Sedgwick, Alfred B.

Leap year; or, The ladies' privilege *see* Buckstone, John Baldwin *in* The modern standard drama, vol. 11

The leap-year proposal *see* Kobbé, Gustav. Two belles to a beau; or, The leap-year proposal *see also in his* Plays for amateurs

Leavitt, Andrew J., 1822-1901.
The academy of stars. An Ethiopian sketch. New York and London: S. French, 187-? 8p. *[joint author: H. W. Eagan]*

The arrival of Dickens. An Ethiopian sketch. New York: S. French, 186-? 8p. (The Ethiopian drama. New series.

no. 5) *[joint author: H. W. Eagan]*

Big mistake *see* White, Charles

The black Ole Bull. An original Ethiopian sketch. New York: S. French, 189-? 8p. The Ethiopian drama. New series) *[joint author: H. W. Eagan]*

The blackest tragedy of all; or, A peep behind the scenes. An Ethiopian sketch. London and New York: S. French, 1878. 8p. *[joint author: H. W. Eagan]*

Blinks and jinks. An original Ethiopian sketch. New York: S. French, 187-? 8p. (The Ethiopian drama. New series) *[joint author: H. W. Eagan]*

Boarding school. An Ethiopian sketch. New York: S. French, 187-? 8p. (The Ethiopian drama. New series) *[joint author: H. W. Eagan]*

The body snatchers. A negro sketch in two scenes. New York: De Witt, c1879. 6p. (De Witt's Ethiopian and comic drama. no. 120)

Bruised and cured *see* White, Charles

The coming man *see* White, Charles

Cousin Joe's visit. An Ethiopian sketch. New York: S. French, 187-? 8p. *[joint author: H. W. Eagan]*

Cremation *see* White, Charles

Deaf as a post. An Ethiopian sketch. New York: S. French, 187-? 8p. (The Ethiopian drama. New series) *[joint author: H. W. Eagan]*

The deserters. An Ethiopian sketch. New York: S. French,

187-? 8p. *[joint author: H. W. Eagan]*

High Jack, the heeler *see* White, Charles

In and out *see* White, Charles

The intelligence office. An Ethiopian sketch in one scene. New York: De Witt, 189-? 5p. *[joint author: H. W. Eagan]*

Jeemes the poet. An Ethiopian sketch. New York: S. French, 187-? 8p. (The Ethiopian drama. New series) *[joint author: H. W. Eagan]*

The lost will *see* White, Charles

The lucky number. An Ethiopian sketch. New York: S. French, 187-? 8p. (The Ethiopian drama. New series. no. 2) *[joint author: H. W. Eagan]*

No pay no cure. A sketch. Chicago: Dramatic Pub. Co., c1882. 7p. (The darkey and comic drama) *[this appears to be a later version of the author's The thumping process]*

No tator; or Man-fish. An Ethiopian sketch. New York: S. French, 187-? 8p. (The Ethiopian drama. New series) *[joint author: H. W. Eagan]*

A remittance from home *see* White, Charles

Rigging a purchase *see* White, Charles

Rip Van Winkle. An original Ethiopian sketch. New York: S. French, 18-? 8p. (The Ethiopian sketch. New series. no. 12) *[joint author: H. W. Eagan]*

The sleep walker *see* White, Charles

Squire for a day *see* White, Charles

The stranger *see* White,
Charles

Ten days in the Tombs. An
Ethiopian sketch. New York:
S. French, 187-? 8p. (The
Ethiopian drama. New series.
no. 13) *[joint author: H. W.
Eagan]*

That wife of mine. A Negro
sketch in one scene. New
York: S. French, 1878. 6p.
(The Ethiopian drama. New
series. no. 25) *[joint
author: H. W. Eagan]*

Them papers *see* White,
Charles

The thumping process. An
original Ethiopian sketch.
New York: S. French, 1877?
8p. (The Ethiopian drama.
New series. no. 26) *[this
appears to be an earlier
version of the author's
No pay no cure]*

A trip to Paris. An Ethiopian
sketch. New York: S. French,
189-? 8p. *[joint author:
H. W. Eagan]*

The two Pompeys. An Ethiopian
sketch. New York: T. H.
French, 187-? 8p.

The upper ten thousand. An
Ethiopian sketch. New York:
S. French, 187-? 8p. (The
Ethiopian drama. New series.
no. 11) *[joint author: H. W.
Eagan]*

Who died first? *see* White,
Charles

Who stole the chickens? An
Ethiopian sketch. New York:
S. French, 189-? 6p. (The
Ethiopian drama. New series)
[joint author: H. W. Eagan]

Leavitt, Burton Emerson.
The frogs of Windham *see*
Leavitt, Nason W.

Leavitt, John McDowell, 1824-
1909.
Afranius [From his: Afranius,
and The Idumean, tragedies,
with The Roman martyrs, and
other poems. New York: n.pub.,
1869] p.1-54.

Ariston [From his: New world
tragedies from old world life.
New York: Harper Bros., 1876.
332p.] p.63-137.

The Idumean [From his: Afranius, and The Idumean, tragedies, with The Roman martyrs,
and other poems. New York:
n.pub., 1869] p.55-105.

The Jewish captives [From his:
New world tragedies from old
world life. New York: Harper
Bros., 1876. 332p.] p.139-197.

The siege of Babylon. A tragedy. New York: Hurd and
Houghton, 1869. 47p.

Leavitt, Nason W.
The frogs of Windham. An
original comic opera in three
acts. New Haven, Conn.: John
J. Kiernan, 1893. 24p.
Libretto. *[music composed by
Burton Emerson Leavitt;
without the music]*

LeBrandt, Joseph, 1864?-1940.
My lady Darrell; or, A strange
marriage. A drama in four
acts. New York: Dick & Fitzgerald, c1898. 62p.

Lebrun, Pierre Antoine, 1785-
1873.
Marie Stuart *see* Marie
Stuart

Le Clercq, Adolphe.
Jalouse *see* Gillette,
William Hooker. Because she
loved him so

Lecocq, Alexandre Charles,
1832-1918.

La fille de Madame Angot
see Sedgwick, Alfred B.
My walking photograph

Fleur-de-thé *see* Byrne,
Charles Alfred. Pearl of
Pekin; or, The dashing tar
outwitted by his wife

Giroflé-Girofla *see*
Sedgwick, Alfred B. The
twin sisters

Le jour et la nuit *see*
Woolf, Benjamin Edward.
Manola; or, The day and
the night

La marjolaine *see* La
marjolaine (The sweet
marjoram)

[The oolah] *see* Rosenfeld,
Sydney

Le petit duc *see* Williams,
Frederick and Sullivan,
Thomas Russell. The little
duke

Ledoux, Albert Reid, 1852-1923.
The delegate. A comedy in
two acts. New York: T. H.
French, c1894. 18p. (French's
minor drama. The acting
edition. no. 357)

Lee, Albert.
The knave of hearts. A Fourth
of July comedietta. New York:
R. H. Russell, 1897. 32p.

Lee, Billy F.
Muldoon's blunders. Farce
comedy in three acts. Clyde,
O.: Ames, c1900. 48p. (Ames'
series of standard and minor
drama. no. 418)

Lee, Franklyn W.
Ali Baba; or, Morgiana and
the forty thieves *see*
Smith, Harry Bache

Lee, Harriet, 1757-1851.
The German's tale [from her

The Canterbury tales] *see*
Byron, George Gordon Noël
Byron, 6th baron. Werner
in The modern standard
drama, vol. 9

Lee, Herbert.
The avenger; or, The Moor of
Sicily. A melo-drama in three
acts. Boston: William V.
Spencer, 1859. 32p. (Spencer's
Boston Theatre. no. 203)
*[Readex has reproduced this
also under the title The
avenger; or, The Moor of
Sicily, q.v.]*

Lee, Sophia, 1750-1824.
The German's tale [from her
The Canterbury tales] *see*
Byron, George Gordon Noël
Byron, 6th baron. Werner
in The modern standard
drama, vol. 9

Le Fanu, Joseph Sheridan, 1814-
1873.
Shamus O'Brien *see* Jessop,
George Henry

Left in charge *see* Bayless,
Bell

A legal wreck *see* Gillette,
William Hooker

A legend of "Norwood"; or,
Village life in New England
see Daly, Augustin

The legend of the Christmas
tree *see* Keatinge, Ella

Legouvé, Gabriel Marie Jean
Baptiste Ernest Wilfrid,
1807-1903.
Adrienne Lecouvreur *see*
Adrienne Lecouvreur *see*
also Schwab, Frederick A.

[Foresight; or, My daughter's
dowry] *see* Delafield,
John H.

Le Grand, Dr.
The genius of liberty *see*
Beadle's dialogues...no. 2

The golden rule *see*
Beadle's dialogues...no. 2

Lehmann, M.
The elf-king; or, Wealth and
poverty. A grand, romantic,
fairy, pantomimic spectacle.
New York: Corbyn and Darcie,
1856. 11p.

Leighton, William, 1833-1911.
At the court of King Edwin.
Philadelphia: J. B. Lippin-
cott, 1878. 157p.

Shakespeare's dream [From
his: Shakespeare's dream and
other poems. Philadelphia:
J. B. Lippincott, 1881.
148p.] p.1-104.

The sons of Godwin. A tragedy. Philadelphia: J. B.
Lippincott, 1877. 188p.

Leland, Oliver Shepard, 1833-
1870.
Beatrice; or, The false and
the true. A play in five
acts. Boston: W. V. Spencer,
1858. 64p. (Spencer's Boston
Theatre, no. 118)

Blue and cherry; or, Appearances are deceitful. A comedietta in one act. Boston:
C. H. Spencer, 1871. 30p.
(Spencer's universal stage.
no. 59)

Caprice; or, A woman's
heart. A comedy in three
acts. New York: S. French,
186-? 59p. (French's standard drama. no. 303)

The rights of man. A comedy
in two acts. New York: S.
French, 1857? 30p. (French's
minor drama. no. 229)

Lem Kettle *see* Carleton,
Henry Guy

Lemaire, Ferdinand.
Samson et Dalila *see*
Barnett, M. J. Samson and
Delilah

Lemon, Mark, 1809-1870.
Grandfather Whitehead *see*
The modern standard drama,
vol. 2

Mind your own business *see*
The modern standard drama,
vol. 12

Lemonade stand *see* Denison,
Thomas Stewart *in his* Wide
awake dialouges

Lemons *see* Daly, Augustin

Lend me five shillings *see*
Morton, John Maddison *in*
The modern standard drama,
vol. 3

Leonia's repentance *see*
Raynor, Verna M. Noel
Carson's oath; or, Leonia's
repentance

Leonor de Guzman *see* Boker,
George Henry

Leonora *see* Fry, Joseph
Reese

Leonora de Castro *see* Opal
(pseud.) *in her* The cloud
of witnesses

Lesaulnier, Louis.
John Park and Dr. Dott's
doings. A moral play in six
scenes. Red Bud, Randolph
Co., Ill.: n.pub., c1879.
37p. *[Readex has assigned
the imprint date of c1879,
whereas the title page of
the work indicates c1872]*

Leslie, Miriam Folline Squier,
1836-1919.
The "demi-monde." A satire on
society. By Mrs. E. G. Squier.
Philadelphia: J. B. Lippin-

cott, 1858. 164p. *[based on
Le demi-monde by Alexandre
Dumas the younger]*

Lessing, Gotthold Aphraim,
1729-1781.
Nathan der Weise *see*
Frothingham, Ellen. Nathan
the wise

A lesson from fairy land *see*
Field, Henrietta Dexter
and Field, Roswell Martin.
Collected works

A lesson from the sunflowers
see Denton, Clara Janetta
Fort. When the lessons are
over

A lesson in elegance; or, The
true art of pleasing *see*
Herbert, Bernard

Lessons from Scripture flowers
see Slade, M. B. C. *in*
Dramatic leaflets

Lessons in cookery *see*
Denison, Thomas Stewart
in his Friday afternoon
series of dialogues

Lessons of life *see* Bliss,
Frank Chapman

Lester, Francis.
Flirtation cured. Farce
comedy in one act. New York:
Dramatic Pub. Co., c1899.
10p. (The wizard series)

The new squire. Comedy in
one act. Chicago: Dramatic
Pub. Co., c1899. 31p.
(Sergel's acting drama.
no. 557)

Our servants. A farce
comedy in one act. New York:
Roxbury Pub. Co., c1899.
12p. (The wizard series)

The skeleton in the closet.
Comedy in one act. New York:
Roxbury Pub. Co., c1899. 32p.

(The wizard series)

Let love but hold the key *see*
Morette, Edgar

Let those laugh who win *see*
Sedgwick, Alfred B.

Leterrier, Eugène, 1842-1884.
La marjolaine *see* La marjolaine (The sweet marjoram)

[The oolah] *see* Rosenfeld,
Sydney

Letter from a presidential
candidate *see* Massey,
Charles. Massey's exhibition
reciter

A letter of introduction *see*
Howells, William Dean

Leupp, Francis Ellington,
1849-1918.
Bagby versus Bagby. A
comedietta in one act. Philadelphia: Penn Pub. Co.,
1912. 40p. *[earlier copyright: 1895]*

Leveaux, Alphonse *see*
Jolly, Alphonse (pseud.)

Lever, Charles, 1806-1872.
Charles O'Malley *see*
Williams, Henry Llewellyn.
Charles O'Malley's aunt

Levy, Clifton Harby, b.1867.
Haman and Mordecai. A
Purim-play in five acts.
Cincinnati: Bloch Pub. and
Print. Co., 1886. 21p.

Lévy, Jules, b.1857.
La douche *see* Daly, Augus-
tin. A wet blanket *in his*
Three preludes to the play

Levy, Samuel Yates, 1827-1888.
The Italian bride. A play in
five acts. Savannah: John
M. Cooper, 1856. 132p.

Lewis, Abbie Goodwin, d.1906.
Caught napping. A one-act
operetta for Christmas eve.
Boston: Oliver Ditson, c1886.
Vocal score. 22p. *[music by
Leo Rich Lewis]*

Lewis, C. M.
Mother earth and her vegetable daughters; or, Crowning
the queen of vegetables *see*
Lewis, E. A. and Lewis, C. M.

Lewis, E. A.
Mother earth and her vegetable daughter's [sic]; or,
Crowning the queen of vegetables. Clyde, O.: Ames,
c1898. 14p. (Ames' series
of standard and minor drama.
no. 397) *[joint author:
C. M. Lewis]*

Lewis, Eliza Gabriella.
The outlaw. A dramatic
sketch [From her: Poems.
Brooklyn: Shannon, 1850]
p.1-51.

Lewis, Estelle Anna Blanche
Robinson, 1824-1880.
The king's stratagem; or,
The pearl of Poland. A
tragedy in five acts. By
Stella (pseud.) London:
Trübner, 1874. Second edition.
94p.

Sappho. A tragedy in five
acts. By Stella (pseud.)
London: Trübner, 1875.
vi, 132, 4p.

Lewis, Leo Rich, 1865-1945.
Caught napping *see*
Lewis, Abbie Goodwin

Lewis, Richard Henry (pseud.)
Robert and Cornelia. A
romantic society tragedy in
five acts and one scene.
Albany, N. Y.: Philip H.
Carroll, c1901. 86p. *[Richard
Henry Lewis is the pseud.
of Philip H. Carroll]*

Licensed snakes. Temperance
dialogue *see* Murray, Ellen
in Dramatic leaflets

The lick skillet wedding *see*
Gibson, Ad. H.

Liddesdale; or, The border
chief *see* Lawson, James

The lieutenant *see* Tiddball,
Walton C.

Life among the little folks
see Payne, John Howard. The
boarding schools; or, Life
among the little folks

Life among the lowly *see*
Aiken, George L. Uncle Tom's
cabin; or, Life among the
lowly

Life at Salt Lake City *see*
English, Thomas Dunn. The
Mormons; or, Life at Salt
Lake City

Life in London *see* Tom and
Jerry; or, Life in London

Life in New York *see* Ritchie,
Anna Cora Ogden Mowatt.
Fashion; or, Life in New York
see also in her Plays

Life in the lobby *see* Piatt,
Donn

The life of an actor *see*
Jessop, George Henry and
St. Maur, J. Edmund Kean;
or, The life of an actor

A life poem *see* Keyes,
Frederick J.

Life-real *see* Stillman,
George A.

The light that always is *see*
Fuller, Henry Blake *in his*
Collected works

A lighter-boy at school *see*
Venable, William Henry *in
his* The school stage

Lights and shadows of the
great rebellion; or, The
hospital nurse of Tennessee
see Dawson, J. H. and
Whittemore, B. G.

Lights of London *see* Brady,
William A.

Like a nettle *see* Denton,
Clara Janetta Fort. When
the lessons are over

Like Caesar's wife *see*
Balch, William Ralston

Like unto like *see* Calvert,
George Henry. Comedies

A likely story *see* Howells,
William Dean

Lilian's last love *see*
Howard, Bronson. The
banker's daughter

Lilliput revels *see* Venable,
William Henry. The white
princess *in his* The school
stage

Lillo, George, 1693?-1739.
George Barnwell *see* The
modern standard drama,
vol. 11

A limb o' the law *see*
Orne, Martha Russell

The Lime-Kiln Club in an
uproar! *see* Williams,
Henry Llewellyn

The Limerick boy; or, Paddy's
mischief *see* Pilgrim,
James

The limit of the law *see*
Adams, Justin

Linda of Chamouni. An opera in
three acts. New York: John
Douglas, 1848. 34p. Libretto.
(The operatic library. no.
23) *[the cover indicates
"music by Bellini," whereas
the title page correctly
signifies "music by Doni-
zetti," as set to Gaetano
Rossi's libretto Linda di
Chamounix; without the music]*

Lindau, Paul, 1839-1919.
Maria und Magdalena *see*
Hollenius, Laurence John.
Maria and Magdalena

Lindner, Albert, 1831-1888.
Katarina die Zweite *see*
Catharina the second

Lindon, Patrick C.
Dr. Baxter's servants. Farce
in one act. Clyde, O.: Ames,
1898. 7p. (Ames' series of
standard and minor drama.
no. 407)

Lindsley, Philip, b.1842.
The humor of the court room;
or, Jones vs. Johnson, a
lawful comedy. Dallas: John
F. Worley, 1899. 79p.

Lines to a favourite actress
see Smith, Richard Penn
in his Dramatic fragments

A lion among the ladies *see*
Macy, William Francis

The lion of the sea *see*
Steele, Silas Sexton

The lion of the West *see*
Paulding, James Kirke

The lion's mouth *see*
Carleton, Henry Guy

Lippmann, Julie Mathilde,
1864-1952.
Cousin Faithful. A comedy

in one act. Philadelphia:
Penn Pub. Co., 1908. 18p.
[earlier copyright: 1897]

The facts in the case.
Farce in one act. Phila-
delphia: Penn Pub. Co.,
1912. 18p. *[earlier copyright: 1897]*

A fool and his money. A
comedy in two acts. Philadelphia: Penn Pub. Co.,
1913. 28p. *[earlier copyright: 1897]*

Listeners hear no good of
themselves *see* Shields,
Sarah Annie Frost *in her*
Parlor charades and proverbs

A literary farce *see* Brazzà-
Savorgnan, Cora Ann Slocomb,
Contesa di

Little barefoot *see* Waldauer,
Augustus

Little bird blue *see* Polding,
Elizabeth. At the fireside;
or, Little bird blue

The little boss *see* Bixby,
Frank L.

A little boys' debate *see*
McBride, H. Elliott *in his*
New dialogues

Little brown jug *see* Baker,
George Melville

The little corporal *see*
Smith, Harry Bache

The little country store *see*
Talladay, Jennie

Little daughter of the regiment
see Rosetti, Joseph

The little dependent *see*
Venable, William Henry *in
his* The school stage

A little dinner in Arcady *see*
Bridges, Robert *in his*
Overheard in Arcady

The little duke *see* Williams,
Frederick and Sullivan,
Thomas Russell

Little Ferrit [sic, Ferritt];
or, The Philadelphia
detective. n.p.: n.pub.,
n.d. Typescript. 33p.

Little Jim *see* Massey,
Charles. Massey's exhibition
reciter

The little glass slipper *see*
Cinderella; or, The glass
slipper *in* Beadle's
dialogues no. 2

The little gleaner *see*
Follen, Eliza Lee Cabot.
Home dramas for young people

Little golden-hair *see*
Silvia and other dramas

Little Goldie; or, The child
of the camp *see* Willard,
Charles O.

Little Italy *see* Fry,
Horace B.

The little joker *see* Coburn,
Carrie W. His last chance;
or, The little joker

Little Lord Fauntleroy *see*
Burnett, Frances Hodgson

The little magician *see*
Keatinge, Ella *in her*
Short plays for children

"The little men" *see* Gould,
Elizabeth Lincoln

The little minister *see*
Fraser, John Arthur

Little Miss Million *see*
Daly, Augustin

The little mischief-makers *see*
Rover, Winnie. The house on
the avenue; or, The little
mischief-makers

Little Miss Nobody *see*
Dumont, Frank

A little misunderstanding
see Arnold, George? and
Cahill, Frank. Parlor
theatricals; or, Winter
evening's entertainment

A little more cider *see*
Baker, George Melville

The little philosophers *see*
Beadle's dialogues...no. 2

Little pitchers *see* Heywood,
Delia A. *in her* Choice
dialogues no. 1

The little red riding hood
see F., W. F.

Little Robinson Crusoe *see*
Smith, Harry Bache

Little Ruby; or, Home jewels
see Wallace, John J.

Little silver hair and the
three bears *see* Venable,
William Henry *in his*
The school stage

Little snow white *see*
Knortz, Karl *in* Venable,
William Henry. The school
stage

Little Snow-White and the
seven dwarfs...Portland,
Me.: D. Tucker, 1869. 12p.
*[title page: "The thread of
incident in this play is
taken...from one of the...
tales of the Brothers Grimm";
the original title was
Schneewittchen]*

Little Sunshine *see* Campbell,
Bartley Theodore

The little tin god-on-wheels
(2nd part of a trilogy) *see*
Grant, Robert *in his* The
little tin god-on-wheels;
or, Society in our modern
Athens

The little tin god-on-wheels;
or, Society in our modern
Athens *see* Grant, Robert

Little trump; or, A Rocky
Mountain diamond *see*
Fisher, Abraham Lincoln

The little tycoon *see*
Spenser, Willard

The little vagrants *see*
Gregg, Helen A.

The little vulgar boy *see*
Hood, Thomas *in* Massey,
Charles. Massey's exhibition
reciter

The little wife *see* Chipman,
Adelbert Z.

The littlest girl *see*
Hilliard, Robert Cochrane

The live injin; or, Jim Crow
see White, Charles

A live woman in the mines; or,
Pike County ahead *see*
Delano, Alonzo

Livingston, Margaret Vere
Farrington, b.1863.
Sauce for the goose. A farce
in one act. Boston: W. H.
Baker, 1899. 11p. (Baker's
edition of plays)

Lloyd, David Demarest, 1851-
1889.
"The senator." New York?:
1889? Typescript, prompt-
book. In four acts. (pag. by

acts.) *[joint author: Sydney Rosenfeld]*

The woman-hater. A farcical comedy in four acts. London, New York: S. French, c1907. 106p. (French's international copyrighted edition of the works of the best authors. no. 131) *[earlier copyright: 1886]*

Local hits; or, High life in New-Orleans. A comedy in one act. New Orleans: Printed at the Office of the Orleanian, 1850. 52p.

Lochinvar *see* Scott, Sir Walter *in* Massey, Charles. Massey's exhibition reciter

Locke, Belle Marshall, 1865-1933.
Breezy Point. A comedy in three acts. Boston: W. H. Baker, c1898. 50p. (Baker's edition of plays)

The great catastrophe. A comedy in two acts. By Nellie M. Locke. Philadelphia: Penn Pub. Co., 1915. 30p. *[earlier copyright: 1895; Nellie M. Locke=Belle Marshall Locke]*

A heartrending affair. A monologue. Philadelphia: Penn Pub. Co., 1911. p.129-132. *[earlier copyright: 1895]*

The Hiartville Shakespeare Club. A farce in one act. Philadelphia: Penn Pub. Co., 1913. p.149-159. (One hundred choice selections. no. 35) *[earlier copyright: 1896]*

Marie's secret. A duologue in one scene. Boston: W. H. Baker, c1893. 8p.

Locke, Nellie M. (pseud.) *see* Locke, Belle Marshall

Locked in a dress-maker's room; or, Mr. Holiday's flirtation *see* Guepner, Willard

Lockroy, Joseph Philippe Simon, called, 1803-1891 (pseud.) Charlot *see* Planché, James Robinson. The follies of a night *in* The modern standard drama, vol. 6

Lockwood, Ingersoll, 1841-1918. Washington. A heroic drama of the revolution in five acts. New York: The author, c1875. 67p.

Lodgings for two *see* Cutler, F. L.

Logan, Algernon Sydney, 1849-1925.
Messalina. A tragedy in five acts. Philadelphia: J. B. Lippincott, 1890. 147p.

Saul. A dramatic poem. Philadelphia: J. B. Lippincott, 1883. 80p.

Logan, Cornelius Ambrosius, 1806-1853.
Yankee land. A comedy in two acts. Boston: W. Spencer, 1856? Prompt-book. 31p. (Spencer's Boston Theatre. no. 70)

Logan, Thomas.
Vermont wool-dealer. A farce in one act. New York: S. French, 1858? 18p. (The minor drama. The acting edition. no. 173) *[Readex reproduced this play also under title]*

Logan, Thomas B.
The cousins; or, The dying requisition. A play in five acts. Philadelphia: Bryson & Cooper, 1848. 39p.

The Lombards at the first crusade. A tragic opera in four acts. New York: John Douglas,

1848. Bilingual text:
English and Italian. 46p.
Libretto. (The operatic
library. no. 26) [music
by Giuseppe Verdi on the
libretto I Lombardi alla
prima crociata by Temistocle
Solera as based on the
romance of the same name by
Tommaso Grossi; without
the music]

London assurance see
Boucicault, Dion in The
modern standard drama,
vol. 4

Lone Tree mine see Hildreth,
David W.

The lonely pollywog of the
mill-pond see Head, M. T.

Long, John Luther, 1861-1927.
Madame Butterfly see
Belasco, David

Longfellow, Henry Wadsworth,
1807-1882.
The blind girl of Castèl-
Cuillè see Morton, Mar-
guerite W. see also
Thompson, Caroline Eunice.
Blind Margaret

Christus. A mystery in three
parts. Boston: James R. Osgood, 1872. vol. 1, 159p.;
vol. 2, 200p.; vol. 3, xvi,
186p.
Contents: The divine
tragedy.--The golden legend.
--The New England tragedies
[cover title for:] John
Endicott.--Giles Corey of
the Salem farms.

Christus. A mystery in
three parts. Boston: James
R. Osgood, 1873. 209p.
Contents: The divine
tragedy.--The golden legend.
--The New England tragedies
[cover title for:] John
Endicott.--Giles Corey of
the Salem farms.

The divine tragedy. Boston:
James R. Osgood, 1871. iv,
150p.

The golden legend. Boston:
Ticknor, Reed, and Fields,
1852. 301p.

King Robert of Sicily see
Furniss, Grace Livingston

The masque of Pandora [From
his: The masque of Pandora
and other poems. Boston:
James R. Osgood, 1875. 146p.]
p.1-54.

Michael Angelo. A dramatic
poem. Boston: Houghton,
Mifflin, 1884 [i.e.1883]
ix, 184p.

The New England tragedies.
London: G. Routledge and
Sons, 1868. 8, 221, 2p.
Contents: Endicott.--Giles
Corey of the Salem farms.

The Spanish student. A play
in three acts. Cambridge:
John Owen, 1843. 183p.

The long-lost nephew see
Meyers, Robert Cornelius V.
in Dramatic leaflets

Look at the clock see
Ingoldsby, Thomas in
Massey, Charles. Massey's
exhibition reciter

Look before you leap; or,
Wooings and weddings see
Lovell, George W. in
The modern standard drama,
vol. 5

Lookup, Alexander (pseud.?)
Excelsior; or, The heir
apparent. New York: Kennedy,
1860. 108p. [caption on
first page: "Party dictators;
or, The rulers of the republic"]

The granddaughter of the
Caesars; or, The hag of the
earth and syren of the

waters. New York: Kennedy,
1860. 107p.

The soldier of the people;
or, The world's deliverer.
New York: Kennedy, 1860.
108p.

Lookup, Thomas, d.1879.
*[Famous abortionist who
"composed plays of question-
able morality, which were
enacted in private; known
as Dr. Evans"--obituary in
New York Times, August 29,
1879, p.2]*
The heart broken lover; or,
A tale of a tragical life.
A pathetic romance in five
acts. New York: Branch,
Thatcher, Universal Pub.
House, 1876. 57p.

A mad match; or, The heartless brother. A tragedy in
three acts. New York:
Universal Pub. Co., 1876.
22p. *[based on Sir Walter
Scott's Bride of Lammermoor]*

Queen Elizabeth; or, Love
and majesty. A tragedy in
five acts. New York: Branch,
Thatcher, Universal Pub.
House, 1876. 21p.

Lord, Alice Emma Sauerwein,
1848-1930.
A vision's quest. A drama
in five acts. Baltimore:
Cushing, 1899. 123p.

Lord, William Wilberforce,
1819-1908.
André. A tragedy in five
acts. New York: C. Scribner,
1856. 138p.

Lord Chumley *see* Belasco,
David and De Mille, Henry
Churchill *see also* De
Mille, Henry Churchill and
Belasco, David *[this is an
instance in which Readex
has entered the same play*

*under each of two joint
authors]*

A lord in Philadelphia *see*
Vanity; or, A lord in
Philadelphia

Lord Ivan and his daughter *see*
Willis, Nathaniel Parker

The lord of Talladega *see*
Schoolcraft, Henry. Alhalla;
or, The lord of Talladega

Lord Timothy Dexter; or, The
greatest man in the east
see Blood, Henry Ames

Lords of creation *see* Thayer,
Ella Cheever

Lortzing, Gustav Albert,
1801-1851.
Zar und Zimmermann *see*
Balatka, Hans. Peter the
Great in Saardam; or, The
Czar and the carpenter

Losada *see* Hopkins, Rufus
Clement

Lost and found *see* The
fortune hunters; or, Lost
and found *see also* Wilkins,
W. Henri. Rock Allen, the
orphan; or, Lost and found

Lost and won *see* Piatt, Donn
in his Various dramatic
works

The lost ball *see* Abbott,
Jacob *in his* Orkney, the
peacemaker; or, The various
ways of settling disputes

The lost child *see* Cushing,
Harry H. *in* Dramatic
leaflets

The lost children *see* Jervey,
Mrs. Lewis

The lost diamond *see* Burgwyn,

Collison Pierrepont Edwards

The lost dog *see* Hunt,
Arzalea

The lost heir; or, The abbé
de L'Épée. An historical
drama in three acts. (From
the German.) New York: Dick
& Fitzgerald, 189-? 27p.
*[based on August Friedrich
Ferdinand von Kotzebue's
Der Taubstumme, which is
founded on Jean Nicholas
Bouilly's L'abbé de L'Épée]*

The lost letter *see* Denton,
Clara Janetta Fort *in her*
From tots to teens

The lost mine *see* Baker,
George Melville. Nevada;
or, The lost mine

The lost New Year *see*
Crane, Eleanor Maud

The lost opportunities *see*
Denison, Thomas Stewart
in his Friday afternoon
series of dialogues

The lost opportunity *see*
Denton, Clara Janetta Fort
in her From tots to teens

Lost; or, The fruits of the
glass *see* Cutler, F. L.

The lost paradise *see*
De Mille, Henry Churchill

The lost "spade"; or, The
grave digger's revenge.
A politico-serio-comedy-
drama. With appendix.
Written by the happy Democratic family, expressly
for the Peace Democracy.
New York: n.pub., 1864. 16p.

The lost will *see* White,
Charles

Lot's wife *see* Saltus,
Francis Saltus

The lottery of love *see*
Daly, Augustin

Louisville Literary Brass Band.
The King of Angelo. A tragico-
comico; or, melo-dramatico
burlesco. Louisville?:
Louisville Literary Brass
Band, 18-? 14p.

Louva, the pauper *see*
Denison, Thomas Stewart

Love *see* Knowles, James
Sheridan *in* The modern
standard drama, vol. 9

Love and astronomy *see*
Kedney, John Steinfort

Love and duty *see* Morris,
Robert. The elopement; or,
Love and duty

Love and jealousy *see* Caughy,
Charles M.

Love and jealousy; or, A
tragedy for the million *see*
Massey, Charles. Massey's
exhibition reciter

Love and law *see* Nobles,
Milton

Love and lockjaw *see* Williams,
Henry Llewellyn

Love and madness; or, The
recluse of the mountain *see*
Steele, Silas Sexton *in his*
Collected works. Book of
plays

Love and majesty *see* Lookup,
Thomas. Queen Elizabeth; or,
Love and majesty

Love and money *see* Basil
(pseud.)

Love and mushrooms *see*
Harris, Francis Augustine.
A majority of one; or,
Love and mushrooms

Love and pride *see* Lytton,
Edward George Earle Lytton
Bulwer-Lytton. The lady of
Lyons; or, Love and pride
in The modern standard
drama, vol. 1

Love and sourkrout *see*
White, Charles. The German
emigrant; or, Love and
sourkrout

Love at sight *see* Fowle,
William Bentley *in his*
Parlor dramas

Love by induction *see*
Heermans, Forbes

The love-chase *see* Knowles,
James Sheridan *in* The
modern standard drama,
vol. 3

Love for love *see* Wallack,
James William

Love in a flue; or, The sweep
and the magistrate *see*
O'Brien, Constance

Love in a lighthouse *see*
Baum, Rosemary

Love in all corners *see*
Dumont, Frank *see also*
Steele, Silas Sexton. Hide
and seek; or, Love in all
corners *in his* Collected
works. Book of plays

Love in death *see* Sharswood,
William. The betrothed; or,
Love in death

Love in harness *see* Daly,
Augustin

Love in '76 *see* Bunce,
Oliver Bell

Love in tandem *see* Daly,
Augustin

Love of a bonnet *see* Baker,
George Melville

The love of a Caliban *see*
Peattie, Elia Wilkinson

The love of a prince; or, The
court of Prussia *see*
Gayler, Charles

The love of gold *see* Wilkins,
W. Henri. The reward of
crime; or, The love of gold

The love of love *see* Fuller,
Henry Blake *in his* Collected works

Love of no politics *see*
Heath, James Ewell, Whigs
and democrats; or, Love of
no politics

Love on crutches *see* Daly,
Augustin

Love; or, The heart's ordeal
see Whitney, Thomas Richard

Love protected by friendship
see Ponte, Lorenzo da. Eliza
and Claudio; or, Love protected by friendship

The love-spell. A comic opera
in two acts. New York: Baker
& Godwin, 1856. 32p. Libretto.
*[music by Gaetano Donizetti
on libretto by Felice Romani]*

Loved and lost *see* Friars,
Austin

Lovell, George William, 1804-
1878.
Look before you leap; or,
Wooings and weddings *see*
The modern standard drama,
vol. 5

Love's sacrifice; or, The
rival merchants *see* The

modern standard drama,
vol. 2

Lovell, Maria Anne Lacy,
1803-1877.
Ingomar, the barbarian *see*
The modern standard drama,
vol. 12 *see also* Sothern,
Edward Hugh and Marlow,
Julia

The lovely Galatea *see* Day,
Willard Gibson

Lover, Samuel, 1791-1868.
Handy Andy *see* Floyd,
William Ralph *see also*
Venable, William Henry.
The Irish valet *in his*
The school stage

The white horse of the
Peppers *see* Massey,
Charles. Massey's exhibition
reciter

A lover and a half *see*
O'Brien, Constance

The lovers *see* Schoolcraft,
Oliver John

The lover's caprice *see*
Bannan, Martha Ridgway.
The fisher maiden [and]
The lover's caprice

The lover's dilemma *see*
Bauman, E. Henri. The
patent washing machine; or,
The lover's dilemma

The lover's ordeal *see* Flora;
or, The lover's ordeal

Love's labor not lost; or,
Cupid's pastime *see*
Andrews, Fred G.

Love's labor saved *see*
Curtis, Herbert Pelham.
Uncle Robert; or, Love's
labor saved

Love's labour's lost *see*
Daly, Augustin

Love's sacrifice; or, The
rival merchants *see* Lovell,
George William *in* The
modern standard drama, vol. 2

Love's stowaway *see* Howells,
William Dean. A sea-change;
or, Love's stowaway

Love's stratagem *see* Hughes,
Louise Marie *see also*
N., S. T. A.

Love's victory *see* Powell,
L. S. and Frank, J. C.
Conn; or, Love's victory

Love's warrant *see* Heermans,
Forbes

Love's young dream *see* Daly,
Augustin. Three preludes to
the play

Loving yet hating *see* Kobbé,
Gustav *see also in his*
Plays for amateurs

Lowell, James Russell, 1819-
1891.
Il pesceballo. Opera seria:
in un atto. Cambridge: Privately printed, 1862. Title
page lacking. Bilingual text:
English and Italian, 31p.
Libretto. *[title page?:
"Musica del Maestro Rossibelli-Donimozarti." Conside-
ring the obvious combination
of names used to manufacture
this "composer" (Gioacchino
Rossini, Vincenzo Bellini,
Gaetano Donizetti, and
Wolfgang Amadeus Mozart), it
is a pity that only the
libretto was made available
to Readex. What fun the
music must have been!]*

A loyal friend *see* Townsend,
Charles

Loyal hearts...founded on the
American and Spanish war of
1898 see Lapoint, William
L.

A loyal lover see File,
Franklin

Lucas, Daniel Bedinger, 1836-
1909.
Collected works. The
dramatic works of...By C. W.
Kent and V. Lucas, editors.
Boston: Richard G. Badger,
1913. x, 6, 271p. (Univer-
sity of Virginia edition)
Contents: The maid of
Northumberland.--Hildebrand.
--Kate McDonald.

The maid of Northumberland.
New York: G. P. Putnam's
Sons, 1879. 184p.

Luce, Grace A.
Brass buttons. A comedy in
three acts. Boston: W. H.
Baker, 1900. 37p. (Baker's
edition of plays) [origi-
nally produced under the
title S. Sutherland Brey-
fogle]

Lucia di Lammermoor. Opera in
three acts. New York: n.pub.,
1856. 16p. Libretto. [music
by Gaetano Donizetti on
libretto by Salvatore Cammarano; without the music;
based on Sir Walter Scott's
Bride of Lammermoor]

Lucian-Lamb see Townsend,
Frederic in his Spiritual
visitors

Lucie of Lammermoor. An opera
in three acts. New York:
Wm. Taylor, 18-? Bilingual
text: English and Italian.
45p. Libretto. (The operatic
library. no. 12) [music by
Gaetano Donizetti on libretto
by Salvatore Cammarano;

without the music; based on
Sir Walter Scott's Bride of
Lammermoor]

Lucifer see Santayana, George

Lucilla; ten scenes in the life
of a lady of fashion see
Walker, James Barr

Lucinda's wedding. An Ethiopian
farce in two scenes. New York:
Happy Hours, 1874. 8p. (The
Ethiopian drama no. 84)

Luck see Clarke, Joseph
Ignatius Constantine

The luck of the golden pumpkin
see Wilson, Olivia W.

A lucky job see White, Charles

The lucky number see Leavitt,
Andrew J. and Eagan, H. W.

Lucretia Borgia. (From the
French of Victor Hugo.) New
York: Metropolitan Print.,
1875. Bilingual text:
English and Italian. 29p.

Lucretia Borgia. n.p.: The
Opera House, 18-? Bilingual
text: English and Italian.
55p. Libretto. [music by
Gaetano Donizetti based on
libretto Lucrezia Borgia by
Felice Romani, founded on
Lucrèce Borgia by Victor
Hugo] see also Calcaterra,
G.

Lucrezia; or, The bag of gold.
A dramatic sketch in five
acts. (Founded on a story
in Roger's poem of Italy.)
By a young gentleman of
Philadelphia. Philadelphia:
Turner & Fischer, 1848. 82p.
[based on Samuel Roger's
Italy; Library of Congress
attributes authorship to
Joseph R. Hopkins]

Lucy of Lammermoor. n.p.:
n.pub., n.d. Title page
lacking. Bilingual text:
Italian and English. 51p.
*[music by Gaetano Donizetti
on libretto by Salvatore
Cammarano; without the
music; based on Sir Walter
Scott's Bride of Lammermoor]*

Lucy's old man *see* McBride,
H. Elliott

Ludekens, Emil.
The Misses Beers. A farce.
Chicago: T. S. Denison,
c1888. 11p. (Amateur series)

Ludlow, Fitz-Hugh, 1836-1870.
Cinderella. New York: John
A. Gray & Green, 1864. 32p.

Cinderella. New York: John
A. Gray & Green, 1864.
Prompt-book with Ms. notes.
34p. (pag. irreg.)

Ludlow, Noah Miller, 1795-1886.
Coriolanus; or, The Roman
matron. A tragedy in five
acts. By William Shakespeare.
Philadelphia: Thomas H. Palmer, 1823. Ludlow's prompt-
book, interleaved with Ms.
notes. 70p.

Lütkenhaus, Anna May Irwin,
b.1874.
Master Skylark. New York:
Century, c1896 & 1914. 31p.
*[a dramatization of John
Bennett's Master Skylark]*

The lunatic *see* Dumont,
Frank

Lunatic asylum *see* White,
Charles. Pompey's patients

Luster, James O.
Dutchey vs. Nigger. An
original farce in one scene.
Clyde, O.: Ames, c1877. 6p.
(Ames' series of standard

and minor drama. no. 220)

Lying will out *see* Curtis,
Herbert Pelham

Lynch, Thomas J.
The rose of Ettrick Vale;
or, The bridal of the borders
see The rose of Ettrick
Vale; or, The bridal of the
borders

Lynd, William John.
Brantley. A drama in five
acts. Golden, Colo.: George
West, Printer, Transcript
Office, 1876. 59p.

Lyons, Joseph Aloysius, b.1838.
The miser. A comedy in three
acts. (From the French of
Molière.) Notre Dame, Ind.:
n.pub., 1886. 36p. *[based on
L'avare by Jean Baptiste
Poquelin Molière]*

Lyons, Julius J., 1843-1920.
The lady or the tiger? *see*
Rosenfeld, Sydney

Lyteria *see* Quincy, Josiah
Phillips

Lytton, Edward George Earle
Lytton Bulwer-Lytton, 1803-
1873.
The Caxtons *see* Venable,
William Henry. Good actions
mend bad actions *in his*
The school stage

Ernest Maltravers *see*
Medina, Louisa H.

Eugene Aram *see* Williams,
Espy William Hendricks

The lady of Lyons; or, Love
and pride *see* The modern
standard drama, vol. 1

The last days of Pompeii
see Medina, Louisa H.

Money *see* The modern
standard drama, vol. 1

Richelieu; or, The conspiracy
see Booth, Edwin. The miscellaneous plays of Edwin
Booth see also The modern
standard drama, vol. 1

M., M.
Uriel Acosta see Uriel
Acosta

Ma Dusenberry and her gearls
see Jaquith, Mrs. M. H.

Mabel's holiday. A comedietta
in one act. New York: Wheat
& Cornett, c1880. p.29-32.
(New York Drama. vol. 5,
no. 56)

Mabel's manoeuvre; or, A
third party see Rosenfeld,
Sydney

MacArdle, John Francis, 1842-
1883.
The marionettes see
Williams, Henry Llewellyn.
The Moko marionettes

Macarthy, Harry.
Barney's courtship; or,
Mollie dear. A musical
interlude in one act.
Chicago: Dramatic Pub. Co.,
c1871. 10p. (The comic
drama. no. 79)

Deeds of darkness. An
intellectual, farcical,
musical, fantastical,
tragical, vocal, instrumen-
tal, lyrical, moral and
laughable Ethiopian extravaganza in one act. New
York: De Witt, c1876. 8p.
(De Witt's Ethiopian and
comic drama. no. 111)

Macbeth see Hinton, Henry L.
Shakespeare's...Macbeth
see also Kelley, Edgar
Stillman. The tragedy of
Macbeth see also Mayo,
Frank see also Shakespeare,

William in Booth, Edwin.
The Shakespearean plays of
Edwin Booth see also
Shakespeare, William in
The modern standard drama,
vol. 7 see also Shakespeare's
...Macbeth

Macbeth travestie see Northall,
William Knight

Macbrayne, Lewis Edward, b.1872.
An engaging position. A comedy
in two acts. Boston: W. H.
Baker, c1898. 25p. (Baker's
edition of plays)

McBride, H. Elliott.
As by fire. A temperance drama
in five acts. Philadelphia:
Penn Pub. Co., 1911. 25p.
[earlier copyright: 1895]

Aunt Susan Jones see
Dramatic leaflets

A bad job. A farce in one act.
Chicago: T. S. Denison, c1878.
p.51-64. (Amateur series)

A big day in Bulger. A farce
in one act. Philadelphia:
Penn Pub. Co., 1912. 13p.
[copyright 1895]

A bitter dose. New York:
National Temperance Society
and Publication House, c1879.
14p. (New temperance dia-
logue)

A boy's rehearsal. New York:
National Temperance Society
and Publication House, 1879.
20p. (New temperance dia-
logue)

The closing of the "Eagle."
A temperance drama in four
acts. New York: Dick & Fitzgerald, c1877. p.136-151.
(Dick's American edition)

The cow that kicked Chicago.
A farce. Chicago: T. S.
Denison, c1882 & 1910. 10p.
(Amateur series)

Don't marry a drunkard to
reform him. A temperance
drama in five acts. New
York: Dick & Fitzgerald,
cl877. p.154-169. (Dick's
American edition)

From Punkin Ridge; or,
Belinda Jane and Jonathan.
An original comedy in one
act. New York: Dick &
Fitzgerald, cl873. 28p.

I'll stay awhile. A farce.
Chicago: T. S. Denison,
cl882. 10p.

The infernal machine see
Dramatic leaflets

Latest dialogues. Chicago:
Henneberry, n.d. 176p.
   Contents: Scene in a
tailor shop.--Separation of
Jeremiah and Seraphena.--
An up-country social circle.
--Girls' debate.--Almost an
elopement.--Trying to raise
the price of butter.--Wrong
Browns.--Miss Arabella
Clipperton's speech.--Baby
show at Skilletville.--Debate
in Squigginsville.--Speaking
extemporaneous speeches.--
Rumpus on Gingerbread Hill.
--Stepping down; or, From
affluence to poverty.--
Opposing the new school-
house.--Out of the tangle.--
Sudden bethrothal.--An intro-
ductory speech.--Frightened
beau.--An infernal machine.--
Temporary 'squire.--Scene in
a jury-room.--Before the
execution.--Pulling a tooth.
--Man under the settee.--
Uncle John.

Lucy's old man. A farce.
Chicago: T. S. Denison,
cl882. 9p. (Amateur series.
no. 203)

Marrying in haste. Boston:
Lee and Shepard, 1872. p.
132-134. Title page lacking.

My Jeremiah. A farce. Chicago:
T. S. Denison, cl882. 12p.
(Amateur series)

New dialogues. New York: Dick
& Fitzgerald, 1883. 178p.
   Contents: A happy woman.--
The somnambulist.--Those
Thompsons.--Playing school.--
Tom and Sally.--Assisting
Hezekiah.--A visit to the
oil regions.--Breaking up the
exhibition.--Turning around.
--A little boy's debate.--
The silver lining.--Restrain-
ing Jotham.--A shoemaker's
troubles.--An uncomfortable
perdicament.--The opening
speech.--The Cucumber Hill
Debating Club.--Married by
the new justice.--Bread on
the waters.--An unsuccessful
advance.--When women have
their rights.--Only another
footprint.--Rosabella's
lovers.--A smart boy.--A
heavy shower.--Master of the
situation.

On the brink; or, The re-
claimed husband. A temperance
drama in two acts. Chicago:
T. S. Denison, cl878. 34p.
(Amateur series)

Out of the depths. A temperance drama in three acts.
New York: Dick & Fitzgerald,
cl877. p.50-61. (Dick's
American edition)

A parlor entertainment see
Denison, Thomas Stewart.
Friday afternoon series of
dialogues

Played and lost. A farce.
Chicago: T. S. Denison,
cl882. 8p.

The poisoned darkys. A temperance interlude in one act.
New York: Dick & Fitzgerald,
cl877. p.31-36.

Ralph Coleman's reformation.
A temperance play in five

acts. New York: Harold
Roorbach, 187-? 12p. (The
amateur stage. no. 66)
*[the title page indicates
this play is in five acts,
whereas it is in only three
acts]*

Stage struck. Boston: Lee
and Shepard, 1872. p.611-614.
Title page lacking. (Original
dialogues)

The stolen child; or, A New
Hampshire man in Boston.
A temperance drama in two
acts. New York: Wehman Bros.,
c1882. 16p.

Striking oil. Philadelphia:
Penn Pub. Co., 1898. p.215-
240. (Keystone edition of
popular plays) *[earlier
copyright: 1888]*

A talk on temperance. New
York: National Temperance
Society and Publication
House, 1879. 7p. (New tem-
perance dialogue)

Two drams of brandy. A
temperance play in one act.
New York: Harold Roorbach,
c1881. 12p. (Roorbach's
acting drama)

Under the curse. A temperance drama in one act. New
York: Dick & Fitzgerald,
c1881. 8p.

The unwelcome guest *see*
Dramatic leaflets

Vanity vanquished *see*
Dramatic leaflets

Well fixed for a rainy day.
A temperance play in one
act. New York: Dick & Fitzgerald, c1882. 13p.

McCabe, J. L.
Maloney's wedding. An Irish
farce comedy in three acts.
Chicago: Goes Lithographing
Co., c1897. Typescript.

Prompt-book with Ms. notes.
43, 32, 22 leaves.

McCarty, William Page, 1839-
1900.
The golden horseshoe. Founded
on the historical accounts
and the legendary account by
Caruthers of the Tramontane
order, or Knights of the
golden horseshoe. Richmond:
F. A. Christian, 1876. 45p.

The prima donna. A comedietta.
n.p.: n.pub., c1892. 10p.

McClain, Billy.
"Before and after the war."
A four act spectacular
comedy. [The evolution of
the Negro. The progress of
the Afro-American...] New
York: n.pub., c1894. Typescript. 35 leaves (numb.
irreg.)

McCloskey, James Joseph, 1827-
1913.
Across the continent; or,
Scenes from New York life and
the Pacific Railroad [From:
America's lost plays. vol. 4.
Princeton: Princeton Univ.
Press, 1940] p.65-114.
[earlier copyright: 1870]

The fatal glass; or, The
curse of drink. A drama in
three acts. London and New
York: Samuel French, 18-?
36p. (French's acting edition.
Late Lacy's)

McConaughy, Julia E. Loomis,
b.1834.
The drunkard's daughter *see*
A collection of temperance
dialogues

MacConnell, Harry T.
The casino girl *see* Smith,
Harry Bache

McCord, Louisa Susannah Cheves,
1810-1880.

Caius Gracchus. New York:
H. Kernot, 1851. 128p.

McCracken, J. L. H.
Earning a living. A comedy
in five acts. By a citizen of
New York (pseud.) New York:
Pudney and Russell, 1849.
63p.

McCullough, John, 1832-1885.
Brutus see Payne, John
Howard, Stark, James, and
McCullough, John in Booth,
Edwin. The miscellaneous
plays of Edwin Booth

Virginius. (Adapted from
J. S. Knowles.) Philadelphia:
Ledger Job Print., 1882.
Title page lacking. 45p.
[adapted from James Sheridan
Knowles' Virginius]

McDermott, J. J.
All in der family. A Dutch
sketch in two scenes. New
York: Happy Hours, c1875.
9p. (The variety stage.
no. 12) [joint author:
Trumble]

"A dark noight's business."
An Irish sketch in one scene.
New York: H. Roorbach, c1875.
9p. (The variety stage)
[joint author: Trumble]

Dot mad tog. A Dutch sketch
in one scene. New York: Dick
& Fitzgerald, c1875. 8p.
(The variety stage) [joint
author: Trumble]

Dot madrimonial adverdisement. A Dutch sketch in one
scene. New York: H. Roorbach,
c1875. 9p. (The variety
stage) [joint author: Trumble]

Dot quied lotgings. A Dutch
sketch in one scene. New York:
H. Roorbach, c1875. 8p. (The
variety stage) [joint author:
Trumble]

A game of billiards. A tem-

perance sketch in one scene.
New York: Happy Hours, c1875.
9p. (The amateur stage. no.
39) [joint author: Trumble]

Mulcahy's cat. An Irish sketch
in one scene. New York: H.
Roorbach, c1875. 8p. (The
variety stage) [joint author:
Trumble]

The ould man's coat tails.
An Irish sketch in one scene.
New York: H. Roorbach, c1891.
8p. (The variety stage)(Roorbach's acting drama) [joint
author: Trumble]

A purty shure cure. An Irish
sketch in one scene. New York:
H. Roorbach, c1875. 10p. (The
variety stage)(Roorbach's
acting drama. no. 14) [joint
author: Trumble]

Who got the pig? An Irish
sketch in one scene. New York:
Dick & Fitzgerald, c1875. 9p.
[joint author: Trumble]

The wrong bottle. A temperance
sketch in one scene. New York:
Dick & Fitzgerald, 1875. 9p.
(The amateur stage) [joint
author: Trumble]

MacDonald, Malcolm.
Guatemozin. A drama. Philadelphia: J. B. Lippincott,
1878. 191p.

MacDonough, Glen, 1866?-1924.
The Algerian. A comedy opera
in three acts. New York:
G. Schirmer, c1893. Vocal
score. 8, 219p. [music by
Reginald DeKoven]

McFadden, Theodore.
Madalena; or, The maids'
mischief. A drama. By Theodore
Davenport Warner (pseud.)
Philadelphia: J. B. Lippincott,
1888. 245p.

McFall, B. G.
Among the moonshiners; or, A

drunkard's legacy. A temperance drama in three acts. Clyde, O.: Ames, c1897. 26p. (Ames' series of standard and minor drama. no. 391)

Joshua Blodgett, from Blodgett's Holler. A comedy in three acts. Clyde, O.: Ames, 1897. 29p. (Ames' series of standard and minor drama. no. 383)

Miss Topsy Turvy; or, The courtship of the deacon. A comedy in three acts. Clyde, O.: Ames, 1899. 31p. (Ames' series of standard and minor drama. no. 411)

McGee, Thomas D'Arcy, 1825-1868.
Sebastian; or, The Roman martyr. A drama in four acts. New York: D. & J. Sadlier, 1861. 52p. *[founded on Nicholas Patrick Stephen Wiseman's Fabiola; or, The Church of the Catacombs]*

McIntosh, Maria Jane, 1803-1878.
[A champion, though no fighter] *see* Venable, William Henry *in his* The school stage

McIntyre, John Thomas, 1871-1951.
Hearts of men. A drama in four acts. Philadelphia: Penn Pub. Co., 1914. 47p. *[earlier copyright: 1899]*

In the toils. A melodrama in five acts. Philadelphia: Penn Pub. Co., 1914. 53p. *[earlier copyright: 1898]*

Mack, John.
Weston, the walkist *see* White, Charles

Mack, Robert Ellice.
Cousin Fannie. A comedy in

three acts. New York: French, 18--. 12p. (French's minor drama. no. 314)

An Irishman's maneuver; or, Mike Donovan's courtship. A comedy in two acts. New York: T. H. French, 18-? 8p. (French's minor drama. no. 313) *[Readex also enters this play under title; taken together, they represent different editions with identical text]*

The masquerade; or, Aunt Hepsaba's fright. A farce in two scenes [From: The New York Drama. New York: Wheat & Cornett, 1878. vol. 4, no. 47] p.349-352.

'Tis the darkest hour before dawn. A petite comedy in one act. New York: S. French, 187-? 12p. (French's minor drama. no. 315)

Mackay, Frank Findley, 1832-1923.
A double life; or, Where there's a will there's a way. An original comedy in three acts. New York: n.pub., c1895. Typescript. 76 leaves.

Mackay, Mary, 1855-1924.
The sorrows of Satan; or, The strange experience of one Geoffrey Tempest, millionaire *see* Creagh, Henry

MacKaye, James Steele, 1842-1894.
An arrant knave & other plays. Princeton, N. J.: Princeton Univ. Press, 1941. xvii, 234p. (America's lost plays, vol. 2) Contents: Rose Michel. A romantic drama in five acts *[founded on Ernest Blum's Rose Michel]*.--Won at last. A play in five acts.--In spite of all. A play in four acts.--An arrant knave. A

medieval comedy in four
acts [originally entitled
Chiqui]

Hazel Kirke. A domestic
comedy-drama in four acts.
New York: M. H. Mallory,
1880. 64p.

Hazel Kirke. A domestic
play in four acts. n.p.:
n.pub., 189-? Typescript,
prompt-book. In four acts
(pag. by acts) with property
plot.

In spite of all. A play in
four acts. Windsor, Vt.:
n.pub., 189-? Photostat of
typescript (pag. by acts)

Money mad. n.p.: n.pub.,
188-? Typescript. In four
acts (pag. by acts)

Paul Kauvar; or, Anarchy.
A play in five acts [From:
Moses, M. J.: Representative
plays by American dramatists.
vol. 3. New York: B. Blom,
1925] p.235-354.

Rose Michel. A romantic play
in five acts. (From the
French of Ernest Blum.) n.p.:
n.pub., 1928. Typescript.
113p. [written in 1875]

MacKaye, Percy, 1875-1956.
A garland to Sylvia. A
dramatic reverie with a
prologue. New York: Macmillan,
1910. xxi, 177p.

A song at the castle see
Sutherland, Evelyn Greenleaf
Baker in her Collected
works. Po' white trash and
other one-act dramas

MacKaye, Steele, 1842-1894
see MacKaye, James Steele

McKee, W. J.
Gettysburg. A drama of the
American Civil War. Pittsburgh: Nevin, Gribbin,
c1879. 87p.

The last witness see Taylor,
W. A. and McKee, W. J.

Mackenzie, James Bovell, 1851-
1919.
Thayendanegea: an historico-
military drama. Toronto: For
the author only by William
Briggs, 1898. 179p.

McKinley, Henry J.
Brigham Young; or, The
prophet's last love. A play
in three acts. San Francisco:
Excelsior Press, Bacon & Co.,
1870. 30p.

McLachlan, Charles.
I dine with my mother. A
comedietta in one act. (From
the French of Decourcelle's
"Je dine chez ma mère.")
New York: S. French, 1857?
15p. (The minor drama. no.
108)

McLellan, Charles Morton
Stewart, 1865-1916.
The belle of New York. A
musical comedy in two acts.
By Hugh Morton [pseud.]
London: Hopewood & Crew,
c1897-98. Vocal score. 213p.
[music by Gustave Kerker]

The girl from up there. A
fantastic musical comedy.
By Hugh Morton [pseud.]
(Also known as The golden
cup.) New York: Rosenfield
Typewriting, 1900? Typescript,
prompt-book. In three acts
(pag. by acts) Libretto.
[music by Gustave Kerker;
without the music]

McLellan, Rufus Charles.
The foundling; or, Yankee
fidelity. A drama in two
acts. Philadelphia: King &
Baird, 1839. 68p.

McMechan, Robert I.
Gracie and Genaro [From his:
Poems and songs. Cincinnati:

Elm Street Print. Co., 1877.
156p.] p.118-126.

McMichael, Clayton Fotterall.
Kenilworth; or, Amy's aims
and Leicester's lesson.
An original burlesque in
two acts. Philadelphia:
Avil Print. Co., 1894. 40p.
[music by Edmond D. Beale;
without the music]

Macomb, Alexander, 1782-1841.
Pontiac; or, The siege of
Detroit. A drama in three
acts. Boston: Samuel Colman,
1835. 60p.

MacSwiney, Paul.
Brian. A tragedy. New York:
Beith Luis Nion Fraternity,
18-? 72p.

Macy, James Cartwright, 1845-
1918.
Der Freyschutz. Grand opera
in three acts. (From the
German of Kind.) Boston:
Oliver Ditson, 1895. 34p.
Libretto. *[music by Karl*
Maria Friedrich Ernst von
Weber; without the music]

Rustic chivalry (Cavalleria
rusticana.) Melodrama in
one act. Boston: Oliver
Ditson, c1892. Vocal score.
Bilingual text: English and
Italian. 135p. *[music by*
Pietro Mascagni on libretto
Cavalleria rusticana by
Giovanni Targioni-Tozzetti
and Guido Menasci]

Macy, William Francis, 1867-
1935.
A lion among the ladies.
A comedy in two acts. Boston:
W. H. Baker, c1890. 24p.
(Baker's edition of plays)

A mad astronomer *see* Sedgwick, Alfred B.

Mad dogs; or, The two Caesars
see Moore, John

A mad match; or, The heartless
brother *see* Lookup, Thomas

A mad philosopher *see* Brown,
John Henry

Madalena; or, The maids' mischief *see* McFadden, Theodore

Madam Piper *see* Morse, Woolson

Madame Butterfly *see* Belasco,
David

Madame devil-may-care *see*
Meltzer, Charles Henry.
Madame sans-gêne

Madame Grundy's dilemma *see*
Sanford, Amelia. Maids,
modes and manners; or,
Madame Grundy's dilemma

Madame Guyon *see* Opal (pseud.)
in her The cloud of witnesses

Madame is abed *see* Woodward,
John A.

Madame Princeton's temple of
beauty *see* Denison, Thomas
Stewart

Madame sans-gêne *see* Meltzer,
Charles Henry

Madame Surratt *see* Rogers,
James Webb

Mad-cap *see* Shields, Sarah
Annie Frost *in her* Parlor
charades and proverbs

Madden, Eva Annie, b.1863.
A noble spy. An historical
play for boys. New York and
Chicago: E. L. Kellogg, 1899.
16p.

Maddox, D. S.

The man from Arizona. A
farce in one act. Philadelphia: Penn Pub. Co., 1899.
10p. (Dramatic library. vol.
1, no. 189)

Madelaine Morel *see* Daly,
Augustin

Madelaine, the bell of Faubourg
see Cunningham, Virginia
Juhan

Mademoiselle de Belle-Isle.
A drama in five acts. (From
the French of Dumas.) New
York: Darcie & Corbyn, 1855.
Bilingual text: French and
English. 71p. *[The original
play was written by Alexandre
Dumas the elder, in colla-
boration with Alexandre
Florian Joseph Colonna
Walewski]*

Mademoiselle's Christmas gifts
see Graham, Mary *in*
Bartlett, George Bradford.
A dream of the centuries
and other entertainments
for parlor and hall

Madmen all; or, The cure of
love *see* Paulding, James
Kirke and Paulding, William
Irving *in their* Collected
works. American comedies

Mae Blossoms reward *see*
Lamson, C. A. Grandmother
Hildebrand's legacy; or,
Mae Blossoms reward

Maeder, Frederick George,
1840-1891.
My sweetheart. An operatic
comic drama in three acts.
London and New York: S.
French, n.d. 40p. (Lacy's
acting edition. vol. 147)
[joint author: William Gill]

The runaway wife *see*
Rankin, McKee and Maeder,

Frederick George

Das maedle und ihr sailor Kerl
see Moss, Alfred Charles.
H. M. S. Pinafore; oder, Das
maedle und ihr sailor Kerl

Maeterlinck, Maurice, 1862-1949.
Alladine et Palomides *see*
Hovey, Richard *in his*
The plays of Maurice Maeter-
linck. Second series *see*
also Porter, Charlotte
Endymion and Clarke, Helen
Archibald

Les aveugles *see* Hovey,
Richard. The blind *in his*
The plays of Maurice
Maeterlinck [First series]
see also Porter, Charlotte
Endymion and Clarke, Helen
Archibald. The sightless

Intérieur *see* Hovey,
Richard. Home *in his* The
plays of Maurice Maeterlinck.
Second series

L'intruse *see* Hovey, Richard.
The intruder *in his* The
plays of Maurice Maeterlinck
[First series]

La mort de Tintagiles *see*
Hovey, Richard *in his* The
plays of Maurice Maeterlinck.
Second series.

Pélleas et Mélisande *see*
Byrne, Charles Alfred *see*
also Hovey, Richard *in his*
The plays of Maurice Maeterlinck. Second series

La princesse Maleine *see*
Hovey, Richard *in his* The
plays of Maurice Maeterlinck
[First series]

Les sept princesses *see*
Hovey, Richard *in his* The
plays of Maurice Maeterlinck
[First series] *see also*
Porter, Charlotte Endymion
and Clarke, Helen Archibald

Maffitt, James Strawbridge,
1832-1897.
The mutton trial see White,
Charles

Magda see Winslow, Charles
Edward Amory

The Magdalen report. A farce
in three acts. By Peter
Pendergrass, senior (pseud.)
New York: n.pub., 1831. 25p.

The magic ball see Pailler,
William

The magic penny see White,
Charles

The magician's troubles see
Charles. The African box;
or, The magician's troubles

The magnetiser; or, Ready for
anybody see Osborn,
Laughton

Magnus, Julian.
A bad case see Bunner,
Henry Cuyler and Magnus,
Julian see also Matthews,
Brander. Comedies for ama-
teur acting

Les Fourchambault. A drama
in five acts [From the New
York Drama. New York: Wheat
& Cornett, 1878. vol. 4,
no. 42] p.161-182. [adapted
from the French of Guillaume
Victor Émile Augier]

A trumped suit. A comedy in
one act. Boston: W. H.
Baker, 1902. 51p. (Baker's
edition of plays) [based on
Eugène Marin Labiche's Les
deux timides; earlier copyright: 1879] see also
Matthews, Brander. Comedies
for amateur acting

Magnus, Maurice, 1876-1920.
Eldyle. An aesthetic drama.
New York: Ego Press, 1898.
28p.

Magpie and the maid see
Coale, George B.

Maguire, John.
Honesty is the best policy;
or, True to the core. A play
in one act and one scene.
New York: C. T. De Witt,
c1877. 8p. (De Witt's acting
plays. no. 211)

Maguire, Walter Haynes.
A scratch race. A comedy in
one act. By Walt Makee
(pseud.) Boston: Walter H.
Baker, 1900. 13p.

"The maid and the marquis" see
Morrison, George Austin.
"Lafayette"; or, "The maid
and the marquis"

The maid and the moonshiner
see Hoyt, Charles Hale

Maid Marion see Smith,
Harry Bache

The maid of Arran see Baum,
Louis F.

The maid of Florence; or, A
woman's vengeance. A pseudo-
historical tragedy in five
acts. Philadelphia: Turner &
Fisher, 18-? 76p. (Turner's
dramatic library of acting
plays. New series. vol. 8,
no. 55) [Readex enters a
different edition of this
play under Virginia Juhan
Cunningham, q.v.]

The maid of honor see Weil,
Oscar

The maid of Munster see Bayly,
Thomas Haynes. Perfection;
or, The maid of Munster in
The modern standard drama,
vol. 4

The maid of Northumberland see
Lucas, Daniel Bedinger see also
his Collected works

The maid of Orleans *see*
Calvert, George Henry

The maid of Saxony; or, Who's
the traitor? *see* Morris,
George Pope

The maid of the lighthouse *see*
Busch, William

Maiden Mona the mermaid *see*
D., F. A.

The maiden who couldn't laugh
see S., E. S. The Princess
Chrysalline; or, The maiden
who couldn't laugh

The maiden wife *see* Goodrich,
Frank Boott and Warden,
Frank L. Romance after
marriage; or, The maiden
wife

The maiden's oath *see* Lawson,
James

The maiden's progress *see*
Hunt, Violet

The maids' mischief *see*
McFadden, Theodore. Madalena;
or, The maids' mischief

Maids, modes and manners; or,
Madame Grundy's dilemma *see*
Sanford, Amelia

Mair, Charles, 1838-1927.
Tecumseh [From his: Tecumseh
...and other Canadian poems.
Toronto: William Briggs,
1901. Second edition. 276p.]
p.8-127, 251-270.

Major, George MacDonald,
fl.1882-1903.
In the god's shadow. New
York: De Vinne Press, 1891.
Limited edition. 88p.

Major Aborn's proposal. A
comedy in one act. New York:
Dick & Fitzgerald, 18-? 20p.

Major John André *see* Haid,
P. Leo

Major Jones courtship; or,
Adventures of a Christmas
Eve *see* Thompson, William
Tappan

A majority of one; or, Love
and mushrooms *see* Harris,
Francis Augustine

Makee, Walt (pseud.) *see*
Maguire, Walter Haynes

Making a hit *see* Dumont, Frank

Making an orator *see* Denton,
Clara Janetta Fort. When the
lessons are over

Malachi and Miranda *see*
Monroe, Jasper R.

Malicious trespass; or, Nine
points of law *see* White,
Charles

Malinche *see* Hopkins, Rufus
Clement

Malloy, Louise.
The prince's wooing. A dramatic poem. Baltimore: American
Job Printing Office, 1894.
31p.

Malone, Walter, 1866-1915.
Claribel [From his: Claribel,
and other poems. Louisville,
Ky.: J. P. Morton, 1882]
p.143-231. *[written when
Malone was between 15 and 16
years old]*

Inez [From his: Claribel, and
other poems. Louisville, Ky.:
J. P. Morton, 1882] p.7-82.
*[written when Malone was
14 years old]*

Maloney's wedding *see* McCabe,
J. L.

The man about town *see* Bowers, E.

Man and wife *see* Daly, Augustin *see also* Webber, Harry A.

Man-fish *see* Leavitt, Andrew J. and Eagan, H. W. No tator; or, Man-fish

The man from Arizona *see* Maddox, D. S.

The man from Maine *see* Townsend, Charles

The man from Mexico *see* Du Souchet, Henry A.

The man from Texas *see* Moore, Bernard Francis

The man-hater *see* Corwin, C. J.

The man in the case *see* Packard, Winthrop

The man Mohammed *see* Stecker, Tom

"The man of mark" *see* Dinsmore, William. His chris cross mark. "The man of mark"

Man of millions *see* Patten, Gilbert. Nan, the mascotte

A man of nerve *see* Tees, Levin C. A rogue's luck; or, A man of nerve

The man of success *see* Cazauran, Augustus R.

The man of ten thousand. A comedy in five acts. (Adapted from Thomas Holcroft.) [From: Alexander's modern acting drama... Philadelphia: Carey & Hart, Hogen & Thompson and W.

Marshall & Co., 1835. vol.3] p.7-80.

The man of the people *see* Simms, William Gilmore. Norman Maurice; or, The man of the people

A man of the world *see* Thomas, Augustus

Man proposes. In several declarations and one act *see* Ford, Paul Leicester

The man under the settee *see* McBride, H. Elliott *in his* Latest dialogues

The man who went to Europe *see* Denton, Clara Janetta Fort

The man with the carpet bag *see* A Beckett, Gilbert Abbott *in* Massey, Charles. Massey's exhibition reciter

The man with the demijohn *see* Baker, George Melville

A manager's trials *see* Fisher, Abraham Lincoln

The mandarin *see* Smith, Harry Bache

The maniac *see* Dawes, Rufus. The battle of Stillwater; or, The maniac

The maniac at the island of St. Domingo. A semi-serious opera in two acts. New York: John Douglas, 1848. Bilingual text: English and Italian. 69p. Libretto. (The operatic library. no. 13) *[music by Gaetano Donizetti on libretto Il furioso all'isola di S. Domingo by Jacopo Ferretti; without the music]*

The maniac wife *see* Hollenbeck, Benjamin W. After

ten years; or, The maniac
wife

Manning, Kathryn.
Francesco Carrara. A drama
in three acts. Chicago:
Dramatic Pub. Co., c1899.
32p. (Sergel's acting drama.
no. 550) [title page: "From
the French"]

Manola; or, The day and the
night see Woolf, Benjamin
Edward

Mansfield, Richard, 1857-1907.
Bouffer and breeze. Opera-
bouffe in one act. New
York?: n.pub., 189-? 15p.

Don Juan. A play in four
acts. New York: Published
for the author by J. W.
Bouton, 1891. 191p.

King Henry V. A history in
five acts. New York:
McClure, Phillips, 1901.
xviii, 124p. [title page:
"by William Shakespeare."]

King Richard the third.
By William Shakespeare. New
York: Metropolitan Job
Print., 18-? 29p.

A mantle of charity see
Phelps, Lavinia Howe in
her Dramatic stories

Many minds in a minute see
Steele, Silas Sexton. The
lawyer, doctor, soldier
and actor; or, Many minds
in a minute in his Collected works. Book of plays

Mappalicus and Bona see
Opal (pseud.) in her The
cloud of witnesses

Maquis, Gaston, b.1860.
C'est le professeur see
Baker, George Melville.
Gustave the professor

Marble, Scott.
Down in Dixie. New York:
n.pub., 1897? Typescript,
prompt-book with Ms. notes.
20, 15, 9, 13 leaves.

The great train robbery.
An original Western drama in
four acts. n.p.: n.pub.,
1896. Typescript, prompt-
book with Ms. notes. 56 leaves.

The stars and stripes. n.p.:
n.pub., 189-. Typescript,
prompt-book. 13, 14, 16
leaves.

The marble bride see Zampa;
or, The marble bride

Marco Bozzaris see Requier,
Augustus Julian

Marcus Aurelius-Howard see
Townsend, Frederic in his
Spiritual visitors

Mardi Gras in New Orleans see
Reynartz, Dorothy. Carnival;
or, Mardi Gras in New Orleans

Mardoche see Knapp, A. Melvin

Maréchalle, Alexandre Marie,
b.1786.
Le deux pénsions see
Payne, John Howard. The
boarding schools; or, Life
among the little folks

Margaret of Anjou see Phelan,
Agnes Vivien

Margery's lovers see Matthews,
Brander

Maria and Magdalena see
Hollenius, Laurence John

Maria Candelaria see Brinton,
Daniel Garrison

Maria Stuart. (From the German
of Schiller.) New York:

Academy of Music, 18-? Bilingual text: English and German. 52p.

Mariamne *see* Osborn, Laughton

Mariana; or, The coquette *see* Morris, Thomas Hollingsworth

Marian's wish *see* Merriman, Effie Woodward *see also in her* Comedies for children

Marie, a woman of the people. The great emotional play in a prologue and five acts. n.p.: n.pub., 1878. Promptbook, interleaved with Ms. notes. 47 leaves.

Marie Antoinette *see* Pray, Isaac Clarke

Marie Antoinette: Queen of France *see* Forrest, Harry

Marie; or, The daughter of the regiment *see* Seguin, Arthur Edward Sheldon

Marie Stuart. A tragedy in five acts. (From the French of Lebrun.) New York: Darcie & Corbyn, 1855. Bilingual text: English and French. 47p. *[based on Pierre Antoine Lebrun's Marie Stuart]*

Marie's secret *see* Locke, Belle Marshall

The mariner's return *see* Putnam, Henry Howell

The mariner's tale *see* Smith, Richard Penn *in his* Dramatic fragments

Marion; or, The reclaimed *see* Hamilton, John R.

Marius (pseud.) *see* For myself alone

La marjolaine (The sweet marjoram.) Opera bouffe in three acts. (From the French of Van Loo and Leterrier.) New York: Metropolitan Job Printing Establishment, 1877. Bilingual text: English and French. 74p. Libretto. *[music by Alexandre Charles Lecocq on libretto by Albert Vanloo and Eugène Leterrier]*

Marjorie Daw *see* Braddon, Mary Elizabeth

Marlow, George. Adrienne Lecouvreur. A tragedy in five acts. New York: n.pub., n.d. Bilingual text: English and German. 38p. *[cover: "by [Heinrich] Grans"]*

Marlowe, Julia. Ingomar the barbarian *see* Sothern, Edward Hugh and Marlowe, Julia

Marplot *see* Shields, Sarah Annie Frost *in her* Parlor charades and proverbs

The marquis *see* Fisher, Abraham Lincoln

Marras, Mowbray. Gabriella *see* Byrne, Charles Alfred and Marras, Mowbray

Marriage by moonlight; or, Hap-hazard *see* Herne, James A. and Belasco, David

The marriage contract *see* Bannister, Nathaniel Harrington. The gentleman of Lyons; or, The marriage contract

A marriage for revenge *see* Howell, S.

The marriage of Georgette *see*

Harrison, William

The marriage of Guenevere *see*
Hovey, Richard

The marriage of Prince
Flutterby *see* Wilson,
Olivia Lovell

Married and single *see*
Poole, John *in* The modern
standard drama, vol. 10

Married bachelors; or,
Pleasant surprises *see*
Rosenfeld, Sydney

Married by the new justice
see McBride, H. Elliott
in his New dialogues

Marry no man if he drinks;
or, Laura's plan and how it
succeeded *see* Bradley,
Nellie H. *see also*
A collection of temperance
dialogues

Marryat, Frederick, 1792-1848.
[A lighter-boy at school]
see Venable, William Henry
in his The school stage

Marrying a fortune *see*
Kavanaugh, Mrs. Russell
in her Original dramas,
dialogues

Marrying in haste *see*
McBride, H. Elliott

Mars, Antony, b.1862.
Les surprises du divorce
see Daly, Augustin. The
lottery of love

Mars and Venus *see* Cobb,
Mary L. Poetical dramas
for home and school

Mars in Mahantango. A play in
five acts. By admirers of
the anthracite drama, and
dedicated to its friends in
Schuylkill County. Potts-
ville, Pa.: Benjamin Bannon,
1852. 100p.

Marsden, Fred (pseud.) *see*
Silver, W. A.

Marshall, Robert, 1863-1910.
His excellency the governor.
A farcical romance in three
acts. Boston: Walter H.
Baker, c1901. 152p.

Marshall, William.
Aarbert. A drama without
stage or scenery, wrought
out through song in many
metres, mostly lyric. New
York: New Amsterdam Book Co.,
1898. 364p. *[prefaced by a
58-page glossary of unusual
and manufactured words used
in the drama]*

Martha's triumph *see* Careo,
Zella. The hidden treasures;
or, Martha's triumph

Martin, Edouard, 1828-1866.
La poudre aux yeux *see*
Fuller, Horace Williams.
False pretensions

Martin, W. H.
Servants vs. master; or, A
father's will. A comedy
drama in three acts. Clyde,
O.: Ames, 1898. 23p. (Ames'
series of standard and
minor drama. no. 404)

The martyrdom of Frederick *see*
Huntington, Gurdon. The
guests of Brazil; or, The
martyrdom of Frederick

The martyrdom of St. Cecily
see Christie, Albany

The martyrs' idol *see* Guiney,
Louise Imogen

The martyrs of Corea *see*
Isoleri, Antonio. Religion
and fatherland; or, The
martyrs of Corea

Mary Queen of Scots *see* Bell, Henry Glassford *in* Massey, Charles. Massey's exhibition reciter

Mary Stuart *see* Ascher, Anton. Scenes from Mary Stuart *see also* Brooks, Edward

Mary, the fisherman's child *see* Herne, James A. Drifting apart; or, Mary, the fisherman's child *see also in his* The early plays of James A. Herne

Mary's birthday; or, The cynic *see* Miles, George Henry

Ma's new boarders *see* Parker, Walter Coleman

Masaniello. (From the French of Scribe.) New York: C. D. Koppel, 1885? Bilingual text: English and German. 33p. Libretto. *[based on Masaniello, ou la muette de Portici, by Augustin Eugène Scribe and Germain Delavigne, as set to music by Daniel François Esprit Auber]*

Mascagni, Pietro, 1863-1945. L'amico Fritz *see* Dole, Nathan Haskell. Friend Fritz

Cavalleria rusticana *see* Day, Willard Gibson *see also* Macy, James Cartwright. Rustic chivalry (Cavalleria rusticana) *see also* Tretbar, Helen D. Rustic chivalry

Zanetto *see* Schmall, Alice F.

The mascot *see* Barker, Theodore T. and Norcross, I. W.

La mascotte *see* Elson, Louis Charles and Norris, J. W.

The mashers mashed *see* Cutler, F. L.

The masked ball *see* Fitch, Clyde *see also* Rattermann, Heinrich Armin. Gustavus III; or, The masked ball

The masked ball; or, The rose-colored domino *see* Steele, Silas Sexton *in his* Collected works. Book of plays

The masonic lodge. A negro initiation. Chicago: Dramatic Pub. Co., c1898. 6 unnumbered pages. (The comic drama. no. 191)

A masque *see* Mitchell, Silas Weir

A masque of culture *see* Trumbull, Annie Eliot

The masque of judgment *see* Moody, William Vaughn

The masque of Pandora *see* Longfellow, Henry Wadsworth

The masque of the gods *see* Taylor, Bayard *see also in his* Collected works. The dramatic works

The masquerade ball *see* Griffin, George W. H. The ticket-taker; or, The masquerade ball *see also* Haskett, Emmett. Bridget Branagan's troubles; or, The masquerade ball

The masquerade; or, Aunt Hepsaba's fright *see* Mack, Robert Ellice

The massacre of St. Bartholomew *see* Jones, Joseph Stevens.

The carpenter of Rouen; or,
The massacre of St. Bartholomew see also Jones,
Joseph Stevens. The surgeon
of Paris; or, The massacre
of St. Bartholomew

Massé, Victor, 1822-1884.
The marriage of Georgette
see Harrison, William

Massenet, Jules Émile Frédéric,
1842-1912.
Werther see Ginty, Eliza-
beth Beall

Massey, Charles.
Massey's exhibition reciter,
and drawing room entertain-
ments. Nos.1-2. New York:
Samuel French, c1856. 186p.
Contents: Little Jim.--
Guy Fawkes; or, A match for
a king.--The mourners (Eliza
Cook).--The man with the
carpet bag (Gilbert Abbott
à Beckett).--Mary Queen of
Scots (Henry Glassford Bell).
--Mesmerism (William Bayle
Bernard).--The little vulgar
boy (Thomas Hood).--The
white horse of the Peppers
(Samuel Lover).--The sea
liberty's emblem.--Against
the American War (Chatham).
--Scotland (Flagg).--Appeal
on behalf of Greece (Lacey).
--Abou Ben Adhem (Leigh
Hunt).--The necessity of
union (Daniel Webster).--
In favor of the American
War (Patrick Henry).--Last
days of Herculaneum (Edwin
Atherstone).--The American
forest girl (Felicia Doro-
thea Browne Hemans).--Love
and jealousy; or, A tragedy
for the million.--The
execution of Montrose (Wm.
Edmonstone Aytoun).--The
Irish tutor (Richard Butler
Glengall).--The soldier
from Bingen (Mrs. Norton).--
Bombastes furioso (William

Barnes Rhodes).--Bernard del
Carpio (Felicia Dorothea
Browne Hemans).--Sylvester
Daggerwood (George Colman).--
Lochinvar (Sir Walter Scott).
--Paddy Dunbar.--The school
for orators.--The dream of
Eugene Aram (Thomas Hood).--
Amateur and professional
acting.--The drunkard's story
(Buckstone).--He was a very
jonteel man for all dat.--
Ginevra (Samuel Rogers).--
The workhouse boy.--Sparticus
to the gladiators at Capua
(E. Kellogg).--Look at the
clock (Thomas Ingoldsby).--
Garrick and the tailor.--
Parrhasius (William Gorman
Wills).--Darkness (George
Gordon Byron).--Daniel v.
Dishcloth (Stevens).--Letter
from a Presidential candidate.
Biglow papers. [In most collections of this type, only
the dramatic works have been
analyzed. Since this is a
typical example of its time,
however, it seemed advisable
to analyze, insofar as
possible, all titles, whether
dramatic works, speeches,
monologues, etc.]

Massey's exhibition reciter,
and drawing room entertainments see Massey, Charles

Massinger, Philip, 1583-1640.
A new way to pay old debts
see The modern standard
drama, vol. 5

Master and slave see Barbauld,
Anna Letitia Aikin in
Follen, Eliza Lee Cabot. Home
dramas for young people

Master Goat, the tailor see
Dulcken, Henry William in
Venable, William Henry. The
school stage

Master of the situation see

McBride, H. Elliott *in his*
New dialogues

Master skylark *see* Lütkenhaus, Anna May Irwin

The mastersingers of Nuremberg
see Jameson, Frederick

The match-box *see* Woodbury,
Alice Gale

A match for a king *see*
Massey, Charles. Guy Fawkes;
or, A match for a king *in*
Massey's exhibition reciter

A match safe *see* Reynolds,
Phineas

Matchmakers *see* Trumbull,
Annie Eliot

A matchmaking father; or,
The bashful suitor *see*
Shettel, James W. and
George, Wadsworth M.

Maternus *see* Spencer, Edward

Mathews, Cornelius, 1817-1889.
Calmstorm, the reformer. A
dramatic comment. New York:
W. H. Tinson, 1853. 71p.

False pretences; or, Both
sides of good society. A
comedy in five acts. New
York: For the author, 1856.
88p.

The politicians. A comedy
in five acts. New York:
n.pub., 1840. 118p.

Witchcraft. A tragedy in
five acts. New York: S.
French, 1852. 99p.

Mathews, Frances Aymar, c1865-
1925.
All for sweet charity.
Comedy for three males and
nine females. New York:
Edgar S. Werner, 1907. 17p.
(Werner edition) *[title*

page: c1889]
American hearts. Comedy for
two males and two females.
New York: Edgar S. Werner,
1907. 13p. (Werner edition)
[title page: c1889]

The apartment. Comedy for
four males and two females.
New York: Edgar S. Werner,
1907. 14p. (Werner edition)
[title page: c1889]

At the Grand Central. Comedy
for two females. New York:
Edgar S. Werner, 1907. 13p.
(Werner edition) *[title page:
c1889]*

Both sides of the counter.
Comedy for one male and two
females. New York: Edgar S.
Werner, 1907. 14p. (Werner
edition) *[title page: c1889]*

Charming conversationalist.
Comedy for one male and two
females. New York: Edgar S.
Werner, 1907. 8p. (Werner
edition) *[title page: c1889;
the Readex microprint omits
the cast and first three
pages of the text]*

The courier. Comedy for two
males and three females.
New York: Edgar S. Werner,
1907. 15p. (Werner edition)
[title page: c1889]

Cousin Frank. A farce in one
act for female characters
only. Boston: Walter Baker,
1896. 9p. (Baker's edition
of plays)

En voyage. Comedy for two
males and two females. New
York: Edgar S. Werner, 1907.
13p. (Werner edition) *[title
page: c1889]*

A finished coquette. A
comedietta in one act. Boston: W. H. Baker, 1895. 16p.
(Baker's edition of plays)

The honeymoon; fourth quarter.

Comedy for two males and
two females. New York:
Edgar S. Werner, 1907. 13p.
(Werner edition) [title
page: c1889]

A knight of the quill.
Comedy for three males and
one female. New York: Edgar
S. Werner, 1907. 13p.
(Werner edition) [title
page: c1889]

On the staircase. Comedy for
one male and one female.
New York: Edgar S. Werner,
1907. 12p. (Werner edition)
[title page: c1889]

Paying the piper. Comedy for
one male and six females.
New York: Edgar S. Werner,
1907. 13p. (Werner edition)
[title page: c1889]

The proposal. Comedy for
one male and two females.
New York: Edgar S. Werner,
1907. 12p. (Werner edition)
[title page: c1889]

Scapegrace. Comedy for one
male and six females. New
York: Edgar S. Werner, 1907.
16p. (Werner edition) [title
page: c1889; this is the
same play as Mathews' Six
to one; or, The scapegrace]

Six to one; or, The scapegrace. A comedietta in one
act. Boston: W. H. Baker,
c1896. 14p. (Baker's edition
of plays) [title page:
c1887; this is the same
play as Mathews' Scapegrace]

Snowbound. Comedy for two
males and two females. New
York: Edgar S. Werner, 1907.
20p. (Werner edition) [title
page: c1889]

Teacups. Comedy for three
males and two females. New
York: Edgar S. Werner, 1907.
13p. (Werner edition) [title
page: c1889]

The title and the money.
Comedy for two males and
two females. New York:
Edgar S. Werner, 1907. 13p.
(Werner edition) [title
page: c1889]

War to the knife. Comedy for
two males and two females.
New York: Edgar S. Werner,
1907. 13p. (Werner edition)
[title page: c1889]

The wedding tour. Comedy for
five males and four females.
New York: Edgar S. Werner,
1907. 14p. (Werner edition)
[title page: c1889]

A woman's forever. Comedy
for one male and one female.
New York: Edgar S. Werner,
1907. 8p. (Werner edition)
[title page: c1889]

Wooing a widow. A comedietta
in one act. Boston: W. H.
Baker, c1895. 12p. (Baker's
edition of plays)

Matilda di Shabran and Corradino; or, The triumph of
beauty see Attinelli,
Joseph

Matilda of Denmark see
Osborn, Laughton in his
The last Mandeville

The matrimonial advertisement
see Augusta, Clara in
Dramatic leaflets see also
Fowler, Egbert Willard

Matrimonial bliss see Buxton,
Ida M.

Matrimony see Shields, Sarah
Annie Frost in her Parlor
charades and proverbs

Matrimony in Scotland see
Gretna Green; or, Matrimony
in Scotland

Matthews, Brander, 1852-1929.

Comedies for amateur acting.
By J. Brander Matthews,
editor. New York: D. Apple-
ton, 1880. 235p. (Appleton's
new handy-volume series)
    Contents: A trumped suit
(Julian Magnus) *[based on
Les deux timides by Eugène
Marin Labiche]*.--A bad case
(Julian Magnus and H. C.
Bunner).--Courtship with
variations (H. C. Bunner).--
A teacher taught (A. H.
Oakes) *[A. H. Oakes is a
pseud. for H. C. Bunner;
based on Le roman d'une
pupille by Paul Ferrier]*.--
Heredity (Arthur Penn)
*[Arthur Penn is a pseud. for
Brander Matthews; based on
La postérité d'une bourg-
mestre by Mario Uchard]*.--
Frank Wylde (J. Brander
Matthews) *[based on Le
serment d'Horace by Henri
Murger]*.

Cuttyback's thunder; or,
Frank Wilde [sic, Wylde].
A comedy in one act. Boston:
W. H. Baker, 1902. 43p.
(Baker's edition of plays)
*[the French original is
Le serment d'Horace by
Henry Murger]*

The decision of the court.
A comedy. New York: Harper,
1893. 60p. (Harper's black
and white series)

Edged tools. A play in four
acts. New York: S. French,
c1873. Prompt-book. 47p.

Frank Wylde *see* Matthews,
Brander. Comedies for
amateur acting *see also
his* Cuttyback's thunder;
or, Frank Wilde [sic, Wylde]

A gold mine. A play in three
acts. New York: S. French,
c1908. 74p. (French's international copyrighted edition
of the works of the best

authors. no. 149) *[joint
author: George Henry Jessop]*

Margery's lovers. An original
comedy in three acts. New
York: n.pub., 1884. Type-
script. 34, 40, 35 leaves.

On probation. A cosmopolitan
comedy [in three acts]. New
York: George W. Kauser,
Typewriter, ca.1890. Typescript. 65, 58, 33 leaves.
*[joint author: George Henry
Jessop]*

Playing a part [From: In
partnership. By Brander
Matthews and H. C. Bunner.
Edinburgh: David Douglas,
1885. 294p.] p.249-271.

The seven conversations of
dear Jones and Baby Van
Rensselaer [From their: In
partnership. Edinburgh:
David Douglas, 1885. 294p.]
p.161-192. *[joint author:
Henry Cuyler Bunner]*

The silent system. A comedy
in one act. (From the French
of Dreyfus.) n.p.: n.pub.,
n.d. p.49-57.

This picture and that. A
comedy. New York: Harper
& Bros., 1894. 77p. (Harper's
black and white series)

Too much Smith; or, Heredity.
A physiological and psychological absurdity in one act.
By Arthur Penn [pseud. for
Brander Matthews] Boston:
Walter H. Baker, 1902. 50p.
*[based on Le postérité d'une
bourgmestre by Mario Uchard;
this play is also in Comedies
for amateur acting by Brander
Matthews, where the author is
given as Arthur Penn and the
title as Heredity, and there
is no indication in that
edition that Arthur Penn is
a pseudonym for Brander
Matthews]*

Matthews, Edith Virginia
Brander.
Six cups of chocolate. A
piece of gossip in one act.
New York and London: Harper
& Bros., c1897. 32p. *[title
page: "Freely Englished
from a 'Kaffeeklatsch' of
E. Schmithof"]*

Maturin, Charles Robert, 1780-
1824.
Bertram; or, The castle of
St. Aldobrand *see* The
modern standard drama,
vol. 7

Melmoth the wanderer *see*
Davidson, Gustav and
Koven, Joseph

Maturin, Edward, 1812-1881.
Viola. A play in four acts.
New York: S. French, 1858.
32p. (French's acting drama.
The acting edition. no. 207)

Maud Muller *see* Merriman,
Effie Woodward

Maud Stanley *see* Coleman,
Mrs. Wilmot Bouton

Maximilian I. A conflict
between the old world and
the new *see* Layman,
Frederick O.

May, Gordon V.
Outwitting the colonel.
A farce in one act. Chicago:
T. S. Denison, c1897. 10p.
(Amateur series)

The May-basket army *see*
Phelps, Lavinia Howe *in
her* Dramatic stories

May Blossom *see* Belasco,
David

May court in Greenwood *see*
Case, Laura U. *in*
Dramatic leaflets

The May queen *see* Denison,
Thomas Stewart *in his*
Friday afternoon series of
dialogues

Mayanni *see* Henley, Anne

Mayo, Frank, 1839-1896.
King Lear. A tragedy in five
acts. By William Shakespeare.
n.p.: n.pub., 18-? Prompt-
book, interleaved with Ms.
notes. 69p. (French's
standard drama. no. 71)

Macbeth. A tragedy in five
acts. By William Shakespeare.
n.p.: n.pub., 1864. Prompt-
book, interleaved with Ms.
notes. 60p. (French's
standard drama. no. 50)

Nordeck. (From the German
novel "Vineta" by Elizabeth
Bürstenbinder.) Chicago:
1884. Prompt-book in Ms.
177p. *[music by Robert
August Stoepel; without
the music; joint author:
John G. Wilson]*

Pudd'nhead Wilson. A play in
prologue and four acts.
(From Mark Twain's book of
the same name.) n.p.: 189-.
Typescript. In a prologue
and four acts.

The royal guard. A romantic
drama in five acts and seven
tableaux. (From the French
of Dumas.) New York: H. A.
Richardson, Typewriter, c1887.
Typescript, prompt-book with
Ms. notes. 68, 59, 38, 35,
56, 34 leaves (pag. by act.)
*[based on Les trois mousque-
taires by Alexander Dumas
the elder]*

Mazeppa *see* White, Charles

Me an' Otis *see* Wells,
Charles Henry

"Me hansom" *see* Wilton, M. J. *bound with his* Waiting for the train

The mechanic's daughter *see* Kavanaugh, Mrs. Russell *in her* Original dramas, dialogues

The mechanic's oath *see* Saunders, Charles Henry. The north end caulker; or, The mechanic's oath

The mechanic's reprieve *see* Murphy, John M.

A medal *see* Mitchell, Silas Weir

Medea. A tragedy in four acts. (From the German of Grillparzer.) New York: Academy of Music, 18-? Bilingual text: English and German. 37p. *see also* Read, Harriette Fanning *in her* Dramatic poems

The Medea of Euripides *see* Patterson, John

Medic, Miles (pseud.) *see* Fales, Willard Henry

"Medica" *see* Engle, Walter K.

Medina, Louise H. Ernest Maltravers. London: J. Dick, 188-? 18p. (Dick's standard plays. no. 379) *[dramatized from the novel of the same name by Edward George Earle Bulwer-Lytton]*

The last days of Pompeii. A dramatic spectacle. New York: S. French, 18-? 31p. (French's standard drama. no. 146) *[dramatized from the novel of the same name by Edward George Earle Bulwer-Lytton]*

Nick of the woods. A drama in three acts. Boston: W. V. Spencer, 185-? 30p. (Spencer's Boston Theatre. no. 62) *[dramatized from the novel of the same name by Robert Montgomery Bird]*

A medley *see* Denton, Clara Janetta Fort. When the lessons are over

Meerschaum (pseud.) Mere sham. A comedy in one act. New York: G. P. Putnam's Sons, 1875. 25p.

A meeting of the young ladies club *see* Latour, Eugene

"Meg" (pseud.) *see* Alcott, Louisa May. Comic tragedies

Meilhac, Henri, 1831-1897. Barbe-bleue *see* Bluebeard

La belle Hélène *see* La belle Hélène

Les brigands *see* Les brigands

Carmen *see* Baker, Theodore

La cigale *see* Delafield, John H.

La cigarette *see* Sullivan, Thomas Russell. A cigarette from Java

Froufrou *see* Daly, Augustin. "Frou Frou" *see also* Frou frou *see also* Schwab, Frederick A. Frou-Frou

La grande duchesse de Gerolstein *see* The grand duchess of Gerolstein

Le petit duc *see* Williams, Frederick and Sullivan, Thomas Russell. The little duke

Le petit hôtel *see* Williams, Henry Llewellyn. The bachelor's box

La veuve *see* Ayer, Harriet Hubbard. The widow

Meleagros *see* Osborn,
Laughton

Mélesville (pseud.) *see*
Duveyrier, Anne Honoré
Joseph

Melmoth, the wanderer *see*
Davidson, Gustav and Koven,
Joseph

Melrose, Thorn.
The commercial drummer.
A comedy in three acts.
Clyde, O.: Ames, c1890. 24p.
(Ames' series of standard
and minor drama. no. 284)

Meltzer, Charles Henry,
1853-1936.
Madame sans-gêne (Madame
devil-may-care.) A comedy
in three acts and a pro-
logue. (From the French of
Sardou and Moreau.) New
York: S. French, c1901.
(French's international
copyrighted edition of the
works of the best authors.
no. 49) *[from the French
of Victorien Sardou and
Adrien Moreau]*

More than queen *see*
Nirdlinger, Charles Frederic
and Meltzer, Charles Henry

The sunken bell. A fairy
play in five acts. (From
the German of Hauptmann.)
New York: Doubleday &
McClure, 1899. Prompt-book
with Ms. notes. 22, 125p.
*[based on Die versunkene
Glocke by Gerhard Hauptmann;
music by Aimé Lachaume]*

The member from Nevada *see*
Blood, Henry Ames. The
Spanish mission; or, The
member from Nevada

Memnon *see* Carleton, Henry
Guy

The memory of a song *see*
Kobbé, Gustav *see also
his* Plays for amateurs

Men and women *see* De Mille,
Henry Churchill and Belasco,
David

The menagerie in the school-
room *see* Hunt, Arzalea

Menasci, Guido, 1867-1925.
Cavalleria rusticana *see*
Day, Willard Gibson *see
also* Macy, James Cartwright.
Rustic chivalry (Cavalleria
rusticana) *see also*
Tretbar, Helen D. Rustic
chivalry

Zanetto *see* Schmall,
Alice F.

Mendes, Henry Pereira, 1852-
1937.
Esther. A Purim play. New
York: Phillip Cowen, 1899.
23p.

Judas Maccabaeus. A Chanukah
play for Sunday school
children. New York: P. Cowen,
1898. 19p.

Mendicant *see* Shields, Sarah
Annie Frost *in her* Parlor
charades and proverbs

Mephistopheles *see* Bangs,
John Kendrick

Mercadante, Saverio, 1795-1870.
Elisa e Claudio, ossia,
L'amore protetto dall'amicizia
see Ponte, Lorenzo da. Eliza
and Claudio; or, Love protected by friendship

Il giuramento *see* Il giuramento; or, The oath

Mercedes *see* Aldrich, Thomas
Bailey

The merchant of Venice *see*

Daly, Augustin *see also*
Hinton, Henry L. *see also*
Shakespeare, William *in*
Booth, Edwin. The Shake-
spearean plays of Edwin
Booth *see also* Shakespeare,
William *in* The modern
standard drama, vol. 8

The merchant of Venice (fourth
act) *see* Shakespeare,
William *in* Dramatic
leaflets

The merchant prince of Cornville *see* Gross, Samuel
Eberly

Mere sham *see* Meerschaum
(pseud.)

Meredith, George [1828-1909],
The household of *see*
Bridges, Robert. Overheard
in Arcady

Mérimée, Prosper, 1803-1870.
Carmen *see* Baker, Theodore

Merington, Marguerite, d.1951.
Captain Lettarblair. A
comedy in three acts. New
York, London: S. French,
c1906. 212p.

Daphne; or, The pipes of
Arcadia. Three acts of
singing nonsense. New York:
Century Co., 1896. 166p.
Libretto.

Meriwether, Elizabeth Avery,
1824-1917.
The devil's dance. A play
for the times. St. Louis:
Hallman Bros., 1886. 67p.

The Ku Klux Klan; or, The
carpet-bagger in New Orleans.
Memphis: Southern Baptist
Pub. Society Print., 1877.
51p.

Merlin revivified and the

hermit *see* Kimball, Hannah
Parker

Merriman, Effie Woodward,
b.1857.
Comedies for children. A
collection of one act plays
...Chicago: Dramatic Pub.
Co., c1898. 100p.
Contents: The drunkard's
family.--The rigmaree.--The
mysterious guest.--Three
newsboys [adapted from "The
little millers"]--The stolen
cat.--What ailed Maudie.--
In Klondyke.--Marian's wish.
--The sick doll.--The quarrel.--The school entertainment.--A Mother Goose comedy.

Diamonds and hearts. A comedy-
drama in three acts. Chicago:
Dramatic Pub. Co., c1897.
40p. (Sergel's acting drama.
no. 418)

The drunkard's family. A
children's play in one act.
Chicago: Dramatic Pub. Co.,
c1898. 14p.

In Klondyke. A children's
drama in one act. Chicago:
Dramatic Pub. Co., c1898.
6p.

The little millers *see her*
Three newsboys *see also her*
Comedies for children

Marian's wish. A children's
play in one act. Chicago:
Dramatic Pub. Co., c1898.
8p.

Maud Muller. A burlesque
entertainment in three acts.
Chicago: Dramatic Pub. Co.,
c1891. p.63-88. (American
amateur drama) [a burlesque
on John Greenleaf Whittier's
Maud Muller]

The mysterious guest. A
children's play in one act.
Chicago: Dramatic Pub. Co.,
c1898. 9p.

A pair of artists. A comedy
in three acts. Chicago:
Dramatic Pub. Co., c1892.
48p. (Sergel's acting drama.
no. 436)

The rigmaree. A children's
play in one act. Chicago:
Dramatic Pub. Co., c1898. 7p.

The sick doll. A children's
play in one act. Chicago:
Dramatic Pub. Co., c1898.
p.67-70.

The stolen cat. A children's
play in one act. Chicago:
Dramatic Pub. Co., c1898. 7p.

Their first meeting. A
comedietta in one act.
Chicago: Dramatic Pub. Co.,
1899. 10p. (American acting
drama)

Three newsboys. A children's
play in one act. Chicago:
Dramatic Pub. Co., c1898.
p.33-39. [adapted from her
The little millers]

Through a matrimonial bureau.
A comedietta in one act.
Chicago: Dramatic Pub. Co.,
c1898. 9p. (Sergel's acting
drama. no. 495)

Tompkins' hired man. A drama
in three acts. Chicago:
Dramatic Pub. Co., c1898.
35p. (Sergel's acting drama.
no. 419)

What ailed Maudie. A children's play in one act.
Chicago: Dramatic Pub. Co.,
c1898. p.49-56.

The merry Christmas of the
old woman who lived in a
shoe see Baker, George
Melville

The merry cobbler see
Fraser, John Arthur

The merry milkmaids see
Gabriel, Charles H.

The merry monarch see Goodwin, John Cheever see also
Payne, John Howard. Charles
II; or, The merry monarch
in The modern standard
drama, vol. 3

The merry war see Elson,
Louis Charles see also
Norcross, I. W.

The merry wives of Windsor see
Daly, Augustin

Mershon, Ralph Smith, 1830-1914.
Saul of Tarsus. A dramatic
poem. Zanesville, O.: Printed
manuscript, c1889. 90 leaves.

Mesmerism see Bernard, William
Bayle in Massey, Charles.
Massey's exhibition reciter

The message boy see Downing,
Laura Case. Defending the
flag; or, The message boy

A message to the children see
Denton, Clara Janetta Fort.
When the lessons are over

Messager, André Charles Prosper,
1853-1929.
Fantine see Woolf, Benjamin
Edward and Field, Roswell
Martin

Messalina see Logan, Algernon
Sydney

Metcalfe, Irving.
A game of chance; or, Allot-
ting the bride. A comedy in
one act. New York: Dramatic
Pub. Co., c1899. 24p. (The
wizard series)

Miss Mary Smith. A comedy in
one act. New York: Dramatic
Pub. Co., c1899. 21p. (The
wizard series)(Sergel's
acting drama. no. 543)

Mettenheimer, H. J.

Our church. A play in five
acts. Cincinnati: Elm Street
Print. Co., 1872. 77p。

A serious flirtation. A play
in four acts. Cincinnati:
Elm Street Print. Co.,
1873. 56p.

Meurice, Paul, 1820-1905.
Fanfan la tulipe *see*
Schönberg, James. True as
steel

Mexico *see* Royle, Edwin
Milton

Meyerbeer, Giacomo, 1791-1864.
L'étoile du Nord *see*
Kellogg, Çlara Louise. The
star of the north

Les Huguenots *see* Kellogg,
Clara Louise. The Huguenots

Meyers, Benjamin F., b.1833.
Collected works [From his:
A drama of ambition and
other pieces of verse。
Harrisburg, Pa。: The Star
Independent, 1901. 300p.]
p.1-60.
Contents: A drama of
ambition.--Orpheus and
Eurydice.--Hermione.

Meyers, Robert Cornelius V.,
1858-1917。
Bill Jepson's wife *see*
Dramatic leaflets

Cassius' whistle. A farce
in one act *see* Dramatic
leaflets

The day before the wedding
see Dramatic leaflets

A desparate encounter *see*
Dramatic leaflets

Did you ever see a ghost?
see Dramatic leaflets

A duel to the death. A
farce in one act. Philadelphia: Penn Pub. Co., 1897.
18p.

A game of chess. A comedietta
in one act. Philadelphia:
Penn Pub. Co., c1889. p.39-56.
(One hundred choice selections.
no. 29)

A lady's note. A farce in one
act. Philadelphia: Penn Pub.
Co., 1912. 13p. *[earlier
copyright: 1895]*

The long lost nephew *see*
Dramatic leaflets

Ze moderne English。 A comedy
in one act. Philadelphia:
Penn Pub. Co., 1912. p.43-54。
(One hundred choice select-
ions。 no. 31) *[earlier copyright: 1891]*

Monsieur. A farce in two acts.
Philadelphia: Penn Pub. Co.,
1911. 23p. *[earlier copyright: 1895]*

A pair of gloves. A farce in
one act. Philadelphia: Penn
Pub. Co., 1909. p.217-229.
(One hundred choice selections.
no. 25) *[earlier copyright:
1888]*

Practical jokes *see* Dramatic
leaflets

A soft black overcoat with a
velvet collar *see* Dramatic
leaflets

Tell your wife. A farce in
three acts. Philadelphia:
Penn Pub. Co., 1912. 28p.
[earlier copyright: 1895]

The top landing *see* Dramatic
leaflets

Under an umbrella *see*
Dramatic leaflets

A well preserved gentleman。
A farce in one act. Philadelphia: Penn Pub. Co., 1899.
17p. (Keystone edition of
popular plays)(Dramatic
library. vol. 1. no. 125)

Where's my hat *see* Dramatic
leaflets

Miantonimo *see* Caverly, Robert Boodey

Michael Angelo *see* Longfellow, Henry Wadsworth

Mickey Free *see* Wilton, M. J.

Mickle, Isaac.
The Old North Tower. Drama in three acts. (From the French of Sorique's Les confrères.) Philadelphia: Townsend Ward, 1846. 80p.
[title page: The Old North Tower; or, The duke for a day. Altered from the suppressed play of Jean Paul Sorique, called Les confrères]

Midnight banquet; or, The castle of Cataldo. A melodrama in two acts. Boston: William V. Spencer, 1857? 28p. (Spencer's Boston Theatre. no. 134)

A midnight bell *see* Hoyt, Charles Hale

The midnight charge *see* Stedman, W. Elsworth

Midnight colic *see* Allyn, Dave E.

The midnight intruder *see* Dumont, Frank

A midnight mistake *see* Munson, A. J.

The mid-night train. A farce in one scene *see* Dumont, Frank *in his* The amateur minstrel

A midsummer madness *see* Townsend, Charles

A midsummer night's dream *see* Daly, Augustin

A midsummer-night's dream. As performed at the Broadway Theatre. New York: S. French, 185-? 48p. (French's American drama. The acting edition. no. 1) *[title page: "By William Shakspeare [sic]"]*

A midsummer-night's dream. As performed at McVicker's Theatre. Chicago: Theatrical Press of W. J. Jefferson, 1888. 55p. *[title page: "By William Shakespeare"]*

Mike Donovan's courtship. A comedietta in two acts. Clyde, O.: Ames, 1888? 9p. (Ames' series of standard and minor drama. no. 356) *[Readex also enters this play under Robert Ellice Mack with the title An Irishman's maneuver; or, Mike Donovan's courtship; they represent different editions with identical text]*

Miladi and the musketeer *see* Barnet, Robert A.

The mild monomaniac *see* Connell, George Stanislaus *in his* The old patroon and other plays

Miles, George Henry, 1824-1871.
Mary's birthday; or, The cynic. A play in three acts. New York: S. French, 186-? 36p. (French's standard drama. The acting edition. no. 242) *[Cover: The cynic; or, Mary's birthday. Title page: Mary's birthday; or, The cynic]*

Mohammed, the Arabian prophet. A tragedy in five acts. Boston: Phillips, Sampson, 1850. viii, 4, 166p. *[this play won a prize of $1,000 in 1850, in a contest sponsored* *by the actor Edwin Forrest]*

Señor Valiente. A comedy in five acts. Baltimore: Henry Taylor, 1859. Prompt-book. 91p.

Señor Valiente; or, The soldier of Chapultepec. A comedy in five acts. Boston: W. V. Spencer, n.d. Prompt-book. 52 leaves. (Spencer's Boston Theatre. no. 193) *[Readex uses the incorrect spelling Chapul-tepee]*

A milk white flag *see* Hoyt, Charles Hale

The milkmaids' convention *see* Rittenhouse, Laura J.

Millard, -----.
Centaurine *see* Gerardy, D.

Millard, Harrison, 1830-1895.
Our heroes *see* Renauld, John B.

Miller, Alice Duer, 1874-1942.
Overheard in a conservatory [and] A dialogue *see* Duer, Caroline

Miller, Charles T.
Frog opera with pollywog chorus. A burletta, founded upon the nursery tale and old song of "A frog he would a wooing go." New York: A. S. Seer's Print. Est., 1876. 16p.

Miller, Chester Gore.
Chihuahua. A new and original social drama in four acts. Chicago: Kehm, Fietsch, & Wilson, 1891. 95p.

Father Junipero Serra. A new and original historical drama in four acts. Chicago: Skeen, Baker, 1894. 160p.

Miller, Cincinnatus Heine *see* Miller, Joaquin

Miller, Frank Justus, 1858-1938. Dido--an epic tragedy. (From the Latin of Vergil.) New York, Boston, Chicago: Silver Burdett, 1900. 88p. *[stage setting, actions, and music by J. Raleigh Nelson]*

Miller, Harry S.
The insurance agent. An eccentric character and comedy sketch. Boston: W. H. Baker, c1898. 9p. (Baker's edition of plays)

Miller, Joaquin, 1841-1913.
The Danites in the Sierras. A drama in four acts. San Francisco: 1882. Typescript. 25p. *[Miller's real name is Cincinnatus Heine Miller]*

'49: Forty-nine. In four acts. An idyl drama of the Sierras. San Francisco: California Pub. Co., 1882. Second edition. 102p.

An Oregon idyl. In four acts [From: Joaquin Miller's poems. San Francisco: Whitaker and Ray, 1910. vol. 6] p.169-244. *[earlier copyright: 1881]*

Tally-ho. A play in three acts [From: Joaquin Miller's poems. San Francisco: Whitaker and Ray, 1910. vol. 6] p.121-167. *[earlier copyright: 1883]*

The miller's daughter *see* Smart, Herbert Durrell. Mine falls; or, The miller's daughter

Millie, the quadroon; or, Out of bondage *see* Elwyn, Lizzie May

Milliet, Paul, b.1858.
Werther *see* Ginty, Elizabeth Beall

The milliner's shop *see* Collyer, Dan

The millionaire *see* Howard,
Bronson. The Henrietta

A millionaire's trials *see*
Cox, Eleanor Rogers. A
duel at dawn

Millöcker, Karl, 1842-1899.
Apajune der Wassermann *see*
Rosenfeld, Sydney. Apajune,
the water sprite

Der Bettelstudent *see*
Schwab, Emil. The beggar
student

Der Feldprediger *see* The
black hussar *see also*
Rosenfeld, Sydney. The
black hussar

Gasparone *see* Rosenfeld,
Sydney

Mills, Elvira L.
Maud Stanley *see* Coleman,
Mrs. Wilmot Bouton

Milman, Henry Hart, 1791-1868.
Fazio; or, The Italian wife
see The modern standard
drama, vol. 1

Milner, Frances S.
Brothers in name. A drama in
six acts. n.p.: n.pub.,
c1899. Typescript, prompt-
book with Ms. notes. 19,
19, 15, 17, 24, 31 leaves.

Milner, Thomas Picton *see*
Picton, Thomas, 1822-1891

Milton, John, 1608-1674.
Paradise lost *see* Taylor,
M. F. and Taylor, John G.

Mind your own business *see*
Lemon, Mark *in* The modern
standard drama, vol. 12

Mine falls; or, The miller's
daughter *see* Smart, Herbert
Durrell

Minette's birthday *see*

André, Richard

The minister's guests *see*
Kavanaugh, Mrs. Russell
in her Original dramas,
dialogues

Minster, Verend (pseud.?)
A carnival of sports. An
entertainment. Philadelphia:
Penn Pub. Co., 1900. p.21-30.
[earlier copyright: 1891]

The Minute Men of 1774-1775 *see*
Herne, James A. *in his* The
early plays

Mirabeau *see* Calvert, George
Henry

The miracle of roses *see*
Polding, Elizabeth. St.
Elizabeth of Thuringia; or,
The miracle of roses

Miralda; or, The justice of
Tacon *see* Ballou, Maturin
Murray

Miriam *see* Hall, Louisa Jane
Park *see also* Williamson,
Eugene F.

Miriam. A drama in three scenes
see Sylvia and other dramas

The misanthrope melted *see*
St. John, Charles Henry

The miscellaneous plays of
Edwin Booth *see* Booth,
Edwin

Mischief *see* Shields, Sarah
Annie Frost *in her* Parlor
charades and proverbs

Mischievous Bob. A comic drama
in one act. New York: Harold
Roorbach, c1891. 18p. (The
amateur stage)

The mischievous Nigger *see*
White, Charles

The miser *see* Lyons, Joseph
Aloysius

Les misérables *see* Griffin,
George W. H.

The miser's gold *see* Moore,
D. H. The New York book
agent; or, The miser's gold

The miser's troubles *see*
Dumont, Frank. The serenade
party; or, The miser's
troubles

Misfortune *see* Shields,
Sarah Annie Frost *in her*
Parlor charades and proverbs

The misfortunes of Ventilator
see Ravel, Jerome. Kim-Ka;
or, The misfortunes of
Ventilator

Miss Arabella Clipperton's
speech *see* McBride, H.
Elliott *in his* Latest
dialogues

Miss Blothingay's blunder *see*
Todd, John W.

Miss Madcap *see* Townsend,
Charles

Miss Manning *see* Runnion,
James B.

Miss Mary Smith *see* Metcalfe,
Irving

Miss Matilda's school *see*
Jones, Gertrude Manly

Miss Mosher of Colorado; or,
A mountain psyche *see*
Richardson, Anna Steese
Sausser

Miss Nonchalance *see*
Schlesinger, Olga Steiner

Miss tom boy *see* Dunne,
Norah

Miss Topsy Turvy; or, The
courtship of the deacon *see*
McFall, B. G.

The Misses Beers *see* Ludekens,
Emil

The missing link *see* Helm,
Charles E. Muolo the monkey;
or, The missing link

The mission of the fairies *see*
Barstow, Ellen M.

A mis-spent life *see* Fore-
paugh, Luella and Fish,
George F. Dr. Jekyll and Mr.
Hyde; or, A mis-spent life

Mistake *see* Shields, Sarah
Annie Frost *in her* Parlor
charades and proverbs

A mistake in identity *see*
Griffith, Benjamin Lease
Crozer

The mistake on both sides *see*
Sanderson, Mary

Mistaken identity *see*
Coes, George H.

Mr. Barnes of New York *see*
Gunter, Archibald Clavering

Mr. Bob *see* Baker, Rachel E.

Mr. Holiday's flirtation *see*
Guepner, Willard. Locked in
a dress-maker's room; or,
Mr. Holiday's flirtation

Mr. Micawber *see* Dialogues
dramatized from the works of
Charles Dickens

Mr. Pecksniff *see* Dialogues
dramatized from the works of
Charles Dickens

Mr. Wilkinson's widows *see*
Gillette, William Hooker

Mr. X *see* Rosenfeld, Sydney

Mrs. Baxter's baby *see*
Lawford, L. E.

Mrs. Didymus' party *see*
Coes, George H.

Mrs. Gamp's tea. A sketch.
(from: Charles Dickens'
Martin Chuzzlewit.) Chicago:
T. S. Denison, 18-? 70p.
(Amateur series. no. 9)
see also Dialogues drama-
tized from the works of
Charles Dickens

Mrs. Mulcahy *see* Hageman,
Maurice

Mistress Nan *see* Norcross,
Frederic Walter

Mistress Nell *see* Hazelton,
George Cochrane

Mrs. Peabody's boarder *see*
Heywood, Delia A. *in her*
Choice dialogues no. 1

Mrs. Peck's pudding *see*
Follen, Eliza Lee Cabot
in her Home dramas for
young people

Mrs. Pepper's ghost *see*
Tees, Levin C.

Mrs. Plodding's nieces; or,
Domestic accomplishments
see Dunne, Norah

Mrs. Smith; or, The wife and
the widow *see* Payne, John
Howard

Mrs. Vatican Smythe's party
see Kavanaugh, Mrs. Russell
in her Original dramas,
dialogues

Mrs. Walthrop's bachelors *see*
Baker, George Melville and
Small, Willard

Mitchell, A.
Under two flags. A romantic
play in two acts. Chicago:
Dramatic Pub. Co., c1892.
31p. (Sergel's acting drama.
no. 346?) *[dramatized from
the novel of the same name
by Marie Louise de la Ramée
(pseud.=Ouida)]*

Mitchell, Langdon Elwyn, 1862-
1935.
Becky Sharp. A play in four
acts [From: America's lost
plays. vol. 16. Princeton,
N. J.: Princeton Univ. Press,
1941] p.197-283. *[dramatized
from William Makepiece
Thackeray's Vanity Fair;
introduction: "Mitchell's
earlier work appeared under
the pseudonym of John Philip
Varley; earlier copyright:
1899]*

Deborah. London?: 1891?
Typescript. In four acts.
(pag. by acts)

In the season. A one act
comedy. London and New York:
S. French, 18-. 17p. (Lacy's
acting edition. vol. 140)

Sylvian. A tragedy. By John
Philip Varley [pseud., see
note above] New York:
Brentano Bros., 1885. 104p.

Mitchell, Silas Weir, 1829-1914.
Barabbas [From his: The
complete poems...New York:
The Century Co., 1914. 447p.]
p.234-256.

The cup of youth [From his:
The complete poems...New
York: The Century Co., 1914.
447p.] p.145-172.

Francis Drake. A tragedy of
the sea. Boston: Houghton,
Mifflin, 1893. 60p.

François Villion [From his:
The complete poems...New York:
The Century Co., 1914. 447p.]
p.194-210.

A masque [From his: A masque and other poems. Boston: Houghton, Mifflin, 1887] p.1-11.

A medal [From his: Complete poems...New York: The Century Co., 1914. 447p.] p.122-125.

Philip Vernon. A tale in prose and verse. New York The Century Co., 1895. 55p.

The violin [From his: The complete poems...New York: The Century Co., 1914. 447p.] p.182-193.

The wager [From his: The wager and other poems. New York: The Century Co., 1900] p.1-14.

Wind and sea [From his: The hill of stones, and other poems. Boston: Houghton, Mifflin, 1883] p.20-32.

Mitchell, T. Berry.
A home by two brides. A play in three acts. n.p.: n.pub., c1872. 37p.

Mitchell, Thomas.
The household tragedy. In four scenes. Albany: Weed, Parsons, 1870. 38p.

Mitsu-yu-nissi; or, The Japanese wedding *see* Scudder, Vida Dutton and Brooks, F. M.

Mneme and Elpis *see* Day, Richard Edwin

Moates, William Gurney.
The changing scales. Baltimore: H. L. Litz, 1897. 64p.

A mock trial *see* Chase, Frank Eugene. A ready-made suit; or, A mock trial

The model house. A comedy in

five acts. Albany: Printing House of C. Van Benthuysen & Sons, 1868. 110p. *[Library of Congress indicates E. P. Hurlburt as the supposed author of this work; this possibly could be Elisha P. Hurlburt, who was writing at the time]*

A model lover *see* Tiffany, Esther Brown

A model pair *see* Abarbanell, Jacob Ralph

Moderation; or, I can take it or leave it alone *see* Ritchie, Thomas *in* A collection of temperance dialogues

A modern Ananias *see* Fraser, John Arthur

The modern Cinderella *see* Field, Henrietta Dexter and Field, Roswell Martin. Collected works

A modern craze *see* Robinson, Charles. Dream camp; or, A modern craze

The modern Job *see* Peterson, Henry

A modern minuet *see* Monroe, Harriet *in her* The passing show

A modern proposal *see* Brown, Marsden

The modern saint *see* Barras, Charles M.

The modern standard drama... edited by E. Sargent... New York: J. Douglass, 1846-8. 12 vols. (pag. by play) *Contents begin on following page*

Contents, vol. 1: Ion.
A tragedy in five acts
(Thomas Noon Talfourd).--
Fazio; or, The Italian wife
(Henry Hart Milman).--The
lady of Lyons; or, Love and
pride (Edward George Earle
Lytton Bulwer-Lytton Lytton).
--Richelieu; or, The con-
spiracy. A play in five acts
(Edward George Earle Lytton
Buler-Lytton Lytton).--
The wife; a tale of Mantus
A play in five acts (James
Sheridan Knowles).--The
honey-moon. A play in five
acts (John Tobin).--The
school for scandal. A comedy
in five acts (Richard Brins-
ley Butler Sheridan).--Money.
A comedy in five acts (Edward
George Earle Lytton Bulwer-
Lytton Lytton).

Contents, vol. 2: The
stranger (based on Menschenhass und Reue by August
Friedrich Ferdinand von
Kotzebue).--Grandfather
Whitehead. An original drama
in two acts (Mark Lemon).--
Richard III (William Shakespeare as arranged by Colley
Cibber).--Love's sacrifice;
or, The rival merchants. A
play in five acts (George
William Lovell).--The gamester (Edward Moore).--A cure
for the heartache. A comedy
in five acts (Thomas Morton).
--The hunchback. A play in
five acts (James Sheridan
Knowles).--Don Caesar de
Bazan. A drama in three
acts (Philippe François
Pinel Dumanoir and Adolphe
Philippe Dennery).

Contents, vol. 3: The
poor gentleman. A comedy in
five acts (George Colman
the younger).--Hamlet
(William Shakespeare as
arranged by John Philip
Kemble).--Charles II; or,
The merry monarch (John

Howard Payne; founded on La
jeunesse de Henry V by
Alexandre Vincent Pineux
Duval).--Venice preserved.
A tragedy in five acts.
(Thomas Otway).--Pizarro
(Richard Brinsley Butler
Sheridan; altered from
Kotzebue's Die Spanier in
Peru [The Spaniards in Peru]).
--The love-chase (James
Sheridan Knowles).--Othello
(William Shakespeare).--Lend
me five shillings. A farce
in one act. (John Maddison
Morton; based on Riche d'-
amour by Joseph Xavier Boni-
face Saintine).

Contents, vol. 4: Virginius
(James Sheridan Knowles).--
The king of the Commons. A
play in five acts. (James
White).--London assurance.
A comedy in five acts. (Dion
Boucicault).--The rent-day
(Douglas William Jerrold "on
an original by David Wilkie"
[Wilkie was not a playwright,
but rather an artist, and two
of his paintings, "Rent-day"
and "Distraining for rent,"
are the inspiration for the
work by Jerrold]).--Two
gentlemen of Verona (William
Shakespeare).--The jealous
wife. A comedy in five acts.
(George Colman the elder).--
The rivals. A comedy in five
acts (Richard Brinsley Butler
Sheridan).--Perfection; or,
The maid of Munster. A farce
in one act. (Thomas Haynes
Bayly).

Contents, vol. 5: A new way
to pay old debts. A comedy in
five acts. (Philip Massinger).
--Look before you leap; or,
Wooings and weddings. A
comedy in five acts. (George
W. Lovell).--King John. A
tragedy in five acts (William
Shakespeare).--The nervous
man and the man of nerve. A
farce in two acts (William

Bayle Bernard).--Damon and Phythias. A play in five acts (John Banim).--The clandestine marriage. A comedy in five acts (George Colman the elder)。--William Tell. A play in three acts (James Sheridan Knowles).-- The day after the wedding. A farce in one act (Marie Thérèse De Camp Kemble [Mrs. Charles Kemble]).
Contents, vol. 6: Speed the plough. A comedy in five acts (Thomas Morton).-- Romeo and Juliet。 A tragedy in five acts (William Shakespeare).--Feudal times; or, The court of James the third. A Scottish historical play (James White)。--Charles the twelfth. An historical drama in two acts (James Robinson Planché).--The bridal. A tragedy in five acts (James Sheridan Knowles as adapted from The maid's tragedy by Francis Beaumont and John Fletcher).--The follies of a night. A vaude-ville comedy in two acts (James Robinson Planché as adapted from the play Char-lot by Joseph Philippe Simon Lockroy, Louis Emile Vander-buch, and Auguste Anicet-Bourgeois)。--The iron chest. A play in three acts (George Colman the younger, as adapted partially from Caleb Williams; or, Things as they are, by William Godwin).--Faint heart never won fair lady. A comedy in one act (James Robinson Planché as translated from the French Vouloir c'est pouvoir).
Contents, vol. 7: The road to ruin. A comedy in five acts (Thomas Holcroft).-- Macbeth. A tragedy in five acts (William Shakespeare).--

Temper. A comedy in five acts (Robert Bell).--Evadue; or, The statue。 A play in five acts (Richard Lalor Sheil; based on James Shirley's Traytor [Traitor])。 --Bertram; or, The castle of St. Aldobrand. A tragedy in five acts (Charles Robert Maturin).--The duenna. An opera in three acts (Richard Brinsley Butler Sheridan; taken in part from William Wycherly's Country wife).-- Much ado about nothing. A comedy in five acts (William Shakespeare).--The critic (presumably Richard Brinsley Butler Sheridan; Readex had not yet issued microprint of this play as of April 1977).
Contents, vol. 8: The apostate。 A tragedy in five acts (Richard Lalor Sheil).-- Twelfth night; or, What you will. A comedy in five acts (William Shakespeare).--Bru-tus; or, The fall of Tarquin. A tragedy in five acts (John Howard Payne).--Simpson and Co. A comedy in two acts (John Poole).--The merchant of Venice. A comedy in five acts (William Shakespeare).-- Old heads and young hearts. A comedy in five acts (Dion Boucicault).--The mountain-eers. A play in three acts (George Colman the younger). --Three weeks after marriage。 A comedy in two acts (Arthur Murphy).
Contents, vol. 9: Love. A play in five acts (James Sheridan Knowles).--As you like it. A comedy in five acts (William Shakespeare).-- The elder brother. A play in five acts (Francis Beaumont and John Fletcher).--Werner (George Gordon Noël Byron Byron, adapted from The Ger-

man's tale from Harriet and Sophia Lee's Canterbury tales).--Gisippus; or, The forgotten friend. A play in five acts (Gerald Griffin). --Town and country. A comedy in five acts (Thomas Morton). --King Lear. A tragedy in five acts (William Shakespeare).--Blue devils (George Colman the younger).

Contents, vol. 10: King Henry VIII. An historical play in five acts (William Shakespeare).--Married and single. A comedy in three acts (John Poole; based on Le célibataire et l'homme marié).--King Henry IV, Part I. A tragedy in five acts (William Shakespeare).--Paul Pry. A comedy in three acts (John Poole).--Guy Mannering; or, The gipsey's prophecy. A musical play in three acts (Daniel Terry as based on the novel by Sir Walter Scott).--Sweethearts and wives. A comedy in three acts (James Kenney).--The serious family. A comedy in three acts (Morris Barnett; adapted from Un mari à la campagne by Jean François Alfred Bayard).--She stoops to conquer. A comedy in five acts (Oliver Goldsmith).

Contents, vol. 11: Julius Caesar. A tragedy in five acts (William Shakespeare).-- The vicar of Wakefield. A comedy in three acts (Joseph Stirling Coyne; dramatization of the work by Oliver Goldsmith).--Leap year; or, The ladies' privilege. A comedy in three acts (John Baldwin Buckstone).--The catspaw. A comedy in five acts (Douglas William Jerrold). --The passing cloud. A romantic drama in two acts (William Bayle Bernard).--The drunkard; or, The fallen saved. A moral

domestic drama in five acts (William Henry Smith *[Sabin (#84781, v.21, p.190) attributes this play to either John Pierpont's The Drunkard or to William Comstock's Rum; or, The first glass; Sabin additionally notes that Smith's original name was Sedley, and a long note explains the change of name (#84786, v.21, p.191)]*).-- Rob Roy MacGregor; or, Auld lang syne. An operatic play in three acts (Isaac Pocock; adapted from Sir Walter Scott's Rob Roy).--George Barnwell. A tragedy in five acts (George Lillo *[Readex failed to underscore the title of this play, so it might be missed easily; it is found on microprint 66]*).

Contents, vol. 12: Ingomar, the barbarian. A play in five acts (Maria Anne Lacy Lovell; adapted from Der Sohn der Wildniss by Eligius Franz Joseph, Freiherr von Münch-Bellinghausen).--Sketches in India. A farce in one act with a portrait and memoir of Mrs. John Seton (Thomas Morton; adapted from the opera The Englishman in India by the same author).--The two friends. A domestic drama in two acts (Michael Rophino Lacy).--Jane Shore. A tragedy in five acts (Nicholas Rowe). --The Corsican brothers. A dramatic romance in three acts and five tableaux (Eugène Grangé and Xavier Aymons, comte de Montépin; adapted from Les frères corses by Alexandre Dumas).--Mind your own business. An original drama in three acts (Mark Lemon).--The writing on the wall. A melo-drama in three acts (Thomas and John Maddison Morton).--The heir at law. A comedy in five acts (George Colman the younger).

A modern tragedy. Not written
by Bacon. n.p.: n.pub., n.d.
15p.

Ze moderne English *see* Meyers,
Robert Cornelius V.

Moelling, Carl Erdwin, b.1838.
Faust's death. A tragedy in
five acts. By Chas. E. Moelling. Philadelphia: J. B.
Lippincott, 1865. 136p.

Mohammed, the Arabian prophet
see Miles, George Henry

The Moko marionettes *see*
Williams, Henry Llewellyn

Molière, Jean Baptiste Poque-
lin, 1622-1673.
L'avare *see* Lyons, Joseph
Aloysius.

Le bourgeois gentilhomme
see Stace, Arthur J. The
upstart

Le Tartuffe *see* Smith,
Solomon Franklin. The hypocrite *see also* Tartuffe;
or, The imposter

Moll Pitcher; or, The fortune
teller of Lynn *see* Jones,
Joseph Stevens

Mollie dear *see* Macarthy,
Harry. Barney's courtship;
or, Mollie dear

Molly Moriarty *see* Sedgwick,
Alfred B.

Moncrieff, William Thomas,
1794-1857.
The Jewess *see* The Jewess

Rochester; or, King Charles
the second's merry days *see*
Fast men of olden time

Money *see* Lytton, Edward
George Earle Lytton Bulwer-
Lytton *in* The modern
standard drama, vol. 1

Money mad *see* MacKaye, James
Steele

Money makes the mare go *see*
Hoyt, Charles Hale. Texas
steer; or, Money makes the
mare go

The monk *see* Osborn, Laughton
in his The last Mandeville

Monkey and madstone *see* Denison, Thomas Stewart *in his*
Wide awake dialogues

Monroe, Harriet, 1860-1936.
After-all. Boston: Poet-Lore,
1900. (vol. 12, no. 3) p.321-
326.

The passing show. Five modern
plays in verse. Boston and
New York: Houghton, Mifflin,
1903. 125p.
Contents: The thunderstorm.
--At the goal.--After all.--
A modern minuet.--It passes
by.

Valeria. A tragedy in a prologue and five acts [From her:
Valeria and other poems.
Chicago: A. C. McClurg, 1892]
p.1-194.

Monroe, Jasper R.
Argo and Irene. A tragedy in
three acts [From his: Dramas
and miscellaneous poems.
Chicago: Knight & Leonard,
1875. 190p.] p.44-80.

An editor who wanted office.
A tragedy in three acts
[From his: Dramas and mis-
cellaneous poems. Chicago:
Knight & Leonard, 1875. 190p.]
p.182-183.

Malachi and Miranda. A drama
in four acts [From his: Dramas
and miscellaneous poems.
Chicago: Knight & Leonard,
1875. 190p.] p.81-114.

Monsieur *see* Meyers, Robert
Cornelius V.

Monsieur Alphonse *see* Daly,
Alphonse

The Montanini *see* Osborn,
Laughton

"Monte Cristo" *see* O'Neill,
James

Montépin, Xavier Aymons, comte
de, 1826-1902.
Les frères corses *see*
Grangé, Eugène and Montépin,
Xavier Aymons, comte de.
The Corsican brothers *see*
The modern standard drama,
vol. 12 *see also* Griffin,
George W. H. Corsican twins

Montgomery, Margaret.
Per telephone. A farce in
one act. Boston: W. H.
Baker, c1893. 17p. (Baker's
edition of plays)

Montgomery, T. M.
Through snow and sunshine.
An original drama in five
acts. Clyde, O.: A. D.
Ames, 1880. 22p. (Ames'
series of standard and
minor drama. no. 105) *[joint
author: T. D. Steed]*

Moody, William Vaughn, 1869-
1910.
The masque of judgment. A
masque-drama in five acts
and a prelude. Boston:
Small, Maynard, 1900p. 127p.

The moonshiner's daughter *see*
Moore, Bernard Francis

The Moor of Sicily *see* The
avenger; or, The Moor of
Sicily *see also* Lee,
Herbert. The avenger; or,
The Moor of Sicily

Moore, A. S.
Cosmos. A play in three acts.
By Drogheda (pseud.) Nash-
ville: Cumberland Presby-

terian Pub. House, 1885. 136p.

Moore, Bernard Francis.
Brother against brother. A
military play in five acts.
Boston: W. H. Baker, c1898.
43p. (Baker's edition of
plays)

Captain Jack; or, The Irish
outlaw. An original Irish
drama in three acts. Boston:
W. H. Baker, c1894. 40p.
(Baker's edition of plays)

"Erin go bragh"; or, The
mountain rebel. An Irish drama
in three acts. New York: Dick
& Fitzgerald, c1896. 40p.

Faugh-a-Ballagh; or, The
wearing of the green. A
romantic Irish play in three
acts. Boston: W. H. Baker,
1899. 39p. (Baker's edition
of plays)

Ferguson, of Troy. A farce
comedy in three acts. Boston:
W. H. Baker, c1900. 50p.
(Baker's edition of plays)

The girl from midway. A farce
comedy in one act. Clyde, O.:
Ames, c1895. 19p. (Ames'
series of standard and minor
drama. no. 359)

The haunted mill; or, Con
O'Ragen's secret. An Irish
drama in three acts. Clyde,
O.: Ames, c1893. 28p. (Ames'
series of standard and minor
drama. no. 314)

The Irish agent. A play of
Irish life in four acts.
Boston: W. H. Baker, c1895.
41p. (Baker's edition of
plays)

A judge by proxy. Farce in
one act. Clyde, O.: Ames,
1898. 12p. (Ames' series of
standard and minor drama.
no. 406)

The man from Texas. A farce

in one act. Boston: W. H.
Baker, c1898. 12p. (Baker's
edition of plays)

The moonshiner's daughter.
A play of mountain life in
three acts. Boston: W. H.
Baker, c1898. 32p. (Baker's
edition of plays)

Poverty flats. A play of
Western life in three acts.
Boston: W. H. Baker, 1899.
35p. (Baker's edition of
plays)

The Rough Rider. A play in
four acts. Boston: W. H.
Baker, c1898. 35p. (Baker's
edition of plays)

The weeping willows. A romantic play in three acts.
Boston: W. H. Baker, 1903.
53p. (Baker's edition of
plays)

Winning a wife. A farce in
one act. Clyde, O.: Ames,
c1898. 13p. (Ames' series of
standard and minor drama.
no. 403)

The wrecker's daughter. A
drama in three acts. Boston:
W. H. Baker, c1896. 32p.
(Baker's edition of plays)

Moore, Charles Leonard, 1854-
1925.
Banquet of Palacios. A comedy. Philadelphia: C. L.
Moore, 1889. 196p.

Ghost of Rosalys. Philadelphia: The author, 1900.
174p.

Moore, D. H.
The New York book agent; or,
The miser's gold. A drama
in four acts. Clyde, O.:
Ames, 1892. 16p. (Ames' series
of standard and minor drama.
no. 298)

Moore, Edward, 1712-1757.
The gamester *see* The modern

standard drama, vol. 2

Moore, Eugene.
Delilah. A tale of olden
times [From his: Delilah...
and miscellaneous verses.
Washington, D.C.: 1888.
174p.] p.5-109.

Moore, Horatio Newton, 1814-
1859.
Orlando; or, A woman's virtue.
A tragedy in five acts. Philadelphia: Frederick Turner,
1835. 60p.

The regicide. An original
tragedy in five acts [From:
The Philadelphia Visitor, and
parlour companion. vol. 3,
nos. 11-12. Philadelphia:
W. B. Rogers, 1838] p.241-254,
265-271.

Moore, J. Owen.
Allatoona *see* Kilpatrick,
Hugh Judson

Moore, James.
Smith, shepherd of the Wissahickon [From his: Shepherd of
the Wissahickon and other
poems. Philadelphia: n.pub.,
1871. 80p.] p.1-4, 5-68.

Moore, John.
Mad dogs; or, The two Caesars.
A farce in one act. New York:
Samuel French, 18-? 15p.

Moorhead, H. C. *see* Moorehead,
Henry Clay

Moorehead, Henry Clay.
Tan-gó-ru-a. An historical
drama in prose. Philadelphia:
T. B. Peterson, 1856. 280p.
*[Readex also enters this
play under title]*

The Moorish bride *see* Hentz,
Caroline Lee Whiting. De Lara;
or, The Moorish bride

The Moorish maiden's vow *see*

Alcott, Louisa May. The cap-
tive of Castile; or, The
Moorish maiden's vow *in her*
Comic tragedies

Moos, H. M. *see* Moos, Herman
M.

Moos, Herman M., 1836-1894.
Mortara; or, The Pope and
his inquisitors. A drama
[From: Mortara...together
with choice poems. By H. M.
Moos. Cincinnati: Black,
1860] p.1-145.

Mordred. A tragedy in five acts
see Campbell, William Wilfred. Collected works. Poetical tragedies

More, Hannah, 1745-1833.
Moses in the bullrushes *see*
Cobb, Mary L. Poetical dramas
for home and school

More, Paul Elmer, 1864-1937.
Prometheus bound (From the
Greek of Aeschylus.) Boston
and New York: Houghton,
Mifflin, c1899. 110p.

More sinned against than sinning
see Carleton, John Louis

More than queen *see* Nirdlinger, Charles Frederic and
Meltzer, Charles Henry

More truth than poetry *see*
Cherrytree, Herr (pseud.)

Moreau, Émile, 1852-1922.
Madame sans-gêne *see*
Meltzer, Charles Henry

Morette, Edgar.
Let love but hold the key.
A musical farce. Chicago:
T. S. Denison, c1900. 39p.
Libretto and vocal score.
(Denison's specialties)
[music by Eugène Fezandié]

Morey, Amos C.
Charlotte Corday. A tragedy
in five acts. New York: Jos.
A. Fraetas, Tribune Job Press,
1844. 48p.

Morgan, Geraldine Woods.
Tannhäuser and the minstrels
tournament on the Wartburg.
Grand romantic opera in three
acts. By Mrs. John P. Morgan.
Berlin: Adolph Fürstner,
c1891. New edition. Bilingual
text: English, 48p.; German,
48p. Libretto. *[music by
Richard Wagner; based on his
Tannhäuser und der Sänger-
krieg auf Wartburg; without
the music]*

Morgiana and the forty thieves
see Smith, Harry Bache. Ali
Baba, jr.; or, Morgiana and
the forty thieves *see also
his* Ali Baba; or Morgiana
and the forty thieves

Morituri: Teias *see* Harned,
Mary

The Mormons; or, Life at Salt
Lake City *see* English,
Thomas Dunn

Morning. A tragedy in five acts
see Campbell, William Wilfred. Collected works. Poetical tragedies

Morning and night *see* Phelps,
Lavinia Howe *in her* Dramatic
stories

Morris, D. L., d.1879.
Dutch justice *see* White,
Charles

Morris, Felix James, 1850-1900.
Circumstantial evidence. A
monologue. Chicago: Dramatic
Pub. Co., c1883. p.7-14.

Electric love (From the

French.) Chicago: Dramatic
Pub. Co., c1883. 9p. (Sergel's acting drama. no. 315)

The old musician. New York:
n.pub., 189-. Typescript.
Prompt-book with Ms. notes.
37 leaves (numb. irreg.)
[title page: From the
French]

Morris, George Pope, 1802-1864.
The maid of Saxony; or, Who's
the traitor? [From his:
Poems. New York: Charles
Scribner, 1854. Third edi-
tion] p.247-350, 365.
[title page: composed by
Charles E. Horn]

Morris, Ramsey, d.1917.
The social trust; or, The
spider's web. New York: Z.
and L. Rosenfield, 18-?
Typescript, prompt-book,
interleaved with Ms. notes.
40, 38, 24, 22 leaves.
[it is possible that Morris'
dates are 1857-1903: see
New York Times, April 10,
1903, p.9, col.2, where the
obituary for one Ramsey
Morris, 1857-1903, indicates
that he had "one play produced"; joint author:
Hillary Bell]

Morris, Robert.
The elopment; or, Love and
duty. A play in three acts.
Philadelphia: Barnard and
Jones, 1860. 67p.

Morris, Thomas Hollingsworth,
1817-1872.
Mariana; or, The coquette.
A comedy in three acts.
Baltimore: James S. Waters &
Sons, 1868. 50p.

Morris, William Smith.
An unconditional surrender.
A comedy in three acts.
Philadelphia: Penn Pub. Co.,

1911. 43p. [earlier copyright:
1892]

Morrison, George Austin, 1864-
1916.
Captain Kidd; or, A peerless
peeress and a haughty pirate.
An original burlesque on
early New York society in
three acts. New York: Trow's
Printing & Bookbinding Co.,
1888. 59p.

"Lafayette"; or, "The maid
and the marquis." An original
burlesque in three acts. New
York: A. E. Chasmar, 1890.
86p.

Morse, Mabel.
A foolish investment. A comedietta in one act. (From the
German.) New York: De Witt,
c1888. 15p. (De Witt's acting
plays. no. 350)

A warm reception. A comediet-
ta in one act. (From the
German "Im Schneegestöber" of
Rudolf Jarosy.) New York:
De Witt, c1890. 11p. (Sergel's
acting drama. no. 345)

Morse, R. G.
Miladi and the musketeer   see
Barnet, Robert A.

Morse, Woolson, 1858-1897.
Cinderella at school. A
musical paraphrase in two
acts. Boston: Louis P.
Goullaud, c1881. Prompt-book
with Ms. notes. 40p. Libretto.
[paraphrased from Aschenbrodel
by Kate Carrington; without
the music]

Madam Piper. Concocted by
Woolson Morse, assisted at
times in the stirring by J.
Cheever Goodwin. New York:
Art Interchange Press, 1884.
35p. [title page: a musical
melange; music composed and
play concocted by...Morse]

The merry monarch *see*
Goodwin, John Cheever

Wang *see* Goodwin, John
Cheever

Mortara; or, The Pope and his
inquisitors *see* Moos,
Herman M.

La morte civile *see* Civil
death

Morter, E. J.
Under ma's thumb. A farce
comedy in three acts. n.p.:
n.pub., c1897. Typescript,
prompt-book. 43, 58, 28
leaves. *[joint author:
Jacob Ralph Abarbanell]*

Morton, Charles H.
Three years in a man-trap.
Temperance drama in five
acts. (Founded on a story
by T. S. Arthur.) Camden,
N. J.: New Republic Print.,
1873. 51p. *[founded on the
story of the same title by
Timothy Shay Arthur; original
copyright: 1872]*

Women of the day. An American
comedy of modern society in
four acts. Philadelphia:
Printed but not published,
1874. 55p.

Morton, Hugh (pseud.) *see*
McLellan, Charles Morton
Stewart

Morton, John Maddison, 1811-
1891.
Declined--with thanks *see*
Williams, Henry Llewellyn

The highest bidder *see*
Belasco, David and Sothern,
Edward Hugh

Lend me five shillings *see*
The modern standard drama,
vol. 3

The writing on the wall *see*

Morton, Thomas and Morton,
John Maddison *in* The modern
standard drama, vol. 12

Morton, Marguerite W.
The blind girl of Castèl-
Cuillé. (From the poem by
Henry W. Longfellow.) New
York: Edgar S. Werner, c1892.
16p. *[title page: poem by
Henry W. Longfellow illustrated tableaux with musical
accompaniment arranged by
Marguerite W. Morton; based
on L'aveugle de Castel-Cuiler
by Jacques Jasmin, translated
by Longfellow]*

Poison. A farce in one scene
for four females. New York:
Edgar S. Werner, 1895. 8p.
*[title page: adapted by Miss
Marguerite Morton]*

The two roses. A farce in two
acts for three males and two
females. New York: Edgar S.
Werner, c1894. 11p.

Morton, Martha, 1865-1925.
A bachelor's romance. An
original play in four acts.
New York: 189-? Typescript,
prompt-book. In four acts
(pag. by acts.)

His wife's father. (From the
German of A. L'Aronge.) New
York: 1865. Typescript,
prompt-book. In four acts
(pag. by acts.) *[handwritten
on title page of copy reproduced by Readex: based on a
central idea in German by
A. L'Aronge [sic, Adolf
L'Arronge]*

Morton, Thomas, 1764-1838.
A cure for the heartache *see*
The modern standard drama,
vol. 2

The Englishman in India *see*
his Sketches in India *in*
The modern standard drama,
vol. 12

Sketches in India   *see*
The modern standard drama,
vol. 12

Speed the plough   *see*
The modern standard drama,
vol. 6

Town and country   *see*
The modern standard drama,
vol. 9

The writing on the wall   *see*
The modern standard drama,
vol. 12

Mosenthal, Salomon Hermann,
Ritter von, 1821-1877.
Deborah   *see*   Daly, Augustin.
Leah: the forsaken   *see also*
Deborah

Isabella Orsini   *see*
Williams, Henry Llewellyn

[Madelaine Morel]   *see*
Daly, Augustin

Moser, Gustav von, 1825-1903.
[An Arabian night in the
nineteenth century]   *see*
Daly, Augustin

Der Bibliothekar   *see*
Hageman, Maurice. Sowing
wild oats

["I shall invite the major"]
see Rosenfeld, Sydney

[The passing regiment]   *see*
Daly, Augustin

Reif-reiflingen   *see* Daly,
Augustin. Our English friend

Ultimo   *see* Daly, Augustin.
The big bonanza

Moses, Anna Jonas.
Esther. A Purim play in five
acts. Cincinnati: Block Pub.
and Print. Co., 1887. 27p.

Moses, David.
The printer and his devils.
An original farce. Clyde, O.:
Ames, c1890. 7p. (Ames'
series of standard and minor

drama. no. 276) *[joint
author: Arthur Blackaller]*

Moses *see* Brown, Charles
Hovey

Moses in Egypt   *see* Parker,
George S. *see also* Ponte,
Lorenzo da *see also* Villa-
rino, Jose J.

Moses in the bullrushes   *see*
More, Hannah *in* Cobb,
Mary L. Poetical dramas for
home and school

Moss, Alfred Charles.
H. M. S. Pinafore: oder, Das
maedle und ihr sailor Kerl.
N'translation fun dem bekannte
Opera. In Pennsylfanist
deutsch. Philadelphia: D. J.
Gallagher, 1885. Bilingual
text: English and Pennsylvania
German. 20p. *[without the
music; earlier copyright:
1882]*

The moth and the flame   *see*
Fitch, Clyde

The mother and the father   *see*
Howells, William Dean

Mother earth and her vegetable
daughter's [sic]; or, Crowning
the queen of vegetables   *see*
Lewis, E. A. and Lewis, C. M.

Mother Goose and her friends
see Venable, William Henry
in his The school stage

A Mother Goose comedy   *see*
Merriman, Effie Woodward
in her Comedies for children

Mother's fool   *see* Wilkins,
W. Henri

A mother's love   *see* Todd,
John W. Arthur Eustace; or,
A mother's love

A mother's love; or, A wreath
for our lady *see* Reynartz,
Dorothy

Motley, John Lothrop, 1814-
1877.
Bluebeard. A story in five
acts [From: The New World.
A weekly journal. New York:
J. Winchester, 1840. vol. 1:
nos. 29, 30; p.449-464, 475-
490] vol. 1: nos. 29, 30;
p.449-452, 478-483. *[trans-*
lated from Johann Ludwig
Tieck's Ritter Blaubart]

The motor bellows *see*
Courtright, William

Mount Savage *see* Payne, John
Howard

Mount Shannon *see* Burke,
James. Shannon boys; or,
Mount Shannon

A mountain pink *see* Bates,
Morgan and Barron, Elwyn
Alfred. Realistic description of life among the
moonshiners of North Carolina. A mountain pink

A mountain psyche *see*
Richardson, Anna Steese
Sausser. Miss Mosher of
Colorado; or, A mountain
psyche

The mountain rebel *see*
Moore, Bernard Francis.
"Erin go bragh"; or, The
mountain rebel

The mountain waif *see*
Townsend, Charles

The mountaineers *see* Colman,
George (1762-1836) *in* The
modern standard drama,
vol. 8

The mountebanks *see* Andrews,
Fred G.

The mourners *see* Cook, Eliza
in Massey, Charles. Massey's
exhibition reciter

The mouse-trap *see* Howells,
William Dean

The mouse-trap. A predicament
see Harrison, Constance Cary
in her Short comedies for
amateur players

The mouth of gold. A series of
dramatic sketches illustrating
the life and times of Chrysostom *see* Johnson, Edwin

Mowatt, Anna Cora *see* Ritchie,
Anna Cora Ogden Mowatt

Mowrey, Phil H.
The musical servant. An
Ethiopian sketch in one
scene. New York: R. M.
De Witt, c1875. 6p. (De Witt's
Ethiopian and comic drama.
no. 44)

Mozart, Wolfgang Amadeus, 1756-
1791.
Don Giovanni *see* Don Giovanni *see also* Sherwood, W.

Much ado about nothing *see*
Daly, Augustin *see also*
Shakespeare, William *in*
Booth, Edwin. The Shakespear-
ean plays of Edwin Booth
see also Shakespeare, Will-
iam *in* The modern standard
drama, vol. 7 *see also*
Wallack, Lester *see also*
Warren, Leslie

Much coin, much care *see*
Jameson, Mrs. *in* Follen,
Eliza Lee Cabot. Home dramas
for young people

Münch-Bellinghausen, Eligius
Franz Joseph, Freiherr von,
1806-1871.
Der Sohn der Wildniss *see*
Anthon, Charles Edward. The

son of the wilderness *see*
also Ingomar the barbarian
see also Lovell, Mary Anne
Lacy. Ingomar the barbarian
in The modern standard
drama, vol. 12

Griseldis *see* Prentiss,
Elizabcth Payson. Griselda

Muldoon's blunders *see*
Lee, Billy F.

Müller, Hugo, 1831-1881.
[Adelaïde; the romance of
Beethoven's life] *see*
Howard, Edmond and Bispham,
David Scull

La muette; or, The dumb girl
of Portic. By G. B. C.
(From the French of Scribe
and Delavigne.) Baltimore:
E. J. Coale, 1831. 46p.
[based on Masaniello, ou la
muette de Portici, by
Augustin Scribe and Germain
Delavigne, as set to music
by Daniel François Esprit
Auber; without the music]

Mulcahy's cat *see* McDermott,
J. J. and Trumble

Mullalt, W. S.
Gentlemen coon's parade *see*
Gentlemen coon's parade
[possibly W. S. Mullally,
1845-1905?]

Mullen, Nicholas.
Janet, the flower girl. A
drawing-room drama in one
act. New York: C. G.
Burgoyne, 1880. 12p.

Mumbo Jum; or, The enchanted
clogs. An Ethiopian extravaganza. New York: Happy
Hours, 1874. Title page
mutilated. 7p. (The Ethiopian drama. no. 82)

Munson, A. J.
A midnight mistake. A melo-

drama in four acts. Clyde, O.:
Ames, c1886. 23p. (Ames'
series of standard and minor
drama. no. 211)

Munson, George A.
An unwelcome return. A comic
interlude in one act. Clyde,
O.: Ames, c1878. 10p. (Ames'
series of standard and minor
drama. no. 65)

Muolo, the monkey; or, The
missing link *see* Helm,
Charles E.

The muder of the Five Field's
Copse *see* Ames, A. D.
The poacher's doom; or, The
murder of the Five Field's
Copse

Murder will out *see* Elwyn,
Lizzie May

Murdoch, Frank Hitchcock, 1843-
1872.
Davy Crockett; or, Be sure
you're right, then go ahead.
By Frank Murdock [sic][From:
America's lost plays. vol. 4.
Princeton, N. J.: Princeton
Univ. Press, 1940] p.115-148.
[earlier copyright: 1872]

Murdoch, James Edward, 1811-
1893.
Laugh when you can. A comedy
in five acts. (From the play
by Frederick Reynolds.)
Louisville: Robert Jones,
1860. Prompt-book, inter-
leaved with Ms. notes. 80p.

Murger, Henri, 1822-1861.
Le serment d'Horace *see*
Matthews, Brander. Cuttybank's
thunder; or, Frank Wilde [sic,
Wylde] *see also* Matthews,
Brander. Frank Wylde *in his*
Comedies for amateur acting

La vie de Bohème *see* Fitch,
Clyde. Bohemia

Murphy, Arthur, 1727-1805.
Three weeks after marriage
see The modern standard
drama, vol. 8

Murphy, Fitzgerald.
A bit o' blarney. An Irish
play of the present time in
three acts. Boston: W. H.
Baker, c1893. 41p. (Baker's
edition of plays)

Murphy, John M.
The mechanics reprieve. A
drama in three acts. Clyde,
O.: Ames, c1899. 30p. (Ames'
series of standard and minor
drama. no. 410)

Murphy, J. Shriver.
A social Judas *see* Tees,
Levin C. and Murphy, J.
Shriver

Murray, Ellen.
Cain, ancient and modern
in Dramatic leaflets

The crusaders *in* Dramatic
leaflets

Esau and Jacob *in* Dramatic
leaflets

Licensed snakes. Temperance
dialogue *in* Dramatic
leaflets

The women of Löwenburg. A
historical comedy in five
scenes. Chicago: T. S.
Denison, c1886. 12p. (The
amateur series)

Muscroft, Samuel J.
The drummer boy; or, The
battlefield of Shiloh. A
new military allegory in
five acts. Mansfield, O.:
L. D. Myers & Bro. Book and
Job Printers, 1872. 31p.

The muses up-to-date *see*
Field, Henrietta Dexter
and Field, Roswell Martin.
Collected works

Music vs. elocution *see* Coes,
George H.

The musical bore. A humorous
farce in one act and one
scene. New York: Dick &
Fitzgerald, c1886. 16p.
(Dick's American edition)

The musical captain; or, The
fall of Vicksburg *see*
Emerson, W. Burt

The musical darkey *see* Cutler,
F. L.

The musical servant *see*
Mowrey, Phil H.

Musset, Alfred de, 1810-1857.
Mardoche *see* Knapp, A.
Melvin

The mutton trial *see* White,
Charles

A mutual friend *see* Waldron,
P. A. Paddy Doyle; or, A
mutual friend

My aunt. A petit comedy in two
acts. Philadelphia: C. Neal,
18-? 27p. Prompt-book. *[Pre-
'56 imprints attributes this
play to Samuel James Arnold,
1774-1852]*

My brother's keeper *see* Baker,
George Melville

My colleen *see* Herne, James A.
The hearthstone; or, My
colleen

My daughter-in-law. A comedy in
three acts. (From the French
of Carré and Bilhaud.) New
York: Z. and L. Rosenfield,
1900. Typescript, prompt-book
with Ms. notes. 42, 54, 38
leaves. *[based on Ma bru by
Fabrice Carré and Paul Bil-
haud]*

My daughter's dowry *see*
Delafield, John H. Foresight;
or, My daughter's dowry

My day & now-a-days *see*
Zediker, N.

My father's will *see*
Abarbanell, Jacob Ralph

My friend from Arkansas *see*
?Sherman, Robert

My friend from India *see*
Du Souchet, Henry A.

My friend Isaac *see* Ford,
Daniel K.

My husband's mirror *see*
Clapp, William Warland

My invalid aunt *see* Chipman,
Adelbert Z. Ruben Rube;
or, My invalid aunt

My Jeremiah *see* McBride,
H. Elliott

My lady Darrell; or, A strange
marriage *see* LeBrandt,
Joseph

My mother-in-law; or, A
divorce wanted *see* Prichard,
Joseph Vila

My mother's gold ring *see*
A collection of temperance
dialogues

My new curate *see* Douglass,
John J.

My pard; or, The fairy of the
tunnel *see* Ward, Lew

My partner *see* Campbell,
Bartley Theodore *see also*
in his The white slave and
other plays

My sister's husband *see*
Brewster, Emma *in her*
Parlor varieties

My uncle, the captain *see*
Baker, George Melville

My walking photograph *see*
Sedgwick, Alfred B.

My wife's mirror *see*
Wilkins, Edward G. P.

My wife's visitors *see*
Dumont, Frank

My youngster's love affair *see*
Connell, George Stanislaus
in his The old patroon and
other plays

Myles, George B.
The winning hand; or, The
imposter. A comedy in four
acts. Clyde, O.: Ames, c1895.
25p. (Ames' series of standard
and minor drama. no. 351)

Myriad-minded man; an imaginary
conversation *see* Block,
Louis James *in his*
Capriccios

Myrtilla *see* Rice, George
Edward

The mysteries of Odd-Fellowship.
A farce in one act. By a
member of the order. Philadelphia: Turner & Fisher,
1836? 32p. (Fisher's
edition of standard farces)

The mysterious artist *see*
Neal, John

A mysterious disappearance *see*
Baker, George Melville

The mysterious guest *see*
Merriman, Effie Woodward
see also in her Comedies
for children

A mysterious kiss *see* A., N.

Mysterious stranger. An Ethiopian sketch in one scene.
New York: Happy Hours, c1874.

6p. (The Ethiopian drama.
no. 75)

The mystery of Oliver's Ferry
see Field, A. Newton.
Bill Detrick; or, The
mystery of Oliver's Ferry

The mystic charm; or, A wonderful cure. A farce in one
act. Clyde, O.: Ames, 189-?
26p. (Ames' series of standard and minor drama. no. 354)

The mystic isle; or, The laws
of average *see* Rosenfeld,
Sydney

The mystic midgets' Liliputian
carnival of nations *see*
Bertram, Eugene and Bassett,
Willard

The mystic spell *see* White,
Charles

N., S. T. A.
A lover's stratagem. A
comedy in three acts. New
York: De Witt, c1884. 15p.
(De Witt's acting plays.
no. 334)

Naaman, the Syrian *see*
Boxer, James *in his*
Sacred dramas

Nack, James, 1809-1879.
The immortal. A dramatic
romance [From his: The
immortal; a dramatic
romance; and other poems.
New York: Stringer and
Townsend, 1850] p.1-83.

The spirit of vengeance.
A drama in three acts
[From his: The romance of
the ring; and other poems.
New York: Delisser & Proc-
ter, 1859] p.37-90.

Najac, Émile de, 1828-1889.
Bébé *see* Babie

Le roi malgré lui *see*
Goodwin, John Cheever. The
merry monarch

The scarlet letter. (From
the novel by Hawthorne.)
n.p.: n.pub., c1877. Prompt-
book in Ms. In five acts,
plus sides for Hester Pyrnne
and musical score (pag. by
acts.) [joint author: Jean
Margaret Landers]

Nan, the mascotte *see* Patten,
Gilbert

Nance Oldfield *see* Aldrich,
Mildred

Nancy and company *see* Daly,
Augustin

Nanka's leap year venture; or,
How she settled her bills *see*
Shettel, James W. and
George, Wadsworth M.

Il nano italiano *see* ?Heywood,
Joseph Converse

Nanon *see* Elson, Louis Charles

Napoleon *see* Adams, Henry
Austin *see also* Dement,
Richmond Sheffield *see also*
Tullidge, Edward Wheelock

Napoleon and Josephine *see*
Dement, Richmond Sheffield

Narcisse the vagrant *see*
Schönberg, James

Narrey, Charles, 1825-1892.
La cigarette *see* Sullivan,
Thomas Russell. A cigarette
from Java

Sophronisba...oh! *see*
Sophronisba...oh!

Nash, Joseph.
Josephine. An historical
drama in four acts. Boston:
F. Wood, 1874. 60p.

Nathan Hale *see* Fitch, Clyde

Nathan the wise *see* Frothingham, Ellen

A natural transformation *see* Osborn, Laughton. The school for critics; or, A natural transformation

Nature's nobleman *see* Pardey, Henry Oake

Naughty Anthony *see* Belasco, David *see also in his* The heart of Maryland and other plays

Neafie, John Andrew Jackson, 1815-1892.
Harolde, the envoye of Artois. A tragic play in five acts. New York: Plaindealer Steam Printing Establishment, 1880. 91p.

Neal, John, 1793-1876.
Duty and safety of emancipation [From: The antislavery offering and picknick...By John A. Collins, compiler. Boston: H. W. Williams, 1843] p.106-110.

Instincts of childhood. A dialogue in two parts [From: The anti-slavery offering and picknick...by John A. Collins, compiler. Boston: H. W. Williams, 1843] p.75-80.

The mysterious artist [From: The anti-slavery offering and picknick...By John A. Collins, compiler. Boston: H. W. Williams, 1843] p.172-177.

Neall, Walter H.
An economical boomerang. A farce in one act. Philadelphia: Penn Pub. Co., 1916. p.143-155. (One hundred choice selections. no. 32) [earlier copyright: 1892]

Raising the wind. A farce in one act. Philadelphia: Penn Pub. Co., 1911. p.163-174. (One hundred choice selections. no. 33) [earlier copyright: 1894]

The necessity of Union *see* Webster, Daniel *in* Massey, Charles. Massey's exhibition reciter

Needles and pins *see* Daly, Augustin

Negative evidence *see* The bat and the ball; or, Negative evidence

Neighbor *see* Arnold, George? and Cahill, Frank. Parlor theatricals; or, Winter evening's entertainment

Neighbor Jackwood *see* Trowbridge, John Townsend

Nelly's rival *see* Reynolds, S. S.

Nelson, D. R.
Armerine, the moonshiner. A tragicomedy in five acts. Portland, Ore.: n.pub., c1899. Title page lacking. 56p.

Nelson, J. Raleigh.
Dido *see* Miller, Frank Justus

Nero *see* Comfort, Richard *see also* Story, William Wetmore

Nero, the parricide *see* Anderson, Edward Lowell

The nervous man and the man of nerve *see* Bernard, William Bayle *in* The modern standard drama, vol. 5

Neuendorff, Adolf, 1843-1897.
Der Rattenfänger von Hameln
see Williams, Frederick. The
rat-charmer of Hamelin

Neumann, Louis.
The flying Dutchman. Romantic
opera in three acts. New York:
Theatre Ticket Office, c1876.
Bilingual text: English, 8p.;
German, 8p.; 5p. Libretto.
*[based on Richard Wagner's
Der fliegende Holländer]*

Nevada; or, The lost mine see
Baker, George Melville

Never again see Pitman,
James R.

Never say die see Baker,
George Melville

Nevin, Arthur Finley, 1871-
1943.
The casino girl see
Smith, Harry Bache

The new and the old see
Beadle's dialogues...no. 2

New boy in school see
Dennison, Thomas Stewart
in his Wide awake dialogues

New brooms sweep clean see
Baker, George Melville

The new calvary see Osborn,
Laughton *in his* Meleagros
[and] The new cavalry

New Christmas see Denton,
Clara Janetta Fort *in her*
From tots to teens

New dialogues see McBride,
H. Elliott

The New England tragedies see
Longfellow, Henry Wadsworth
see also *in his* Christus

The New Englanders see

Davison, E. Mora

The new governess see Walker,
Janet Edmondson

The "New Hagodoh Shel Pesach"
see Bien, Herman Milton.
Easter eve; or, The "New
Hagodoh Shel Pesach"

New Hampshire gold see Rand,
Katharine Ellen

A New Hampshire man in Boston
see McBride, H. Elliott.
The stolen child; or, A New
Hampshire man in Boston

The new King Arthur see
Fawcett, Edgar

The new Magdalen see Field,
A. Newton

The new moon see André,
Richard

The new Pandora see Robinson,
Harriet Jane Hanson

The new partner see Tees,
Levin C.

The new south see Greene,
Clay Meredith and Grismer,
Joseph Rhode

The new squire see Lester,
Francis

The new system see Davis,
Mary Evelyn Moore

A new travesty on Romeo and
Juliet see Soule, Charles
Carroll

A new way to pay old debts
Massinger, Philip *in* The
modern standard drama, vol. 5

The new woman see Denison,
Thomas Stewart
Rugg, George

The new woman's husband *see*
Dumont, Frank

The new world *see* Read,
Harriette Fanning *in her*
Dramatic poems

New-year morning; a petit
opera, in one act. As
performed...on the first
of January, 1831...By the
carrier. n.p.: n.pub., 1831.
1p. Broadside.

New Year's calls *see*
Griffin, George W. H.

New Years in New York; or,
The German baron *see*
Spangler, W. H.

A New Year's masque *see*
Thomas, Edith Matilda

A new year's reception *see*
Smith, Hubbard Taylor

The New York book agent; or,
The miser's gold *see*
Moore, D. H.

New York by gaslight *see*
White, Charles. Streets of
New York; or, New York by
gaslight

Newport *see* Rae, Robert

News of the night; or, A trip
to Niagara *see* Bird,
Robert Montgomery *in his*
The cowled lover and other
plays

Newton, Charles E. (pseud.)
see Perine, Charles E.

Newton, William Wilberforce,
1843-1914.
Troublesome children, their
ups and downs *see* Fessen-
den, Helen May Trott.
Troublesome children; or,
The unexpected voyage of
Jack and Pen

A nice quiet chat *see*
Williams, Marie Josephine

Nicholas of the Flue. The
savior of the Swiss Republic
see Schaad, John Christian

Nick of the woods *see* Medina,
Louisa H.

Nick Whiffles *see* Robinson,
John Hovey

Nieuwenhuysen, Gustave, 1812-
1862.
La favorita *see* La favorita
see also The favorite *see*
also Révoil, Bénèdict Henry.
La favorite

The nigger and the Yankee *see*
Vautrot, George S. Black vs.
white; or, The nigger and the
Yankee

Nigger boarding-house *see*
Wenlandt, Oliver

The Nigger night school *see*
Barnes, Thomas

A night in a strange hotel *see*
White, Charles

A night in Buenos Ayres *see*
Bushby (pseud.)

A night of knights. New York:
n.pub., 1900? Typescript,
prompt-book. 22 leaves.

A night off; or, A page from
Balzac *see* Daly, Augustin

A night with Brudder Bones.
An Ethiopian comicality in
one scene. New York: Happy
Hours, c1874. 7p. (The
Ethiopian drama. no. 64)

A night with Charles XII of
Sweden; or, A soldier's
wife's fidelity *see* De
Peyster, John Watts

293 NOBLES

The nightingale and the lark
see Keatinge, Ella see
also her Short plays for
children

Nigri, Julius von St. Albino,
1849-1895.
Pfingsten in Florenz see
Goldmark, George and Rosenfeld, Sydney. Amorita

Nine points of law see
White, Charles. Malicious
trespass; or, Nine points
of law

Nino's revenge see Dugan,
Caro Atherton in her
Collected works

The ninth anniversary of the
New York Mirror, July, 1831
see Woodworth, Samuel

Nip and tuck see Switzer,
Marvin D.

Nip and Tuck see White,
Charles. The serenade

Nirdlinger, Charles Frederic,
1862-1940.
More than queen. (From the
French of Bergerat.) New
York: n.pub., 1899. Type-
script. Title page lacking.
30, 20, 30, 25, 20 leaves.
[based on Plus que reine by
Émile Bergerat; joint author:
Charles Henry Meltzer]

No cure, no pay see Griffin,
George W. H.

No king in America see
Colman, Julia

No pay no cure see Leavitt,
Andrew J.

No peddlers wanted. Comic
dialogue. Lebanon, O.: March
Bros., 18-? 8p.

No questions asked see
Rosenfeld, Sydney and
Bisson, Alexandre Charles
Auguste

No tator; or, Man-fish see
Leavitt, Andrew J. and
Eagan, H. W.

No use crying for spilled milk
see Robinson, Lucy Catlin
Bull in her Various
dramatic works

Nobility; or, The alcalde of
Zalamea see Pierra, Adolfo

A noble outcast see Fraser,
John Arthur

The noble savages see Dumont,
Frank

A noble spy see Madden, Eva
Annie

Nobles, Milton, 1847-1924.
The actor; or, A son of
Thespis. An original comedy-
drama in four acts. Philadelphia: Ledger Job Print.,
1891. 104p.

From sire to son; or, The
hour and the man. An original
drama in four acts. Philadelphia: Ledger Job Print.,
1887. Prompt-book, inter-
leaved. 85p.

Interviews; or, Bright
Bohemia. An American comedy
in four acts. Philadelphia:
Ledger Job Print., 1881.
Prompt-book, interleaved.
77p.

Love and law. An original
comedy-drama in four acts.
Philadelphia: Ledger Job
Print., 1884. 78p.

The phoenix. A drama in four
acts. Chicago: Dramatic Pub.
Co., 1900. 128p. (Green-room

edition of copyrighted plays) *[earlier copyright: 1875]*

Nobody's Moke *see* Gray, William W.

Nobody's money *see* Furness, Horace Howard

Nobody's son *see* Griffin, George W. H.

Noel Carson's oath; or, Leonia's repentance *see* Raynor, Verna M.

Nomad (pseud.)
"Caught at last." [From: "Caught at last." By Nomad [bound with] The blue stocking. By D. Joseph. New York: De Witt, c1884. 11p.] p.1-7. (De Witt's acting plays. no. 333) *[Readex has reproduced only the play by Nomad; Nomad is the pseud. of Adéle Crafton Smith]*

Nona, Francis.
The fall of the Alamo. An historical drama in four acts...concluded with an epilogue entitled "The battle of San Jacinto." New York: G. P. Putnam's Sons, 1879. 257p. *[music composed by the author]*

Non-committal *see* The school for politicans; or, Non-committal

None so deaf as those who won't hear *see* Curtis, Herbert Pelham

Nonsense; or, Two ways of training boys *see* Venable, William Henry *in his* The school stage

Nora Darling *see* Roberts, T. W.

Norah's good-bye *see* Dumont, Frank

Norcross, Frédéric Walter.
Hadley. A Bucks County romance in five acts. [From his: Plays and poems...London: For the author, Chiswick Press, 1902. 163p.] p.1-2, 1, 82-159. *[earlier copyright: 1898]*

Mistress Nan. A drama of the American revolution in three acts. [From his: Plays and poems...London: For the author, Chiswick Press, 1902. 163p.] p.1-9, 15-68, 1. *[earlier copyright: 1898; this play was to have been produced starring Fanny Davenport, who died before it could be produced]*

Norcross, I. W.
Gillette; or, Count and countess. Boston: Oliver Ditson, c1884. Vocal score. 206p. *[title page: J. W. Norcross [sic, I. W. Norcross]; music by Edmond Audran on the libretto Gillette de Narbonne by Henri Chivot and Alfred Duru]*

The mascot *see* Barker, Theodore T. and Norcross, I. W.

The merry war. New York: n.pub., c1882. Title page lacking. Vocal score. 28p. *[music by Johann Strauss on the libretto Der lustige Krieg by F. Zell (pseud. of Camillo Wälzel) and Richard Genée]*

Nordeck *see* Mayo, Frank and Wilson, John G.

Norma *see* Fry, Joseph Reese

Norman Maurice; or, The man of the people *see* Simms, William Gilmore

Normand, Jacques Clary Jean,
1848-1931.
La goutte d'eau *see* Coale,
George B. The drop of water

Norna; or, The witch's curse
see Alcott, Louisa May
in her Comic tragedies

Norris, J. W.
La mascotte *see* Elson,
Louis Charles and Norris,
J. W.

The North End caulker; or,
The mechanic's oath *see*
Saunders, Charles Henry

Northall, William Knight.
Macbeth travestie. New
York: S. French, 184-?
36p. (The minor drama.
no. 36)

Northern lights *see* Fuller,
Henry Blake *in his* Collected works

Norton, Mrs.
The soldier from Bingen
see Massey, Charles.
Massey's exhibition reciter

Norton, Jessie.
Sappho. A classical historical play for girls. New
York: Edgar S. Werner, c1894.
28p.

Norton, Morilla Maria, b.1865.
Gloria Victis. Warner,
N. H.: E. C. Cole, 1900. 50p.

Not a man in the house *see*
Smith, S. Jennie

Not as deaf as he seems. An
Ethiopian farce in one act
for two characters. Clyde,
O.: Ames, 18-. 6p. (Ames'
series of standard and minor
drama. no. 61)

Not at home *see* Griffith,
Benjamin Lease Crozer

Notes and notices [From: The
Collegian. No. 5. Cambridge:
Hilliard and Brown, 1830]
p.242-248.

Nothing to nurse *see* Walcot,
Charles Melton

Notre-Dame of Paris *see* Fry,
Joseph Reese

Novice *see* Shields, Sarah
Annie Frost *in her* Parlor
charades and proverbs

Nowak, A.
The lady or the tiger? *see*
Rosenfeld, Sydney

Nugent, John Charles, 1878-
1947.
An Indiana romance. A drama
in four acts. n.p.: n.pub.,
189-? Typescript. In four
acts (pag. by acts)

Nugget Nell; or, Claim ninety-
six *see* Ward, Lew. Claim
ninety-six

Nugget Nell, the pet of Poker
Flat *see* Cowley, E. J. and
Bennette, Wilson T. Craw-
ford's claim; or, Nugget
Nell, the pet of Poker Flat

Number two *see* Friars, Austin

Nuts to crack--no. 1 *see*
Denton, Clara Janetta Fort.
When the lessons are over

Nuts to crack--no. 2 *see*
Denton, Clara Janetta Fort.
When the lessons are over

O Hanu San *see* Rosse, Jeanie
Quinton. The Japanese girl
(O Hanu San)

Oakes, A. H.
A teacher taught. A comedy
in one act. Boston: W. H.
Baker, 1902. 26p. (Baker's
edition of plays) [A. H.

*Oakes is the pseud. of
Henry Cuyler Bunner; based
on Le roman d'une pupille
by Paul Ferrier; earlier
copyright: 1879] see also*
Matthews, Brander. Comedies
for amateur acting

The oath *see* Furber, Pierce
see also Il giuramento;
or, The oath

Oath bound; or, Faithful unto
death *see* Hanshew,
Thomas W.

The oath of office *see*
Cannon, Charles James
see also his Collected
works. Dramas

Obedience; or, Too mindful by
far *see* Lambla, Hattie
Lena

The obedient servants *see*
Denton, Clara Janetta Fort.
When the lessons are over

Obeying orders *see* White,
Charles

An object lesson *see*
Heywood, Delia A.
Choice dialogues. no. 1

An object lesson in history
see Colclough, Emma Shaw

O'Brien, Constance.
Cross purposes. A comedietta
in four scenes. New York:
De Witt, 189-? 38p. (De
Witt's acting plays. no. 382)

Love in a flue; or, The
sweep and the magistrate.
A comedy in two scenes.
New York: De Witt, 189-?
35p. (De Witt's acting
plays. no. 385)

A lover and a half. A
comedy in two acts. New
York: De Witt, 18-? 30p.

(De Witt's acting plays.
no. 384)

The wager. A comedy in one
act. New York: De Witt,
189-? 27p. (De Witt's acting
plays. no. 383)

O'Brien, Daniel Webster *see*
Bryant, Daniel

O'Brien, Fitz-James, 1828-1862.
A gentleman from Ireland.
A comedy in three acts. New
York: Samuel French, c1858.
20p. (The minor drama. no.
156) *[Readex's entry indicates that this play is in
three acts, whereas actually
it is in two acts]*

An obstinate Romeo *see*
Latour, Eugene. Tricks of
trade; or, An obstinate
Romeo

Octavia Bragaldi; or, The
confession *see* Barnes,
Charlotte Mary Sanford

O'Day, the Alderman *see*
Ryan, Samuel E.

The oddity *see* Fowle,
William Bentley *in his*
Parlor dramas

Odds with the enemy *see*
Denison, Thomas Stewart

Off the stage *see* Rosenfeld,
Sydney

Off to the war! *see* Woolf,
Benjamin Edward

Offenbach, Jacques, 1819-1880.
Barbe-bleue *see* Bluebeard

La belle Hélène *see* La
belle Hélène

Les brigands *see* Les
brigands

Geneviève de Brabant *see*

Bailey, G. see also
Sedgwick, Alfred B. Leap
year

La grande duchesse de
Gerolstein see The grand
duchess of Gerolstein

Madame l'archiduc see
Sedgwick, Alfred B. A single
married man

Orphée aux enfers see
Orpheus and Eurydice

La princesse de Trébizonde
see Sedgwick, Alfred B.
The queerest courtship

The office in an uproar see
Steele, Silas Sexton. The
stage struck clerk; or, The
office in an uproar in his
Collected works. Book of
plays

Ogden, Octavius Nash, b.1852.
Dominic You. A tragedy in
three acts. New Orleans:
E. P. Brandao, 1895. 56p.

Oh! hush!; or, The Virginny
cupids! see White, Charles

Oh, well, it's no use see
Coes, George H.

Ohnet, Georges, 1848-1918.
Le maître des forges see
Prichard, Joseph Vila.
The iron master

Old Acre folk see Stevens,
Dana J.

Old and young; or, Both alike
see Salmon, John

Old Block (pseud.) see
Delano, Alonzo

The old Catholics at Cologne
see Fröhlich, Herr (pseud.)

Old clothes see Back from
Californy; or, Old clothes

The (old clothes) merchant of
Venice; or, The young judge
and old jewry. A burlesque
sketch for the drawing-room.
New York: De Witt, 189-?
15p. (De Witt's acting
plays. no. 331) ["an adaptation" of a work by W.
Shakespeare]

The old country store see
Hiland, Frank E.

Old Dad's cabin see
White, Charles

The old fashioned husking bee
see Pelham, Nettie H.

Old foes with new faces see
Bowers, Elizabeth. The black
agate; or, Old foes with
new faces

Old Glory in Cuba see
Beaty, Thomas R.

Old heads and young hearts see
Boucicault, Dion in The
modern standard drama,
vol. 8

The old homestead see
Thompson, Denman and Ryer,
George W.

Old Hunks, the miser. An
Ethiopian comicality.
Chicago: T. S. Denison, 18-?
9p. (The Ethiopian drama)

The old Kentucky home. A
darkey sketch in three
scenes. New York: Harold
Roorbach, c1874. 8p. (The
Ethiopian drama. no. 80)

The old lady's will see
Beadle's...dialogues no. 2
see also A collection of
temperance dialogues

The old love and the new see
Howard, Bronson. The banker's
daughter

Old love letters *see*
Howard, Bronson

The old maid's association
see Wilson, Louise Latham

The old maid's conference
see Schell, Stanley

The old maid's convention
see Parsons, Laura Matilda
Stephenson *see also* The
spinsters' convention

The old maid's triumph *see*
Beck, William L. Captured;
or, The old maid's triumph

An old maid's wooing *see*
Orne, Martha Russell

The old man's pocket-book *see*
Kavanaugh, Mrs. Russell
in her Original dramas,
dialogues

Old Mrs. Williams' dance *see*
White, Charles. Going for
the cup; or, Old Mrs.
Williams' dance

The old musician *see* Morris,
Felix James

Old New York; or, Democracy
in 1689 *see* Smith, Elizabeth Oakes Prince

The old North Tower *see*
Mickle, Isaac

The old parson *see* Coes,
George H.

The old patroon *see* Connell,
George Stanislaus *in his*
The old patroon and other
plays

Old photograph album *see*
Denison, Thomas Stewart
in his Wide awake dialogues

An old plantation night *see*

Hazard, Eleanor and Hazard,
Elizabeth

An old play in a new garb.
Hamlet, Prince of Denmark
see Rice, George Edward

Old Pompey *see* Cutler, F. L.

Old Poz *see* Edgeworth, Maria
in Follen, Eliza Lee Cabot.
Home dramas for young people

The old seventy-sixer *see*
Jaimson, George. The Revolutionary soldier

Old times made new *see*
Chronothanatoletron; or,
Old times made new

The old toll house mystery *see*
Coes, George H. That dorg;
or, The old toll house
mystery

The old trunk in the garret
see Keatinge, Ella

An old vagabond *see* Heermans,
Forbes

The old Wayside Inn *see*
Crary, J. E.

The old woman who lived in a
shoe *see* Wilson, Olivia W.
in her The luck of the
golden pumpkin

Olea *see* Ruhland, Mildred
Amelie

O'Leary, James.
Ellie Laura; or, The border
orphan. New York: P. O'Shea,
c1871. 41p.

Oleomargarine *see* Wilton,
M. J.

The olive merchants of Bagdat
see Follen, Eliza Lee Cabot.
Home dramas for young people

Oliver Cromwell *see* Donoho, Thomas Seaton

Olivet; or, A rare Teutonic specimen *see* Crary, J. E.

Olivette. Opera comique in three acts. By T. L. (From Farnie's play of the same title.) Boston: Oliver Ditson, c1881. 64p. Libretto and vocal score. *[music by Edmond Audran on libretto Les noces d'Olivette by Henri Chivot and Alfred Duru as based on Olivette by Henry Brougham Farnie]*

Olivia. Vicar of Wakefield *see* Davenport, Fanny Lily Gypsy

Oluph; a tragedy. New York: Osborn & Buckingham, 1836. 105p.

Olwine, Isaac Wayne *see* Olwine, Wayne

Olwine, Wayne.
Camille; or, The fate of a coquette. A tragic play in five acts. By a gentleman of Philadelphia. Edited by Wayne Olwine. (From the French of A. Dumas.) New York: O. A. Roorbach, 1856. 64p. *[based on La dame aux camélias by Alexandre Dumas the younger]*

Camille; or, The fate of a coquette. A tragic play in five acts. By Wayne Olwine, editor. New York: Wheat & Cornett, c1877. (New York Drama, vol. 2, no. 24, p.1-21)

Om. Mammon *see* Elshemus, Louis Michael

The Omnibus. A farce in one act. (From Pocock's play of the same title.) New York: Wm. Taylor, 1848? 23p. (The minor drama. no. 26) *[from Isaac Pocock's The Omnibus as based on Cherry Bounce by Richard John Raymond]*

On both sides *see* Heermans, Forbes

On bread and water *see* Rosenfeld, Sydney

On guard *see* Townsend, Charles

On his devoted head *see* Coale, George B.

On parole *see* Shipman, Louis Evan

On probation *see* Matthews, Brander and Jessop, George Henry

On the Bowery *see* Stephens, Robert Neilson

On the brink; or, The reclaimed husband *see* McBride, H. Elliott

On the mountain top *see* Block, Louis James *in his* Capriccios

On the staircase *see* Mathews, Frances Aymar

On the whirlwind *see* Fuller, Henry Blake *in his* Collected works

On to victory *see* Buxton, Ida M.

Once on a time *see* Baker, George Melville

One coat for two suits *see* Walcot, Charles Melton

One glass of wine *see* Elwyn, Lizzie May. Dot, the miner's daughter; or, One glass of wine

One hundred for thirty *see* Dumont, Frank. Get-rich-quick society; or, One hundred for thirty

One hundred years ago; or, Our boys of 1776 *see* Baker, George Melville

100th night of Hamlet *see* White, Charles

One lie leads to another *see* Runnion, James B. Champagne and oysters; or, One lie leads to another

One must hurry *see* Ritch, C. W.

One night in a bar room *see* White, Charles

One night in a medical college *see* Dumont, Frank

One of our girls *see* Howard, Bronson

One question. New York: Brentanos, 1889. 122p. *[Pre-'56 imprints attributes this play to Austice Curtis]*

One, two, three *see* White, Charles

One year *see* Enéleh, H. B.

O'Neal the great; or, Cogger na Caille [sic, Caillie] *see* Belden, N. H.

O'Neil the Great *see* Rizy, F. X.

O'Neill, James, 1849-1920. "Monte Cristo." By Charles Fechter. Revised by James O'Neill. [From: Monte Cristo ...By J. B. Russak, editor.

Princeton, N. J.: Princeton Univ. Press, 1941. America's lost plays, vol. 16. 360p.] p.1-70. *[based on Le comte de Monte-Cristo by Alexandre Dumas the elder]*

Onions. A parody on "Carrots" *see* Smith, Edgar McPhail

Only a flirtation *see* Hervey, Alfreton

Only another footprint *see* McBride, H. Elliott *in his* New dialogues

Only cold tea *see* Denison, Thomas Stewart

An only daughter *see* Denison, Thomas Stewart

The only young man in town. A comedy in eleven scenes. Boston: W. H. Baker, 189-? 16p. (Baker's edition of plays)

The onward march to freedom *see* Busch, William. Sorosis; or, The onward march to freedom

The oolah *see* Rosenfeld, Sydney

Opal (pseud.) The cloud of witnesses. New York: J. Miller, 1874. 522p. Contents: The creation.-- Abel's widow.--The Benedicite.--St. Paul in Athens.-- Rome.--Mappalicus and Bona. --The snow-flake.--Chosroes the second.--John the almoner. --The venerable Bede.--Alphage, Archbishop of Canterbury.--The true cross.--The Bruce.--Joan of Arc.--Bishop Hooper.--Bucer.--Captain John Smith.--Madame Guyon.--Leonora de Castro.--The death of Novalis.--Herder.

An open secret *see* Campbell, Marian D.

The opening speech *see* McBride, H. Elliott *in his* New dialogues

Opera mad; or, The scream-a-donna *see* Steele, Silas Sexton *in his* Collected works. Book of plays

Oppenheim, Charles. The wig-maker and his servants. An Ethiopian farce in one scene. Clyde, O.: Ames, c1885. 7p. (Ames' series of standard and minor drama. no. 156)

Opposing the new school-house *see* McBride, H. Elliott *in his* Latest dialogues

Optic, Oliver (pseud. of William Taylor Adams). The deamons of the glass *see* Dramatic leaflets

The orator of Zepata City *see* Davis, Richard Harding

Orbesson, Fernand d' *see* Dorbesson, Fern

The Order of the Sons of Mars *see* Hiland, Frank E. The curtain lifted; or, The Order of the Sons of Mars

Ordonneau, Maurice, 1854-1916. La plantation Thomasin *see* Gillette, William Hooker. Too much Johnson

An Oregon idyl *see* Miller, Joaquin

O'Reilly, Augustine J. The double triumph. Drama in two acts. Dramatized from the story of Placidus, in the "Martyrs of the Coliseum." New York: D. & J.

Sadlier, 1875. 66p.

Orestes; or, The avenger *see* Koopman, Harry Lyman

The organist. A domestic drama in one act. (Adapted from Henry A. Jones', Harmony.) n.p.: n.pub., 1892. Typescript, prompt-book. 28 leaves.

The original John Schmidt *see* Barry, S. The persecuted Dutchman; or, The original John Schmidt

An original widow's pension; or, The fugitive fortune *see* Van Harlingen, Katherine

Orkney the peacemaker; or, The various ways of settling disputes *see* Abbott, Jacob

Orlando; or, A woman's virtue *see* Moore, Horatio Newton

Ormusd's triumph; or, The fall of Ahriman. New York: Alexander V. Blake, 1842. vii, 100p.

Orne, Martha Russell. A black diamond. A comic drama in two acts. Boston: Walter H. Baker, c1890. 24p. (Baker's edition of plays)

The country school. An entertainment in two scenes. Boston: W. H. Baker, c1890. 20p. (Baker's novelty list)

The donation party; or, Thanksgiving Eve at the parsonage. A comedy in three acts. Boston: W. H. Baker, c1894. 43p. (Baker's edition of plays)

A limb o' the law. A comedy in two acts. Boston: W. H. Baker, c1892. 18p. (Baker's edition of plays)

An old maid's wooing. A

drama in two acts. Boston:
Walter H. Baker, c1899. 22p.
(Baker's edition of plays)

Timothy Delano's courtship.
A comedy in two acts. New
York: Dick & Fitzgerald,
c1892. 27p.

The orphan boys; or, The poisoned draught *see* Steele,
Silas Sexton *in his* Collected works. Book of plays

Orpheus *see* Field, Annie
Adams *see also* Lazarus,
Emma *see also* Raymond,
Fanny Malone

Orpheus and Eurydice (Orphée
aux enfers.) Opera bouffe
in three acts. New York:
Edward E. Rice, 18-? iv,
33p. Libretto. *[music by
Jacques Offenbach on the
libretto Orphée aux enfers
by Hector Jonathan Crémieux
and.Ludovic Halévy] see
also* Meyers, Benjamin F.
in his Collected works

Orpheus and Eurydice; or,
The wandering minstrel *see*
Arnold, George? and Cahill,
Frank. Parlor theatricals;
or. Winter evening's enter-
tainment

Orton, Jason Rockwood, 1806-
1867.
Arnold [From his: Arnold,
and other poems. New York:
Partridge & Brittan, 1854]
p.7-101.

Osborn, Laughton, 1809-1878.
(Dramatic series, vol. 1)
Bianca Capello. New York:
Moorhead, Simpson & Bond,
1868. p.200-419.

Calvary--Virginia; tragedies.
New York: Doolady, 1867.
200p.
    Contents: Calvary.--Vir-

ginia.

The critique of the vision of
Rubeta. A dramatic sketch in
one act. By Autodicus (pseud.)
Philadelphia: Printed for the
trade, 1838. 32p.

(Dramatic series, vol. 2)
The last Mandeville, the
heart's sacrifice, The monk,
Matilda of Denmark; tragedies.
New York: American News, 1870.
p.273-605.

The magnetiser [and] The
prodigal. New York: James
Miller, 1869. 231p.
    Contents: The magnetiser;
or, Ready for anybody.--
The prodigal; or, A vice and
virtue.

(Dramatic series, vol. 6)
Mariamne. New York: Henry L.
Hinton, 1873. p.167-269.

Meleagros [and] The new
calvary. New York: American
News, 1871. 58, 164p.

The Montanini. New York:
J. Miller, 1868. p.266-397.

The school for critics; or,
A natural transformation.
[From his: Dramatic works.
New York: James Miller, 1868.
vol. 4. 517p. (Comedies)]
p.399-517.

The silver head, The double
deceit; comedies. New York:
Doolady, 1867. 262p.
    Contents: The silver head.--
The double deceit; or, The
husband-lovers.

Ugo da este--Uberto--The Cid
of Seville; tragedies. New
York: J. Miller, 1869. 269p.

Osborn, Merit.
Farmer Larkin's boarders. An
original comedy in two acts.
Clyde, O.: Ames, c1897. 25p.
(Ames' series of standard and
minor drama. no. 388)

Oscar the half-blood *see*
Schönberg, James

Osgood, Harry O.
The baby. An original come-
dietta in one act. Boston:
W. H. Baker, 1899. 16p.
(Baker's edition of plays)

Osgood, L. W.
The Union spy; or, The
battle of Weldon railroad.
A military drama in five
acts. Woburn, Mass.: J. L.
Parker, 1871. 32p. (Parker's
amateur player)

Ossawattomie Brown; or, The
insurrection at Harper's
Ferry *see* Swayze, Mrs.
J. C.

Othello *see* Forrest, Edwin
see also Griffin, George
W. H. *see also* Shakespeare,
William *in* Booth, Edwin.
The Shakespearean plays of
Edwin Booth *see also*
Shakespeare, William *in*
The modern standard drama,
vol. 3

Othello. As performed by
Salvini. New York: George
F. Nesbitt, 1873. Bilingual
text: English and Italian.
135p. *[title page: By Wm.
Shakespeare]*

Othello. By William Shakespeare.
As played at the Park Theatre.
New York: William Taylor,
1846. 74p. (Modern standard
drama. no. 23)

Othello. By William Shakespeare.
As performed by Salvini and
Booth. New York: n.pub.,
1886. Title page lacking.
64p.

Othello and Darsdemoney. A
negro burlesque. Chicago:
T. S. Denison, n.d. 6p.

Othello the Moor of Venice
see Hinton, Henry L.
Shakespeare's...Othello
the Moor of Venice

The other fellow *see* Horne,
Mary Barnard

Other people's children *see*
Field, A. Newton

Other people's troubles *see*
Dumont, Frank

Otway, Thomas, 1652-1685.
Venice preserved *see*
The modern standard drama,
vol. 3

Ouchilanca; or, The rancher's
fate *see* Skiff, Frank D.

Ouida (pseud.) *see* De La
Ramée, Marie Louise

The ould man's coat tails *see*
McDermott, J. J. and Trumble

An ounce of prevention *see*
Wilstach, Paul

Our Aunt Robertina *see* Dallas,
Mary Kyle

Our awful aunt *see* Buxton,
Ida M.

Our best society *see* Browne,
Irving

Our boarding house *see* Grover,
Leonard

Our boys of 1776 *see* Baker,
George Melville. One hundred
years ago; or, Our boys of
1776

Our church *see* Mettenheimer,
H. J.

Our colored conductors *see*
Coes, George H.

Our country *see* Denison,
Thomas Stewart

Our country aunt; or, Aunt
Jerusha's visit. A domestic
drama in two acts. Clyde,
O.: Ames, 1899? 9p. (Ames'
series of standard and
minor drama. no. 347)
[the copy reproduced by
Readex begins on the fourth
page of the drama, and
therefore omits the cast
of characters]

Our daughters *see* Greenwood,
Frederick L.

Our English friend *see* Daly,
Augustin

Our family umbrella *see*
Cleveland, E. E.

Our folks *see* Baker, George
Melville

Our gal *see* Johnson,
Samuel D.

Our girls in camp *see*
Tiffany, Esther Brown.
Anita's trial; or, Our
girls in camp

Our heroes *see* Renauld,
John B.

Our hopeful son *see* Ingraham,
C. F. Jimmie Jones; or, Our
hopeful son

Our hotel; or, Rats, the bell
boy *see* Brunnhofer, Will
H.

Our Jack *see* Stenman, C. A.

Our Jemimy; or, Connecticut
courtship *see* Conway,
H. J.

Our Jim *see* Fowler, Egbert
Willard

Our Kittie *see* Polson,
Minnie

Our national finances. A
serious comedy. This comedy
never was played, and
probably never will be played;
it always has been played,
and always will be played and
may become a tragedy. New
York: The author, 1864. 36p.

Our new minister *see* Thompson,
Denman and Ryer, George W.

Our servants *see* Lester,
Francis

Our society *see* Stuart,
Clinton

Our starry banner *see* Fraser,
John Arthur

Our summer boarder's [sic];
or, The jolly tramp *see*
Rawley, Bert C.

Our utopia *see* Hope, Kate

Our war correspondent *see*
Buzzell, Arthur L. Captain
Dick; or, Our war corres-
pondent

Out at sea *see* Perine,
Charles E.

Out in the streets *see* Cook,
S. N.

Out of bondage *see* Elwyn,
Lizzie May. Millie, the
quadroon; or, Out of bondage

Out of his sphere *see*
Hildreth, David W.

Out of sight *see* Risdon,
Davis. A black trump

Out of the depths *see*
McBride, H. Elliott

Out of the question *see*
Howells, William Dean

Out of the shadow *see*
Vatter, August and Spencer,
John E.

Out of the tangle *see*
McBride, H. Elliott *in his*
Latest dialogues

Out on the world. A drama in
three acts. Clyde, O.: Ames,
c1880. 23p. (Ames' series
of standard and minor drama.
no. 83)

The outcast's daughter *see*
Delanoy, Mary Frances
Hanford

The outlaw. (From the Italian
of P. Giacometti.) New
York: J. J. Little, 1890.
Bilingual text: Italian
and English. 99p. Libretto
[sic, see note below]
*[title page: La morte civile.
Readex incorrectly has
called this a libretto; The
outlaw is a play in which
Tommaso Salvini played as an
actor, not an opera singer]*
see also Lewis, Eliza
Gabriella

Outwitting the colonel *see*
May, Gordon V.

Over the cliff *see* Hornett,
Stephen Francis. In the
way; or, Over the cliff

Over the garden fence *see*
Chapman, W. F.

Over the garden wall *see*
Felter, Will D.

Overheard in a conservatory
see Duer, Caroline [and]
Miller, Alice Duer

Overheard in Arcady *see*

Bridges, Robert

Owen, Orville Ward, 1854-1924.
Robert, Earl of Essex. The
tragical historie of our late
brother...deciphered from the
works of Sir Francis Bacon.
Detroit and London: Howard
Pub. Co. and Gay and Bird,
1895. 104p. *[title page:
"By the author of Hamlet,
Richard III, Othello, As You
Like It, etc. and of the
newly discovered tragedy,
Mary, Queen of Scots." This
is an example of Shakespeare's
works being attributed to
Bacon]*

Owen, Robert Dale, 1801-1877.
Pocahontas. A historical
drama in five acts. New York:
G. Dearborn, 1837. 240p.

Owens, Garrett W.
And all about nothing. A
pathetico-comical drama in
one act. New York: Edgar S.
Werner, 1895. 24p.

The Oxford affair *see* Cobb,
Josephine H. and Paine,
Jennie E.

Oxygen! a Mount Desert pastoral
see Grant, Robert *in his*
The little tin gods-on-wheels;
or, Society in our modern
Athens

P. P. P. Podge *see* White,
Charles. The stage-struck
couple

Pacini, Giovanni, 1796-1867.
Saffo *see* Sappho

Packard, Hannah James, 1815-
1831.
The choice. A tragedy [From
her: The choice...with other
miscellaneous poems. Boston:
Leonard C. Bowles, 1832.
142p.] p.3-99.

Packard, Winthrop, 1862-1943.
The man in the case. A
comedy in three acts for
female characters only.
Boston: W. H. Baker, c1896.
37p.

Paddy Doyle; or, A mutual
friend *see* Waldron, P. A.

Paddy Dunbar *see* Massey,
Charles. Massey's exhibition
reciter

Paddy McFling's experience
see Hildreth, David W.
Joining the Tinpanites; or,
Paddy McFling's experience

Paddy Miles the Limerick boy
see Pilgrim, James

Paddy the piper *see* Pilgrim,
James

Paddy's mischief *see* Pilgrim, James. The Limerick
boy; or, Paddy's mischief

Page, G. T.
Blind Margaret *see*
Thompson, Caroline Eunice

A page from Balzac *see*
Daly, Augustin. A night
off; or, A page from Balzac

Pailler, William.
The magic bell. A fairy play
for children in three acts.
Chicago and New York: Drama-
tic Pub. Co., 1899. 37p.
(Children's plays)

Pailleron, Édouard Jules Henri,
1834-1899.
L'étincelle *see* Williams,
Henry Llewellyn. Sparking

[Subtleties of jealousy]
see Rosenfeld, Sydney

[The triumph of youth] *see*
Robertson, Donald

Paine, Jennie E.
The Oxford affair *see*
Cobb, Josephine H. and Paine,
Jennie E.

Paine, John Knowles, 1839-1906.
Azára. Opera in three acts.
Leipzig, New York: Breitkopf
und Härtel, c1901. Vocal
score. Bilingual text: English
and German. 372p. *[Libretto
by the composer]*

The painter's apprentice *see*
Dumont, Frank

The painter's studio; or, Art
and artifice *see* Steele,
Silas Sexton *in his*
Collected works. Book of
plays

A pair of artists *see* Merriman, Effie Woodward

A pair of gloves *see* Meyers,
Robert Cornelius V.

A pair of shoes *see* Rosenfeld,
Sydney

Palmer, John Williamson, 1825-
1906.
The queen's heart. A comedy
in three acts. Boston: W. V.
Spencer, 1858. Prompt-book.
80p. (Spencer's Boston
theatre. vol. 23, no. 179)

Palomita; or, The veiled
songstress *see* Glover,
Howard

Pamela's prodigy *see* Fitch,
Clyde

Pan, the wood-god *see*
Caldcleugh, William George

Pandora *see* Crumpton, M.
Nataline *see also* Dugan,
Caro Atherton *in her*
Collected works *see also*
Field, Annie Adams

Papa's bulldog *see* Parker, Walter Coleman

The paper don't say *see* Denison, Thomas Stewart *in his* Friday afternoon series of dialogues

Paradise lost *see* Taylor, M. F. and Taylor, John G.

The parasite; or, How to make one's fortune. A comedy in five acts. Philadelphia: J. B. Lippincott, 1872. 78p. *[Based on Médiocre et rampant by Louis Benoît Picard]*

Parasol drill *see* Denton, Clara Janetta Fort. When the lessons are over

Pardey, Henry Oake, 1808-1865. Nature's nobleman. A comedy in five acts. New York: Wm. Taylor, 1853? 79p. (Modern standard drama. no. 100)

The parish priest *see* Hart, Daniel L.

Parisina. Lyric drama in three acts. New York: Snowden, 1850. Bilingual text: English and Italian. 71p. Libretto. *[music by Gaetano Donizetti on libretto by Felice Romani; without the music]*

Parker, George S. Moses in Egypt. Boston: Oliver Ditson, 1855. Vocal score. Bilingual text: English and Italian. 160p. *[music by Gioacchino Rossini on libretto adapted by Luigi Balocchi and Victor Joseph Étienne Jouy from that of Rossini's oratorio, Mosè in Egitto, by Andrea Leone Tottola]*

Parker, Harry. Gertrude Wheeler, M. D. A comedy in one act. Chicago: Dramatic Pub. Co., c1889. 18p. (Sergel's acting drama. no. 544)

Parker, Lottie Blair, 1858?-1937. Way down east. A drama in four acts. n.p.: 189-? Typescript. 80p. *[a hand-written note on the copy reproduced by Readex indicates that the play was "elaborated" by Joseph Rhode Grismer]*

Parker, Walter Coleman. All a mistake. A farce comedy in three acts. Chicago: T. S. Denison, c1903. 54p. (Alta series) *[earlier copy-right: 1898]*

Finnegan and Flanagan. A vaudeville sketch in one act. New York: Fitzgerald, c1899. 11p.

Jimmy the newsboy. Boston, New York, Chicago: White-Smith Music Pub. Co., c1893. Vocal score. 18p. *[music by the author]*

Kissing the wrong girl. A vaudeville sketch in one set. New York: Fitzgerald, c1899. 10p.

Ma's new boarders. A vaude-ville sketch in one act. New York: Dick & Fitzgerald, c1899. 15p.

Papa's bulldog. A vaudeville sketch in one act. New York: Dick & Fitzgerald, c1899. 9p.

A proposal by proxy. A vaude-ville sketch in one act. New York: Dick & Fitzgerald, c1899. 12p.

Those dreadful twins. A farce comedy. Chicago: T. S.

Denison, c1901. 46p. (Alta series)

Parkington. (Charade) *see* Follen, Eliza Lee Cabot. Home dramas for young people

Parliamentary law *see* Denton, Clara Janetta Fort *in her* From tots to teens

The parlor car *see* Howells, William Dean

Parlor charades and proverbs *see* Shields, Sarah Annie Frost

Parlor dramas *see* Fowle, William Bentley

A parlor entertainment *see* McBride, H. Elliott *in* Denison, Thomas Stewart. Friday afternoon series of dialogues

A parlor match *see* Hoyt, Charles Hale

Parlor theatricals; or, Winter evening's entertainment *see* Arnold, George? and Cahill, Frank

Parlor varieties *see* Brewster, Emma E.

A paroxysm of passion *see* Busch, William. That guilty pair; or, A paroxysm of passion

Parrhasius; or, Thriftless ambition *see* Williams, Espy William Hendricks

Parrhasius *see* Wills, William Gorman *in* Massey, Charles. Massey's exhibition reciter

Parsimony *see* Caldor, M. T. *in his* Social charades

Parson Poor's donation party *see* Jaquith, Mrs. M. H.

Parsons, Laura Matilda Stephenson, 1855-1925.
The district school at Blueberry Corners. A farcical entertainment in three scenes. Boston: Walter H. Baker, c1894. 22p. (Baker's edition of plays)

The old maid's convention. An entertainment in one scene. Boston: Walter H. Baker, c1899. 18p. (Baker's edition of plays)

A partial eclipse *see* Wilstach, Paul

Party dictators; or, The rulers of the Republic *see* Lookup, Alexander (pseud.) Excelsior; or, The heir apparent

Passe Rose *see* Paul, Anne Marie

The passing cloud *see* Bernard, William Bayle *in* The modern standard drama, vol. 11

The passing regiment *see* Daly, Augustin

The passing show *see* Monroe, Harriet

Passions *see* Dey, F. Marmaduke

Passion's dream *see* Sample, Walter Boyd

Passion's tempests *see* Tillson, Jesse Paxon *in his* Collected works

Past redemption *see* Baker, George Melville

Pastil *see* Arnold, George? and Cahill, Frank. Parlor

theatricals; or, Winter
evening's entertainment

Pat McFree, the Irish patentee
see Perkins, George

Patchwork see Pelham, Nettie
H. The belles of Blackville
[bound with] Patchwork

The patent right agent see
Denison, Thomas Stewart
in his Friday afternoon
series of dialogues

The patent washing machine;
or, The lover's dilemma see
Bauman, E. Henri

Patriot (Charade) see
Follen, Eliza Lee Cabot.
Home dramas for young people

Pat's dilemma; or, Too much of
a good thing. A funny Irish
dialect farce. New York:
Dick & Fitzgerald, c1886.
16p. (Dick's American
edition)

Patsy O'Wang see Denison,
Thomas Stewart

Patten, Gilbert, 1866-1945.
Clover farm. A farce comedy
in three acts. Boston: Walter
H. Baker, c1898. 52p. (Baker's
edition of plays) [Gilbert
Patten is the form of name
used by Readex; Library of
Congress uses William George
Patten]

Nan, the mascotte. A comedy
drama in four acts. (Originally produced under title
of Man of Millions.) Boston:
Walter H. Baker, c1898. 56p.
(Baker's edition of plays)

Patten, William George see
Patten, Gilbert

The pattern man. A comedy in

five acts. Albany, N. Y.:
J. Munsell, 1868. 107p.
[Pre-'56 imprints: In manu-
script on title-page, "E. P.
Hurlburt, Esq." Therefore,
Hurlburt is considered the
supposed author]

Patterson, John.
The Medea of Euripides.
Louisville: John P. Morton,
c1894. 81p.

Paul, Anne Marie.
Passe Rose. By Anne Marie
Paul, Frances Marsh Bancroft,
Susan Edmond Coyle and Ada
Elizabeth Herrick. n.p.:
n.pub., 1894. 40p. [a drama-
tization of Arthur Sherburne
Hardy's Passe Rose; the
authors were graduates of
the class of 1894 of Smith
College]

Paul and Virginia; or, The
runaway slave see
Ringwalt, Jessie Elder,
Mrs. J. L.

Paul Forrester. A play in
four acts. (From the French
of Augier.) New York: New
York Print. Co., 1871. 110p.

Paul Jones see Berger,
William

Paul Kauvar; or, Anarchy see
MacKaye, James Steele

Paul Pry see Poole, John in
The modern standard drama,
vol. 10

Paulding, James Kirke, 1778-
1860.
Collected works. American
comedies. Philadelphia:
Carey and Hart, 1847. 295p.
[joint author: William Irving
Paulding]
Contents: The Bucktails;

or, Americans in England.--
The noble exile.--Madmen
all; or, The cure of love.
--Antipathies; or, The
enthusiasts by the ears.

The lion of the West. A
farce in two acts. Retitled
The Kentuckian; or, A trip
to New York. (Rev. by John
A. Stone and Wm. B. Ber-
nard). Stanford, Calif.:
Stanford Univ. Press, 1954.
54p. *[first produced in
1831; the manuscript was
lost for over 100 years,
and the search for it is
detailed in a lengthty
preface]*

Madmen all *see* How to
write "popular" stories *in*
Beadle's...dialogues no. 2

Paulding, William Irving,
1825?-1890.
Collected works. American
comedies *see* Paulding,
James Kirk and Paulding,
William Irving

Pauline. Drama in five acts
and seven tableaux. New
York: S. French, 18-? 42p.
(French's American drama.
The acting edition. no. 135)
*[translated and adapted from
Pauline by Alexandre Dumas]*

Pauline Pavlovna *see* Aldrich,
Thomas Bailey

Pawn ticket no. 210 *see*
Greene, Clay Meredith and
Belasco, David

Paying the piper *see*
Mathews, Frances Aymar

Payne, John Howard, 1791-1852.
The boarding schools; or,
Life among the little folks
[From: Trial without jury &
other plays. By C. Hislop
and W. R. Richardson, edi-

tors. Princeton, N. J.:
Princeton Univ. Press, 1940.
264p.] (America's lost plays.
vol. 5, p.91-111) *[based on
Les deux pensions by Alexandre
Marie Maréchalle and Charles
Hubert]*

Brutus *see* Booth, Edwin.
The miscellaneous plays of
Edwin Booth

Brutus; or, The fall of
Tarquin *see* The modern
standard drama, vol. 8

Charles II; or, The merry
monarch *see* The modern
standard drama, vol. 3

Mrs. Smith; or, The wife and
the widow. A farce in one
act. London: T. H. Lacy,
18-. 20p. (Lacy's acting
edition. vol. 84)

Mount Savage [From: Trial
without jury & other plays.
By C. Hislop and W. R.
Richardson, editors. Princeton, N. J.: Princeton Univ.
Press, 1940. 264p.] (America's
lost plays. vol. 5, p.55-89)
*[title page: The solitary of
Mount Savage; or, The fate
of Charles the Bold; adaptation of René Charles
Guilbert de Pixérécourt's Le
mont sauvage; ou Le solitaire]*

Scenes from an unpublished
play [From: Life and writings
of...By Gabriel Harrison,
editor. Albany, N. Y.: J.
Munsell, 1875. 410p.] p.293-
296.

The Spanish husband; or,
First and last love [From:
Trial without jury & other
plays. By C. Hislop and
W. R. Richardson, editors.
Princeton, N. J.: Princeton
Univ. Press, 1940. 264p.]
(America's lost plays, vol. 5,
p.205-264) *[adapted from Le
peintre de son déshonneur*

by Laurent Angliviel de la Beaumelle, which is a prose translation of Pedro Calderón de la Barca's El pintor de su deshonra]

The two galley slaves. A melo-drama in two acts. (From the French) New York: S. French, 184-? 29p. (French's acting edition)

Woman's revenge [From: The last duel in Spain & other plays. By C. Hislop and W. R. Richardson, editors. Princeton, N. J.: Princeton Univ. Press, 1940. 265p.] (America's lost plays, vol. 6, p.57-84)

Peabody, Josephine Preston, 1874-1922.
Fortune and men's eyes. A drama in one act [From her: Fortune and men's eyes. New poems with a play. Boston: Houghton, Mifflin, c1900] p.1-49.

The pea-green glazed cambric *see* Kavanaugh, Mrs. Russell *in her* Original dramas, dialogues

A peace maker *see* Denton, Clara Janetta Fort. When the lessons are over

Peace or war *see* Cobb, Mary L. Poetical dramas for home and school

A peaceful assault *see* Atherton, George

The Peak sisters *see* Horne, Mary Barnard

Peake, Richard Brinsley *see* Peake, Robert Brinsley

Peake, Robert Brinsley, 1792-1847.
The bottle imp *see* The bottle imp

Pearl of Pekin; or, The dashing tar outwitted by his wife *see* Byrne, Charles Alfred

The pearl of Poland *see* Lewis, Estelle Anna Blanche Robinson. The king's stratagem; or, The pearl of Poland

The pearl of Savoy. A domestic drama in five acts. New York: Samuel French, 18-? 44p. (French's standard drama. The acting edition. no. 337) *[translation and adaptation of Gaetano Rossi's Linda di Chamounix]*

The peasant, the princess and the prophet *see* Brooks, Elbridge Streeter. David the son of Jesse; or, The peasant, the princess and the prophet

Peattie, Elia Wilkinson, 1862-1935.
The love of a Caliban. A romantic opera in one act. Wausau, Wisc.: Van Vechten & Ellis, 1898. Limited edition. 41p.

Peck, Elizabeth Weller.
Nathaniel Hawthorne's *Scarlet Letter* dramatized. A play in five acts. Boston: Franklin Press, Rand, Avery, 1876. 72p.

The peddler of Very Nice *see* Baker, George Melville

A peep at the vices and virtues of country and city life *see* Howe, J. Burdette. The woman of the world; or, A peep at the vices and virtues of country and city life

A peep behind the scenes *see* Leavitt, Andrew J. and Eagan, H. W. The blackest tragedy of all; or, A peep behind the scenes

The peer and the peasant *see*
Ritchie, Anna Cora Ogden
Mowatt. Armand; or, The
peer and the peasant *see*
also her Plays

A peerless peeress and a haughty
pirate *see* Morrison, George
Austin. Captain Kidd; or, A
peerless peeress and a haughty
pirate

Peleg and Peter; or, Around the
Horn *see* Cutler, F. L.

Pelham, Nettie H.
The belles of Blackville
[bound with] Patchwork. New
York: H. Roorbach, c1897.
20p. *[title page: The belles
of Blackville. A negro minstrel entertainment for
young ladies concluding with
a specialty farce entitled
"Patchwork"]*

The Christmas ship. A Christ-
mas entertainment. Chicago:
T. S. Denison, c1888. 10p.
(Denison's specialties)

The old fashioned husking
bee. An old folks' enter-
tainment in one scene.
Boston: W. H. Baker, 1891.
17p. (Baker's edition of
plays)

The realm of time. A pageant
for young people and children. Chicago: T. S. Denison,
1890. 20p.

The white caps. Chicago:
T. S. Denison, 1891. 12p.

Pélléas and Mélisande *see*
Byrne, Charles Alfred *see
also* Hovey, Richard *in his*
The plays of Maurice Maeterlinck. Second series

Pellico, Silvio, 1789-1854.
Euphemio di Messina *see*
Eliot, Elizabeth Fried
Lummis. Euphemio of Messina

Pemberton, Thomas Edgar,
1849-1905.
Sue *see* Harte, Bret and
Pemberton, Thomas Edgar

The pen and the press *see*
Greenly, William Jay *in his*
The three drunkards

The pendant *see* Fowle,
William Bentley *in his*
Parlor dramas

Pendergrass, Peter, Sr. (pseud.)
The Magdalen report *see*
The Magdalen report

Penelope's symposium *see*
Pratt, Sarah H.

Penikeese; or, Cuisine and
cupid *see* Buel, David
Hillhouse

Penitent *see* Shields, Sarah
Annie Frost *in her* Parlor
charades and proverbs

The penitent's return *see*
Reid, Charles S.

Penmark Abbey *see* Williams,
Henry Llewellyn

Penn, Arthur.
Heredity. A physiological and
psychological absurdity in
one act *see* Matthews,
Brander. Comedies for amateur
acting

Penn, Arthur *see also*
Matthews, Brander

Penn Hapgood; or, The Yankee
schoolmaster *see* Chase,
George B.

Pennsylvania Dutch Rip Van
Winkle *see* Rauch, Edward H.

A Pennsylvania kid; or, A
soldier's sweetheart *see*
Taylor, Frederic W.

The people's lawyer *see*
Jones, Joseph Stevens
see also his Solon Shingle;
or, The people's lawyer

Pepita, the gipsy girl of
Andalusia *see* Dramatic
leaflets

Pepper, George, fl.1835.
Kathleen O'Neil; or, A picture of feudal times in Ireland. A national melodrama of
the fourteenth century in
three acts. Philadelphia:
Thomas Town, 1832. 84p.

Pepusch, John Christopher,
1667-1752.
The beggar's opera *see*
Harrison, William

Per telephone *see* Montgomery,
Margaret

Percival, James Gates, 1795-
1856.
The sister spirits [From
his: The dream of a day and
other poems. New Haven:
S. Babcock, 1843. 264p.]
p.182-185.

The perfection of beauty *see*
Kavanaugh, Mrs. Russell *in
her* Original dramas,
dialogues

Perfection; or, The maid of
Munster *see* Bayly, Thomas
Haynes *in* The modern
standard drama, vol. 4

Pericles-Hamilton *see*
Townsend, Frederic *in his*
Spiritual visitors

Perils of a great city *see*
Townsend, Charles

Perils of moderate drinking
see Heywood, Delia A. *in
her* Choice dialogues. no. 1

Perine, Charles E.

Cast upon the world. An
entirely original drama in
five acts. By Charles E.
Newton (pseud.) Chicago:
Dramatic Pub. Co., c1869.
40p. (Sergel's acting drama.
no. 175)

Henry the Fifth. A historical
play in five acts. By William
Shakspeare [sic] By Charles
E. Newton (pseud.) Chicago:
Dramatic Pub. Co., c1875. 63p.
(Sergel's acting drama. no.
180)

Out at sea. An entirely
original romantic drama in a
prologue and four acts. By
Charles E. Newton (pseud.)
New York: Dramatic Pub. Co.,
c1872. 40p. (De Witt's acting
plays. no. 178)

Perkins, George, 1844-1926.
Pat McFree, the Irish paten-
tee. A farce in one act.
Clyde, O.: Ames, c1898. 12p.
(Ames' series of standard and
minor drama. no. 392)

A perplexing predicament *see*
Coes, George

A perplexing situation *see*
Smith, S. Jennie

The perplexity of Monsieur
Victor *see* Knapp, A. Melvin.
The industrious moth; or,
The perplexity of Monsieur
Victor

The persecuted Dutchman; or,
The original John Schmidt
see Barry, S.

The Persian queen *see* Goldschmidt, William. Hadassah;
or, The Persian queen

The Persian slave *see* Ritchie,
Anna Cora Ogden Mowatt.
Gulzara; or, The Persian slave

A personal matter *see* Chase,

Frank Eugene

Il pesceballo *see* Lowell,
James Russell

The pet of Parsons' ranch
see Felch, William Farrand

The pet of the camp *see*
Cutler, F. L. Joe, the waif;
or, The pet of the camp

Pete and the peddler *see*
Dumont, Frank *in his* The
amateur minstrel *see also*
White, Charles

Peter Pan, a respectful burlesque on *see* Stewart,
Grant. A respectful bur-
lesque on Peter Pan

Peter the Great in Saardam;
or, The Czar and the carpenter *see* Balatka, Hans

Peterson, Henry, 1818-1891.
Caesar. A dramatic study in
five acts. Philadelphia:
H. Peterson, 1879. 72p.

Columbus. In six acts.
Cincinnati: Walter Peterson,
1893. 65p.

The modern Job. Philadel-
phia: H. Peterson, 1869.
124p.

Le petit chaperon rouge *see*
F., W. F. The little red
riding hood

Pets of society *see*
Denison, Thomas Stewart

Pflueger, Carl, 1850-1901.
"1492" *see* Barnet,
Robert A.

Phaedra. (From the French of
Racine.) New York: Darcie &
Corbyn, 1855. Bilingual
text: English and French.
36p.

Phaedra. As performed by Fanny
Janaushek. (From the German
of Schiller.) New York:
Fanny Janaushek, 186-? Bilingual text: English and German.
32p. *[title page: "A tragedy
...by Racine, translated into
German by Friedrich von
Schiller"]*

Phan-Tom *see* Cahill, Frank
in Arnold, George? and
Cahill, Frank. Parlor
theatricals; or, Winter
evening's entertainment

Pheelim O'Rooke's curse *see*
Simms, George A.

Phelan, Agnes Vivien.
Margaret of Anjou. Chicago:
Donohue & Henneberry, 1888.
48p.

Phelps, Ellsworth C., 1827-1913.
David the son of Jesse; or,
The peasant, the princess and
the prophet *see* Brooks,
Elbridge Streeter

Phelps, Lavinia Howe.
Dramatic stories. For home
and school entertainment.
Chicago: S. C. Griggs, 1874.
262p.
Contents: The mantle of
charity.--A picnic.--Candy-
pulling.--A golden wedding.--
The dandy prince.--Shenstone
society.--Bringing back the
sunshine.--The bumblebee.--
Am I one?--The birch.--The
gold snuff-box.--Catnip tea.
--What makes a man?--Morning
and night.--The bootblack.--
Blind Eva.--The May-basket
army.--A game of nuts.--The
kernel of corn.--The pocket-
book.--The tangled thread.--
Sorrowing Nettie.--What
Christmas means.--Three ways
of keeping Christmas.--A
substantial Christmas wish.
--A Christmas address.

Phelps, Merridan.
The first violin *see* Clarke,
Joseph Ignatius Constantine
and Phelps, Merridan

Phelps, Pauline.
A cyclone for a cent. A
farce in one act. Boston:
W. H. Baker, 1894. 17p.
(Baker's edition of plays)

A Shakespearian conference.
New York: Edgar S. Werner,
c1899. 15p.

Phidias-Raphael *see* Townsend,
Frederic *in his* Spiritual
visitors

The Philadelphia detective
see Little Ferritt; or,
The Philadelphia detective

Philip of Pokanoket *see*
Furman, Alfred Antoine

Philip Vernon *see* Mitchell,
Silas Weir

Phillips, Henry, 1838-1895.
Faust. A dramatic sketch.
(From the German of Adalbert
von Chamisso.) Philadelphia:
For private circulation,
1881. Limited edition. 23p.

Phillips, Ida Orissa.
The bright and dark sides of
girl-life in India. Boston:
Morning Star Pub. House,
1891. 32p.

Phillips, Jonas B., d.1867.
Camillus; or, The self-
exiled patriot. A tragedy
in five acts. New York,
Philadelphia: E. B. Clayton;
C. Neal, 1833. 59p. *[title
page: Clayton's edition]*

The evil eye. A melo-drama
in two acts. New York: S.
French, 1831. 16p. (The
minor drama. The acting
edition. no. 134) *[note at*

*end of list of characters:
founded on the story of the
Evil eye published in London
Keepsake of 1830]*

The evil eye. New York and
Philadelphia: E. B. Clayton;
C. Neal, 1831. Title page
lacking. 27p. *[joint author:
George Jones; also see note
above; no mention is made of
Jones in the edition cited
previously]*

Zamira [From his: Zamira, a
dramatic sketch, and other
poems. New York: G. A. C.
Van Beuren, 1835] p.7-19.

Phillips, Watts, 1825-1874.
Camilla's husband *see* Herne,
James A. and Belasco, David.
Marriage by moonlight; or,
Hap-hazard

Philo: an evangeliad *see*
Judd, Sylvester

Phintias and Damon *see* Ross,
Joseph M.

Phocion *see* Doyle, Edwin Adams

The phoenix *see* Nobles, Milton

Phyllis, the beggar girl *see*
Siegfried, W. A.

Piatt, Donn, 1819-1891.
Life in the lobby. A comedy
in five acts. Washington:
Judd & Detweiler, 1875. Title
page lacking. 78p.

Various dramatic works [From
his: Poems and plays. Cincinnati: Robert Clarke, 1893.
360p.] p.115-360.
Contents: Lost and won.--A
king's love.--Emotional insanity. A comedy in one act.--
Blennerhassett's island.

Piave, Francesco Maria, 1810-
1876.
Ernani *see* Ernani

Picard, Louis Benoît, 1769-
1828.
Médiocre et rampant *see*
The parasite; or, How to
make one's fortune

A picked-up dinner *see*
Hanlon, Henry Oldham

Pickett, A. St. J.
The sublime tragedy of the
lost cause. A tragic poem
of the War. In four acts.
Columbus: Westbote Print.
Co., 1884. 238p.

Pickett, Haskell.
The rake's lesson; or,
Taming a husband. A comic
drama in two acts. n.p.:
n.pub., 185-? Prompt-book
in Ms. 88 leaves.

A picnic *see* Phelps,
Lavinia Howe *in her*
Dramatic stories

Picton, Thomas, 1822-1891.
Cupid's eye-glass. A
comedy in one act. New
York: De Witt, 1874. 9p.
(De Witt's acting plays.
no. 152) *[author's original
name: Thomas Picton Milner]*

A hard case. A farce in one
act. New York: De Witt,
1874. 13p. (De Witt's
acting plays. no. 151)

A tell-tale heart. A
comedietta in one act.
New York: De Witt, 1874.
15p. (De Witt's acting
plays. no. 150)

A tempest in a tea pot.
A petite comedy in one act.
Chicago: Dramatic Pub. Co.,
c1871. 12p. (American acting
drama)

There's no smoke without a
fire. A comedietta in one
act. New York: De Witt,
c1873. 15p. (De Witt's
acting plays. no. 146)

'Tis better to live than to
die. A petite comedy in one
act. New York: De Witt,
c1874. 12p. (De Witt's
acting plays. no. 153)

The picture gallery *see*
White, Charles. Daguerreotypes;
or, The picture gallery

A picture of feudal times in
Ireland *see* Pepper, George.
Kathleen O'Neil; or, A picture
of feudal times in Ireland

Pidgin, Charles Felton, 1844-
1923.
Blennerhassett; or, The irony
of fate. A dramatic romance
in a prologue and four acts.
Boston: C. M. Clarke, 1901.
69p.

Pierce, G. H.
Gertie's vindication. A drama
in two acts. Clyde, O.: Ames,
c1888. 16p. (Ames' series of
standard and minor drama.
no. 255)

The pierced eye. Musical
extravaganza in three acts.
(From the French of Hervé.)
New York: John A. Gray &
Green, 1869. Bilingual text:
English and French. 38p.
Libretto. *[cover: L'oeuil
crevé, words and music by
Hervé]*

Pierpont, John, 1785-1866.
The drunkard *see* Smith,
W. H. The drunkard; or, The
fallen saved

Pierra, Adolfo.
The Cuban patriots. A drama
of the struggle for independence actually going on in
the gem of the Antilles. In
three acts. (Written in
English by a native Cuban.)
Philadelphia: n.pub., 1873.
45p.

Nobility; or, The alcalde
of Zalamea. A drama in three
acts. (From the Spanish of
Calderón de la Barca.)
Philadelphia: Wm. F. Fell,
1885. 48p. *[based on Calderón de la Barca's Alcalde
de Zalamea]*

Piestre, Pierre Étienne,
1811-1903.
Une cause célèbre *see*
Cazauran, Augustus R.
A celebrated case

Les deux orphelines *see*
Jackson, N. Hart. The two
orphans *see also* Stevenson,
Kate Claxton Cone. Two
orphans *see also* The two
orphans

The pigeons; or, The bonnie
lass of Brittany *see*
Hardman, Richard

Pigtail *see* Arnold, George?
and Cahill, Frank. Parlor
theatricals; or, Winter
evening's entertainment

Pike county ahead! *see*
Delano, Alonzo. A live
woman in the mines; or,
Pike county ahead!

Pilgrim, James, 1825-1879.
Eveleen Wilson, the flower
of Erin. An original drama
in three acts. Boston: W. V.
Spencer, 1853? Prompt-book.
32 leaves. (Spencer's Boston
theatre. no. 77)

The female highwayman; or,
The blighted lily. A drama
in three acts. New York:
1852. Prompt-book in Ms.
In three acts (pag. by acts)

Ireland and America; or,
Scenes in both. A drama in
two acts. New York: S.
French, 1856? Title page
mutilated. 27p.

Irish assurance and Yankee
modesty. An original farce
in two acts. New York: S.
French, 187-? 24p. (French's
American drama. The acting
edition. no. 64)

Jeanie Deans; or, The heart
of Mid-Lothian. A Scottish
drama in three acts. (From
the novel by Sir Walter
Scott.) n.p.: n.pub., 18-?
Prompt-book in Ms. 69p.

Katty O'Sheal. A farce in
two acts. New York: S. French,
1870? 22p. (French's minor
drama. The acting edition.
no. 295)

The Limerick boy; or, Paddy's
mischief. An original farce
in one act. Boston: W. V.
Spencer, 1856? 16p. (Spencer's
Boston theatre. no. 16)
*[This is the same play as
Pilgrim's Paddy Miles the
Limerick boy]*

Paddy Miles the Limerick boy.
A farce in one act. London:
T. H. Lacy, 18-. 16p. (Lacy's
acting edition. vol. 95)
*[This is the same play as
Pilgrim's The Limerick boy;
or, Paddy's mischief]*

Paddy the piper. A comic
drama in one act. New York:
S. French, 18-. 16p. (French's
American drama. The acting
edition. no. 62)

Robert Emmet, the martyr of
Irish liberty. An historical
drama in three acts. Boston:
W. V. Spencer, 1857? 28p.
(Spencer's Boston theatre.
no. 123)

Servants by legacy. A farce
in one act. Boston: William
V. Spencer, 185-? 10p.
(Spencer's Boston theatre.
no. 178)

Shandy Maguire; or, The bould

boy of the mountain. In two
acts. Boston: W. V. Spencer,
1855? Prompt-book. 38p.
(Spencer's Boston theatre.
no. 24)

Wild Irish girl. A drama
in three acts. New York:
S. French, 18-? 31p.
(French's minor drama.
The acting edition. no. 336)

Yankee Jack; or, The
buccaneer of the Gulf. A
nautical drama in three
acts. n.p.: 18-? Prompt-
book in Ms. 93p.

The pilgrim's choice *see*
Caldor, M. T. *in his*
Social charades

Pindar-Drake *see* Townsend,
Frederic *in his* Spiritual
visitors

Pine, M. S. (pseud.) *see*
Finn, Sister Mary Paulina

The pine tree's choice *see*
Denton, Clara Janetta
Fort. When the lessons
are over

Pinkopki, Phillip.
A colonel's mishap. A farce
comedy in one act. Clyde,
O.: Ames, c1891. 8p. (Ames'
series of standard and
minor drama. no. 289)

Pipes and perdition *see*
Prichard, Joseph Vila

The pipes of Arcadia *see*
Merington, Marguerite.
Daphne; or, The pipes of
Arcadia

Pique *see* Daly, Augustin

The pirate *see* Bradbury,
Sophia Louise Appleton
see also Ponte, Lorenzo da

The pirate of the isles *see*
Belden, N. H.

The pirate's legacy *see*
Saunders, Charles Henry
see also his The pirate's
legacy; or, The wrecker's
fate

Pirsson, Joseph P.
The discarded daughter. A
comedy in five acts. New
York: William Stodart, 1832.
64p.

Pistols for two *see* Cutter,
Rollin

"Pistols for seven" *see*
Howard, Bronson. Saratoga;
or, "Pistols for seven"

Pitman, James R., 1844-1914.
Never again. A comedy scene.
n.p.: n.pub., 189-? Type-
script, prompt-book. 30 leaves.

Pitt, George Dibdin, 1799-1855.
The poacher's doom; or, The
murder of the Five Field's
Copse *see* Ames, A. D.

Pixérécourt, René Charles
Guilbert de, 1773-1844.
Le Mont Sauvage; ou Le soli-
taire *see* Payne, John
Howard. Mount Savage

Pizarro *see* Sheridan, Richard
Brinsley Butler *in* The
modern standard drama, vol. 3

Pizzi, Emilio, 1861-1940.
Gabriella *see* Byrne,
Charles Alfred and Marras,
Mowbray

Placer gold; or, How Uncle
Nathan lost his farm *see*
Hildreth, David W.

The plague of my life *see*
Daveau, Illion

Planché, James Robinson, 1796-1880.
Charles the Twelfth *see* The modern standard drama, vol. 6

Faint heart never won fair lady *see* The modern standard drama, vol. 6

The follies of a night *see* The modern standard drama, vol. 6

Fortunio and his seven gifted servants *see* Fortunio and his seven gifted servants

The Garrick fever *see* Williams, Henry Llewellyn. The black Forrest

Plantation bitters *see* Horne, Mary Barnard

Plautus, Titus Maccius, 254?-184 B.C.
The two captives *see* The two captives

Played and lost *see* McBride, H. Elliott

Playing a part *see* Matthews, Brander

Playing cat and dog *see* Abbott, Jacob *in his* Orkney the peacemaker; or, The various ways of settling disputes

Playing married *see* Denison, Thomas Stewart *in his* Wide awake dialogues

Playing school *see* McBride, H. Elliott *in his* New dialogues

The playwright *see* Landis, Leonard Lincoln

A plea for the pledge *see* A collection of temperance dialogues

Pleasant companions *see* Dumont, Frank

Pleasant surprises *see* Rosenfeld, Sydney. Married bachelors; or, Pleasant surprises

Pleasant wedding guests *see* Ritchie, Fannie

A pleasaunt comedie of the life of Will Shakespeare *see* Smith, Harry Bache

A pleasure trip *see* Chisnell, Newton

The pleroma *see* Chittenden, Ezra Porter

The plutocrat *see* Schupphaus, Otto Frederick

Po' white trash. A study of a little-known phase of American life *see* Sutherland, Evelyn Greenleaf Baker *in her* Collected works. Po' white trash and other one-act dramas

The poacher's doom; or, The murder of the Five Field's Copse *see* Ames, A. D.

Pocahontas *see* Byers, Samuel Hawkins Marshall *see also* Hendrick, Welland *see also* Owen, Robert Dale

The pocket-book *see* Phelps, Lavinia Howe *in her* Dramatic stories

Pocock, Isaac, 1782-1835.
The Omnibus *see* The Omnibus

Rob Roy MacGregor; or, Auld lang syne *see* The modern standard drama, vol. 11

The podesta's daughter *see*
Boker, George Henry

Poe, Edgar Allan, 1809-1849.
The gold bug *see* Hagarty,
W. H.

The poet *see* Sprague,
Achsa W.

Poet and musician *see*
Bullock, Cynthia. Dialogue.
Poet and musician

Poetical dramas for home and
school *see* Cobb, Mary L.

The poet's offering *see*
Benedict, Frank *in his*
The shadow worshiper

Poison *see* Baker, George
Melville *see also* Morton,
Marguerite W.

The poisoned darkys *see*
McBride, H. Elliott

The poisoned draught *see*
Steele, Silas Sexton. The
orphan boys; or, The poisoned
draught *in his* Collected
works. Book of plays

The polar bear *see* Dumont,
Frank

Polding, Elizabeth.
At the fireside; or, Little
bird blue. A play for
children in three acts.
Chicago: Dramatic Pub. Co.,
c1898. 12p.

The dawn of redemption; or,
The adoration of the Magi
kings. A Christmas play in
four acts. Chicago: Dramatic
Pub. Co., c1899. 11p. (Sergel's acting drama. no. 576)

A harmonious family. Play
for children in three acts.
Chicago: Dramatic Pub. Co.,
c1899. 12p. (Children's
plays)

St. Elizabeth of Thuringia;
or, The miracle of roses. A
legendary drama in five acts
for young ladies. New York:
Joseph F. Wagner, c1899. 33p.

The police court *see* Coes,
George H.

The policy players *see*
White, Charles

The Polish Jew *see* Williams,
Henry Llewellyn. The bells;
or, The Polish Jew

Political dialogues. Soldiers
on their right to vote, and
the men they should support.
Washington, D. C.: Chronicle
Print., 1864? 16p.

A political pull *see* Jackson,
John Jasper

The politicians *see* Mathews,
Cornelius

A politician's breakfast *see*
Tees, Levin C. A row in the
kitchen [bound with] A
politician's breakfast

Polson, Minnie.
Our Kittie. A comedy drama
in three acts. Clyde, O.:
Ames, c1894. 20p. (Ames'
series of standard and minor
drama. no. 333)

Wild Mab. A border drama in
four acts. Clyde, O.: Ames,
c1891. 19p. (Ames' series of
standard and minor drama.
no. 290)

Poltroonius *see* Head, Edward
Francis

Polyeuctes, the martyr. A
Christian tragedy in five
acts. (From the French of
Corneille.) New York: Darcie
& Corbyn, 1855. Bilingual
text: English and French.

45p. *[based on Polyeucte,*
martyr; tragédie chrétienne
by Pierre Corneille]

Pomp Green's snakes *see*
Shettel, James W. and
George, Wadsworth M.

Pompey's patients *see* White,
Charles

Pomp's pranks *see* Cutler,
F. L.

Ponte, Lorenzo da, 1749-1839.
[Library of Congress and
other bibliographical
sources enter the name
under Da Ponte, Lorenzo;
Readex indicates a death
date of 1838]
Don Giovanni *see* Don
Giovanni *see also* Sher-
wood, W.

Eliza and Claudio; or, Love
protected by friendship. New
York: For Lorenzo da Ponte,
J. H. Turney, Printer 1832.
Bilingual text: English and
Italian. 77p. Libretto.
[music by Saverio Mercadante]

Eliza and Claudio; or, Love
protected by friendship. New
York: For Lorenzo da Ponte,
J. H. Turney, Printer, 1833.
(Second edition, revised.)
Bilingual text: English and
French [sic, Italian]. 77p.
Libretto. *[music by Saverio*
Mercadante; Readex indicates
that this is a bilingual
libretto in English and
French, whereas in reality
it is in English and Italian]

Moses in Egypt. New York:
For Lorenzo da Ponte, J. H.
Turney, printer, 1832. Bi-
lingual text: English and
Italian. 55p. Libretto.
[music by Gioacchino Rossini
on libretto adapted by Luigi
Balocchi and Victor Joseph

Étienne Jouy from that of
Rossini's oratorio, Mosè in
Egitto, by Andrea Leone
Tottola; without the music]

The pirate. A melodrama in
two acts. (From the Italian
of Romani.) New York: W. E.
Dean, 1832. Bilingual text:
English and Italian. 71p.
[music by Vincenzo Bellini
on Felice Romani's libretto,
Il pirata]

Pontia: the daughter of Pilate
see Felix, V. Rev. F.

Pontiac; or, The siege of
Detroit *see* Macomb,
Alexander

Poole, John, 1768?-1872.
Married and single *see*
The modern standard drama,
vol. 10

Paul Pry *see* The modern
standard drama, vol. 10

Simpson and Co. *see* The
modern standard drama, vol. 8

The poor gentleman *see*
Colman, George *in* The
modern standard drama, vol. 3

The poor girl *see* Babcock, J.
Frederick. Floret; or, The
poor girl

Poor Peter *see* Brewster,
Emma E. *in her* Parlor
varieties

The pop-corn man *see* Field,
A. Newton

The Pope and his inquisitors
see Moos, Herman M. Mortara; or, The Pope and his
inquisitors

Popping by proxy *see* Young,
O. E.

Port wine vs. jealousy *see* White, Charles

Porter, Charlotte Endymion, 1859-1942.
Alladine and Palomides. (From the German of Maurice Maeterlinck.) Boston: Poet-Lore, 1895. (vol. 7, nos. 6 and 7.) p.281-301. *[based on Maurice Maeterlinck's Alladine und Palomides; joint author: Helen Archibald Clarke]*

The seven princesses. (From the German of Maurice Maeterlinck.) Boston: Poet-Lore, 1894. (vol. 4, nos. 1-3.) p.29-32, 87-93, 150-161. *[based on Maurice Maeterlinck's Die sieben Prinzessinnen; joint author: Helen Archibald Clarke]*

The sightless. (From the German of Maurice Maeterlinck.) Boston: Poet-Lore, 1893. (vol. 5, nos. 3, 4, 5, 6-9.) p.159-163, 218-221, 273-277, 442-452. *[based on Maurice Maeterlinck's Die Blinden; joint author: Helen Archibald Clarke]*

Porter's troubles; or, The Fifth Ave. Hotel *see* Harrigan, Edward

The portrait painter *see* White, Charles

Possumfat. An Ethiopian opera in two scenes. New York: Happy Hours, 1874. 7p. (The Ethiopian drama. no. A3)

Potter, Paul Meredith, 1853-1921.
Trilby *see* Smith, Edgar McPhail. "Trilby"

The pound of flesh *see* Shylock, the Jew; or, The pound of flesh [from Shake-speare, William. The merchant of Venice] *in* Steele, Silas Sexton. Collected works. Book of plays

Pousse cafe *see* Smith, Edgar McPhail and De Lange, Louis

Poverty flats *see* Moore, Bernard Francis

Powell, H. Arthur.
The widow Mullin's Christmas *see* Beach, Stanley Yale and Powell, H. Arthur

Powell, L. S.
Conn; or, Love's victory. A drama of the strikes. Clyde, O.: Ames, c1885. 28p. (Ames' series of standard and minor drama. no. 160) *[joint author: J. C. Frank]*

Power, Thomas F.
The Virginia veteran. A military drama in four acts. Boston: Baker, c1874. 57p.

The power of woman's influence *see* Bradley, Nellie H. The first glass; or, The power of woman's influence

Powers, Francis.
The first born. A Chinese drama in one act. n.p.: n.pub., n.d. Typescript. 37p.

Poyas, Catharine Gendron, 1813-1882.
The convert [From her: The Huguenot daughters and other poems. Charleston: John Russell, 1849. 167p.] p.145-148.

The Huguenot daughters; or, Reasons for adherence to the faith [From her: The Huguenot daughters and other poems. Charleston: John Russell, 1849. 167p.] p.5-21.

Practical jokes *see* Meyers,

Robert Cornelius V. *see*
Dramatic leaflets

Pratt, R. Horace.
West Point; or, A tale of
treason (epilogue) *see*
Breck, Joseph

Pratt, Sarah H.
Penelope's symposium. A
dialogue illustrating life
in ancient Greece. Chicago:
T. S. Denison, c1891. 16p.

Pratt, Silas Gamaliel, 1846-
1916.
Zenobia, Queen of Palmyra.
Lyric opera in four acts.
Boston: Oliver Ditson,
c1882. Vocal score. 206p.
*[music composed by the
author]*

Pratt, William W.
Ten nights in a bar-room.
A drama in five acts. (From
T. S. Arthur's novel of the
same name.) Boston: W. H.
Baker, c1889. 37p. (Baker's
edition of plays)

Ten nights in a bar-room.
A temperance drama in five
acts. New York, London: S.
French, 18-? Revised edition.
46p. (French's standard
drama. The acting edition.
no. 339)

Pray, Isaac Clarke, 1813-1869.
Angelo the tyrant of Padua.
(From the French of Victor
Hugo.) New York: John A.
Gray & Green, 1866. Bilin-
gual text: English and
Italian. 40p. *[based on
Victor Hugo's Angelo, tirano
de Pádue, and translated by
Francisco Asenjo y Barbieri
under the title Angelo,
tiranno di Padova]*

The idiot boy. A dramatic
sketch [From his: Prose and

verse from the portfolio of
an editor. Boston: Russell,
Shattuck, 1836. 186p.]
p.80-85.

Julietta Gordini, the miser's
daughter. A play in five
acts. New York: 1839. Prompt-
book. 40 leaves.

Marie Antoinette. A drama in
a prologue, five acts, and
epilogue. (Written for
Madame Adelaide Ristori by
Paolo Giacometti. The
English translation by
Isaac C. Pray.) New York:
Theatre Francais, 1867. 82p.
Bilingual text: Italian and
English.

Sor Teresa; or, Isabella
Suarez. (From the Italian of
Luigi Camoletti.) New York:
John A. Gray & Green, 1868.
Bilingual text: English and
Italian. 51p.

The premature proposal *see*
Bradley, A. F. *in* Dramatic
leaflets

The Prentice knights *see*
Dialogues dramatized from the
works of Charles Dickens

Prentiss, Elizabeth Payson,
1818-1878.
Griselda. A dramatic poem in
five acts. New York: Young
Woman's Christian Assoc.,
c1876. 152p. *[based on Münch-
Bellinghausen's Griseldis]*

Preposition vs. proposition
Kavanaugh, Mrs. Russell *in*
her Original dramas, dia-
logues

President Cromwell *see*
Townsend, George Alfred

Preston, Daniel Swann, 1838-
1893.

Columbus; or, A hero of the new world. An historical play. New York and London: G. P. Putnam's Sons, 1887. viii, 103p.

A pretty piece of property *see* Brewster, Emma E. *in her* Parlor varieties

Preuss, Henry Clay. Fashions and follies of Washington's life. A play in five acts. Washington, D. C.: The author, 1857. 75p.

Prevention better than cure *see* The temperance school dialogues

A previous engagement *see* Howells, William Dean

Priam, King of Troy *see* Bailey, William Entriken. Dramatic poems

Prichard, Joseph Vila. Daniel Rochat. A comedy in five acts. (From the French of Sardou.) New York and London: Samuel French, c1880. 76p. (French's standard drama. The acting edition. no. 379) *[because of an error on the title page, Readex has entered this play incorrectly under Pritchard; it should read Prichard, as given above]*

The great Hindoo secret. A comedy in three acts. New York: De Witt, c1884. 46p. (De Witt's acting plays. no. 335)

The iron master. A drama in four acts. n.p.: n.pub., 19-? Prompt-book, interleaved with Ms. notes. 63p. Title page mutilated. *[based on Le maître des forges by Georges Ohnet]*

My mother-in-law; or, A divorce wanted. A comedy in three acts. (From the French of "Le procés veradieux.") New York and London: S. French, c1876. 47p. (French's parlor comedies. no. 8) *[adapted from Le procés veauradieux by Alfred Charlemagne Lartigue Delacour]*

Pipes and perdition. A comedy in one act. New York: Harold Roorbach, c1881. 15p. (The acting edition. no. 147) *[title page: adapted from the French]*

The pride of Company G *see* Hildreth, David W. The volunteers; or, The pride of Company G

Pride punished *see* Corner, Julia. Cinderella; or, Pride punished *in* Venable, William Henry. The school stage

The prima donna *see* McCarty, William Page

Primary class (Washington's birthday) *see* Denton, Clara Janetta Fort. From tots to teens

Prince Deukalion *see* Taylor, Bayard *see also in his* Collected works. The dramatic works

Prince Karl *see* Gunter, Archibald Clavering

The Prince of Gilead's vow *see* Alexander, William. Ella; or, The Prince of Gilead's vow

The Prince of Palermo *see* Smith, Dexter. Boccaccio; or, The Prince of Palermo

Prince of Palermo; or, The students of Florence *see* Smith, Dexter

Prince Pedro *see* Garnier, John Hutchinson

Prince Prettywitz and little Cinderella *see* Smith, Harry Bache. The crystal slipper; or, Prince Prettywitz and little Cinderella

Prince pro tem *see* Barnet, Robert A.

The prince's wooing *see* Malloy, Louise

The princess *see* Haughwout, L. May

The Princess Adelaide *see* Bergen, Helen Corinne

The Princess Chic *see* La Shelle, Kirke

The Princess Chrysalline; or, The maiden who couldn't laugh *see* S., E. S.

The Princess Elizabeth *see* Williams, Francis Howard

The princess far-away *see* Renauld, Charles. La princesse lointaine

Princess Maleine *see* Hovey, Richard *in his* The plays of Maurice Maeterlinck [First series]

La princesse lointaine *see* Renauld, Charles

Principles form character *see* Wehner, J. H.

The printer and his devils *see* Moses, David and Blackaller, Arthur

Pritchard, Joseph Vila *see* Prichard, Joseph Vila

Pritchard, Polly Ann *see* Heywood, Delia A.

Private boarding *see* Courtright, William

The privateer of '76 *see* Howe, J. Burdette. The Golden Eagle; or, The privateer of '76

Pro tem *see* Griffith, Benjamin Lease Crozer

The prodigal; or, A vice and virtue *see* Osborn, Laughton *in his* The magnetiser

Prof. Baxter's great invention *see* Horne, Mary Barnard

Prof. Black's phunnygraph; or, Talking machine *see* Hockenbery, Frank

The professor is interrupted *see* Heywood, Delia A. *in her* Choice dialogues. no. 1

Prof. James' experience teaching a country school *see* Jamieson, Guy Arthur

Professor Robinson *see* Hageman, Maurice

The professor's present *see* Denton, Clara Janetta Fort *in her* From tots to teens

Prologue for the theatre *see* Lazarus, Emma

Prometheus (pseud.) *see* Busch, William

Prometheus bound *see* More, Paul Elmer

Proof positive *see* File, Franklin

The prophecy *see* Bunce, Oliver Bell. Fate; or, The prophecy

The prophet *see* Taylor, Bayard *see also in his* Collected works. The dramatic works

The prophet of St. Paul's *see* Brown, David Paul

The prophet's last love *see* McKinley, Henry J. Brigham Young; or, The prophet's last love

The proposal *see* Mathews, Frances Aymar

A proposal by proxy *see* Parker, Walter Coleman

A proposal under difficulties *see* Bangs, John Kendrick

Pseudo--a charade *see* Heywood, Delia A. *in her* Choice dialogues. no. 1

Psyche, M. D. *see* Barnard, Charles

A public benefactor *see* Baker, George Melville

The public meeting *see* Beadle's...dialogues no. 2

Pudd'nhead Wilson *see* Mayo, Frank

Pürner, Charles, b.1849. "Thrilby" *see* Herbert, Joseph W.

Pug and the baby. Farce-comedy in one act. Clyde, O.: Ames, c1889. 13p. (Ames' series of standard and minor drama. no. 265)

The pull back *see* Denison, Thomas Stewart

Pullen, Elizabeth Jones, b.1894. Algernon in London. A tragedy. Portland, Me.: William M. Marks, 1880. 16p.

Pulling a tooth *see* McBride, H. Elliott *in his* Latest dialogues

Pulling teeth by steam *see* Von Culin, Everett. The dentist's clerk; or, Pulling teeth by steam

Pulsky, Mrs. The sleeper awakened *see* Follen, Eliza Lee Cabot. Home dramas for young people

Punch and Judy. New York: C. F. A. Hinrichs, 1873? 14p.

Purim *see* Bien, Herman Milton

Puritan's daughter. New York: "Season" Print, 1869. 55p. Libretto. *[libretto by John Vipon Bridgeman]*

The purse *see* Harris, Theodore

Purse-proud *see* Shields, Sarah Annie Frost *in her* Parlor charades and proverbs

A purty shure cure *see* McDermott, J. J. and Trumble

Putkins. Heir to--Castles in the air *see* Emerson, William R.

Putnam, Henry Howell, b.1868. The mariner's return. A drama in three acts. New York: S. French, c1888. 31p. (French's standard drama. The acting edition. no. 303)

Putnam, M. L. *see* Putnam, Mary Trail Spence Lowell

Putnam, Mary Trail Spence
Lowell, 1810-1898.
The bondmaid. Boston: J.
Munroe, 1844. 112p. *[title
page: By Fredrika Bremer...
translated from the Swedish
by M. L. Putnam]*

Tragedy of errors. Boston:
Ticknor and Fields, 1862.
249p.

Tragedy of success. Boston:
Ticknor and Fields, 1862.
191p.

Putnam, the iron son of '76
see Bannister, Nathaniel
Harrington

The puzzled Dutchman *see*
White, Charles. The bogus
talking machine; or, The
puzzled Dutchman

The quack *see* Denison,
Thomas Stewart *in his*
Friday afternoon series of
dialogues

The quack doctor *see*
Smith, John Washington

Quaker quiddities; or, Friends
in council *see* Congdon,
James Bunker

The Quakers *see* Arthur,
Robert

The quarrel *see* Merriman,
Effie Woodward *in her*
Comedies for children

Quarrelsome servants *see*
Griffin, George W. H.

Queen Anne cottages *see*
Davis, Mary Evelyn Moore

Queen Elizabeth; or, Love and
majesty *see* Lookup, Thomas

Queen Esther *see* Bliss,
Frank Chapman

Queen Helen *see* Cheney, John
Vance

The queen of a day. A comic
opera in two acts. Boston:
J. H. Eastburn's, 1855. 33p.
Libretto. *[music by Edward
Francis Fitzwilliam to the
libretto by John Baldwin
Buckstone]*

The queen of beauty *see*
Dramatic leaflets

The queen of Cyprus *see*
Révoil, Bénèdict Henry

Queen of hearts *see* Greenough,
James Bradstreet

The queen of Sheba *see*
Hanssen, C. J.

Queen Vashti *see* Cobb, Mary L.
Poetical dramas for home and
school

The queens *see* Aldémah. The
queens

The queen's coffer *see* Dugan,
Caro Atherton *in her*
Collected works

The queen's heart *see* Palmer,
John Williamson

The queen's lace handkerchief
see Elson, Louis Charles

The queen's musketeers *see*
Révoil, Bénèdict Henry

A queer fit *see* Dramatic
leaflets

Queer, quaint and quizzical
questions *see* Dumont,
Frank *in his* The amateur
minstrel

The queerest courtship *see*
Sedgwick, Alfred B.

The quest of Merlin *see*
Hovey, Richard

A question of honor *see*
Franklin, Sidney

The quicksands of Gotham *see*
Brooke, Van Dyke

A quilting party in the thirties. An outline sketch for
music *see* Sutherland,
Evelyn Greenleaf Baker *in*
her In office hours and
other sketches for vaude-
ville or private acting

Quincy, Josiah Phillips,
1829-1910.
Charicles...By the author of
Lyteria. Boston: Ticknor &
Fields, 1856. 106p.

Lyteria. Boston: Ticknor &
Fields, 1854. 123p.

Quinn, Richard.
Called away. A drama in four
acts. New York: Samuel
French, c1891. 38p. (French's
standard drama. The acting
edition. no. 423)

Innisfail; or, The wanderer's
dream. A drama of Irish life
in four acts. Boston: W. H.
Baker, c1890. 53p. (Baker's
edition of plays)

Quite correct *see* Smith,
Richard Penn

Quits *see* Brown, Abbie Farwell *see also* Tibbetts,
Martie E. Two Aunt Emilys;
or, Quits

Quizzing a quack *see* Heywood,
Delia A. *in her* Choice
dialogues. no. 1

R., H. *[Library of Congress:*
H. R.=Horace Russ]
The headsman. New York: Jas.
Van Norden, 1840. 78p.
[p.5-8 missing]

Race for a wife *see* Fothergill, F.

The race track *see* Dumont,
Frank *in his* The amateur
minstrel

Rachel, the fire waif *see*
Elwyn, Lizzie May

Racine, Jean Baptiste, 1639-
1699.
Andromache *see* Andromache

Athalie *see* Sumichrast,
Frederick Caesar John Martin
Samuel Roussy de

Bajazet *see* Bajazet

Phèdra *see* Phaedra

Les plaideurs *see* Browne,
Irving. The suitors

A racing romance *see* Toler,
Sallie F. Handicapped; or,
A racing romance

Rae, Robert.
Newport. A play in six acts.
Chicago: Hazlitt & Reed,
1877. 75p.

A rag baby *see* Hoyt, Charles
Hale

The rag-picker's child *see*
Adams, Justin

Rags and bottles; or, The two
waifs *see* Taylor, Malcolm
Stuart

The railroad explosion. An act
in two scenes [and] The echo.
Scene for banjoist and mock
banjo ("Bones.") New York:
S. French, 18-?. 20, 7p.
(French's acting edition.
no. 42)

The railroad of love *see*
Daly, Augustin

The rainbow *see* Beadle's...
dialogues no. 2

Raising the wind *see* Neall,
Walter H.

The rake's lesson; or, Taming
a husband *see* Pickett,
Haskell

Ralph Coleman's reformation
see McBride, H. Elliott

Ramona *see* Dillaye, Ina

Ramanzo, the conscience
stricken brigand *see*
Smith, John N.

The rancher's fate *see*
Skiff, Frank D. Ouchilanca;
or, The rancher's fate

Rand, Katharine Ellen.
New Hampshire gold. A comedy
drama in three acts. Boston:
Walter H. Baker, c1897. 40p.
(Baker's edition of plays)

Randall, William W.
Snowflake and the seven
gnomes *see* Bert, Frederick
W.

A rank deception *see* Smith,
Lilli Huger

Ranken, Frederic [i.e. Frede-
rick], 1869-1905.
"The ameer." A comic opera
in three acts. New York,
Chicago: M. Witmark, c1899.
Vocal score. 205p. *[joint
author: Kirke La Shelle;
music by Victor Herbert]*

Rankin, McKee, 1841-1914.
The runaway wife. n.p.:
n.pub., c1888. Typescript,
prompt-book. 42p. *[joint
author: Frederick George
Maeder]*

A rare Teutonic specimen *see*
Crary, J. E. Olivet; or,
A rare Teutonic specimen

The rat-charmer of Hamelin
see Williams, Frederick

Rats, the bell boy *see*
Brunnhofer, Will H. Our
hotel; or, Rats, the bell
boy

Rattermann, Heinrich Armin,
1832-1923.
Gustavus III; or, The masked
ball. Grand tragic opera in
five acts, with ballet.
(From the French of Scribe.)
Cincinnati: Volksfreund,
1869. Bilingual text: English
and German. 40p. Libretto.
*[music by Daniel François
Auber on libretto Gustave
III, ou Le bal masque by
Augustin Eugène Scribe;
Rattermann's German title:
Gustav III; oder, Der Masken-
ball; without the music]*

Rauch, Edward H., 1826-1902.
Pennsylvania Dutch Rip Van
Winkle. A romantic drama in
two acts. Mauch Chunk, Pa.:
E. H. Rauch, 1883. 32p.
*[written in Pennsylvania
Dutch and based on Washington
Irving's Rip Van Winkle]*

Raux, Eugene.
The road to fortune. A new
American comedy in four acts.
Philadelphia: G. B. Zieber,
1846. 52p.

Ravel, Jerome, 1814?-1890.
Kim-Ka; or, The misfortunes
of Ventilator. A grand
Chinese pantomime. New York:
n.pub., 1852. 12p.

The raw recruit; or, A day with
the National Guard *see*
Ingraham, Jean

Rawley, Bert C.
Andy Freckles, the mischievous boy. Farce comedy in

one act. Clyde, O.: Ames, c1898. 13p. (Ames' series of standard and minor drama. no. 393)

Badly mixed. A farce in one act. Clyde, O.: Ames, c1894. 7p. (Ames' series of standard and minor drama. no. 344)

A crazy lot. Farce in one scene. Clyde, O.: Ames, c1901. 12p. (Ames' series of standard and minor drama. no. 426)

Deacon Jones' wife's ghost. A farce in one act. Clyde, O.: Ames, c1894. 8p. (Ames' series of standard and minor drama. no. 345) *[for some reason, Readex does not here use the middle initial "C" in Rawley's name, whereas it does in all other entries]*

The Freeman mill strike. A comedy drama in three acts. Clyde, O.: Ames, c1897. 21p. (Ames' series of standard and minor drama. no. 385)

Our summer boarder's [sic]; or, The jolly tramp. A farce comedy in two scenes. Clyde, O.: Ames, c1896. 15p. (Ames' series of standard and minor drama. no. 370)

Stupid cupid. Farce in one act. Clyde, O.: Ames, 1896. 10p. (Ames' series of standard and minor drama. no. 365)

Trixie; or, The wizard of Fogg Island. A drama in three acts. Clyde, O.: Ames, c1896. 18p. (Ames' series of standard and minor drama. no. 364)

Uncle Jed's fidelity; or, The returned cowboy. A comedy drama in three acts. Clyde, O.: Ames, c1898. 27p. (Ames' series of standard and minor drama. no. 396)

Raymond, Fanny Malone. Orpheus. A grand opera in four acts. New York: Published at the Academy of Music, c1863. Bilingual text: English and French. 14, 4p. Libretto. *[music by Christoph Willibald von Gluck on libretto Orfeo ed Euridice by Ranieri de' Calsabigi; without the music]*

Raymond, George Lansing, 1839-1929. The Aztecs. By Walter Warren (pseud.) Boston: Arena Pub. Co., 1894. 126p. *[also published under the title The Aztec god, see below]*

Collected works. The Aztec god and other dramas. New York and London: G. P. Putnam's Sons, 1900. 447p. Contents: The Aztec god *[also published under the title The Aztecs, see above]*. --Columbus *[also published under the title Columbus the discoverer [see below]*. --Cecil the seer.

Columbus the discoverer. By Walter Warren (pseud.) Boston: Arena Pub. Co., 1893. 164p. *[also published under the title Columbus (see above); Readex has reproduced this play under Raymond's pseudonym, Walter Warren]*

Raymond, George Lansing, 1839-1929 *see also* Warren, Walter

Raymond, Richard John. Cherry Bounce *see* The Omnibus

Raynor, Verna M. The Bird family and their friends. A comedy in three acts. Clyde, O.: Ames, c1898. 38p. (Ames' series of standard and minor drama. no. 394)

Noel Carson's oath; or,
Leonia's repentance. A
drama in four acts. Clyde,
O.: Ames, 1889. 30p. (un-
numbered) (Ames' series of
standard and minor drama.
no. 408)

Read, Harriette Fanning,
fl. 1848-1860.
Dramatic poems. Boston:
Wm. Crosby & H. P. Nichols,
1848. 297p.
Contents: Medea.--Erminia:
a tale of Florence.--The
New World.

Read, Thomas Buchanan, 1822-
1872.
The alchemist's daughter
[From his: Lays and ballads.
Philadelphia: George S.
Appleton, 1849. 140p.]
p.69-91.

A vision of death. An
extract [From his: Lays and
ballads. Philadelphia:
George S. Appleton, 1849.
140p.] p.108-114.

Reade, Charles, 1814-1884.
Art: a dramatic tale *see*
Aldrich, Mildred. Nance
Oldfield

White lies *see* Turner,
Cyril

Ready answers *see* The
temperance school dialogues

Ready for anybody *see* Osborn,
Laughton. The magnetiser; or,
Ready for anybody

A ready made suit; or, A mock
trial *see* Chase, Frank
Eugene

A real Thanksgiving *see*
Schell, Stanley

Realistic description of life
among the moonshiners of

North Carolina. *A mountain
pink see* Bates, Morgan and
Barron, Elwyn Alfred

The realm of time *see* Pelham,
Nettie H.

Reasons for adherence to the
faith *see* Poyas, Catharine
Gendron. The Huguenot daughters; or, Reasons for
adherence to the faith

Rebecca's triumph *see* Baker,
George Melville

The rebellion *see* Denton,
Clara Janetta Fort *in her*
From tots to teens

The rebellion of '61 *see*
Baker, Delphine P. Solon;
or, The rebellion of '61

A rebuff *see* Denton, Clara
Janetta Fort *in her*
From tots to teens

The reception of the months
see Alexander, Louis

The reclaimed *see* Hamilton,
John R. Marion; or, The
reclaimed

The reclaimed husband *see*
McBride, H. Elliott. On the
brink; or, The reclaimed
husband

Reclaimed; or, The danger of
moderate drinking *see*
Bradley, Nellie H.

The recluse of the mountain
see Steele, Silas Sexton.
Love and madness; or, The
recluse of the mountain *in
his* Collected works. Book
of plays

Reconciliation *see* Appleton,
Nathan

The recruiting office *see*
White, Charles

The recruiting officer *see*
Daly, Augustin

The red chignon *see* Baker,
George Melville

A red-hot massage *see* Tees,
Levin C.

The red knight *see* Broadhurst, George Howells

A red letter day *see* Fuller,
Horace Williams

Red or white? *see* Browne,
William Maynadier

The red rock wave *see* Brown,
Charles Hovey

The red rock wave cruiser
see Brown, Charles Hovey.
Elfins and mermaids; or,
The red rock wave cruiser

Red Rover [prologue only]
see Smith, Richard Penn
in his Dramatic fragments

The Red Seal--scenes from an
unpublished play *see*
Holmes, Oliver Wendell.
Scenes from an unpublished
play

Reece, Robert, 1838-1891.
The highest bidder *see*
Belasco, David and Sothern,
Edward Hugh

Rees, James, 1802-1885.
The dwarf. A dramatic poem.
New York: F. Saunders, 1839.
62p.

Reeves, George.
The slave's strategy. A
comedy in three acts. Memphis: Free Trader Pub. Co.,
1882. 59p.

A reformer in ruffles *see*
Williams, Francis Howard

The reformer of Geneva *see*
Shields, Charles Woodruff

The reformer reformed *see*
Howie, Hellen Morrison

The refreshmenting room *see*
Dialogues dramatized from
the works of Charles Dickens

The regicide *see* Moore,
Horatio Newton

The regicides *see* Caverly,
Robert Boodey

The register *see* Howells,
William Dean

The registered letter. A
comedy in one act. (From
the French of Droz.) By
members of the Bellevue
Dramatic Club of Newport.
Boston: Walter H. Baker,
1901. 23p. (Baker's edition
of plays) *[earlier copyright:
1878; based on Un paquet de
lettres by Gustave Droz]*

The rehearsal; or, Barry's
old man *see* White, Charles

Rehearsing a tragedy *see*
Daly, Augustin

Reid, Bertha Belle Westbrook,
d.1939.
The prince of the world. The
great Christian play *see*
Reid, James Halleck and
Reid, Bertha Belle Westbrook

Reid, Charles S.
Joe Simpson's double. A
sketch in one act for male
characters only. Boston:
W. H. Baker, c1892. 9p.
(Baker's edition of plays)

The penitent's return. A

comedietta in one act.
Philadelphia: Penn Pub. Co.,
1908. 11p. *[earlier copyright: 1895]*

Reid, James Halleck, 1862-1920.
The prince of the world.
The great Christian play.
New York: n.pub., 1900.
Typescript, prompt-book with
Ms. notes. 72 leaves (numb.
irreg.) *[joint author:
Bertha Belle Westbrook Reid]*

Rejected; or, The tribulations
of authorship *see* Denison,
Thomas Stewart

Relief. A humorous drama. By
a Chicago lady. Chicago:
University Pub. Co., 1872.
68p.

The Relief Aid Sewing Society;
or, Mrs. Jones's vow *see*
Kavanaugh, Mrs. Russell
in her Original dramas,
dialogues

Religion and fatherland; or,
The martyrs of Corea *see*
Isoleri, Antonio

A remittance from home *see*
White, Charles

Renan, Ernest, 1823-1890.
L'abbesse de Jouarre *see*
Delon, Georges and Rhodes,
James F. The abbess of
Jouarre

Renard, Jules, 1864-1910.
Poil de carotte *see*
Smith, Edgar McPhail. Onions

Renauld, Charles.
Cyrano de Bergerac. An
heroic comedy in five acts.
New York: Frederick A.
Stokes, c1899. xviii, 214p.
*[translated from Cyrano de
Bergerac by Edmond Rostand]*

La princesse lointaine. (The
princess far-away.) A play
in four acts in verse. (From
the French of Rostand.) New
York: Frederick A. Stokes,
c1899. 110p.

Socrates and his wife. A
one-act comedy in verse.
New York: Marinoni Press,
c1889. xii, 2, 39p. *[based
on Socrate et sa femme by
Théodore Faullain de Banville]*

The wanderer. A one-act
comedy in verse. New York:
George F. Nesbitt, c1890.
x, 2, 20p. *[based on Le
passant by François Coppée;
in the first production of
this play (Paris, 1869) Sarah
Bernhardt played the role of
Zanetto]*

Renauld, John B.
Our heroes. A military play
in five acts. New York:
R. M. De Witt, 1873. 46p.
*[musical numbers by Harrison
Millard]*

The renegade [and] More truth
than poetry *see* Cherrytree,
Herr (pseud.)

The reprobate *see* James,
Henry

Requier, Augustus Julian,
1825-1887.
Marco Bozzaris. A play in
three acts [From his: Poems.
Philadelphia: J. B. Lippincott, 1860] p.127-190.

Rescued *see* Gilbert, Clayton
H.

A respectful burlesque on Peter
Pan *see* Stewart, Grant

Restraining Jotham *see*
McBride, H. Elliott *in his*
New dialogues

The return of Persephone *see*
Field, Annie Adams。 Sophocles
[and] The return of Persephone

Return of Sol Gills *see*
Dialogues dramatized from
the works of Charles Dickens

The returned cowboy *see*
Rawley, Bert C. Uncle Jed's
fidelity; or, The returned
cowboy

Retz, Jean François Paul de
Gondi, cardinal de, 1614-
1679.
Le conjuration du conte
Jean-Louis de Fiesque *see*
Elliott, William. Fiesco

A reunion *see* Heywood,
Delia A. *in her* Choice
dialogues. no. 1

The Reverend Griffith Davenport *see* Herne, James A.
in his The early plays
*[Act IV only, with a summary
of missing acts; founded on
Helen H. Gardener's novel,
An unofficial patriot]*

Reverses *see* Field, A. Newton

Révoil, Bénèdict Henry, 1816-
1882。
La favorite. (The king's
mistress.) New York: Herald
Book and Job Print。 Office,
1845。 Bilingual text:
English and French. 22p.
Libretto. *[music by Gaetano
Donizetti on libretto by
Alphonse Royer, Jean Nicolas
Gustave von Nieuwenhuysen
and Augustin Scribe; without
the music]*

Gemma of Vergy. A tragic
opera in two acts. New York:
John Douglas, 1848. Bilingual
text: English and Italian。
51p。 Libretto. (The operatic
library。 no. 22) *[music by

Gaetano Donizetti on libretto
by Emmanuele Bidera; without
the music]*

The queen of Cyprus。 Grand
opera in five acts。 New York:
Herald Book and Job Print。
Office, 1845。 Bilingual text:
English and French. 30 unnum-
bered pages。 Libretto. *[music
by Jacques François Fromental
Élie Halévy on libretto La
reine de Chypre by Jules
Henri Vernoy de Saint-Georges]*

The queen of Cyprus. New
Orleans: J。 L. Sollée's Book
& Job Print。 Office, 1857.
Third edition (revised.)
Bilingual text: English and
French. 36p. Libretto.
*[music by Jacques François
Fromental Élie Halévy on
libretto La reine de Chypre
by Jules Henri Vernoy de
Saint-Georges; without the
music]*

The queen's musketeers。 Comic
opera in three acts. New
York: Herald Book and Job
Print。 Office, 1846。 Bilingual text: English and
French. 44p. Libretto。
*[music by Jacques François
Fromental Élie Halévy on
libretto Les mousquetaires
de la reine by Jules Henri
Vernoy de Saint-Georges;
without the music]*

The revolt of the bees *see*
Baker, George Melville

The Revolution *see* Allen,
Ethan. Washington; or,
The Revolution

A revolutionary marriage *see*
Donnell, Florence T。

The Revolutionary soldier; or,
The old seventy-sixer *see*
Jaimson, George

The revolving wedge *see*

Ware, Thornton M. and
Baker, George P.

The reward of crime; or, The
love of gold *see* Wilkins,
W. Henri

Reymond: a drama of the
American Revolution *see*
Cronkhite, Henry McLean

Reynartz, Dorothy.
Carnival; or, Mardi Gras in
New Orleans. A comedy in one
act. (From the French.) New
York: J. F. Wagner, c1899.
16p. (Sergel's acting drama.
no. 558)

A cup of coffee. Comedy in
one act for young ladies.
Chicago: Dramatic Pub. Co.,
c1899. 22p. (Sergel's acting
drama. no. 526)

It is never too late to mend.
Comedy in one act for young
ladies. Chicago: Dramatic
Pub. Co., c1899. 8p. (Sergel's acting drama. no. 559)

A mother's love; or, A
wreath for our lady. A play
in one act for children.
New York: Joseph F. Wagner,
c1899. 21p. Libretto. (The
wizard series)

Two mothers. Drama in four
acts for young ladies. New
York: Joseph F. Wagner,
c1899. 30p. (The wizard
series)

Reynolds, Fin *see* Reynolds,
Phineas

Reynolds, Frederic, 1764-1841.
Laugh when you can *see*
Murdoch, James Edward

Reynolds, Phineas.
A match safe. A farce comedy
in three acts. By Fin Reynolds. Pittsburgh: n.pub.,
c1898. Typescript. 71 leaves.

Reynolds, S. S.
Nelly's rival. A sketch in
one act. Boston: Walter H.
Baker, c1898. 8p. (Baker's
edition of plays) *[arranged
from François Coppée's
Rivales]*

Reynolds, William C., 1836-1911.
An American pasha. An original
comedy in three acts. Chicago:
Chicago Legal News, 1883.
Title page lacking. 50p.

The Rhinegold *see* Jameson,
Frederick

Rhodes, James F.
The abbess of Jouarre *see*
Delon, Georges and Rhodes,
James F.

Rhodes, William Barnes, 1772-
1826.
Bombastes furioso *see*
Massey, Charles. Massey's
exhibition reciter

Rhodes, William Henry, 1822-
1876.
Theodosia, the pirate's
prisoner. A tragedy in three
acts [From his: The Indian
gallows and other poems.
New York: Edward Walker,
1846. 153p.] p.51-100.

Rice, George Edward, 1822-1863.
Blondel. A historic fancy
in two acts. Boston: Ticknor,
Reed & Fields, 1854. 51p.

Myrtilla. A fairy extravaganza in one act. Boston:
Ticknor, Reed & Fields, 1854.
35p.

An old play in a new garb in
three acts. *Hamlet, Prince of
Denmark.* Boston: Ticknor,
Reed & Fields, 1852. 59p.
*[preface: "The following
bagatelle being a version of
the play of Hamlet, was made
by the writer for the purpose*

of amusing himself, while
he was confined to the house
convalescent after an illness; and he submits this
as an apology for his
levity." Readex also enters
this same play under title]

Rice, James, 1846-1882.
The golden butterfly see
Griffith, Frank Carlos see
also A streak of luck

Rice, Walter F.
Winning ways. A farce in
one act. Boston: Walter H.
Baker, c1899. 12p. (Baker's
edition of plays)

A rice pudding see Tiffany,
Esther Brown

The rich Miss Poor see
Townsend, Charles

Richard II see Shakespeare,
William in Booth, Edwin.
The Shakespearean plays of
Edwin Booth

Richard III see Shakespeare,
William in Booth, Edwin.
The Shakespearean plays of
Edwin Booth see also
Shakespeare, William in
The modern standard drama,
vol. 2

Richard Carvel see Rose,
Edward Everett

Richard-Henry (pseud.)
A happy day see Williams,
Henry Llewellyn

Richards, Bert.
Colored senators. An
Ethiopian burlesque in one
scene. Clyde, O.: Ames,
c1887. 8p. (Ames' series
of standard and minor
drama. no. 222)

Cupid's capers. A farce-
comedy in three acts. Clyde,

O.: Ames, 1887. 21p. (Ames'
series of standard and
minor drama. no. 225)

Fooling with the wrong man.
A farce in one act. Clyde,
O.: Ames, 1887. 11p. (Ames'
series of standard and
minor drama. no. 224)

Hallabahoola, the medicine
man; or, The squirtgun
treatment. An original
farce in one scene. Clyde,
O.: Ames, c1892. 9p. (Ames'
series of standard and minor
drama. no. 307)

The spellin' skewl; or,
Friday afternoon at Deestrick
No. 4. An original burlesque
in one scene. Clyde, O.:
Ames, c1891. 13p. (Ames'
series of standard and minor
drama. no. 295)

Richardson, Abbey Sage, 1837-
1900.
Americans abroad. (From the
French of Sardou.) New York:
Z. & L. Rosenfield, 1892.
Typescript, prompt-book with
Ms. notes. 58, 61, 51 leaves.
[based on Les américaines à
l'étranger by Sardou]

A colonial girl see Hill,
Grace Livingston and Richardson, Abbey Sage

Richardson, Anna Steese Sausser,
1865-1949.
Miss Mosher of Colorado; or,
A mountain psyche. A comedy-
drama in four acts. New York:
Dick & Fitzgerald, c1899. 48p.

Richardson, John, 1796-1852.
Wacousta; a tale of the
Pontiac conspiracy see
Jones, R.? Wacousta; or,
The curse

Richardson, Warren.
The rise and fall of Mark
Reynolds. A domestic play

in five acts. Boston:
Printed by the author,
1868. 44p.

Richelieu; or, The conspiracy
see Lytton, Edward George
Earle Lytton Bulwer-Lytton
in Booth, Edwin. The miscellaneous plays of Edwin
Booth *see also* Lytton,
Edward George Earle Lytton
Bulwer-Lytton *in* The
modern standard drama,
vol. 1

Rickey, Sam (pseud.), d.1885.
*[Sam Rickey is a pseudonym
for Richard T. Higgins]*
Ambition *see* White,
Charles

Bad whiskey *see* White,
Charles

The rehearsal; or, Barry's
old man *see* White, Charles

Ricord, Elizabeth Stryker,
1788-1865.
Zamba; or, The insurrection.
A dramatic poem in five acts.
Cambridge: J. Owen, 1842.
139p.

Rideal, Charles Frederick,
b.1858.
The cross of honor. A military dramalette in one act.
New York: Abbey Press, c1900.
38p. *[joint author: C. Gordon
Winter]*

Rides, Quid (pseud.)
The widow's maid and the
bachelor's man; or, How to
get rid of them *see* The
widow's maid and the bachelor's man; or, How to get
rid of them

Riegen, Julian (pseud.) *see*
Nigri, Julius von St. Albino

Riego; or, The Spanish martyr
see Robertson, John

The rifle ball *see* Wallack,
Lester. Rosedale *see also
his* Rosedale; or, The rifle
ball

Rigging a purchase *see* White,
Charles

The rights of man *see* Leland,
Oliver Shepard

The rigmaree *see* Merriman,
Effie Woodward *see also
her* Comedies for children

Rigmarole *see* Venable,
William Henry *in his* The
school stage

Riley, James Whitcomb, 1849-
1916.
The flying islands of the
night. Indianapolis: Bowen-
Merrill, 1892. 88p.

Rimbaud, Théophile, 1824-1867.
Les deux couronnes *see*
The two crowns

Rinaldo, the doctor of Florence
see Lacy, Ernest

Ring rule and ring ruin *see*
Carter, Alfred G. W.

Ringwalt, Jessie Elder, Mrs.
J. L.
Paul and Virginia; or, The
runaway slave. A play in
three acts. Philadelphia:
Ringwalt & Brown, 1864. 35p.
*[dramatized from Paul et
Virginie by Jacques Henri
Bernardin de Saint-Pierre]*

Rio Grande *see* Townsend,
Charles

Rip Van Winkle *see* Jefferson,
Joseph and Boucicault, Dion
see also Leavitt, Andrew J.
and Eagan, H. W. *see also*
Shannon, J. W. *see also*
Wainwright, John Howard

Rip Van Winkle; a legend of
the Catskills *see* Burke,
Charles

Rip Van Winkle, Pennsylvania
Dutch *see* Rauch, Edward H.
Pennsylvania Dutch Rip Van
Winkle

Ripples *see* Browne, W. Gault

Risdon, Davis.
A black trump. A negro comedy
in two acts. (Originally published under the title, Out
of sight.) Boston: Walter H.
Baker, c1899. 22p. (Baker's
edition of plays)

The rise and fall of Mark
Reynolds *see* Richardson,
Warren

The rise and fall of the
Confederate States *see*
The tragedy of Abraham
Lincoln; or, The rise and
fall of the Confederate
States

The rise in Harlem. A comedy
in five acts. New York:
Baker & Goodwin, 1864. 67p.
*[Readex also enters this
play under Benjamin Fordyce
Barker, q.v.]*

Rishell, Dyson, b.1858.
Elfrida. Philadelphia: J. B.
Lippincott, 1883. 146p.

Risifi's daughter *see* Green,
Anna Katharine

Ritch, C. W.
One must marry. A comedy in
one act. Translated by C. W.
Ritch. (From the German of
Zechmeister.) New York:
Harold Roorbach, 1891. 18p.
(Roorbach's acting drama.
no. 144) *[title page: "From
the German of A. Wilhelmi";*

*based on Einer muss heiraten
(?) by Alexander Victor Zechmeister (pseud.=A. Wilhelmi)]*

Ritchie, Anna Cora Ogden Mowatt,
1819-1870.
Armand; or, The peer and the
peasant. A play in five acts.
New York: Stringer & Townsend,
1851. 60p.

Armand; or, The peer and the
peasant. A play in five acts.
New York: Stringer & Townsend,
1851. Prompt-book. 60p.

Fashion; or, Life in New York.
A comedy in five acts. New
York: S. French & Son, 1854?
62p. (French's standard drama.
no. 215)

Fashion; or, Life in New York.
A comedy in five acts. London:
W. Newberry, 1850. Prompt-
book. 62p.

Gulzara; or, The Persian
slave. By Anna Cora Mowett
[sic][From: The New World.
A weekly journal. New York:
J. Winchester, 1841. vol. 2,
no. 17] p.259-264. *[Readex
errs in using Mowett; the
name on the title page
correctly reads Mowatt]*

Plays. Boston: Ticknor &
Fields, 1855. 60, 62p.
Contents: Armand; or, The
peer and the peasant. A play
in five acts.--Fashion; or,
Life in New York. A comedy
in five acts.

Ritchie, Fannie.
Pleasant wedding guests.
Comedy in one act. Chicago:
Dramatic Pub. Co., c1899.
22p. (Sergel's acting drama.
no. 566)

Ritchie, Thomas.
Moderation; or, I can take it
or leave it alone *in* A collection of temperance dialogues

Rittenhouse, Laura J.
   The milkmaids' convention.
   Burlesque entertainment.
   Chicago: Dramatic Pub. Co.,
   c1898. 22p.

Rival artists *see* White,
   Charles

The rival barber shops *see*
   Dumont, Frank

A rival by request *see*
   Griffith, Benjamin Lease
   Crozer

The rival fairies *see* Corbyn,
   Wardle. Blanche; or, The
   rival fairies

The rival lovers *see* White,
   Charles

The rival merchants *see*
   Lovell, George. Love's
   sacrifice; or, The rival
   merchants *in* The modern
   standard drama, vol. 2

The rival poets *see* Baker,
   George Melville

Rival tenants *see* White,
   Charles

The rivals *see* Jefferson,
   Joseph *see also* Sheridan,
   Richard Brinsley Butler *in*
   The modern standard drama,
   vol. 4

The rivals [scene from] *see*
   Sheridan, Richard Brinsley
   Butler *in* Dramatic leaf-
   lets

Rives, Amélie *see* Troubetzkoy, Amélie Rives Chanler

Riviere, Louise.
   The little lady *see* Den-
   ton, Clara Janetta Fort *in*
   From tots to teens

Rizy, F. X.
   O'Neil the Great. Dramatic
   poem in two parts. Hartford:
   n.pub., c1879. 16p.

Rizzio *see* Cannon, Charles
   James

The road and the riders *see*
   Howe, J. Burdette. Scarlett
   Dick; the King's highwayman
   [or; The road and the riders]

The road to fortune *see* Raux,
   Eugene

The road to ruin *see* Holcroft,
   Thomas *in* The modern
   standard drama, vol. 7

Rob Roy *see* Smith, Harry
   Bache

Rob Roy MacGregor; or, Auld
   lang syne *see* Pocock, Isaac
   in The modern standard
   drama, vol. 11

Rob Roy; or, The thistle and
   the rose *see* Smith, Harry
   Bache

Rob, the hermit; or, The black
   chapel of Maryland *see*
   Adams, Charles Frederick

Robert, M.
   Blanche; or, The rival
   fairies *see* Corbyn, Wardle

Robert and Cornelia *see* Lewis,
   Richard Henry

Robert, Earl of Essex *see*
   Owen, Orville Ward

Robert Emmet, a tragedy of
   Irish history *see* Clarke,
   Joseph Ignatius Constantine

Robert Emmet, the martyr of
   Irish liberty *see* Pilgrim,
   James

Robert Make-airs; or, The
two fugitives *see* Warden,
Edward

Robert of Sicily *see*
Furniss, Grace Livingston

Roberts, T. W.
Kathleen O'Neil. A play in
four acts. n.p.: n.pub.,
c1892. 35 leaves.

Nora Darling. A play in
three acts. n.p.: n.pub.,
c1891. 34 leaves.

Waldeck; or, The haunted
dell. A play in four acts.
Chicago: n.pub., c1890.
58 leaves.

Robertson, Donald, 1860-1926.
The triumph of youth; or,
The white mouse. A comedy
in three acts. (From the
French of Pailleron.)
Chicago: Dramatic Pub. Co.,
c1907. 99p. (Sergel's
acting drama. no. 601)

Robertson, John, 1787-1873.
Riego; or, The Spanish
martyr. A tragedy in five
acts. Richmond: P. D.
Bernard, 1850. 106p.

Riego; or, The Spanish
martyr. (Reconstructed
and greatly abridged.)
Richmond: J. W. Randolph,
1872. 67p.

Robertson, Thomas William,
1829-1871.
David Garrick *see*
Sullivan

Robin Hood *see* Smith,
Harry Bache

Robins, Mary Ellis.
The forerunners. Woodstock,
N. Y.: Maverick Press,
18-? 82p.

Robinson, Charles.
Dream camp; or, A modern
craze. Rochester: Gelhaar,
Fleming and Bigelow, 1890.
47p. Libretto. *[title page:
"composed by Walter S.
Bigelow"]*

Ye gods and goddesses; or,
The apple of discord. A
mythical medley. Rochester:
E. R. Andrews, 1889. 48p.
Libretto. *[title page:
"composed by John H. Strong"]*

Robinson, Fayette, d.1859.
The Cardinal. A tragedy in
five acts. n.p.: n.pub.,
c1848. p.309-348.

Robinson, Harriet Jane Hanson,
1825-1911.
Captain Mary Miller. Boston:
W. H. Baker, 1877. 47p.
(The Globe drama) *[though
nearly illegible, the copyright date at the bottom of
the cover of the copy reproduced by Readex appears to
read 1876; the date at the
bottom of the page listing
the cast of characters reads
1887]*

The new Pandora. A drama in
five acts. New York and
London: G. P. Putnam's Sons,
1889. 151p.

Robinson, John Hovey, b.1825.
Nick Whiffles. A drama in
three acts. New York: S.
French, c1858. 35p. (French's
standard drama. no. 353)
*[Wallace gives a birth date
of 1835 for Robinson]*

Robinson, Lucy Catlin Bull,
1861-1903.
Various dramatic works [From
her: A child's poem. Hartford: Case Lockwood & Brainard, 1872. 171p.] p.129-171.

Contents: A rolling stone
gathers no moss.--No use
crying for spilled milk.--
Victor, the king of fairy-
land.

Robinson, T. S.
The student's frolic. A
laughable farce in one act.
New York: Dick & Fitzgerald,
18-? 28p. (Dick's American
edition)

Robinson Crusoe see Godoy,
José Francisco see also
Jenks, Almet F.

Robinsonade see Childs,
Nathaniel

Robjohn, William James, 1843-
1920.
The flying Dutchman. Romantic
opera in three acts. By
Caryl Florio (pseud.) Baltimore: Sun Printing Establishment, c1876. 33p. Libretto.
[libretto to Richard Wagner's
Der fliegende Holländer]

Rocchietti, Joseph.
Charles Rovellini. A drama
of the disunited states of
North America. New York:
n.pub., 1875. 69p. [a long
Preface presents an interesting tirade against Lincoln
and also against most of the
press of the time]

Rock Allen, the orphan; or,
Lost and found see Wilkins,
W. Henri

A Rocky Mountain diamond see
Fisher, Abraham Lincoln.
Little trump; or, A Rocky
Mountain diamond

Rodebaugh, T. Wilson.
John Winchester; or, Between
love and duty. A drama in
four acts. Clyde, O.: Ames,

c1895. 32p. (Ames' series of
standard and minor drama.
no. 362)

Rodenberg, Julius, 1831-1914.
The tower of Babel. A sacred
opera in one act. Cleveland
and Chicago: S. Brainard's
Sons, c1879. Vocal score.
159p. [based on Anton Rubinstein's Der Thurm zu Babel]

Roeckel, Joseph Leopold,
1838-1923.
A bird in hand see Schell,
Stanley. An old maid's conference

Roger (pseud.) see Ascher,
Anton

Rogers, James Webb, 1822-1896.
Madame Surratt. A drama in
five acts. Washington, D. C.:
Thomas J. Brashears, 1879.
148p.

Madame Surratt. New York:
William Abbatt, 1912. (Extra
no. 20...The Magazine of
history.) 8, 161p.

Rogers, Samuel, 1763-1855.
Ginevra see Massey,
Charles. Massey's exhibition
reciter

Italy see Lucrezia; or,
The bag of gold

The vision of Columbus see
Speed, Belle Lewis. Columbia

A rogue's luck; or, A man of
nerve see Tees, Levin C.

Rohan the silent. A romantic
drama in one act see
Sutherland, Evelyn Greenleaf
Baker in her Collected
works. Po' white trash and
other one-act dramas

Rohlfs, Mrs. Charles see
Green, Anna Katharine

A rolling stone gathers no
moss *see* Robinson, Lucy
Catlin Bull *in her*
Various dramatic works

The rolling year *see* Cobb,
Mary L. Poetical dramas
for home and school

Rollingpin, Commodore (pseud.)
see Carter, John Henton

The Roman martyr *see* McGee,
Thomas D'Arcy. Sebastian;
or, The Roman martyr

The Roman martyrs *see*
Codman, Henry

The Roman matron *see* Ludlow,
Noah Miller. Coriolanus;
or, The Roman matron

Romance after marriage; or,
The maiden wife *see* Good-
rich, Frank Boott and
Warden, Frank L.

Romani, Felice, 1788-1865.
L'elisir d'amore *see*
The elixir of love *see also*
The love-spell *see also*
Weil, Oscar. Adina; or, The
elixir of love

Lucrezia Borgia *see*
Calcaterra, G. *see also*
Lucretia Borgia

Norma *see* Fry, Joseph
Reece

Parisina *see* Parisina

Il pirata *see* Ponte,
Lorenzo da. The pirate

La sonnambula *see* The
somnambulist

Rome *see* Opal (pseud.) *in*
her The cloud of witnesses

Romeo and Juliet. By William
Shakespeare. New York: R. H.
Russell, 1899. 110p. (Maude

Adams' acting edition) *see*
also Cornell, John *see also*
Hinton, Henry L. *see also*
Shakespeare, William *in*
The modern standard drama,
vol. 6 *see also* Williams,
Frederick

Romeo and Juliet (balcony
scene) *see* Shakespeare,
William. Romeo and Juliet
in Dramatic leaflets

Romeo and Juliet, a new travesty
on *see* Soule, Charles
Carroll. A new travesty on
Romeo and Juliet

Romeo and Juliet restored *see*
Baker, George Melville. Capuletta; or, Romeo and Juliet
restored

A Romeo on "the gridiron" *see*
Williams, Henry Llewellyn

Romer, King of Norway *see*
Welcker, Adair *in his*
Romer, King of Norway and
other dramas

Rongé [or Ronger], Florimond
see Hervé, Florimond
Rongé

Rookwood *see* Bannister,
Nathan Harrington

Room forty-five *see* Howells,
William Dean

Room 44 *see* Simms, George A.

Rooms to let without board
see Griffin, George W. H.
and Denier, Tony

Rooney's restaurant *see*
Hiland, Frank E.

Root, George Frederick, 1820-
1895.
The flower queen; or, The
coronation of the rose *see*

Crosby, Frances Jane

The haymakers. An operatic cantata in two parts. New York: Mason Bros., 1860. 16p. Libretto. *[music by the author; without the music]*

Rosabella's lovers. A burlesque in five acts *see* McBride, H. Elliott *in his* New dialogues

Rosberry Shrub, sec. *see* Drake, Frank C.

Roscius-Kemble *see* Townsend, Frederic *in his* Spiritual visitors

Rose, Con., Jr.
Dead Sea fruit. A comedy drama in five acts and eight tableaux. Washington: n.pub., 1875. 78p.

Rose, Edward Everett, 1862-1939.
Janice Meredith. New York and London: S. French, 1927. 112p. *[based on the novel Janice Meredith by Paul Leicester Ford]*

Richard Carvel. (From the novel of W. Churchill.) New York: Z. and L. Rosenfield, 1900. Typescript. Prompt-book with Ms. notes. 53, 41, 35, 30 leaves.

Rose, G. B., b.1860.
Sebastian; a dramatic poem. Buffalo: Charles Wells Moulton, 1894. 93p.

The rose *see* Fiske, Minnie Maddern Davey

The rose and the ring *see* Greenough, James Bradstreet

The rose-colored domino *see* Steele, Silas Sexton. The

masked ball; or, The rose colored domino *in his* Collected works. Book of plays

Rose Dale *see* Griffin, George W. H.

Rose Michel *see* MacKaye, James Steele *see also* MacKaye, James Steele An arrant knave & other plays

The rose of Ettrick Vale; or, The bridal of the borders. A drama in two acts. (Adapted from Thomas Lynch's play.) New York: Samuel French, 18-? Prompt-book. 31p. (French's American drama. The acting edition. no. 62)

Rosedale *see* Wallack, Lester

Rosedale; or, The rifle ball *see* Wallack, Lester

Rosen, Julius, 1833-1892.
Halbe Dichter *see* Daly, Augustin. Nancy and company

[Lemons] *see* Daly, Augustin

Starke Mitteln *see* Daly, Augustin. Needles and pins

Rosenfeld, Sydney, 1855-1931.
Amorita *see* Goldmark, George and Rosenfeld, Sydney

Apajune, the water sprite. A comic opera in three acts. New York: Willis Woodward, c1885. 39p. Libretto. *[music by Karl Millöcker to libretto Apajune der Wassermann by Camillo Wälzel and Richard Genée; without the music]*

The black hussar. In three acts. New York: Brentano Bros., 1885. 51p. Libretto. *[music by Karl Millöcker to libretto Der Feldprediger by Alois Wohlmuth and Hugo Wittmann; without the music]*

The bridal trap. New York:
Willis Woodward, 1886. 63,
46p. Libretto. *[cover:*
"original text written by
Sydney Rosenfeld to the
music of 'Le serment d'am-
our.'"; without the music]

The club friend; or, A
fashionable physician. An
original comedy in four
acts. New York: Dramatic
Pub. Co., c1897. 89p.
(Green-room edition of copyrighted plays)

Gasparone. Romantic comic
opera in three acts. (From
the German of Zell and
Genée.) New York: Hermann
Bartsch, Job, Book and
Music Typographer, 1885.
23p. Libretto. *[music by*
Karl Millöcker to libretto
by Camillo Wälzel (pseud.=
F. Zell) and Richard Genée]

The hair apparent; or, The
treacherous wig. (From the
German of Grandjean.)
Chicago: Dramatic Pub. Co.,
c1876. 10p. *[based on Rote*
Haare by Moritz Anton Grand-
jean]

Her only fault. A comedietta
in one act. (From the German
of Goerlitz.) Chicago: Dramatic Pub. Co., c1882. 13p.
(Sergel's acting drama.
no. 303) *[based on Eine*
volkommense Frau (?) by
Karl Görlitz]

High C. A comedietta in one
act. A free adaptation from
the German of M. A. Grandjean. New York: Robert M.
De Witt, c1875. 17p. (De
Witt's acting plays. no.
1911) *[based on Das hohe C*
by Moritz Anton Grandjean]

"I shall invite the major."
A petite comedy in one act.
(From the German of G. von
Moser.) New York: R. M. De

Witt, c1875. 16p. (De Witt's
acting plays. no. 177)

The lady or the tiger?, text
of songs...An original musical comedy-drama in three
acts. New York: F. V. Strauss,
c1888. 32p. *[cover: "founded*
on the incident contained in
the sketch of the same name,
by contract with Mr. Frank
R. Stockton"; music by Julius
J. Lyons and A. Nowak;
without the music]

Mabel's manoeuvre; or, A
third party. A parlor interlude in one scene. (From the
German of Benedix.) New York:
R. M. De Witt, c1876. 10p.
(De Witt's acting plays.
no. 210) *[based on Der Dritte*
by Julius Roderich Benedix]

Married bachelors; or,
Pleasant surprises. A come-
dietta in one act. (From the
German of Benedix.) Chicago:
Dramatic Pub. Co., c1876.
11p. (De Witt's acting plays.
no. 208) *[based on Die*
Eifersüchtigen by Julius
Roderich Benedix]

Mr. X. A farce in one act.
Chicago: Dramatic Pub. Co.,
c1875. 17p. (Sergel's acting
drama. no. 188)

The mystic isle; or, The
laws of average. An entirely
original comic drama in two
acts. Philadelphia: Dunlap &
Clarke, 1886. 32p. Libretto.
[music by John B. Grant;
without the music]

No questions asked. A farce
in three acts. (From the
French of Bisson.) New York:
n.pub., n.d. Typescript,
prompt-book with Ms. notes.
35, 42, 29 leaves.

Off the stage. An original
comedietta in one act. New
York: R. M. De Witt, c1875.

26p. (De Witt's acting plays. no. 173)

On bread and water. A musical farce in one act, imitated from the German. Chicago: Dramatic Pub. Co., c1875. 12p. (Sergel's acting drama. no. 176)

The oolah. Comic opera in three acts. (Music by C. Lecocq.) New York: R. A. Saalfield, c1887. 44p. Libretto. *[original text of songs adapted by Sydney Rosenfeld to fit the music of Alexandre Charles Lecocq; libretto by Eugène Leterrier and Albert Vanloo; without the music]*

A pair of shoes. A farce in one act. New York: Dramatic Pub. Co., c1882. 12p. (De Witt's acting plays. no. 305)

The senator *see* Lloyd, David Demarest and Rosenfeld, Sydney

Subtleties of jealousy. (From the French of Pailleron.) New York: n.pub., 1898. Typescript, prompt-book with Ms. notes. 33 leaves. *[based on the French of Édouard Jules Henri Pailleron]*

The ulster. A farcical comedy in three acts. New York: De Witt, c1882. 46p. (De Witt's acting plays. no. 307) *[cover: "in part adapted from the German, and in part original"]*

Rosetti, Joseph.
Household affairs; or, A cause for divorce. Comedy in one act. New York: Dramatic Pub. Co., c1899. 16p. (The wizard series)

In the forest. A play for children in three acts. Chicago: Dramatic Pub. Co.,

c1899. 11p. (Children's plays)

Little daughter of the regiment. A play for children in two acts. Chicago: Dramatic Pub. Co., c1899. 10p. (Children's plays)

Rosina Meadows, the village maid; or, Temptations unveiled *see* Saunders, Charles Henry

Rosita; or, Boston and banditti *see* Woodward, Matthew C.

Roskoten, Robert.
Carlotta. A tragedy in five acts. Peoria, Ill.: J. W. Franks & Sons, 1880. 123p.

Rosmersholm *see* Carmichael, Montgomery

Ross, Joseph M.
Phintias and Damon. Morristown, N. J.: C. D. Platt, 1897. 76p.

Rosse, Jeanie Quinton.
The Egyptian princess. A romantic operetta in two acts for women's voices. Boston: Boston Music Co., c1899. Vocal score. 106p. *[music by Charles John Vincent]*

The Japanese girl (O Hanu San.) An operetta in two acts for ladies. Boston: Boston Music Co., c1899. Vocal score. 74p. *[music by Charles John Vincent]*

Rossi, F.
Grand historical spectacular [sic, spectacle] masterpiece America *see* Kiralfy, Imre

Rossi, Gaetano, 1780-1855.
Il giuramento *see* Il giuramento; or, The oath

Linda di Chamounix *see*

Linda of Chamouni *see also*
The pearl of Savoy

Semiramide *see* Semiramis

Rossibelli-Donimozarti,
Maestro (pseud.)
Il pesceballo *see* Lowell,
James Russell

Rossini, Gioacchino Antonio,
1792-1868.
Il barbiere di Siviglia
see The barber of Seville

La cenerentola *see* Cinderella; or, The fairy and
little glass slipper

La gazza ladra *see* Coale,
George B. Magpie and the
maid *see also* The thieving
magpie

Matilda di Shabran; ossia,
Il trionfo della beltà *see*
Attinelli, Joseph. Matilda
di Shabran and Corradino

Mosé in Egitto *see* Parker,
George S. Moses in Egypt
see also Ponte, Lorenzo da.
Moses in Egypt *see also*
Villarino, Jose J. Moses
in Egypt

Semiramide *see* Semiramis

Rostand, Edmond, 1868-1918.
Cyrano de Bergerac *see*
Renauld, Charles *see also*
Smith, Harry Bache

La princesse lointaine *see*
Renauld, Charles

Roth, Edward, 1826-1911.
The gray tigers of Smithville; or, He would and he
wouldn't. A school extravaganza in three acts. Philadelphia: n.pub., 1887. 80p.
(American school and college
plays. no. 1)

The rough diamond *see*
Buckstone, John Baldwin *in*
Dramatic leaflets *see also*

Steele, Silas Sexton. The
country cousin; or, The
rough diamond *in his*
Collected works. Book of
plays

The Rough Rider *see* Moore,
Bernard Francis

The rounders *see* Smith,
Harry Bache

Rover, Winnie.
The houses on the avenue; or,
The little mischief-makers.
A drama in six scenes. New
York: Catholic Pub. Soc.,
1877. 62p.

A row in the kitchen *see*
Tees, Levin C.

Rowe, Bolton.
Impulse. A play in five acts.
Boston: n.pub., 1880. 80p.

Rowe, Nicholas, 1674-1718.
Jane Shore *see* The modern
standard drama, vol. 12

Royal, Ralph (pseud.) *see*
Abarbanell, Jacob Ralph

The royal guard *see* Mayo,
Frank and Wilson, John G.

The royal revenge *see* Hayes,
Maude Blanche

Royer, Alphonse, 1803-1875.
La favorita *see* La favorita
see also The favorite *see*
also Révoil, Bénédict Henry.
La favorite (The king's
mistress)

Royle, Edwin Milton, 1862-1942.
Mexico. A romantic drama in
four acts. New York: Z. and
L. Rosenfield Typewriting,
1895. Typescript, prompt-
book. 12, 42, 31, 36 leaves.

Ruben Rube; or, My invalid

aunt *see* Chipman, Adelbert Z.

Rubens-Cole *see* Townsend, Frederic *in his* Spiritual visitors

Rubinstein, Anton Grigorievitch, 1829-1894。 Der Thurm zu Babel *see* Rodenberg, Julius。 The tower of Babel

Rugg, George. The new woman。 A farcical sketch with one act, one scene and one purpose. Boston: W. H. Baker, c1896. 6p. (Baker's edition of plays)

Ruhland, Mildred Amelie. Olea. New York: Kalkhoff, 19-? 64p.

The rulers of the Republic *see* Lookup, Alexander (pseud.) Excelsior; or, The heir apparent

Rum; or, The first glass *see* Comstock, William

A rumpus on Gingerbread Hill *see* McBride, H。 Elliott *in his* Latest dialogues

Rumpus Romali Remique *see* Grinnell, Charles Edward. Jurgium Geminorum; or, Rumpus Romali Remique

Rumsey, Mrs. B。 C. A St. Augustine episode. A drama in three acts. Buffalo: n.pub。, 1884. 39p.

A run on the bank *see* Blaney, Charles E.

The runaway slave *see* Ringwalt, Jessie Elder, Mrs. J. L. Paul and Virginia; or, The runaway slave

The runaway wife *see* Rankin, McKee and Maeder, Frederick George

The runaways *see* Baker, George Melville *see also* Denison, Thomas Stewart *in his* Friday afternoon series of dialogues

Running to waste; the story of a tomboy *see* Baker, George Melville。 Our folks

Runnion, James B. Champagne and oysters; or, One lie leads to another. A farce in three acts。 Chicago: Dramatic Pub. Co., c1906。 51p. (Sergel's acting drama. no。 584)

Hearts and diamonds. A comedy in three acts. Chicago?: Printed as Ms. for the use of the stage, and not published, c1875。 59p.

Miss Manning. Nutley, N. J.: Frank Weston, 189-? Typescript, prompt-book. Title page missing. 58, 53, 47 leaves.

A rural ruse *see* Winston, Mary A.

Rush, James, 1786-1869. Hamlet. A dramatic prelude in five acts. Philadelphia: Key & Biddle, 1834。 122p。 *["A prelude to Shakespeare's Hamlet"]*

Russ, Horace *see* R。, H。

Russ, William Ward. The strike; or, Under the shadow of a crime. A drama in five acts. Clyde, O.: Ames, c1900。 32p. (Ames' series of standard and minor drama。 no。 423)

Russell, Charles Walcott.
A turn in the market. A
drama in one act. Boston:
W. H. Baker, 1895. 12p.
(Baker's edition of plays)

The water-melon cure. Knock-
about farce in one act.
Chicago: Dramatic Pub. Co.,
n.d. 16p. *[on the microprint
for this play, Readex in-
correctly gives the author's
name as Charles Wolcott
Russell]*

Russell, G. Frederick.
What's in a name? A farce
in one act. Philadelphia:
Penn Pub. Co., 1912. 13p.
[earlier copyright: 1895]

A Russian honeymoon *see*
Harrison, Constance Cary

Rustic chivalry (Cavalleria
rusticana) *see* Macy,
James Cartwright *see also*
Tretbar, Helen D.

Ruth *see* Browne, Frances
Elizabeth

Ruy Blas *see* Hugo, Victor
Marie *in* Booth, Edwin.
The miscellaneous plays of
Edwin Booth

Ryan, Samuel E.
O'Day, the Alderman. A
comedy drama in four acts.
Boston: Baker, 1901. 64p.
(Baker's edition of plays)

Ryer, George W.
The old homestead *see*
Thompson, Denman and Ryer,
George W.

Our new minister *see*
Thompson, Denman and Ryer,
George W.

Ryley, Madeleine Lucette,
1868-1934.
An American citizen. An

original comedy in four acts.
New York, London: S. French,
c1895. 63p.

Christopher junior. Comedy
in four acts. New York: S.
French, c1889. 65p. (French's
standard library edition)

Ryman, John Addison, 1837?-1896.
Julius the snoozer; or, The
conspirators of Thompson
Street *see* White, Charles

S., C. W.
Every-day life *see* Every-
day life

S., E. S.
The Princess Chrysalline;
or, The maiden who couldn't
laugh. St. Louis: Little &
Becker, 1882. 38p. *[E. S. S.
is Mrs. S. E. Sells]*

S., N. S.
Armada days. A dramatic
sketch. Cambridge, Mass.:
University Press, c1898.
92p. *[N. S. S. is Nathaniel
Southgate Shaler]*

S. H. A. M. Pinafore *see*
Wilkins, W. Henri

S. Sutherland Breyfogle *see*
Luce, Grace A. Brass buttons

Sabel, Sigmund.
Hadassah; or, The Persian
queen *see* Goldschmidt,
William

Sacred dramas *see* Boxer,
James

The sacrifice of Iphigenia
see Bailey, William Entriken.
Dramatic poems

Sadlier, Mary Anne Madden,
1820-1903.
The invisible hand. A drama
in two acts. By Mrs. J.

Sadlier. New York: D. & J.
Sadlier, c1873. 36p.

The secret. By Mrs. J.
Sadlier. New York: D. & J.
Sadlier, 1873, 32p.

The talisman. A drama in one
act. By Mrs. J. Sadlier.
New York: D. & J. Sadlier,
18-? 33p.

Safford, De Forest.
Watertown in '75. A scenic
dialogue in five parts.
Mt. Auburn: Published at
the Memorial Office, 1860.
32p.

Sag Harbor *see* Herne,
James A.

A sailor's life on the raging
main *see* Hart, George G.
E. C. B. Susan Jane; or,
A sailor's life on the
raging main

The sailor's return *see*
Baker, George Melville.
The tempter; or, The
sailor's return

A St. Augustine episode *see*
Rumsey, Mrs. B. C.

St. Clair, Clarence.
Fear of scandal. A play in
four acts. New York?: A.
Freeman, c1900. Typescript,
prompt-book. 49 leaves.

St. Elizabeth of Thuringia;
or, The miracle of roses
see Polding, Elizabeth

Saint-Georges, Jules Henri
Vernoy de, 1799-1875.
La fille du régiment *see*
The child of the regiment
see also The daughter of
the regiment *see also* La
figlia del reggimento *see
also* Seguin, Arthur Edward

Sheldon. Marie; or, The
daughter of the regiment

Les mousquetaires de la
reine *see* Révoil, Bénèdict
Henry. The queen's musketeers

La reine de Chypre *see*
Révoil, Bénèdict Henry. The
queen of Cyprus

Le val d'Andorre *see*
The valley of Andorre

St. John, Charles Henry.
The misanthrope melted. A
scene from an unfinished
drama [From his: Poems.
Boston: A. Williams, 1859.
144p.] p.121-127.

St. Mark; or, A husband's
sacrifice *see* Wilkins,
John H. Signor Marc

St. Maur, J.
Kean; ou, désordre et génie
see Jessop, George Henry.
Edmund Kean; or, The life
of an actor

St. Patrick's Eve *see*
Kathleen Mavourneen; or, St.
Patrick's Eve

St. Paul in Athens *see* Opal
(pseud.) *in her* The cloud
of witnesses

Saint-Pierre, Jacques Henri
Bernardin de, 1737-1814.
Paul et Virginie *see*
Ringwalt, Jessie Elder,
Mrs. J. L. Paul and Virginia;
or, The runaway slave

Saint-Saëns, Camille, 1835-1921.
Samson et Dalila *see*
Barnett, M. J. Samson and
Delilah

St. Valentine's day *see*
Trumbull, Annie Eliot

Saintine, Joseph Xavier Boni-

face, known as, 1798-1865.
Riche d'amour *see* Morton,
John Maddison. Lend me five
shillings *in* The modern
standard drama, vol. 3

Salmon, John.
Old and young; or, Both
alike. A comedy in two acts.
Boston: W. V. Spencer, 1856?
30p. (Spencer's Boston
theatre. no. 97)

Salmonsen, Morris, 1843-1913.
We mortals. A play in three
acts. Chicago: J. M. W.
Jones Stationery and Print.
Co., 1897. 147p.

Salome *see* Heywood, Joseph
Converse

Salome, the daughter of
Herodias *see* Heywood,
Joseph Converse

Saltus, Francis Saltus,
1849-1889.
Bel-Shar-Uzzar [From his:
The witch of En-dor and
other poems. Buffalo:
Charles Wells Moulton,
1891. 331p.] p.183-279.

Carthage [From his: The
witch of En-dor and other
poems. Buffalo: Charles
Wells Moulton, 1891. 331p.]
p.145-182.

Dolce far niente [and] An
answer [From his: Dreams
after sunset. Buffalo:
Charles Wells Moulton,
1892. Limited edition.
256p.] p.54-64, 232-255.

Lot's wife [From his: The
witch of En-dor and other
poems. Buffalo: Charles
Wells Moulton, 1891. 331p.]
p.281-331.

Sam Weller's visit. (From
Dickens' Pickwick Papers.)
New York: Wheat & Cornett,

c1877. p.31-32. (New York
Drama, vol. 3, no. 29)

Sambo's return. An Ethiopian
sketch in one scene. New
York: H. Roorbach, c187-?
6p. (The Ethiopian drama.
no. 73)

The same thing over again *see*
Cutler, F. L. Kitty and
Patsy; or, The same thing
over again

Sam'l of Posen; or, The
commercial drummer *see*
Jessop, George Henry

Sample, Walter Boyd.
Passions's dream. New York:
G. W. Dillingham, 1895. 122p.

Sam's courtship *see* White,
Charles

Samson. A play in five acts.
(From the Italian of
Ippolito D'Aste.) New York:
George F. Nesbitt, 1873.
Bilingual text: English and
Italian. 79p. *see also*
Howells, William Dean

Samson and Delilah *see*
Barnett, M. J.

Samson and Delilah; or, Dagon
stoops to Sabaoth *see*
Bien, Herman Milton

Sand, George, 1803-1876.
Le petit Fadette *see*
Waldauer, Augustus. Fanchon,
the cricket

Sandeau, Jules, 1811-1883.
Mademoiselle de la Seig-
lière *see* Hélène de la
Seiglière

Sanderson, Mary.
The mistake on both sides.
A petite comedy in one act.
New York: Baker, Godwin

1852. 12p. *[this play was written when the author was ten years old]*

Sands, Robert C.
Waldimar *see* Bailey, John J.

Sands, Robert Charles, 1799-1832.
Isaac; a type of redeemer [From his: The writings of ...New York: Harper & Bros., 1834. vol. 1, 395p.; vol. 2, 408p.] vol.1, p.117-135.

Sanford, Amelia.
The advertising girls. A masque of very fly leaves in two scenes. Boston: W. H. Baker, c1900. 18p. (Baker's edition of plays)

The ghost of an idea. A comedietta in one act and three scenes. Philadelphia: Penn Pub. Co., 1898. 13p. (Keystone edition of popular plays)

Maids, modes and manners; or, Madame Grundy's dilemma. Philadelphia: Penn Pub. Co., 1911. 14p. *[earlier copyright: 1896]*

Sanford, Myron Reed, d.1939.
Temporibus hominis Arpinatis. Middlebury, Vt.: Register Co., c1900. 45p. *[text in Latin and English]*

Santa Claus' daughter *see* Elliott, Everett and Hardcastle, F. W.

Santa Claus' frolics *see* Baker, George Melville

Santa Claus the first *see* Chase, Frank Eugene

Santayana, George, 1863-1952.
Lucifer. A theological

comedy. Chicago: H. S. Stone, 1899. 187p. *[this is the first edition of Santayana's work later (1924) entitled Lucifer; or, The heavenly truce]*

Santiago; or, For the red, white and blue *see* Fraser, John Arthur

Saphar, Will D.
The German volunteer. A military allegory and comedy drama in four acts. Philadelphia: U. S. Grant Post No. 5, 188-? 30p.

Sapolio *see* Smith, Edgar McPhail and Smith, Harry Bache

Sappho. A tragic opera in three acts. New York: M. Douglas, 18-? Bilingual text: English and Italian. 48p. Libretto. *[music by Giovanni Pacini on libretto Saffo by Salvatore Cammarano; without the music]*

Sappho *see* Fitch, Clyde *see also* Frothingham, Ellen *see also* Ginty, Elizabeth Beall *see also* Lewis, Estelle Anna Blanche Robinson *see also* Norton, Jessie

Saratoga: a dramatic romance of the revolution *see* Dailey, W. B.

The Saratoga fairies *see* Walworth, Reubena Hyde. Where was Elsie; or, The Saratoga fairies

Saratoga; or, "Pistols for seven" *see* Howard, Bronson

Sarcey, Francisque, 1827-1899.
Est-ce trop cher? *see* Is it too dear?

Sardou, Victorien, 1831-1908.
Les américaines à l'étranger
see Richardson, Abby Sage.
Americans abroad

Daniel Rochat *see* Prichard,
Joseph Vila

Dora *see* Williams, Henry
Llewellyn. Diplomates

Fernanda *see* Schönberg,
James. Fernande *see also*
Williams, Henry Llewellyn.
Fernanda; or, Forgive and
forget

Madame sans-gêne *see*
Meltzer, Charles Henry

Nos bons villageois *see*
Daly, Augustin. Hazardous
ground

La papillonne *see* Daly,
Augustin and Wood, Frank.
Taming a butterfly

La Tosca *see* Davenport,
Fanny Lily Gypsy

Sargent, Epes, 1831-1880.
The candid critic [From
his: Songs of the sea, with
other poems. Boston: J.
Munroe, 1847] p.159-194,
207-208.

The lampoon [From his: Songs
of the sea, with other poems.
Boston: J. Munroe, 1847]
p.195-201, 208

Velasco. A tragedy in five
acts. New York: Harper &
Bros., 1839. 110p. Title
page mutilated

Satan: a libretto *see*
Cranch, Christopher Pearse

Satane, Bimet, 1827-1899 *see*
Sarcey, Francisque (pseud.)

A satire on trial by jury
see Bailey, George W.
Diagram of a modern law suit;
or, A satire on trial by jury

Satterlee, Clarence.
A Christmas carol. In seven
staves. By Charles Dickens.
Dramatized by Clarence
Satterlee. Chicago: Dramatic
Pub. Co., 1886. 22p. (Ser-
gel's acting drama. no. 343)

Sauce for the goose *see*
Livingston, Margaret Vere
Farrington

Saul *see* Coxe, Arthur
Cleveland *see also* Iliowizi,
Henry *see also* Logan,
Algernon Sydney

Saul of Tarsus *see* Mershon,
Ralph Smith

Saunders, Charles Henry,
1818-1857.
The North End caulker; or,
The mechanic's oath. A story
of Boston Harbor and the Rio
Grande in five acts. Boston:
1851. Prompt-book in Ms. 47
leaves.

The pirate's legacy. n.pl.:
18-? Prompt-book in Ms. In
two acts (pag. by acts)
*[this is the same play as
the printed edition which
appeared under the title
The pirate's legacy; or,
The wrecker's fate (see
below)]*

The pirate's legacy; or, The
wrecker's fate. A drama in
two acts. New York: S. French
& Son, 187-? 26p. (French's
standard drama. The acting
edition. no. 321) *[this is
the same play as the prompt-
book version which appeared
under the title The pirate's
legacy (see above)]*

Rosina Meadows, the village
maid; or, Temptations un-
veiled. A local domestic
drama in three acts. (From
the novel by William B.

English.) Boston: W. V.
Spencer, 18-? Prompt-book.
52 leaves. (Spencer's
Boston theatre. no. 11)

The sausage makers *see*
White, Charles

Savage, John, 1828-1888.
Dreaming by moonlight
[From his: Faith and fancy.
New York: James B. Kirke,
1864. 118p.] p.85-106.

Sybil. A tragedy in five
acts. New York: J. B.
Kirker, 1865. 105p.

Saved *see* Dramatic leaflets
see also Hotchkiss, Zort P.
see also Tardy, Edwin

Saved at last *see* Bradley,
Nellie H. The first glass;
or, The power of woman's
influence *see also* The
wine cup; or, Saved at last

Saved from the wreck *see*
Serrano, Thomas K.

Saxe, John Godfrey, 1816-1887.
A connubial eclogue *see*
Beadle's...dialogues no. 2

The ugly aunt *see* Call,
S. C.

Sayings and singings. A frag-
ment of a farce [From:
American comic annual. By
Henry J. Finn, editor.
Boston: Richardson, Lord &
Holbrook, 1831. 220p.]
p.49-59.

A scale with sharps and flats
see Cutler, F. L.

Scampini *see* White, Charles

Scan mag!; or, The village
gossip. n.pl.: n.pub., n.d.
Title page lacking. 34p.

Scandinavia *see* Denison,
Thomas Stewart *in his*
Friday afternoon series of
dialogues

Scapegrace *see* Mathews,
Frances Aymar *see also* her
Six to one; or, The scape-
grace

Scarlet Dick; the King's
highwayman [or, The road and
the riders] *see* Howe, J.
Burdette

The scarlet letter *see*
Andrews, George H. *see also*
Harrison, Gabriel *see also*
Lathrop, George Parsons
see also Najac, Émile de
and Landers, Jean Margaret
see also Peck, Elizabeth
Weller

The scarlet stigma *see* Smith,
James Edgar

Scene from Faust *see* Lazarus,
Emma

Scene from unpublished play
see Holmes, Oliver Wendell

Scene in a jury-room *see*
McBride, H. Elliott *in his*
Latest dialogues

A scene in a tailor shop *see*
McBride, H. Elliott *in his*
Latest dialogues

Scene of Blanchette *see*
Aldrich, Thomas Bailey.
IV. Scene of Blanchette

Scenes at Gurney's. New York:
Happy Hours, 187-? 8p. (The
Ethiopian drama. no. 54)

Scenes at the fair. Boston:
James B. Dow, 1833. 14p.

Scenes from American history

see Barnes, William Horatio.
The drama of secession; or,
Scenes from American history

Scenes from an unpublished
play *see* Payne, John
Howard

Scenes from Mary Stuart *see*
Ascher, Anton

Scenes from New York life and
the Pacific Railroad *see*
McCloskey, James Joseph.
Across the continent; or,
Scenes from New York life
and the Pacific Railroad

Scenes in a sanctum *see*
Coes, George H.

Scenes in Athens *see* Ford,
Alfred. The five hour law;
or, Scenes in Athens

Scenes in both *see* Pilgrim,
James. Ireland and America;
or, Scenes in both

Scenes in Congress, July 4th,
1776 *see* Howe, C. E. B.
Signing the Declaration of
Independence; or, Scenes
in Congress, July 4th, 1776

Scenes in front of a clothing
store *see* Dumont, Frank

Scenes on the Mississippi *see*
White, Charles

Schaad, John Christian, fl.
1856-1866.
Nicholas of the Flue. The
savior of the Swiss Republic.
A dramatic poem in five acts.
Washington, D. C.: McGill &
Witherow, 1866. 144p.

Schell, Stanley.
An old maid's conference.
A humorous entertainment in
two scenes for any number of
males and females. New York:

Edgar S. Werner, 1900. 44p.
Libretto. *[Contains two
songs: A bird in hand (words
by Frederick Edward Weatherly and music by Joseph
Leopold Roeckel) and 'Twas
surely fate (words by Clifton
Bingham and music by Dotie
Davies [pseud.=Hope Temple])]*

Schell, Stanley.
Cinderella *see* Henley,
Anne and Schell, Stanley

A real Thanksgiving [and]
A Thanksgiving lesson. By
Eva Lyle Dickinson. New
York: Edgar S. Werner,
c1899. (Werner's Magazine.
vol. 24) p.153-161.

The scheme that failed *see*
Tubbs, Arthur Lewis

Schiller, Johann Christoph
Friedrich von, 1759-1805.
Don Carlos *see* Calvert,
George Henry

Maria Stuart *see* Ascher,
Anton. Scenes from Mary
Stuart *see also* Brooks,
Edward. Mary Stuart *see
also* Maria Stuart

Phädra *see* Phaedra

Wilhelm Tell *see* Brooks,
Charles Timothy. William
Tell *see also* Griffin,
George W. H. William Tell

Schindler, Anthony J.
Knaves and fools. Comedy in
one act for male characters.
New York: J. Fischer & Bro.,
c1897. 24p. (Fischer's
edition. no. 1456)

Schleiffarth, George M.,
d.1921.
Rosita; or, Boston and
banditti *see* Woodward,
Matthew C.

Schlesinger, Olga Steiner,
b.1865.

The fortune-teller. A farce
comedy in one act. By Olga
Steiner. Chicago and New
York: Dramatic Pub. Co.,
c1899. 13p. (Sergel's acting
drama. no. 505)

The ghost in the boarding
school. A comedy in one act
for young ladies. By Olga
Steiner. Chicago and New
York: Dramatic Pub. Co.,
c1899. 9p. (Sergel's acting
drama. no. 452)

Hard of hearing. A comedy in
one act for young ladies.
Chicago and New York: Dramatic Pub. Co., c1899. 18p.
(Sergel's acting drama.
no. 451)

Miss Nonchalance. A comedy
in one act. By Olga Steiner.
Chicago and New York: Dramatic Pub. Co., c1899. 16p.
(Sergel's acting drama.
no. 538)

Schmall, Alice F.
Zanetto [and] At sunset.
New York?: n.pub., 18-?
Title page lacking. 23p.
Libretto.
   Contents: Zanetto [based
on La passant by François
Coppée; opera in one act
by Pietro Mascagni on
libretto by Guido Menasci].
--At sunset [opera in one
act by Gaetano Coronaro]

Schmithof, E.
Kaffeeklatsch see Matt-
hews, Edith Virginia
Brander. Six cups of chocolate

Schmucker, Samuel Mosheim
see Smucker, Samuel M.

Schnapps see Clifton, Mary
A. Delano

Schönberg, James.

Fernande. A story of the
period. New York: Burnton,
1870. 81p. (Burnton's
library and acting drama.
no. 1) [adapted from the
French of Victorien Sardou]

Narcisse the vagrant. A
tragedy in five acts. London
and New York: S. French,
18-. 48p. (Lacy's acting
edition. vol. 107) [adapted
from Narciss by Albert Emil
Brachvogel]

Oscar the half-blood. A
sensational play in a prologue and four acts. London:
Dick's Standard Plays, 1883?
28p. (Dick's standard plays.
no. 474)

True as steel. A romantic
military drama in five acts
and six tableaux. London:
Dick's Standard Plays, 1883.
24p. (Dick's standard plays.
no. 482) [adapted from Fanfan la tulipe by Paul
Meurice]

Schoenthan, Franz von, 1849-
1913.
[The great unknown] see
Daly, Augustin

[An international match] see
Daly, Augustin

Komtesse Guckerl see Daly,
Augustin. The countess Gucki

[The last word] see Daly,
Augustin

[A night off; or, A page from
Balzac] see Daly, Augustin

[The passing regiment] see
Daly, Augustin

[The railroad of love] see
Daly, Augustin

Der Schwabenstreich see
A kettle of fish

[7-20-8; or, Casting a
boomerang] see Daly,
Augustin

Schoenthan, Paul, 1853-1905.
[A night off; or, A page
from Balzac] *see* Daly,
Augustin

Scholar, Barney, 1839-1886
Ambition *see* White,
Charles

School *see* Field, A. Newton

The school bell *see* Denton,
Clara Janetta Fort. When
the lessons are over

The school entertainment *see*
Merriman, Effie Woodward
in her Comedies for
children

The school for critics; or,
A natural transformation
see Osborn, Laughton

The school for orators *see*
Massey, Charles *in*
Massey's exhibition reciter

The school for politicians;
or, Non-committal. A comedy
in five acts. (From Scribe's
"Bertrand et Raton; ou, L'art
de conspirer.") New York:
Carvill, 1840. 179p.

The school for politics *see*
Gayarré, Charles Étienne
Arthur

The school for scandal *see*
Daly, Augustin *see also*
Sheridan, Richard Brinsley
Butler *in* The modern
standard drama, vol. 1

The school for scandal
(quarrel scene) *see*
Sheridan, Richard Brinsley
Butler *in* Dramatic leaflets

School is out *see* Denton,
Clara Janetta Fort. When
the lessons are over

The school ma'am *see* Denison,
Thomas Stewart

The school of Queen Mab *see*
Durfee, Job

The school stage *see* Venable,
William Henry

Schoolcraft, Henry Rowe, 1793-
1861.
Alhalla; or, The lord of
Talladega. A tale of the
Greek war [From: Alhalla...
with some selected miscellanies...By Henry Rowe Col-
craft. New York and London:
Wiley & Putnam, 1843. 116p.]
p.1-4, 1-83.

Schoolcraft, Oliver John.
The lovers. A fragment [From
his: Arsiesis and other
poems. New York: G. P. Putnam's Sons, 1881. 113p.]
p.73-86.

The schoolmaster abroad *see*
A collection of temperance
dialogues

Schrader, August.
Die Grille; oder, kleine
Fadette *see* Waldauer,
Augustus. Fanchon, the
cricket

Schupphaus, Otto Frederick.
The plutocrat. A drama in
five acts. New York: A.
Lovell, 1892. 103p.

Schwab, Emil.
The beggar student. Comic
opera in three acts. Boston,
New York, Chicago: White,
Smith, 18-? Vocal score.
183p. *[music by Karl Millöcker on libretto Der Bettelstudent by Camillo Wälzel
(pseud.=F. Zell) and Rudolf
Genée; also known in America
and England as The student
beggar]*

The beggar student. (Music by C. Milloecker.) Boston and Chicago: White, Smith, c1883. 42p. Libretto. *[see note on previous entry]*

Schwab, Frederick A., 1844?-1927.
Adrienne Lecouvreur [sic, Lecouvreur] A play in five acts. New York: F. Rullman at The Theatre Ticket Office, c1880. Bilingual text: English and French. 48p. *[originally by Augustin Eugène Scribe and Gabriel Marie Jean Baptiste Legouvé]*

Euryanthe. A romantic opera in three acts. (From the German of Von Chézy.) New York: n.pub., c1887. Bilingual text: English and German. 16, 16p. Libretto. *[music by Carl Maria von Weber on words by Wilhelmine Christiane von Chézy]*

Frou-Frou. A comedy in five acts. New York: F. Rullman at The Theatre Ticket Office, c1880. Bilingual text: English and French. 49p. *[based on Froufrou by Henri Meilhac and Ludovic Halévy]*

Le sphinx. New York: F. Rullman at the Theatre Ticket Office, c1880. Bilingual text: English and French. 29p. *[based on Le sphinx by Octave Feuillet]*

Schwalm, Francis.
Christmas dramatic plays. By Francis Schwalm of Folsom, Sacramento County, California, U. S. A. n.pl.: n.pub., c1882. 32p. *[despite the title, this publication contains only one play, and it is not a Christmas play!)*

The scientific country school

see Wilson, Louise Latham

Scintillate see Denison, Thomas Stewart *in* Friday afternoon series of dialogues

Scipio Africanus. An Ethiopian extravaganza in three scenes. New York: Happy Hours, c1874. 8p. (The Ethiopian drama. no. 90)

Scotland see Flagg, ? Massey, Charles. Massey's exhibition reciter

Scott, W. Atkins.
Cupid in shirt sleeves. A farce comedy in one act. New York: Dramatic Pub. Co., c1899. 18p. (The wizard series)

An L. A. W. rest. A farce in one act. New York: Roxbury Pub. Co., c1899. 14p. (The wizard series)

Scott, Sir Walter, 1771-1832.
The bride of Lammermoor see Lookup, Thomas. A mad match; or, The heartless brother see also Lucia di Lammermoor see also Lucie of Lammermoor see also Lucy of Lammermoor

Guy Mannering see Terry, Daniel *in* The modern standard drama, vol. 10

The heart of Midlothian see Pilgrim, James. Jeanie Deans; or, The heart of Midlothian

Lady of the lake see Cobb, Mary L. Poetical dramas for home and school see also Steele, Silas Sexton. Blanche of Devan; or, The death of Roderick Dhu *in his* Collected works. Book of plays see also Thomson, Mortimer Neal

Lochinvar *see* Massey,
Charles. Massey's exhibition
reciter

Rob Roy *see* Pocock, Isaac.
Rob Roy MacGregor; or, Auld
lang syne *in* The modern
standard drama, vol. 11
see also Smith, Harry Bache
see also Smith, Harry Bache.
Rob Roy; or, The thistle
and the rose

The scout of the Philippines
see Dumont, Frank

Scoville, Nesbit Stone.
A country kid. A rural merry
comedy in three acts. New
York: S. French, c1900.
Prompt-book. 62p. (French's
American acting edition.
no. 1)

A scratch race *see* Maguire,
Walter Haynes

The scream-a-donna *see*
Steele, Silas Sexton. Opera
mad; or, The scream-a-donna
in his Collected works.
Book of plays

Scribble, Sam (pseud.)
The king of the beavers.
A new, original, political,
allegorical, burlesque
extravaganza. Montreal:
M. Longmoore, 1865. Prompt-
book with Ms. notes. 20p.

Scribe, Augustin Eugène,
1791-1861.
Adrienne Lecouvreur *see*
Adrienne Lecouvreur *see also*
Schwab, Frederick A.

Bertrand et Raton, ou, L'art
de conspirer *see* The
school for politicians; or,
Non-committal

La dame blanche *see* The
white lady

L'étoile du nord *see*

Kellogg, Clara Louise. The
star of the north

La favorita *see* La favorita *see also* The favorite
see also Révoil, Bénèdict
Henry. La favorite

Fra Diavolo *see* Fra-Diavolo; or, The inn of Terracina

Gustave III, ou Le bal masque
see Rattermann, Heinrich
Armin. Gustavus III; or, The
masked ball

Les Huguenots *see* Kellogg,
Clara Louise. The Huguenots

La lune de Miel *see*
Harrison, Constance Cary. A
Russian honeymoon

Masaniello, ou la muette de
Portici *see* Masaniello
see also La muette; or, The
dumb girl of Portic

Le philtre *see* Weil, Oscar.
Adina; or, The elixir of love

Les premières amours, ou
Les souvenirs d'enfance *see*
Hollenius, Laurence John.
First love

Scribner, Lizzie B.
Beresford benevolent society
see Brewster, Emma E. and
Scribner, Lizzie B.

Scudder, Vida Dutton, 1861-
1954.
Mitsu-yu-nissi; or, The
Japanese wedding. Chicago:
T. S. Denison, c1887. 20p.
(Denison's specialties)
(Young's standard series of
plays) *[joint author: F. M.
Brooks]*

The sculptor's daughter *see*
Cannon, Charles James.
Collected works. Dramas

The sculptor's triumph *see*
Baker, George Melville

A sea-change; or, Love's
stowaway *see* Howells,
William Dean

Sea drift *see* Houston,
Harry

The sea liberty's emblem
see Massey, Charles *in*
Massey's exhibition reciter

The sea of ice; or, A thirst
for gold, and the wild
flower of Mexico. A romantic drama in five tableaux.
New York: S. French, 18-?
40p. (French's American
drama. The acting edition.
no. 30)

A sea of troubles *see* Baker,
George Melville

Sea serpent vs. mermaid *see*
Denison, Thomas Stewart
in his Wide awake dia-
logues

Seaman, Abel (pseud.) *see*
Chase, Frank Eugene

The seance *see* Denison,
Thomas Stewart *in his* Wide
awake dialogues

Search for a wardrobe *see*
Heywood, Delia A. *in her*
Choice dialogues. no. 1

Seawell, J.
Volentia. A play in five
acts. Mobile: Farrow &
Dennett, 1859. 93p.

Sebastian *see* Rose, G. B.

Sebastian; or, The Roman
martyr *see* McGee,
Thomas D'Arcy

Second, Albéric, 1817-1887.
[A mysterious kiss] *see*
A., N. A mysterious kiss

Second floor, Spoopendyke *see*
Furniss, Grace Livingston

Second sight; or, Your fortune
for a dollar *see* Herbert,
Bernard

The secret *see* Sadlier,
Mary Anne Madden

The secret; or, The hole in the
wall. A farce in one act.
New York, London: S. French,
185-? 22p. (French's minor
drama. no. 17)

The secret order of the Confrierie *see* Jones, Joseph
Stephens. The carpenter and
his apprentice; or, The
secret order of the Con-
frierie *in* Steele, Silas
Sexton. Collected works.
Book of plays

Secret Service *see* Gillette,
William Hooker. An American
drama arranged in four acts
and entitled *Secret service*
[Readex also enters this
play under its title, Secret
service; the two editions
are identical]

The secretary *see* Denison,
Thomas Stewart *in his*
Friday afternoon series of
dialogues

Sedgwick, Alfred B.
The big banana. A comical
musical sketch. New York:
Happy Hours, 1875. 5, 3p.
Libretto and vocal score.
(The variety stage. no. 1)
[music by the author]

The charge of the hash
brigade *see* Skelly,
Joseph P.

Circumstances alter cases.
Comic operetta. (From the
French of Tourte.) New York:

Robert M. De Witt, 1876.
Vocal score. 33p. (De Witt's
acting plays. no. 205)
*[based on the French of
François Tourte; music
composed by the author]*

The decree of divorce.
A musical sketch. New York:
Happy Hours, 1875. 16p.
Libretto and vocal score.
(The variety stage. no. 18)
*[music composed by the
author]*

Estranged. An operetta in
one act. (Adapted from
Charles Sears Lancaster's
comedietta Advice to
husbands. Music selected
from the finest melodies
in Verdi's celebrated opera,
"Il travatore [sic]") New
York: R. M. De Witt, 1876.
Vocal score. 30p. (De Witt's
acting plays. no. 200)

Gambrinus, king of lager
beer *see* Dumont, Frank

I love your wife. A musical
sketch. New York: Happy
Hours, 1875. 15p. (The
variety stage. no. 16)
*[music composed by the
author]*

The law allows it. A musical
monologue. New York: Happy
Hours, 1875. 5, 3p. (The
variety stage. no. 4)
*[music composed by the
author]*

Leap year. Musical duality.
Music selected and adapted
from Offenbach's celebrated
opera, Geneviève de Brabant.
New York: Robert M. De
Witt, 1875. Vocal score.
15p. (De Witt's acting
plays. no. 189)

Let those laugh who win.
A musical sketch. New York:
Happy Hours, 1875. 10p.
(The variety stage. no. 19)

A mad astronomer. A musical
sketch. New York: Happy
Hours, c1875. Libretto. 9p.
(The variety stage. no. 14)
*[music composed by the
author]*

Molly Moriarty. An Irish
musical sketch. Chicago:
Dramatic Pub. Co., c1876.
Libretto. 9p. *[music composed
by the author]*

My walking photograph. Musical
duality in one act. Music
selected and arranged...from
Le Cocq's opera "La fille
de Madame Angot." Chicago:
Dramatic Pub. Co., c1876.
Libretto. 26p.

The queerest courtship. Comic
operetta in one act. Music
selected and arranged from
Offenbach's celebrated opera
"La princesse de Trébizonde."
New York: Robert M. De Witt,
1876. Vocal score. 31p. (De
Witt's acting plays. no. 196)

A single married man. Comic
operetta in one act. Music
selected from the most popular melodies in Offenbach's
celebrated opera bouffe,
"Madame l'archiduc." New
York: De Witt, c1883. Vocal
score. 43p.

Sold again and got the money.
Comic operetta. New York:
Robert M. De Witt, 1876.
Vocal score. 27p. (De Witt's
acting plays. no. 207)
*[music composed by the
author]*

The spelling match. A comic
musical duality. New York:
Happy Hours, c1875. Libretto.
4, 4p. (The variety stage.
no. 6) *[Readex makes a typographical error by ascribing
this work to Alfred W. instead of Alfred B. Sedgwick]*

There's millions in it. A

musical and dramatic sketch.
New York: Happy Hours,
c1875. 7, 3p. (The acting
drama. no. 162)(The variety
stage) *[music composed by
the author]*

Tootle, tootle, too; or, The
Frenchman and his pupil.
A musical sketch. New York:
Happy Hours, 1875. 5, 5p.
(The variety stage. no. 8)
*[music composed by the
author]*

The twin sisters. Comic
operetta in one act. Music
selected from the most
popular numbers in Le Cocq's
...''Giroflé-Girofla.'' New
York: De Witt, c1876. 36p.
Libretto.

Sedgwick, Alfred W. *[typo-
graphical error by Readex]
see* Sedgwick, Alfred B.
The spelling match

Sedley, William Henry *see*
Smith, William Henry

Seeing Bosting *see* Cutler,
F. L.

Seeing the elephant *see*
Baker, George Melville

Seguin, Arthur Edward Sheldon,
1809-1852.
Marie; or, The daughter of
the regiment. A comic opera
in two acts. (From the French
of A. Jaëll.) Boston: White
& Potter, 1850. 34p. *[music
by Gaetano Donizetti on
libretto La fille du regiment by Jules Henri Vernoy
de Saint-Georges and Jean
François Alfred Bayard;
without the music]*

Seguin, Edward *see* Seguin,
Arthur Edward Sheldon

Seitz, B. Frank.

Effervescing. A comedy in
four acts. Newville, Pa.:
n.pub., 1896. 68p.

The Seldarte craze *see*
Baker, George Melville *see
also* Baker, George Melville.
Forty minutes with a crank;
or, The Seldarte craze

The select school *see*
Stanton, F. J.

Self *see* Bateman, Mrs.
Sidney Frances Cowell

The self-exiled patriot *see*
Phillips, Jonas B. Camillus;
or, The self-exiled patriot

Sells, Mrs. S. E. *see*
S., E. S.

Semiramis. New York: Houel &
Macoy, 1845. Bilingual text:
English and Italian. 60/61p.
Libretto. *[music by Gioac-
chino Rossini on libretto by
Gaetano Rossi; without the
music]*

The senator *see* Lloyd,
David Demarest and Rosenfeld,
Sydney

Señor Valiente *see* Miles,
George Henry

Señor Valiente; or, The
soldier of Chapultepec *see*
Miles, George Henry

A sensation at last *see*
Beadle's...dialogues no. 2

The separation of Jeremiah and
Seraphena *see* McBride, H.
Elliott *in his* Latest
dialogues

The serenade *see* Smith,
Harry Bache *see also*
White, Charles

The serenade party; or, The
miser's troubles *see*
Dumont, Frank

The sergeant's wife. A drama
in two acts. Boston: William
V. Spencer, 1855. 29p。
(Spencer's Boston theatre。
no. 19)

The serious family *see*
Barnett, Morris *in* The
modern standard drama,
vol. 10

A serious flirtation *see*
Mettenheimer, H. J.

Serrano, Thomas K.
Between two fires. A comedy
drama in three acts。 New
York: Dick & Fitzgerald,
c1888. 50p.

Saved from the wreck。 A
drama in three acts。 New
York: Dick & Fitzgerald,
c1888. 48p.

Sertrew, Saul.
Awful girls; or, Big results.
Comedy farce in one act.
New York: A。 J. Fisher,
c1879. Title-page lacking.
24p. (The variety stage.
no. 13)

The bachelor's prize. Comic
sketch for two characters.
New York: A. J. Fisher,
c1879. 4p。

Servants by legacy *see*
Pilgrim, James

Servants vs. master; or, A
father's will *see* Martin,
W. H.

Served him right *see* Denton,
Clara Janetta Fort. When
the lessons are over

The set of turquoise *see*
Aldrich, Thomas Bailey

Seth Greenback *see* Denison,
Thomas Stewart

The seven ages *see* Baker,
George Melville

The seven conversations of
dear Jones and Baby Van
Rensselaer *see* Matthews,
Brander and Bunner, Henry
Cuyler

The seven dwarfs; or, Harlequin
in the world of wonders *see*
Foster, Joseph C.

The seven old ladies of Lavender Town *see* Bunner,
Henry Cuyler *see also in*
his Three operettas

The seven princesses *see*
Hovey, Richard *in his* The
plays of Maurice Maeterlinck
[First series] *see also*
Porter, Charlotte Endymion
and Clarke, Helen Archibald

7-20-8; or, Casting a boomerang
see Daly, Augustin

Seven years of a soldier's life
see Howe, J. Burdette. The
British slave; or, Seven
years of a soldier's life

A sewing circle of the period
see Buxton, Ida M.

The sewing machine agents *see*
Dumont, Frank. Unlimited
cheek; or, The sewing machine
agents

Seymour, Charles W。
Home, sweet home. A grim
farce in three acts。 New
York: For the author by
Flockhart, Hooper, 1879. 70p。

Seymour, Harry, 1819?-1883.
Aunt Dinah's pledge. A tem-
perance drama in two acts.
New York: Happy Hours,

18-? New edition. 19p.
(The acting drama. no. 57)

The temperance doctor. A
moral drama in two acts.
New York: S. French, 18-?
24p. (French's standard
drama. no. 356)

Sforza see Heywood, Joseph
Converse

Shackell, G.
Chops. An Ethiopian farce
in one act. Clyde, O.:
Ames, 1886. 10p. (Ames'
series of standard and
minor drama. no. 214)

Shades of Shakespeare's women
see West, A. Laurie

Shadow castle see Felch,
William Farrand

The shadow of the law see
Fulton, Harry Clifford.
Jean Valjean; or, The shadow
of the law

The shadow worshiper see
Benedict, Frank Lee

The Shah's bride see Brunswick, Herman. Amina; or,
The Shah's bride

The Shaker lovers see
Johnson, Samuel D.

Shakespeare, William, 1564-
1616.
Antony and Cleopatra see
Sothern, Edward Hugh

As you like it see Daly,
Augustin see also The
modern standard drama,
vol. 9

The comedy of errors see
The comedy of errors

Coriolanus see Coriolanus
see also Ludlow, Noah
Miller

Hamlet see Batchelder,
Samuel Francis. Hamlet; or,
The sport, the spook, and
the spinster see also
Booth, Edwin. The Shake-
spearean plays of Edwin
Booth see also Gay, Walter
see also Griffin, George
W. H. Hamlet the dainty see
also Hamlet see also
Hamlet, Prince of Denmark
see also Hinton, Henry L.
Shakespeare's...Hamlet see
also The modern standard
drama, vol. 3 see also
Rice, George Edward. An old
play in a new garb. Hamlet,
Prince of Denmark see also
Rush, James see also
Soule, Charles Carroll.
Hamlet revamped

Hamlet (ghost scene) see
Dramatic leaflets

Henry IV, Part I see The
modern standard drama, vol.
10

Henry IV (boasting scene)
see Falstaff's boasting in
Dramatic leaflets

Henry V see Mansfield,
Richard see also Perine,
Charles E.

Henry VIII see Booth,
Edwin. The Shakespearean
plays of Edwin Booth see
also The modern standard
drama, vol. 10

Julius Caesar see Booth,
Edwin. The Shakespearean
plays of Edwin Booth see
also The modern standard
drama, vol. 11 see also
Shakespeare's...Julius
Caesar

Julius Caesar (scene) see
The two Romans in Beadle's
...dialogues no. 2

King John see The modern
standard drama, vol. 5

King Lear *see* Booth,
Edwin. The Shakespearean
plays of Edwin Booth *see
also* Forrest, Edwin *see
also* Mayo, Frank *see also*
The modern standard drama,
vol. 9 *see also* Shake-
speare's King Lear *see also*
Sothern, Edward Hugh

Love's labour's lost *see*
Daly, Augustin

Macbeth *see* Booth, Edwin.
The Shakespearean plays of
Edwin Booth *see also* Hin-
ton, Henry L. Shakespeare's
...Macbeth *see also*
Kelley, Edgar Stillman. The
tragedy of Macbeth *see also*
Mayo, Frank *see also* The
modern standard drama, vol.
7 *see also* Northall,
William Knight. Macbeth
travestie *see also*
Shakespeare's...Macbeth

The merchant of Venice *see*
Baker, George Melville.
The peddler of Very Nice
see also Booth, Edwin. The
Shakespearean plays of Edwin
Booth *see also* Daly,
Augustin *see also* Griffin,
George W. H. Shylock *see
also* Hinton, Henry L. *see
also* The modern standard
drama, vol. 8 *see also*
The (old clothes) merchant
of Venice; or, The young
judge and old jewry

The merchant of Venice
(scene) *see* Shylock, the
Jew; or, The pound of
flesh *in* Steele, Silas
Sexton. Collected works.
Book of plays

The merchant of Venice
(fourth act) *see* Dramatic
leaflets

The merry wives of Windsor
see Daly, Augustin

A midsummer night's dream

see Daly, Augustin *see also*
A midsummer night's dream

Much ado about nothing *see*
Booth, Edwin. The Shakespear-
ean plays of Edwin Booth *see
also* Daly, Augustin *see also*
The modern standard drama,
vol. 7 *see also* Wallack,
Lester *see also* Warren,
Leslie

Othello *see* Booth, Edwin.
The Shakespearean plays of
Edwin Booth *see also*
Forrest, Edwin *see also*
Griffin, George W. H. *see
also* Hinton, Henry L.
Shakespeare's...Othello the
Moor of Venice *see also*
The modern standard drama,
vol. 3 *see also* Othello.
As performed by Salvini *see
also* Othello. As performed
by Salvini and Booth *see
also* Othello. As played at
the Park Theatre

Richard II *see* Booth,
Edwin. The Shakespearean
plays of Edwin Booth

Richard III *see* Booth,
Edwin. The Shakespearean
plays of Edwin Booth *see
also* Hinton, Henry L. King
Richard III *see also*
Mansfield, Richard *see
also* The modern standard
drama, vol. 2

Romeo and Juliet *see* Baker,
George Melville. Capuletta;
or, Romeo and Juliet restored
see also Cornell, John Henry
see also Hinton, Henry L.
see also The modern standard
drama, vol. 6 *see also*
Romeo and Juliet *see also*
Soule, Charles Carroll. A
new travesty on Romeo and
Juliet *see also* Williams,
Frederick

Romeo and Juliet (balcony
scene) *see* Dramatic
leaflets

The taming of the shrew
see Bangs, John Kendrick.
Katharine see also Booth,
Edwin. The Shakespearean
plays of Edwin Booth.
Katherine and Petruchio
see also Daly, Augustin

The tempest see Barry,
Thomas see also Daly,
Augustin

Twelfth night; or, What
you will see Daly,
Augustin see also The
modern standard drama,
vol. 8

The two gentlemen of Verona
see Daly, Augustin see
also The modern standard
drama, vol. 4

The Shakespeare water-cure.
By "The Larks." New York:
Dick & Fitzgerald, c1897.
42p. [earlier copyright:
1883]

The Shakespeare wooing. A
play of shreds and patches
see Taylor, M. M.

The Shakespearean plays of
Edwin Booth see Booth,
Edwin

Shakespeare's dream see
Hartmann, Theodore. The
Christmas fairies; or,
Shakespeare's dream see
also Leighton, William

Shakespeare's...Julius Caesar.
New York: Henry L. Hinton,
187-? (As performed by
Lawrence Barrett.) 20p.

Shakespeare's...King Lear.
New York: n.pub., 188-?
Bilingual text: English
and Italian. 55p.

Shakespeare's...Macbeth. New
York: Sanford, Harroun, 1866.

Bilingual text: English and
Italian. 36p.

A Shakespearian conference
see Phelps, Pauline

Shaler, Nathaniel Southgate
see S., N. S.

Shall our mothers vote? see
Baker, George Melville

The sham doctor see White,
Charles

The sham professor see Cutler, F. L.

Shamus O'Brien see Jessop,
George Henry

Shandy Maguire; or, The bould
boy of the mountain see
Pilgrim, James

Shannon, J. W.
Rip Van Winkle. Grand
romantic opera in three acts.
New York: G. Schirmer, c1882.
Vocal score. 297p. [music
by George Frederick Bristow
on libretto by John Howard
Wainwright, "reconstructed"
by J. W. Shannon, founded
on Rip Van Winkle by Washington Irving]

Shannon boys; or, Mount Shannon
see Burke, James

Shapley, Rufus Edmonds, 1840-
1906.
Under the wheels. A play in
five acts. (Founded on the
novel, "Le drame de la Rue
de la Paix," by A. Beloit.)
Philadelphia: Printed for
the author's private use,
1873. 58p.

Sharswood, William, b.1836.
The betrothed; or, Love in
death. A play in five acts.

Philadelphia: Ashmead &
Evans, 1865. 79p. *[a portion
of one scene in the fourth
act is adapted loosely from
the French of Alphonse Karr]*

A shattered idol *see*
Townsend, Charles

Shaun Aroon *see* Townsend,
Charles

Shaw, J. S. R.
How Sister Paxley got her
child baptized. An Ethiopian
farce in one scene. Clyde,
O.: Ames, 1880. 7p. Last
page mutilated. (Ames'
series of standard and
minor drama. no. 103)

She stoops to conquer. A
comedy in five acts. New
York: Robert M. De Witt,
c1876. Libretto. 51p. (De
Witt's acting plays. no.
203) *[by Oliver Goldsmith;
Readex's designation of
"libretto" seems inappropriate
since this is Goldsmith's
play with the single addition
of one song] see also*
Goldsmith, Oliver *in* The
modern standard drama, vol. 10

She wou'd and she wou'd not
see Daly, Augustin

She would be a widow; or,
Butternut's bride *see*
Tees, Levin C.

Sheddan, W. B.
The joke on Squinim. (The
black statue, revised.)
Chicago: T. S. Denison,
c1883. 11p.

Sheil, Richard Lalor, 1791-
1851.
The apostate *see* The
modern standard drama,
vol. 8

Evadue; or, The statue *see*
The modern standard drama,
vol. 7

Shelland, Harry E.
Fun in a school-room. A
farcical sketch in one act.
By Henry E. Shelland. New
York: Dick & Fitzgerald,
c1908. 13p.

The great libel case. A
mock trial. New York: Dick &
Fitzgerald, c1900. 31p.
(Dick's American edition)

Shenandoah *see* Howard,
Bronson

Shenstone society *see* Phelps,
Lavinia Howe *in her* Dramatic stories

Shepard, Thomas Griffin, 1848-
1905.
Penikeese; or, Cuisine and
cupid *see* Buel, David
Hillhouse

The shepherdess of Lourdes;
or, The blind princess *see*
Felix, V. Rev. F.

Sheridan, Richard Brinsley
Butler, 1751-1816.
The critic; or, A tragedy
rehearsed *see* Daly,
Augustin. Rehearsing a
tragedy *see also* The
modern standard drama, vol. 7

The duenna *see* The modern
standard drama, vol. 7

The forty thieves *see*
Forty thieves

Pizarro *see* The modern
standard drama, vol. 3

The rivals *see* Jefferson,
Joseph *see also* The modern
standard drama, vol. 4

The rivals (scene) *see*
Dramatic leaflets

The school for scandal
see Daly, Augustin *see*
also The modern standard
drama, vol. 1

The school for scandal
(quarrel scene) *see*
Dramatic leaflets

Sheridan-Fry, Emma.
In far Bohemia *see*
Sutherland, Evelyn Green-
leaf Baker *in her* Col-
lected works. Po' white
trash and other one-act
dramas

Roham the silent *see*
Sutherland, Evelyn Green-
leaf Baker *in her* Col-
lected works. Po' white
trash and other one-act
dramas

Sherlock Holmes *see*
Gillette, William Hooker
and Doyle, Arthur Conan

Sherman, Helen Hoyt.
The lady from Philadelphia.
A farce in one act. Philadelphia: Penn Pub. Co.,
1912. 16p. *[earlier copyright: 1896]*

Sherman, Robert [supposed
author]
My friend from Arkansas.
n.p.: n.pub., c1899. Typescript. 18, 15, 16, 13
leaves.

Sherwood, W.
Don Giovanni. New York:
George F. Nesbitt, 1872.
40p. Libretto. *[music by
Mozart on libretto by
Lorenzo da Ponte; without
the music]*

Shettel, James.
A coincidence. An Ethiopian
farce in one act. By Shettel
and George. Clyde, O.: Ames,
c1893. 7p. (Ames' series of

standard and minor drama.
no. 325) *[joint author:
Wadsworth M. George]*

A matchmaking father; or,
The bashful suitor. A farce
in one act. Clyde, O.: Ames,
c1892. 7p. (Ames' series of
standard and minor drama.
no. 313) *[joint author:
Wadsworth M. George]*

Nanka's leap year venture;
or, How she settled her bills.
A comedietta in one act.
Clyde, O.: Ames, 1891. 17p.
(Ames' series of standard
and minor drama. no. 296)
*[joint author: Wadsworth M.
George]*

Pomp Green's snakes. An
Ethiopian farce in one act.
Clyde, O.: Ames, 1891. 10p.
(Ames' series of standard
and minor drama. no. 297)
*[joint author: Wadsworth M.
George]*

Shields, Charles Woodruff,
1825-1904.
The reformer of Geneva. An
historical drama. New York:
G. P. Putnam's Sons, 1898.
125p.

Shields, Lottie.
Kate's infatuation. A comedy
in one act for young ladies.
New York: Dramatic Pub. Co.,
c1899. 16p. (The wizard
series)

When the cat's away. A comedy
in one act for young ladies.
Chicago and New York: Dramatic Pub. Co., c1890. 14p.
(Sergel's acting drama.
no. 454)

Shields, Sarah Annie Frost,
fl.1859-1889.
Aladdin; or, The wonderful
lamp. A fairy tale drama for
the little folks. New York:
Dick & Fitzgerald, 1899. 16p.

All's well that ends well.
A petite comedy in one act.
New York: Dick & Fitzgerald,
n.d. 17p. (Dick's American
edition)

Blue Beard. A melodramatic
travesty. New York: Dick &
Fitzgerald, n.d. 13p. (Dick's
American edition)

Bolts and bars. A comedy in
one act. New York: Dick &
Fitzgerald, n.d. 28p.
(Dick's American edition)

Parlor charades and proverbs.
Philadelphia: J. B. Lippincott, 1859. 262p.
    Matrimony.--Misfortune.--
Stage struck.--Marplot.--
Mad-cap.--Inconstant.--
Domestic.--Purse-proud.--
Bridegroom.--Mistake.--
Charades in tableaux vivants:
Falsehood.--Penitent.--
Mendicant.--Novice.--Washing-
ton.--Knighthood.--Mischief.
--Proverbs in tableaux: When
the cat's away, the mice will
play.--There's no rose without a thorn.--Killing two
birds with one stone.--It
is no use to cry over spilt
milk.--Listeners hear no
good of themselves.--Do not
trifle with edge tools.--
Charity begins at home [end
of proverbs in tableaux].--
Faint heart never won fair
lady.--There's many a slip
'twixt the cup and the lip.
--When poverty comes in at
the door, love flies out at
the window.--All that
glitters is not gold.--The
heyden.

The train to Mauro. An
original interlude in one
act. By S. A. Frost (pseud.)
New York: Dick & Fitzgerald,
c1870. 9p.

The ship comes in *see* Fuller,

Henry Blake *in his* Collected works

Shipman, Louis Evan, 1869-1933.
D'Arcy of the guards; or,
The fortunes of war. A comedy
in four acts. Berkeley:
n.pub., 1898. Typescript,
prompt-book with Ms. notes.
26, 33, 24, 23 leaves.

On parole. An original comedy
in four acts. n.p.: n.pub.,
19-? Typescript, prompt-book
with Ms. notes. 32, 40, 32,
24 leaves.

The shipwrecked strangers; or,
Wanted and not wanted *see*
The temperance school dia-
logues

Shirley, James, 1596-1666.
The traitor *see* Sheil,
Richard Lalor. Evadue; or,
The statue *in* The modern
standard drama, vol. 7

Shoemaker, Dora Adèle.
A fighting chance; or, For
the blue or the gray. A play
in three acts for female
characters. Boston: W. H.
Baker, 1900. 46p. (Baker's
edition of plays)

The shoemaker of Toulouse; or,
The avenger of humble life
see Hill, Frederic Stanhope

A shoemaker's troubles *see*
McBride, H. Elliott *in*
New dialogues

Shooting stars; or, The battle
of the comets *see* Woodworth,
Samuel

Shore Acres *see* Herne, James
A.

Short comedies for amateur
players *see* Harrison,
Constance Cary

A shot from the kitchen
range *see* Echols, Walter
Jarrell. The general manager;
or, A shot from the kitchen
range

The shot in the dark *see*
Hanshew, Thomas W. Will-o'-
the-wisp; or, The shot in
the dark

The show at Wilkins' Hall; or,
A leaf from the life of
Maria Jane *see* Wilson,
Bertha M.

The showman's ward *see*
Fraser, John Arthur

A shrewd guess *see* Heywood,
Delia A. *in her* Choice
dialogues. no. 1

Shylock *see* Griffin, George
W. H.

Shylock, the Jew; or, The
pound of flesh *see* Shakespeare, William. The mer-
chant of Venice (scene) *in*
Steele, Silas Sexton. Collected works. Book of plays

Siamese twins *see* White,
Charles

Siberia *see* Campbell,
Bartley Theodore

Sibyl *see* Gildenhaus,
Charles *in his* Plays

The sick doll *see* Keatinge,
Ella *in her* Short plays
for children *see also*
Merriman, Effie Woodward
see also in her Comedies
for children

Sickly sentimentalism *see*
Heywood, Delia A. *in her*
Choice dialogues. no. 1

Sidney Lear *see* Wright,
Caleb Earl

The siege of Babylon *see*
Leavitt, John McDowell

The siege of Berwick *see*
Townsend, Eliza. The wife of
Seaton; or, The siege of
Berwick

The siege of Detroit *see*
Macomb, Alexander. Pontiac;
or, The siege of Detroit

The siege of Syracuse *see*
Leahy, William Augustine

Siegfried, W. A.
Phyllis, the beggar girl.
A romantic melo-drama in
three acts. Clyde, O.: Ames,
1890. 11p. (Ames' series of
standard and minor drama.
no. 5)

Tom Blossom; or, The spider's
web. A romantic drama in
a prologue and four acts.
Clyde, O.: Ames, 1891. 19p.
(Ames' series of standard
and minor drama. no. 293)

Siegfried *see* Jameson,
Frederick

The sightless *see* Porter,
Charlotte Endymion and
Clarke, Helen Archibald

Signing an actor *see* Ward,
Lew

Signing the Declaration of
Independence; or, Scenes in
Congress, July 4th, 1776 *see*
Howe, C. E. B.

Signing the pledge *see*
Dramatic leaflets

Signor Marc *see* Wilkins,
John H.

Silence in the ranks. A comedy
in one act. (From the French
of E. D'Hervilly.) By members
of the Bellevue Dramatic Club

of Newport. Boston: Walter
H. Baker, 1902. 24p. (Baker's
edition of plays) *[earlier
copyright: 1878; based on
Silence dans les rangs! by
Ernest d'Hervilly]*

The silent system *see*
Matthews, Brander

The silent witness *see*
Heermans, Forbes. Down the
Black Cañon; or, The silent
witness

Silsbee, Alice M.
Jolly Joe's lady minstrels.
Boston: W. H. Baker, c1893.
33p. *[joint author: Mary
Bernard Horne]*
Contents: Jolly Joe's
lady minstrels.--Bells in
the kitchen.

Silver, W. A.
Clouds. An original American
comedy in four acts. By Fred
Marsden [pseud. of W. A.
Silver] New York: R. M.
De Witt, c1873. Prompt-book.
64p.

The Kerry Gow [By Frederick
Marsden, pseud. of W. A.
Silver] Typescript. In four
acts (various pagination)

The silver dollar *see*
Barnard, Charles

The silver head *see* Osborn,
Laughton

The silver lining *see*
McBride, H. Elliott *in his*
New dialogues

The silver slipper *see*
Hubner, Charles William.
Cinderella; or, The silver
slipper

The silver spoon *see* Jones,
Joseph Stevens

Silverstone's wager *see*
Andrews, R. R.

Silvia *see* Silvia and other
dramas

Silvia and other dramas. For
the young. New York: P. M.
Haverty, 1874. 173p. *[Readex
enters another edition of
The sisters of Alhama under
the author, Eugene F. William-
son]*
Contents: Silvia.--Silvia's
jubilee.--Miriam.--Little
Golden-Hair.--The sisters of
Alhama [by Eugene F. William-
son]

Silvia's jubilee *see* Silvia
and other dramas

Simmie (pseud.) *see* Simon,
Ferdinant Peter

Simms, George A.
Pheelim O'Roorke's curse.
An Irish drama in four acts.
Clyde, O.: Ames, 1890. 25p.
(Ames' series of standard
and minor drama. no. 280)

Room 44. An original farce
in one act. Clyde, O.: Ames,
1889. 7p. (Ames' series of
standard and minor drama.
no. 267)

Unjust justice. An original
farce in one act. Clyde, O.:
Ames, 1889. 7p. (Ames' series
of standard and minor drama.
no. 269)

Simms, William Gilmore, 1806-
1870.
Atalantis. A story of the
sea in three parts. New York:
J. & J. Harper, 1832. 80p.

Atalantis; a story of the
sea. Philadelphia: Carey and
Hart, 1848. 72p.

Bertram [From his: Poems,

descriptive, dramatic,
legendary, and contemplative.
New York: Redfield, 1853]
vol.2, p.312-328.

Caius Marius [From his:
Poems, descriptive, dramatic,
legendary, and contemplative.
New York: Redfield, 1853]
vol.2, p.300-311.

The death of Cleopatra [From
his: Poems, descriptive,
dramatic, legendary, and
contemplative. New York:
Refield, 1853] vol.2,
p.329-333.

Norman Maurice; or, The man
of the people. An American
drama in five acts. Richmond:
Jno. R. Thompson, 1851. 31p.

Simon, Ferdinant Peter.
Antony and Hero. By Simmie
(pseud.) New Haven: F. Simon,
1899. 61p.

Simple Silas; or, The detective
from Plunketsville see
Chase, George B.

Simpson see Brownson,
Orestes Augustus

Simpson and Co. see Poole,
John in The modern
standard drama, vol. 8

Sims, George Robert, 1847-1922.
The lights o' London see
Brady, William A.

Sinbad lyrics see Smith,
Harry Bache

The sincere mourner see
Venable, William Henry in
his The school stage

The singing girl see Smith,
Harry Bache

A singing school of ye olden
time see Horne, Mary
Barnard

A single married man see
Sedgwick, Alfred B.

Sir Harry Vane. Drama in five
acts. Boston: Printed, not
published, 1883. 93p.
[Dramatic compositions copyrighted in the United States
gives E. H. Clement as the
author; though the title of
this drama is Sir Harry Vane,
the leading character is Sir
Henry Vane]

Siraudin, Paul, 1813-1883.
Les femmes qui pleurent see
Weeping wives in Harrison,
Constance Cary. Short comedies
for amateur players see also
What tears can do

The sirens and the muses see
Cobb, Mary L. Poetical
dramas for home and school

The sister spirits see
Pervical, James Gates

The sisters of Alhama see
Silvia and other dramas
see also Williamson,
Eugene F.

Sisters of Mercy, Meriden,
Conn. see The grand baby
show

A sister's sacrifice see
Daly, Augustin

Sitting up for husbands to
come home see Denison,
Thomas Stewart in his Wide
awake dialogues

Six cups of chocolate see
Matthews, Edith Virginia
Brander

The six degrees of crime; or,
Wine, women, gambling, theft,
murder and the scaffold see
Hill, Frederick Stanhope

Six to one; or, The scapegrace *see* Mathews, Frances
Aymar

16,000 years ago. An Ethiopian
act in one scene. New York:
Dick & Fitzgerald, 187-?
8p. *[Readex enters another
edition of this play under
the author, Henry Llewellyn
Williams, under the complete
title, Dem good ole times;
or, Sixteen thousand years
ago, q.v.]*

The skeleton in the closet
see Lester, Francis

Skelly, Joseph P., ca.1853-
1895.
The charge of the hash
brigade. Comic Irish musical
sketch. New York: De Witt,
c1876. 15p. (De Witt's
Ethiopian and comic drama.
no. 108) *[includes the music
"arranged for the piano by
Alfred B. Sedgwick"]*

Sketches in India *see* Morton,
Thomas *in* The modern standard drama, vol. 12

Skiff, Frank D.
Ouchilanca; or, The rancher's
fate. A play in three acts.
Cincinnati: T. J. Smith,
1864. 66p. [p.63-66 missing]

Slade, M. B. C.
Lessons from scripture
flowers *see* Dramatic
leaflets

The trees of the Bible *see*
Dramatic leaflets

The slave's strategy *see*
Reeves, George

The sleep walker *see*
White, Charles

The sleeper awakened *see*

Pulsky, Mrs. *in* Follen,
Eliza Lee Cabot. Home dramas
for young people

The sleeping beauty *see*
Dugan, Caro Atherton *in her*
Collected works

The sleeping car *see* Howells,
William Dean

Slick and Skinner; or, The
barber pards *see* Gibson,
Ad. H.

A slippery day *see* White,
Charles

Sloane, A. Baldwin, 1873?-1925.
Jack and the bean-stalk *see*
Barnet, Robert A.

Slocomb, Cora *see* Brazzà-
Savorgnan, Cora Ann Slocomb,
contesa di

Slow beau and fast beau *see*
Denison, Thomas Stewart *in
his* Wide awake dialogues

Small, Willard.
Mrs. Walthrop's bachelors
see Baker, George Melville

Smart, Herbert Durrell.
Mine falls; or, The miller's
daughter (an idyl of Yankee-
land.) A rural comedy drama
in five acts. New York and
London: S. French, c1902.
77p. (French's American
acting edition. no. 2)

The village belle. A romantic
comedy drama in three acts.
New York and London: S.
French, c1900. 59p. (French's
American acting edition.
no. 3)

A smart boy *see* McBride,
H. Elliott *in his* New
dialogues

Smiley, Robert Watt.
What's next? An original
farcical comedy in three
acts. By Bob Watt (pseud.)
New York: Fitzgerald Pub.
Corp., c1895. 55p.

Smith, Adèle Crafton   see
Nomad (pseud.)

Smith, Bessie Blair.
A considerable courtship.
A farce in one act. Philadelphia: Penn Pub. Co.,
1914. 11p. *[earlier
copyright: 1900]*

Smith, Dexter, 1842-1909.
Blanks and prizes. A come-
dietta in one act. Boston:
Walter H. Baker, c1889. 16p.
(Baker's edition of plays)
(Spencer's universal stage.
no. 11)

Boccaccio; or, The Prince
of Palermo. Comic opera in
three acts. Boston: Oliver
Ditson, c1880. Vocal score.
246p. *[music by Franz von
Suppé on libretto Boccaccio
by Camillo Wälzel (pseud.=
F. Zell) and Richard Genée]*

Prince of Palermo; or, The
students of Florence. Comic
opera in three acts adapted
from Suppé's Boccaccio.
Boston: Oliver Ditson, c1800.
30p. Libretto. *[music by
Franz von Suppé on libretto
Boccaccio by Camillo Wälzel
(pseud.=F. Zell) and Richard
Genée; without the music;
the parts of Boccaccio and
Leonetto, and those of all
the Florentine students,
though male, were interpreted
by females in this edition]*

Smith, Edgar McPhail, 1857-
1938.
"Catherine." A burlesque of
the play of the same title.

New York: Rosenfield Stenography and Typewriting,
1899. Typescript, prompt-
book. 19, 15 leaves. *[based
on Catherine by Henri Léon
Émile Lavedan]*

Editha's burglar   see Thomas,
Augustus and Smith, Edgar
McPhail

Hurly burly   see Smith, Harry
Bache and Smith, Edgar McPhail

Onions. A parody on "Carrots."
n.p.: n.pub., 189-? Type-
script. 2, 19 leaves. *[based
on Poil de carotte by Jules
Renard]*

Pousse cafe. A dramatic im-
possibility. New York: n.pub.,
1898. Typescript, prompt-
book. 39 leaves. *[joint
author: Louis De Lange; music
by John Stromberg; without
the music]*

Sapolio. In one act and four
scenes. New York: Rosenfield,
18-? Typescript, prompt-book
with Ms. notes. 11, 4, 11, 23,
13 leaves. *[joint author:
Harry Bache Smith; burlesque
on Sapho by Alphonse Daudet
and Adolphe Belot; New York
Public Library attributes this
play to Edgar Valentine Smith,
not Edgar McPhail Smith]*

"The three musketeers." A
burlesque fragment. n.p.:
n.pub., 189-? Typescript.
20 leaves. *[based on Les
trois mousquetaires by
Alexandre Dumas]*

Travesty upon "Arizona." New
York: Witmark Music Library
and Agency, 1900. Typescript.
2, 14, 1, 26 leaves (pag. by
scene) *[handwritten opposite
the names of the characters
on the copy photographed by
Readex are the names of the
members of the cast, which
included Lillian Russell,*

Fay Templeton, Lou Fields, Jos. Weber, and De Wolf Hopper]

"Trilby." A burlesque of the play of the same title. (From Paul Meredith Potter.) n.p.: n.pub., n.d. Typescript, prompt-book with Ms. notes. 21p. *[a burlesque on Trilby by Paul Meredith Potter, which was based on Trilby by George Louis Palmella Busson Du Maurier]*

"Waffles." A travesty upon "Raffles." New York: Rosenfield Stenography and Typewriting, 189-? Typescript, prompt-book with Ms. notes. 19, 8 leaves (pag. irreg.) *[based on Raffles by Ernest William Hornung]*

Smith, Edgar Valentine.
Sapolio *see* Smith, Edgar McPhail and Smith, Harry Bache

Smith, Elizabeth Oakes Prince, 1806-1893.
Old New York; or, Democracy in 1689. A tragedy in five acts. New York: Stringer & Townsend, 1853. 65p.

Smith, Harry Bache, 1860-1936.
Ali Baba; or, Morgiana and the forty thieves. A spectacular extravaganza in four acts. By Harry B. Smith, Franklyn W. Lee and John Gilbert. n.p.: n.pub., 1892. Typescript. 28, 5, 20, 9, 7, 18 leaves. *[handwritten on copy reproduced by Readex: "music by W. H. Batchelor and others"; the copy photographed by Readex is incomplete, and the missing pages are indicated on the microprint]*

Ali Baba, jr.; or, Morgiana and the forty thieves. A spectacular extravaganza in four acts. n.p.: n.pub., 1892. Typescript. Scenario. 9p. *[handwritten on copy reproduced by Readex: "music by W. H. Batchelor and others"; without the music]*

The ambassador. (Scenario of the play) [By John Halliwell Hobbes] (From the French of *Monsieur de la Palisse* by De Fleurs and De Caillavet.) New York: Rosenfield Typewriting, n.d. Typescript. 19p. *[music by Claude Terrasse; without the music]*

The bells of Bohemia (verses from.) A musical comedy in two acts. New York?: n.pub., 1900. 30p. *[music by Ludwig Engländer on libretto by Harry B. Smith]*

The casino girl. Music by Ludwig Engländer. London: E. Ascherberg, c1900. 140p. *[interpolated music by Harry T. MacConnell and Arthur Nevin, with additional music by Arthur Cyril Gordon Weld and Reginald DeKoven]*

The crystal slipper; or, Prince Prettywitz and little Cinderella. Spectacular burlesque in three acts and fourteen tableaux. By Alfred Thompson and Harry B. Smith. Chicago: Press of "America," 1888. 31p. Libretto. *[music by Fred J. Eustis; without the music]*

Cyrano de Bergerac. Comic opera in three acts. (Music by V. Herbert.) New York: M. Witmark & Sons, 1899. Vocal score. 220p. *[based on Cyrano de Bergerac by Edmond Rostand]*

Don Quixote. A comic opera in three acts founded upon Cervantes' novel. Music by Reginald DeKoven. New York: G. Schirmer, c1890. 198p.

(G. Schirmer's edition。
no. 243)

The fencing master. A comic
opera in three acts. Music
by Reginald DeKoven。 Buffalo:
Baker, Jones, 1892. 74p.
Libretto。 [without the
music]

"The fortune teller." New
York: n.pub。, 1898。 Type-
script, prompt-book。 18p。
Title page lacking。 Libretto。
[music by Victor Herbert;
without the music; shortened
version]

Foxy Quiller。 Comic opera
in three acts. Music by
Reginald DeKoven。 New York
and London: E。 Schuberth,
c1900。 Vocal score. 234p。

The highwayman. Romantic
comic opera in three acts.
Music by R. DeKoven. New
York: T. B. Harms, c1898.
Vocal score. 223p.

Hurly burly. New York:
n。pub., 1898. Typescript,
prompt-book in two acts
(pag. by act。) Libretto。
[joint author: Edgar McPhail
Smith]

The idol's eye。 Comic opera
in three acts. Music by V.
Herbert. New York: E. Schuberth, c1897。 Vocal score。
161p.

Jupiter; or, The cobbler and
the king. Comic opera in two
acts. Music by Julian
Edwards. Cincinnati, New
York, Chicago: John Church,
c1893。 Vocal score. 169p.

The Knickerbockers。 A comic
opera in three acts. Chicago:
n.pub., c1891. 47p. Libretto。
[music by Reginald DeKoven;
without the music]

The Knickerbockers. A comic
opera in three acts. Music

by Reginald DeKoven. New
York: G. Schirmer, c1892.
258p.

The little corporal. A comic
opera in three acts. New
York and London: Breitkopf &
Härtel, c1898. 33p. Libretto。
[music by Ludwig Engländer;
without the music]

Little Robinson Crusoe. A
burlesque in three acts.
n.p。: n.pub., 1895. Type-
script. 76 leaves. [leaf 6
is missing from the copy
reproduced by Readex]

Maid Marian. Comic opera in
three acts. Music by Reginald
DeKoven。 New York and London:
E. Schuberth, c1901。 Vocal
score. 303p.

The mandarin。 A comic opera
in three acts. Music by
Reginald DeKoven. New York?:
n.pub。, c1896。 58p. Libretto.
[without the music]

A pleasaunt comedie of the
life of Will Shakespeare.
Chicago: Dial Journal, 1893。
xxviii, 116p.

Rob Roy. Romantic comic
opera。 Music by R. DeKoven.
New York: G。 Schirmer, c1894.
Vocal score. 311p. [based on
the novel by Sir Walter
Scott]

Rob Roy; or, The thistle and
the rose. An opera in three
acts。 Chicago: Stone and
Kimball, 1894. 197p。 Libretto.
[music by Reginald DeKoven;
without the music; based on
the novel by Sir Walter
Scott entitled Rob Roy]

Robin Hood。 A comic opera
in three acts. Music by
Reginald DeKoven。 New York:
Burr Print。 House, 1896,
c1890. 46p。 Libretto. [with-
out the music]

Rosita; or, Boston and banditti *see* Woodward, Matthew C.

The rounders. A vaudeville in three acts. (From the French.) (Music by L. Engländer.) New York: E. Schuberth, c1899. Vocal score. 154p.

Sapolio *see* Smith, Edgar McPhail and Smith, Harry Bache

The serenade. Comic opera in three acts. (Music by V. Herbert.) New York: E. Schuberth, c1897. Vocal score. 210p.

Sinbad lyrics. Chicago: National Print. and Eng. Co., 1893. 9 leaves. Libretto.

The singing girl. Comic opera in three acts. (Music by V. Herbert.) New York: M. Witmark, c1899. Vocal score. 242p.

The tar and the tartar. A comic opera. (Music by Adam Itzel, Jr.) New York: Hitchcock and McCargo Pub. Co., c1891. Vocal score. 16 leaves.

The three dragoons. Comic opera in three acts. (Music by Reginald DeKoven.) Cincinnati, New York, Chicago, Leipsic: John Church, c1899. Vocal score. 313p.

The tzigane. A Russian comic opera in three acts. (Music by Reginald DeKoven.) New York: Brooklyn Citizen Job Print. Off., c1895. 39p. Libretto.

The viceroy. Comic opera in three acts. (Music by V. Herbert.) New York: M. Witmark & Sons, c1900. Vocal score. 178p.

The wizard of the Nile. (Music by Victor Herbert.) New York: n.pub., 1895. Typescript with Ms. notes. 15p. Libretto. [Prompt-book]

Smith, Hubbard Taylor. A new year's reception. Comic opera in two acts. Washington, D. C.: John F. Ellis, c1886. 44p. Libretto. *[music composed by the author]*

Smith, James Edgar. The scarlet stigma. A drama in four acts. Washington, D. C.: James J. Chapman, 1899. 88p. *[based on The scarlet letter by Nathaniel Hawthorne]*

Smith, John N. Ramanzo, the conscience stricken brigand. New York: For the author, 1840. 74p.

Smith, John Washington, c1815-1877. The quack doctor. A negro farce in one act and one scene. New York: S. French, 1855? 22p. (The Ethiopian drama)

Smith, Lilli Huger. A rank deception. A farce in two acts. Boston: W. H. Baker, c1899. 28p. (Baker's edition of plays)

Smith, Richard Penn, 1799-1854. Caius Marius. A tragedy. Edited with introduction by N. M. Westlake. Philadelphia: University of Pennsylvania Press, 1968. 152p. *[this is the first published edition; it was first presented in Philadelphia on January 12, 1831, with Edwin Forrest]*

Dramatic fragments [From: The miscellaneous works of... By Horace W. Smith, editor. Philadelphia: H. W. Smith,

1856. 326p.] p.17-32, 65-73.
    Contents: The mariner's
tale.--Prologue to the "Red
Rover."--Lines to a favourite actress.--Song of mortality.

Quite correct. A comedy in
two acts. [From: Alexander's
modern acting drama...Phila-
delphia: Carey & Hart, Hogan
& Thompson and W. Marshall,
1835. vol. 2. 277p.] p.117-
155. *[based on Doubts and
fears by Theodore Edward
Hook (first series of Sayings
and doings), which was
originally a French farce,
L'hôtel garni; ou La leçon
singulière by Marc Antoine
Madeleine Desaugiers and
Michel Joseph Gentil de
Chavagnac]*

Smith, S. Decatur, Jr.
    Grandpa. A farce-comedy in
one act. Philadelphia: Penn
Pub. Co., 1912. 15p. *[earlier
copyright: 1900]*

Smith, S. Jennie.
    A free knowledge-ist; or,
Too much for one head. A
comedy in two acts. Chicago:
T. S. Denison, c1893. 12p.
(Amateur series)

Not a man in the house. A
comedy in two acts. Chicago:
T. S. Denison, c1897. 21p.
(Amateur series)

A perplexing situation. A
comedy in two parts. Philadelphia: Penn Pub. Co.,
1916. 19p. *[earlier copyright: 1895]*

Smith, Solomon Franklin, 1801-
1869.
    The hypocrite. A comedy in
three acts. New York: W.
Taylor, 18-? Prompt-book.
44p. (Modern standard drama.
no. 55) *[altered from The*

*hypocrite by Isaac Bicker-
staff, which was based on
The non-juror by Colley
Cibber, itself based on
Le tartuffe by Molière]*

Smith, William Henry, 1806-
1872.
    The drunkard; or, The fallen
saved. A moral domestic drama
in five acts. Boston: Jones's
Pub. House, 1847. 50p.
(Boston museum edition of
American acting drama. no. 1)
*[Sabin (#84781, v.21, p.190)
attributes this play to
either John Pierpont's The
Drunkard or to William Comstock's Rum; or, The first
glass. Sabin additionally
notes that Smith's original
name was Sedley, and a long
note explains the change of
name (#84786, v.21, p.191)]*

The drunkard; or, The fallen
saved. A moral domestic drama
in five acts. New York:
S. French, 1860? Prompt-book.
64p. (French's standard drama.
no. 86) *[see note above]*

The drunkard; or, The fallen
saved *see also* The modern
standard drama, vol. 11

The Smith mystery *see* Wilson,
Louise Latham

Smith, shepherd of the Wissahickon *see* Moore, James

Smithdeal, J. D.
    The mystic midgets' Liliputian
carnival of nations *see*
Bertram, Eugene and Bassett,
Willard

The smoking car *see* Howells,
William Dean

Smucker, Samuel M., 1823-1863.
    The Spanish wife. A play in
five acts. New York: W.
Taylor, 1854. 96p. (The

American drama. no. 1)
*[Wallace indicates that the
author's real name is
Samuel Mosheim Schmucker]*

Snider, Denton Jacques, 1841-
1925.
Clarence. A drama in three
acts. St. Louis: E. F.
Hobart, 1872. 45p.

Snobson's stag party *see*
Tees, Levin C.

Snow Ball, a colored valet
see Emerson, M. Burt

Snow-bound *see* Baker, George
Melville

Snowbound *see* Matthews,
Frances Aymar

The snow-cap sisters *see*
Stuart, Ruth McEnery

The snow-flake *see* Opal
(pseud.) *in her* The cloud
of witnesses

Snowflake and the seven
gnomes *see* Bert, Frederick
W.

Snyder, Charles McCoy, b.1859.
The false prophet *see* Knox,
John Armoy and Snyder,
Charles McCoy

Soane, George, 1790-1860.
Undine; or, The spirit of
the waters *see* Undine;
or, The spirit of the
waters

Social charades *see* Caldor,
M. T.

The social glass; or, Victims
of the bottle *see* Wood-
ward, T. Trask

A social Judas *see* Tees,

Levin C. and Murphy, J.
Shriver

A social outcast *see* Townsend, Charles

The social trust; or, The
spider's web *see* Morris,
Ramsay and Bell, Hillary

The social war of 1900; or,
The conspirators and lovers
see Landis, Simon Mohler

Society acting *see* Dumont,
Frank

The society for doing good, but
saying bad *see* Beadle's...
dialogues no. 2

The society for the suppression
of gossip *see* Denison,
Thomas Stewart *in his*
Friday afternoon series of
dialogues

Society in our modern Athens
see Grant, Robert. The little
tin gods-on-wheels; or,
Society in our modern Athens

Socrates and his wife *see*
Renauld, Charles

A soft black overcoat with a
velvet collar *see* Meyers,
Robert Cornelius V. *in*
Dramatic leaflets

Sogård, Peder Thyge Jesper,
b.1844.
A glove. (From the Norwegian
of Björnstjerne Björnson.)
Boston: Poet-Lore, 1892.
(vol. 4, nos. 1-7) p. 7-13,
70-81, 128-135, 204-212,
254-261, 332-360.

Sold again and got the money
see Sedgwick, Alfred B.

The soldier from Bingen *see*

Norton, Mrs. *in* Massey, Charles. Massey's exhibition reciter

The soldier of Chapultepec *see* Miles, George Henry. Señor Valiente; or, The soldier of Chapultepec

A soldier of fortune *see* Brier, Warren Judson

The soldier of the people; or, The world's deliverer *see* Lookup, Alexander (pseud.?)

Soldiers on their right to vote, and the men they should support *see* Political dialogues. Soldiers on their right to vote, and the men they should support

A soldier's sweetheart *see* Taylor, Frederick W. A Pennsylvania kid; or, A soldier's sweetheart

A soldier's wife's fidelity *see* De Peyster, John Watts. A night with Charles XII of Sweden; or, a soldier's wife's fidelity

The soldier's wife; or, A bride in a barrack room *see* Steele, Silas Sexton *in his* Collected works. Book of plays

Solèra, Temistocle, 1815-1878. Attila *see* Attila

I lombardi alla prima crociata *see* The Lombards at the first crusade

Solid silver *see* Barnes, William Henry Linow

The solitary of Mount Savage; or, The fate of Charles,

the Bold *see* Payne, John Howard

Sollogub, Vladimir Aleksandrovich, 1814-1882. Sa canne et son chapeau *see* His hat and cane

Solomon, Edward, 1853-1895. The maid and the moonshiner *see* Hoyt, Charles Hale

Solon; or, The rebellion of '61 *see* Baker, Delphine P.

Solon Shingle; or, The people's lawyer *see* Jones, Joseph Stevens

Some noted characters *see* Denton, Clara Janetta Fort *in her* From tots to teens

Some talk about poets *see* Halpine, Charles Graham

Something to be thankful for *see* Denton, Clara Janetta Fort. When the lessons are over

The somnambulist. An opera in three acts. As performed... at the Broadway Theatre. New York: Samuel French, 1854. Libretto. 30p. *[music by Vincenzo Bellini on libretto by Felice Romani]* *see also* McBride, H. Elliott *in his* New dialogues

The son of the night *see* Gayler, Charles

The son of the wilderness *see* Anthon, Charles Edward

A son of Thespis *see* Nobles, Milton. The actor; or, A son of Thespis

A song at the castle. A romantic comedy in one act *see*

Sutherland, Evelyn Greenleaf
Baker *in her* Collected
works。 Po' white trash and
other one-act dramas

Song of mortality *see* Smith,
Richard Penn *in his* Dramatic fragments

The song of songs *see*
Daland, William Clinton

Sonneborn, Hilton Burnside.
The wedding trip. A comedy
in two acts。 (From the
German of Benedix。) Chicago:
T. S。 Denison, c1890。 33p。
(The amateur series) *[based
on Die Hochzeitsreise by
Julius Roderich Benedix]*

Who told the lie? A comedy
in one act. (From the
German of Benedix.) Chicago:
T. S. Denison, c1890. 17p.
*[based on Die Lügnerin by
Julius Roderich Benedix]*

The woman hater. A farce in
one act. (From the German of
Benedix.) Chicago: T. S.
Denison, 1890. 16p. *[based
on Der Weiberfeind by Julius
Roderich Benedix]*

Sonnleithner, Joseph von,
1765-1835.
Fidelio, oder die eheliche
Liebe *see* Fidelio; or,
Constancy rewarded

The sons of Godwin *see*
Leighton, William, Jr.

The sons of Usna *see* Chivers,
Thomas Holley

Sophocles, 496?-406 B.C.
Electra *see* Brincklé,
J。 G。 The Electra of
Sophocles

Sophocles *see* Field, Annie
Adams

Sophronisba。。。oh! A comedy in
one act。 By Charles Narrey.
Translated by members of the
Bellevue Dramatic Club of
Newport。 Boston: W。 H。 Baker,
1901。 33p. *[earlier copyright:
1878]*

Sor Teresa; or, Isabella Suarez
see Pray, Isaac Clarke

Sorique, Jean Paul。
Les confrères *see*
Mickle, Isaac. The old North
Tower

Sorosis; or, The onward march
to freedom *see* Busch,
William

Sorrowing Nettie *see* Phelps,
Lavinia Howe *in her*
Dramatic stories

The sorrows of Satan *see*
Creagh, Henry

Sothern, Edward Hugh, 1859-
1933.
Antony and Cleopatra. By
William Shakespeare。 n.p.:
n.pub., n.d. Prompt-book
with Ms. notes. 115p.

The highest bidder *see*
Belasco, David and Sothern,
Edward Hugh

Ingomar the barbarian. A
play in three acts. n.p.:
n.pub., 18-? Prompt-book
with Ms。 notes。 38 leaves。
*[joint author: Julia Mar-
lowe; based on Ingomar the
barbarian by Maria Anne Lacy
Lovell]*

King Lear。 By William
Shakespeare. New York: William
Harris, 189-? Prompt-book in
Ms. 102 unnumbered leaves.

Soule, Charles Carroll, 1842-
1913.
Hamlet revamped. A travesty

without a pun! Modernized and
set to music. St. Louis: G.
I. Jones, 1880. 48p. *[the
music used was from popular
airs of the time]*

A new travesty on Romeo and
Juliet, as presented before
the University Club of St.
Louis, Jan. 16, 1877. St.
Louis: G. I. Jones, 1877.
50p. *[the music used was from
popular airs of the time,
including "Dixie"]*

Soumet, Alexandre, 1788-1845.
Jeanne d'Arc *see* Joan of
Arc

Sousa, John Philip, 1854-1932.
The bride-elect. Comic
opera in three acts. Cin-
cinnati, New York, Chicago:
John Church, c1897. Vocal
score. 255p.

A southern rose *see* Brown,
J. S.

Southworth, Emma Dorothy
Eliza Nevitte, 1819-1899.
The hidden hand *see* Jones,
Robert

Sowing wild oats; or, Uncle
John's private secretary
see Hageman, Maurice

The Spagnoletto *see* Lazarus,
Emma

Spangler, W. H.
New Years in New York; or,
The German baron. An original
comedy in two acts. Clyde,
O.: Ames, c1883. 27p. (Ames'
series of standard and minor
drama. no. 149)

The Spanish and Aztec races
see Cuevas, José de Jesús.
The heart and the sword; or,
The conquerors and conquered;
or, The Spanish and Aztec
races

The Spanish gypsy *see* Eliot,
George *in* Cobb, Mary L.
Poetical dramas for home
and school

The Spanish husband; or, First
and last love *see* Payne,
John Howard

The Spanish martyr *see*
Robertson, John. Riego; or,
The Spanish martyr

The Spanish mission; or, The
member from Nevada *see*
Blood, Henry Ames

The Spanish student *see*
Longfellow, Henry Wadsworth

The Spanish wife *see* Smucker,
Samuel M.

Sparking *see* Williams, Henry
Llewellyn

The sparkling cup *see*
Denison, Thomas Stewart

Sparks, Peter (pseud.)
Upside down. An original
philosophical and mythological comedy, in five acts
with appropriate tableaux.
New Orleans: Printed at
the Commercial Bulletin
Office, 1871. 31p.

The sparrow of Lesbia. A
comedy in one act. (From the
French of Barthet.) New
York: Darcie & Corbyn, 1855.
Bilingual text: French and
English. 22p. (Darcie &
Corbyn's edition of Mlle.
Rachel's plays) *[based on
Le moineau de Lesbie by
Armand Barthet]*

Sparticus to the gladiators
at Capua *see* Kellogg, E.
in Massey, Charles.
Massey's exhibition reciter

Speaking extemporaneous
  speeches *see* McBride,
  H. Elliott *in his* Latest
  dialogues

Speed, Belle Lewis.
  Columbia. Drama in one act
  for 31 females. By Belle
  Tevis [sic, Lewis] Speed.
  New York: Edgar S. Werner,
  1894. 15p. *[compiled and
  arranged principally from
  The vision of Columbus by
  Samuel Rogers and The
  Columbiad by Joel Barlow]*

Speed the plough *see* Morton,
  Thomas *in* The modern
  standard drama, vol. 6

The spellin' skewl; or,
  Friday afternoon at Deestrick
  No. 4 *see* Richards, Bert

The spelling lesson *see*
  Kavanaugh, Mrs. Russell *in*
  her Original dramas,
  dialogues

The spelling match *see*
  Sedgwick, Alfred B.

Spencer, Bella Zilfa, 1840-
  1867.
  The two wives of Lynn. An
  original play in five acts.
  San Francisco: Alta California Print. House, 1866. 42p.

Spencer, Edward, 1834-1883.
  Electric light *see* Hazel-
  ton, William B. and Spencer,
  Edward

  Maternus. A tragedy in five
  acts. Baltimore: J. F.
  Weishampel, Jr., 1876. 89p.

Spencer, John E.
  Out of the shadow *see*
  Vatter, August and Spencer,
  John E.

Spenlow & Jorkins *see* Dia-

logues dramatized from the
works of Charles Dickens

Spenser, Willard, 1852-1933.
  The little tycoon, words of
  the songs and choruses of.
  An original American-Japanese
  comic opera. n.p.: n.pub.,
  c1886. Libretto. 24p. *[music
  composed by the author;
  without the music]*

Le sphinx *see* Schwab,
  Frederick A.

The spider's web *see* Morris,
  Ramsay and Bell, Hillary.
  The social trust; or, The
  spider's web *see also*
  Siegfried, W. A. Tom Blossom;
  or, The spider's web

The spinsters' convention. An
  evening's entertainment in
  one scene. (The original "Old
  maid's convention.) Chicago:
  Dramatic Pub. Co., c1900. 32p.

The spirit of seventy-six; or,
  The coming woman *see* Curtis,
  Ariana Randolph Wormeley

The spirit of the pine *see*
  Tiffany, Esther Brown

The spirit of the waters *see*
  Undine; or, The spirit of
  the waters

The spirit of vengeance *see*
  Nack, James

Spiritual visitors *see*
  Townsend, Frederic

The sport, the spook, and the
  spinster *see* Batchelder,
  Samuel Francis. Hamlet;
  or, The sport, the spook, and
  the spinster

Sport with a sportsman. An
  Ethiopian extravaganza in

one scene. London and New
York: S. French, 18-? Title
page lacking. p.11-24.
*[Readex also enters this
play under Henry Llewellyn
Williams, q.v.]*

Sports on a lark *see* Griffin,
George W. H.

Sprague, Achsa W., 1827-1862.
The poet [From her: The
poet and other poems.
Boston: W. White, 1865]
p.i-xxiii, 1-189.

Spring, Retlaw.
Women's rights. A comedietta
in two acts. New York: Happy
Hours, 18-? 12p. (The
amateur stage. no. 43)

The spy of Atlanta *see* Ames,
A. D. and Bartley, C. G.

The spy of Gettysburg *see*
Townsend, Charles

Squeer's school *see* Dialogues
dramatized from the works of
Charles Dickens

Squier, Mrs. E. G. *see*
Leslie, Miriam Folline Squier

Squire for a day *see* White,
Charles

The squire's daughter *see*
Walker, Will L.

The squirtgun treatment *see*
Richards, Bert. Hallabahoola,
the medicine man; or, The
squirtgun treatment

Stace, Arthur J.
The upstart. A comedy in
three acts. (From the French
of Molière.) Notre Dame,
Ind.: "Ave Maria," 18-? A
new edition. 45p. *[founded
on Le bourgeois gentilhomme
by Molière and arranged for
male characters only]*

Stafford, J. Benson.
"Her trump card." A farce in
one act. New York: n.pub.,
189-? Typescript, promt-book.
25 unnumbered leaves.

Stage struck *see* McBride,
H. Elliott *see also*
Shields, Sarah Annie Frost
in her Parlor charades and
proverbs

Stage struck barber *see*
White, Charles. The stage-
struck couple

The stage struck clerk; or,
The office in an uproar *see*
Steele, Silas Sexton *in his*
Collected works. Book of
plays

The stage-struck couple *see*
White, Charles

The stage-struck darkey. An
interlude in one act. New
York: Harold Roorbach, c1891.
8p.

The stage-struck Yankee *see*
Durivage, Oliver Everett

"Stand by the flag" *see*
Baker, George Melville

Stanford, Charles Villers,
1852-1924.
Shamus O'Brien *see* Jessop,
George Henry

Stanley and his African dwarfs
see Van Wart, F. B. Stanley's dwarfs

Stanley's dwarfs *see* Van
Wart, F. B.

Stanton, F. J.
The select school. An Ethiopian farce in one act. Clyde,
O.: Ames, c1883. 6p. (Ames'
series of standard and minor
drama. no. 122)

Stanton, William J.
King Alfred *see* Van
Rensselaer, Henry and
Stanton, William J.

Staples, H. A.
Joseph in bondage. Buffalo:
Bigelow Bros., 18-? 24p.
Libretto. *[music composed
by J. M. Chadwick; without
the music]*

Stapleton, John.
A bachelor's honeymoon. An
original farce comedy. New
York: n.pub., 1897. Type-
script, prompt-book. 60, 48,
37 leaves.

Star Amaranth--Twenty-ninth
hundred birthday of Homer
see Townsend, Frederic *in
his* Spiritual visitors

The star of Bethlehem *see*
Finn, Sister Mary Paulina
in her Alma mater; or, The
Georgetown Centennial

The star of the north *see*
Kellogg, Clara Louise

The star of union and liberty
see Clark, William Adolphus.
Gen. Grant; or, The star of
union and liberty

Stark, James.
Brutus *see* Payne, John
Howard, Stark, James, and
McCullough, John *in* Booth,
Edwin. The miscellaneous
plays of Edwin Booth

The starring system *see*
Straws; or, The starring
system

The stars and stripes *see*
Marble, Scott

Starting in life *see* A
collection of temperance
dialogues

The statue *see* Sheil, Richard
Lalor. Evadue; or, The
statue *in* The modern
standard drama, vol. 7

Stecker, Tom.
The man Mohammed. A dramatic
character-sketch. Cambridge,
Mass.: Co-operative Press,
1900. 73p.

Stedman, W. Elsworth.
The Confederate spy. A mili-
tary drama in five acts. New
York: S. French, 1887. 51p.
(French's standard drama.
The acting edition. no. 402)

The confidential clerk. A
stirring play in four acts.
New York: T. H. French; S.
French, c1892. 51p. (French's
standard drama. The acting
edition. no. 414)

The midnight charge. A grand
military play in four acts.
New York and London: S.
French, c1892. 56p. (French's
standard drama. The acting
edition. no. 413)

The Yankee detective. A drama
in three acts. Chicago: T. S.
Denison, c1886. 32p. (Amateur
series)

Steed, T. D.
Through snow and sunshine
see Montgomery, T. M. and
Steed, T. D.

Steele, Silas Sexton.
The brazen drum; or, The
Yankee in Poland. A national
drama in two acts. Philadelphia: Turner & Fisher, 186-?
42p. (Turner's dramatic
library. no. 78)

Collected works. Book of
plays. Being a collection of
original, altered, and
selected tragedies, plays,
dramas, comedies, farces,
burlesques, charades, lec-

tures, etc. Philadelphia:
George G. Evans, 1859. 349p.
  Contents: The well of
death; or, The brothers of
Padua *[from The Matricide]*.
--Blanche of Devan; or,
The death of Roderick Dhu
*[dramatized from Scott's
poem The lady of the lake]*.
--Love and madness; or, The
recluse of the mountain.
A romantic play in one act
and one scene *["...conden-
sation of a popular musical
play by Colman the Younger,
the leading subject of which
is taken from the celebrated
Spanish poet, Cervantes"]*.
--The wizard's warning; or,
The warrior's faith. A play
in one scene *[by Thomas
Campbell]*.--The youth of
Argos. A scene in the classical tragedy of Ion. By
T. Noon Talford *[sic,
Talfourd]*.--Shylock, the
Jew; or, The pound of flesh.
In one act and one scene
*[from Shakespeare's Merchant
of Venice]*.--The carpenter
and his apprentice; or, The
secret order of the Con-
frierie. A thrilling episode
of "Initiation" in one act
and one scene *[from J. S.
Jones' Carpenter of Rouen]*.
--The masked ball; or, The
rose-colored domino. A play
in two acts, two scenes,
and two tableaux.--The
orphan boys; or, The poi-
soned draught. A play in
one scene and one act.--
The Yankee tar's return;
or, The boy and the purse.
A play in one act and one
scene.--The youth who never
saw a woman. A farce on one
act and one scene.--The
soldier's wife; or, A bride
in a barrack room. A play of
hearts in one act and one
scene.--The hypochondriac;
or, A cure for the "blues."

A farce in one act and one
scene.--Two families in one
room; or, The boundary line.
A comic play in two acts
and one scene.--A kiss in
the dark. A ludicrous farce
in one act and one scene.--
A conjugal lesson. A comic
play in one act and one
scene *[by H. Danvers]*.--
The country cousin; or, The
rough diamond. A drawing-
room farce in one act and
one scene.--The lawyer,
doctor, soldier and actor;
or, Many minds in a minute.
A play in one act and one
scene.--Fairly taken in. A
comic interlude in one act
and one scene *[by Mrs.
Charles Kemble]*.--The
stranger's kiss; or, Who
speaks first? A drawing-room
farce in one act and one
scene.--Hide and seek; or,
Love in all corners. A
stirring and laughable
interlude in one act and one
scene.--The stage struck
clerk; or, The office in an
uproar. A spirited farce in
one act and one scene.--
The tailor of Tipperary; or,
The Irish lion. A glorious
drawing-room farce in one
act and one scene.--Opera
mad; or, The scream-a-donna.
An extravaganza in one act
and one scene.--The painter's
studio; or, Art and artifice.
A play for portraits and
postures in one act and many
pictures.--The house that
Jack built. A comical and
operatic charade in one act
and one scene.--Christmas
charades, etc.--Advice to
fools in pouring water on a
duck's back.--Apples. An
original negro lecture.
*[note: a series of poems and
monologues have been omitted
from the above contents
listing]*

The crock of gold; or, The toiler's trials [From: Metamora and other plays. By E. R. Page, editor. Princeton: Princeton Univ. Press, 1941. (America's lost plays, vol. 14) 399p.] p.175-233. *[dramatized from the tale of the same name by Martin Farquhar Tupper]*

The lion of the sea. A nautical drama in three acts. n.p.: n.pub., 186-? Promptbook in Ms. 69p.

Steell, Willis, 1866-1941.
The death of the discoverer. Philadelphia: H. Murray, c1892. 89p.

Steiner, Emma Roberto, 1857-1929.
The Viking *see* Clayton, Estelle

Steiner, Olga *see* Schlesinger, Olga Steiner

Stella (pseud.) *see* Lewis, Estelle Anna Blanche Robinson

Stenman, C. A.
Our Jack. A drama in three acts. Clyde, O.: Ames, c1900. 28p. (Ames' series of standard and minor drama. no. 419)

Stephania *see* Story, William Wetmore

Stephens, Robert Neilson, 1867-1906.
"The alderman." New York: For Thomas H. Davis, 1895. Typescript, prompt-book. 24, 25, 11 leaves.

An enemy to the king. San Francisco: Ayres' Copying Bureau, 18-? Typescript, prompt-book. 43, 42, 37, 29 leaves.

Girl wanted. A farce in three acts. n.p.: n.pub., 19-? Title page lacking. Typescript, prompt-book. 30, 32, 14 leaves.

On the Bowery. New York: n.pub., 1895? Title page lacking. Typescript, prompt-book with Ms. notes. 24, 39, 3, 18 leaves.

Stepping down; or, From affluence to poverty *see* McBride, H. Elliott *in his* Latest dialogues

Sterling, Sara Hawkins.
Hamlet's brides *see* Taylor, M. M. The Shakespeare wooing--a play of shreds and patches

Stern, Edwin M.
Hick'ry farm. A comedy-drama of New England life in two acts. Chicago: Dramatic Pub. Co., c1891. 28p. (American acting drama)

Stern, Herman Isidore, 1854-1926. *[Readex enters under H. I. Stern]*
Evelyn Gray; or, The victims of our western Turks. A tragedy in five acts. New York: John B. Alden, 1890. 236p.

Stevens, -----.
Daniel v. Dishcloth *see* Massey, Charles. Massey's exhibition reciter

Stevens, Dana J.
Old Acre folk. A rustic drama in two acts. Boston: W. H. Baker, 1902. 36p. (Baker's edition of plays)

Stevens, David Kilburn, b.1860.
Miladi and the musketeer *see* Barnet, Robert A.

Stevenson, Kate Claxton Cone.
Two orphans. A play in six
acts. New York?: Printed not
published, 187-? 70p. *[based
on Les deux orphelines by
Adolphe Philippe Dennery
and Pierre Étienne Piestre
(pseud.=Eugène Cormon);
Readex has reproduced the
same edition of this play
under three different
entries: N. Hart Jackson,
Kate Claxton Cone Stevenson,
and The two orphans (title
entry)]*

Stevenson, Robert Louis
Balfour, 1850-1894.
The strange case of Dr.
Jekyll and Mr. Hyde *see*
Forepaugh, Luella and
Fish, George F. Dr. Jekyll
and Mr. Hyde; or, A mis-
spent life

Stevenson, Robert Louis
Balfour, The household of
see Bridges, Robert *in his*
Overheard in Arcady

Stewart, Grant, 1866-1929.
A respectful burlesque on
Peter Pan. n.p.: n.pub.,
189-? Typescript, prompt-
book. 15 leaves. *[based on
Sir James Matthew Barrie's
Peter Pan]*

Stewart, J. C. [pseud. for
John Stewart Crossy]
The baby elephant. A negro
sketch in two scenes.
Chicago: Dramatic Pub. Co.,
c1875. 9p.

Eh? What is it? An Ethiopian
sketch. New York: De Witt,
c1871. 7p.

The elopement. An original
farce in three scenes. New
York: De Witt, 1876. 7p.
(De Witt's Ethiopian and
comic drama. no. 98)

Hemmed in. An Ethiopian
sketch. New York: De Witt,
1871. 6p. (De Witt's
Ethiopian and comic drama.
no. 3)

The last of the Mohicans.
An Ethiopian sketch. New
York: De Witt, 1870? 6p.

3, A. M. An original sketch
in two scenes. New York:
De Witt, c1876. 7p.

The three chiefs. An original
sketch in two scenes. New
York: De Witt, c1876. 7p.
(De Witt's Ethiopian and
comic drama. no. 100)

Tricks. An Ethiopian sketch.
Chicago: T. S. Denison, 18-?
8p.

The two black roses. An
Ethiopian sketch. New York:
De Witt, 1871. 7p. (De Witt's
Ethiopian and comic drama.
no. 5)

The wrong man in the right
place. A negro sketch in two
scenes [By John Stewart
Crossy] Chicago: Dramatic
Pub. Co., c1876. 7p.

Stillman, George A.
Life-real. New York: J. C.
Derby, 1855. 137p.

Stinson, J. Frederic Jessup,
1855-1943.
Two passions and a cardinal
virtue. A comedy of two
London Junes [From his:
The sentimental calendar.
By J. S. of Dale. New York:
Charles Scribner's Sons,
1886. 280p.] p.105-156.

A stitch in time saves nine
see Baker, George Melville.
Ignorance is bliss [and] A
stitch in time

Stobitzer, Heinrich, b.1856.

[Love on crutches] *see*
Daly, Augustin

Stockade *see* Denison, Thomas
Stewart *in his* Friday
afternoon series of dialogues

Stocks up! Stocks down! A duo-
logue in one scene. Chicago:
Dramatic Pub. Co., 19-? 6p.
(Comic drama. no. 121)
*[Readex also enters this
play under Henry Llewellyn
Williams, q.v.]*

Stockton, Frank Richard,
1834-1902.
The lady or the tiger? *see*
Rosenfeld, Sydney

Stockton, Frank Richard, The
household of *see* Bridges,
Robert *in his* Overheard
in Arcady

Stoddard, Lorimer, 1864-1901.
In the palace of the king.
A dramatization in four
acts. (From the novel by
F. Marion Crawford.) New
York: n.pub., 1900. Type-
script, prompt-book, interleaved. Act IV lacking (pag.
irreg.) *[though there is
much similarity, this is a
different play from that of
the same title by Paul
Kester]*

Stoepel, Robert August, 1821-
1887.
The false prophet *see*
Knox, John Armoy and Snyder,
Charles McCoy

Nordeck *see* Mayo, Frank
and Wilson, John G.

The stolen cat *see* Merriman,
Effie Woodward *see also her*
Comedies for children

The stolen child; or, A New
Hampshire man in Boston

see McBride, H. Elliott

Stolen dispatches *see* Brown,
S. J. In the enemy's camp;
or, Stolen dispatches

Stolen pocketbook *see*
Denison, Thomas Stewart *in
his* Wide awake dialogues

Stolen sweets *see* Denison,
Thomas Stewart *in his*
Wide awake dialogues

Stolen watermelons *see*
Denison, Thomas Stewart *in
his* Wide awake dialogues

The stolen will *see* Tilden,
Len Ellsworth

Stone, John Augustus, 1801-1834.
The Kentuckian; or, A trip
to New York *see* Paulding,
James Kirke. The lion of the
West

Storming the fort *see* White,
Charles

Story, William Wetmore, 1819-
1895.
Nero. Edinburgh: W. Blackwood and Sons, 1875. viii,
275p.

Stephania. A tragedy in five
acts, with a prologue. Edinburgh: William Blackwood and
Sons, 1875. 109p.

The story of a famous wedding.
An outline sketch for music
and dancing *see* Sutherland,
Evelyn Greenleaf Baker *in
her* In office hours and
other sketches for vaudeville
or private acting

The story spinner *see* Fuller,
Henry Blake *see* Collected
works

Stout, George L.

Coalheaver's revenge *see*
White, Charles

Rival tenants *see* White,
Charles

Stowe, Harriet Elizabeth
Beecher, 1811-1896.
Christian slave (extracts)
see Follen, Eliza Lee
Cabot. Home dramas for young
people

Dred; a tale of the great
Dismal Swamp *see* Conway,
H. J.

Uncle Tom's cabin *see*
Aikin, George L. *see also*
Townsend, Charles

Strakosch, Moritz, 1825-1887.
Giovanna di Napoli *see*
Watson, Henry C. Giovanna
of Naples

The strange adventures of Jack
and the bean-stalk *see*
Barnet, Robert A. Jack and
the bean-stalk, The strange
adventures of

A strange marriage *see*
LeBrandt, Joseph. My lady
Darrell; or, A strange
marriage

The stranger *see* Kotzebue,
August Friedrich Ferdinand
von *in* The modern standard
drama, vol. 2 *see also*
White, Charles

The stranger within the gates
see Fuller, Henry Blake
in his Collected works

The stranger's kiss; or, Who
speaks first? *see* Steele,
Silas Sexton *in his*
Collected works. Book of
plays

The stranglers of Paris *see*
Belasco, David *see also*

his The heart of Maryland
and other plays

Stratton, George William,
b.1830.
The fairy grotto. An operetta
in four acts. Boston, London:
G. W. Stratton; Chappell,
c1872. Vocal score. 122p.
[music composed by the author]

Laila. Operetta in three
parts. Boston, London: G. W.
Stratton, c1867. Vocal score.
72p. *[music composed by the
author]*

Strauss, Johann, 1825-1899.
Der lustige Krieg *see*
Elson, Louis Charles. The
merry war *see also* Norcross, I. W. The merry war

Das Spitzentuch der Königin
see Elson, Louis Charles.
The queen's lace handkerchief

Strawberry shortcake *see*
Hunter, Wesley J.

A strawman *see* Aborn, Edward

Straws; or, "The starring
system." A grand romantic
antic sketch in one act.
Philadelphia: Turner &
Fisher, 1841. 14p. Title
page lacking. (Fisher's
edition of standard farces)

A streak of luck. An American
comedy in five tableaux.
New York: n.pub., 1879. 48p.
*[adapted from The golden
butterfly by Walter Besant
and James Rice]*

The streets of New York *see*
Williams, Frederick

Streets of New York; or, New
York by gaslight *see*
White, Charles

Strife *see* Dale, Horace C.

The strike; or, Under the
shadow of a crime *see*
Russ, William Ward

Striking oil *see* McBride,
H. Elliott

Stromberg, John.
Pousse cafe *see* Smith,
Edgar McPhail and De Lange,
Louis

Strong, John H.
Ye gods and goddesses; or,
The apple of discord *see*
Robinson, Charles

Struck by lightning *see*
Cutler, F. L.

A struggle for life and
liberty *see* Cornish,
O. W. Foiled; or, A struggle for life and liberty

Stuart, Clinton, 1852-1937.
Our society. A comedy in
three acts. New York: M. M.
Williams, Typewriter, 1886.
Typescript, prompt-book.
56 leaves.

Stuart, Ruth McEnery, 1849-
1917.
The snow-cap sisters. A
burlesque. New York and
London: Harper & Bros.,
1901. 32p. *[earlier copyright: 1897]*

Stubs; or, The fool from
Boston *see* Willard,
Charles O.

The student and his neighbor
see Woodward, N. A. *in*
Dramatic leaflets

The student beggar *see*
Schwab, Emil. The beggar
student

The student prince *see* Hay,
Henry Hanby

The student's frolic *see*
Robinson, T. S.

The students of Florence *see*
Smith, Dexter. Prince of
Palermo; or, The students
of Florence

The stumbling block; or, Why a
deacon gave up his wine *see*
Bradley, Nellie H.

Stupid cupid *see* Rawley,
Bert C.

Stupid servant *see* Dumont,
Frank *in his* The amateur
minstrel *see also* White,
Charles

Suardon, P. (pseud.) *see*
Dole, Nathan Haskell. Friend
Fritz

Sublime and ridiculous *see*
Coes, George H.

The sublime tragedy of the
lost cause *see* Pickett,
A. St. J.

The subrunners of '63-4 *see*
Hildreth, David W. Forced
to the war; or, The sub-
runners of '63-4

A substantial Christmas wish
see Phelps, Lavinia Howe
in her Dramatic stories

Subtleties of jealousy *see*
Rosenfeld, Sydney

A sudden betrothal *see*
McBride, H. Elliott *in his*
Latest dialogues

A sudden shower *see* Daly,
Augustin. Three preludes to
the play

Sudermann, Hermann, 1857-1928.
Johannes *see* Harned, Mary
and Harned, W. H.

Magda *see* Winslow, Charles
Edward Amory

Morituri: Teja *see* Harned,
Mary. Morituri: Teias

Sue *see* Harte, Bret and
Pemberton, Thomas Edgar

The suitors *see* Browne,
Irving

Sullivan, Sir Arthur Seymour,
1842-1909.
H. M. S. Pinafore *see*
Dey, F. Marmaduke. H. M. S.
Plum *see also* Moss,
Alfred. H. M. S. Pinafore;
oder, Das maedle und ihr
sailor Kerl *see also*
Wilkins, W. Henri. S. H. A.
M. Pinafore

Sullivan, Thomas Russell,
1849-1916.
A cigarette from Java.
Comedy in one act. Boston:
Walter H. Baker, 1892. 20p.
(Baker's edition of plays)
*[based on La cigarette by
Henri Meilhac and Charles
Narrey]*

The little duke *see*
Williams, Frederick and
Sullivan, Thomas Russell

Sullivan. ("David Garrick.")
A play in three acts. (From
the French of Duveyrier.)
New York: Seer's Print.
Establishment, 1880. 83p.
*[bilingual text: Italian
and English; Thomas William
Robertson's play David
Garrick was adapted from
Duveyrier's Sullivan]*

Sullivan the slugger. A farce
in one act. (From the
English of M. Williams and
F. C. Burnand.) Boston:
W. H. Baker, c1889. 16p.
(Baker's edition of plays)
[based on Sullivan the

*slugger by Montagu Stephen
Williams and Sir Francis
Cowley Burnand]*

The sulphur bath *see* Dumont,
Frank

Sumichrast, Frederick Caesar
John Martin Samuel Roussy
de, 1845-1933.
Athaliah. A tragedy drawn
from Holy Scripture. (From
the French of Racine.) By
F. C. de Sumichrast. Cam-
bridge: Co-operative Print.
Society, 1897. Bilingual
text: English and French.
xxvii, 189p. *[based on
Athalie by Jean Baptiste
Racine]*

Sunbonnets *see* Campbell,
Marian D.

The sunken bell *see* Harned,
Mary *see also* Meltzer,
Charles Henry

Sunlight; or, The diamond
king *see* Hamilton, George H.

Sunshine follows rain. Comedy
in one act. (From the French
of Girardin.) New York:
F. Rullman, at the Theatre
Ticket Office, c1888. Bilingual text: English and
French. 27p. *[based on La
joie fait peur by Delphine
Gay de Girardin]*

Suppé, Franz von, 1819-1895.
Boccaccio *see* Boccaccio
see also Smith, Dexter
see also Smith, Dexter.
Prince of Palermo; or, The
students of Florence

Fatinitza *see* Barker,
Theodore T. and Baxter,
Sylvester *see also*
Fatinitza

Die schöne Galathea *see*
Day, Willard Gibson. The
lovely Galatea

A supper in Dixie *see*
Triplet, James

Supremacy *see* File,
Franklin and Call, Edward P.

The surgeon of Paris *see*
Jones, Joseph Stevens

The surgeon of Paris; or,
The massacre of St. Bartho-
lomew *see* Jones, Joseph
Stevens

Surprised *see* Denton, Clara
Janetta Fort

"Surrender!" *see* Thomas,
Augustus

Sutherland, Evelyn Greenleaf
Baker, 1855-1908.
At the barricade. An episode
of the Commune of '71. n.p.:
n.pub., 1900? Title page
lacking. p.187-211.

Collected works. Po' white
trash and other one-act
dramas. Chicago: Herbert S.
Stone, 1900. 232p.
Contents: Po' white trash.
--In far Bohemia. Written
in collaboration with Mrs.
Emma Sheridan-Fry.--The end
of the way.--A comedie
Royall.--A bit of instruc-
tion.--A song at the castle.
In collaboration with Percy
Wallace MacKaye.--Rohan the
silent.--At the barricade.--
Galatea of the toy-shop.

In office hours and other
sketches for vaudeville or
private acting. Boston:
Walter H. Baker, 1900. 61p.
Contents: In office hours.
--A quilting party in the
thirties.--In Aunt Chloe's
cabin.--The story of a
famous wedding.

Sutphen, William Gilbert Van
Tassel, 1861-1945.

First aid to the injured. A
farce in one act. New York:
Harper & Bros., c1896. 32p.

In the dark. A society farce.
Chicago: T. S. Denison,
1886. 9p. (The amateur
series)

Swanwick, Catherine.
Eva [and] A tragic poem. In
one scene [From her: Plays
and poems of L. New York:
Delisser & Procter, 1859.
98p.]
Contents: Eva. In one
scene.--A tragic poem. In
three acts. *[Readex also
enters these plays under
Miss L. B. Adams]*

Swayze, Mrs. J. C. *[Kate Lucy
Edwards Swayze]*, 1834-1862.
Ossawattomie Brown; or, The
insurrection at Harper's
Ferry. A drama in three acts.
New York: S. French, 1860?
27p. (French's standard
drama. The acting edition.
no. 226)

Swayze, Kate Lucy Edwards *see*
Swayze, Mrs. J. C.

The sweep and the magistrate
see O'Brien, Constance. Love
in a flue; or, The sweep and
the magistrate

Sweepstakes *see* Arnold,
George? and Cahill, Frank.
Parlor theatricals; or,
Winter evening's entertain-
ment

The Sweet family *see* Felter,
Will D.

The sweet girl graduate *see*
Curzon, Sarah Anne

The sweet marjoram *see* La
marjolaine (The sweet
marjoram)

Sweetbrier; or, The flower
girl of New York *see*
Elwyn, Lizzie May

Sweethearts and wives *see*
Kenney, James *in* The
modern standard drama,
vol. 10

Switched off *see* Elwyn,
Lizzie May

Switzer, Marvin D.
Nip and tuck. Farce in one
act. Clyde, O.: Ames, c1898.
8p. (Ames' series of standard
and minor drama. no. 395)

The sword *see* Follen, Eliza
Lee Cabot. Home dramas for
young people

Sybil *see* Savage, John

Sylvester Daggerwood *see*
Colman, George *in* Massey,
Charles. Massey's exhibition
reciter

Sylvian *see* Mitchell, Langdon Elwyn

Sylvia's soldier *see* Baker,
George Melville

The tables turned *see* Fowle,
William Bentley *in his*
Parlor dramas

Taggs, the waif; or, Uncle
Seth *see* Ward, Lew

The tailor of Tipperary; or,
The Irish lion *see* Steele,
Silas Sexton *in his* Col-
lected works. Book of plays

The tailor's strike *see*
Highest price for old
clothes; or, The tailor's
strike

Taken in and done for *see*

Kemble, Marie Thérèse De
Camp *in* Beadle's...dia-
logues no. 2

Taking the census *see* Buxton,
Ida M. *see also* Denison,
Thomas Stewart *in his*
Friday afternoon series of
dialogues

A tale of a tragical life *see*
Lookup, Thomas. The heart
broken lover; or, A tale of
a tragical life

A tale of treason *see* Breck,
Joseph. West Point; or, A
tale of treason

Talfourd, Thomas Noon, 1795-
1854.
Ion *see* The modern standard
drama, vol. 1

Ion (scene: The youth of
Argos) *see* Steele, Silas
Sexton. Collected works.
Book of plays

The youth of Argos *see*
Steele, Silas Sexton.
Collected works. Book of
plays

Taliesin *see* Hovey, Richard

The talisman *see* Sadlier,
Mary Anne Madden

The talisman; or, The fairy's
favor. A grand fairy spectacle *see* Conway, H. J.

A talk on temperance *see*
McBride, H. Elliott

Talking machine *see* Hockenbery, Frank. Prof. Black's
phunnygraph; or, Talking
machine

Talladay, Jennie.
The little country store. In
one act. Auburn, N. Y.:

Wm. J. Moses, 1894. 36p.

Tally-ho *see* Miller, Joaquin

Tally Rhand (pseud.)
Guttle and Gulpit. A farce
in two acts. New York: W.
Taylor, 1853. 36p. (The
American drama, no. 3)

Tamayo *see* Yellott, George

Taming a butterfly *see* Daly,
Augustin and Wood, Frank

Taming a husband *see*
Pickett, Haskell. The
rake's lesson; or, Taming
a husband

Taming of the shrew *see*
Daly, Augustin *see also*
Shakespeare, William.
Katharine and Petruchio
(The taming of the shrew)
in Booth, Edwin. The
Shakespearean plays of
Edwin Booth

Tammie, Carrie.
The birthday cake. A comedy
in two acts. Chicago:
Dramatic Pub. Co., c1899.
19p. (Sergel's acting
drama, no. 551)

A tangled skein, in three
knots *see* Dyer, Elizabeth

The tangled thread *see*
Phelps, Lavinia Howe *in*
her Dramatic stories

Tan-gó-ru-a. An historical
drama in prose. Philadel-
phia: T. B. Peterson,
1856. 280p. *[Readex also
enters this same play under
H. C. Moorhead, q.v.]*

Tannhäuser *see* Byars,
William Vincent

Tannhäuser and the minstrels

tournament on the Wartburg
see Morgan, Geraldine Woods

The tar and the tartar *see*
Smith, Harry Bache

Tardy, Edwin.
Saved. A temperance sketch
in one act. Clyde, O.: Ames,
18-. 6p. (Ames' series of
standard and minor drama.
no. 59)

Targioni-Tozzetti, Giovanni,
1868-1934.
Cavalleria rusticana *see*
Day, Willard Gibson *see
also* Macy, James Cartwright.
Rustic chivalry (Cavalleria
rusticana) *see also* Tretbar, Helen D. Rustic chivalry

Tarleton *see* Venable, William
Henry *in his* The school
stage

Tartuffe; or, The imposter.
A comedy in five acts. (From
the French of Molière.) New
York: F. Rullman at the
Theatre Ticket Office,
c1888. Bilingual text:
French and English. 43p.

Tassin, Algernon De Vivier,
1869-1941.
A class-day conspiracy. A
comedy in one act. Boston:
Walter H. Baker, c1895. 18p.
(Baker's edition of plays)

Tatters, the pet of Squatters'
Gulch *see* Tees, Levin C.

The tattler *see* Kavanaugh,
Mrs. Russell *in her* Original dramas, dialogues
*["dramatized from a story
which appeared in T. S.
Arthur's popular magazine
in 1863"]*

Taurus-Vertus (pseud.)
Vendetta. A semi-local tra-

gedy. New Orleans: n.pub.,
1870. 30p.

Tayleure, Clifton W., 1830-
1891.
The boy martyrs of Sept. 12,
1814. A local historical
drama in three acts. New
York: French, 1859. 30p.
(French's standard drama.
no. 249)

Horseshoe Robinson; or, The
battle of King's Mountain.
A legendary patriotic drama
in three acts. New York:
S. French, c1858. 40p.
(French's standard drama.
The acting edition. no. 213)

Horseshoe Robinson; or, The
battle of King's Mountain.
London: S. French, c1858.
Prompt-book. 40 leaves.
(French's standard drama.
The acting edition. no. 213)

Won back. A play in four
acts. Chicago: Dramatic
Pub. Co., c1892. 48p.
(Sergel's acting drama)

Taylor, Bayard, 1825-1878.
Collected works. The drama-
tic works of Bayard Taylor.
Boston: Houghton, Mifflin,
1880. 345p.
    Contents: The prophet.--
The masque of the gods.--
Prince Deukalion.

La damnation de Faust *see*
La damnation de Faust

Faust. (From the German of
Goethe.) Boston: Fields,
Osgood, 1871. In two parts.
vol. 1, xviii, 405p.; vol.
2, xvi, 536p.

The masque of the gods.
Boston: James R. Osgood,
1872. 47p.

Prince Deukalion. A lyrical
drama. Boston: Houghton,
Osgood, 1878. 171p.

The prophet. A tragedy.
Boston: J. R. Osgood, 1874.
300p.

Taylor, C. W.
The drunkard's warning. A
temperance drama in three
acts. New York: Happy Hours,
18-? New edition. 41p. (The
acting drama. no. 54)

Taylor, Frederic W.
A Pennsylvania kid; or, A
soldier's sweetheart. A
comedy drama in four acts.
Boston: Walter H. Baker,
c1894. 42p. (Baker's edition
of plays)

Taylor, Howard P., 1838-1916.
Snowflake and the seven
gnomes *see* Bert, Frederick
W.

Taylor, John G.
Paradise lost *see* Taylor,
M. F. and Taylor, John G.

Taylor, M. F.
Paradise lost. A drama from
Milton's great poem. Denver:
Rocky Mountain News Print.
Co., 1878. 27p. *[joint
author: John G. Taylor]*

Taylor, M. M.
The Shakespeare wooing. A
play of shreds and patches
...[bound with] Hamlet's
brides by Sara Hawkins
Sterling. Boston: Walter H.
Baker, 1915. 14, 19p.
(Baker's edition of plays)
    Contents: The Shakespeare
wooing. A play of shreds and
patches taken from the works
of William Shakespeare by
M. M. Taylor. *[earlier copyright: 1892].*--Hamlet's
brides. A Shakespearean burlesque in one act by Sara
Hawkins Sterling. *[earlier
copyright: 1900].*

Taylor, Malcolm Stuart.
Aar-u-ag-oos; or, An east
Indian drug. An entirely
original farce in one act.
Clyde, O.: Ames, c1884.
12p. (Ames' series of
standard and minor drama.
no. 129) *[Readex makes
a typographical error by
entering this particular
work under Malcom Stuart
Taylor]*

The afflicted family; or, A
doctor without a diploma.
A farce comedy in four acts.
By Malcolm Stewart Taylor.
Clyde, O.: Ames, c1883. 46p.
(Title page mutilated)
(Ames' series of standard
and minor drama. no. 124)
*[the title page of this
work gives the author's
middle name as Stewart,
whereas in reality it is
Stuart]*

Auld Robin Gray. An emotional
drama in five acts. Clyde,
O.: Ames, 1881. 53p. (Ames'
series of standard and minor
drama. no. 125) *[from Auld
Robin Gray by Lady Anne
Lindsay Barnard]*

A honeymoon eclipse. A comedy
in one act. New York: H.
Roorbach, c1900. 13p.

Rags and bottles; or, The
two waifs. An original comedy
in two acts. By M. Stewart
[sic, Stuart] Taylor. Clyde,
O.: Ames, c1887. 18p. (Ames'
series of standard and minor
drama. no. 219)

Taylor, Tom, 1817-1880.
The fool's revenge *see*
Booth, Edwin. The miscella-
neous plays of Edwin Booth

Retribution *see* Williams,
Espy William Hendricks. The
husband

Taylor, W. A.
The last witness. An American
drama of politics and society.
Pittsburgh: n.pub., 1878.
55p. *[joint author: W. J.
M'Kee]*

Tea at four o'clock *see*
Harrison, Constance Cary *in*
her Short comedies for
amateur players

The tea party *see* Denison,
Thomas Stewart *in his*
Friday afternoon series of
dialogues *see also* Fowle,
William Bentley *in his*
Parlor dramas *see also*
Heywood, Delia A. *in her*
Choice dialogues. no. 1

A teacher taught *see* Oakes,
A. H. *see also* Oakes, A. H.
in Matthews, Brander.
Comedies for amateur acting

Teacher wanted *see* Crosby,
Frank *in* Dramatic leaflets

Teacups *see* Mathews, Frances
Aymar

The tear *see* Fowle, William
Bentley *in his* Parlor dramas

The tearful and tragical tale
of the tricky troubadour;
or, The truant tracked *see*
Broughall, George

The teasing brothers *see*
Abbott, Jacob *in his*
Orkney the peacemaker; or,
The various ways of settling
disputes

Tecumseh *see* Mair, Charles

Tecumseh and the prophet of
the west *see* Jones,
George

Tecumseh; or, The battle of
the Thames *see* Emmons,
Richard

Tees, Levin C.
Baby coach parade. A sketch.
Chicago: T. S. Denison,
1894. 7p.

Botany Bay. A melodrama in
three acts. Philadelphia:
Penn Pub. Co., 1914. 51p.
[earlier copyright: 1893;
founded on Great expecta-
tions by Charles Dickens]

Hypnotizing a landlord. A
sketch in one scene. Chicago:
Dramatic Pub. Co., c1899.
6p. (The comic drama)

Mrs. Pepper's ghost. An
Ethiopian farce in one
scene. Philadelphia: Penn
Pub. Co., 1916. 8p.
[earlier copyright: 1894]

The new partner. A comedy
drama in three acts. New
York: Dick & Fitzgerald,
c1895. 53p. (Title page
mutilated)

A politican's breakfast
see A row in the kitchen
[bound with] A politician's
breakfast

A red-hot massage. An
Ethiopian farce in one
scene. Philadelphia: Penn
Pub. Co., 1915. 8p. *[earlier*
copyright: 1894]

A rogue's luck; or, A man
of nerve. A farce comedy in
three acts. New York: Dick &
Fitzgerald, c1909. 46p.

A row in the kitchen [bound
with] A politician's breakfast. Chicago: T. S. Denison,
c1894. 9p.

She would be a widow; or,
Butternut's bride. An original farce-comedy in three
acts for laughing purposes

only. New York: Harold
Roorbach, c1897. 49p.

Snobson's stag party. A
farce in one act for male
characters only. New York:
Dick & Fitzgerald, c1899.
23p.

A social Judas. A society
drama in three acts. Philadelphia: Penn Pub. Co.,
1912. 47p. *[earlier copy-*
right: 1896; joint author:
J. Shriver Murphy]

Tatters, the pet of Squatters'
Gulch. A border drama in
three acts. Philadelphia:
Penn Pub. Co., 1912. 38p.
[earlier copyright: 1893]

This paper for sale. A farce
in one act. Philadelphia:
Penn Pub. Co., 1911. 13p.
[earlier copyright: 1895]

Tegner, Esaias, 1782-1846.
[Fridthof's Saga] *see*
Hanson, Carl Fredrik

Teias *see* Harned, Mary.
Morituri: Teias

Telemachus *see* Gildenhaus,
Charles *in his* Plays

Tell-tale *see* Bartlett,
George Bradford *in his*
A dream of the centuries
and other entertainments
for parlor and hall

A tell-tale eyebrow *see*
Tiffany, Esther Brown

Tell tale eyes; or, Daisy and
Don *see* Busch, William

A tell-tale heart *see*
Picton, Thomas

Tell your wife *see* Meyers,
Robert Cornelius V.

Temper *see* Bell, Robert *in* The modern standard drama, vol. 7

The temperance doctor *see* Seymour, Harry

A temperance pcinic with the old woman who lived in a shoe *see* Bradley, Nellie H.

The temperance school dialogues. New York: Henry J. Wehman, c1892. 90p.
Contents: The shipwrecked strangers; or, Wanted and not wanted.--A cure for a bad appetite.--Why don't you drink?--Keeping the cold out.--Eyes and no eyes.--First and last.--The unexpected convert.--The evening party.--Which will you give up?--Two sides: "which are you on?"--The two alphabets: alcohol and water.--Ready answers.--Water or wine?--How to get below par.--To the right or left?--A glass of double X.--The two roads.--Prevention better than cure.

A temperance town *see* Hoyt, Charles

The tempest *see* Barry, Thomas *see also* Daly, Augustin

A tempest in a tea pot *see* Picton, Thomas

Tempest tossed *see* Enéleh, H. B.

Temple, Hope (pseud.) *see* Davies, Dotie

A temporary 'squire *see* McBride, H. Elliott *in his* Latest dialogues

Temporibus hominis Arpinatis *see* Sanford, Myron Reed

Temptation resisted *see* Denison, Thomas Stewart *in his* Friday afternoon series of dialogues

Temptations unveiled *see* Saunders, Charles Henry. Rosina Meadows, the village maid; or, Temptations unveiled

The tempter; or, The sailor's return *see* Baker, George Melville

Ten days in the Tombs *see* Leavitt, Andrew J. and Eagan, H. W.

Ten nights in a bar-room *see* Pratt, William W.

Ten scenes in the life of a lady of fashion *see* Walker, James Barr. Lucilla; ten scenes in the life of a lady of fashion

A $10,000 wager *see* Wood, J. M. G.

Tenants *see* James, Henry

A tender attachment *see* Baker, George Melville

Tennyson, Alfred, 1809-1892. A dream of fair women *see* Winn, Edith Lynwood. A vision of fair women

Enoch Arden *see* Cook, S. N. The wanderer's return

The princess *see* Haughwout, L. May

Tent and throne *see* Wilson, John G.

Teresa Contarini *see* Elliott, Elizabeth Fries Lummis

Terra Mariae *see* Finn,
Sister Mary Paulina. The
Angel's meeting; or, Terra
Mariae *in her* Alma mater;
or, The Georgetown Centennial

Terrasse, Claude, 1867-1923.
The ambassador *see* Smith,
Harry Bache

A terrible threat *see*
Denton, Clara Janetta Fort
in her From tots to teens

Terry, Daniel, c1780-1829.
Guy Mannering; or, The
gipsey's prophecy *see*
The modern standard drama,
vol. 10

A test case; or, Grass versus
granite *see* Daly, Augustin

Testing hearts *see* Cook,
S. N. Uncle Jack; or,
Testing hearts

Tevis, Belle *see* Speed,
Belle Lewis

A Texan mother-in-law *see*
Gibson, Ad. H.

A Texas steer *see* Hoyt,
Charles Hale

Texas steer; or, Money makes
the mare go *see* Hoyt,
Charles Hale

Thacher, John Boyd, 1847-1909.
Charlecote; or, The trial of
William Shakespeare. New
York: Dodd, Mead, 1895. xx,
125p. Plates interleaved.
*[based on Walter Savage
Landor's Citation of
William Shakespeare]*

Thackeray, Thomas James,
1796-1877.
L'Abbaye de Penmarque *see*
Williams, Henry Llewellyn.

Penmark Abbey.

Thackeray, William Makepiece,
1811-1863.
L'Abbaye de Penmarque *see*
Williams, Henry Llewellyn.
Penmark Abbey

Christmas pantomime *see*
Greenough, James Bradstreet.
The rose and the ring

Vanity Fair *see* Mitchell,
Langdon Elwyn. Becky Sharp

Thanksgiving Eve at the
parsonage *see* Orne, Martha
Russell. The donation party;
or, Thanksgiving Eve at the
parsonage

That American woman *see*
Brann, William Cowper

That box of cigarettes *see*
Baum, Rosemary

That boy Sam *see* Cutler,
F. L.

That dorg; or, The old toll
house mystery *see* Coes,
George H.

That guilty pair; or, A
paroxysm of passion *see*
Busch, William

That mysterious bundle *see*
Lambla, Hattie Lena

That nose *see* Woolf, Benjamin
Edward

That other fourth *see* Denton,
Clara Janetta Fort *in her*
From tots to teens

That rascal Pat *see* Grover,
J. Holmes

That Patrick! *see* Tiffany,
Esther Brown

That wife of mine *see*

Leavitt, Andrew J. and
Eagan, H. W.

Thatcher, George, 1846-after
1909.
Gentlemen coon's parade *see*
Gentleman coon's parade

Thaxter, Adam Wallace, 1832-
1864.
The grotto nymph; or, Fairy
favor. A fantastico-musical
morceau of absurdity in one
consecutive act and a tableau. Boston: W. V. Spencer,
1858? 21p. (Spencer's Boston
theatre. no. 187)

Thayendanegea *see* Mackenzie,
J. B.

Thayer, Ella Cheever.
Lords of creation. Woman
suffrage drama in three
acts. Boston: W. H. Baker,
c1883. 39p. (Baker's edition
of plays)

Thayer, Julia M.
Fighting the rum-fiend *see*
Dramatic leaflets

Thayer, William Roscoe, 1859-
1923.
Hesper; an American drama.
Cambridge: Charles W.
Sever, 1888. 107p.

Théaulon de Lambert, Marie
Emmanuel Guillaume Margue-
rite, 1787-1841.
Nanon, Ninon et Maintenon!
see Elson, Louis Charles.
Nanon

Le petit chaperon rouge
see F., W. F. The little
red riding hood

Their first meeting *see*
Merriman, Effie Woodward

Their graduating essays *see*
West, Emma Elise

Thekla, a fairy drama *see*
Toler, Mrs. H. M.

Them papers *see* White,
Charles

Theodosia, the pirate's
prisoner *see* Rhodes,
William Henry

Théophile *see* Greene,
Henry Copley

There is no rose without
thorns *see* Arnold, George
in Arnold, George? and
Cahill, Frank. Parlor
theatricals; or, Winter
evening's entertainment

There's many a slip 'twixt
the cup and the lip *see*
Shields, Sarah Annie Frost
in her Parlor charades and
proverbs

There's millions in it *see*
Sedgwick, Alfred B.

There's no rose without a
thorn *see* Shields, Sarah
Annie Frost *in her* Parlor
charades and proverbs

There's no smoke without a
fire *see* Picton, Thomas

Theseus *see* Crumpton, M.
Nataline

Thiboust, Lambert, 1826-1867.
Les femmes qui pleurent *see*
Weeping wives *in* Harrison,
Constance Cary. Short
comedies for amateur players
see also What tears can do

Thief of time *see* Baker,
George Melville

Thiele, Richard.
Débutantes in the culinary
art; or, A frolic in the

cooking class *see* Allen,
Lucy

Thieves at the mill *see*
White, Charles

The thieving magpie. A semi-
serious opera in two acts.
New York: M. Douglas, 18-?
Bilingual text: English and
Italian. Libretto. 77p.
*[music by Gioacchino Rossini
on libretto La gazza ladra
by Giovanni Gherardini,
based on the French melo-
drama La pie voleuse by
Jean Marie Théodore Baudouin
and Louis Charles Caigniez;
the title page incorrectly
attributes the music to
Donizetti]*

A third party *see* Rosenfeld,
Sydney. Mabel's manoeuvre;
or, A third party

$34.12; a farce *see* Goodwin,
John Cheever

Thirty hours for three thousand
years; or, Heresy and planets
see Kastelic, George Anton

Thirty minutes for refreshments
see Baker, George Melville

A thirst for gold, and the wild
flower of Mexico *see* The
sea of ice; or, A thirst for
gold, and the wild flower of
Mexico

This paper for sale *see*
Tees, Levin C.

This picture and that *see*
Matthews, Brander

The thistle and the rose *see*
Smith, Harry Bache. Rob Roy;
or, The thistle and the
rose

Thomas, Augustus, 1857-1934.

Alabama. A drama in four
acts. New York: n.pub.,
1891? Typescript, prompt-
book (pag. by act)

Alabama. A drama in four
acts. Chicago: Dramatic Pub.
Co., 1905. 148p. *[earlier
copyright: 1898]*

Arizona. A drama in four
acts. Chicago: Dramatic Pub.
Co., c1899. 155p. (Sergel's
acting drama. no. 571) *see
also* Smith, Edgar McPhail.
Travesty upon "Arizona"

The capitol. n.p.: n.pub.,
1895. Typescript. 88 leaves
(pag. irreg.)

Don't tell her husband. New
York: Rosenfield Stenography
and Typewriting, 1897. Title
page lacking. Typescript,
prompt-book with Ms. notes.
38, 56, 35 leaves.

Editha's burglar. A dramatic
sketch in one act. New York:
n.pub., 189-? Typescript,
prompt-book. 19 leaves.
*[joint author: Edgar McPhail
Smith; based on the short
story of the same title by
Frances Hodgson Burnett]*

A man of the world. A new and
original comedietta in one
act. n.p.: n.pub., 1889?
In ms. 29 leaves.

"Surrender!" A comedy of war.
New York?: n.pub., 189-?
Typescript. 32, 39, 30, 32
leaves.

Thomas, Edith Matilda, 1854-
1925.
A New Year's masque [From
her: A New Year's masque and
other poems. Boston: Houghton, Mifflin, 1885. 138p.]
p.1-8.

Thomas, F. J.
Commercial infidelity; or,

Burglar to slow music. A
play in three acts. Detroit:
Free Press Book and Job
Print. House, 1873. 31p.

Thomas, Lewis Foulk, 1808-1868.
Cortez, the conqueror. A
tragedy in five acts.
Washington, D. C.: B. W.
Ferguson, 1857. 73p.

Thomas, Theodore, 1835-1905.
Alceste *see* Alceste

Thomas à Becket *see* Bleckley,
Paul *see also* Hamilton,
Alexander *see also* Hollis-
ter, Gideon Hiram

Thompson, Alfred.
The crystal slipper; or,
Prince Prettywitz and little
Cinderella *see* Smith,
Harry Bache and Thompson,
Alfred

Thompson, Caroline Eunice.
Blind Margaret. A dramatic
sketch. Chicago: T. S.
Denison, c1890. Libretto.
12p. *["music by G. T. Page
(Harvard '92)"; based on
The blind girl of Castèl-
Cuillè by Henry Wadsworth
Longfellow, which is a
translation of Jacques
Jasmin's poem L'aveugle de
Castel-Culier]*

Thompson, Denman, 1833-1911.
The old homestead. New York:
n.pub., 1887. Typescript.
41 leaves. *[joint author:
George W. Ryer]*

Our new minister. New York:
n.pub., 1903. Typescript.
43 leaves. *[an earlier
copyrighted edition appeared
in 1893 under the title Our
new minister, a Yankee comedy
in four acts]*

Thompson, Lewis Sabin, 1868-
1908.

Prince pro tem *see* Barnet,
Robert A.

Thompson, William Tappan,
1812-1882.
Major Jones' courtship; or,
Adventures of a Christmas
Eve. A domestic comedy in two
acts. By Major Jones (pseud.)
Savannah: Edward J. Purse,
1850. 61p.

Thomson, Mortimer Neal, 1831-
1875.
The lady of the lake. A
travestie in one act. New
York: S. French, c1860.
35p. (The minor drama. no.
176) *[a travesty on Sir Walter Scott's The lady of the
lake]*

Thor *see* Day, Richard Edwin

A thorn among the roses *see*
Baker, George Melville

A thoroughbred *see* Woodhull,
Aaron H.

Thorp, Philip.
Young America's dream. A
discoursory interview between
the spirits of liberty,
tyranny and a citizen of the
world. An allegory. New York:
Abbe & Yates, 1854. 32p.

Those awful boys *see* Field,
A. Newton

Those dreadful twins *see*
Parker, Walter Coleman

Those Thompsons *see* MaBride,
H. Elliott *in his* New
dialogues

3, A. M. *see* Stewart, J. C.

Three black Smiths *see*
Williams, Henry Llewellyn

The three brothers; or, Crime

Readex entry, given above, is in error; the author's name as given on the title page is Tidball]

The tie that binds *see* Wells, David Dwight and Cook, Charles Emerson

Tieck, Johann Ludwig, 1773-1853.
Ritter Blaubart *see* Motley, John Lothrop. Bluebeard

Tiffany, Esther Brown, b.1858.
Anita's trial; or, Our girls in camp. A comedy in three acts for female characters. Boston: W. H. Baker, c1889. 42p. (Baker's edition of plays)

Apollo's oracle. An entertainment in one act. Boston: Walter H. Baker, 1897. Libretto. 8p. (Baker's novelties) *[music from Iphigénie en Tauride by Christoph Willibald Gluck]*

An autograph letter. A comedy in three acts. Boston: W. H. Baker, c1889. 42p. (Baker's edition of plays)

Bachelor maids. A comedy in one act for female characters. Boston: W. H. Baker, c1897. 12p. (Baker's edition of plays)

A blind attachment. A comedy in one act. Boston: W. H. Baker, 1895. 17p. (Baker's edition of plays)

A borrowed umbrella. A comedietta in one act. Boston: W. H. Baker, c1893. 7p. (Baker's edition of plays)

A model lover. A comedy in two acts. Boston: W. H. Baker, c1893. 22p. (Baker's edition of plays)

A rice pudding. A comedy in two acts. Boston: W. H. Baker, c1889. 30p. (Baker's edition of plays)

The spirit of the pine. A Christmas masque. Boston: L. Prang, c1890. 12p.

A tell-tale eyebrow. A comedy in two acts. Boston: W. H. Baker, c1889. 23p. (Baker's edition of plays)

That Patrick! A comedy in one act. Boston: W. H. Baker, c1886. 13p. (Baker's edition of plays)

The way to his pocket. A comedy in one act. Boston: W. H. Baker, c1889. 24p. (Baker's edition of plays)

Young Mr. Pritchard. A comedy in two scenes. Boston: W. H. Baker, c1886. 17p. (Baker's edition of plays)

Tilden, Len Ellsworth.
The emigrant's daughter. A border drama in three acts. Clyde, O.: Ames, c1884. 28p. (Ames' series of standard and minor drama. no. 143)

The finger of fate; or, The death letter. A melodrama in three acts. Boston: Walter H. Baker, 1893. 32p. (Baker's edition of plays)

The stolen will. A comedy drama in three acts. Boston: W. H. Baker, c1881. 58p. (Baker's edition of plays)

The stolen will. A comedy drama in three acts. Marlboro, N. H.: The author, 1881. 53p.

Tillson, Jesse Paxon, b.1870.
Collected works. The dramatic works of a new author. Toledo, O.: B. F. Wade,

1896. 135p.
  Contents: Passion's tem-
  pests.--Don Seiglemon.--
  Chas. Wengleigh, the Duke.--
  Jacob Busby.--Geewhilekins.

Tilmon Joy, the emancipator
  see Warren, Horatio N.

Tim Carty's trial; or, Whist-
  ling at landlords see
  Cusack, Sister Mary Frances
  Clare

Tim Flannigan; or, Fun in a
  grocery store see Gordinier, Charles A.

Tim M'Quain's bother see
  Jeffries, L. Q.

Timayenis, Telemachus Thomas,
  b.1853.
  The two corporals. Springfield, Mass.: J. D. Gill,
  1876. 92p. [cover: translated from the Greek]

Timon-Swift see Townsend,
  Frederic in his Spiritual
  visitors

Timothy Delano's courtship
  see Orne, Martha Russell

A tin soldier see Hoyt,
  Charles Hale

The Tipperary warbler; or, The
  fraud of the dry goods boxes.
  An historical and operatic
  play in three acts. Rochester, N. Y.: Parish, 1865.
  51p.

'Tis all a farce. A farce in
  two acts. (Adapted from
  J. T. Allingham.) Philadelphia: R. H. Lenfestey,
  1834. 30p. [adapted from
  John Till Allingham]

'Tis all a notion see Bird,

Robert Montgomery. 'Twas
  all for the best; or, 'Tis
  all a notion in his The
  cowled lover and other plays

'Tis an ill wind that blows
  nobody good see Cahill,
  Frank in Arnold, George?
  and Cahill, Frank. Parlor
  theatricals; or, Winter
  evening's entertainment

'Tis better to live than to
  die see Picton, Thomas

'Tis the darkest hour before
  dawn see Mack, Robert
  Ellice

Tit for tat see Ascher,
  Anton. Scenes from Mary
  Stuart [bound with] Tit
  for tat see also Buxton,
  Ida M.

Titania see Baker, George
  Melville

The title and the money see
  Mathews, Frances Aymar

Titterwell, Timothy (pseud.)
  see Kettell, Samuel

To meet Mr. Thompson see
  Denton, Clara Janetta Fort

To rent see Hageman, Maurice

To the right or left? see
  The temperance school dialogues

Tobin, John, 1770-1804.
  The honey-moon see The
  modern standard drama,
  vol. 1

Todd, John W.
  Arthur Eustace; or, A mother's love. A temperance drama
  in five acts. By J. W. Todd.
  Clyde, O.: Ames, c1891. 40p.

(Ames' series of standard and minor drama. no. 294)

Miss Blothingay's blunder. A comedy in three scenes. Clyde, O.: Ames, c1894. 15p. (Ames' series of standard and minor drama. no. 341)

The toiler's trials *see* Steele, Silas Sexton. The crock of gold; or, The toiler's trials

Toler, Mrs. H. M.
Eh? What did you say? A farce in three scenes. Clyde, O.: Ames, c1885. 10p. (Ames' series of standard and minor drama. no. 148)

Thekla. A fairy drama in three acts. Clyde, O.: Ames, c1884. 14p. (Ames' series of standard and minor drama. no. 144)

Waking him up. A farce in one act. Clyde, O.: Ames, c1885. 9p. (Ames' series of standard and minor drama. no. 147)

Toler, Sallie F.
Bird's Island. A drama in four acts. Chicago: Dramatic Pub. Co., c1897. 42p. (American acting drama)

Handicapped; or, A racing romance. An original comedy in two acts. New York: De Witt, c1894. 13p. (De Witt's acting plays. no. 399)

Tom and Jerry; or, Life in London. A burletta of fun, frolic and flash in three acts. Philadelphia: Chestnut Street Theatre, 1849. Prompt-book, interleaved with Ms. notes. 61p. *[the above imprint was taken from a handwritten page. The imprint on the published title page reads: Baltimore: Printed and published by J. Robinson, 1825. The British Museum Catalog (v. 239, col. 907) indicates that this work may be an adaptation of Life in London by Pierce Egan]*

Tom and Sally *see* McBride, H. Elliott *in his* New dialogues

Tom Blossom; or, The spider's web *see* Siegfried, W. A.

Tompkins' hired man *see* Merriman, Effie Woodward

Tom's arrival. A play for girls in one act. New York: Dick & Fitzgerald, 18-? 9p.

Tony the convict *see* Townsend, Charles

Too late for the train *see* Baker, George Melville

Too little vagrants; or, Beware of tramps *see* Dumont, Frank

Too mindful by far *see* Lambla, Hattie Lena. Obedience; or, Too mindful by far

Too much for one head *see* Smith, S. Jennie. A free knowledge-ist; or, Too much for one head

Too much Johnson *see* Gillette, William Hooker

Too much of a good thing *see* Denison, Thomas Stewart *see also* Pat's dilemma; or, Too much of a good thing

Too much Smith; or, Heredity *see* Matthews, Brander

Tooley, Larry.
The Dutchman's ghost *see*
White, Charles

The German immigrant; or,
Love and sourkrout *see*
White, Charles

Tooth, William.
Facts and fancies. A serio-
comico musical libretto in
two acts. Chicago: J. S.
Thompson, 1858. 36p. *[music
by William H. Currie;
without the music]*

Tootle, tootle, too; or, The
Frenchman and his pupil
see Sedgwick, Alfred B.

The top landing *see* Meyers,
Robert Cornelius V. *in*
Dramatic leaflets

Topp's twins *see* Denison,
Thomas Stewart

Torquato Tasso *see* Algernon
(pseud.)

Torrey, John, 1796-1873 *or*
Torrey, Mary Cutler, b.1831.
*[John Torrey was a botanist
who lived during the dates
noted above; Mary Cutler
Torrey was a poet, born in
Burlington, Vermont, in
1831, but with an unknown
death date]*
America: A dramatic poem.
(Ascribed to both authors.)
New York: Anson D. F. Ran-
dolph, 1863. 110p.

Torrey, Mary Cutler, b.1831.
America: a dramatic poem
see Torrey, John *or*
Torrey, Mary Cutler

Torrie, Hiram D. *[supposed
author]*
The tragedy of Abraham
Lincoln; or, The rise and
fall of the Confederate
States

Tortesa the usurer *see*
Willis, Nathaniel Parker
see also his Two ways of
dying for a husband

La Tosca *see* Davenport,
Fanny Lily Gypsy

Tottola, Andrea Leone, d.1831.
Mosé in Egitto *see* Parker,
George S. Moses in Egypt
see also Ponte, Lorenzo da.
Moses in Egypt *see also*
Villarino, Jose J.

The touchstone of truth; or,
The harlequin travellers.
n.p.: n.pub., 18-? Prompt-
book in Ms. 28 unnumbered
leaves.

The tournament of Idylcourt
see Baker, George Melville

Tournemine, Pierre, 1760?-1846.
L'Abbaye de Penmarque *see*
Williams, Henry Llewellyn.
Penmark Abbey

Tourte, François, 1747-1835.
[Circumstances alter cases]
see Sedgwick, Alfred B.

The tower of Babel *see*
Rodenberg, Julius

Town and country *see* Morton,
Thomas *in* The modern
standard drama, vol. 9

A town meeting *see* Hiland,
Frank E.

Townsend, Charles, 1857-1914.
Border land. An original
drama in three acts.
Chicago: Dramatic Pub. Co.,
c1889. 25p. (Sergel's acting
drama. no. 352)

A breezy call. An original
comedietta in one act.
Chicago: T. S. Denison,
c1891. 10p. (Amateur series)

Broken fetters. An original drama in five acts. Chicago: Dramatic Pub. Co., c1890. 32p. (Sergel's acting drama. no. 356)

Capt. Racket. A comedy in three acts. Chicago: Dramatic Pub. Co., c1898. 40p. (Sergel's acting drama. no. 414)

The captain's wager. A comedietta. Chicago: Dramatic Pub. Co., 1900? 9p. (American acting drama) *[earlier copyright: 1899]*

The dark tragedian. A negro farce in one act. Chicago: Dramatic Pub. Co., c1898. 7p. (The darkey and comic drama)

The darkey tragedian. An Ethiopian sketch in one scene. New York: Dick & Fitzgerald, c1874. Title page mutilated. 7p. *[Readex has also entered this play under its title]*

The darkey wood dealer. A farce in one act. New York: Wehman Bros., c1890. 11p.

Deception. An original farce in one act. Chicago: T. S. Denison, c1891. 15p. (Amateur series)

The doctor. An original comic drama in three acts. Boston: W. H. Baker, 1896. 41p. (Baker's edition of plays)

Down in Dixie. A drama in four acts. Chicago: T. S. Denison, 1894. Author's edition. 54p.

Early vows. A comedy in two acts. By C. F. Townsend. Chicago: T. S. Denison, c1889. 28p. (Alta series)

A family affair. A comedy in three acts. Adapted from

"Preté [sic] moi ta femme." Philadelphia: Penn Pub. Co., 1916. 41p. *[earlier copyright: 1898; based on the work of Georges Léon Jules Marie Feydeau]*

Finnigan's fortune. An original comic Irish play in three acts. Boston: W. H. Baker, c1893. Author's edition. 38p.

Four A. M. A satirical sketch. Philadelphia: Penn Pub. Co., 1914. 9p. *[earlier copyright: 1897]*

A gilded youth. A comedy in three acts. Boston: Walter H. Baker, c1896. 35p. (Baker's edition of plays)

The golden gulch. An original drama in three acts. New York: Fitzgerald Pub. Corp., c1893. 42p. *[the complete name of the publisher is Dick & Fitzgerald]*

The iron hand. A drama in four acts. Chicago: T. S. Denison, c1897. 39p. (Alta series)

The jail bird. A drama in five acts. New York: Dick & Fitzgerald, c1893. 46p.

A loyal friend. A comedy-drama in four acts. Philadelphia: Penn Pub. Co., 1915. 40p. *[earlier copyright: 1898]*

The man from Maine. An original drama in five acts. Author's edition. New York: Dick & Fitzgerald, c1893. 42p.

A midsummer madness. A vaudeville sketch in one act. Chicago: Dramatic Pub. Co., c1898. 9p. (Sergel's acting drama. no. 408)

Miss Madcap. A comedietta in one act. New York: H.

Roorbach, c1890. 12p. (Roorbach's American edition of acting plays. no. 23) 12p.

The mountain waif. An original drama in four acts. Boston: Walter H. Baker, c1892. 42p. (Baker's edition of plays)

On guard. A farce in one act. By Col. C. F. Townsend. Chicago: T. S. Denison, c1889. 11p. (Amateur series)

Perils of a great city. A melodrama in four acts. Author's edition. Philadelphia: Penn Pub. Co., 1911. 47p. [earlier copyright: 1899]

The rich Miss Poor. A financial romance in one act. New York: De Witt, c1899. 12p. (De Witt's acting plays. no. 410)

Rio Grande. An original drama in three acts. Boston: W. H. Baker, c1891. Author's edition. 44p. (Baker's edition of plays)

A shattered idol. A petite comedy in one act. New York: De Witt, c1896. 7p. (De Witt's acting plays. no. 405)

Shaun Aroon. An original Irish drama in three acts. New York: Dick & Fitzgerald, c1893. Author's edition. 37p.

A social outcast. A domestic drama in one act. Chicago and New York: Dramatic Pub. Co., c1895. 11p. (Sergel's acting drama. no. 403)

The spy of Gettysburg. An original drama in four acts. Boston: W. H. Baker, c1891. Author's edition. 38p. (Baker's edition of plays)

Tony, the convict. A drama in five acts. Chicago: T. S. Denison, c1893. 60p.

Uncle Josh. A drama in four acts. Chicago: T. S. Denison, 1891, 1919. 54p. (Alta series)

Uncle Rube. An original drama in four acts. Chicago: Dramatic Pub. Co., c1899. 56p. (Sergel's acting drama. no. 430)

Uncle Tom's cabin. A melodrama in five acts. New York: Fitzgerald Pub. Corp., c1889. 44p. [the complete name of the publisher is Dick & Fitzgerald; based on the novel by Harriet Beecher Stowe]

Under a cloud. An original comedy drama in two acts. New York: Harold Roorbach, c1890. 29p. (Roorbach's American edition of acting plays. no. 48)

Vacation. An original comedy in two acts. Chicago: Dramatic Pub. Co., c1893. 24p. Author's edition. (Sergel's acting drama. no. 398)

The vagabonds. An original drama in three acts. Boston: W. H. Baker, c1895. Author's edition. 31p. (Baker's edition of plays)

Wanted: a hero. A petite comedy. Chicago: T. S. Denison, c1897. 10p. (Amateur series)

A White Mountain boy. An original drama in five acts. Philadelphia: Penn Pub. Co., 1914. 47p. [earlier copyright: 1896]

A wonderful letter. A farce in one act. By Col. C. F. Townsend. Chicago: T. S. Denison, c1889. 8p. (Amateur series)

The woven web. An original drama in four acts. New York: Dick & Fitzgerald, c1889. 45p.

Townsend, Eliza, 1788-1854.
The wife of Seaton; or, The
siege of Berwick. An historic tragedy [From her: Poems
and miscellanies...Boston:
George C. Rand & Avery, 1856.
355p.] p.193-260.

Townsend, Frederic.
Spiritual visitors. New
York: John S. Taylor, 1854.
346, 11p.
Contents: Alcibiades-
Sheridan.--Henry Dandolo-
Peter Stuyvesant.--Rubens-
Cole.--Pindar-Drake.--Star
Amaranth: Twenty-ninth
hundreth birthday of Homer.
--Diogenes-Rabelais.--Aris-
tides-Jay.--Chrysostom-
Channing.--Amphion-Bellini.
--Roscius-Kemble.--Archi-
medes-Fulton.--Marcus Aure-
lius-Howard.--Corinna-Lady
Jane Grey.--Ben Jonson-Sam
Johnson.--Julius Caesar-
Zachary Taylor.--Timon-
Swift.--John Smith-Sydney
Smith.--Lucian-Lamb.--Father
Nile-Father Mississippi.--
Pericles-Hamilton.--Phidias-
Raphael.

Townsend, George Alfred,
1841-1914.
President Cromwell. A drama
in four acts. New York:
E. F. Bonaventure, c1884.
94p.

Townsend, Miss M. G.
The ugliest of seven see
Dramatic leaflets

The toy shop see Isham,
Frederic Stewart and
Weitzel, Edward Winfield

Tracy, George Lowell.
Miladi and the musketeer
see Barnet, Robert A.

Tracy, J. Perkins.
Harlequin old bogey; or, The

imps of the school and the
secret of the old oak chest.
A nautical, melo-dramatical,
sensational, pantomimical
burlesque uproar, in three
acts. San Francisco: Dramatic
Pub. Co., 1878. 50p. [title
page: "Music composed and
arranged by Prof. Henry
Hoffmann"; without the music;
an eleven-page history of
pantomime is included]

A tragedy for the million see
Massey, Charles. Love and
jealousy; or, A tragedy for
the million in Massey's
exhibition reciter

A tragedy in a New York flat
see Hartmann, Sadakichi

The tragedy of Abraham Lincoln;
or, The rise and fall of the
Confederate States. New York:
Dr. C. W. Selden, c1881. 64p.
[possibly an edition of a
work by Hiram D. Torrie]

Tragedy of errors see Putnam,
Mary Trail Spence Lowell

The tragedy of Macbeth see
Kelley, Edgar Stillman

Tragedy of success see
Putnam, Mary Trail Spence
Lowell

A tragic poem see Adams,
Miss L. B. Eva [bound with]
A tragic poem see also
Swanwick, Catherine in her
Eva [and] A tragic poem

The train to Mauro see
Shields, Sarah Annie Frost

The traveler see Denison,
Thomas Stewart in his
Friday afternoon series of
dialogues

Travesty upon "Arizona" see

Smith, Edgar McPhail

The treacherous wig *see*
Rosenfeld, Sydney. The
hair apparent; or, The
treacherous wig

The treason of West Point *see*
Hubbell, Horatio. Arnold;
or, The treason of West
Point

A treasure from Egypt *see*
Ward-Base, H.

The trees of the Bible *see*
Slade, M. B. C. *in* Dramatic leaflets

Tréfeu, Étienne, 1821-1903.
Geneviève de Brabant *see*
Bailey, G.

Treitschke, Georg Friedrich,
1776-1842.
Fidelio, oder die eheliche
Liebe *see* Fidelio; or,
Constancy rewarded

Tretbar, Helen D.
Rustic chivalry (Cavalleria
rusticana.) Melodrama in
one act. By Helen F. Tretbar. New York: Richard A.
Saalfield, 189-? Vocal
score. Bilingual text:
English and Italian. 146p.
*[music by Pietro Mascagni
on libretto by Giovanni
Targioni-Tozzetti and
Guido Menasci, based on
the story of the same name
by Giovanni Verga]*

The trial of alcohol *see*
A collection of temperance
dialogues

The trial of William Shakespeare *see* Thacher, John
Boyd. Charlecote; or, The
trial of William Shakespeare

Trialogues *see* Griffith,

William

The trials of a country
editor *see* Anderson,
Thomas F. *see also*
Heywood, Delia A. *in her*
Choice dialogues. no. 1

The tribulations of authorship
see Denison, Thomas Stewart.
Rejected; or, The tribulations of authorship

Tricks *see* Stewart, J. C.

Tricks in a doctor's shop *see*
Venable, William Henry *in his*
The school stage

Tricks of trade; or, An obstinate Romeo *see* Latour,
Eugene

Tricks upon travellers *see*
Coes, George H.

The tricky nig *see* Hall,
J. Griffin. The crowded
hotel; or, The tricky nig

Tried and true *see* Furlong,
John Ryan

Trilby *see* Smith, Edgar
McPhail

A trilogy in miniature *see*
Connell, George Stanislaus
in his The old patroon and
other plays

A trip to Cambridge. An acting
comedietta in one act. New
York: Happy Hours, 1879.
11p. (The acting drama.
no. 76)

A trip to Chinatown *see*
Hoyt, Charles Hale *see also*
his A trip to Chinatown;
or, An idyl of San Francisco

A trip to New York *see* The
Kentuckian; or, A trip to
New York

A trip to Niagara *see*
Bird, Robert Montgomery.
News of the night; or, A
trip to Niagara *in his*
The cowled lover and other
plays

A trip to Paris *see* Leavitt,
Andrew J. and Eagan, H. W.

The triple wedding *see*
Barnard, Charles

Triplet, James.
Call at number 1-7. A farce
in one act. New York: S.
French, 1864? 16p.

A supper in Dixie. A farce
in one act. New York: S.
French, c1865. 16p. (French's
minor drama. The acting
edition. no. 296)

T'riss; or, Beyond the Rockies
see Adams, Justin

The triumph of beauty *see*
Attinelli, Joseph. Matilda
di Shabran and Corradino;
or, The triumph of beauty

The triumph of virtue *see*
Henry, Sarepta Myrendal
Irish. Victoria; or, The
triumph of virtue

The triumph of youth; or, The
white mouse *see* Robertson,
Donald

Trixie; or, The wizard of Fogg
Island *see* Rawley, Bert C.

Troubet, Amélie Rives *see*
Troubetzkoy, Amélie Rives
Chanler

Troubetzkoy, Amélie Rives
Chanler, 1863-1945.
Athelwold. Drama in five
acts. New York: Harper &
Bros., 1893. 118p.

Herod and Mariamne. (Reprint:

Lippincott's Monthly Magazine. Sept., 1888.) Philadelphia: J. B. Lippincott,
c1888. p.305-394. *[title
page: "by Amélie Rives"
with Troubet handwritten
following]*

The trouble at Satterlee's *see*
Wilson, Louise Latham

De trouble begins at nine. An
act for bones and banjoist.
Boston: W. H. Baker, 1894.
8p. (Baker's darkey plays)
*[Readex enters an earlier
edition of this same play
under Charles White, q.v.]*

Trouble in the garden *see*
Field, Henrietta Dexter and
Field, Roswell Martin. Col-
lected works

Troubled by ghosts *see* Vane,
Larry

Troublesome children; or, The
unexpected voyage of Jack
and Pen *see* Fessenden,
Helen May Trott

The troublesome kid *see*
Bennett, W. L. Katie's
deception; or, The troublesome kid

The troublesome servant *see*
Griffin, George W. H.

Trovatore, Il Seignior Maestro
Infelice (pseud.)
Trovatore *see* Heywood,
Joseph Converse

Trowbridge, John Eliot, b.1845.
The heroes of '76 *see* Cobb,
Charles E.

Trowbridge, John Townsend,
1827-1916.
Coupon bonds. A play in four
acts. Boston: W. H. Baker,
c1876. 39p. (Baker's edition
of plays)

Cudjo's cave *see* Chase, George B. Penn Hapgood; or, The Yankee schoolmaster

Neighbor Jackwood. A domestic drama in five acts. Boston: Phillips, Sampson, 1857. 72p. *[based on the novel of the same name by the same author]*

The truant tracked *see* Broughall, George. The tearful and tragical tale of the tricky troubadour; or, The truant tracked

True! *see* Laidlaw, F. Allan

The true art of pleasing *see* Herbert, Bernard. A lesson in elegance; or, The true art of pleasing

True as steel *see* Schönberg, James

The true cross *see* Opal (pseud.) *in her* The cloud of witnesses

True hearts *see* Benedict, Frank Lee *in his* The shadow worshiper

True to the core *see* Maguire, John. Honesty is the best policy; or, True to the core

True to the last *see* Ames, A. D. Driven to the wall; or, True to the last

True wealth *see* Latour, H. J.

Trumbell, David. The death of Capt. Nathan Hale. A drama in five acts. Hartford: E. Geer, 1845. 32p.

Trumble, -----. All in der family *see* McDermott, J. J. and Trumble

A dark noight's business *see* McDermott, J. J. and Trumble

Dot mad tog *see* McDermott, J. J. and Trumble

Dot madrimonial adverdisement *see* McDermott, J. J. and Trumble

Dot quied lotgings *see* McDermott, J. J. and Trumble

A game of billards *see* McDermott, J. J. and Trumble

Mulcahy's cat *see* McDermott, J. J. and Trumble

The ould man's coat tails *see* McDermott, J. J. and Trumble

A purty shure cure *see* McDermott, J. J. and Trumble

Who got the pig? *see* McDermott, J. J. and Trumble

The wrong box *see* McDermott, J. J. and Trumble

Trumbull, Annie Eliot, 1857-1949. Green-room rivals. A comedietta in one act. By Annie Eliot (pseud.) New York: Edgar S. Werner, c1894. 16p. (Werner edition of plays)

A masque of culture. By Annie Eliot (pseud.) Hartford: Press of Case, Lockwood & Brainard, 1893. 54p.

Matchmakers. A comedy in one act. By A. E. Boston: W. H. Baker, 1895. 30p. (Baker's edition of plays)

St. Valentine's day. A comedy in one act for female characters. By Annie Eliot (pseud.) Boston: W. H. Baker, c1892. Prompt-book. 17p.

The wheel of progress. Hartford: Press of Case, Lockwood & Brainard, 1898. 50p.

A trumped suit *see* Magnus, Julian *see also* Magnus, Julian *in* Matthews, Brander. Comedies for amateur acting

The trustee *see* Browne, William Maynadier

Trusty and true *see* Dramatic leaflets

The try company *see* Bowler, Rev. G. *in* A collection of temperance dialogues

Try it on *see* Vane, Larry

Trying the characters *see* Beadle's...dialogues. no. 2

Trying the new teacher *see* Denison, Thomas Stewart *in his* Wide awake dialogues

Trying to raise the price of butter *see* McBride, H. Elliott *in his* Latest dialogues

Tubbs, Arthur Lewis, 1867-1946.
Dinner at six. A comedy in two acts. Philadelphia: Penn Pub. Co., 1914. 18p. *[earlier copyright: 1895]*

A double deception. A comedy in one act. Boston: W. H. Baker, 1900. 24p. (Baker's edition of plays)

The fruit of his folly. A drama in five acts. Philadelphia: Penn Pub. Co., 1916. 58p. *[earlier copyright: 1894]*

The heart of a hero. A domestic drama in four acts. Philadelphia: Penn Pub. Co., 1916. 44p. *[earlier copyright: 1897]*

The scheme that failed. A comedy in one act. Phila-

delphia: Penn Pub. Co., 1916. 24p. *[earlier copyright: 1895]*

Tullidge, Edward Wheelock, 1829-1894.
Ben Israel; or, From under the curse. Salt Lake City: J. C. Graham, 1815. 52p. *[music by George Edward Percy Careless]*

Elizabeth of England. A play in five epochs. Salt Lake City: n.pub., 1880? 67p.

Napoleon. Salt Lake City: n.pub., 1888. (Western Galaxy. vol. 1, no. 2) p.251-287 (pag. irreg.)

Tulu *see* Furniss, Grace Livingston

Tupper, Martin Farquhar, 1810-1889.
The crock of gold *see* Steele, Silas Sexton; or, The toiler's trials

Turkeys in season. An original Ethiopian whimsicality in two scenes. New York: Samuel French, 18-? 8p. (The Ethiopian drama. no. 62)

A turn in the market *see* Russell, Charles Walcott

The turn of the tide; or, Wrecked in port *see* Wilkins, W. Henri

Turner, Cyril.
White lies. A drama in three acts. New York: O. A. Roorbach, Jr., 1858. 36p. *[based on the novel of the same name by Charles Reade]*

Turner, J. M., d.1907.
Don't get weary; or, Johnny, you've been a bad boy *see* Don't get weary; or, Johnny,

you've been a bad boy *see also* Gentlemen coon's parade...and Don't get weary; or, Johnny, you've been a bad boy

Turning around *see* McBride, H. Elliott *in his* New dialogues

Twain, Mark (pseud.) *see* Clemens, Samuel Langhorne

Twain's dodging *see* Field, A. Newton

'Twas all for the best; or, 'Tis all a notion *see* Bird, Robert Montgomery *in his* The cowled lover and other plays

Twelfth night; or, What you will *see* Daly, Augustin *see also* Shakespeare, William *in* The modern standard drama, vol. 8

The twin sisters *see* Sedgwick, Alfred B.

'Twixt love and money *see* Fraser, John Arthur

The two alphabets--alcohol and water *see* The temperance school dialogues

Two Aunt Emilys; or, Quits *see* Tibbetts, Martie E.

The two awfuls *see* Dumont, Frank

Two belles to a beau; or, The leap-year proposal *see* Kobbé, Gustav *see also in* his Plays for amateurs

The two black roses *see* Stewart, J. C.

The two cadis *see* Eichberg, Julius

The two Caesars *see* Moore, John. Mad dogs; or, The two Caesars

The two captives. (From the Latin of Plautus.) New York: n.pub., 1893. Bilingual text: English and Latin. xx, 101p.

Two centuries ago *see* Barnes, Charlotte Mary Sanford. The forest princess; or, Two centuries ago

The two corporals *see* Timayenis, Telemachus Thomas

The two crowns. A drama in one act for young ladies. (From the French of Rimbault [sic, Rimbaut]) Baltimore: John Murphy, 1870. 30p. *[based on Les deux couronnes by Théophile Rimbaut]*

Two drams of brandy *see* McBride, H. Elliott

The two elopements *see* Crary, J. E. Johanes Blatz's mistake; or, The two elopements

Two families in one room; or, The boundary line *see* Steele, Silas Sexton *in his* Collected works. Book of plays

The two friends *see* Lacy, Michael Rophino *in* The modern standard drama, vol. 1

The two fugitives *see* Warden, Edward. Robert Make-airs; or, The two fugitives

The two galley slaves *see* Payne, John Howard

The two gentlemen of Verona *see* Daly, Augustin *see also* Shakespeare, William *in* The modern standard drama, vol. 4

Two ghosts in white *see*
Denison, Thomas Stewart

Two lives *see* Vickers,
George M. *in* Dramatic
leaflets

Two men of Sandy Bar *see*
Harte, Bret

The two moschetoes *see*
Kettell, Samuel

Two mothers *see* Reynartz,
Dorothy

Two negatives make an affirmative *see* Heermans,
Forbes

Two of a kind *see* Wilson,
Louise Latham

The two orphans. A play in
six acts. (As played by Kate
Claxton.) New York?: Printed
not published, 187-? 70p.
[based on Les deux orphe-
lines by Adolphe Philippe
Dennery and Pierre Étienne
Piestre (pseud.=Eugène
Cormon); Readex has repro-
duced the same edition of
this play under three
different entries: N. Hart
Jackson, Kate Claxton Cone
Stevenson, and The two
orphans (title entry)]

Two out of time *see* Herford,
Oliver

Two passions and a cardinal
virtue *see* Stinson, J.
Frederic Jessup

The two philosophers. A quaint
sad comedy *see* Chapman,
John Jay

The two Pompeys *see* Leavitt,
Andrew J. and Eagan, H. W.

The two roads *see* The tem-

perance school dialogues

The two Romans *see* Beadle's
...dialogues no. 2

The two roses *see* Morton,
Marguerite W.

Two sides--"which are you on?"
see The temperance school
dialogues

Two strings to her bow *see*
Harrison, Constance Cary
see also in her Short
comedies for amateur players

Der two subprises *see* Clifton,
Mary A. Delano

$2,000 reward; or, Done on both
sides *see* Cutler, F. L.

Two veterans *see* Hageman,
Maurice

The two waifs *see* Taylor,
Malcolm Stuart. Rags and
bottles; or, The two waifs

Two ways of dying for a husband
see Willis, Nathaniel Parker

Two ways of training boys *see*
Venable, William Henry. Nonsense; or, Two ways of
training boys *in his*
The school stage

The two wives of Lynn *see*
Spencer, Bella Zilfa

Two women: 1862 *see* Woolson,
Constance Fenimore

The tyrant of New Orleans. By
an ex-Confederate officer.
Atlanta: Herald Pub. Co.,
1873. 46p.

The tyrant of Padua *see*
Angelo; or, The tyrant of
Padua

Tyrolean queen *see* French,
Arthur W.

The Tyrolean queen revised
see French, Arthur W.
Gipsy queen (The Tyrolean
queen revised)

Tyrrel *see* Howard, George H.

The tzigane *see* Smith,
Harry Bache

Uberto *see* Osborn, Laughton
in his Ugo da Este

Uchard, Mario, 1824-1893.
La fiammina *see* Clapp,
William Warland

La postérité d'un bourg-
mestre *see* Matthews,
Brander. Too much Smith;
or, Heredity *see also*
Penn, Arthur. Heredity
Matthews, Brander. Comedies
for amateur acting

The ugliest of seven *see*
Townsend, Miss M. G. *in*
Dramatic leaflets

The ugly aunt; or, Falsehood
and truth *see* Call, S. C.

Ugo da Este *see* Osborn,
Laughton

The ulster *see* Rosenfeld,
Sydney

Unappreciated talent *see*
White, Charles. Guide to
the stage; or, Unappreciated
talent

Uncle Caleb's home *see*
Collyer, Dan. Christmas Eve
in the South; or, Uncle
Caleb's home

Uncle Dick's mistake *see*
Whalen, E. C.

Uncle Eph's dream *see* White,
Charles

Uncle Ethan *see* Cook, S.

Uncle Jack; or, Testing hearts
see Cook, S. N.

Uncle Jed's fidelity; or, The
returned cowboy *see* Rawley,
Bert C.

Uncle Jeff *see* White, Charles

Uncle John *see* McBride, H.
Elliott *in his* Latest
dialogues

Uncle John's private secretary
see Hageman, Maurice. Sowing
wild oats; or, Uncle John's
private secretary

Uncle Josh *see* Townsend,
Charles

Uncle Robert; or, Love's labor
saved *see* Curtis, Herbert
Pelham

Uncle Rube *see* Townsend,
Charles

Uncle Seth *see* Ward, Lew.
Taggs, the waif; or, Uncle
Seth

Uncle Tom. An Ethiopian inter-
lude in one scene. New York:
Happy Hours, 1874. 6p. (The
Ethiopian drama. no. 97)

Uncle Tom up to date *see*
Browne, M. C. The landlord's
revenge; or, Uncle Tom up
to date

Uncle Tom's cabin *see* Townsend, Charles

Uncle Tom's cabin; or, Life
among the lowly *see* Aiken,
George L.

Uncle Tom's freedom *see* Arnold, James Oliver. Historical drama and tableaux, *Uncle Tom's freedom*

Uncle Tony's mistake *see* Allyn, Dave E. "In for it"; or, Uncle Tony's mistake

An uncomfortable perdicament *see* McBride, H. Elliott *in his* New dialogues

An unconditional surrender *see* Morris, William Smith

Under a cloud *see* Townsend, Charles

Under a spell *see* Gibbs, Julia De Witt

Under an umbrella *see* Meyers, Robert Cornelius V. *in* Dramatic leaflets

Under de kerosene. An Ethiopian interlude. New York: Happy Hours, 1874. 7p. (The Ethiopian drama. no. 74)

Under ma's thumb *see* Morter, E. J. and Abarbanell, Jacob Ralph

Under protest *see* Bidwell, Jeanne Raymond

Under the American flag *see* Coon, Hilton

Under the curse *see* McBride, H. Elliott

Under the gaslight *see* Daly, Augustin

Under the greenwood tree *see* Huse, Carolyn Evans

Under the laurels *see* Denison, Thomas Stewart

Under the polar star *see* Belasco, David and Greene, Clay, Meredith

Under the shadow of a crime *see* Russ, William Ward. The strike; or, Under the shadow of a crime

Under the spell *see* Whalen, E. C.

Under the wheel *see* Garland, Hamlin

Under the wheels *see* Shapley, Rufus Edmonds

Under two flags *see* Mitchell, A.

The undertaker's daughter *see* Dumont, Frank

Undine *see* Dugan, Caro Atherton *in her* Collected works

Undine; or, The spirit of the waters. A drama in three acts. By George Soane. (Altered and adapted for...Holiday Street Theatre, Baltimore.) New York: S. French, 1858. 30p. (French's standard drama. no. 202) *[based on George Soane's Undine, which was translated from the German of Friedrich Heinrich Karl La Motte Foqué's Undine]*

The unexpected convert *see* The temperance school dialogues

The unexpected guests *see* Howells, William Dean

An unexpected legacy *see* Fowler, Egbert Willard

Unexpected visitors *see* Dumont, Frank

The unexpected voyage of Jack
and Pen *see* Fessenden,
Helen May Trott. Troublesome
children; or, The unexpected
voyage of Jack and Pen

An unhappy pair *see* Griffin,
George W. H.

The Union sergeant; or, The
battle of Gettysburg. A
historical drama of the War
founded on facts. Written
by a veteran of the war for
the Union. Springfield,
Mass.: Geo. W. Sargent,
1873. xii, 70, 7p.

The Union spy; or, The battle
of Weldon railroad *see*
Osgood, L. W.

United States mail *see* White,
Charles *see also his*
Gettin' de bag to hold; or,
The United States mail

Unjust justice *see* Simms,
George A.

The unknown heir *see* Bingham, Frank Lester. Henry
Granden; or, The unknown
heir

The unknown rival *see*
Emerson, William D.

Unlimited cheek; or, The sewing
machine agents *see* Dumont,
Frank

The unloved wife; or, Woman's
faith *see* Alcott, Louisa
May *in her* Comic tragedies

An unsuccessful advance *see*
McBride, H. Elliott *in his*
New Dialogues

The unwelcome guest *see*
McBride, H. Elliott *in*
Dramatic leaflets

An unwelcome return *see*
Munson, George A.

An up-country social circle
see McBride, H. Elliott in
his Latest dialogues

Up head! An Ethiopian interlude
in one scene. New York:
Happy Hours, 1874? 6p. (The
Ethiopian drama. no. 99)

The upstart *see* Stace,
Arthur J.

The upper ten thousand *see*
Leavitt, Andrew J. and Eagan,
H. W.

Upside down *see* Sparks,
Peter (pseud.)

Uriel Acosta. A tragedy in
five acts. (From the German
of Karl Gützkow.) By M. M.
New York: M. Ellinger, 1860.
92p. (pag. irreg.) *see also*
Hovey, Richard and Jones,
François Stewart

Ursula of Brittany. A school
play based on the legend of
Saint Ursula. New York: The
Ursulines of St. Teresa's,
c1894. 35p.

Using the weed *see* Baker,
George Melville

The usurper; or, The Americans
in Tripoli *see* Jones,
Joseph Stevens

Vacation *see* Townsend, Charles

Vacation days *see* Card,
Evelyn G. Whiting. A con-
fidence game

Vaez, Gustave (pseud.) *see*
Nieuwenhuysen, Jean Nicolas
Gustave van

The vagabonds *see* Townsend, Charles

Valabrègue, Albin, 1853-1937. [Love in harness] *see* Daly, Augustin

Valentine, Laura Jewry, d.1889. Games for family parties and children *see her* Diamonds and toads *in* Venable, William Henry. The school stage

Valeria *see* Monroe, Harriet

A valet's mistake *see* Cook, Sherwin Lawrence

The Valkyrie *see* Jameson, Frederick

The valley of Andorre. A comic opera in three acts. (From the French of St. Georges.) Boston: J. H. Eastburn's Press, 1856. 43p. Libretto. *[music by Jacques François Fromental Élie Halévy; based on Le Val d'Andorre by Jules Henri Vernoy de Saint-Georges; without the music]*

Vanderburch, Louis Émile, 1794-1862. Charlot *see* Planché, James Robinson. The follies of a night *in* The modern standard drama, vol. 6

Le sergent Frédéric *see* Gayler, Charles. The love of a prince; or, The court of Prussia

Vane, Larry. Troubled by ghosts. A burlesque. Chicago: T. S. Denison, c1899. 8p. (The Ethiopian drama)

Try it on. A farce. Chicago: Dramatic Pub. Co., c1899. 20p. (Sergel's acting drama. no. 417)

Van Harlingen, Katherine. An original widow's pension; or, The fugitive fortune. A comedy in four acts. n.p.: n.pub., 1898. Typescript, prompt-book. 120 leaves.

Vanity; or, A lord in Philadelphia. Corrected by J. B. Addis. Philadelphia: T. K. and P. G. Collins, 1854. 54p.

Vanity vanquished *see* McBride, H. Elliott *in* Dramatic leaflets

Vanloo, Albert, 1844-1920. La marjolaine *see* La marjolaine (The sweet marjoram)

[The oolah] *see* Rosenfeld, Sydney

Van Rensselaer, Henry. King Alfred. An historical drama. New York: Cincinnati and St. Louis: Benziger Bros., 1886. 48p. *[joint author: William J. Stanton]*

Van Wart, F. B. Stanley's dwarfs. An original entertainment in one act for male characters. New York, London: S. French, c1888. 23p. *[the complete title of this play is Stanley and his African dwarfs]*

Van Waters, George, fl.1841-59. Azon, the invader of Eden; or, Immortality snatched from the Tree of life. New York: Published by the author, 1858. 161p.

Van Winkle, Edgar Simeon. Dramatic fragments [From his: A memento. New York: F. B. Patterson, 1876. 281p.] p.226-249.

Varieties of American life *see* Campbell, Amelia Pringle.

The great house; or, Varieties of American life

The various ways of settling disputes *see* Abbott, Jacob. Orkney the peacemaker; or, The various ways of settling disputes

Varley, John Philip (pseud.) *see* Mitchell, Langdon Elwyn

Varrie, Vida.
The coming man; or, Fifty years hence. Philadelphia: E. C. Markley & Sons, 1872. 37p.

Vatter, August.
Out of the shadow. A drama in three acts. (Altered from the original version entitled "A noble sacrifice.") Boston: W. H. Baker, c1889. 48p. (Baker's edition of plays) *[joint author: John E. Spencer]*

Vautrot, George S.
At last. A temperance drama in three acts. Clyde, O.: Ames, c1879. 19p. (Ames' series of standard and minor drama. no. 73)

Black vs. white; or, The nigger and the Yankee. An original farce in one act. Clyde, O.: Ames, 1880. 19p. (Ames' series of standard and minor drama. no. 86)

The false friend. A drama in two acts. Clyde, O.: Ames, c1879. 38p. (Ames' series of standard and minor drama. no. 67)

Vegiard, J. T.
The Dutch recruit; or, The blue and gray. An original allegorical drama of the Civil War in five acts.

Clyde, O.: Ames, c1879. 49p. (Ames' series of standard and minor drama. no. 242)

The veiled priestess *see* Case, Laura U. *in* Dramatic leaflets

The veiled songstress *see* Glover, Howard. Palomita; or, The veiled songstress

Vela of Alava *see* Cergrinn, H. H.

Velasco *see* Sargent, Epes

Venable, William Henry, 1836-1920.
Parlor plays for parlor actors *see* Little silver hair and the three bears *in his* The school stage

The school stage. A collection of juvenile acting plays. Cincinnati, New York: Wilson, Hinkle, c1873. 234p.
Contents: The sincere mourner.--Dolly's doctor [from Henry William Dulcken's Rhyme and reason].--Master Goat, the tailor [adapted from Henry William Dulcken's Rhyme and reason].--Mother Goose and her friends.--Chinese damsel [adapted from the work of Charlotte Mary Yonge].--Little silver hair and the three bears [from Parlor plays for parlor actors].--A champion though no fighter [dramatized from Maria Jane McIntosh].--A lighter-boy at school [dramatized from Captain Frederick Marryat].--Lazy Lawrence; or, Industry and idleness contrasted [adapted from Maria Edgeworth].--Diamonds and toads [from Mrs. Valentine's Games for children].--Tarleton [dramatized from Tarlton by Maria Edgeworth].--The

white princess [slightly
altered from Lilliput rev-
els].--Good actions mend
bad actions [adapted from
Bulwer's The Caxtons].--
Nonsense; or, Two ways of
training boys.--Cinderella;
or, Pride punished [from
Julia Corner's Little plays].
--Rigmarole [adapted from
Louisa May Alcott's Little
women].--The fag's revolt
[dramatized from Thomas
Hughes' School days at
Rugby].--Tricks in a doctor's
shop.--The little dependent
[dramatized from Charlotte
Brontë's Jane Eyre].--Con-
tentment [adapted from
Louisa May Alcott's Little
women].--The Irish valet
[from Samuel Lover's Handy
Andy].--Imaginary possessions.--A colored witness.--
Irish equivocations [adapted
from George Barrington's
Personal sketches].--Grit as
well as manners.--Alfred the
king [Anna Letitia Aikin
Barbauld].--Little snow
white [by Karl Knortz].

Venanzi, Angelo.
Grand historical spectacular
[sic, spectacle] masterpiece
America *see* Kiralfy, Imre

Vendetta *see* Tarus-Vertus
(pseud.)

The veneered savage *see*
Furniss, Grace Livingston

The Venerable Bede *see* Opal
(pseud.) *in her* The cloud
of witnesses

Venice preserved *see* Otway,
Thomas *in* The modern
standard drama, vol. 3

Verconsin, Eugene, 1823-1892.
[A drawing-room car] *see*
A drawing-room car

Verdi, Giuseppe, 1813-1901.
Attila *see* Attila

Ernani *see* Ernani

I lombardi alla prima
crociata *see* The Lombards
at the first crusade

Il trovatore *see* Broughall,
George. The tearful and
tragical tale of the tricky
troubadour; or, The truant
tracked *see also* Sedgwick,
Alfred B. Estranged

Verga, Giovanni, 1840-1922.
Cavalleria rusticana *see*
Day, Willard Gibson *see also*
Tretbar, Helen D. Rustic
chivalry

Vergil *see* Vergilius Maro,
Publius

Vergilius Maro, Publius, 70-19
B. C.
The Aenid *see* Miller, Frank
Justus. Dido

Vermont wool-dealer. A farce
in one act. New York: S.
French, 18-. 18p. (The minor
drama. The acting edition.
no. 173) *[Readex also enters
this play under Thomas Logan,
q.v.]*

Verne, Jules, 1828-1905.
Around the world in eighty
days *see* Around the world
in eighty days

The very age! *see* Gould,
Edward Sherman

The veteran of 1812; or, Kesiah
and the scout *see* Woodward,
T. Trask

The veteran; or, France and
Algeria *see* Wallack, Lester

Vezin, Hermann, 1829-1910.
Cruel to be kind. A drama in

five acts. n.p.: n.pub.,
1872? 53 leaves. *[title
page: "from the German"]*

The vicar of Wakefield *see*
Coyne, Joseph Stirling *in*
The modern standard drama,
vol. 11

A vice and virtue *see* Osborn,
Laughton. The prodigal; or,
A vice and virtue *in his*
The magnetiser

Vice versa *see* Glenn, M. L.
see also Goodfellow, Mrs.
E. J. H.

The viceroy *see* Smith, Harry
Bache

Vickers, George M.
Two lives *see* Dramatic
leaflets

The victims of our western
Turks *see* Stern, H. I.
Evelyn Gray; or, The victims
of our western Turks

Victims of the bottle *see*
Woodward, T. Trask. The
social glass; or, Victims
of the bottle

Victor, Frances A., 1826-1902.
Azlea. By Frances A. Fuller
(pseud.) New York: A. S.
Barnes, 1851 (From: Poems of
sentiment and imagination
with dramatic and descriptive
pieces) 35p. p.133-166.

Victor Durand *see* Carleton,
Henry Guy

Victor, the king of fairy-land
see Robinson, Lucy Catlin
Bull *in her* Various dramatic works

Victoria; or, The triumph of
virtue *see* Henry, Sarepta
Myrendal Irish

Victory *see* Kimball, Hannah
Parker

The victory of faith, and hope,
and love *see* Austin, J. J.
The golden age to come; or,
The victory of faith, and
hope, and love

The Viking *see* Barron, Elwyn
Alfred *see also* Clayton,
Estelle

The village belle. A romantic
drama in four acts. New York:
Happy Hours, c1877. 12p.
(The amateur stage. no. 54)
see also Smart, Herbert
Durrell

The village gossip *see* Scan
mag!; or, The village gossip

Village life in New England
see Daly, Augustin. A legend
of "Norwood"; or, Village
life in New England

The village postmaster *see*
Ives, Alice Emma and Eddy,
Jerome H.

Villarino, Jose J.
Moses in Egypt. Sacred
tragedy in four acts. Boston:
Eastburn's Press, 1847. 26p.
*[music by Gioacchino Rossini;
libretto adapted by Luigi
Balocchi and Victor Joseph
Étienne Jouy from that of
Rossini's oratorio, Mosé in
Egitto, by Andrea Leone
Tottola; without the music]*

Villetard de Prunières,
Charles Edmond, 1828-1889.
Le testament de César Giro-
dot *see* Walcot, Maria
Grace. The cup and the lip

Vilikens and Dinah *see*
White, Charles

Villikins and his Diniah *see*

Griffin, Caroline Stearns

Vincent, Charles John, 1852-
1924.
The Egyptian princess *see*
Rosse, Jeanie Quinton

The Japanese girl (O Hanu
San) *see* Rosse, Jeanie
Quinton

Vinegar bitters *see* White,
Charles

Viola *see* Maturin, Edward

The violent remedy *see*
Curtis, Ariana Randolph
Wormeley. Doctor Mondschein;
or, The violent remedy

The violin *see* Mitchell,
Silas Weir

Virginia. A tragedy in five
acts. (From the French of
Latour.) New York: Darcie &
Corbyn, 1855. Bilingual text:
French and English. 47p.
*[based on Virginie by Isi-
dore Latour de Saint-Ybars]*
see also Osborn, Laughton.
Cavalry--Virginia: tragedies

The Virginia veteran *see*
Power, Thomas F.

The Virginian *see* Campbell,
Bartley Theodore *in his*
The white slave and other
plays

Virginius *see* Knowles, James
Sheridan *in* The modern
standard drama, vol. 4 *see
also* McCullough, John

The Virginny cupids! *see*
White, Charles. Oh! hush!;
or, The Virginny cupids!

The Virginny mummy *see*
White, Charles

The virtues *see* Beadle's...
dialogues no. 2 *see also*
A collection of temperance
dialogues

A vision of death. An extract
see Read, Thomas Buchanan

A vision of fair women *see*
Winn, Edith Lynwood

The visions of freedom *see*
Baker, George Melville

A vision's quest *see* Lord,
Alice Emma Sauerwein

A visit from Mother Goose *see*
Davidson, Belle L.

A visit to the oil regions
see McBride, H. Elliott
in his New dialogues

A visit to the zoological
gardens *see* Dumont, Frank
in his The amateur minstrel

The vocation of St. Aloysius.
A drama in three acts. (From
the Italian of Padre Boero.)
New York: Joseph F. Wagner,
18-? 32p. *[based on La
vocazione di San Luigi
Gonzaga alla compagnia de
Gesù by Giuseppe Boero]*

Vogelsang, G.
The creator. Drama in five
acts. Baltimore: n.pub.,
1864. 7p.

Vogt, Harry V.
By force of impulse. An
original drama in five acts.
New York: Dick & Fitzgerald,
c1887. 92p.

The voice of the sea *see*
Fairman, James

Volentia *see* Seawell, J.

The volunteers; or, The pride
of Company G *see* Hildreth,
David W₀

Von Culin, Everett.
The dentist's clerk; or,
Pulling teeth by steam₀
A farce in one act. New
York and London: S. French,
1877? 17p.

The vow of the Ornani *see*
Gotthold, Newton

W₀, E₀ C₀ *see* Wilson, Ella
Calista Handy

W., J₀ M₀
A brown paper parcel₀ New
York: S. French, c1899₀ 9p.
(French's international
copyrighted edition of the
works of the best authors.
no₀ 26) *[Readex also enters
this same play under Marie
Josephine Williams]*

"W. H₀" *see* Denton, Clara
Janetta Fort

Wacousta; or, The curse *see*
Jones, R.?

Wälzel, Camillo, 1829-1895₀
[pseud.=F. Zell]
Apajune der Wassermann *see*
Rosenfeld, Sydney₀ Apajune,
the watersprite

Der Bettelstudent *see*
Schwab, Emil. The beggar
student

Boccaccio *see* Boccaccio
see also Smith, Dexter₀
Boccaccio; or, The Prince
of Palermo

Gasparone *see* Rosenfeld,
Sydney

Der lustige Krieg *see*
Elson, Louis Charles₀ The
merry war *see also*
Norcross, I. W. The merry
war

Nanon *see* Elson, Louis
Charles

"Waffles₀" A travesty upon
"Raffles" *see* Smith,
Edgar McPhail

The wager *see* Kitchel,
Mrs. Francis W₀ *see also*
Mitchell, Silas Weir *see also*
O'Brien, Constance

The wages of sin *see* Brady,
William A.

Wagner, Richard, 1813-1883.
Der fliegende Holländer *see*
Neumann, Louis₀ The flying
Dutchman *see also* Robjohn,
William James. The flying
Dutchman

Die Götterdämmerung *see*
Jameson, Frederick. Dusk of
the gods

Die Meistersinger von Nürn-
berg *see* Jameson, Frederick. The mastersingers of
Nuremberg

Das Rheingold *see* Jameson,
Frederick. The Rhinegold

Siegfried *see* Jameson,
Frederick

Tannhäuser und der Sänger-
krieg auf Wartburg *see*
Morgan, Geraldine Woods₀
Tannhäuser and the minstrels
tournament on the Wartburg

Die Walküre *see* Jameson,
Frederick₀ The Valkyrie

Wainwright, D. Wadsworth.
Wheat and chaff. A comedy in
five acts₀ New York: Charles
Roe, 1858₀ 83p.

Wainwright, John Howard.
Rip Van Winkle. An original
American grand opera in
three acts₀ New York: Wardle
Corbyn, 1855. Prompt-book
with Ms₀ notes. 37p. Libretto.

*[music by George Frederick
Bristow, adapted from the
story of the same name by
Washington Irving; without
the music]* see also
Shannon, J. W.

Waiting for the train *see*
Wilton, M. J.

Wake up, William Henry *see*
White, Charles

Waking him up *see* Toler,
Mrs. H. M.

Walcot, Charles Melton, 1815-
1868 *[originally Charles
Walcot Melton]*
"A good fellow." A petite
comedy in one act. New York:
S. French, c1856. 15p.
(French's American drama.
The acting edition. no. 89)

Hiawatha; or, Ardent spirits
and laughing water. A musical extravaganza in two
acts. New York: S. French,
c1856. 32p. (The minor drama.
no. 109)

Nothing to nurse. An original farce in one act. London:
T. H. Lacy, 1857. 19p. (Amateur Theatre. vol. 10)

One coat for two suits. An
entirely original comic
drama in two acts. New York:
S. French, c1857. 26p.
(The minor drama. no. 113)

Walcot, Maria Grace.
The cup and the lip. (From
the French of Belot and
Villetard.) New York:
Samuel French, 1860? 48p.
(French's standard drama.
no. 227) *[based on Le
testament de César Girodot,
by Adolphe Belot and Edmond
Villetard]*

Waldauer, Augustus.

Fanchon, the cricket. A
domestic drama in five acts.
(From the German version of
a tale by George Sand.) New
York: S. French, 186-? 48p.
(French's standard drama.
The acting edition. no. 334)
*[George Sand's work Le petit
Fadette was later translated
by August Schrader under the
title Die grille; oder,
kleine Fadette, which Waldauer has here translated
into English]*

The female cavalier.
(Altered from [Colley]
Cibber's "She would and she
would not.") Philadelphia:
n.pub., 18-? Title-page
lacking. Prompt-book,
interleaved, with Ms. notes.
20p.

Little barefoot. A domestic
drama in five acts. (From
the German.) New York: S.
French, 1864. 42p. (French's
standard drama. The acting
edition. no. 335) *["companion
piece of 'Fanchon, the
cricket.'"]*

Waldeck; or, The haunted dell
see Roberts, T. W.

Waldimar *see* Bailey, John J.

Waldron, P. A.
Paddy Doyle; or, A mutual
friend. An Irish farce in
one act and one scene.
New York: Dick & Fitzgerald,
c1898. 16p. (Dick's American
edition)

Waleski, Alexandre Florian
Joseph Colonna, 1810-1868.
Mademoiselle de Belle-Isle
see Mademoiselle de Belle-
Isle

Walker, Alfred.
Giorgione, the painter of

Venice. A tragedy in five
acts. Cambridge: Riverside
Press, 1869. 196p. (Walker's
plays. vol. 1)

Walker, Horace Eaton, b.1852.
Acrisius, King of Argos
[From his: Acrisius...and
other poems. Claremont,
N. H.: Geo. I. Putnam,
1895. 95p.] p.4-62.

Walker, James Barr, 1805-1887.
Lucilla; ten scenes in the
life of a lady of fashion
[From his: Immortality and
worth of the soul...Chicago:
Henry A. Sumner, 1871.
211p.] p.54-105.

Walker, Janet Edmondson.
The new governess. A comedy
in one act. Chicago:
Dramatic Pub. Co., c1899.
16p. [cover: "adapted from
the German"]

Walker, Will L.
The squire's daughter. A
comedy drama in three acts.
Clyde, O.: Ames, c1894. 36p.
(Ames' series of standard
and minor drama. no. 336)

The walking delegate see
Cook, Charles Emerson

Wall, Annie.
Is lying easy? A comedy.
(From the German of Benedix.)
St. Louis: G. I. Jones,
1877. 72p.

Wallace, F. K.
Pete and the peddler see
White, Charles

Wallace, John J., 1831-1892?
Little Ruby; or, Home
jewels. A domestic drama in
three acts. New York: Dramatic Pub. Co., c1872. Author's
edition. 38p. (De Witt's
acting plays. no. 164)

Wallace, Lewis, 1827-1905.
Commodus [From his: The
wooing of Malkatoon...New
York and London: Harper &
Bros., 1898. 167p.] p.81-167.

Wallack, James William,
1791?-1864.
Congreve's...Love for love.
Revised and altered by James
W. Wallack. New York: D.
Appleton, 1854. 88p.

Wallack, Lester, 1820-1888.
Much ado about nothing. A
comedy in six acts. By
William Shakespeare. New
York: Samuel French, 1869.
61p. (French's standard
drama. no. 55)

Rosedale. (Based on the
novel "Lady Lee's widow-
hood.") Prompt-book in Ms.
in five acts. Acts 1 and 5
only. New York: n.pub.,
1863. [the complete title
of this play is Rosedale;
or, The rifle ball, which
was based on Sir Edward
Bruce Hamley's Lady Lee's
widowhood]

Rosedale; or, The rifle ball.
(From: America's lost plays.
vol. 4. Princeton, N. J.:
Princeton Univ. Press, 1940)
p.3-64. [based on Sir Edward
Bruce Hamley's Lady Lee's
widowhood] see also
Griffin, George W. H. Rose
Dale

The veteran; or, France and
Algeria. A drama in six
tableaux. New York: S.
French, 1859. 63p. (French's
standard drama. no. 220)
[based on James Grant's
novel, Frank Hilton; or,
The queen's own]

Wallberg, Anna Cornjelm.
Fridthjof's Saga see
Hanson, Carl Fredrik.
Fridthjof and Ingerborg

Waller, Daniel Wilmarth,
1824?-1882.
Into the world. Drama in
three acts. New York: Laura
Keene Theatre, 1862. Prompt-
book in Ms. 109 leaves.

The wallflowers [1st part of
a trilogy] *see* Grant,
Robert *in his* The little
tin gods-on-wheels; or,
Society in our modern Athens

Walsh, John.
Irish inspiration. New
York: n.pub., 1891. Title
page lacking. Typescript,
prompt-book, interleaved,
with Ms. notes. 25, 21,
23, 23 leaves. *[possible
dates for John Walsh:
1847-1919; see Wallace]*

Walsh, Joseph P.
The actor's scheme; or,
How we got our dinner. A
farce. Clyde, O.: Ames,
c1891. 8p. (Ames' series
of standard and minor
drama. no. 291)

Walsh, Townsend, d.1941.
The boys of Kilkenny. New
York: n.pub., 1897. Title
page lacking. Typescript,
prompt-book with Ms. notes.
150 unnumbered leaves.

Walworth, Reubena Hyde.
Where was Elsie; or, The
Saratoga fairies. A come-
dietta in one act. New
York: Edgar S. Werner,
1900. 15p. *[possibly a
daughter of Reuben Hyde
Walworth, 1788-1867]*

The wanderer *see* Renauld,
Charles

The wanderer's dream *see*
Quinn, Richard. Innisfail;
or, The wanderer's dream

The wanderer's return *see*
Cook, S. N.

The wandering minstrel *see*
Orpheus and Eurydice; or,
The wandering minstrel *in*
Arnold, George? and Cahill,
Frank. Parlor theatricals;
or, Winter evening's enter-
tainment

Wang *see* Goodwin, John
Cheever

Wanted: a confidential clerk
see Chapman, W. F.

Wanted: a correspondent *see*
Denison, Thomas Stewart

Wanted: a hero *see* Townsend,
Charles

Wanted a husband *see* Cutler,
F. l.

Wanted, a male cook *see* Baker,
George Melville

Wanted--a nurse *see* Kobbé,
Gustav *see also his* Plays
for amateurs *see also*
White, Charles

Wanted--a valet *see* Griffith,
Benjamin Lease Crozer

Wanted and not wanted *see*
The shipwrecked strangers;
or, Wanted and not wanted
in The temperance school
dialogues

The war of the roses *see*
Baker, George Melville

War to the knife *see* Mathews, Frances Aymar

Ward, Cyrenus Osborne, 1832-
1902.
The great rebellion. Remi-
niscences of the struggle

that cost a million lives.
A drama in five acts. New
York: n.pub., 1881. 126p.

Ward, Elizabeth Stuart Phelps,
1844-1911.
The gates between *see her*
Within the gates

Within the gates. Boston and
New York: Houghton Mifflin,
1901. 150p. *[taken from an
original story The gates
between by the same author]*

Ward, L. L. (pseud.)
Ward, Lew

Ward, Lew.
Claim ninety-six. A border
drama in five acts. By Len
Ware (pseud.) Clyde, O.:
Ames, c1893. 42p. (Ames'
series of standard and
minor drama. no. 310)
*[originally published in
1892 under the title Nugget
Nell; or, Claim ninety-six]*

Gyp, the heiress; or, The
dead witness. A drama in
four acts. By L. L. Ward
(pseud.) Clyde, O.: Ames,
1892. 31p. (Ames' series of
standard and minor drama.
no. 311)

My pard; or, The fairy of
the tunnel. A western drama
in four acts. By L. L.
Ware (pseud.) Clyde, O.:
Ames, c1895. 29p. (Ames'
series of standard and minor
drama. no. 355) *[the title
page of this publication
gives Ward's pseudonym as
Leo Ware, not L. L. as
indicated by Readex]*

Signing an actor. Specialty
sketch in one act. By Len
Ware (pseud.) Clyde, O.:
Ames, c1894. 10p. (Ames'
series of standard and
minor drama. no. 346)

Taggs, the waif; or, Uncle
Seth. A drama in five acts.
By Len Ware (pseud.) Clyde,
O.: Ames, c1896. 40p. (Ames'
series of standard and minor
drama. no. 369)

Ward, Thomas, 1807-1873.
The fair truant. An operetta
in two acts founded on fact.
New York: French & Wheat,
1869. 23p. Libretto. *[music
by the author; without the
music]*

Flora; or, The gipsy's
frolic. A pastoral opera in
three acts. New York: French
& Wheat, 1858. 54p. Libretto.
*[music by the author; with-
out the music]*

Ward-Base, H.
A treasure from Egypt. A
farce. Chicago: T. S.
Denison, c1897. 26p. (Star
series)

Warden, Edward.
Robert Make-airs; or, The
two fugitives. A burlesque.
London & New York: Samuel
French, 18-? 10p. (French's
acting edition. Late Lacy's)

Scampini *see* White, Charles

Warden, Frank L.
Romance after marriage; or,
The maiden wife *see*
Goodrich, Frank Boott and
Warden, Frank L.

Ware, Eugene Fitch, 1841-1911.
The Kansas bandit; or, The
fall of Ingalls [From his:
Some of the rhymes of Ironquill (pseud.) Topeka: Crane,
1900. Tenth edition. 344p.]
p.282-304.

Ware, Henry, 1794-1843.
The feast of tabernacles *see*
Cobb, Mary L. Poetical
dramas for home and school

Ware, L. L. (pseud.) *see*
Ward, Lew

Ware, Len (pseud.) *see*
Ward, Lew

Ware, Leo (pseud.) *see*
Ward, Lew

Ware, Thornton M.
The revolving wedge. A
football romance in one
act. Boston: W. H. Baker,
c1896. 31p. (Baker's edition
of plays) *[joint author:
George Pierce Baker]*

A warm reception *see* Morse,
Mabel

Warner, Theodore Davenport
(pseud.) *see* McFadden,
Theodore

Warren, Horatio N., b.1838.
Tilmon Joy; the emancipator.
War drama in four acts
[From his: The declaration
of independence and war
history...Buffalo: Courier
Co., Printers, 1894. 189p.]
p.173-189. *[music by the
author; without the music]*

Warren, Leslie.
Much ado about nothing.
Arranged in two acts for
amateur representation. By
William Shakespeare. Boston:
Walter H. Baker, c1894. 22p.
(Baker's edition of plays)

Warren, Nathan Boughton, 1815-
1898.
Hidden treasure; or, The
good St. Nicholas. A Twelfth
Night play in three acts.
Troy, N. Y.: n.pub., 1881.
35p. *[Readex has entered an
operetta version of this
play under title]*

Warren, Walter (pseud.) *see
also* Raymond, George Lansing

Warren, Walter (pseud.)
Columbus the discoverer.
Boston: Arena Pub. Co.,
1893. vi, 164p. *[the real
name of Walter Warren is
George Lansing Raymond,
1839-1929; Readex also
enters this play under
Raymond]*

The warrior's faith *see*
Campbell, Thomas. The
wizard's warning; or, The
warrior's faith *in* Steele,
Silas Sexton. Collected
works. Book of plays

Washington *see* Lockwood,
Ingersoll *see also*
Shields, Annie Frost *in her*
Parlor charades and proverbs

Washington; or, The Revolution
see Allen, Ethan

Washington reconstructed *see*
Fast, Edward Gustavus.
The gentleman of the color;
or, Washington reconstructed

Washington's birthday *see*
Denton, Clara Janetta Fort
in her From tots to teens

The water-melon cure *see*
Russell, Charles Walcott

Water or wine? *see* The
temperance school dialogues

Waters, Roland.
The home-made bonnet. A
narrative-play in one act.
Baltimore: Guggenheimer &
Weil, c1878. 56p.

Watertown in '75 *see* Safford,
De Forest

Watson, Henry C.
Giovanna of Naples. New York:
Snowden, 1850. Bilingual text:
English and Italian. 57p.
Libretto. *[music by Moritz
Strakosch; without the music]*

Watt, Bob (pseud.) *see*
Smiley, Robert Watt

Wax works at play *see*
Williams, Henry Llewellyn

Way down east *see* Parker,
Lottie Blair

The way of life *see* Baily,
Jno. Jay

The way to his pocket *see*
Tiffany, Esther Brown

The way to win him *see*
Daly, Augustin. The inconstant; or, The way to win
him

We mortals *see* Salmonsen,
Morris

Wealth and poverty *see*
Lehmann, M. The elf-king;
or, Wealth and poverty

The wearing of the green *see*
Moore, Bernard Francis.
Faugh-a-Ballagh; or, The
wearing of the green

The weathercock *see* Allingham, John Till *in* Dramatic
leaflets

Weatherly, Frederic Edward,
1848-1929.
A bird in hand *see* Schell,
Stanley. An old maid's conference

Weaver, Addison, c1833-1903.
Young scamp *see* White,
Charles

A web of lies *see* Edgcome,
John

Webb, Charles.
The Corsican brothers *see*
Griffin, George W. H.
Corsican twins

Webber, Harry A.
Man and wife. A drama in
five acts. (From the novel
by Wilkie Collins.) Clyde,
O.: Ames, 1873. Prompt-book.
48p. Title page mutilated.
(Ames' series of standard
and minor drama. no. 46)

Weber, Karl Maria Friedrich
Ernst von, 1786-1826.
Euryanthe *see* Schwab,
Frederick A.

Der Freischütz *see* Burk-
hardt, Charles B. *see also*
Der Freischütz *see also*
Macy, James Cartwright. Der
Freyschütz

Webster, Daniel, 1782-1852.
The necessity of Union *see*
Massey, Charles. Massey's
exhibition reciter

Wedded and parted *see* Goddard, Edward. By force of
love; or, Wedded and parted

The wedding feast *see* Leahy,
William Augustine

A wedding notice *see* Hunt,
Arzalea

The wedding tour *see* Mathews,
Frances Aymar

The wedding trip *see* Sonneborn, Hilton Burnside

The weed and the boy *see*
Denton, Clara Janetta Fort.
When the lessons are over

The weeping willows *see*
Moore, Bernard Francis

Weeping wives. A comedietta
see Harrison, Constance
Cary *in her* Short comedies
for amateur players

Wehman's burnt cork; or, The

amateur minstrel *see*
Dumont, Frank. The amateur
minstrel

Wehner, J. H.
Principles form character.
A comedy in three acts. New
York: Samuel French, c1859.
23p. (The minor drama. The
acting edition. no. 175)

Weil, Oscar, 1839-1921.
Adina; or, The elixir of
love. Boston: Alfred Mudge &
Son, 1886. 40p. Libretto.
[music by Gaetano Donizetti
on libretto by Felice Romani,
based on Le Philtre by
Eugène Scribe; without the
music]

Bobby Shaftoe *see* Bunner,
Henry Cuyler *in his* Three
operettas

The maid of honor. Opera
comique. (From the French
of Halévy.) Boston: Alfred
Mudge & Son, 1886. 43p.
Libretto.

The seven old ladies of
Lavender Town *see* Bunner,
Henry Cuyler *see also in*
his Three operettas

The three little kittens of
the land of Pie *see* Bunner,
Henry Cuyler *in his* Three
operettas

Weitzel, Edward Winfield.
The toy shop *see* Isham,
Frederic Stewart and
Weitzel, Edward Winfield

Welcker, Adair, 1858-1926.
Flavia. Berkeley, Calif.:
The author, c1885. 118p.

Welcker, Adair, 1858-1926.
Romer, King of Norway and
other dramas. Sacramento:
Press of Lewis and Johnston,
1885. 245p.
Contents: The bitter end.--

Flavia.--Dream of realms
beyond us.--Romer, King of
Norway.

Weld, Arthur Cyril Gordon,
1862-1914.
The casino girl *see* Smith,
Harry Bache

Well fixed for a rainy day *see*
McBride, H. Elliott

The well of death; or, The
brothers of Padua *see*
Steele, Silas Sexton *in his*
Collected works. Book of
plays

The well of St. Keyne *see*
Fowle, William Bentley *in*
his Parlor dramas

A well preserved gentleman
see Meyers, Robert Cornelius V.

Wells, Charles Henry.
Me an' Otis. An original
drama in four acts. Boston:
W. H. Baker, c1897. 35p.
(Baker's edition of plays)

Wells, David Dwight, 1868-1900.
The tie that binds. A come-
dietta. Philadelphia: Penn
Pub. Co., 1909. 18p. *[earlier*
copyright: 1896; joint author:
Charles Emerson Cook]

Wenlandt, Oliver.
A holy terror. A farce in one
act for four male characters.
New York: Dick & Fitzgerald,
c1896. 19p.

Nigger boarding-house. A
screaming farce in one act
and one scene for six male
burnt-cork characters. New
York: Fitzgerald, c1898.
24p. Title page mutilated.

The wept of the Wish-ton-wish.
A drama in two acts from

J. Fennimore [sic, Fenimore]
Cooper's celebrated novel
of the same name. New York:
S. French, 185-? Prompt-
book with Ms. notes. 26p.
(French's standard drama.
The acting edition. no. 154)

"We're all teetotalers" *see*
Baker, George Melville

Werner *see* Byron, George
Gordon Noël Byron, 6th
baron *in* The modern
standard drama, vol. 9

Werther *see* Ginty, Elizabeth
Beall

West, A. Laurie.
Shades of Shakespeare's
women. Entertainment in ten
scenes. New York: Edgar S.
Werner, c1894-96. 32p.
(Werner's plays)

West, Emma Elise.
Their graduating essays.
A comedietta in one scene
for two young ladies. New
York: Edgar S. Werner, 1900.
11p.

West Point *see* Baker,
George Melville

West Point; or, A tale of
treason *see* Breck, Joseph

Westcott, Edward Noyes, 1847-
1898.
David Harum *see* Hitchcock,
James Ripley Wellman and
Hitchcock, Martha Wolcott
Hall

Weston, Effie Ellsler, 1858-
1942.
A wolf in sheep's clothing.
n.p.: n.pub., 18-? Title
page lacking. Typescript,
prompt-book with Ms. notes.
56, 38, 47 leaves.

Weston, the walkist *see*
White, Charles

A wet blanket *see* Daly,
Augustin. Three preludes
to the play

Whalen, E. C.
Documentary evidence. A
farce. Chicago: T. S.
Denison, c1899. 16p. (Amateur series)

A double election. A farce
in one act. Clyde, O.: Ames,
c1887. 13p. (Ames' series of
standard and minor drama.
no. 249)

From Sumter to Appomattox.
A war drama in four acts.
Chicago: T. S. Denison,
c1889. 59p. (Alta series)

Uncle Dick's mistake. A
farce in one act. Chicago:
T. S. Denison, c1889. 13p.
(Amateur series)

Under the spell. A temperance
play in four acts. Chicago:
T. S. Denison, c1890. 70p.
[music composed by the author]

What ailed Maudie *see* Merriman, Effie Woodward *see also*
in her Comedies for children

What became of Parker *see*
Hageman, Maurice

What bird would you be? *see*
Denison, Thomas Stewart *in*
his Wide awake dialogues

What Christmas means *see*
Phelps, Lavinia Howe *in her*
Dramatic stories

What happened to Jones *see*
Broadhurst, George Howells

What is a gentleman? *see*
Denton, Clara Janetta Fort
in her From tots to teens

What makes a man? *see*
Phelps, Lavinia Howe *in her*
Dramatic stories

What shall I take? *see*
Dumont, Frank

What tears can do. A comedietta
in one act. (From the French
of Siraudin and Thiboust.)
New York: De Witt, c1883.
18p. (De Witt's acting
plays. no. 311) *[translated
from Les femmes qui pleurent
by Paul Siraudin and Lambert
Thiboust]*

What they will do *see* Denton,
Clara Janetta Fort *in her*
From tots to teens

What you will *see* Daly,
Augustin. Twelfth night; or,
What you will *see also*
Shakespeare, William.
Twelfth night; or, What you
will *in* The modern stan-
dard drama, vol. 8

What's in a name? *see*
Russell, G. Frederick

What's next? *see* Smiley,
Robert Watt

Wheat and chaff *see* Wainwright, D. Wadsworth

The wheel of progress *see*
Trumbull, Annie Eliot

The wheelbarrow *see* Abbott,
Jacob *in his* Orkney the
peacemaker; or, The various
ways of settling disputes

Wheeler, Esther Gracie Lawrence, fl.1875-93.
A cup of tea drawn from
1773. By Mrs. W. L. Wheeler.
Cambridge: Riverside Press,
1875. 21p.

Wheeler, Mrs. W. L. *see*

Wheeler, Esther Gracie
Lawrence

When I am a woman *see* Denison,
Thomas Stewart *in his* Wide
awake dialogues *see also*
Denton, Clara Janetta Fort.
When the lessons are over

When I come back *see* Blumenthal, Oscar and Kadelburg,
Gustav

When poverty comes in at the
door, love flies out at the
window *see* Shields, Sarah
Annie Frost *in her*
Parlor charades and proverbs

When the cat's away *see*
Shields, Lottie

When the cat's away the mice
will play *see* Arnold,
George *in* Arnold, George?
and Cahill, Frank. Parlor
theatricals; or, Winter
evening's entertainment
see also Shields, Sarah
Annie Frost *in her* Parlor
charades and proverbs

When the lessons are over *see*
Denton, Clara Janetta Fort

When women have their rights
see McBride, H. Elliott
in his New dialogues

When women weep *see* Gotthold,
J. Newton

Where there's a will there's a
way *see* Browne, Irving.
Doctor Polyanthus; or, Where
there's a will there's a way
see also Mackay, Frank
Findley. A double life; or,
Where there's a will there's
a way

Where was Elsie; or, The
Saratoga fairies *see* Walworth, Reubena Hyde

Where's my hat *see* Meyers,
Robert Cornelius V. *in*
Dramatic leaflets

Which will have him? *see*
Woodward, John A.

Which will you give up? *see*
The temperance school
dialogues

Whigs and Democrats; or, Love
of no politics *see* Heath,
James Ewell

While the joy goes on *see*
Denton, Clara Janetta Fort.
When the lessons are over

Whistling at landlords *see*
Cusack, Sister Mary Frances
Clare. Tim Carty's trial;
or, Whistling at landlords

Whitaker, Lily C., b.1850.
Young American Progressive
Hobby Club. A farce in one
scene. New York: Edgar S.
Werner, 1896. 20p.

White, Charles, 1821-1891.
*[Some bibliographic sources,
including the Harvard Theatre
Collection Catalog of Engrav-
ed Dramatic Portraits, the
New York Public Library
Theatre Collection Catalog
(Part III), and Edward
LeRoy Rice in his Monarchs
of Minstrelsy, give Charles
White a middle initial of
"T." Most sources, however,
including Readex, do not
use a middle initial. They
are one and the same author]*
The African box; or, The
magician's troubles. A bur-
lesque on the box mystery
in two scenes. Arranged by
C. White. Chicago: Dramatic
Pub. Co., c1897. 6p. (The
comic drama. no. 73)

All's well that ends well

see his The serenade

Ambition. A pleasing farce
in one act. By Sam Rickey
and Master Barney. Arranged
by C. White. New York: R. M.
De Witt, c1877. 6p. (De Witt's
Ethiopian and comic drama.
no. 116) *[Sam Rickey's real
name is Richard T. Higgins;
Master Barney's real name is
Barney Scholar]*

Bad whiskey. A comic Irish
sketch in one scene. By Sam
Rickey and Master Barney.
Arranged by Charles White.
New York: De Witt Pub. House,
c1875. 6p. (De Witt's
Ethiopian and comic drama.
no. 42) *[see note immediately
above]*

Big mistake. A Negro sketch.
By A. J. Leavitt. Arranged by
Charles White. Chicago and
New York: Dramatic Pub. Co.,
1875. 6p. (The darkey and
comic drama) *[by Andrew J.
Leavitt]*

The black chemist. An Ethiop-
ian sketch in one scene.
Chicago and New York:
Dramatic Pub. Co., c1874. 6p.
(The comic drama)

The black shoemaker. A Negro
farce. London and New York:
S. French, 188-? p.43-51.
(French's acting edition.
no. 45)

The black statue. A negro
farce in one act and one
scene. London and New York:
S. French, 18-? 12p.
(French's acting edition)

Black-ey'd William. A nautical Ethiopian sketch in two
scenes. New York: Dramatic
Pub. Co., c1874. 6p. (De
Witt's Ethiopian and comic
drama. no. 11)

The bogus injun. A very

laughable sketch in four scenes. New York: R. M. De Witt, c1875. 6p. (De Witt's Ethiopian and comic drama. no. 78)

The bogus talking machine; or, The puzzled Dutchman. A negro farce in one scene. By Griffan [sic, Griffin] Hall. Arranged by Charles White. Chicago, New York: Dramatic Pub. Co., c1876. 6p. (The comic drama. no. 89)

Bone squash. A comic opera in two acts and eight scenes. London and New York: S. French, 1881? 24p. (French's acting edition. no. 77)

Bruised and cured. A Negro burlesque sketch in one scene. By A. J. Leavitt. Arranged by C. White. New York: De Witt, c1874. 5p. (De Witt's Ethiopian and comic drama. no. 24)

Coalheaver's revenge. A negro sketch. By George L. Stout. Arranged by Charles White. Chicago: Dramatic Pub. Co., c1874. 7p. (The comic drama)

The coming man. An Ethiopian sketch in two scenes. By A. J. Leavitt. Arranged by C. White. New York: C. T. De Witt, c1877. 6p. (De Witt's Ethiopian and comic drama. no. 112)

The Coopers. A farce in one act and one scene. New York: Happy Hours, 187-? 16p. (The Ethiopian drama. no. 5)

Cremation. An Ethiopian sketch. By A. J. Leavitt. Arranged by Charles White. New York: R. M. De Witt, c1875. 6p. (De Witt's Ethiopian and comic drama. no. 41)

Daguerreotypes; or, The picture gallery. An Ethiopian sketch in one scene. New York: De Witt, c1874. 6p. (De Witt's Ethiopian and comic drama. no. 12)

Damon and Pythias. A negro burlesque sketch in two scenes. Chicago: Dramatic Pub. Co., c1875. 5p. (The darkey and comic drama)

The darkey's stratagem. A negro sketch in one act. Arranged by C. White. Chicago: Dramatic Pub. Co., c1875. 9p. (The comic drama. no. 63)

The draft. A negro sketch in one act and two scenes. New York: R. M. De Witt, c1875. 6p. (De Witt's Ethiopian and comic drama. no. 50)

Dutch justice. A very laughable sketch in one scene. By D. L. Morris. Arranged by Charles White. (First edition entitled, Police court. Written by Brosse Fanning.) Chicago: Dramatic Pub. Co., c1876. 8p. (The comic drama. no. 95)

The Dutchman's ghost. By Larry Tooley. Arranged by Charles White. Chicago: Dramatic Pub. Co., c1875. 6p. (The comic drama)

Excise trials. A burlesque Negro sketch in one scene. Arranged by C. White. New York: R. M. De Witt, c1875. 6p. (De Witt's Ethiopian and comic drama. no. 52)

The fellow that looks like me. A laughable interlude in one scene. By Oliver Durevarge. Arranged by Charles White. Chicago: Dramatic Pub. Co., c1847. 7p. (The comic drama)

The first night. A very
pleasing farce in one act.
By James Budworth. Arranged
by Charles White. New York:
R. M. De Witt, c1876. 16p.
(De Witt's Ethiopian and
comic drama. no. 88)

Fisherman's luck. An Ethiopian sketch in one scene.
Chicago: Dramatic Pub. Co.,
c1875. 5p. (The comic drama.
no. 51)

The German emigrant; or,
Love and sourkrout. By
Larry Tooley. Arranged by
Charles White. Chicago:
Dramatic Pub. Co., c1876.
7p. (The darkey and comic
drama)

Gettin' de bag to hold;
or, The United States mail.
An Ethiopian farce. Chicago:
T. S. Denison, 18-? 8p.
(The Ethiopian drama)

Getting square on the call
boy. A humorous sketch in
one scene. Chicago: Dramatic
Pub. Co., c1875. 5p. (The
comic drama)

The ghost. An Ethiopian
sketch in one scene. Chi-
cago: Dramatic Pub. Co.,
c1874. 5p. (The comic drama)

Glycerine oil. An Ethiopian
sketch in two scenes. By
John Arnold, and arranged by
Charles White. New York:
R. M. De Witt, 1874. 5p.
(De Witt's Ethiopian and
comic drama. no. 31)

Going for the cup; or, Old
Mrs. Williams' dance. An
Ethiopian interlude in one
scene. New York: Robert M.
De Witt, c1874. 8p. (De
Witt's Ethiopian and comic
drama. no. 20)

Good night's rest. A sketch
in one scene. Arranged by C.
White. New York: R. M. De

Witt, c1876. 7p. (De Witt's
Ethiopian and comic drama.
no. 82)

Gripsack. A negro sketch in
one scene. By John Arnold.
Arranged by Charles White.
New York: R. M. De Witt,
c1876. 5p. (De Witt's
Ethiopian and comic drama.
no. 86)

Guide to the stage; or,
Unappreciated talent. Chicago:
Dramatic Pub. Co., c1875. 6p.

The happy couple. A short
humorous farce. Chicago and
New York: Dramatic Pub. Co.,
c1875. 7p. (The darkey and
comic drama)

Hard times. A Negro extra-
vaganza in one scene. By
D. D. Emmett. Arranged by C.
White. Chicago and New York:
Dramatic Pub. Co., c1874.
9p. [by Daniel Decatur
Emmett]

High Jack, the heeler. An
Ethiopian sketch in one
scene. By A. J. Leavitt
and arranged by Charles
White. New York: De Witt
Pub. House, 1875. 6p. (De
Witt's Ethiopian and comic
drama. no. 48)

Hippotheatron; or, Burlesque
circus. An extravagant funny
sketch. New York: De Witt
Pub. House, c1875. 6p. (De
Witt's Ethiopian and comic
drama. no. 68)

The hop of fashion. A Negro
farce in one act and two
scenes. New York: Happy
Hours, 187-? 21p. (The
Ethiopian drama. no. 21)

In and out. A Negro sketch
in one scene. By A. J.
Leavitt. Arranged by C.
White. New York: De Witt
Pub. House, c1875. 4p. (De
Witt's Ethiopian and comic
drama. no. 71)

Jealous husband. A Negro sketch. Arranged by C. White. New York: R. M. De Witt, c1874. 6p. (De Witt's Ethiopian and comic drama. no. 33)

The jolly millers. A negro farce in one act and one scene. New York: Happy Hours, 188-? 13p.

Julius the snoozer; or, The conspirators of Thompson Street. An Ethiopian burlesque in three scenes. By A. Ryman. Arranged by C. White. New York: R. M. De Witt, c1876. 8p. (De Witt's Ethiopian and comic drama. no. 94) *[by John Addison Ryman]*

Laughing gas. A Negro burlesque sketch. As arranged by Charles White. New York: R. M. De Witt, c1874. 5p. (De Witt's Ethiopian and comic drama. no. 36)

The live injin; or, Jim Crow. A comical Ethiopian sketch in four scenes. By Dan Bryant. Arranged by Charles White. Chicago: Dramatic Pub. Co., 18-? 7p. (The comic drama) *[Dan Bryant's real name is Daniel Webster O'Brien]*

The lost will. A Negro sketch. (Formerly called "Government despatches.") By A. J. Leavitt. Arranged by Charles White. New York: De Witt Pub. House, c1875. 7p. (De Witt's Ethiopian and comic drama. no. 60)

A lucky job. A Negro farce. New York: R. M. De Witt, c1874. 12p. (De Witt's Ethiopian and comic drama. no. 37)

Lunatic asylum *see his* Pompey's patients

The magic penny. A Nigger melodrama in one act. London and New York: S. French, 18-? Title page lacking. 18p. (French's acting edition (Late Lacy's) no. 55)

Malicious trespass; or, Nine points of law. A sketch in one scene. New York: R. M. De Witt, c1874. 7p. (De Witt's Ethiopian and comic drama. no. 19)

Mazeppa. An equestrian burlesque in two acts. Transposed and arranged by C. White. New York: S. French, 186-? 12p. (The Ethiopian drama. no. 3)

The mischievous Nigger. A Negro farce. New York: H. Roorbach, 187-? 31p.

The mutton trial. An Ethiopian sketch in two scenes. By James Maffitt. Arranged by Charles White. New York: De Witt Pub. House, c1874. 7p. (De Witt's Ethiopian and comic drama. no. 8)

The mystic spell. A pantomime in seven scenes. New York: F. A. Brady, 1856. 15p. (Brady's Ethiopian drama. no. 12)

Nip and Tuck *see his* The serenade

A night in a strange hotel. A laughable Negro sketch in one scene. Chicago: Dramatic Pub. Co., c1875. 5p. (The comic drama. no. 49)

Obeying orders. Ethiopian military sketch in one scene. By John Arnold. Arranged by C. White. New York: R. M. De Witt, c1874. 6p. (De Witt's Ethiopian and comic drama. no. 22)

Oh! hush!; or, The Virginny cupids! An operatic olio

in one act and three scenes.
New York: Happy Hours, 1873?
21p. (The Ethiopian drama.
no. 19)

Old Dad's cabin. A Negro
farce in one act and one
scene. Clyde, O.: Ames,
189-. 10p. (Ames' series of
standard and minor drama.
no. 234)

One night in a bar room.
A burlesque sketch. New
York: R. M. De Witt, c1874.
7p. (De Witt's Ethiopian
and comic drama. no. 30)

100th night of Hamlet. A
Negro sketch. Arranged by
Charles White. New York:
R. M. De Witt, c1874. 6p.
(De Witt's Ethiopian and
comic drama. no. 27)

One, two, three. A Negro
sketch in one scene. (Sometimes called "Bounce.")
By John Wild. Arranged by
Charles White. New York:
R. M. De Witt, c1875. 6p.
(De Witt's Ethiopian and
comic drama. no. 76) *[first
introduced in Detroit in
1861 under the title of
Conner's dramatic agency]*

P. P. P. Podge *see*
The stage-struck couple

Pete and the peddler. A
Negro and Irish sketch in
one scene. By F. K. Wallace.
Arranged by Charles White.
Chicago: Dramatic Pub. Co.,
c1876. 6p. (The darkey and
comic drama)

The policy players. An
Ethiopian sketch in one
scene. New York: R. M.
De Witt, c1874. 6p. (De
Witt's Ethiopian and comic
drama. no. 9)

Pompey's patients. A laughable interlude in two scenes.
Sometimes called Lunatic

asylum. Chicago and New York:
Dramatic Pub. Co., c1875. 6p.
(The darkey and comic drama)

Port wine vs. jealousy. A
highly amusing sketch. By
William Carter. Arranged by
C. White. New York: De Witt
Pub. House, c1875. 8p. (De
Witt's Ethiopian and comic
drama. no. 66)

The portrait painter. A
pantomimic farce in one act
and one scene. New York: S.
French, 187-? 25p. (The
Ethiopian drama. no. 20)

The recruiting office. An
Ethiopian sketch in two
scenes. New York: De Witt
Pub. House, c1874. 5p. (De
Witt's Ethiopian and comic
drama. no. 14)

The rehearsal; or, Barry's
old man. A laughable Irish
farce in two scenes. By Sam
Rickey and Master Barney.
Arranged by Charles White.
Chicago: Dramatic Pub. Co.,
c1876. 6p. (The comic drama.
no. 105) *[Sam Rickey's real
name is Richard T. Higgins;
Master Barney's real name
is Barney Scholar]*

A remittance from home. An
Ethiopian sketch in one scene.
By A. J. Leavitt. Arranged by
C. White. New York: R. M.
De Witt, c1875. 5p. (De Witt's
Ethiopian and comic drama.
no. 45)

Rigging a purchase. A Negro
sketch in one scene. By
A. J. Leavitt. Arranged by
C. White. New York: R. M.
De Witt, c1875. 7p. (De
Witt's Ethiopian and comic
drama. no. 55)

Rival artists. A Negro sketch
in one scene. Arranged by
Charles White. New York:
R. M. De Witt, c1876. 7p. (De

Witt's Ethiopian and comic drama. no. 81)

The rival lovers. A Negro farce in one act and one scene. New York: O. A. Roorbach, 186-? 18p. (The Ethiopian drama. no. 7)

Rival tenants. A Negro sketch. By Geo. L. Stout. Arranged by Charles White. Chicago and New York: Dramatic Pub. Co., c1874. 6p. (The darkey and comic drama)

Sam's courtship. An Ethiopian farce in one act. New York: Dramatic Pub. Co., c1874. 7p. (De Witt's Ethiopian and comic drama. no. 15)

The sausage makers. A Negro burlesque sketch in two scenes. Arranged by Charles White. New York: De Witt Pub. House, c1875. 5p. (De Witt's Ethiopian and comic drama. no. 59)

Scampini. An anti-tragical, comical, magical, and laughable pantomime. By Edward Warden. Arranged by Charles White. Chicago: Dramatic Pub. Co., c1874. 8p. (The darkey and comic drama)

Scenes on the Mississippi. A real (Southern) darkey sketch in two scenes. By Buckley's minstrels. Chicago: Dramatic Pub. Co., c1875. 5p. (The comic drama. no. 80)

The serenade. A Negro sketch in two scenes. (Sometimes called "All's well that ends well," and "Nip and Tuck.") New York: R. M. De Witt, 1876. 5p. (De Witt's Ethiopian and comic drama. no. 84)

The sham doctor. A Negro

farce in one act and three scenes. New York: Happy Hours, 187-? 17p. (The Ethiopian drama. no. 8)

Siamese twins. A Negro burlesque sketch. Arranged by C. White. New York: R. M. De Witt, c1874. 6p. (De Witt's Ethiopian and comic drama. no. 38)

The sleep walker. An Ethiopian sketch in two scenes. By A. J. Leavitt. Arranged by Charles White. New York: Robert M. De Witt, c1875. 5p. (De Witt's Ethiopian and comic drama. no. 74)

A slippery day. An Ethiopian sketch in one scene. By Robert Hart, as arranged by Charles White. New York: R. M. De Witt, 1875. 7p. (De Witt's Ethiopian and comic drama. no. 46)

Squire for a day. A Negro sketch in one scene. By Andrew J. Leavitt. Arranged by C. White. New York: R. M. De Witt, c1875. 7p. (De Witt's Ethiopian and comic drama. no. 69)

Stage struck barber *see his* The stage-struck couple

The stage-struck couple. A laughable interlude in one scene. (Sometimes called "Stage struck barber," "P. P. Podge," &c.) New York: R. M. De Witt, 1875. 5p. (De Witt's Ethiopian and comic drama. no. 56)

Storming the fort. An Ethiopian burlesque sketch in one scene. New York: R. M. De Witt, c1874. 4p. (De Witt's Ethiopian and comic drama. no. 16)

The stranger. A burlesque Negro sketch in one scene. By A. J. Leavitt, as arranged

by Charles White. Chicago:
Dramatic Pub. Co., c1875.
4p. (The darkey and comic
drama)

Streets of New York; or,
New York by gaslight. An
Ethiopian sketch in one
scene. New York: Dramatic
Pub. Co., c1874. 6p. (De
Witt's Ethiopian and comic
drama. no. 13)

Stupid servant. An Ethiopian
sketch in one scene. Chicago:
Dramatic Pub. Co., c1874. 7p.
(The darkey and comic drama)

Them papers. An Ethiopian
sketch in one scene. By
A. J. Leavitt and arranged
by Charles White. New York:
De Witt Pub. House, 1875.
6p. (De Witt's Ethiopian and
comic drama. no. 54)

Thieves at the mill. A comic
Ethiopian drama in one act
and four scenes. New York:
S. French, 18-? 19p. (The
Ethiopian drama. no. 24)

Three strings to one bow.
An Ethiopian sketch. Arranged
by C. White. New York: R. M.
De Witt, c1874. 5p. (De
Witt's Ethiopian and comic
drama. no. 34)

De trouble begins at nine.
A Darkey interlude. Boston:
Walter H. Baker, c1889. 8p.
(Baker's edition of plays)
[title page: "an act for
bones and banjoist." Readex
enters a later edition of
this same play under title]

Uncle Eph's dream. An original Negro sketch in two
scenes and two tableaux.
New York: R. M. De Witt,
1874. 6p. (De Witt's Ethiopian and comic drama. no. 28)

Uncle Jeff. A Negro farce in
one act and five scenes.
Arranged by C. White. New

York: Harold Roorbach, 1891.
25p. (Roorbach's acting
drama)

United States mail. A farce
in one act. New York: S.
French, 187-? 19p. (The
Ethiopian drama. no. 4)

Vilikens and Dinah. A Negro
farce in one act and one
scene. New York: Happy Hours,
187-. 13p. (The Ethiopian
drama. no. 10) [the cover
gives title as Villikins and
his Dinah, whereas the title
page gives Vilikens and
Dinah. This play is based on
Sir Francis Cowley Burnand's
Villikins and his Dinah.
Another edition is entered
by Readex under Caroline
Stearns Griffin, Villikins
and his Diniah]

Vinegar bitters. A Negro
sketch in one scene. By
Frank Dumont. Arranged by
Charles White. New York:
De Witt, c1875. 5p. (De
Witt's Ethiopian and comic
drama. no. 62)

The Virginny mummy. A Negro
farce in one act and four
scenes. New York: Happy
Hours, 187-? 16p. (The
Ethiopian drama. no. 23)
[the cover gives "Virginia
..." and the title page gives
"Virginny"]

Wake up, William Henry.
Revised and arranged by
Charles White. New York:
De Witt Pub. House, 1874.
6p. (De Witt's Ethiopian and
comic drama. no. 32) [title
page: "a Negro sketch known
as Psychological experiments,
Psychology, Bumps and Lumps,
Bumpology, etc."]

Wanted, a nurse. A laughable
sketch. New York: R. M.
De Witt, c1874. 5p. (De Witt's
Ethiopian and comic drama.
no. 39)

Weston, the walkist. A very amusing sketch in one scene. By John Mack, arranged by Charles White. New York: R. M. De Witt, 1875. 7p. (De Witt's Ethiopian and comic drama. no. 75)

Who died first? A Negro sketch. By A. J. Leavitt, arranged by Charles White. Chicago: Dramatic Pub. Co., c1874. 9p. (The comic drama. no. 29)

The wreck. A nautical negro farce in one act and one scene. New York: Happy Hours, 187-? 19p. (The Ethiopian drama. no. 18)

Young scamp. A Darkey sketch in one scene. By Add[ison] Weaver. Arranged by Charles White. New York: De Witt Pub. House, c1876. 5p. (De Witt's Ethiopian and comic drama. no. 85)

White, George.
Kathleen's honor. An original melo-drama in five acts. Philadelphia: Music and Drama Co., 1892. 25p.

White, James, 1803-1862.
Feudal times; or, The court of James the third *see* The modern standard drama, vol. 6

The king of the Commons *see* The modern standard drama, vol. 4

White, John Blake, 1781-1859.
The forgers. A dramatic poem. Reprinted from the "Southern Literary Journal," March, 1837. New York?: n.pub., 1899. 59p.

The white caps *see* Pelham, Nettie H.

The white horse of the Peppers

see Lover, Samuel *in* Massey, Charles. Massey's exhibition reciter

The white lady. A comic opera in three acts. (From the French of Scribe.) New York: Baker & Godwin, 1866. Bilingual text: English and French. 37, 8p. Libretto. *[music by Adrien Boieldieu on libretto La dame blanche by Augustin Eugène Scribe]*

A white lie *see* Dale, Horace C. *see also* Keatinge, Ella

White lies *see* A collection of temperance dialogues *see also* Turner, Cyril

A White Mountain boy *see* Townsend, Charles

The white mouse *see* Robertson, Donald. The triumph of youth; or, The white mouse

The white princess *see* Venable, William Henry *in his* The school stage

The white slave *see* Campbell, Bartley Theodore *see also* *in his* The white slave and other plays

White sulphur; or, A day at the springs *see* Callahan, Charles E.

Whiting, Evelyn G. *see* Card, Evelyn G. Whiting

Whitley, Thomas W.
The Jesuit; or, The amours of Capt. Effingham and the Lady Zarifa [From United States Democratic Review. Washington, D. C.: March, May, 1850. 244, 450p.] p.235-244, 439-450.

Whitney, Thomas Richard,
1804-1858.
Love; or, The heart's
ordeal [From his: Evening
hours; a collection of
poems. New York: Leavitt,
Trow, 1844. 118p.] p.7-30.

Whittemore, B. G.
Lights and shadows of the
great rebellion; or, The
hospital nurse of Tennessee
see Dawson, J. H. and
Whittemore, B. G.

Whittier, John Greenleaf,
1807-1892.
Maud Muller see Merriman,
Effie Woodward

Who caught the count see
Hiland, Frank E.

Who died first? see White,
Charles

Who got the pig see McDermott,
J. J. and Trumble

Who paid for the supper see
Kaler, James Otis. A devil
of a scrape; or, Who paid
for the supper

Who speaks first? see Steele,
Silas Sexton. The stranger's
kiss; or, Who speaks first?
in his Collected works.
Book of plays

Who stole the chicken? see
Leavitt, Andrew J. and
Eagan, H. W.

Who told the lie? see
Sonneborn, Hilton Burnside

Who's the actor? see Dumont,
Frank

Who's the traitor? see Morris,
George Pope. The maid of
Saxony; or, Who's the traitor?

Who's to inherit? An original
comedy in one act. New York:
Dick & Fitzgerald, 18-? 18p.

Whose baby is it? see
Dumont, Frank

Why a deacon gave up his wine
see Bradley, Nellie H.
The stumbling block; or,
Why a deacon gave up his
wine

Why don't you drink? see
The temperance school
dialogues

Why Smith left home see
Broadhurst, George Howells

Why they joined the Rebeccas
see Buxton, Ida M.

Wickersham, James Alexander,
b. 1851.
Aliso and Acne. New York:
Brentano's Literary Emporium,
c1881. 116p.

Wide awake dialogues see
Denison, Thomas Stewart

Wide awake Nell see Dumont,
Frank. The girl from Klondike;
or, Wide awake Nell

Wide enough for two see
Denison, Thomas Stewart

The widow see Ayer, Harriet
Hubbard

Widow Freeheart; or, The woman
haters see Hardy, Edward
Trueblood

The widow from the West; or,
The late Mr. Early see
Coon, Hilton

The widow Mullin's Christmas
see Beach, Stanley Yale
and Powell, H. Arthur

The widower's trials *see*
Dow, James M.

The widow's maid and the
bachelor's man; or, How to
get rid of them. A petite
comedy in two acts. By
Quid Rides (pseud.) Cin-
cinnati: U. P. James,
1859. 33p.

The widow's marriage *see*
Baker, George Henry

The widow's proposals *see*
Felter, Will D.

The wife *see* Belasco, David
and De Mille, Henry Churchill

The wife; a tale of Mantus
see Knowles, John Sheridan
in The modern standard
drama, vol. 1

The wife and the widow *see*
Payne, John Howard, Mrs.
Smith; or, The wife and
the widow

A wife by advertisement *see*
Cliffe, Clifton

The wife of Seaton; or, The
siege of Berwick *see*
Townsend, Eliza

The wig-maker and his servants
see Oppenheim, Charles

The wig makers. An Ethiopian
farce in one act. New York:
S. French, 18-? 8p. (French's
acting drama. Late Lacy's)

Wild, John, 1843-1898.
Conner's dramatic agency
see White, Charles. One,
two, three

One, two, three *see* White,
Charles

Wild Irish girl *see* Pilgrim,
James

Wild Mab *see* Polson, Minnie

Wildenbruch, Ernst von,
1845-1909.
Harold *see* Clarke, Hugh
Archibald

Wilder, J. A.
Hamlet; or, The sport, the
spook, and the spinster *see*
Batchelder, Samuel Francis

Wiley, Sara King, 1871-1909.
Cromwell. An historical
play in five acts [From her:
Poems lyrical and dramatic,
to which is added Cromwell:
an historical play. London:
Chapman & Hall, 1900] p.97-
214.

Wilhelmi, A. (pseud.) *see*
Zechmeister, Alexander Victor

Wilkie, David, 1785-1841.
The rent-day *see* Jerrold,
Douglas William *in* The
modern standard drama,
vol. 4

Wilkins, Edward G. P., d.1861.
My wife's mirror. A comedy
in one act. New York: S.
French, 1856. 16p. (French's
American drama. The acting
edition. no. 97)

Young New York. A comedy in
three acts. New York: S.
Perry, c1856. 36p. (French's
standard drama. no. 185)

Wilkins, John H., 1826?-1853.
Signor Marc. A play in five
acts. (Also known as St.
Marc; or, A husband's sacrifice.) [From: America's lost
plays. Edited by Eugene Page.
Princeton, N. J.: Princeton
Univ. Press, 1941. vol. 14,
p.261-341]

Wilkins, W. Henri.
Hash! An original farce in
one act. Clyde, O.: Ames,

1880? 10p. (Ames' series of standard and minor drama. no. 116)

Mother's fool. A farce in one act. Clyde, O.: Ames, c1879. 12p. (Ames' series of standard and minor drama. no. 69)

The reward of crime; or, The love of gold. A drama of Vermont in two acts. Clyde, O.: Ames, c1880. 20p. (Ames' series of standard and minor drama. no. 71)

Rock Allen, the orphan; or, Lost and found. A comedy drama in two acts. Clyde, O.: Ames, 1871. 17p. (Ames' series of standard and minor drama. no. 45)

S. H. A. M. Pinafore. An original operatic burlesque and parody in one act. Clyde, O.: Ames, c1882. 12p. (Ames' series of standard and minor drama. no. 115) *[a burlesque on Sir William Schwenck Gilbert's H. M. S. Pinafore]*

Three glasses a day; or, The broken home. A moral and temperance drama in three acts. Clyde, O.: Ames, 1878. 16p. (Ames' series of standard and minor drama. no. 63)

The turn of the tide; or, Wrecked in port. A nautical and temperance drama in three acts. Clyde, O.: Ames, c1880. Prompt-book, interleaved with Ms. notes. 25p. (Ames' series of standard and minor drama. no. 102)

The will *see* Fowle, William Bentley *in his* Parlor dramas

The will and the way *see* Calvert, George Henry. Comedies

Will-o'-the-wisp; or, The shot in the dark *see* Hanshew, Thomas W.

Will you marry me? *see* Julian, Robert

Willard, Charles O. Little Goldie; or, The child of the camp. A Western comedy drama in four acts. Clyde, O.: Ames, c1893. 28p. (Ames' series of standard and minor drama. no. 330)

Stubs; or, The fool from Boston. A farce comedy in four acts. Clyde, O.: Ames, c1895. 34p. (Ames' series of standard and minor drama. no. 363)

Willard, Edward. Julius Caesar. An historical tragedy in five acts. Philadelphia: H. Willard, c1890. 116p.

William Henry *see* Chaney, Mrs. George L.

William Tell. An Ethiopian interlude. London and New York: S. French, 1881? 8p. *see also* Brooks, Charles Timothy *see also* Fowle, William Bentley *in his* Parlor dramas *see also* Griffin, George W. H. *see also* Knowles, James Sheridan *in* The modern standard drama, vol. 5

Williams, Barney, 1823-1876. Alive and kicking. New York: n.pub., 1846. Title page lacking. Prompt-book in Ms. 40 unnumbered leaves. *[Barney Williams is really Bernard Flaherty (or O'Flaherty)]*

Williams, Charles. The elopement; or, The disinherited son. A petite comedy in two acts [Bound with: Gonsalvo...and other poems] Philadelphia: T. K. and P. G. Collins, 1848. [163p.] p.83-108.

Gonsalvo; or, The corsair's doom [From his: Gonsolvo... The elopement...and other poems. Philadelphia: T. K. and P. G. Collins, 1848. 163p.] p.1-7, 12-81.

Williams, Espy William Hendricks, 1852-1908.
The atheist. A modern masque. New Orleans: n.pub., 189-? 13p.

Eugene Aram. A play in five acts. New Orleans: Amos S. Collins, 1874. Private edition. 73p. [based on Bulwer-Lytton's novel Eugene Aram]

The husband. A society play in four acts. New Orleans: Theo. A. Ray, 1898. 89p. [founded in part on Retribution by Tom Taylor]

Parrhasius; or, Thriftless ambition. A dramatic poem. New Orleans: Southern Pub. Co., 1879. 26p.

Witchcraft; or, The witch of Salem. A legend of old New England in five acts. New Orleans: E. A. Brandao, 1886. 53p.

Williams, Francis Howard, 1844-1922.
The higher education. A comedy in two acts. Philadelphia: Collins, 1882? 41p.

The Princess Elizabeth. A lyric drama. Philadelphia: Claxton, Remsen, & Haffelfinger, 1880. 212p.

A reformer in ruffles. A comedy in three acts. Philadelphia: For the author by Collins, c1883. 56p.

Williams, Frederick.
The little duke (Le petit duc.) Comic opera in three acts. Boston: Oliver Ditson, c1879. Vocal score. 116p. [music by Alexander Charles Lecocq on libretto Le petit duc by Henri Meilhac and Ludovic Halévy; joint author: Thomas Russell Sullivan]

The little duke. A comic opera in three acts. (From the French of Lecocq.) Boston: Oliver Ditson, c1879. 64p. Libretto. [see note immediately above]

The rat-charmer of Hamelin. Comic opera in four acts. New York: Edward Schuberth, c1381. Vocal score. Bilingual text: English and German. 198p. [music by Adolf Neuendorff on libretto Der Rattenfänger von Hameln by Heinrich Italiener]

Romeo and Juliet. By William Shakespeare. New York: n.pub., 1899. 158p. Prompt-book, interleaved, with Ms. notes.

The streets of New York. A drama in five acts. (From Boucicault's The poor of New York.) Boston: Boston Museum, 18-? Prompt-book interleaved with Ms. notes. 45p. (pag. irreg.) (French's standard drama. The acting edition. no. 189)

Williams, George W.
Cleveland's reception party. An original farce in three scenes. Clyde, O.: Ames, c1892. 9p. (Ames' series of standard and minor drama. no. 317)

Williams, Henry Llewellyn, b.1842.
L'article 47; or, Breaking

the ban. A drama in three acts. (Translated from the French of Adolphe Belot.) New York: De Witt, c1872. 42p. (De Witt's acting plays. no. 137)

B. B. *see his* The black chap from Whitechapel

The bachelor's box. A comedietta in one act. (From the French of Meilhac and Halevy.) New York: For the trade by De Witt, 1880. 18p. *[based on Le petit hôtel by Henri Meilhac and Ludovic Halévy]*

The bells; or, The Polish Jew. A romantic, moral drama in three acts. (From the French of Erckmann and Chatrain [sic, Chatrian]) New York: De Witt, 1872. 33p. *[based on Le Juif polonais by Émile Erckmann and Alexandre Chatrian]*

The black chap from Whitechapel. An eccentric Negro piece. Chicago: Dramatic Pub. Co., c1871. 14p. (The comic drama. no. 6) *[based on Sir Francis Cowley Burnand's B. B.]*

The black Forrest. An Ethiopian farce. New York: De Witt, c1882. 10p. (De Witt's Ethiopian and comic drama. no. 146) *[based on James Robinson Planché's The Garrick fever]*

De black magician; or, The wonderful beaver. An Ethiopian comicality in one scene. Chicago and New York: Dramatic Pub. Co., c1876. 16p. (The darkey and comic drama)

Bobolino, the black bandit. A musical farce. Chicago: Dramatic Pub. Co., c1880. 8p. (The comic drama)

Challenge dance. London and New York: S. French, 18-? Title page lacking. p.38-46. (French's acting edition. Late Lacy's. no. 43) *[Readex also enters this same play under title]*

Charles O'Malley's aunt. A comedietta in one scene. Chicago: T. S. Denison, c1897. 27p. (Denison's acting plays) *[based on the novel of the same name by Charles Lever]*

Dancing attendance. A comedietta in one act. New York: De Witt, c1894. 13p. (De Witt's acting plays. no. 401)

The darkey sleep-walker; or, Ill-treated ill somnambulo. An original nigger act in one scene. New York: Published for the trade by De Witt, 1880. 12p. (De Witt's Ethiopian and comic drama. no. 113)

Dar's de money. Burlesque on "Othello.") London and New York: S. French, 18-? Title page lacking. *[Williams is the presumed author]*

Deaf--in a horn. An Ethiopian sketch in one act. Chicago: T. S. Denison, 18-? 6p. (The Ethiopian drama) *[Readex enters another edition of this play under title]*

Declined--with thanks. An original farcical comedietta in one act and one scene. (From the English of J. M. Morton.) Chicago: Dramatic Pub. Co., c1886. 17p. (Sergel's acting drama. no. 342) *[based on the work of John Maddison Morton]*

Dem good ole times; or, Sixteen thousand years ago. An Ethiopian act in one scene. Chicago: T. S. Denison, 18-? 7p. (The Ethiopian drama)

[Readex enters another edition of this play under the title Sixteen thousand years ago]

Diplomates. A comedy in four acts. (From the French of Sardou.) Chicago: T. S. Denison, 1894. 84p. (Denison's series. vol. 5. no. 35) *[based on Dora by Victorien Sardou]*

Fernanda; or, Forgive and forget. A drama in three acts. (From the French of Sardou.) New York: De Witt, c1870. 56p.

Fetter Lane to Gravesend; or, A dark romance from the "Railway library." London and New York: S. French, 18-? Title page lacking. p.21-28.

The fifth wheel. A comedy in three acts. New York: De Witt, c1869. 42p. (De Witt's acting plays. no. 99)

Go and get tight. An Ethiopian farce in one scene. New York: De Witt, 1880. 9p. (De Witt's Ethiopian and comic drama. no. 130)

A happy day. A domestic farce in one act. By Richard-Henry (pseud.) Adapted by H. L. Williams. New York: De Witt, c1886. 15p. (De Witt's acting plays. no. 347)

Isabella Orsini. A romantic drama in four acts. (From the German of Mosenthal.) New York: De Witt, c1870. 51p. (De Witt's acting plays. no. 122)

The Lime-Kiln Club in an uproar! An Ethiopian drollery in one scene. Chicago: Dramatic Pub. Co., c1891. 8p. (The darkey and comic drama. no. 9)

Love and lockjaw. A black-face farce in one scene. New York: De Witt, c1895. 15p. (De Witt's Ethiopian and comic drama. no. 163)

Marjorie Daw see Braddon, Mary Elizabeth

Moko marionettes. An Ethiopian eccentricity in one act and two scenes. (Founded on "The Marionettes" by J. F. MacArdle.) New York: Published for the trade, 1880. 13p. (De Witt's Ethiopian and comic drama. no. 129)

Penmark Abbey. A nautical melodrama in two acts. (From the French of W. M. Thackeray.) New York: De Witt, c1884. 34p. (De Witt's acting plays. no. 320) *[Although attributed to William Makepiece Thackeray, this work actually was written by Thomas James Thackeray and co-authored by Pierre Tournemine under the title L'Abbaye de Penmarque; see Henry Sayre Van Duzer's A Thackeray library (Port Washington, N. Y.: Kennikat Press, 1965, p.100)]*

A Romeo on "the gridiron." A monologue for a lady. New York: De Witt, c1883. 6p. (De Witt's acting plays. no. 316)

Sparking. A comedietta in one act and one scene. Chicago: Dramatic Pub. Co., c1882. 19p. (American acting drama) *[founded on L'étincelle by Édouard Pailleron]*

Sport with a sportsman. New York and London: S. French, 18-? Title page lacking. p.11-24. (French's acting edition. Late Lacy's) *[Readex also enters this same play under title]*

Stocks up! Stocks down! A
duologue in one scene.
Chicago: Dramatic Pub. Co.,
18-? 6p. (The comic drama)
[Readex also enters this
same play under its title]

Three black Smiths. An original Ethiopian eccentricity
in one scene. London and New
York: S. French, 18-? Title
page lacking. p.25-36.
(French's acting edition.
Late Lacy's)

Wax works at play. Chicago:
T. S. Denison, 1894. 12p.
(The Ethiopian drama)

Williams, Marie Josephine.
A brown paper parcel. New
York: S. French, c1899. 9p.
(French's international
copyrighted...edition of the
works of the best authors.
no. 26) [Readex also enters
this same play under W.,
J. M.]

A nice quiet chat. London:
S. French, c1899. 8p.
(French's international
copyrighted...edition of the
works of the best authors.
no. 25)

Williams, Montagu Stephen,
1835-1892.
Sullivan the slugger see
Sullivan the slugger

Williamson, Eugene F.
Miriam. A drama in three
scenes. Pittsburgh: Stevenson, Foster & Co., 1879.
32p.

The sisters of Alhama.
Pittsburgh: Stevenson,
Foster & Co., 1880. 72p.
see also Silvia and other
dramas

Willis, Nathaniel Parker,
1806-1867.
Bianca Visconti; or, The

heart overtasked. New York:
Samuel Colman, 1839. 108p.
(Colman's dramatic library)
see also Dying to lose him;
or, Bianca Visconti in his
Two ways of dying for a
husband

Lord Ivan and his daughter
[From his: Melanie and
other poems. New York:
Saunders and Otley, 1837.
Second edition. 242p.]
p.23-46.

Tortesa the usurer. New York:
S. Colman, 1839. 149p.
(Colman's dramatic library)

Two ways of dying for a
husband. 1: Dying to keep
him; or, Tortesa the usurer.
2: Dying to lose him; or,
Bianca Visconti. London:
H. Cunningham, 1839. 245p.

Willner, Wolff, b.1863.
The book of Esther. Drama-
tized by Rev. W. Willner.
Cincinnati: American Hebrew
Pub. House, 1892. 32p.

Wills, William Gorman, 1828-
1891.
Olivia see Davenport,
Fanny Lily Gypsy

Parrhasius see Massey,
Charles. Massey's exhibition
reciter

Wilson, Bertha M.
A Chinese wedding. A representation of the wedding
ceremony in China, arranged
as a costume pantomime in
seven scenes. Philadelphia:
Penn Pub. Co., 1895. 23p.
(Keystone edition of popular
plays)

The show at Wilkins' Hall;
or, A leaf from the life of
Maria Jane. Arranged for
either a lady or a gentleman
in female costume. New York:

Dick & Fitzgerald, c1895.
8p. *[a "take-off" on Del-
sarteans]*

Wilson, Ella Calista Handy,
b.1851.
The bachelor's Christmas.
A Christmas entertainment.
By E. C. W. Boston: W. H.
Baker, c1889. 31p. (Baker's
edition of plays)

Wilson, John G., 1832-1914.
Nordeck *see* Mayo, Frank
and Wilson, John G.

The royal guard *see* Mayo,
Frank and Wilson, John G.

Tent and throne. A romantic
play in five acts. Monmouth,
Ill.: G. G. McCosh, 1879.
51 unnumbered leaves.

Wilson, Louise Latham.
A case of suspension. A
comedietta in one act.
Philadelphia: Penn Pub. Co.,
1916. 20p. *[earlier copyright: 1899]*

The old maids' association.
A farcical entertainment.
Philadelphia: Penn Pub. Co.,
1916. 17p. *[earlier copyright: 1900]*

The scientific country
school. A farcical enter-
tainment. Philadelphia:
Penn Pub. Co., 1916. 28p.
[earlier copyright: 1899]

The Smith mystery. A comedy
in one act. Chicago: Dramatic Pub. Co., c1899. 12p.
(Sergel's acting drama.
no. 503)

The trouble at Satterlee's.
A farce in one act. Philadelphia: Penn Pub. Co.,
1911. 16p. *[earlier copyright: 1899]*

Two of a kind. A comedy.
Chicago: T. S. Denison,
c1899. 20p. (Amateur series)

The wreck of Stebbins pride.
A comedy in two acts. Philadelphia: Penn Pub. Co.,
1912. 27p. *[earlier copyright: 1899]*

Wilson, Olivia Lovell.
The luck of the golden
pumpkin [bound with] The
old woman who lived in a shoe
[and] Christmas [From:
Christmas entertainments for
home and school...By Jay
Kaye. Boston: W. H. Baker,
c1887. 104p.] p.57-99.

The marriage of Prince
Flutterby. A comedy for
children in one act. Boston:
Walter H. Baker, 1886. 20p.
(Baker's edition of plays)

Wilstach, Paul, 1870-1952.
A game for two. An episode
in one act for a man and
his wife. Washington, D. C.:
n.pub., c1896. Typescript,
prompt-book with Ms. notes.
31 leaves (numb. irreg.)

An ounce of prevention.
A comedy in one act. New
York: n.pub., 189-. Type-
script, prompt-book. 25
leaves.

A partial eclipse. In one
act. New York: n.pub.,
c1896. Typescript, prompt-
book. 24 leaves.

Wilton, M. J.
Fun in a cooper's shop.
An original Ethiopian sketch.
New York: De Witt, 188-.
9p. (De Witt's Ethiopian
and comic drama. no. 152)

How to pay the rent. An
original farce in one scene.
New York: De Witt, c1883.
8p. (De Witt's Ethiopian
and comic drama. no. 150)

Mickey Free. A sketch in one
scene. New York: De Witt,
188-? 8p. (De Witt's Ethiop-

ian and comic drama. no.
151)

Oleomargarine. An Ethiopian
sketch in one scene.
Chicago: Dramatic Pub. Co.,
c1892. 8p. (The comic drama)

Waiting for the train. An
original sketch in one scene
for male character [bound
with] Me hanson [sic, han-
som] New York: P. J. Kenedy,
Excelsior Pub. House, 1888.
11p. (Kenedy's new series
of plays) *[Me hansom is a
solo recitation]*

Wind and sea *see* Mitchell,
Silas Weir

Wine as a medicine; or,
Abbie's experience *see*
Bradley, Nellie H.

The wine cup; or, Saved at
last. A temperance sketch
in two scenes. New York:
Happy Hours, c1876. 8p.
(The amateur stage. no. 47)

Wine, women, gambling, theft,
murder and the scaffold *see*
Hill, Frederick Stanhope.
The six degrees of crime;
or, Wine, women, gambling,
theft, murder and the
scaffold

Wink, Frederick.
Amina; or, The Shah's bride
see Brunswick, Herman

Winkle, William.
A great success. A comedy
in three acts. New York:
De Witt, 18-? 46p. (De Witt's
acting plays. no. 306)

Winkley, Rev. S. H.
The coming of the Messiah
see Cobb, Mary L. Poetical
dramas for home and school

Winn, Edith Lynwood, 1868-1933.

A vision of fair women. A
dramatic paraphrase based on
Tennyson's Dream of fair
women. Boston: Walter H.
Baker, c1891. 15p. (Baker's
edition of plays)(Baker's
novelty list)

Winning a wife *see* Moore,
Bernard Francis

The winning hand; or, The
imposter *see* Myles,
George B.

Winning ways *see* Rice,
Walter F.

Winslow, Catherine Mary Reignolds, d.1911.
Broken trust. A drama in
five acts. Boston: n.pub.,
c1886. Typescript, prompt-
book with Ms. notes. Title
page lacking. 21 leaves.

Winslow, Charles Edward Amory,
1877-1957.
Magda. A play in four acts.
(From the German of Suder-
mann.) New York, London:
S. French, c1895. 161p.

Winston, Mary A.
A rural ruse. A comedy in
one act. Boston: Walter H.
Baker, c1893. 14p. (Baker's
edition of plays)

Winter, C. Gordon.
The cross of honor *see*
Rideal, Charles Frederick
and Winter, C. Gordon

Winter, William, 1834-1917.
The inconstant; or, The way
to win him *see* Daly,
Augustin

Winter evening's entertainment
see Arnold, George and
Cahill, Frank. Parlor theatricals; or, Winter evening's
entertainment

Winters, Elizabeth.
Columbia, the gem of the
ocean. Chicago: A. Flanagan,
1899. 12p.

Wiseman, Nicholas Patrick
Stephen, 1802-1865.
Fabiola; or, The church of
the Catacombs *see* McGee,
Thomas D'Arcy. Sebastian;
or, The Roman martyr

Wiske, Mortimer.
His chris cross mark. "The
man of mark" *see* Dinsmore,
William

The witch of bramble hollow
see Côté, Marie

The witch of Salem *see*
Williams, Espy William Hendricks. Witchcraft; or, The
witch of Salem

Witchcraft *see* Mathews,
Cornelius

Witchcraft; or, The witch of
Salem *see* Williams, Espy
William Hendricks

The witch's curse *see*
Alcott, Louisa May. Norna;
or, The witch's curse *in her*
Comic tragedies

The witch's secret *see*
Dale, Horace C. Imogene;
or, The witch's secret

Within an inch of his life
see Hearne, James A. *in his*
The early plays

Within the gates *see* Ward,
Elizabeth Stuart Phelps

Wittmann, Hugo, 1839-1923.
Der Feldprediger *see* The
black hussar

The wizard of Fogg Island *see*
Rawley, Bert C. Trixie; or,

The wizard of Fogg Island

The wizard of the Nile *see*
Smith, Harry Bache

The wizard of the sea *see*
Jones, Joseph Stevens.
Captain Kyd; or, The wizard
of the sea

The wizard's warning; or, The
warrior's faith *see* Campbell, Thomas *in* Steele,
Silas Sexton. Collected
works. Book of plays

Wohlmuth, Alois, b.1852.
Der Feldprediger *see* The
black hussar

A wolf in sheep's clothing *see*
Weston, Effie Ellsler

The woman-hater *see* Lloyd,
David Demarest *see also*
Sonneborn, Hilton Burnside

The woman haters *see* Hardy,
Edward Trueblood. Widow Freeheart; or, The woman haters

The woman of the world; or, A
peep at the vices and virtues
of country and city life *see*
Howe, J. Burdette

Woman's faith *see* Alcott,
Louisa May. The unloved wife;
or, Woman's faith *in her*
Comic tragedies

A woman's forever *see* Mathews,
Frances Aymar

A woman's heart *see* Leland,
Oliver Shepard. Caprice; or,
A woman's heart

A woman's honor *see* Fraser,
John Arthur

Woman's lefts *see* Ele, Rona

Woman's revenge *see* Payne,
John Howard

Woman's rights *see* Fowle,
William Bentley *in his*
Parlor dramas *see also*
Drey, Sylvan

A woman's vengeance *see*
Cunningham, Virginia Juhan.
The maid of Florence; or,
A woman's vengeance *see also*
The maid of Florence; or,
A woman's vengeance

A woman's virtue *see* Moore,
Horatio Newton. Orlando;
or, A woman's virtue

Woman's vows and Mason's oaths
see Duganne, Augustine
Joseph Hickey

Woman's will *see* Koopman,
Harry Lyman

The women of Löwenburg *see*
Murray, Ellen

Women of the day *see* Morton,
Charles H.

Women rule *see* Ingersoll,
Charles

Women's rights *see* Spring,
Retlaw

Won at last *see* MacKaye,
James Steele *in his* An
arrant knave & other plays

Won back *see* Tayleure,
Clifton W.

Won by strategy *see* Chapman,
W. F.

The wonder! A woman keeps a
secret *see* Daly, Augustin

The wonderful beaver *see*
Williams, Henry Llewellyn.
De black magician; or, The
wonderful beaver

A wonderful cure *see* The
mystic charm; or, A wonderful cure

A wonderful cure. A farce in
one act for female characters
only. Boston: Walter H.
Baker, c1889. 21p. (Baker's
edition of plays)

The wonderful lamp *see*
Aladdin; or, The wonderful
lamp *see also* Shields,
Sarah Annie Frost

A wonderful letter *see* Townsend, Charles

The wonderful telephone *see*
Dumont, Frank *see also his*
The amateur minstrel *see*
also Haskett, Emmett

Wood, C. A. F.
The Irish broom-maker; or,
A cure for dumbness. A farce
in one act. New York: S.
French, 185-? 18p. (French's
American drama. The acting
edition. no. 75)

Wood, Frank.
Taming a butterfly *see*
Daly, Augustin and Wood,
Frank

Wood, I. M. G. *see*
Wood, J. M. G.

Wood, J. M. G.
A case of jealousy. A comedy
in two acts. By I. M. G.
[i.e., J. M. G.] Wood. Clyde,
O.: Ames, c1896. 15p. (Ames'
series of standard and minor
drama. no. 368)

A $10,000 wager. Farce in
two acts. By I. M. G. [i.e.,
J. M. G.] Wood. Clyde, O.:
Ames, c1890. 16p. (Ames'
series of standard and minor
drama. no. 367)

The wood fairies *see* Hunt,
Arzalea

Woodbury, Alice Gale.
The match-box. An original
comedy in two acts. Chicago:
Dramatic Pub. Co., c1894.
15p. (Sergel's acting drama.
no. 400)

Woodhull, Aaron H.
A thoroughbred. A society
comedy in three acts. New
York: Riverside Printing,
1901. 45p.

Woodhull, Mary G.
For old love's sake. A comedy
in two acts. Philadelphia:
Penn Pub. Co., 1900. 12p.
[earlier copyright: 1896]

Woods, Virna, 1864-1903.
The Amazons. A lyrical drama.
Meadville, Penn.: Flood and
Vincent, 1891. 73p.

Woodville, Henry.
"Confederates." A drama in
one act. New York: S. French,
c1899. 27p. (French's international copyrighted...edit-
ion of the works of the best
authors. no. 18)

"Confederates." London and
New York: S. French, c1899.
27p. (Lacy's acting edition.
vol. 144)

Woodward, John A.
Bouquet. A comedietta in one
act. Boston: Charles H.
Spencer, Agent, c1871. 20p.
(Spencer's universal stage.
no. 54) *[cover: "adapted
from the French"]*

Madame is abed. Vaudeville
in one act and one scene.
Boston: C. H. Spencer, Agent,
1871. 16p. (Spencer's universal stage. no. 63) *[cover:
"translated and adapted by
John A. Woodward"]*

Which will have him? A vaudeville in one act and one

scene. Boston: Charles H.
Spencer, 1871. 12p. (Spencer's universal stage. no.
62) *[cover: "translated and
adapted by John A. Woodward"]*

Woodward, Matthew C.
Rosita; or, Boston and banditti. An original comic
opera in two acts. Chicago:
Bowen & Schleiffarth, 1887.
42p. Libretto. *[music by
George M. Schleiffarth,
lyrics by Harry Bache Smith;
without the music]*

Woodward, N. A.
The student and his neighbors
see Dramatic leaflets

Woodward, T. Trask.
The social glass; or, Victims
of the bottle. The great
sensational temperance drama
in five acts. New York and
London: S. French, c1887.
46p. (French's standard
drama. The acting edition.
no. 385)

The veteran of 1812; or,
Kesiah and the scout. A
romantic military drama in
five acts. New York: Dramatic
Pub. Co., c1883. 32p. (De
Witt's acting plays. no. 317)

Woodworth, Samuel, 1785-1842.
The forest rose; or, American
farmers. A drama in two acts.
Boston: W. Spencer, 1855.
Prompt-book. 32p. (Boston
theatre. no. 2)

The ninth anniversary of the
New York Mirror, July, 1831
[From his: Poetical works.
Edited by his son. New York:
C. Scribner, 1861. vol. 2]
p.193-216.

Shooting stars; or, The
battle of the comets [From
his: Poetical works. Edited
by his son. New York: C.

Scribner, 1861. vol. 2]
p.217-249. [originally
published: 1834]

Wooing a widow see Mathews,
Frances Aymer

The wooing of Penelope see
Field, Henrietta Dexter
and Field, Roswell Martin.
Collected works

Wooing under difficulties
see Douglass, John T.

Wooings and weddings see
Lovell, George W. Look
before you leap; or, Wooings
and weddings in The modern
standard drama, vol. 5

Woolf, Benjamin Edward, 1836-
1901.
Djakh and Djill. n.p.:
n.pub., 1800 [sic, 1880?]
Title page lacking. 16p.
Libretto.

The doctor of Alcantara.
Comic opera in two acts.
Boston: O. Ditson, c1879.
30p. Libretto. [music by
Julius Eichberg; without
the music]

Don't forget your opera-
glasses. An original farce
in one act. New York and
London: Samuel French, 18-?
15p. (French's minor drama.
The acting edition. no. 211)

Fantine. A comic opera in
three acts. Boston: Oliver
Ditson, c1884. Vocal score.
224p. [joint author: Roswell
Martin Field; music by
Firmin Bernicat and André
Charles Prosper Messager
on libretto by Ernest
Dubreuil, Albert Humbert,
and Urbain Rocoux, called
Paul; first performed in
1883 in Paris under the
title François les Bas-Bleus]

Manola; or, The day and the
night. Comic opera in three
acts. Boston: Oliver Ditson,
c1882. 64p. Libretto. [music
composed by Charles Lecocq
under the title Le jour et
la nuit; libretto by Albert
Vanloo and Eugène Leterrier;
without the music]

Off to the war! An original
farce for the times in one
act. Boston: W. V. Spencer,
1861. 23p. (Spencer's Boston
theatre)

That nose. An original farce
in one act. New York: Samuel
French, 186-? 16p. (French's
minor drama. The acting
edition. no. 279)

Woolson, Constance Fenimore,
1840-1894.
Two women: 1862. A poem [in
dramatic form] (Reprinted
from Appleton's Journal.)
New York: D. Appleton, 1877.
92p.

The workhouse boy see Massey,
Charles in Massey's exhibition reciter

The world a mask see Boker,
George Henry. Glaucus and
other plays

A world's affair. A comedy for
children. Notre Dame, Ind.:
Office of the "Ave Maria,"
189-? 20p.

The world's deliverer see
Lookup, Alexander (pseud.?)
The soldier of the people;
or, The world's deliverer

The world's own see Howe,
Julia Ward

The woven web see Townsend,
Charles

A wreath for our lady see

Reynartz, Dorothy. A mother's love; or, A wreath for our lady

The wreath of virtue *see* Kavanaugh, Mrs. Russell *in her* Original dramas, dialogues

The wreck *see* White, Charles

The wreck of Stebbins pride *see* Wilson, Louise Latham

Wrecked *see* Ames, A. D.

Wrecked in port *see* Wilkins, W. Henry. The turn of the tide; or, Wrecked in port

The wrecker's daughter *see* Moore, Bernard Francis

The wrecker's fate *see* Saunders, Charles Henry. The pirate's legacy; or, The wrecker's fate

Wright, Caleb Earl, b.1810. Sidney Lear. A metrical romance. Wilkes-Barre, Pa.: R. Baur & Son, 1889. 128p.

Wright, Henry Clarke, 1797-1870. Dick Crowninshield, the assassin and Zachary Taylor, the soldier. n.p.: n.pub., 1848. 12p.

Wright, J. B. Jonathan in England. A comedy in three acts. (Altered from Coleman's "Who wants a guinea?") Boston: William V. Spencer, 1859? 32p. (Spencer's Boston theatre. no. 200)

Wright, M. L. Fielding manor. A drama in a prologue and four acts. Clyde, O.: Ames, c1883. 37p.

(Ames' series of standard and minor drama. no. 162) *[based on Edgar Fawcett's story The false friend; according to the New York Public Library, the publication date should read 1885]*

Writing a book *see* Denton, Clara Janetta Fort *in her* From tots to teens

The writing on the wall *see* Morton, Thomas and Morton, John Maddison *in* The modern standard drama, vol. 12

The wrong bottle *see* McDermott, J. J. and Trumble

The wrong box *see* Clifton, Mary A. Delano

The wrong Browns *see* McBride, H. Elliott *in his* Latest dialogues

The wrong Mister Wright *see* Broadhurst, George Howells

The wrong woman in the right place *see* Stewart, J. C.

Wuttke, Hermann. Crown jewels. A drama in four acts. New York?: n.pub., 1897. Typescript, promptbook. 84 unnumbered leaves.

Wycherley, William, 1640?-1716. The country-wife *see* Daly, Augustin. The country girl *see also* Sheridan, Richard Brinsley Butler. The duenna *in* The modern standard drama, vol. 7

Wyeth, Albert Lang. Cupid on wheels. A comedy in two acts. Philadelphia: Penn Pub. Co., 1900. 21p. *[earlier copyright: 1897]*

Wyke, Byam, d.1944.
The doctor's assistant. A
farce. Chicago: Dramatic
Pub. Co., c1898. 7p. (The
comic drama)

The Xlanties; or, Forty
thieves. A musical, satirical & quizzical burlesque
in two acts. By the C. A. P.
& Co. Philadelphia: M'Laugh-
lin Brothers' Steam-power
Print. Off., 1857. 43p.

Yacob's hotel experience see
Eberhart, B. F.

Yaddo: an autumn masque see
Lathrop, George Parsons

The Yankee detective see
Stedman, W. Elsworth

The Yankee duelist see
Field, A. Newton

Yankee fidelity see McLellan,
Rufus Charles. The foundling;
or, Yankee fidelity

The Yankee in Poland see
Steele, Silas Sexton. The
brazen drum; or, The Yankee
in Poland

Yankee Jack; or, The buccaneer
of the Gulf see Pilgrim,
James

Yankee land see Logan,
Cornelius Ambrosius

The Yankee schoolmaster see
Chase, George B. Penn
Hapgood; or, The Yankee
schoolmaster

The Yankee tar's return; or,
The boy and the purse see
Steele, Silas Sexton in
Collected works. Book of
plays

Ye gods and goddesses; or,

The apple of discord see
Robinson, Charles

Ye quest. New York: n.pub.,
1884. 8p.

Yellott, George, b.1819?
Tamayo. A tragedy in five
acts. Baltimore: Bull &
Tuttle, 1857. 32p.

The yellow kid who lived in
Hogan's alley see Dumont,
Frank

Yonge, Charlotte Mary, 1823-
1901.
[Chinese damsel] see
Venable, William Henry in
his The school stage

Young, Margaret.
Kitty. A dramatic sketch
for two female characters.
Chicago: Dramatic Pub. Co.,
18-? 11p. (Sergel's acting
drama. no. 563) (The wizard
series)

Kitty. A dramatic sketch
for female characters. New
York: Roxbury Pub. Co.,
18-? 11p. (The wizard series)

Young, O. E.
Popping by proxy. A farce in
one act. Boston: Walter H.
Baker, c1899. 28p. (Baker's
edition of plays)

Young American Progressive
Hobby Club see Whitaker,
Lily C.

Young America's dream see
Thorp, Philip

Young Dr. Devine see Goodfellow, Mrs. E. J. H.

The young folk's minstrels see
Bangs, John Kenneth

A young gentleman of Philadelphia *see* Lucrezia; or, The bag of gold

The young judge and old jewry *see* The (old clothes) merchant of Venice; or, The young judge and old jewry

The young man about town *see* Chase, Lucien B.

Young Mr. Pritchard *see* Tiffany, Esther Brown

Young Mrs. Winthrop *see* Howard, Bronson

Young New York *see* Wilkins, Edward G. P.

Young scamp *see* White, Charles

The young teetotaler; or, Saved at last *see* Bradley, Nellie H. The first glass; or, The power of woman's influence

Your fortune for a dollar *see* Herbert, Bernard. Second sight; or, Your fortune for a dollar

The youth of Argos *see* Talfourd, Thomas Noon *in* Steele, Silas Sexton. Collected works. Book of plays

The youth who never saw a woman *see* Steele, Silas Sexton *in his* Collected works. Book of plays

Zacharias' funeral *see* Courtright, William

Zamba; or, The insurrection *see* Ricord, Elizabeth Stryker

Zamira *see* Phillips, Jonas B.

Zampa; or, The marble bride. A comic opera in three parts. (Music by Hérold.) New York: Academy of Music, 18-? Bilingual text: English and Italian. Libretto. 33p. *[libretto by Anne Honoré Joseph Duveyrier (pseud.= Mélesville); without the music]*

Zanetto *see* Schmall, Alice F.

Zechmeister, Alexander Victor, 1817-1877. Einer muss heiraten *see* Ritch, C. W. One must marry

Zediker, N. Family discipline. A monologue in one scene for a child. Clyde, O.: Ames, c1886. 5p. (Ames' series of standard and minor drama. no. 184)

Kittie's wedding cake. An original farce in one act. Clyde, O.: Ames, c1886. 9p. (Ames' series of standard and minor drama. no. 182)

My day & Now-a-days. A monologue in one scene for a child. Clyde, O.: Ames, c1886. 5p. (Ames' series of standard and minor drama. no. 186)

Zell, F. (pseud.) *see* Wälzel, Camillo

Zenobia, Queen of Palmyra *see* Pratt, Silas Gamaliel

Zerubbabel's second wife *see* Brewster, Emma E. *see also her* Parlor varieties

Zion *see* Hollenbeck, Benjamin W.

APPENDIX I: SERIES

Series noted in the main entry for each play are here
arranged alphabetically by the name of the series, and then
numerically when applicable. As remarked in the "Preface,"
series notations often appeared on the cover and not on the
title page of the publication. Since many covers were lacking
from copies reproduced by Readex, or were not photographed,
it is possible that certain series notations might have been
omitted unintentionally.

THE ACTING DRAMA
18. Aladdin; or, The wonderful
lamp
54. Taylor, C. W. The drunkard's warning
56. Allen, John Henry. The
fruits of the wine cup
57. Seymour, Harry. Aunt
Dinah's pledge
63. The drunkard's home
76. A trip to Cambridge
100. Howe, J. Burdette. The
woman of the world; or,
A peep at the vices and
virtues of country and
city life
101. Adams, Charles Frederick.
Rob the hermit; or, The
black chapel of Maryland
116. Diplomacy
120. Cross purposes
135. Delafield, John H. Foresight; or, My daughter's
dowry
147. Prichard, Joseph Vila.
Pipes and perdition
162. Sedgwick, Alfred B.
There's millions in it
174. Hope, Kate. Our utopia

ALTA SERIES
Brier, Warren Judson. Jedediah
Judkins, J. P.
Denison, Thomas Stewart. It's
all in the pay-streak
---- Topp's twins
Parker, Walter Coleman. All a
mistake

---- Those dreadful twins
Townsend, Charles. Early vows
---- The iron hand
---- Uncle Josh
Whalen, E. C. From Sumter to
Appomattox

THE AMATEUR DRAMA
Baker, George Melville. Above
the clouds
---- Bonbons
---- The Boston dip
---- Capuletta; or, Romeo and
Juliet restored
---- A Christmas carol
---- A close slave
---- Coals of fire
---- "A drop too much"
---- The duchess of Dublin
---- Enlisted for the war; or,
The home-guard
---- Freedom of the press
---- The greatest plague in
life
---- A little more cider
---- Love of a bonnet
---- My uncle the captain
---- Never say die
---- New brooms sweep well
---- A public benefactor
---- The red chignon
---- The rival poets
---- The runaways
---- The sculptor's triumph
---- The seven ages
---- "Stand by the flag"
---- Sylvia's soldier
---- Thief of time

---- A thorn among the roses
---- Too late for the train
---- Using the weed
---- The visions of freedom
---- The war of the roses
---- "We're all teetotalers"
11. Baker, George Melville.
One hundred years ago;
or, Our boys of 1776

AMATEUR SERIES
Brier, Warren Judson. A sol-
dier of fortune
Denison, Thomas Stewart. A
convention of papas
---- A dude in a cyclone
---- A first-class hotel
---- The great doughnut cor-
poration
---- The great pumpkin case
of Guff vs. Muff
---- Madame Princeton's
temple of beauty
---- The new woman
---- Patsy O'Wang
---- Rejected; or, The tribu-
lations of authorship
---- Too much of a good thing
---- Wide enough for two
Felch, William Farrand. The
pet of Parson's ranch
Frank, J. C. Homeopathy; or,
The family cure
Griffith, Benjamin Lease
Crozer. A mistake in
identity
---- Not at home
Hendrick, Welland. Pocahontas
Hyde, Elizabeth A. An engaged
girl
Ludekens, Emil. The Misses
Beers
McBride, H. Elliott. A bad
job
---- The cow that kicked
Chicago
---- My Jeremiah
May, Gordon V. Outwitting
the colonel
Murray, Ellen. The women of
Löwenburg
Smith, S. Jennie. A free
knowledge-ist; or, Too
much for one head

---- Not a man in the house
Sonneborn, Hilton Burnside.
The wedding trip
Sutphen, William Gilbert Van
Tassel. In the dark
Townsend, Charles. A breezy
call
---- Deception
---- On guard
---- Wanted; a hero
---- A wonderful letter
Whalen, E. C. Documentary
evidence
---- Uncle Dick's mistake
Wilson, Louise Latham. Two of
a kind
9. Mrs. Gamp's tea
203. McBride, H. Elliott.
Lucy's old man
408. Denison, Thomas Stewart.
Pets of society

THE AMATEUR STAGE
The harvest storm
McDermott, J. J. and Trumble.
The wrong bottle
39. McDermott, J. J. and
Trumble. A game of bill-
iards
43. Spring, Retlaw. Women's
rights
46. Delafield, John H. The
last drop
47. The wine cup; or, Saved
at last
51. All's fair in love and
war
54. The village belle
66. McBride, H. Elliott.
Ralph Coleman's refor-
mation

AMATEUR THEATRE
vol. 10. Walcot, Charles Melton. Nothing to nurse

AMERICAN ACTING DRAMA
Carleton, John Louis. More
sinned against than
sinning
Cliffe, Clifton. A wife by
advertisement
Dumont, Frank. The girl from
Klondike; or, Wide awake
Nell

Emerson, William D. The
  unknown rival
Fraser, John Arthur. A noble
  outcast
---- 'Twixt love and money
Friars, Austin. Loved and
  lost
Fuller, Horace Williams. Bad
  advice
Hageman, Maurice. Professor
  Robinson
---- To rent
---- Two veterans
Hilliard, Robert Cochrane.
  The littlest girl
Merriman, Effie Woodward.
  Their first meeting
Picton, Thomas. A tempest in
  a tea pot
Stern, Edwin M. Hick'ry Farm
Toler, Sallie F. Bird's Island
Townsend, Charles. The cap-
  tain's wager
Williams, Henry Llewellyn.
  Sparking

AMERICAN AMATEUR DRAMA
André, Richard. Food for powder
---- A handsome cap
---- Minette's birthday
Brown, Marsden. A modern
  proposal
Fraser, John Arthur. Bloomer
  girls; or, Courtship in
  the twentieth century
---- A delicate question
---- The showman's ward
Merriman, Effie Woodward.
  Maud Muller

AMERICAN DRAMA
  1. Smucker, Samuel M. The
     Spanish wife
  3. Tally Rhand (pseud.).
     Guttle and Gulpit

AMERICAN DRAMATIC LIBRARY
vol. 1. Dawes, Rufus. Athenia
  of Damascus

AMERICAN SCHOOL AND COLLEGE
PLAYS
  1. Roth, Edward, ed. The

gray tigers of Smithville;
  or, He would and he
  wouldn't

AMERICA'S LOST PLAYS
vol. 2. MacKaye, James Steele.
  An arrant knave & other
  plays
vol. 4. Grover, Leonard. Our
  boarding house
---- Jessop, George Henry.
  Sam'l of Posen; or, The
  commercial drummer
---- McCloskey, James Joseph.
  Across the continent; or,
  Scenes from New York life
  and the Pacific Railroad
---- Murdoch, Frank Hitchcock.
  Davy Crockett; or, Be
  sure you're right, then
  go ahead
---- Wallack, Lester. Rosedale;
  or, The rifle ball
vol. 5. Payne, John Howard.
  The boarding school; or,
  Life among the little
  folks
---- ---- Mount Savage
---- ---- The Spanish husband;
  or, First and last love
vol. 6. Payne, John Howard.
  Woman's revenge
vol. 7. Herne, James A. The
  early plays of James A.
  Herne
vol. 9. Hoyt, Charles Hale.
  A bunch of keys; or, The
  hotel
---- ---- A midnight bell
---- ---- A milk white flag
---- ---- A temperance town
---- ---- A trip to Chinatown
vol. 10. Howard, Bronson. The
  banker's daughter
---- ---- Baron Rudolph
---- ---- Hurricanes
---- ---- One of our girls
---- ---- Old love letters
vol. 14. Dawes, Rufus [or]
  Conway, H. J. The battle
  of Stillwater; or, The
  maniac
---- Field, Joseph M. Job and
  his children

---- Jones, Joseph Stevens.
The usurper; or, The
Americans in Tripoli
---- Steele, Silas Sexton.
The crock of gold; or,
The toiler's trials
---- Wilkins, John H. Signor
Marc
vol. 16. Hazelton, George
Cochrane. Mistress Nell
---- Mitchell, Langdon Elwyn.
Becky Sharp
---- O'Neill, James. "Monte
Cristo"
vol. 18. Belasco, David. The
heart of Maryland and
other plays
vol. 19. Campbell, Bartley
Theodore. The white
slave
vol. 20. Daly, Augustin.
Divorce
---- ---- Man and wife

AMES AND HOLGATE'S SERIES OF
STANDARD AND MINOR DRAMA
5. Gotthold, J. Newton.
When women weep
7. Gotthold, J. Newton.
The vow of the Ornani

AMES' SERIES OF STANDARD AND
MINOR DRAMA
4. Field, A. Newton. Twain's
dodging
5. Siegfried, W. A. Phyllis,
the beggar girl
7. Haskett, Emmett. The
wonderful telephone
18. Ames, A. D. The poacher's
doom; or, The murder of
the Five Field's Copse
38. Lambla, Hattie Lena.
The bewitched closet
40. ---- That mysterious
bundle
43. Kinnaman, C. F. Arrah
de Baugh
44. Lambla, Hattie Lena.
Obedience; or, Too mind-
ful by far
45. Wilkins, W. Henri. Rock
Allen, the orphan; or,
Lost and found

46. Webber, Harry A. Man and
wife
47. Clifton, Mary A. Delano.
The wrong box
48. ---- Schnapps
49. ---- Der two subprises
50. Buxton, Ida M. How she has
her own way
51. Gilbert, Clayton H.
Rescued
52. Bingham, Frank Lester.
Henry Granden; or, The
unknown heir
58. Ames, A. D. Wrecked
59. Tardy, Edwin. Saved
60. Ames, A. D. Driven to the
wall; or, True to the last
61. Not as deaf as he seems
63. Wilkins, W. Henri. Three
glasses a day; or, The
broken home
64. Cutler, F. L. That boy
Sam
65. Munson, George A. An
unwelcome return
66. Cutler, F. L. Hans, the
Dutch J. P.
67. Vautrot, George S. The
false friend
68. Cutler, F. L. The sham
professor
69. Wilkins, W. Henri. Mother's
fool
71. ---- The reward of crime;
or, The love of gold
73. Vautrot, George S. At last
75. Babcock, Charles W. Adrift
79. Ames, A. D. and Bartley,
C. G. The spy of Atlanta
82. Killing time
83. Out of the world
86. Vautrot, George S. Black
vs. white; or, The nigger
and the Yankee
95. Burton, James. In the
wrong clothes
102. Wilkins, W. Henri. The
turn of the tide; or,
Wrecked in port
103. Shaw, J. S. R. How Sister
Paxey got her child bap-
tized
104. Cutler, F. L. Lost!; or,
The fruits of the glass

105. Montgomery, T. M. and
Steed, T. D. Through
snow and sunshine
106. Cutler, F. L. Lodgings
for two
107. Field, A. Newton. School
108. ---- Those awful boys
109. ---- Other people's
children
110. ---- Reverses
111. ---- The Yankee duelist
112. ---- The new Magdalen
113. ---- Bill Detrick; or,
The mystery of Oliver's
Ferry
114. Dey, F. Marmaduke.
Passions
115. Wilkins, W. Henri.
S. H. A. M. Pinafore
116. ---- Hash!
117. Andrews, Fred G. Hal
Hazard; or, The federal
spy
118. Field, A. Newton. The
pop-corn man
120. Dey, F. Marmaduke.
H. M. S. Plum
121. Hanshew, Thomas W.
Will-o'-the-wisp; or,
The shot in the dark
122. Stanton, F. J. The select
school
123. Chisnell, Newton. A
thrilling item
124. Taylor, Malcolm Stuart.
The afflicted family;
or, A doctor without a
diploma
125. ---- Auld Robin Gray
126. Greenwood, Frederick L.
Our daughters
127. Gibson, Ad. H. The lick
skillet wedding
128. Cutler, F. L. The musical
darkey
129. Taylor, Malcom [sic, Mal-
colm] Stuart. Aar-u-ag-
oos; or, An east Indian
drug
131. Chisnell, Newton. The
cigarette
132. Cutler, F. L. Actor and
servant

133. ---- Seeing Bosting
134. ---- Pomp's pranks
135. Dow, James M. The widower's trials
137. Buxton, Ida M. Taking the
census
138. ---- A sewing circle of
the period
139. ---- Matrimonial bliss
141. Careo, Zella. The hidden
treasures; or, Martha's
triumph
142. Buxton, Ida M. Tit for tat
143. Tilden, Len Ellsworth.
The emigrant's daughter
144. Toler, Mrs. H. M. Thekla,
a fairy drama
145. Cutler, F. L. Cuff's luck
146. Buxton, Ida M. Our awful
aunt
147. Toler, Mrs. W. H. Waking
him up
148. ---- Eh? What did you say?
149. Spangler, W. H. New Years
in New York; or, The
German baron
150. Cutler, F. L. Old Pompey
151. ---- Wanted a husband
152. Dunn, Herb H. Driven from
home; or, A father's curse
154. Bauman, E. Henri. Fun in
a post office
155. Buxton, Ida M. Why they
joined the Rebeccas
156. Oppenheim, Charles. The
wig-maker and his servants
160. Powell, L. S. and Frank,
J. C. Conn; or, Love's
victory
162. Wright, M. L. Fielding
manor
164. Hollenbeck, Benjamin W.
After ten years; or, The
maniac wife
166. Gibson, Ad. H. A Texan
mother-in-law
168. Chisnell, Newton. A
pleasure trip
174. Andrews, Fred G. Love's
labor not lost; or,
Cupid's pastimes
180. Browne, W. Gault. Ripples
182. Zediker, N. Kittie's

276. Moses, David and Black-
     aller, Arthur. The
     printer and his devils
277. Emerson, W. Burt. The
     musical captain; or,
     The fall of Vicksburg
280. Simms, George A. Pheelim
     O'Rooke's curse
281. Tibbetts, Martie E. Two
     Aunt Emilys; or, Quits
283. Chase, George B. Haunted
     by a shadow; or, Hunted
     down
284. Melrose, Thorn. The
     commercial drummer
285. Cutler, F. L. The
     mashers mashed
287. ---- Cousin Josiah
289. Pinkopki, Phillip. A
     colonel's mishap
290. Polson, Minnie. Wild Mab
291. Walsh, Joseph P. The
     actors' scheme; or, How
     we got our dinner
292. Gordinier, Charles A.
     Tim Flannagan; or, Fun
     in a grocery store
293. Siegfried, W. A. Tom
     Blossom; or, The spider's
     web
294. Todd, John W. Arthur
     Eustace; or, A mother's
     love
295. Richard, Bert. The
     spellin' skewl; or,
     Friday afternoon at
     Deestrick No. 4
296. Shettel, James W. and
     George, Wadsworth M.
     Nanka's leap year ven-
     ture; or, How she settled
     her bills
297. ---- Pomp Green's snakes
298. Moore, D. H. The New
     York book agent; or, The
     miser's gold
299. Ingraham, C. F. Jimmie
     Jones; or, Our hopeful
     son
300. Lamson, C. A. Grandmother
     Hildebrand's legacy; or,
     Mae Blossoms reward

301. Cutler, F. L. Peleg and
     Peter; or, Around the
     horn
302. Guepner, Willard. Locked
     in a dress-maker's room;
     or, Mr. Holiday's flir-
     tation
304. Echols, Walter Jarrell.
     The general manager; or,
     A shot from the kitchen
306. Chisnell, Newton. The
     three hats
307. Richards, Bert. Hallaba-
     hoola, the medicine man;
     or, The squirtgun treat-
     ment
308. Crary, J. E. The Irish
     squire of Squash Ridge
309. Elliott, Everett and
     Hardcastle, F. W. Santa
     Claus' daughter
310. Ward, Lew. Claim ninety-
     six
311. ---- Gyp, the heiress; or,
     The dead witness
312. Cook, S. Uncle Ethan
313. Shettel, James W. and
     George, Wadsworth M.
     A matchmaking father;
     or, The bashful suitor
314. Moore, Bernard Francis.
     The haunted mill; or,
     Con O'Ragen's secret
317. Williams, George W.
     Cleveland's reception
     party
318. Emerson, W. Burt. The
     adventuress; or, Lady
     Evelyn's triumph
319. Allyn, Dave E. "In for
     it"; or, Uncle Tony's
     mistake
321. Barr, E. Nelson. Broken
     links
322. Ingraham, Jean. The raw
     recruit; or, A day with
     the National Guard
323. Crary, J. E. Johannes
     Blatz's mistake; or, The
     two elopements
324. Hoefler, Henry A. A day
     in a doctor's office

325. Shettel, James and
George, Wadsworth M.
A coincidence
328. Browne, M. C. The landlord's revenge; or, Uncle
Tom up to date
329. Cook, Sherwin Lawrence.
A valet's mistake
330. Willard, Charles O.
Little Goldie; or, The
child of the camp
331. Crary, J. E. The old
Wayside Inn
333. Polson, Minnie. Our Kittie
334. Crary, J. E. Olivet; or,
A rare Teutonic specimen
336. Walker, Will L. The
squire's daughter
340. Brunnhofer, Will H. Our
hotel; or, Rats the bell
boy
341. Todd, John W. Miss Blothingay's blunder
342. Downing, Laura Case.
Defending the flag; or,
The message boy
343. Davis, Edwin Abraham.
Daisy Garland's fortune
344. Rawley, Bert C. Badly
mixed
345. ---- Deacon Jones' wife's
ghost
346. Ward, Lew. Signing an
actor
347. Our country aunt; or,
Aunt Jerusha's visit
350. Goddard, Edward. By
force of love; or, Wedded
and parted
351. Myles, George B. The
winning hand; or, The
imposter
352. Haskett, Emmett. Bridget
Branagan's troubles;
or, The masquerade ball
354. The mystic charm; or, A
wonderful cure
355. Ward, Lew. My pard; or,
The fairy of the tunnel
356. Mike Donovan's courtship
358. Emerson, M. Burt. Snow
Ball, a colored valet

359. Moore, Bernard Francis.
The girl from midway
361. Haskett, Emmett. Jake
and Snow
362. Rodebaugh, T. Wilson.
Josh Winchester; or,
Between love and duty
363. Willard, Charles O.
Stubs; or, The fool from
Boston
364. Rawley, Bert B. Trixie;
or, The wizard of Fogg
Island
365. ---- Stupid Cupid
366. Hamilton, George H.
Hotel Healthy
367. Wood, J. M. G. A $10,000
wager
368. ---- A case of jealousy
369. Ward, Lew. Taggs, the
waif; or, Uncle Seth
370. Rawley, Bert C. Our
summer boarder's [sic];
or, The jolly tramp
372. Hamilton, George H.
Sunlight; or, The diamond
king
374. Farrell, John Rupert.
Hearts of gold
377. Eberhart, B. F. Home rule
---. ---- Yacob's hotel
experience
379. Haskett, Emmett. The
Dutchman's picnic
380. Bennett, W. L. Katie's
deception; or, The
troublesome kid
381. Cleveland, E. E. Our
family umbrella
383. McFall, B. G. Joshua
Blodgett, from Blodgett's
Holler
385. Rawley, Bert C. The
Freeman mill strike
386. Jordon, Clifton E. Hazel
Adams
388. Osborn, Merit. Farmer
Larkin's boarders
389. Cutler, F. L. Kitty and
Patsy; or, The same thing
over again
391. McFall, B. G. Among the

moonshiners; or, A
drunkard's legacy
392. Perkins, George. Pat
McFree, the Irish
patentee
393. Rawley, Bert C. Andy
Freckles, the mischievous
boy
394. Raynor, Verna M. The Bird
family and their friends
395. Switzer, Marvin D. Nip
and Tuck
396. Rawley, Bert C. Uncle
Jed's fidelity; or, The
returned cowboy
397. Lewis, E. A. and Lewis,
C. M. Mother earth and
her vegetable daughter's
[sic]; or, Crowning the
queen of vegetables
398. Farrell, John Rupert.
The haunted hat
402. Cutler, F. L. Joe, the
waif; or, The pet of the
camp
403. Moore, Bernard Francis.
Winning a wife
404. Martin, W. H. Servants
vs. master; or, A
father's will
405. Beaty, Thomas R. Old
Glory in Cuba
406. Moore, Bernard Francis.
A judge by proxy
407. Lindon, Patrick C.
Dr. Baxter's servants
408. Raynor, Verna M. Noel
Carson's oath; or,
Leonia's repentance
409. Brown, J. S. A southern
rose
410. Murphy, John M. The
mechanics reprieve
411. McFall, B. G. Miss Topsy
Turvy; or, The courtship
of the deacon
413. Elwyn, Lizzie May.
Switched off
415. Coon, Hilton. Under the
American flag
416. Chipman, Adelbert Z.
Ruben Rube; or, My
invalid aunt

417. ---- The little wife
418. Lee, Billy F. Muldoon's
blunders
419. Stenman, C. A. Our Jack
420. Elwyn, Lizzie May.
Rachel, the fire waif
421. Kinnaman, C. F. In a
spider's web
422. Chenoweth, Lawrence.
After the circus
423. Russ, William Ward. The
strike; or, Under the
shadow of a crime
426. Rawley, Bert C. A crazy
lot!

APPLETON'S NEW HANDY-VOLUME SERIES
Matthews, Brander. Comedies
for amateur acting

BAKER'S DARKEY PLAYS
Bowers, E. The man about town
Coes, George H. Badly sold
---- Black blunders
---- Everyday occurences
---- The faith cure
---- A finished education
---- The intelligence office
---- Oh, well, it's no use
---- The police court
---- Scenes in a sanctum
---- Sublime and ridiculous
---- That dorg; or, The old
toll house mystery
---- Tricks upon travellers
De trouble begins at nine
Hiland, Frank E. Careless
Cupid

BAKER'S EDITION OF PLAYS
Aborn, Edward. A strawman
Adams, Justin. At the picket-
line
---- Down east
---- The limit of the law
---- The rag-picker's child
---- T'riss; or, Beyond the
Rockies
Addison, Julia de Wolff Gibbs.
Blighted buds
Aldrich, Mildred. Nance Old-
field

Arnold, Alexander Streeter.
    In the nick of time
Baker, George Melville.
    Among the breakers
---- Better than gold
---- Bread on the waters
---- The champion of her sex
---- Comrades
---- Down by the sea
---- The fairy of the fountain;
    or, Diamonds and toads
---- A Grecian bend
---- Humors of the strike
---- The hypochondriac
---- The last loaf
---- Little brown jug
---- My brother's keeper
---- A mysterious disappear-
    ance
---- Nevada; or, The lost mine
---- Our folks
---- Rebecca's triumph
---- The tempter; or, The
    sailor's return
---- A tender attachment
---- Thirty minutes for
    refreshments
---- Wanted, a male cook
Baker, Rachel E. After taps
---- Bachelor Hall [joint
    author: Robert Melville
    Baker]
---- Mr. Bob
Baker, Robert Melville. An
    awkward squad
Barnard, Charles. Psyche,
    M. D.
Bates, Arlo. A gentle jury
Bates, Ella Skinner. The
    convention of the Muses
Baum, Rosemary. Love in a
    lighthouse
---- That box of cigarettes
Beach, Stanley Yale and
    Powell, H. Arthur. The
    widow Mullin's Christmas
Bidwell, Jeanne Raymond.
    Under protest
Bixby, Frank L. The little
    boss
Brewster, Emma E. Beresford
    Benevolent Society
    [joint author: Lizzie B.

    Scribner]
---- A dog that will fetch will
    carry
---- Eliza's bona-fide offer
---- How the colonel proposed
---- Zerubbabel's second wife
Brooke, Van Dyke. The quick-
    sands of Gotham
Brown, Abbie Farwell. Quits
Browne, William Maynadier.
    A fool for luck
---- Red or white?
---- The trustee
Bunner, Henry Cuyler and
    Magnus, Julian. A bad
    case
Campbell, Marian D. A Chinese
    dummy
---- Sunbonnets
Card, Evelyn G. Whiting. A
    confidence game
Chase, Frank Eugene. The bat
    and the ball; or, Negative
    evidence
---- The great umbrella case
---- In the trenches
---- Santa Claus the first
Coburn, Carrie W. His last
    chance; or, The little
    joker
Coes, George H. A perplexing
    predicament
Coolidge, Henry Dingley. Dead
    reckoning
Coon, Hilton. The widow from
    the West; or, The late
    Mr. Early
Cowley, E. J. The Bohemians
Crumpton, M. Nataline. Ceres
---- Pandora
---- Theseus
Curtis, Herbert Pelham. Uncle
    Robert; or, Love's labor
    saved
Dallas, Mary Kyle. Our Aunt
    Robertina
A dead heat
Denton, Clara Janetta Fort.
    All is fair in love
---- A change of color
---- The man who went to
    Europe
---- To meet Mr. Thompson

---- "W. H."

Dix, Beulah Marie. Cicely's cavalier

Enebuske, Sarah Folsom. A detective in petticoats

An equal chance

Fisher, Abraham Lincoln. Little trump; or, A Rocky Mountain diamond

Fowler, Egbert Willard. A matrimonial advertisement

---- Our Jim

---- An unexpected legacy

Furniss, Grace Livingston. A box of monkeys

---- The corner lot chorus

---- The flying wedge

---- Second floor, Spoopendyke

Gaddess, Mary L. The Ivy Queen

Getchell, Wendell P. A fisherman's luck

Gibbs, Julia De Witt. A false note

The governess

Griffith, Benjamin Lease Crozer. A rival by request

Hanlon, Henry Oldham. A double shuffle

---- Facing the music

---- A picked-up dinner

Harris, Francis Augustine. Class day

---- A majority of one; or, Love and mushrooms

Hiland, Frank E. Blundering Bill

---- Broken bonds

---- Captain Swell

---- Dr. McBeatem

---- The lady lawyer

---- The old country store

---- Rooney's restaurant

---- A town meeting

---- Who caught the count

Hildreth, David W. Bound by an oath

---- Forced to the war; or, The subrunners of '63-4

---- The granger; or, Caught in his own trap

---- Out of his sphere

---- Placer gold; or, How Uncle Nathan lost his farm

His hat and cane

Horne, Mary Barnard. The ladies of Cranford

---- Prof. Baxter's great invention

---- A singing school of ye olden time

Humphrey, Lewis D. A bachelor's banquet; or, An indigestible romance

Hurd, St. Clair. Counsel for the plaintiff

Jones, Gertrude Manly. Miss Matilda's school

Jones, Joseph Stevens. Solon Shingle; or, The people's lawyer

Jones, Robert. The hidden hand

A kettle of fish

Knapp, Lizzie Margaret. An afternoon rehearsal

Lawrence, F. N. Lanty's luck; or, Falsely accused

Livingston, Margaret Vere Farrington. Sauce for the goose

Locke, Belle Marshall. Breezy Point

Luce, Grace A. Brass buttons

Macbrayne, Lewis Edward. An engaging position

Macy, William Francis. A lion among the ladies

Magnus, Julian. A trumped suit

Mathews, Frances Aymar. Cousin Frank

---- A finished coquette

---- Six to one; or, The scapegrace

---- Wooing a widow

Matthews, Brander. Cuttybank's thunder; or, Frank Wilde [sic, Wylde]

Miller, Harry S. The insurance agent

Montgomery, Margaret. Per telephone

Moore, Bernard Francis. Brother against brother

---- Captain Jack; or, The Irish outlaw

---- Faugh-a-Ballagh; or, The
wearing of the green
---- Ferguson, of Troy
---- The Irish agent
---- The man from Texas
---- The moonshiner's daughter
---- Poverty flats
---- The Rough Rider
---- The weeping willows
---- The wrecker's daughter
Murphy, Fitzgerald. A bit o'
blarney
Oakes, A. H. A teacher taught
The only young man in town
Orne, Martha Russell. A black
diamond
---- The donation party; or,
Thanksgiving Eve at the
parsonage
---- A limb o' the law
---- An old maid's wooing
Osgood, Harry O. "The baby"
Packard, Winthrop. The man
in the case
Parsons, Laura Matilda
Stephenson. The district
school at Blueberry
Corners
---- The old maids' convention
Patten, Gilbert. Clover farm
---- Nan, the mascotte
Pelham, Nettie H. The old
fashioned husking bee
Phelps, Pauline. A cyclone
for a cent
Pratt, William W. Ten nights
in a bar-room
Quinn, Richard. Innisfail; or,
The wanderer's dream
Rand, Katharine Ellen. New
Hampshire gold
The registered letter
Reid, Charles S. Joe Simpson's
double
Reynolds, S. S. Nelly's rival
Rice, Walter F. Winning ways
Risdon, Davis. A black trump
Rugg, George. The new woman
Russell, Charles Walcott.
A turn in the market
Sanford, Amelia. The adver-
tising girls

Shoemaker, Dora Adèle. A
fighting chance; or, For
the blue or the gray
Silence in the ranks
Smith, Dexter. Blanks and
prizes
Smith, Lilli Huger. A rank
deception
Sullivan, Thomas Russell. A
cigarette from Java
Sullivan the slugger
Tassin, Algernon De Vivier.
A class-day conspiracy
Taylor, Frederic W. A Pennsyl-
vania kid; or, A soldier's
sweetheart
Taylor, M. M. The Shakespeare
wooing--a play of shreds
and patches
Thayer, Ella Cheever. Lords
of creation
Tiffany, Esther Brown. Anita's
trial; or, Our girls in
camp
---- An autograph letter
---- Bachelor maids
---- A blind attachment
---- A borrowed umbrella
---- A model lover
---- A rice pudding
---- A tell-tale eyebrow
---- That Patrick!
---- The way to his pocket
---- Young Mr. Pritchard
Tilden, Len Ellsworth. The
finger of fate; or, The
death letter
---- The stolen will
Townsend, Charles. The doctor
---- Finnigan's fortune
---- A gilded youth
---- The mountain waif
---- Rio Grande
---- The spy of Gettysburg
---- The vagabonds
Trowbridge, John Townsend.
Coupon bonds
Trumbull, Annie Eliot. Match-
makers
---- St. Valentine's day
Tubbs, Arthur Lewis. A double
deception

Vatter, August and Spencer,
    John E. Out of the shadow
Ware, Thornton M. and Baker,
    George P. The revolving
    wedge
Warren, Leslie. Much ado
    about nothing
Wells, Charles Henry. Me an'
    Otis
White, Charles. De trouble
    begins at nine
Wilson, Ella Calista Handy.
    The bachelor's Christmas
Wilson, Olivia Lovell. The
    marriage of Prince
    Flutterby
Winn, Edith Lynwood. A vision
    of fair women
Winston, Mary A. A rural ruse
A wonderful cure
Young, O. E. Popping by proxy

BAKER'S NOVELTIES
The grand baby show
Hildreth, David W. Joining
    the Tinpanites; or, Paddy
    McFling's experience
Horne, Mary Barnard. The last
    of the Peak sisters; or,
    The great moral dime
    show
---- The Peak sisters
Orne, Martha Russell. The
    country school
Tiffany, Esther Brown.
    Apollo's oracle

BAKER'S NOVELTY LIST
Winn, Edith Lynwood. A vision
    of fair women

BOOTH'S SERIES OF ACTING PLAYS
1. Hinton, Henry L. Shake-
    speare's...Hamlet. As
    produced by Edwin Booth
2. ---- King Richard III
3. ---- Shakespeare's...
    Othello the Moor of
    Venice
5. ---- Romeo and Juliet

BOSTON MUSEUM EDITION OF

AMERICAN ACTING DRAMA
1. Smith, William Henry. The
    drunkard; or, The fallen
    saved

THE BOSTON THEATRE
1. Hill, Frederick Stanhope.
    The six degrees of crime;
    or, Wine, women, gambling,
    theft, murder and the
    scaffold
2. Woodworth, Samuel. The
    forest rose; or, American
    farmers

BURNTON'S LIBRARY AND ACTING
DRAMA
1. Schönberg, James. Fernande

THE CATHOLIC AMERICAN PLAY OF
THE YEAR
Hartnedy, M. M. A. Christopher
    Columbus

CHILDREN'S PLAYS
Pailler, William. The magic
    bell
Polding, Elizabeth. At the
    fireside; or, Little
    bird blue
---- A harmonious family
Rosetti, Joseph. In the forest
---- Little daughter of the
    regiment
18. Debenham, L. Grannie's
    picture

COLMAN'S DRAMATIC LIBRARY
Dawes, Rufus. Athenia of
    Damascus
Willis, Nathaniel Parker.
    Bianca Visconti; or, The
    heart overtasked
---- Tortesa the usurer

THE COMIC DRAMA
Dumont, Frank. Absent minded
---- The rival barber shops
Tees, Levin C. Hypnotizing
    a landlord
White, Charles. The black
    chemist

---- Coalheaver's revenge
---- The Dutchman's ghost
---- The fellow that looks
   like me
---- Getting square on the
   call boy
---- The ghost
---- The live injin; or, Jim
   Crow
Williams, Henry Llewellyn.
   Stocks up! Stocks down!
Wilton, M. J. Oleomargarine
Wyke, Byam. The doctor's
   assistant
  6. Williams, Henry Llewellyn.
   The black chap from Whitechapel
 29. White, Charles. Who died
   first?
 49. ---- A night in a strange
   hotel
 51. ---- Fisherman's luck
 63. ---- The darkey's stratagem
 67. Harrigan, Edward. The
   editor's troubles
 73. White, Charles. The
   African box; or, The
   magician's troubles
 79. Macarthy, Harry. Barney's
   courtship; or, Mollie
   dear
 80. White, Charles. Scenes on
   the Mississippi
 89. ---- The bogus talking
   machine; or, The puzzled
   Dutchman
 90. Dumont, Frank. The lunatic
 95. White, Charles. Dutch
   justice
105. ---- The rehearsal; or,
   Barry's old man
114. Dumont, Frank. One night
   in a medical college
121. Stocks up! Stocks down!
142. Dumont, Frank. Happy
   Uncle Rufus
169. ---- The lady barber
171. ---- Other people's
   troubles
191. The masonic lodge
193. Dumont, Frank. Too little

vagrants; or, Beware of
   tramps

DARCIE & CORBYN'S EDITION OF
M'LLE RACHEL'S PLAYS
Adrienne Lecouvreur
Andromache
Angelo; or, The tyrant of Padua
The sparrow of Lesbia

THE DARKEY AND COMIC DRAMA
The demon phonograph; or, The
   battery and the assault
Don't get weary; or, Johnny,
   you've been a bad boy
Dumont, Frank. The cake walk
---- Dodging the police; or,
   Enforcing the Sunday law
---- Get-rich-quick society;
   or, One hundred for thirty
---- How to get a divorce
---- Jack Sheppard and Joe
   Blueskin; or, Amateur road
   agents
---- Love in all corners
---- Norah's good-bye
---- The serenade party; or,
   The miser's troubles
---- Society acting
---- The undertaker's daughter
---- The unexpected visitors
---- Who's the actor?
---- Whose baby is it?
A Dutchman in Ireland
Gentlemen coon's parade
Leavitt, Andrew J. No pay no
   cure
Townsend, Charles. The dark
   tragedian
White, Charles. Big mistake
---- Damon and Pythias
---- The German emigrant; or,
   Love and sourkrout
---- The happy couple
---- Pete and the peddler
---- Pompey's patients
---- Rival tenants
---- Scampini
---- The stranger
---- Stupid servant
Williams, Henry Llewellyn. De
   black magician; or, The
   wonderful beaver

9. Williams, Henry Llewellyn.
The Lime-Kiln Club in an
uproar!

DENISON'S ACTING PLAYS
Williams, Henry Llewellyn.
Charles O'Malley's aunt

DENISON'S ACTING PLAYS.
AMATEUR SERIES
Hendrick, Welland. Pocahontas

DENISON'S SERIES
vol. 5, no. 35. Williams,
Henry Llewellyn. Diplo-
mates
vol. 7, no. 46. Denton, Clara
Janetta Fort. From tots
to teens

DENISON'S SPECIALTIES
Morette, Edgar. Let love but
hold the key
Pelham, Nettie H. The Christmas ship
Scudder, Vida Dutton and
Brooks, F. M. Mitsu-yu-
nissi; or, The Japanese
wedding

DE WITT'S ACTING PLAYS
99. Williams, Henry Llewellyn.
The fifth wheel
122. ---- Isabella Orsini
137. ---- L'article 47; or,
Breaking the ban
146. Picton, Thomas. There's
no smoke without a fire
150. ---- A tell-tale heart
151. ---- A hard case
152. ---- Cupid's eye-glass
153. ---- 'Tis better to live
than to die
164. Wallace, John J. Little
Ruby; or, Home jewels
173. Rosenfeld, Sydney. Off
the stage
177. ---- "I shall invite
the major"
178. Perine, Charles E. Out
at sea
189. Sedgwick, Alfred B. Leap
year

194. Comstock, William. Rum;
or, The first glass
196. Sedgwick, Alfred B. The
queerest courtship
200. ---- Estranged
203. She stoops to conquer
204. A drawing-room car
207. Sedgwick, Alfred B. Sold
again and got the money
208. Rosenfeld, Sydney.
Married bachelors; or,
Pleasant surprises
210. ---- Mabel's manoeuvre;
or, A third party
211. Maguire, John. Honesty is
the best policy; or, True
to the core
213. Ayer, Harriet Hubbard.
The widow
302. Abarbanell, Jacob Ralph.
A model pair
305. Rosenfeld, Sydney. A pair
of shoes
306. Winkle, William. A great
success
307. Rosenfeld, Sydney. The
ulster
311. What tears can do
316. Williams, Henry Llewellyn.
A Romeo on "the gridiron"
317. Woodward, T. Trask. The
veteran of 1812; or,
Kesiah and the scout
320. Williams, Henry Llewellyn.
Penmark Abbey
322. For myself alone
325. Laidlaw, F. Allan. True!
327. Friars, Austin. Number two
332. ---- Loved and lost
333. Nomad (pseud.) "Caught at
last"
334. N., S. T. A. A lover's
stratagem
335. Prichard, Joseph Vila.
The great Hindoo secret
337. Enéleh, H. B. Tempest
tossed
338. Braddon, Mary Elizabeth.
Marjorie Daw
347. Williams, Henry Llewellyn.
A happy day
349. Fuller, Horace Williams.
A red letter day

85. ---- Young scamp
86. ---- Gripsack
88. ---- The first night
92. Dumont, Frank. The polar bear
93. ---- What shall I take?
94. White, Charles. Julius the snoozer; or, The conspirators of Thompson Street
98. Stewart, J. C. The elopement
100. ---- The three chiefs
103. Brown, J. H. Katrina's little game
106. Dumont, Frank. Gambrinus, king of lager beer
107. ---- Africanus Bluebeard
108. Skelly, Joseph P. The charge of the hash brigade
109. Dumont, Frank. Making a hit
111. Macarthy, Harry. Deeds of darkness
112. White, Charles. The coming man
113. Williams, Henry Llewellyn. The darkey sleepwalker; or, Ill-treated ill somnambulo
116. White, Charles. Ambition
---. Courtright, William. Zacharias' funeral
117. ---- The motor bellows
119. Dumont, Frank. My wife's visitors
120. Leavitt, Andrew J. The body snatchers
129. Williams, Henry Llewellyn. The Moko marionettes
130. ---- Go and get tight
132. Dumont, Frank. The noble savages
134. ---- Unlimited cheek; or, The sewing machine agents
135. ---- Pleasant companions
139. ---- A desperate situation
143. ---- The wonderful telephone
144. Hall, J. Griffin. The crowded hotel; or, The tricky nig

146. Williams, Henry Llewellyn. The black Forrest
147. Collyer, Dan. The milliner's shop
148. ---- Christmas Eve in the South; or, Uncle Caleb's home
150. Wilton, M. J. How to pay the rent
151. ---- Mickey Free
152. ---- Fun in a cooper's shop
154. Dumont, Frank. The sulphur bath
157. Don't get weary; or, Johnny, you've been a bad boy
---. Gentlemen coon's parade... and Don't get weary; or, Johnny, you've been a bad boy
160. Dumont, Frank. Scenes in front of a clothing store
163. Williams, Henry Llewellyn. Love and lockjaw
164. Dumont, Frank. The yellow kid who lived in Hogan's Alley

DICK'S AMERICAN EDITION
The billet doux
Chapman, W. F. Won by strategy
McBride, H. Elliott. The closing of the "Eagle"
---- Don't marry a drunkard to reform him
---- Out of the depths
The musical bore
Pat's dilemma; or, Too much of a good thing
Robinson, T. S. The student's frolic
Shelland, Harry E. The great libel case
Shields, Sarah Annie Frost. All's well that ends well
---- Blue Beard
---- Bolts and bars
Waldron, P. A. Paddy Doyle; or, A mutual friend

DICK'S LONDON ACTING EDITION OF
STANDARD ENGLISH PLAYS AND

COMIC DRAMAS
460. Aldridge, Ira. The black
doctor

DICK'S STANDARD PLAYS
379. Medina, Louisa H. Ernest
Maltravers
474. Schönberg, James. Oscar
the half-blood
482. ---- True as steel

DIVERSIONS FOR STUDENTS
1. Greenough, James Brad-
street. Queen of hearts

DRAMATIC LIBRARY
43. Hughes, Louise Marie.
Love's stratagem
109. Cobb, Josephine H. and
Paine, Jennie E. The
Oxford affair
125. Meyers, Robert Cornelius
V. A well preserved
gentleman
180. Griffith, Helen Sherman.
The burglar alarm
185. Howie, Hellen Morrison.
After the matinée
187. ---- The reformer reformed
188. Franklin, Sidney. A
question of honor
189. Maddox, D. S. The man
from Arizona

DUNCOMBE'S EDITION
The Jewess

THE ETHIOPIAN DRAMA
Hockenberry, Frank. Prof.
Black's phunnygraph; or,
Talking machine
Old Hunks, the miser
Smith, John Washington. The
quack doctor
Vane, Larry. Troubled by
ghosts
White, Charles. Gettin' de bag
to hold; or, The United
States mail
Williams, Henry Llewellyn.
Deaf--in a horn
---- Dem good ole times; or,
Sixteen thousand years ago

---- Wax works at play
2. Christy, Edwin Byron.
Box and Cox
3. White, Charles. Mazeppa
4. ---- United States mail
5. ---- The Coopers
7. ---- The rival lovers
8. ---- The sham doctor
10. ---- Vilikens and Dinah
18. ---- The wreck
19. ---- Oh! hush!; or, The
Virginny cupids!
20. ---- The portrait painter
21. ---- The hop of fashion
23. ---- The Virginny mummy
24. ---- Thieves at the mill
26. Griffin, George W. H.
Les misérables
33. ---- The hypochondriac
34. ---- William Tell
36. ---- Feast
37. ---- The Fenian spy; or,
John Bulls [sic, Bull]
in America [joint author:
George Christy]
38. ---- Jack's the lad
39. ---- Othello
40. ---- Camille
44. ---- Shylock
49. ---- Hamlet the dainty
50. ---- Corsican twins
54. Scenes at Gurney's
62. Turkeys in season
64. A night with Brudder Bones
73. Sambo's return
74. Under de kerosene
75. Mysterious stranger
78. Griffin, George W. H.
Hunk's wedding day
80. The old Kentucky home
82. Mumbo Jum; or, The enchanted clogs
84. Lucinda's wedding
90. Scipio Africanus
97. Uncle Tom
99. Up head!
109. Dancing mad

THE ETHIOPIAN DRAMA. NEW SERIES
Leavitt, Andrew J. and Eagan,
H. W. Blinks and jinks
---- Boarding school
---- Deaf as a post

---- Jeemes the poet
---- No tator; or, Man-fish
---- Who stole the chickens?
2. Leavitt, Andrew J. and
Eagan, H. W. The lucky
number
5. ---- The arrival of
Dickens
11. ---- The upper ten thousand
12. ---- Rip Van Winkle
13. ---- Ten days in the Tombs
25. ---- That wife of mine
26. Leavitt, Andrew J. The
thumping process
A3. Possumfat

THE EVERGREEN
vol. 1. Holmes, Oliver Wendell.
Scene from unpublished
play

FISCHER'S EDITION
1456. Schindler, Anthony J.
Knaves and fools

FISHER'S EDITION OF STANDARD
FARCES
The mysteries of Odd-Fellowship
Straws; or, The starring system

FRENCH'S ACTING DRAMA. LATE
LACY'S
The wig makers

FRENCH'S ACTING EDITION.
[titles preceded by asterisks
(*) are further designated by
"Late Lacy's" on the title page
or cover of the publications]
*Black mail
Daly, Augustin. Leah, the
forsaken
*Deaf in a horn
*McCloskey, James Joseph. The
fatal glass; or, The
curse of drink
Payne, John Howard. The two
galley slaves
*Warden, Edward. Robert Make-
airs; or, The two fugi-
tives

White, Charles. The black
statue
*Williams, Henry Llewellyn.
Sport with a sportsman
*---- Three black Smiths
27. Griffin, George W. H.
Quarrelsome servants
42. The railroad explosion
[and] The echo
*43. Challenge dance.
*--. Williams, Henry Llewellyn.
Challenge dance [Readex
enters the same edition of
this play twice, once under
title, once under author]
45. White, Charles. The black
shoemaker
50. Griffin, George W. H.
An unhappy pair
*55. White, Charles. The magic
penny
65. Griffin, George W. H. The
ticket taker; or, The
masquerade ball
77. White, Charles. Bone
squash
83. Griffin, George W. H.
The black crook burlesque
157. Howard, Bronson. The
Henrietta
207. Maturin, Edward. Viola
*698. Howe, J. Burdette. Hand-
some Jack

FRENCH'S AMERICAN ACTING
EDITION
1. Scoville, Nesbit Stone.
A country kid
2. Smart, Herbert Durrell.
Mine falls; or, The
miller's daughter
3. ---- The village belle

FRENCH'S AMERICAN DRAMA. THE
ACTING EDITION
1. A midsummer-night's dream
16. Brian O'Linn
30. The sea of ice; or, A
thirst for gold, and the
wild flower of Mexico
35. Jones, Joseph Stevens.
The carpenter of Rouen;

FRENCH'S PARLOR COMEDIES
8. Prichard, Joseph Vila.
My mother-in-law; or,
A divorce wanted
9. Abarbanell, Jacob Ralph.
My father's will

FRENCH'S STANDARD DRAMA
Drake, Frank C. Rosberry
Shrub, sec.
Every-day life
50. Mayo, Frank. Macbeth
55. Wallack, Lester. Much
ado about nothing
71. Mayo, Frank. King Lear
86. Smith, W. H. The drunkard;
or, The fallen saved
146. Medina, Louisa H. The
last days of Pompeii
163. Bateman, Mrs. Sidney
Frances Cowell. Self
164. Cinderella; or, The
fairy and the little
glass slipper
168. Gayler, Charles. The
love of a prince; or,
The court of Prussia
169. ---- The son of the night
171. Howe, J. Burdette. The
Golden Eagle; or, The
privateer of '76
185. Wilkins, Edward G. P.
Young New York
202. Undine; or, The spirit
of the waters
215. Ritchie, Anna Cora Ogden
Mowatt. Fashion; or, Life
in New York
217. Aiken, George L. Uncle
Tom's cabin; or, Life
among the lowly [possibly
no. 218 of the series]
218. [see 217 above]
220. Wallack, Lester. The
veteran; or, France and
Algeria
227. Walcot, Maria Grace.
The cup and the lip
232. Jones, Joseph Stevens.
Moll Pitcher; or, The
fortune teller of Lynn

249. Tayleure, Clifton W. The
boy martyrs of Sept. 12,
1814
263. Johnson, Samuel D. The
fireman
303. Leland, Oliver Shepard.
Caprice; or, A woman's
heart
352. Kathleen Mavourneen; or,
St. Patrick's Eve
353. Robinson, John Hovey.
Nick Whiffles
356. Seymour, Harry. The
temperance doctor
358. Hardy, Edward Trueblood.
Widow Freeheart; or, The
woman haters
359. Daly, Augustin. "Frou
Frou"
376. Kilpatrick, Hugh Judson
and Moore, J. Owen. Alla-
toona

FRENCH'S STANDARD DRAMA. THE
ACTING EDITION
154. The wept of the Wish-ton-
wish
174. Burke, Charles. Rip van
Winkle
187. Goodrich, Frank Boott and
Warden, Frank. Romance
after marriage; or, The
maiden wife
189. Williams, Frederick. The
streets of New York
205. English, Thomas Dunn. The
Mormons; or, Life at Salt
Lake City
206. Burnett, James Gilbert.
Blanche of Brandywine
208. Deseret deserted; or, The
last days of Brigham Young
209. Americans in Paris; or,
A game of dominoes
---. Hurlbert, William Henry.
Americans in Paris; or, A
game of dominoes
213. Tayleure, Clifton W.
Horseshoe Robinson; or,
The battle of King's
Mountain

216. Baker, Benjamin Archibald. A glance at New York
226. Swayze, Mrs. J. C. Ossawattomie Brown; or, The insurrection at Harper's Ferry
242. Miles, George Henry. Mary's birthday; or, The cynic
253. Hill, Frederic Stanhope. The shoemaker of Toulouse; or, The avenger of humble life
279. Faust and Marguerite
303. Putnam, Henry Howell. The mariner's return
321. Saunders, Charles Henry. The pirate's legacy; or, The wrecker's fate
331. Belden, N. H. O'Neal the great; or, Cogger no Caille [sic, Caillie]
332. Floyd, William Ralph. Handy Andy
333. Belden, N. H. The pirate of the isles
334. Waldauer, Augustus. Fanchon, the cricket
335. ---- Little barefoot
337. The pearl of Savoy
339. Pratt, William W. Ten nights in a bar-room
351. Clark, William Adolphus. Gen. Grant; or, The star of union and liberty
369. Howard, Bronson. Saratoga; or, "Pistols for seven"
379. Prichard, Joseph Vila. Daniel Rochat
385. Woodward, T. Trask. The social glass; or, Victims of the bottle
402. Stedman, W. Elsworth. The Confederate spy
413. ---- The midnight charge
414. ---- The confidential clerk
421. Drey, Sylvan. Cupid and cupidity
423. Quinn, Richard. Called away

442. Cazauran, Augustus R. A celebrated case

FRENCH'S STANDARD LIBRARY EDITION
Broadhurst, George Howells. What happened to Jones
---- Why Smith left home
---- The wrong Mister Wright
Du Souchet, Henry A. The man from Mexico
Gillette, William Hooker. An American drama arranged in four acts and entitled *Secret service*
Ives, Alice Emma and Eddy, Jerome H. The village postmaster
Ryley, Madeleine Lucette. Christopher junior

THE GLOBE DRAMA
Babie
Baker, George Melville. The flowing bowl
---- Forty minutes with a crank; or, The Seldarte craze
---- Gustave the professor
---- Mrs. Walthrop's bachelors [joint author: Willard Small]
---- Past redemption
---- Snow-bound
Chase, Frank Eugene. A personal matter
Fales, Willard Henry. The cool collegians
Robinson, Harriet Jane Hanson. Captain Mary Miller

GODEY'S MAGAZINE AND LADY'S BOOK
vol. 42. Hale, Sarah Josepha Buell. The judge

THE GREEN-ROOM EDITION OF COPYRIGHTED PLAYS
Nobles, Milton. The phoenix
Rosenfeld, Sydney. The club friend; or, A fashionable physician

GREENROOM EDITION OF PLAYS
Boker, George Henry. Francesca
    da Rimini

HARPER'S BLACK AND WHITE
SERIES
Freeman, Mary Eleanor Wilkins.
    Giles Corey, yeoman
Howells, William Dean. The
    Albany depot
---- Evening dress
---- A letter of introduction
---- The unexpected guests
Matthews, Brander. The decis-
    ion of the court
---- This picture and that

HARPER'S STORY BOOKS
vol. 10. Abbott, Jacob.
    Orkney the peacemaker;
    or, The various ways of
    settling disputes

KENEDY'S NEW SERIES OF PLAYS
Cox, Eleanor Rogers. A duel
    at dawn
Wilton, M. J. Waiting for
    the train [bound with]
    "Me hansom"

KEYSTONE EDITION OF POPULAR
PLAYS
Dumont, Frank. A girl of the
    century
Griffith, Benjamin Lease
    Crozer. Between the acts
Hughes, Louise Marie. Love's
    stratagem
McBride, H. Elliott. Striking
    oil
Meyers, Robert Cornelius V.
    A very well preserved
    gentleman
Sanford, Amelia. The ghost of
    an idea
Wilson, Bertha M. A Chinese
    wedding

LACY'S ACTING EDITION OF PLAYS
83. Conrad, Robert Taylor.
    Jack Cade, the captain of
    the commons
--. Forrest, Harry. Marie

Antoinette: Queen of
    France
84. Payne, John Howard. Mrs.
    Smith; or, The wife and
    the widow
95. Pilgrim, James. Paddy
    Miles the Limerick boy
107. Schönberg, James. Narcisse
    the vagrant
110. Campbell, Bartley Theo-
    dore. Little sunshine
114. Howe, J. Burdette. Hand-
    some Jack
---. ---- Scarlet Dick; the
    King's highwayman [or, The
    road and the riders]
134. Golden, William Echard
    Michael. Hearts
---. Isham, Frederic Stewart
    and Weitzel, Edward
    Winfield. The toy shop
140. Mitchell, Langdon Elwyn.
    In the season
144. Woodville, Henry. "Con-
    federates"
147. Maeder, Frederick George
    and Gill, William. My
    sweetheart

MAUDE ADAMS' ACTING EDITION
Romeo and Juliet

THE MINOR DRAMA
26. The Omnibus
36. Northall, William Knight.
    Macbeth travestie
78. Johnson, Samuel D. Our gal
107. ---- In and out of place
108. McLachlan, Charles. I dine
    with my mother
109. Walcot, Charles Melton.
    Hiawatha; or, Ardent
    spirits and laughing
    water
111. Bunce, Oliver Bell. Love
    in '76
113. Walcot, Charles Melton.
    One coat for two suits
117. Hall, Abraham Oakey.
    A coroner's inquisition
176. Thomson, Mortimer Neal.
    The lady of the lake

THE MINOR DRAMA. THE ACTING
EDITION
130. Delano, Alonzo. A live
    woman in the mines; or,
    Pike county ahead
134. Phillips, Jonas B. The
    evil eye
151. Barry, S. The Dutchman's
    ghost; or, All right
152. ---- The persecuted
    Dutchman; or, The origi-
    nal John Schmidt
156. O'Brien, Fitz-James.
    A gentleman from Ireland
166. Hoppin, William Jones.
    The lady of the bed-
    chamber
170. Conway, H. J. Hiram
    Hireout; or, Followed by
    fortune
173. Logan, Thomas. Vermont
    wool-dealer
---. Vermont wool-dealer
174. La Bree, Lawrence.
    Ebenezer Venture; or,
    Advertising for a wife
175. Wehner, J. H. Principles
    form character

MODERN STANDARD DRAMA
23. Othello...As played at
    the Park Theatre
55. Smith, Solomon Franklin.
    The hypocrite
100. Pardey, Henry Oake.
    Nature's nobleman

NEW TEMPERANCE DIALOGUES
Bradley, Nellie H. The first
    glass; or, The power of
    woman's influence
---- Marry no man if he drinks;
    or, Laura's plan, and how
    it succeeded
---- Reclaimed; or, The danger
    of moderate drinking
---- The stumbling block; or,
    Why a deacon gave up his
    wine
---- Wine as a medicine; or,
    Abbie's experience
McBride, H. Elliott. A bitter
    dose

---- A boy's rehearsal
---- A talk on temperance

NEW YORK DRAMA
vol. 1. no. 6. Daveau, Illion.
    The plague of my life
vol. 2. no. 24. Olwine, Wayne.
    Camille; or, The fate of
    a coquette
vol. 3. no. 29. Sam Weller's
    visit
vol. 4, no. 47. Mack, Robert
    Ellice. The masquerade;
    or, Aunt Hepsaba's fright
vol. 5. no. 56. Gabrielle de
    Belle Isle
---- Mabel's holiday

ONE HUNDRED CHOICE SELECTIONS
25. Meyers, Robert Cornelius
    V. A pair of gloves
29. ---- A game of chess
31. ---- Ze moderne English
32. Neall, Walter H. An
    economical boomerang
33. ---- Raising the wind
35. Locke, Belle Marshall.
    The Hiartville Shakespeare
    club

THE OPERATIC LIBRARY
1. La favorita
6. The barber of Seville
12. Lucie of Lammermoor
13. The maniac at the island
    of St. Domingo
21. Il giuramento; or, The
    oath
22. Révoil, Bénédict Henry.
    Gemma of Vergy
23. Linda of Chamouni
24. The elixir of love
26. The Lombards at the
    first crusade
29. Don Giovanni

ORIGINAL DIALOGUES
McBride, H. Elliott. Stage
    struck

PARKER'S AMATEUR PLAYER
Osgood, L. W. The Union spy;
    or, The battle of Weldon
    railroad

PARLOR PLAYS FOR HOME
PERFORMANCE
  10. Dark deeds

PLAYS FOR CHILDREN
  1. Jervey, Mrs. Lewis. The
  lost children

POET LORE
vol. 4. nos. 1-3. Porter,
  Charlotte Endymion and
  Clarke, Helen Archibald.
  The seven princesses
vol. 4. nos. 1-7. Sogård,
  Peder Thyge Jesper. A
  glove
vol. 4. nos. 3-9. Porter,
  Charlotte Endymion and
  Clarke, Helen Archibald.
  The sightless
vol. 7. nos. 6-7. ---- Alla-
  dine and Palomides

ROORBACH'S ACTING DRAMA
Highest price for old clothes;
  or, The tailor's strike
McBride, H. Elliott. Two drams
  of brandy
McDermott, J. J. and Trumble.
  The ould man's coat tails
White, Charles. Uncle Jeff
  14. McDermott, J. J. and
  Trumble. A purty shure
  cure

ROORBACH'S AMERICAN EDITION
OF ACTING PLAYS
  23. Townsend, Charles. Miss
  Madcap
  47. Herbert, Bernard. Second
  sight; or, Your fortune
  for a dollar
  48. Townsend, Charles. Under
  a cloud
  49. Dale, Horace C. Strife

SERGEL'S ACTING DRAMA
Coale, George B. The drop of
  water
Delanoy, Mary Frances Hanford.
  The outcast's daughter
Tayleure, Clifton W. Won back
102. Cornish, O. W. Foiled;

  or, A stuggle for life
  and liberty
175. Perine, Charles E. Cast
  upon the world
176. Rosenfeld, Sydney. On
  bread and water
180. Perine, Charles E. Henry
  the Fifth
188. Rosenfeld, Sydney. Mr. X
192. Hollenius, Laurence John.
  A game of cards
283. Hart, George G. E. C. B.
  Susan Jane; or, A sailor's
  life on the raging main
303. Rosenfeld, Sydney. Her
  only fault
308. Abarbanell, Jacob Ralph.
  All on account of a
  bracelet
314. Fraser, John Arthur.
  Santiago; or, For the
  red, white and blue
315. Morris, Felix James.
  Electric love
319. Enéleh, H. B. One year
342. Williams, Henry Llewellyn.
  Declined--with thanks
343. Satterlee, Clarence.
  A Christmas carol
345. Morse, Mabel. A warm
  reception
346. Fuller, Horace Williams.
  False pretentions
---. Mitchell, A. Under two
  flags
352. Townsend, Charles. Border
  land
356. ---- Broken fetters
357. Heermans, Forbes. Down
  the Black Cañon; or, The
  silent witness
361. Fraser, John Arthur. A
  modern Ananias
362. ---- The merry cobbler
379. Heermans, Forbes. Two
  negatives make an affirmative
380. ---- In the fire-light
381. ---- Love's warrant
398. Townsend, Charles.
  Vacation
400. Woodbury, Alice Gale.
  The match-box

557. Lester, Francis. The new squire
558. Reynartz, Dorothy. Carnival; or, Mardi Gras in New Orleans
559. ---- It is never too late to mend
560. Edgcome, John. The last coat
563. Young, Margaret. Kitty
565. Edgcome, John. A web of lies
566. Ritchie, Fannie. Pleasant wedding guests
571. Thomas, Augustus. Arizona
576. Polding, Elizabeth. The dawn of redemption; or, The adoration of the Magi kings
584. Runnion, James B. Champagne and oysters; or, One lie leads to another
601. Robertson, Donald. The triumph of youth; or, The white mouse
836. Coale, George B. On his devoted head

SPENCER'S BOSTON THEATRE
Woolf, Benjamin Edward. Off to the war!
6. Jones, Joseph Stevens. Captain Kyd; or, The wizard of the sea
11. Saunders, Charles Henry. Rosina Meadows, the village maid; or, Temptations unveiled
16. Pilgrim, James. The Limerick boy; or, Paddy's mischief
19. The sergeant's wife
24. Pilgrim, James. Shandy Maguire; or, The bould boy of the mountain
34. The comedy of errors
36. Jones, Joseph Stevens. The surgeon of Paris
62. Medina, Louisa H. Nick of the woods
70. Logan, Cornelius Ambrosius. Yankee land
77. Pilgrim, James. Eveleen Wilson, the flower of Erin
90. Aladdin; or, The wonderful lamp
97. Salmon, John. Old and young; or, Both alike
106. Howe, J. Burdette. The British slave; or, Seven years of a soldier's life
123. Pilgrim, James. Robert Emmet, the martyr of Irish liberty
134. Midnight banquet; or, The castle of Cataldo
156. Bannister, Nathaniel Harrington. Putnam, the iron son of '76
169. Ballou, Maturin Murray. Miralda; or, The justice of Tacon
178. Pilgrim, James. Servants by legacy
179. Palmer, John Williamson. The queen's heart
187. Thaxter, Adam Wallace. The grotto nymph; or, Fairy favor
193. Miles, George Henry. Señor Valiente; or, The soldier of Chapultepec
200. Wright, J. B. Jonathan in England
203. The avenger; or, The Moor of Sicily
---. Lee, Herbert. The avenger; or, The Moor of Sicily
205. Jaimson, George. The Revolutionary soldier

SPENCER'S BOSTON THEATRE.
NEW SERIES
32. Jones, Joseph Stevens. The people's lawyer

SPENCER'S UNIVERSAL STAGE
11. Smith, Dexter. Blanks and prizes
49. Andrews, R. R. Silverstone's wager
54. Woodward, John A. Bouquet
59. Leland, Oliver Shepard. Blue and cherry; or, Appearances are deceitful

62. Woodward, John A. Which
    will have him?
68. ---- Madame is abed

THE STAR DRAMA
Denison, Thomas Stewart.
    Under the laurels
1363. ---- Louva, the pauper

STAR SERIES
Houston, Harry. Sea drift
Ward-Base, H. A treasure
    from Egypt

TURNER'S ACTING STAGE
Gretna Green; or, Matrimony
    in Scotland

TURNER'S DRAMATIC LIBRARY
78. Steele, Silas Sexton.
    The brazen drum; or,
    The Yankee in Poland

**TURNER'S DRAMATIC LIBRARY OF
ACTING PLAYS. NEW SERIES**
vol. 8. no. 55. The Maid of
    Florence; or, A woman's
    influence

THE VARIETY STAGE
Head, M. T. The lonely polly-
    wog of the mill-pond
McDermott, J. J. and Trumble.
    A dark noight's business
---- Dot mad tog
---- Dot madrimonial adver-
    disement
---- Dot quied lotgings
---- Mulcahy's cat
---- The ould man's coat tails
Sedgwick, Alfred B. There's
    millions in it
  1. ---- The big banana
  4. ---- The law allows it
  6. ---- The spelling match
  8. ---- Tootle, tootle, too;
    or, The Frenchman and
    his pupil
 12. McDermott, J. J. and
    Trumble. All in der
    family
 13. Sertrew, Saul. Awful
    girls; or, Big results

14. Sedgwick, Alfred B.
    A mad astronomer
16. ---- I love your wife
18. ---- The decree of divorce
19. ---- Let those laugh who
    win

THE VAUDEVILLE STAGE
Coes, George H. Here she goes
    and there she goes
---- Mrs. Didymus' party

WALKER'S PLAYS
  1. Walker, Alfred. Giorgione,
    the painter of Venice

WEMYSS' ACTING DRAMA
Daly, Augustin. Under the
    gaslight
  3. ---- Griffith Gaunt; or,
    Jealousy
  4. ---- Hazardous grounds

WERNER EDITION
Mathews, Frances Aymar.
    All for sweet charity
---- American hearts
---- The apartment
---- At the Grand Central
---- Both sides of the counter
---- A charming conversation-
    alist
---- The courier
---- En voyage
---- The honeymoon; fourth
    quarter
---- A knight of the quill
---- On the staircase
---- Paying the piper
---- The proposal
---- Scapegrace
---- Snowbound
---- Teacups
---- The title and the money
---- War to the knife
---- The wedding tour
---- A woman's forever
Trumbull, Annie Eliot. Green-
    room rivals

WERNER'S PLAYS
West, A. Laurie. Shades of
    Shakespeare's women

WERNER'S READINGS AND
RECITATIONS
   4. Daly, Augustin. A sister's
     sacrifice

WESTERN GALAXY
vol. 1. no. 2. Tullidge,
    Edward Wheelocks.
    Napoleon

THE WILLIAM WARREN EDITION
OF STANDARD PLAYS
Jones, Joseph Stevens. The
    silver spoon

THE WIZARD SERIES
The fortune hunters; or, Lost
    and found
Latour, Eugene. Adorable
    Elizabeth
---- An affection of the
    heart
---- Tricks of trade; or, An
    obstinate Romeo
Lester, Francis. Flirtation
    cured
---- Our servants
---- The skeleton in the
    closet
Metcalfe, Irving. A game of·
    chance; or, Allotting
    the bride
---- Miss Mary Smith
Reynartz, Dorothy. A mother's
    love; or, A wreath for
    our lady
---- Two mothers
Rosetti, Joseph. Household
    affairs; or, A cause
    for divorce
Scott, W. Atkins. Cupid in
    shirt sleeves
---- An L. A. W. rest
Shields, Lottie. Kate's
    infatuation
Young, Margaret. Kitty

YOUNG'S STANDARD SERIES OF
PLAYS
Scudder, Vida Dutton and
    Brooks, F. M. Mitsu-yu-
    nissi; or, The Japanese
    wedding

APPENDIX II: ETHNIC/RACIAL

Due to the importance of drama in attitude-formation during the nineteenth century, a playwright's utilization of ethnic characters is highly significant. This appendix arranges all plays containing such characters into categories which reflect racial and ethnic origin. When a character is removed from his or her own national or ethnic environment, it is here considered an ethnic one. If the setting of a play is Dublin, for instance, the play ordinarily will not be listed under the heading "Irish in cast." In a few instances where an American has written a play involving characters in their own homeland, the play has been included in this ethnic/racial list since the emphasis is on how the American writer *interpreted* the foreign character. In this volume, "Blacks in cast" includes black-face, as in minstrel plays: again, it is the *attitude* toward various ethnic groups which is being stressed. It is hoped that no group will take offense at the listings in this appendix, for, if anything, this list demonstrates why we are a nation with still-unhealed prejudices.

AMERICANS IN CAST

Gunter, Archibald Clavering. Prince Karl

Horne, Mary Barnard. The other fellow

McLellan, Rufus Charles. The foundling; or, Yankee fidelity

Matthews, Brander and Jessop, George Henry. A gold mine

---- On probation

Mickle, Isaac. The old North Tower

Morris, Felix James. Electric love

Murphy, Fitzgerald. A bit o' blarney

Paulding, James Kirke and Paulding, William Irving. The Bucktails; or, Americans in England *in their* Collected works. American comedies

Pierra, Adolfo. The Cuban patriots

Ranken, Frederic and La Shelle, Kirke. "The ameer"

Richardson, Abby Sage. Americans abroad

The registered letter

Rosse, Jeanie Quinton. The Japanese girl (O Hanu San)

Scudder, Vida Dutton and Brooks, F. M. Mitsu-yu-nissi; or, The Japanese wedding

Simms, George A. Pheelim O'Rooke's curse

Tally Rhand (pseud.) Guttle and Gulpit

Warren, Nathan Boughton. Hidden treasure; or, The good St. Nicholas

Whitley, Thomas W. The Jesuit; or, The amours of Capt. Effingham and the Lady Zarifa

Williams, Henry Llewellyn. Diplomates

Woodward, Matthew C. Rosita; or, Boston and banditti

Wright, J. B. Jonathan in England

Wright, M. L. Fielding manor

ARABIANS IN CAST

Winters, Elizabeth. Columbia, the gem of the ocean

ARGENTINES IN CAST
Winters, Elizabeth. Columbia,
the gem of the ocean

AUSTRALIANS IN CAST
Harte, Bret. Two men of Sandy
Bar
Shields, Sarah Annie Frost.
All's well that ends well
Tees, Levin C. and Murphy,
J. Shriver. A social Judas

AUSTRIANS IN CAST
Fowle, William Bentley.
William Tell *in his* Parlor
dramas
Gayler, Charles. The love of
a prince; or, The court of
Prussia
Howard, Bronson. Aristocracy
King Friedrich Wilhelm First
Kinney, Elizabeth Clementine
Dodge. Bianca Cappello
Lazarus, Emma. The Spagnoletto
Lloyd, David Demarest and
Rosenfeld, Sydney. The
senator
The pattern man
Roskoten, Robert. Carlotta
Williams, Henry Llewellyn.
Diplomates

BLACKS IN CAST
Abbott, Jacob. All against the
grain *in* Abbott, Jacob.
Orkney the peacemaker; or,
The various ways of settling
disputes
Aiken, George L. Uncle Tom's
cabin; or, Life among the
lowly
Aldridge, Ira. The black doctor
Alexander, William. Fall of
Palmyra
Allyn, Dave E. "In for it";
or, Uncle Tony's mistake
An American wife
Ames, A. D. and Bartley, C. G.
The spy of Atlanta
Andrews, Fred G. Hal Hazard;
or, The federal spy
Angelo; or, The tyrant of
Padua

Appleton, Nathan. Centennial
movement, 1876
Arnold, James Oliver. Historical
drama and tableaux, *Uncle
Tom's freedom*
Babcock, Charles W. Adrift
Back from Californy; or, Old
clothes
Bajazet
Baker, George Augustus. West
Point
Baker, George Melville. Among
the breakers
---- Better than gold
---- A close shave
---- Enlisted for the war; or,
The home-guard
---- The flowing bowl
---- Forty minutes with a
crank; or, The Seldarte craze
---- Gentlemen of the jury
---- The man with the demijohn
---- My uncle the captain
---- Nevada; or, The lost mine
---- One hundred years ago; or,
Our boys of 1776
---- Past redemption
---- Rebecca's triumph
---- The Seldarte craze
---- Shall our mothers vote?
---- "Stand by the flag"
---- Thirty minutes for
refreshments
Baker, Rachel E. After taps
---- Bachelor Hall [joint
author: Robert Melville
Baker]
Baker, Robert Melville. Black
magic
Bangs, John Kendrick. The
young folk's minstrels
Barbauld, Anna Letitia Aikin.
Master and slave *in* Follen,
Eliza Lee Cabot. Home dramas
for young people
Barker, Benjamin Fordyce. The
rise in Harlem
Barking up the wrong tree; a
darkey sketch
Barnes, James. The black
barber; or, Humours of
Pompey Suds' shaving saloon
---- The darkey breach of
promise case

---- The darkey phrenologist
---- Doctor Snowball
Barnes, Thomas. The Nigger
  night school
Barnes, William Horatio. The
  drama of secession; or,
  Scenes from American history
Barr, E. Nelson. Broken links
Bateman, Mrs. Sidney Frances
  Cowell. Self
Bates, Morgan and Barron,
  Elwyn Alfred. Realistic
  description of life among
  the moonshiners of North
  Carolina. A mountain pink
Baum, Rosemary. Love in a
  lighthouse
Bauman, E. Henri. Everybody
  astonished
---- Fun in a post office
---- Lauderbach's little
  surprise
---- The patent washing
  machine; or, The lover's
  dilemma
Bayless, Bell. Left in charge
Belasco, David. The heart of
  Maryland
---- May Blossom
La belle Hélène
Bennett, W. L. Katie's decep-
  tion; or, The troublesome
  kid
Bien, Herman Milton. Easter
  eve; or, The "New Hagodoh
  Shel Pesach"
Bixby, Frank L. In the wilds
  of Tennessee
---- The little boss
The black bachelor
Black mail
Blackie, George. The excursion
  of 4th July, 1860
Blood, Henry Ames. How much I
  loved thee!
---- The Spanish mission; or,
  The member from Nevada
Booth, Edwin. Othello in
  The Shakespearean plays of
  Edwin Booth
Boothman, William. His last
  scout
Bowers, E. The man about town

Brewster, Emma E. A bunch of
  buttercups in her Parlor
  varieties
Brier, Warren Judson. A
  soldier of fortune
Brown, J. S. A southern rose
---- In the enemy's camp; or,
  Stolen despatches
Browne, M. C. The landlord's
  revenge; or, Uncle Tom up
  to date
Buxton, Ida M. Carnival of days
---- Our awful aunt
---- Tit for tat
Buzzell, Arthur L. Captain
  Dick; or, Our war corres-
  pondent
Callahan, Charles Edward.
  White sulphur; or, A day at
  the springs
Campbell, Amelia Pringle. The
  great house; or, Varieties
  of American life
Campbell, Bartley Theodore.
  A brave man
---- Fairfax in his The white
  slave and other plays
---- Little sunshine
---- The white slave
---- The white slave in his
  The white slave and other
  plays
Carleton, Henry Guy. A gilded
  fool
Carter, John Henton. The blood-
  stained boot-jack; or, The
  chambermaid's revenge
Challenge dance
Chandler, A. N. Crimp's trip
  to the Centennial
Chapman, W. F. Over the garden
  fence
Chase, Frank Eugene. The bat
  and the ball; or, Negative
  evidence
---- In the trenches
---- A ready-made suit; or, A
  mock trial
Chase, George B. Penn Hapgood;
  or, The Yankee schoolmaster
---- Simple Silas; or, The
  detective from Plunketsville
Childs, Nathaniel. Robinsonade

Chipman, Adelbert Z. The little
  wife
Christy, Edwin Byron. Box and
  Cox
Cinderella *in* Caldor, M. T.
  Social charades
Clark, William Adolphus.
  Gen. Grant; or, The star of
  union and liberty
Clifton, Mary A. Delano. The
  wrong box
Coes, George H. Badly sold
---- Black blunders
---- Everyday occurences
---- The faith cure
---- A finished education
---- Here she goes and there
  she goes
---- The intelligence office
---- Mistaken identity
---- Mrs. Didymus' party
---- Music vs. elocution
---- Oh, well, it's no use
---- The old parson
---- Our colored conductors
---- A perplexing predicament
---- The police court
---- Scenes in a sanctum
---- Sublime and ridiculous
---- That dorg; or, The old
  toll house mystery
---- The three o'clock train;
  or, The haunted house
---- Tricks upon travellers
Collyer, Dan. Christmas Eve
  in the South; or, Uncle
  Caleb's home
---- The milliner's shop
Connell, George Stanislaus.
  The old patroon *in his* The
  old patroon and other plays
Conway, H. J. Dred; a tale of
  the great Dismal Swamp
---- Our Jemimy; or, Connec-
  ticut courtship
Cook, S. N. Out in the streets
Cook, Sherwin Lawrence. A
  valet's mistake
Copcutt, Francis. Edith
Corsican twins
Courtright, William. Zacharias'
  funeral
Cowan, Frank. The three-fold
  love

Cronkhite, Henry McLean.
  Reymond: a drama of the
  American Revolution
Curzon, Sarah Anne. Laura
  Secord
Cutler, F. L. Cuff's luck
---- Joe, the waif; or, The
  pet of the camp
---- The mashers mashed
---- The musical darkey
---- Old Pompey
---- Peleg and Peter; or,
  Around the Horn
---- Pomp's pranks
---- A scale with sharps and
  flats
---- Seeing Bosting
---- The sham professor
---- That boy Sam
Dale, Horace C. The deacon
---- The deacon's tribulations
---- Josiah's courtship
---- Strife
---- A white lie
Daly, Augustin. Divorce
---- Horizon
---- A legend of "Norwood";
  or, Village life in New
  England
---- A test case; or, Grass
  versus granite
---- Under the gaslight
Dancing mad
Darcy, Fred. The devil's mine
D'Arcy, James J. Dark before
  dawn
The darkey tragedian
Dawson, J. H. and Whittemore,
  B. G. Lights and shadows of
  the great rebellion; or,
  The hospital nurse of Tennes-
  see
Dazey, Charles Turner. In old
  Kentucky
Deaf in a horn
The demon phonograph; or, The
  battery and the assault
Denison, Thomas Stewart.
  Borrowing trouble
---- A domestic wanted *in his*
  Friday afternoon series of
  dialogues
---- The Kansas immigrants;
  or, The great exodus

---- Louva, the pauper
---- Odds with the enemy
---- Our country
---- Topp's twins
---- Under the laurels
---- Wide enough for two
Denton, Clara Janetta Fort.
The man who went to Europe
Don't get weary; or, Johnny,
you've been a bad boy
Don't get weary; or, Johnny,
you've been a bad boy *in*
Gentlemen coon's parade...
and Don't get weary; or,
Johnny, you've been a bad
boy
Downing, Laura Case. Defending
the flag; or, The message
boy
Duganne, Augustine Joseph
Hickey. Woman's vows and
Mason's oaths
Dumont, Frank. Absent minded
---- Absent-minded *in his*
The amateur minstrel
---- Africanus Bluebeard
---- An awful plot
---- The black brigands
---- The cake walk
---- The case of Smythe vs.
Smith
---- The Cuban spy
---- Cupid's frolics
---- Cupid's frolics *in his*
The amateur minstrel
---- A desperate situation
---- A desperate situation
in his The amateur minstrel
---- Election day
---- False colors
---- Gambrinus, king of lager
beer
---- The girl from Klondike;
or, Wide awake Nell
---- Happy Uncle Rufus *in his*
The amateur minstrel
---- Helen's funny babies
---- How to get a divorce
---- Little Miss Nobody
---- Making a hit
---- The midnight intruder
---- The mid-night train *in*
his The amateur minstrel

---- My wife's visitors
---- The noble savages
---- One night in a medical
school
---- Other people's troubles
---- The painter's apprentice
---- Pete and the peddler *in*
his The amateur minstrel
---- Pleasant companions
---- The polar bear
---- Queer, quaint and quizzical
questions *in his* The amateur
minstrel
---- The race track *in his* The
amateur minstrel
---- The rival barber shops
---- Scenes in front of a
clothing store
---- The scout of the Philip-
pines
---- The serenade party; or,
The miser's troubles
---- Society acting
---- Stupid servant *in his*
The amateur minstrel
---- The sulphur bath
---- Too little vagrants; or,
Beware of tramps
---- The two awfuls
---- Unexpected visitors
---- Unlimited cheek; or, The
sewing machine agents
---- A visit to the zoological
gardens *in his* The amateur
minstrel
---- What shall I take?
---- Who's the actor?
---- Whose baby is it?
---- The wonderful telephone
---- The wonderful telephone
in his The amateur minstrel
---- The yellow kid who lived
in Hogan's Alley
Duncan, Florence I. Ye last
sweet thing in corners.
Being ye faithful drama of
ye artists' vendetta
Easton, William Edgar. Dessa-
lines: a dramatic tale
The echo *in* The railroad
explosion [and] The echo
An elephant on ice
Elwyn, Lizzie May. Dot, the

miner's daughter; or, One
glass of wine
---- Millie, the quadroon;
or, Out of bondage
---- Murder will out
---- Rachel, the fire waif
---- Sweetbrier; or, The
flower girl of New York
Emerson, M. Burt. Snow Ball,
a colored valet
---- The adventuress; or,
Lady Evelyn's triumph
Emery, E. The gypsy's secret
Engle, Walter K. "Medica"
Eshobel, Raymond. How much I
loved thee!
Fales, Willard Henry. The
cool collegians
Fantasma
Field, A. Newton. Other
people's children
---- The pop-corn man
---- School
---- Those awful boys
---- Twain's dodging
Finn, Sister Mary Paulina.
Heart of gold, true and
tried *in her* Alma mater;
or, The Georgetown Centen-
nial
Fisher, Abraham Lincoln. A
manager's trials
Fiske, Minnie Maddern Davey.
The rose
Fitch, Anna Mariska. Items
Fitch, Clyde. Barbara Freitchie
[sic], the Frederick girl!
---- Nathan Hale
Flewellyn, Julia Collitan.
It is the law
Ford, Harriet and De Mille,
Beatrice M. The greatest
thing in the world
Forrest, Edwin. Othello
Fox, George Washington
Lafayette. Jack and Gill
went up the hill
Fraser, John Arthur. Because
I love you
---- Dewey, the hero of Manila
---- The merry cobbler
---- Our starry banner
---- Santiago; or, For the
red, white and blue

---- A woman's honor
Freeman, Mary Eleanor Wilkins.
Giles Corey, yeoman
The fugitives
Furlong, John Ryan. Tried and
true
Gailey, Florence Louise. Ez-
Zahra
Gallus Jake
Gentlemen coon's parade
Gibson, Ad. H. Slick and
Skinner; or, The barber pards
---- A Texan mother-in-law
Gillette, William Hooker. An
American drama arranged in
four acts and entitled *Secret
Service*
---- Held by the enemy
Glenn, M. L. Vice versa
Godoy, José Francisco. Robinson
Crusoe
Goode, George W. Ebony flats
and black sharps
Goodrich, Frank Boott. Flir-
tation, and what comes of it
Gray, William W. Nobody's Moke
Great cry and little wool
Greene, Clay Meredith.
Forgiven
---- The new south [joint
author: Joseph Rhode Grismer]
Griffin, George W. H. The actor
and the singer; or, Gaily the
troubadour
---- The black crook burlesque
---- Camille
---- Corsican twins
---- Feast
---- The Fenian spy; or, John
Bulls [sic, Bull] in America
[joint author: George Christy]
---- Fighting for the union
---- The great arrival
---- Hamlet the dainty
---- Hunk's wedding day
---- The hypochondriac
---- Jack's the lad
---- Les misérables
---- New Year's calls
---- No cure, no pay
---- Nobody's son
---- Othello
---- Quarrelsome servants
---- Rooms to let without

board [joint author: Tony
Denier]
---- Rose Dale
---- Shylock
---- Sports on a lark
---- The ticket-taker; or, The
masquerade ball
---- The troublesome servant
---- An unhappy pair
---- William Tell
Griffith, Benjamin Lease
Crozer. Wanted--a valet
Grimm, Edward. The king's
judges
Grinnell, V. B. The heroic
Dutchman of seventy-six
Gross, Samuel Eberly. The
merchant prince of Cornville
Grover, Leonard. Our boarding
house
Hagarty, W. H. The gold bug
Hageman, Maurice. A crazy
idea
Haid, P. Leo. Major John
André
Hall, J. Griffin. The crowded
hotel; or, The tricky nig
Hamilton, George H. Sunlight;
or, The diamond king
Handy Andy
Harrigan, Edward. The editor's
troubles
Hart, George G. E. C. B.
Susan Jane; or, A sailor's
life on the raging main
Harte, Bret and Pemberton,
Thomas Edgar. Sue
Haskett, Emmett. Jake and Snow
---- The wonderful telephone
Haunted house
Hazard, Eleanor and Hazard,
Elizabeth. An old plantation
night
Hazelton, William B. and
Spencer, Edward. Electric
light
Heath, James Ewell. Whigs and
Democrats; or, Love of no
politics
Heller, Robley Eugene.
Appomattox
Helm, Charles E. Muolo, the
monkey; or, The missing link

Hendrick, Welland. Pocahontas
Herne, James A. The Reverend
Griffith Davenport in his
The early plays of James A.
Herne
Highest price for old clothes;
or, The tailor's strike
Hiland, Frank E. Broken bonds
---- Captain Swell
---- Careless Cupid
---- Dr. McBeatem
---- A town meeting
Hildreth, David W. Bound by an
oath
---- The granger; or, Caught
in his own trap
Hinton, Henry L. Shakespeare's
...Othello the Moor of Venice
Hockenbery, Frank. Prof. Black's
phunnygraph; or, Talking
machine
Hollenbeck, Benjamin W. Zion
Horne, Mary Barnard. The
darktown bicycle club scandal
---- The last of the Peak
sisters; or, The great moral
dime show
---- Plantation bitters
---- A singing school of ye
olden time
Howard, Bronson. Hurricanes
---- Saratoga; or, "Pistols
for seven"
---- Shenandoah
Howells, William Dean. The
Albany depot
---- The parlor car
---- The sleeping car
Hoyt, Charles Hale. A Texas
steer
---- Texas steer; or, Money
makes the mare go
Hunter, Wesley J. Strawberry
shortcake
Ingraham, C. F. The best cure
Ingraham, Jean. The raw
recruit; or, A day with the
National Guard
Jaimson, George. The Revolutio-
nary soldier
Jenks, Almet F. Robinson Crusoe
Jervey, Mrs. Lewis. The lost
children

Johnson, Samuel D. The fireman
Jones, Joseph Stevens. Captain
  Kyd; or, The wizard of the
  sea
Jones, Robert. The hidden hand
Jordon, Clifton E. Hazel Adams
Julian, Robert. Burglars
Jumbo-Jum!
Kavanaugh, Mrs. Russell. The
  elopement *in her* Original
  dramas, dialogues
---- The mechanic's daughter
  in her Original dramas,
  dialogues
---- The pea-green glazed
  cambric *in her* Original
  dramas, dialogues
Kidder, Jerome. The drama of
  earth
The kidnapped clergyman; or,
  Experience the best teacher
Kilpatrick, Hugh Judson and
  Moore, J. Owen. Allatoona
Kinnaman, C. F. In a spider's
  web
Lamson, C. A. Grandmother
  Hildebrand's legacy; or, Mae
  Blossoms reward
Latour, H. J. True wealth
Lawson, James. The maiden's
  oath
Leavitt, Andrew J. and Eagan,
  H. W. The academy of stars
---- The arrival of Dickens
---- The black Ole Bull
---- The blackest tragedy of
  all; or, A peep behind the
  scenes
---- Blinks and jinks
---- Boarding school
---- The body snatchers [with-
  out Eagan]
---- Cousin Joe's visit
---- Deaf as a post
---- The deserters
---- The intelligence office
---- Jeemes the poet
---- The lucky number
---- No tator; or, Man-fish
---- Rip Van Winkle
---- Ten days in the Tombs
---- That wife of mine
---- A trip to Paris

---- The two Pompeys
---- The upper ten thousand
---- Who stole the chickens?
Leavitt, Nason W. The frogs of
  Windham
Lee, Billy F. Muldoon's blunders
Lindon, Patrick C. Dr. Baxter's
  servants
Lippmann, Julie Mathilde. A
  fool and his money
Lloyd, David Demarest and
  Rosenfeld, Sydney. The
  senator
Local hits; or, high life in
  New-Orleans
Lockwood, Ingersoll. Washington
Lucas, Daniel Bedinger. Hilde-
  brand *in his* Collected works
---- Kate McDonald *in his*
  Collected works
---- The maid of Northumber-
  land
---- The maid of Northumber-
  land *in his* Collected works
Lucinda's wedding
Luster, James O. Dutchey vs.
  Nigger
Lynd, William John. Brantley
Macarthy, Harry. Deeds of
  darkness
McBride, H. Elliott. The
  Cucumber Hill debating club
  in his New dialogues
---- Married by the new justice
  in his New dialogues
---- Master of the situation
  in his New dialogues
---- My Jeremiah
---- The poisoned darkys
---- A rumpus on Gingerbread
  Hill *in his* Latest dialogues
---- A temporary 'squire *in*
  his Latest dialogues
---- Well fixed for a rainy
  day
McCarty, William Page. The
  golden horseshoe
McClain, Billy. Before and
  after the war
McCloskey, James Joseph.
  Across the continent; or,
  Scenes from New York life
  and the Pacific Railroad

McFall, B. G. Miss Topsy Turvy;
or, The courtship of the
deacon
McIntyre, John Thomas. Hearts
of men
Mack, Robert Ellice. An
Irishman's maneuver
---- 'Tis the darkest hour
before dawn
McKee, W. J. Gettysburg
The maniac at the island of
St. Domingo
Marble, Scott. Down in Dixie
The masonic lodge
Mayo, Frank. Pudd'nhead Wilson
Melrose, Thorn. The commercial
drummer
Meriwether, Elizabeth Avery.
The Ku Klux Klan; or, The
carpetbagger in New Orleans
Merriman, Effie Woodward.
Diamonds and hearts
Mike Donovan's courtship
Miller, Chester Gore. Chi-
huahua
Miller, Joaquin. '49: Forty-
nine. An idyl drama of the
Sierras
Mitchell, T. Berry. A home
by two brides
The model house
Monroe, Jasper R. Argo and
Irene
---- Malachi and Miranda
Moore, Bernard Francis. The
Rough Rider
Morris, William Smith. An
unconditional surrender
Mowrey, Phil H. The musical
servant
Mumbo Jum; or, The enchanged
clogs
Munson, A. J. A midnight
mistake
Munson, George A. An unwelcome
return
Muscroft, Samuel J. The drummer
boy; or, The battlefield of
Shiloh
Mysterious stranger
Neal, John. Duty and safety
of emancipation
---- The mysterious artist

A night with Brudder Bones
Norcross, Frederic Walter.
Mistress Nan
Not as deaf as he seems
Old Hunks, the miser
The old Kentucky home
Oppenheim, Charles. The wig-
maker and his servants
Orne, Martha Russell. A black
diamond
---- The donation party; or,
Thanksgiving Eve at the
parsonage
---- A limb o' the law
---- Timothy Delano's courtship
Orton, Jason Rockwood. Arnold
Osgood, L. W. The Union spy;
or, The battle of Weldon
railroad
Othello. As performed by
Salvini
Othello...As performed by
Salvini and Booth
Othello...As played at the
Park Theatre
Othello and Darsdemoney
Parker, Walter Coleman. Those
dreadful twins
The pattern man
Paulding, James Kirke. The
lion of the West
Pelham, Nettie H. The belles
of Blackville
---- The old fashioned husking
bee
---- "Patchwork" *in her* The
belles of Blackville [bound
with] "Patchwork"
Perkins, George. Pat McFree,
the Irish patentee
Piatt, Donn. Blennerhassett's
island *in his* Various
dramatic works
---- Life in the lobby
---- Lost and won *in his*
Various dramatic works
Pickett, A. St. J. The sublime
tragedy of the lost cause
Pidgin, Charles Felton.
Blennerhassett; or, The
irony of fate
Pierce, G. H. Gertie's vin-
dication

Pierra, Adolfo. The Cuban
  patriots
Pilgrim, James. Ireland and
  America; or, Scenes in both
---- Paddy the piper
---- Servants by legacy
---- Yankee Jack; or, The
  buccaneer of the Gulf
Polson, Minnie. Our Kittie
---- Wild Mab
Possumfat
Power, Thomas F. The Virginia
  veteran
Preuss, Henry Clay. Fashions
  and follies of Washington
  life
 Putnam, Henry Howell. The
  mariner's return
Putnam, Mary Trail Spence
  Lowell. Tragedy of errors
---- Tragedy of success
The railroad explosion
Raux, Eugene. The road to
  fortune
Rawley, Bert C. Badly mixed
---- A crazy lot!
---- Deacon Jones' wife's
  ghost
---- The Freeman mill strike
---- Stupid Cupid
---- Trixie; or, The wizard
  of Fogg Island
---- Uncle Jed's fidelity;
  or, The returned cowboy
Raymond, George Lansing.
  Cecil the seer in his
  Collected works
Raynor, Verna M. Noel Carson's
  oath; or, Leonia's repent-
  ance
Reeves, George. The slave's
  strategy
Reid, Charles S. Joe Simpson's
  double
Renauld, John B. Our heroes
Reynolds, William C. An
  American pasha
Richards, Bert. Colored
  senators
---- Cupid's capers
---- Hallabahoola, the medicine
  man; or, The squirtgun
  treatment

Ricord, Elizabeth Stryker.
  Zamba; or, The insurrection
Ringwalt, Jessie Elder, Mrs.
  J. L. Paul and Virginia; or,
  The runaway slave
Risdon, Davis. A black trump
The rise in Harlem
Ritchie, Anna Cora Ogden Mowatt.
  Fashion; or, Life in New York
---- Fashion; or, Life in New
  York in her Plays
Robinson, John Hovey. Nick
  Whiffles
Rose, Edward Everett and Ford,
  Paul Leicester. Janice
  Meredith
Rosenfeld, Sydney. A pair of
  shoes
Royle, Edwin Milton. Mexico
Rumsey, Mrs. B. C. A St.
  Augustine episode
Russell, Charles Walcott. The
  water-melon cure
Ryan, Samuel E. O'Day, the
  Alderman
Saltus, Francis Saltus.
  Carthage
Sambo's return
Sanford, Amelia. The ghost of
  an idea
Saphar, Will D. The German
  volunteer
Saunders, Charles Henry. The
  North End caulker; or, The
  mechanic's oath
---- The pirate's legacy
---- The pirate's legacy; or,
  The wrecker's fate
Scenes at Gurney's
Schönberg, James. Oscar the
  half-blood
Scipio Africanus
Seitz, B. Frank. Effervescing
Sertrew, Saul. Awful girls;
  or, Big results
Seymour, Harry. Aunt Dinah's
  pledge
Shackell, G. Chops
Shakespeare, William. Othello
---- Othello in Booth, Edwin.
  The Shakespearean plays of
  Edwin Booth
Shaw, J. S. R. How Sister

Paxey got her child baptized

Sheddan, W. B. The joke on Squinim

Shelland, Harry E. The great libel case

Shettel, James W. and George, Wadsworth M. A coincidence

---- Pomp Green's snakes

Shields, Sarah Annie Frost. Aladdin; or, The wonderful lamp

Shipman, Louis Evan. D'Arcy of the guards; or, The fortunes of war

---- On parole

Shoemaker, Dora Adèle. A fighting chance; or, For the blue or the gray

Siegfried, W. A. Phyllis, the beggar girl

---- Tom Blossom; or, The spider's web

Silsbee, Alice M. and Horne, Mary Barnard. Bells in the kitchen in their Jolly Joe's lady minstrels

Simms, George A. Room 44

16,000 years ago

Smart, Herbert Durrell. Mine falls; or, The miller's daughter

Smith, John Washington. The quack doctor

Sport with a sportsman

Stace, Arthur J. The upstart

The stage-struck darkey

Stanton, F. J. The select school

Stecker, Tom. The man Mohammed

Stedman, W. Elsworth. The Confederate spy

---- The confidential clerk

---- The midnight charge

---- The Yankee detective

Steele, Silas Sexton. Apples in his Collected works. Book of plays

Stewart, J. C. The baby elephant

---- Eh? What is it?

---- Hemmed in

---- The last of the Mohicans

---- The two black roses

---- The wrong woman in the right place

Stocks up! Stocks down!

Stowe, Harriet Elizabeth Beecher. Christian slave [extracts] in Follen, Eliza Lee Cabot. Home dramas for young people

Stuart, Ruth McEnery. The snowcap sisters

Sutherland, Evelyn Greenleaf Baker. In Aunt Chloe's cabin in her In office hours and other sketches for vaudeville or private acting

---- In office hours in her In office hours and other sketches for vaudeville or private acting

---- Po' white trash in her Collected works. Po' white trash and other one act dramas

Switzer, Marvin D. Nip and tuck

Taurus-Vertus (pseud.) Vendetta

Tayleure, Clifton W. The boy martyrs of Sept. 12, 1814

Taylor, W. A. and M'Kee, W. J. The last witness

Tees, Levin C. Mrs. Pepper's ghost

---- The new partner

---- A red-hot massage

---- Snobson's stag party

---- Tatters, the pet of Squatters' Gulch

---- This paper for sale

Thomas, Augustus. Alabama

---- The capitol

Thompson, William Tappan. Major Jones courtship; or, Adventures of a Christmas Eve

Tibbetts, Martie E. Two Aunt Emilys; or, Quits

Tidball, Walton C. The lieutenant

The Tipperary warbler; or, The fraud of the dry goods boxes

Toler, Sallie F. Handicapped; or, A racing romance

Townsend, Charles. Border
land
---- The dark tragedian
---- The darkey tragedian
---- The darkey wood dealer
---- Down in Dixie
---- A family affair
---- The golden gulch
---- The man from Maine
---- A midsummer madness
---- The spy of Gettysburg
---- Tony, the convict
---- Uncle Josh
---- Uncle Tom's cabin
---- Vacation
---- The vagabonds
---- The woven web
The tragedy of Abraham Lincoln;
or, The rise and fall of the
Confederate States
Triplet, James. A supper in
Dixie
De trouble begins at nine
Trumbell, David. The death
of Capt. Nathan Hale
Tubbs, Arthur Lewis. The
fruit of his folly
Turkeys in season
Uncle Tom
Under de kerosene
The Union sergeant; or, The
battle of Gettysburg
Up head!
Vane, Larry. Troubled by
ghosts
---- Try it on
Van Harlingen, Katherine. An
original widow's pension;
or, The fugitive fortune
Van Wart, F. B. Stanley's
dwarfs
Vautrot, George S. At last
---- Black vs. white; or,
The nigger and the Yankee
Vegiard, J. T. The Dutch
recruit; or, The blue and
gray
Venable, William Henry. A
colored witness *in his*
The school stage
Von Culin, Everett. The
dentist's clerk; or, Pulling
teeth by steam

Ward, Cyrenus Osborne. The
great rebellion
Ward, Lew. Claim ninety-six
Ward, Thomas. The fair truant
Warden, Edward. Robert Make-
airs; or, The two fugitives
Warren, Horatio N. Tilmon Joy,
the emancipator
Wenlandt, Oliver. A holy terror
---- Nigger boarding-house
Whalen, E. C. From Sumter to
Appomattox
Wheeler, Esther Gracie Lawrence.
A cup of tea drawn from 1773
White, Charles. The African
box; or, The magician's
troubles
---- Big mistake
---- The black chemist
---- Black-ey'd William
---- The black shoemaker
---- The black statue
---- The bogus injun
---- The bogus talking machine;
or, The puzzled Dutchman
---- Bone squash
---- Bruised and cured
---- Coalheaver's revenge
---- The coming man
---- The Coopers
---- Cremation
---- Daguerreotypes; or, The
picture gallery
---- Damon and Pythias
---- The darkey's stratagem
---- The draft
---- Dutch justice
---- Excise trials
---- The fellow that looks
like me
---- Fisherman's luck
---- The German emigrant; or,
Love and sourkrout
---- Gettin' de bag to hold;
or, The United States mail
---- Getting square on the
call boy
---- The ghost
---- Glycerine oil
---- Going for the cup; or,
Old Mrs. Williams' dance
---- Good night's rest
---- Gripsack

---- Guide to the stage; or,
Unappreciated talent
---- The happy couple
---- Hard times
---- High Jack, the heeler
---- Hippotheatron; or,
Burlesque circus
---- The hop of fashion
---- In and out
---- Jealous husband
---- The jolly millers
---- Julius the snoozer; or,
The conspirators of Thompson
Street
---- Laughing gas
---- The live injin; or, Jim
Crow
---- The lost will
---- A lucky job
---- The magic penny
---- Malicious trespass; or,
Nine points of law
---- Mazeppa
---- The mischevious Nigger
---- The mutton trial
---- The mystic spell
---- A night in a strange
hotel
---- Obeying orders
---- Oh! hush!; or, The
Virginny Cupids!
---- Old Dad's cabin
---- 100th night of Hamlet
---- One, two, three
---- Pete and the peddler
---- The policy players
---- Port wine vs. jealousy
---- The portrait painter
---- Pompey's patients
---- The recruiting office
---- A remittance from home
---- Rigging a purchase
---- Rival artists
---- The rival lovers
---- Rival tenants
---- Sam's courtship
---- The sausage makers
---- Scampini
---- Scenes on the Mississippi
---- The serenade
---- The sham doctor
---- Siamese twins
---- The sleep walker

---- A slippery day
---- Squire for a day
---- The stage-struck couple
---- Storming the fort
---- The stranger
---- Streets of New York; or,
New York by gaslight
---- Stupid servant
---- Them papers
---- Thieves at the mill
---- Three strings to one bow
---- De trouble begins at nine
---- Uncle Eph's dream
---- Uncle Jeff
---- United States mail
---- Vilikens and Dinah
---- Vinegar bitters
---- The Virginny mummy
---- Wake up, William Henry
---- Wanted a nurse
---- Weston, the walkist
---- Who died first?
---- The wreck
---- Young scamp
White, George. Kathleen's honor
The wig makers
Wilkins, W. Henri. Hash!
---- Mother's fool
---- S. H. A. M. Pinafore
---- The turn of the tide; or,
Wrecked in port
William Tell
Williams, George W. Cleveland's
reception party
Williams, Henry Llewellyn. The
black chap from Whitechapel
---- The black Forrest
---- De black magician; or,
The wonderful beaver
---- Bobolino, the black bandit
---- Challenge dance
---- The darkey sleep-walker;
or, Ill-treated ill somnambulo
---- Dar's de money
---- Deaf--in a horn
---- Dem good ole times; or,
Sixteen thousand years ago
---- Fetter Lane to Gravesend;
or, A dark romance from the
"Railway library"
---- Go and get tight
---- The Lime-Kiln Club in an
uproar!

---- Love and lockjaw
---- The Moko marionettes
---- Sport with a sportsman
---- Stocks up! Stocks down!
---- Three black Smiths
---- Wax works at play
Wilton, M. J. Fun in a cooper's
  shop
---- Oleomargarine
Winkle, William. A great
  success
Wood, J. M. G. A case of
  jealousy
---- A $10,000 wager
Woodward, T. Trask. The
  veteran of 1812; or, Kesiah
  and the scout
Woolf, Benjamin Edward. Off
  to the war!
The Xlanties; or, Forty thieves
Zediker, N. Kittie's wedding
  cake

BRAZILIANS IN CAST
Matthews, Brander and Jessop,
  George Henry. On probation
Richardson, Abbey Sage.
  Americans abroad

CAMBODIANS IN CAST
Goodwin, John Cheever. Wang

CHINESE IN CAST
Andrews, Fred G. The mounte-
  banks
Appleton, Nathan. Centennial
  movement, 1876
Baker, George Melville.
  Nevada; or, the lost mine
---- New brooms sweep clean
Brewster, Emma E. A bunch of
  buttercups *in her* Parlor
  varieties
Caldor, M. T. Curiosity *in*
  his Social charades
---- Elocution *in his* Social
  charades
Campbell, Bartley Theodore.
  My partner
---- My partner *in his* The
  white slave and other plays
Cowley, E. J. and Bennette,
  Wilson T. Crawford's claim;

or, Nugget Nell, the pet of
  Poker Flat
Daly, Augustin. Horizon
Denison, Thomas Stewart.
  Patsy O'Wang
Dr. Kearny
Dumont, Frank. Conrad; or, The
  hand of a friend
---- Little Miss Nobody
---- The scout of the Philip-
  pines
Hanshew, Thomas W. The 'forty-
  niners
Harte, Bret. Two men of Sandy
  Bar
Hildreth, David W. Lone Tree
  mine
Horne, Mary Barnard. The last
  of the Peak sisters; or, The
  great moral dime show
Hoyt, Charles Hale. A trip to
  Chinatown
Hunt, Arzalea. The lost dog
McCloskey, James Joseph.
  Across the continent; or,
  Scenes from New York life
  and the Pacific Railroad
Marble, Scott. The stars and
  stripes
Moore, Bernard Francis.
  Poverty flats
Myles, George B. The winning
  hand; or, The imposter
Pelham, Nettie H. The old
  fashioned husking bee
Powell, L. S. and Frank, J. C.
  Conn; or, Love's victory
Powers, Francis. The first born
Ravel, Jerome. Kim-Ka; or,
  The misfortunes of Ventilator
Smith, Edgar McPhail. Travesty
  upon "Arizona"
Stuart, Ruth McEnery. The snow-
  cap sisters
Todd, John W. Arthur Eustace;
  or, A mother's love
Townsend, Charles. The golden
  gulch
Trumbull, Annie Eliot. A masque
  of culture
Ward, Lew. Gyp, the heiress;
  or, The dead witness
Williams, Henry Llewellyn.

Wax works at play
Wilson, Bertha M. A Chinese
wedding
The Xlanties; or, Forty thieves

CUBANS IN CAST
Chase, Frank Eugene. In the
trenches
Dumont, Frank. The Cuban spy
Fraser, John Arthur. Santiago;
or, For the red, white and
blue
---- A woman's honor
Lapoint, William W. Loyal
hearts
Moore, Bernard Francis. The
Rough Rider
Morrison, George Austin.
"Lafayette"; or, "The maid
and the marquis"
Picton, Thomas. A tempest in
a tea pot
Williams, Henry Llewellyn.
Diplomates

DANES IN CAST
MacSwiney, Paul. Brian
Van Rensselaer, Henry and
Stanton, William J. King
Alfred

DUTCH IN CAST [see also
Germans in cast. During the
period, the terms "Dutch"
and "Germans" often were
used interchangeably. For
instance, in Thomas Stewart
Denison's Wide enough for
two (see below), there is a
character named Fritz who,
in the list of characters,
is noted as "a very funny
Dutchman," while in the
costume description, he is
called an "ordinary German
laborer"]
Ames, A. D. and Bartley, C. S.
The spy of Atlanta
Baker, George Melville. One
hundred years ago; or, Our
boys of 1776
Barry, S. The Dutchman's ghost;
or, All right

---- The persecuted Dutchman;
or, The original John Schmidt
Brewster, Emma E. A bunch of
buttercups in her Parlor
varieties
---- The free ward in her
Parlor varieties
Brooks, E. S. A dream of the
centuries in Bartlett, George
Bradford. A dream of the
centuries and other enter-
tainments for parlor and hall
Brown, J. H. Katrina's little
game
Burke, Charles. Rip Van Winkle
Burnett, James Gilbert. Blanche
of Brandywine
Chase, George B. Penn Hapgood;
or, The Yankee schoolmaster
Clifton, Mary A. Delano. Der
two subprises
Crary, J. E. The Irish squire
of Squash Ridge
---- Jacob Shlaff's mistake
---- Johanes Blatz's mistake;
or, The two elopements
---- The old Wayside Inn
Cutler, F. L. Actor and servant
---- The Dutch prize fighter
---- Hans, the Dutch J. P.
---- Lodgings for two
---- $2,000 reward; or, Done
on both sides
---- Wanted a husband
The days of the know nothings
Denison, Thomas Stewart. A
first-class hotel
---- Pets of society
---- Topp's twins
---- Wide enough for two
Dumont, Frank. The Cuban spy
---- Little Miss Nobody
A Dutchman in Ireland
Fisher, Abraham Lincoln. A
manager's trials
Fraser, John Arthur. The
showman's ward
Gibson, Ad. H. Slick and
Skinner; or, The barber pards
Gordinier, Charles A. Tim
Flannigan; or, Fun in a
grocery store
Grinnell, V. B. The heroic
Dutchman of seventy-six

Hall, J. Griffin. The crowded hotel; or, The tricky nig

Harrigan, Edward. Porter's troubles; or, The Fifth Ave. Hotel

Haskett, Emmett. The Dutchman's picnic

Howe, J. Burdette. Scarlet Dick, the King's highwayman [or, The road and the riders]

Hunt, Arzalea. The lost dog

Ingraham, C. F. Hans Brummel's cafe

Jefferson, Joseph and Boucicault, Dion. Rip Van Winkle

Jones, Joseph Stevens. Captain Kyd; or, The wizard of the sea

Kavanaugh, Mrs. Russell. The dancing Dutchman *in her* Original dramas, dialogues

Kinnaman, C. F. In a spider's web

Lover, Samuel. The white horse of the Peppers *in* Massey, Charles. Massey's exhibition reciter

Luster, James O. Dutchey vs. Nigger

McBride, H. Elliott. A baby show at Skilletsville *in his* Latest dialogues

---- The cow that kicked Chicago

---- Lucy's old man

---- The man under the settee *in his* Latest dialogues

---- Opposing the new schoolhouse *in his* Latest dialogues

---- Out of the tangle *in his* Latest dialogues

---- A rumpus on Gingerbread Hill *in his* Latest dialogues

---- Scene in a jury-room *in his* Latest dialogues

---- A scene in a tailor shop *in his* Latest dialogues

---- A smart boy *in his* New dialogues

---- Trying to raise the price of butter *in his* Latest dialogues

McCloskey, James Joseph. Across the continent; or, Scenes from New York life and the Pacific Railroad

McDermott, J. J. and Trumble. All in der family

---- Dot mad tog

---- Dot madrimonial adverdisement

---- Dot quied lotgings

Maeder, Frederick George and Gill, William. My sweetheart

Morrison, George Austin. Captain Kidd; or, A peerless peeress and a haughty pirate

Owen, Robert Dale. Pocahontas

Shannon, J. W. Rip Van Winkle

Shelland, Harry E. Fun in a school-room

Shettel, James W. and George, Wadsworth M. Nanka's leap year venture; or, How she settled her bills

Smith, Elizabeth Oakes Prince. Old New York; or, Democracy in 1689

Smith, Harry Bache. The Knickerbockers

Stedman, W. Elsworth. The Confederate spy

Stephens, Robert Neilson. The alderman

---- Girl wanted

Stewart, J. C. The three chiefs

Thomas, F. J. Commercial infidelity; or, Burglar to slow music

Todd, John W. Arthur Eustace; or, A mother's love

Townsend, Charles. Finnigan's fortune

---- The mountain waif

---- Henry Dandolo-Peter Stuyvesant *in his* Spiritual visitors

Vane, Larry. Troubled by ghosts

---- Try it on

Vegiard, J. T. The Dutch recruit; or, The blue and gray

Von Culin, Everett. The dentist's clerk; or, Pulling teeth by steam

Wainwright, John Howard. Rip
Van Winkle
Warren, Horatio N. Tilmon
Joy, the emancipator
Whalen, E. C. From Sumter to
Appomattox
---- Under the spell
White, Charles. The bogus
talking machine; or, The
puzzled Dutchman
---- Dutch justice
---- The Dutchman's ghost
---- Excise trials
---- The first night
---- The mystic spell
---- One night in a bar room
---- Wanted, a nurse
Wilkins, W. Henri. Mother's
fool
Winters, Elizabeth. Columbia,
the gem of the ocean
Woodward, N. A. The student
and his neighbor in Dramatic
leaflets

ENGLISH IN CAST
Appleton, Nathan. Centennial
movement, 1876
---- Reconciliation
Balatka, Hans. Peter the great
in Saardem; or, The Czar and
the carpenter
Brewster, Emma E. Elizabeth
Carisbrooke with a "P" in her
Parlor varieties
Broadhurst, George Howells.
The wrong Mister Wright
Brooke, Van Dyke. The quick-
sands of Gotham
Brown, Charles Hovey. Elfins
and mermaids; or, The red
rock wave cruiser
---- The red rock wave
Brown, John Henry. A mad
philosopher
Browne, William Maynadier.
A fool for luck
Burgwyn, Collison Pierrepont
Edwards. The lost diamond
Burnett, James Gilbert.
Blanche of Brandywine
Campbell, Bartley Theodore.

Little sunshine
---- My partner
---- My partner in his The
white slave and other plays
---- The white slave
Carleton, Henry Guy. The
butterflies
---- A gilded fool
Chapman, W. F. Won by strategy
Chenoweth, Lawrence. After the
circus
Colburn, Carrie W. His last
chance; or, The little joker
Cowan, Frank. The three-fold
love
Cox, Eleanor Rogers. A million-
aire's trials in her A duel
at dawn
Crane, Eleanor Maud. "Just for
fun"
Dallas, Mary Kyle. Our Aunt
Robertina
Daly, Augustin. Horizon
---- An international match
---- Lemons
---- Madelaine Morel
---- The passing regiment
---- A wet blanket in his
Three preludes to the play
Davis, Mary Evelyn Moore.
A bunch of roses
Davison, E. Mora. The New
Englanders
Denison, Thomas Stewart. The
new woman
---- Our country
Denton, Clara Janetta Fort.
New Christmas in her From
tots to teens
---- That other fourth in her
From tots to teens
Donnelly, Henry Grattan. The
American girl
Ele, Rona. Woman's lefts
Emmons, Richard. Tecumseh; or,
The battle of the Thames
The English traveler in
Beadle's...dialogues no. 2
Fawcett, Edgar. Americans
abroad
Felter, Will D. Over the
garden wall

For myself alone

Ford, Paul Leicester. "The best laid plans"

Fraser, John Arthur. A modern Ananias

Furniss, Grace Livingston. A box of monkeys

---- The Jack trust

Gayarré, Charles Étienne Arthur. Dr. Bluff in Russia; or, The Emperor Nicholas and the American doctor

Glover, Stephen E. The cradle of liberty; or, Boston in 1775

Great cry and little wool

Griffith, Benjamin Lease Crozer. Not at home

---- A rival by request

Grinnell, V. B. The heroic Dutchman of seventy-six

Gunter, Archibald Clavering. The fighting troubadour

---- Prince Karl

Hamilton, C. J. The four-leaved shamrock

Herne, James A. The Minute Men of 1774-1775 *in his* The early plays of James A. Herne

Hill, Grace Livingston and Richardson, Abbey Sage. A colonial girl

Holcomb, Willard. A gilded brick

Holland, Elihu Goodwin. The highland treason

Horne, Mary Barnard. The four-leaved clover

Howard, Bronson. Aristocracy

---- The Henrietta

Hubbell, Horatio. Arnold; or, The treason of West Point

The hunter of Monadnoc

Jaimson, George. The Revolutionary soldier

Kidder, Kathryn. The heart of her husband

King Friedrich Wilhelm First

Kobbé, Gustav. Wanted--a nurse

---- Wanted--a nurse *in his* Plays for amateurs

Leavitt, Nason W. The frogs of Windham

Lynd, William John. Brantley

McBride, H. Elliott. Striking oil

McFall, B. G. Miss Topsy Turvy; or, The courtship of the deacon

McIntyre, John Thomas. In the toils

McLellan, Rufus Charles. The foundling; or, Yankee fidelity

Macomb, Alexander. Pontiac; or, The siege of Detroit

Madden, Eva Annie. A noble spy

Mathews, Frances Aymar. The courier

---- En voyage

Meyers, Benjamin F. A drama of ambition *in his* Collected works

Moore, Bernard Francis. Captain Jack; or, The Irish outlaw

---- "Erin go bragh"; or, The mountain rebel

---- Faugh-a-Ballagh; or, The wearing of the green

---- The Irish agent

Morris, Robert. The elopement; or, Love and duty

Nobles, Milton. Love and law

Norcross, Frederic Walter. Mistress Nan

Orton, Jason Rockwood. Arnold

Osborn, Laughton. Matilda of Denmark *in his* The last Mandeville

---- The prodigal; or, A vice and virtue *in his* The magnetiser

Osgood, Harry O. "The baby"

Pardey, Henry Oake. Nature's nobleman

The pattern man

Paulding, James Kirke. The lion of the West

Piatt, Donn. Blennerhassett's island *in his* Various dramatic works

---- Lost and won *in his* Various dramatic works

Pilgrim, James. Ireland and America; or, Scenes in both

---- Jeanie Deans; or, The heart of Mid-Lothian

Ranken, Frederic and La
Shelle, Kirke. "The ameer"
Rankin, McKee and Maeder,
Frederick George. The
runaway wife
Richardson, Abbey Sage.
Americans abroad
Richardson, Anna Steese
Sausser. Miss Mosher of
Colorado; or, A mountain
psyche
Roberts, T. W. Kathleen O'Neil
Rose, Edward Everett. Janice
Meredith [joint author:
Paul Leicester Ford]
---- Richard Carvel
Rosenfeld, Sydney. Mr. X
Rumsey, Mrs. B. C. A St.
Augustine episode
Safford, De Forest. Watertown
in '75
St. Clair, Clarence. Fear of
scandal
Shipman, Louis Evan. D'Arcy
of the guards; or, The
fortunes of war
Smith, Harry Bache. The bells
of Bohemia
---- The idol's eye
---- Rob Roy
---- Rob Roy; or, The thistle
and the rose
---- The rounders
Spangler, W. H. New Years in
New York; or, The German
baron
Spenser, Willard. The little
tycoon
Steele, Silas Sexton. The
brazen drum; or, The Yankee
in Poland
A streak of luck
Sutherland, Evelyn Greenleaf
Baker. In far Bohemia in her
Collected works. Po' white
trash and other one-act
dramas
---- A song at the castle in
her Collected works. Po'
white trash and other one-
act dramas
Tayleure, Clifton W. The boy
martyrs of Sept. 12, 1814

---- Horseshoe Robinson; or,
The battle of King's Mountain
Tees, Levin C. Snobson's stag
party
---- A social Judas [joint
author: J. Shriver Murphy]
Tillson, Jesse Paxon. Chas.
Wengleigh, the Duke in his
Collected works
---- Jacob Busby in his
Collected works
Toler, Sallie F. Bird's Island
Townsend, Charles. The man
from Maine
Triblet, James. A supper in
Dixie
Trumbull, Annie Eliot. A
masque of culture
Vanity; or, A lord in Phila-
delphia
Van Winkle, Edgar Simeon.
Dramatic fragments
Venbale, William. Chinese
damsel in his The school
stage
White, Charles. Excise trials
Williams, Francis Howard. The
higher education
Williams, Henry Llewellyn.
Fernanda; or, Forgive and
forget
Winters, Elizabeth. Columbia,
the gem of the ocean
Wright, M. L. Fielding manor

FRENCH IN CAST
Americans in Paris; or, A
game of dominoes
Appleton, Nathan. Centennial
movement, 1876
---- Reconciliation
Baker, George Melville. Bonbons
---- The Boston dip
---- Down by the sea
---- A tender attachment
---- Wanted, a male cook
Baker, Rachel E. The chaperon
Balatka, Hans. Peter the great
in Saardam; or, The Czar and
the carpenter
Brewster, Emma E. A bunch of
buttercups in her Parlor
varieties

Broadhurst, George Howells.
Why Smith left home
Brown, John Henry. A mad
philosopher
Browne, William Maynadier.
The trustee
Brownson, Orestes Augustus.
Simpson
Burnett, Frances Hodgson and
Gillette, William Hooker.
Esmeralda
Caldor, M. T. Elocution *in
his* Social charades
Campbell, Bartley Theodore.
The galley slave *in his*
The white slave and other
plays
Campbell, William Wilfred.
Daulac *in his* Collected
works. Poetical tragedies
Carleton, Henry Guy. Victor
Durand
Chisnell, Newton. The three
hats
Coon, Hilton. The widow from
the West; or, The late Mr.
Early
Dallas, Mary Kyle. Aroused
at last
Daly, Augustin. The great
unknown
---- Love in harness
---- Man and wife
Denison, Thomas Stewart.
Our country
---- Scandinavia *in his*
Friday afternoon series
of dialogues
Enéleh, H. B. Tempest tossed
Fawcett, Edgar. Americans
abroad
Felter, Will D. Over the
garden wall
Field, A. Newton. The new
Magdalen
Fisher, Abraham Lincoln.
A manager's trials
---- The marquis
Fiske, Minnie Maddern Davey.
The rose
Fowle, William Bentley. Love
at sight *in his* Parlor dramas
---- The tear *in his* Parlor
dramas

Gillette, William Hooker.
Too much Johnson
Goodwin, John Cheever. Wang
Graham, Mary. Mademoiselle's
Christmas gifts *in* Bartlett,
George Bradford. A dream of
the centuries and other
entertainments for parlor
and hall
Griffith, Benjamin Lease
Crozier. Between the acts
Griffith, Helen Sherman. A
fallen idol
Gross, Samuel Eberly. The
merchant prince of Cornville
Gunter, Archibald Clavering.
The fighting troubadour
---- Mr. Barnes of New York
Holcomb, Willard. A gilded
brick
Howard, Bronson. Aristocracy
---- The banker's daughter
Howe, J. Burdette. Handsome
Jack
Hunt, Violet. The maiden's
progress
Hurlbert, William Henry.
Americans in Paris; or, A
game of dominoes
Jessop, George Henry. Sam'l
of Posen; or, The commercial
drummer
Johnson, Samuel D. In and out
of place
Keatinge, Ella. A white lie
Knapp, Lizzie Margaret. An
afternoon rehearsal
The last of the Mohicans
Lee, Billy F. Muldoon's blun-
ders
Lippmann, Julie Mathilde. The
facts in the case
Locke, Belle Marshall. Breezy
Point
---- Marie's secret
Lockwood, Ingersoll. Washington
Lucas, Daniel Bedinger. Kate
McDonald *in his* Collected
works
Mackay, Frank Findley. A double
life; or, Where there's a
will there's a way
MacKaye, James Steele. In spite
of all

---- In spite of all *in his*
An arrant knave & other
plays
---- Won at last *in his* An
arrant knave & other plays
McKinley, Henry J. Brigham
Young; or, The prophet's
last love
McLellan, Charles Morton
Stewart. The belle of New
York
Macomb, Alexander. Pontiac;
or, The siege of Detroit
Mathews, Cornelius. False
pretences; or, Both sides
of good society
Mathews, Frances Aymar. A
finished coquette
---- Scapegrace
---- Six to one; or, The
scapegrace
Matthews, Edith Virginia
Brander. Six cups of
chocolate
Meyers, Robert Cornelius V.
Ze moderne English
---- Monsieur
Miller, Joaquin. An Oregon
idyl
Milner, Frances S. Brothers
in name
Morrison, George Austin.
"Lafayette"; or, "The maid
and the marquis"
Orton, Jason Rockwood. Arnold
Osborn, Laughton. The magne-
tiser; or, Ready for
anything *in his* The magne-
tiser
---- The prodigal; or, A vice
and virtue *in his* The
magnetiser
Packard, Hannah James. The
choice
Packard, Winthrop. The man in
the case
Parker, Walter Coleman. Ma's
new boarders
Patten, Gilbert. Clover farm
The pattern man
Pilgrim, James. Wild Irish
girl
Raux, Eugene. The road to
fortune

Ritchie, Anna Cora Ogden
Mowatt. Fashion; or, Life
in New York
---- Fashion; or, Life in New
York *in her* Plays
Roskoten, Robert. Carlotta
St. Clair, Clarence. Fear of
scandal
The sea of ice; or, A thirst
for gold, and the wild flower
of Mexico
Sedgwick, Alfred B. Circum-
stances alter cases
---- Tootle, tootle, too; or,
The Frenchman and his pupil
Shettel, James W. and George,
Wadsworth M. Nanka's leap
year venture; or, How she
settled her bills
Shields, Charles Woodruff.
The reformer of Geneva
Shields, Sarah Annie Frost.
Misfortune *in her* Parlor
charades and proverbs
Shoemaker, Dora Adèle. A
fighting chance; or, For the
blue or the gray
Smith, Edgar McPhail. "Waffles"
A streak of luck
Stuart, Ruth McEnery. The snow-
cap sisters
Sutherland, Evelyn Greenleaf
Baker. A song at the castle
in her Collected works. Po'
white trash and other one-
act dramas
Tees, Levin C. She would be a
widow; or, Butternut's bride
Townsend, Charles. Finnigan's
fortune
---- Uncle Josh
Triplet, James. A supper in
Dixie
Ward, Lew. Taggs, the waif;
or, Uncle Seth
White, Charles. The mischievous
Nigger
Williams, Francis Howard. The
higher education
Williams, Henry Llewellyn. The
bells; or, The Polish Jew
Wilson, Louise Latham. The old
maids' association
Woodward, John A. Which will
have him?

Woolson, Constance Fenimore.
Two women: 1862

GERMANS IN CAST *[see note
under Dutch in cast]*
Appleton, Nathan. Centennial
movement, 1876
Baker, George Augustus. West
Point
Baker, George Melville. Forty
minutes with a crank; or,
The Seldarte craze
---- The Seldarte craze
---- A tender attachment
Baker, Robert Melville. An
awkward squad
Bauman, E. Henri. Lauderbach's
little surprise
Black justice; or, Half an
hour in a Kentucky court
house
The bottle imp
Broadhurst, George Howells.
Why Smith left home
Campbell, William Wilfred.
Hildebrand *in his* Collected
works. Poetical tragedies
Chase, Frank Eugene. A ready-
made suit; or, A mock trial
Chenoweth, Lawrence. After
the circus
Clifton, Mary A. Delano.
Schnapps
Cowan, Frank. The three-fold
love
Cutler, F. L. Peleg and Peter;
or, Around the Horn
Dale, Horace C. Strife
Daly, Augustin. Love in harness
Dawson, J. H. and Whittemore,
B. G. Lights and shadows of
the great rebellion; or,
The hospital nurse of
Tennessee
Delanoy, Mary Frances Hanford.
The outcast's daughter
Denison, Thomas Stewart. A
domestic wanted *in his*
Friday afternoon series of
dialogues
---- Hans von Smash
Dumont, Frank. Get-rich-quick
society

---- The rival barber shops
---- The scout of the Philip-
pines
---- The yellow kid who lived
in Hogan's Alley
Du Souchet, Henry A. The man
from Mexico
---- My friend from India
Eberhart, B. F. Yacob's hotel
experience
English, Thomas Dunn. The
Mormons; or, Life at Salt
Lake City
Fast, Edward Gustavus. The
gentleman of the color;
or, Washington reconstructed
Field, A. Newton. The new
Magdalen
Fraser, John Arthur. The merry
cobbler
---- Our starry banner
Garland, Hamlin. Under the
wheel
Gayler, Charles. The love of
a prince; or, The court
of Prussia
Gorman, Richard. Half a day
off
Gunter, Archibald Clavering.
Prince Karl
Hageman, Maurice. What became
of Parker?
Hamilton, George H. Hotel
Healthy
Harrigan, Edward. Porter's
troubles; or, The Fifth Ave.
Hotel
Heermans, Forbes. Down the
Black Cañon; or, The silent
witness
Herbert, Joseph W. "Thrilby"
Heywood, Delia A. Pseudo *in
her* Choice dialogues no. 1
Hiland, Frank E. Who caught
the count
Hildreth, David W. Out of his
sphere
Holbrook, Amelia Weed. Jack,
the commodore's grandson
Horne, Mary Barnard. The
four-leaved clover
Howard, Bronson. Baron Rudolph
Howells, William Dean. Bride
roses

In quod; or, Courting the
wrong lass
Johnson, Samuel D. In and
out of place
Lee, Billy F. Muldoon's
blunders
McCabe, J. L. Maloney's
wedding
McDermott, J. J. and Trumble.
Dot madrimonial adverdise-
ment
MacKaye, James Steele. In
spite of all
---- In spite of all *in his*
An arrant knave & other
plays
---- Money mad
---- Won at last *in his* An
arrant knave & other plays
Mathews, Frances Aymar. A
finished coquette
---- Paying the piper
Matthews, Edith Virginia
Brander. Six cups of
chocolate
Meyers, Robert Cornelius V.
A lady's note
Monroe, Jasper R. An editor
who wanted office
Osborn, Laughton. The
prodigal; or, A vice and
virtue *in his* The magnetiser
Prichard, Joseph Vila. The
great Hindoo secret
Putnam, Mary Trail Spence
Lowell. Tragedy of errors
Renauld, John B. Our heroes
Richards, Bert. Cupid's capers
---- Hallabahoola, the medicine
man; or, The squirtgun treat-
ment
Rogers, James Webb. Madame
Surratt
Rose, Edward Everett and
Ford, Paul Leicester. Janice
Meredith
Runnion, James B. Champagne
and oysters; or, One lie
leads to another
Saphar, Will D. The German
volunteer
Sedgwick, Alfred B. The big
banana

Seymour, Charles W. Home,
sweet home
Shelland, Harry E. The great
libel case
Siegfried, W. A. Tom Blossom;
or, The spider's web
Smith, Harry Bache. The bells
of Bohemia
---- The rounders
Sonneborn, Hilton Burnside.
Who told the lie?
Spangler, W. H. New Years in
New York; or, The German
baron
Stapleton, John. A bachelor's
honeymoon
Story, William Wetmore.
Stephania
Tees, Levin C. Snobson's stag
party
Tiffany, Esther Brown. A
model lover
---- That Patrick!
Townsend, Charles. A wonderful
letter
White, Charles. The German
emigrant; or, Love and
sourkrout
---- The rival lovers
Wilkins, W. Henry. S. H. A. M.
Pinafore
Wilton, M. J. How to pay the
rent
---- Waiting for the train
The Xlanties; or, Forty thieves

GREEKS IN CAST
Horne, Mary Barnard. The last
of the Peak sisters; or,
The great moral dime show
Trumbull, Annie Eliot. A
masque of culture

HESSIANS IN CAST
Burnett, James Gilbert.
Blanche of Brandywine
Shipman, Louis Evan. D'Arcy
of the guards; or, The
fortunes of war

HUNGARIANS IN CAST
Herbert, Bernard. Second
sight; or, Your fortune for
a dollar

INDIANS (NORTH AMERICAN) IN CAST

Appleton, Nathan. Centennial movement, 1876

Bannister, Nathaniel Harrington. Putnam, the iron son of '76

Barnes, Charlotte Mary Sanford. The forest princess; or, Two centuries ago

Belasco, David and Fyles, Franklin. The girl I left behind me *in* Belasco, David. The heart of Maryland and other plays

Bingham, Frank Lester. Henry Granden; or, The unknown heir

Brinton, Daniel Garrison. Maria Candelaria

Brooks, E. S. A dream of the centuries *in* Bartlett, George Bradford. A dream of the centuries and other entertainments for parlor and hall

Byers, Samuel Hawkins Marshall. Pocahontas

Caverly, Robert Boodey. Chocorua in the mountains

---- King Philip

---- The last night of a nation

---- Miantonimo

---- The regicides

Cherrytree, Herr. More truth than poetry

---- The renegade [and] More truth than poetry

Clarke, Joseph Ignatius Constantine. Luck

Cobb, Mary L. Home *in her* Poetical dramas for home and school

Cummings, G. D. The history of Geronimo's summer campaign in 1885

Curzon, Sarah Anne. Laura Secord, the heroine of 1812

Dailey, W. B. Saratoga: a dramatic romance of the revolution

Daly, Augustin. Horizon

Dillaye, Ina. Ramona

Dumont, Frank. The girl from Klondike; or, Wide awake Nell

---- Society acting

Duvar, John Hunter. De Roberval

Emmons, Richard. Tecumseh; or, The battle of the Thames

English, Thomas Dunn. The Mormons; or, Life at Salt Lake City

Furman, Alfred Antoine. Philip of Pokanoket

Hamilton, Alexander. Canonicus

Harrison, Gabriel. The scarlet letter

Hartnedy, M. M. A. Christopher Columbus

Hendrick, Welland. Pocahontas

Herne, James A. The Minute Men of 1774-1775 *in his* The early plays of James A. Herne

Heywood, Delia A. Kindness softens even savage hearts *in her* Choice dialogues no. 1

Hunter-Duvar, John. De Roberval

In quod; or, Courting the wrong lass

Jones, George. Tecumseh and the prophet of the west

Jones, R.? Wacousta; or, The curse

The last of the Mohicans

Leavitt, Nason W. The frogs of Windham

McCarty, William Page. The golden horseshoe

McCloskey, James Joseph. Across the continent; or, Scenes from New York life and the Pacific Railroad

Mackenzie, James Bovell. Thayendanegea

Macomb, Alexander. Pontiac; or, The siege of Detroit

Mair, Charles. Tecumseh

Marble, Scott. The great train robbery

Medina, Louisa H. Nick of the woods

Miles, George Henry. Señor Valiente

---- Señor Valiente; or,
The soldier of Chapultepec
Moorehead, Henry Clay. Tan-
gó-ru-a
Najac, Émile de and Landers,
Jean Margaret. The scarlet
letter
O'Leary, James. Ellie Laura;
or, The border orphan
Owen, Robert Dale. Pocahontas
Piatt, Donn. Blennerhassett's
island *in his* Various
dramatic works
Preston, Daniel Swann. Colum-
bus; or, A hero of the new
world
Preuss, Henry Clay. Fashions
and follies of Washington
life
Raymond, George Lansing.
Columbus *in his* Collected
works
---- Columbus the discoverer
Read, Harriette Fanning. The
new world *in her* Dramatic
poems
Robinson, John Hovey. Nick
Wiffles
Schoolcraft, Henry Rowe,
Alhalla; or, The lord of
Talladega
Sir Harry Vane
Tan-gó-ru-a
Tees, Levin C. Tatters, the
pet of Squatters' Gulch
Tilden, Len Ellsworth. The
emigrant's daughter
Townsend, Charles. Border land
---- The golden gulch
Van Winkle, Edgar Simeon.
Dramatic fragments
Walcot, Charles Melton.
Hiawatha; or, Ardent spirits
and laughing water
The wept of the Wish-ton-wish
White, Charles. The bogus
injun
---- The rehearsal; or, Barry's
old man

INDIANS (INDIA) IN CAST
Osborn, Laughton. The prodigal; or, A vice and virtue

in his The magnetiser

IRISH IN CAST
Adams, Justin. The limit of
the law
Addison, Julia de Wolff Gibbs.
Blighted buds
Ames, A. D. Driven to the
wall; or, True to the last
Andrews, Fred G. The mounte-
banks
Arnold, George. When the cat's
away the mice will play *in*
Arnold, George and Cahill,
Frank. Parlor theatricals;
or, Winter evening's enter-
tainment
Babcock, Charles W. Adrift
Baker, George Melville. Among
the breakers
---- The champion of her sex
---- A close shave
---- Coals of fire
---- "A drop too much"
---- The duchess of Dublin
---- The flowing bowl
---- Forty minutes with a
crank; or, The Seldarte craze
---- Freedom of the press
---- Gentlemen of the jury
---- The greatest plague in
life
---- A Grecian bend
---- Humors of the strike
---- The hypochondriac
---- Love of a bonnet
---- New brooms sweep clean
---- Our folks
---- Rebecca's triumph
---- A sea of troubles
---- Seeing the elephant
---- The Seldarte craze
---- Shall our mothers vote?
---- A tender attachment
---- Thief of time
---- A thorn among the roses
---- Wanted, a male cook
Baker, Rachel E. After taps
---- Bachelor Hall [joint
author: Robert Melville
Baker]
---- The chaperon
Baker, Robert Melville. An
awkward squad

Barnard, Charles. Psyche,
M. D.

Barney the baron

Barr, E. Nelson. Broken links

---- Clearing the mists [joint
author: J. M. Hogan]

Baum, Louis F. The maid of
Arran

Bauman, E. Henri. Fun in a
post office

Bausman, William. Early
California

Beck, William L. Beyond
pardon; or, The Countess of
Lynn

Belasco, David and Greene,
Clay Meredith. Under the
polar star

Belden, N. H. O'Neal, the
great; or, Cogger na Caille
[sic, Caillie]

Bernard, William Bayle.
Mesmerism *in* Massey, Charles.
Massey's exhibition reciter

---- The nervous man and the
man of nerve *in* The modern
standard drama, vol. 5

The billet doux

Bixby, Frank L. In the wilds
of Tennessee

---- The little boss

Brewster, Emma E. A bunch of
buttercups *in her* Parlor
varieties

---- The free ward *in her*
Parlor varieties

---- How the colonel proposed

---- How the colonel proposed
in her Parlor varieties

Brian O'Linn

Bridges, Robert. The household of Rudyard Kipling
in his Overheard in Arcady

Broadhurst, George Howells.
What happened to Jones

---- Why Smith left home

Brown, J. S. A southern rose

---- In the enemy's camp; or,
Stolen despatches

Browne, W. Gault. Ripples

Browne, William Maynadier.
The trustee

Brownson, Orestes Augustus.
Simpson

Burgwyn, Collison Pierrepont
Edwards. The lost diamond

Burke, James. Shannon boys;
or, Mount Shannon

Buzzell, Arthur L. Captain
Dick; or, Our war corres-
pondent

Cahill, Frank. 'Tis an ill
wind that blows nobody good
in Arnold, George and
Cahill, Frank. Parlor
theatricals; or, Winter
evening's entertainment

Caldor, M. T. College Ned *in
his* Social charades

---- Parsimony *in his* Social
charades

Campbell, Amelia Pringle.
The great house; or,
Varieties of American life

Cannon, Charles James. Better
late than never *in his*
Collected works. Dramas

Carleton, John Louis. More
sinned against than sinning

Caverly, Robert Boodey. The
last night of a nation

---- Miantonimo

---- The regicides

Cazauran, Augustus R. A
celebrated case

Chapman, W. F. Wanted: a
confidential clerk

Chase, Frank Eugene. The
great umbrella case

---- A ready-made suit; or,
A mock trial

Chase, George B. Haunted by a
shadow; or, Hunted down

Chase, Lucien Bonapart. The
young man about town

Clifton, Mary A. Delano. The
wrong box

Cobb, Josephine H. and Paine,
Jennie E. The Oxford affair

Coes, George H. The faith cure

---- The intelligence office

Colburn, Carrie W. His last
chance; or, The little joker

Cook, S. N. Uncle Jack; or,
Testing hearts

Coon, Hilton. Under the American flag

Cowan, Frank. The three-fold
love
Cowley, E. J. and Bennette,
Wilson T. Crawford's claim;
or, Nugget Nell, the pet of
Poker Flat
Crane, Eleanor Maud. "Just for
fun"
Crary, J. E. The Irish squire
of Squash Ridge
---- The old Wayside Inn
Cusack, Sister Mary Frances
Clare. Tim Carty's trial;
or, Whistling at landlords
Cushing, Harry H. The lost
child *in* Dramatic leaflets
Cutler, F. L. Hans the Dutch
J. P.
---- Kitty and Patsy; or,
The same thing over again
---- $2,000 reward; or, Done
on both sides
Dale, Horace C. Breaking his
bonds
---- Imogene; or, The witch's
secret
---- Josiah's courtship
Daly, Augustin. A flash of
lightning
---- The great unknown
---- Lemons
---- Love in tandem
---- Under the gaslight
Davis, Mary Evelyn Moore.
Christmas boxes
The days of the know nothings
Dean, Frank J. Joe Ruggles;
or, The girl miner
Delanoy, Mary Frances Hanford.
The outcast's daughter
Denison, Thomas Stewart. The
babes in the woods; or, The
ferocious uncle and the
avenging robins
---- A convention of papas
---- The danger signal
---- A domestic wanted *in his*
Friday afternoon series of
dialogues
---- Hans von Smash
---- The Irish linen peddler
---- Lessons in cookery *in his*

Friday afternoon series of
dialogues
---- Patsy O'Wang
---- The school ma'am
---- Seth Greenback
---- Two ghosts in white
Denton, Clara Janetta Fort.
All is fair in love
---- A change of color
Douglass, John J. My new curate
Dow, James M. The widower's
trials
Dumont, Frank. The case of
Smythe vs. Smith
---- Conrad; or, The hand of
a friend
---- The Cuban spy
---- Dodging the police; or,
Enforcing the Sunday law
---- Little Miss Nobody
---- Norah's goodbye
---- The rival barber shops
---- The yellow kid who lived
in Hogan's Alley
Dunne, Norah. Mrs. Plodding's
nieces; or, Domestic
accomplishments
Du Souchet, Henry A. The man
from Mexico
A Dutchman in Ireland
Elliott, Everett and Hard-
castle, F. W. Santa Claus'
daughter
Elwyn, Lizzie May. Murder will
out
---- Rachel, the fire waif
---- Sweetbrier; or, The flower
girl of New York
---- Switched
Emerson, W. Burt. The musical
captain; or, The fall of
Vicksburg
English, Thomas Dunn. The
Mormons; or, Life at Salt
Lake City
Every-day life
Fales, Willard Henry. The cool
collegians
Felch, William Farrand. The pet
of Parsons' ranch
Fisher, Abraham Lincoln. A
manager's trials
Fitch, Clyde. Beau Brummel

Flewellyn, Julia Collitan.
It is the law
Floyd, William Ralph. Handy
Andy
Ford, Daniel K. The bacterio-
logist
Forepaugh, Luella and Fish,
George F. Dr. Jekyll and Mr.
Hyde; or, A mis-spent life
The fortune hunters; or, Lost
and found
Fothergill, F. Race for a
wife
Fowle, William Bentley.
Country cousins *in his*
Parlor dramas
---- The double ghost *in his*
Parlor dramas
---- The tea party *in his*
Parlor dramas
---- Woman's rights *in his*
Parlor dramas
Fox, George Washington
Lafayette. Jack and Gill
went up the hill
Frank, J. C. Homeopathy; or,
The family cure
Frank Glynn's wife; or, An
American harem
Fraser, John Arthur. Because
I love you
---- The merry cobbler
---- Our starry banner
---- Santiago; or, For the
red, white and blue
A frightened lodger *in*
Dramatic leaflets
Furniss, Grace Livingston.
The flying wedge
Garland, Hamlin. Under the
wheel
Gibson, Ad. H. A Texan mother-
in-law
Gilbert, Clayton H. Rescued
Glengall, Richard Butler,
Earl of. The Irish tutor
in Massey, Charles. Massey's
exhibition reciter
Goddard, Edward. By force of
love; or, Wedded and parted
Goodfellow, Mrs. E. J. H.
Vice versa
Gordinier, Charles A. Tim

Flannigan; or, Fun in a
grocery store
Green, John B. Circumstantial
evidence
Griffin, George W. H. The
ticket-taker; or, The
masquerade ball
Griffith, Helen Sherman.
A borrowed luncheon
---- The burglar alarm
Grinnell, V. B. The heroic
Dutchman of seventy-six
Grover, J. Holmes. That rascal
Pat
Grover, Leonard. Our boarding
house
Gunter, Archibald Clavering.
The fighting troubadour
Hageman, Maurice. Mrs. Mulcahy
Hall, J. Griffin. The crowded
hotel; or, The tricky nig
Hamilton, C. J. The four-leaved
shamrock
Hamilton, George H. Sunlight;
or, The diamond king
Hanlon, Henry Oldham. A
picked-up dinner
Hanshew, Thomas W. The
'forty-niners
Harrigan, Edward. Porter's
troubles; or, The Fifth Ave.
Hotel
Harrison, Constance Cary. Tea
at four o'clock *in her*
Short comedies for amateur
players
Hart, Daniel L. The parish
priest
Hart, George G. F. C. B.
Susan Jane; or, A sailor's
life on the raging main
Hartnedy, M. M. A. Christopher
Columbus
Haskett, Emmett. Bridget
Branagan's troubles; or, The
masquerade ball
---- The wonderful telephone
Heermans, Forbes. Down the
Black Cañon; or, The silent
witness
Herbert, Bernard. Second
sight; or, Your fortune for
a dollar

Herne, James A. The hearth-
stone; or, My colleen
Heywood, Delia A. Mrs. Pea-
body's boarder *in her*
Choice dialogues no. 1
Hiland, Frank E. Dr. McBeatem
---- The lady lawyer
---- Rooney's restaurant
---- A town meeting
Hildreth, David W. The granger;
or, Caught in his own trap
---- Joining the Tinpanites;
or, Paddy McFling's exper-
ience
---- Lone Tree mine
---- Placer gold; or, How
Uncle Nathan lost his farm
---- The volunteers; or, The
pride of Company G
Hoefler, Henry A. A day in
a doctor's office
Hollenbeck, Benjamin W. After
ten years; or, The maniac
wife
Hoppin, William Jones. The
lady of the bed-chamber
Horne, Mary Barnard. The
last of the Peak sisters;
or, The great moral dime
show
---- Prof. Baxter's great
invention
Howe, C. E. B. Signing the
Declaration of Independence;
or, Scenes in Congress,
July 4th, 1776
Howe, J. Burdette. Handsome
Jack
Howells, William Dean. The
Albany depot
---- Out of the question
Hunt, Arzalea. The lost dog
---- A wedding notice
In quod; or, Courting the
wrong lass
Jackson, John Jasper. A
politican pull
Jackson, N. Hart. The bottom
of the sea
Jeffries, L. Q. Tim M'Quain's
bother
Jervey, Mrs. Lewis. The lost
children

Jessop, George Henry. Shamus
O'Brien
Johnson, Samuel D. Brian
O'Linn
---- The fireman
---- In and out of place
Kavanaugh, Mrs. Russell. The
minister's guests *in her*
Original dramas, dialogues
Kinnaman, C. F. Arrah de Baugh
Kobbe, Gustav. Loving yet
hating
---- Loving yet hating *in his*
Plays for amateurs
Lamson, C. A. Grandmother
Hildebrand's legacy; or,
Mae Blossom's reward
Landis, Simon Mohler. The
social war of 1900; or,
The conspirators and lovers
Lapoint, William W. Loyal
hearts
Lawrence, F. N. Lanty's luck;
or, Falsely accused
Lee, Billy F. Muldoon's
blunders
Lester, Francis. Our servants
Lippmann, Julie Mathilde.
Cousin Faithful
---- The facts in the case
Locke, Belle Marshall. The
Hiartville Shakespeare Club
Macarthy, Harry. Barney's
courtship; or, Mollie dear
McBride, H. Elliott. As by
fire
---- A baby show at Skillets-
ville *in his* Latest dia-
logues
---- A big day in Bulger
---- The cow that kicked Chi-
cago
---- I'll stay awhile
---- My Jeremiah
---- Opposing the new school-
house *in his* Latest dialogues
---- A rumpus on Gingerbread
Hill *in his* Latest dialogues
---- Scene in a jury-room *in
his* Latest dialogues
---- The somnambulist *in his*
New dialogues
---- Striking oil

---- A sudden bethrothal *in his* Latest dialogues

---- A temporary 'squire *in his* Latest dialogues

---- Trying to raise the price of butter *in his* Latest dialogues

---- Vanity vanquished *in his* Dramatic leaflets

McCabe, J. L. Maloney's wedding

McCloskey, James Joseph. Across the continent; or, Scenes from New York life and the Pacific Railroad

McDermott, J. J. and Trumble. A dark noight's business

---- Dot mad tog

---- Dot quied lotgings

---- A game of billards

---- Mulcahy's cat

---- The ould man's coat tails

---- A purty shure cure

---- Who got the pig?

---- The wrong bottle

McIntyre, John Thomas. In the toils

Mack, Robert Ellice. An Irishman's maneuver

---- The masquerade; or, Aunt Hepsaba's fright

---- 'Tis the darkest hour before dawn

McKee, W. J. Gettysburg

McMichael, Clayton Fotterall. Kenilworth; or, Amy's aims and Leicester's lesson

The Magdalen report

Maguire, John. Honesty is the best policy; or, True to the core

Martin, W. H. Servants vs. master; or, A father's will

Massey, Charles. The school for orators *in* Massey's exhibition reciter

Mathews, Frances Aymar. The apartment

Matthews, Brander and Jessop, George Henry. A gold mine

---- On probation

Merington, Marguerite. Captain Lettarblair

Meriwether, Elizabeth Avery. The devil's dance

Metcalfe, Irving. Miss Mary Smith

Meyers, Robert Cornelius V. A lady's note

Mike Donovan's courtship

Miller, Joaquin. Tally-ho

A millionaire's trials *in* Cox, Eleanor Rogers. A duel at dawn

Moates, William Gurney. The changing scales

Monroe, Jasper R. Malachi and Miranda

Montgomery, Margaret. Per telephone

Moore, Bernard Francis. Brother against brother

---- Ferguson, of Troy

---- The girl from midway

---- The haunted mill; or, Con O'Ragen's secret

---- A judge by proxy

---- The moonshiner's daughter

---- Poverty flats

---- The Rough Rider

---- Winning a wife

---- The wrecker's daughter

Moore, D. H. The New York book agent; or, The miser's gold

Morton, Charles H. Three years in a man-trap

Morton, Marguerite W. The two roses

Munson, George A. An unwelcome return

Murphy, John M. The mechanics reprieve

Neall, Walter H. An economical boomerang

---- Raising the wind

New-year morning

Nobles, Milton. Love and law

O'Brien, FitzJames. A gentleman from Ireland

The Omnibus

Osborn, Merit. Farmer Larkin's boarders

Out of the world

Packard, Winthrop. The man in the case

Parker, Harry. Gertrude
Wheeler, M. D.
Parker, Walter Coleman.
All a mistake
---- Finnegan and Flanagan
---- Those dreadful twins
Patriot in Follen, Eliza Lee
Cabot. Home dramas for
young people
Pat's dilemma; or, Too much
of a good thing
The pattern man
Pelham, Nettie H. The old
fashioned husking bee
Phelps, Pauline. A cyclone
for a cent
Piatt, Donn. Life in the lobby
Pickett, A. St. J. The sublime
tragedy of the lost cause
Pierce, G. H. Gertie's vin-
dication
Pilgrim, James. Ireland and
America; or, Scenes in both
---- Irish assurance and
Yankee modesty
---- Katty O'Sheal
---- Servants by legacy
---- Wild Irish girl
Pirsson, Joseph P. The
discarded daughter
Polding, Elizabeth. At the
fireside; or, Little bird
blue
---- A harmonious family
Powell, L. S. and Frank, J. C.
Conn; or, Love's victory
Quinn, Richard. Called away
Rawley, Bert C. Stupid Cupid
---- Trixie; or, The wizard
of Fogg Island
Raynor, Verna M. Noel Carson's
oath; or, Leonia's repen-
tance
Relief
Renauld, John B. Our heroes
Richards, Bert. Cupid's capers
---- Fooling with the wrong man
---- Hallabahoola, the medicine
man; or, The squirtgun
treatment
The rise in Harlem
Rosenfeld, Sydney. The ulster
Runnion, James B. Champagne

and oysters; or, One lie
leads to another
Russ, William Ward. The strike;
or, Under the shadow of a
crime
Ryan, Samuel E. O'Day, the
Alderman
Sadlier, Mary Anne Madden.
The secret
Saphar, Will D. The German
volunteer
Schindler, Anthony J. Knaves
and fools
Schupphaus, Otto Frederick.
The plutocrat
Sedgwick, Alfred B. The
spelling match
Seitz, B. Frank. Effervescing
Serrano, Thomas K. Between
the fires
Seymour, Charles W. Home,
sweet home
Shelland, Harry E. The great
libel case
Shettel, James W. and George,
Wadsworth M. Nanka's leap
year venture; or, How she
settled her bills
Shields, Sarah Annie Frost.
Domestic in her Parlor
charades and proverbs
---- Inconstant in her Parlor
charades and proverbs
---- Matrimony in her Parlor
charades and proverbs
Shoemaker, Dora Adèle. A
fighting chance; or, For
the blue or the gray
Siegfried, W. A. Tom Blossom;
or, The spider's web
Simms, George A. Pheelim
O'Rooke's curse
---- Unjust justice
Skelly, Joseph P. The charge
of the hash brigade
Smart, Herbert Durrell.
Mine falls; or, The miller's
daughter
Smiley, Robert Watt. What's
next?
Smith, Harry Bache. The bells
of Bohemia
---- The highwayman

---- The idol's eye
---- Little Robinson Crusoe
---- The rounders
---- The three dragoons
Smith, S. Jennie. A free
  knowledge-ist; or, Too much
  for one head
---- Not a man in the house
---- A perplexing situation
Sonneborn, Hilton Burnside.
  Who told the lie?
Stedman, W. Elsworth. The
  Confederate spy
---- The confidential clerk
---- The midnight charge
Steele, Silas Sexton. The
  tailor of Tipperary; or, The
  Irish lion *in his* Collected
  works. Book of plyas
Stephens, Robert Neilson.
  The alderman
---- Girl wanted
---- On the Bowery
Stern, Edwin M. Hick'ry Farm
Stern, H. I. Evelyn Gray; or,
  The victims of our western
  Turks
Stewart, J. C. The three
  chiefs
Switzer, Marvin D. Nip and
  Tuck
Talladay, Jennie. The little
  country store
Tees, Levin C. A politician's
  breakfast *in his* A row in
  the kitchen [bound with]
  A politician's breakfast
---- A row in the kitchen
  [bound with] A politician's
  breakfast
---- She would be a widow;
  or, Butternut's bride
---- Snobson's stag party
Tibbetts, Martie F. Two Aunt
  Emilys; or, Quits
Tiffany, Esther Brown. A rice
  pudding
Tilden, Len Ellsworth. The
  emigrant's daughter
The Tipperary warbler; or,
  The fraud of the dry goods
  boxes
Todd, John W. Arthur Eustace;
  or, A mother's love

Toler, Sallie F. Bird's Island
Townsend, Charles. Border land
---- Broken fetters
---- Deception
---- Down in Dixie
---- Finnigan's fortune
---- The golden gulch
---- A loyal friend
---- The mountain waif
---- On guard
---- Rio Grande
---- Shaun Aroon
---- A social outcast
---- Uncle Josh
---- Vacation
---- The vagabonds
---- The woven web
A trip to Cambridge
Triplet, James. Call at
  number 1-7
Trumbell, David. The death
  of Capt. Nathan Hale
Tubbs, Arthur Lewis. The
  scheme that failed
Vanity; or, A lord in
  Philadelphia
Varrie, Vida. The coming man;
  or, Fifty years hence
Vautrot, George S. The false
  friend
Vegiard, J. T. The Dutch
  recruit; or, The blue and
  gray
Venable, William Henry. The
  Irish valet *in his* The
  school stage
---- Tricks in a doctor's
  shop *in his* The school
  stage
Von Culin, Everett. The
  dentist's clerk; or, Pulling
  teeth by steam
Walcot, Charles Melton. One
  coat for two suits
Waldron, P. A. Paddy Doyle;
  or, A mutual friend
Walker, Will L. The squire's
  daughter
Ward, Elizabeth Stuart Phelps.
  Within the gates
Ward, Lew. My pard; or, The
  fairy of the tunnel
Ward-Base, H. A treasure from
  Egypt

Warren, Horatio N. Tilmon
Joy, the emancipator
Wehner, J. H. Principles
form character
Whalen, E. C. Under the spell
White, Charles. Ambition
---- Bad whiskey
---- Coalheaver's revenge
---- Dutch justice
---- Excise trials
---- The hop of fashion
---- The mischievous Nigger
---- Pete and the peddler
---- The rehearsal; or,
Barry's old man
---- The rival lovers
---- Siamese twins
---- Vinegar bitters
---- The Virginny mummy
White, George. Kathleen's
honor
Whitley, Thomas W. The Jesuit;
or, The amours of Capt.
Effingham and the Lady
Zarifa
Wilkins, W. Henri. S. H. A. M.
Pinafore
Willard, Charles O. Little
Goldie; or, The child of
the camp
Williams, Barney. Alive and
kicking
Williams, Henry Llewellyn.
Charles O'Malley's aunt
---- The fifth wheel
Wilson, Louise Latham. A
case of suspension
---- The Smith mystery
---- The trouble at Satterlee's
Wilton, M. J. How to pay the
rent
---- Mickey Free
---- Waiting for the train
Winkle, William. A great
success
Wood, C. A. F. The Irish
broom-maker; or, A cure
for dumbness
Woodbury, Alice Gale. The
match-box
Woodhull, Aaron H. A thorough-
bred
Woodward, N. A. The student

and his neighbors *in* Dramatic leaflets

ITALIANS IN CAST

Appleton, Nathan. Centennial
movement, 1876
Bridges, Robert. The household
of F. Marion Crawford *in his*
Overheard in Arcady
Brooke, Van Dyke. The quick-
sands of Gotham
Brown, Charles Hovey. Elfins
and mermaids; or, The red
rock wave cruiser
---- The red rock wave
Cahill, Frank. Honor among
thieves *in* Arnold, George
and Cahill, Frank. Parlor
theatricals; or, Winter
evening's entertainment
Chase, Frank Eugene. A ready-
made suit; or, A mock trial
Copcutt, Francis. Edith
Daly, Augustin. "Frou Frou"
---- 7-20-8; or, Casting a
boomerang
The days of the know nothings
Dumont, Frank. Dodging the
police; or, Enforcing the
Sunday law
Every-day life
Fawcett, Edgar. Americans
abroad
Fry, Horace B. Little Italy
Grover, Leonard. Our boarding
house
Howells, William Dean. A sea-
change; or, Love's stowaway
Hoyt, Charles Hale. A tin
soldier
Leland, Oliver Shepard.
Beatrice; or, The false and
the true
McCloskey, James Joseph.
Across the continent; or,
Scenes from New York life
and the Pacific Railroad
Marie, a woman of the people
Mathews, Frances Aymar. A
finished coquette
Moates, William Gurney. The
changing scales
Nobles, Milton. Love and law

Osborn, Laughton. The magnetiser; or, Ready for
anybody *in his* The magnetiser
Parker, Walter Coleman. Ma's
new boarders
Shettel, James W. and George,
Wadsworth M. Nanka's leap
year venture; or, How she
settled her bills
Smith, Harry Bache. The
tzigane
Stephens, Robert Neilson. The
alderman
Talladay, Jennie. The little
country store
Tiffany, Esther Brown. Anita's
trial; or, Our girls in camp
Trumbull, Annie Eliot. A masque
of culture
Wilkins, Edward G. P. Young New
York

JAPANESE IN CAST
Appleton, Nathan. Centennial
movement, 1876
Carter, Alice P. The fairy
steeplecrown
Cook, Charles Emerson. The
Koreans; or, The ancestors
of King-Ki-Too
---- The walking delegate
Horne, Mary Barnard. The last
of the Peak sisters; or, The
great moral dime show
MacKaye, James Steele. Money
mad
Robinson, Charles. Dream camp;
or, A modern craze
Smith, Harry Bache. Foxy
Quiller
Tiffany, Esther Brown. Bachelor
maids
Winters, Elizabeth. Columbia,
the gem of the ocean

JAVANESE IN CAST
Chisnell, Newton. The cigarette
Sullivan, Thomas Russell. A
cigarette from Java

JEWS IN CAST
Alexander, William. Ella; or,
The Prince of Gilead's vow
Baker, George Melville.
Conjuration
---- The peddler of Very Nice
Bien, Herman Milton. Easter
eve; or, The "New Hagodoh
Shel Pesach"
Bixby, Frank L. The little boss
The bottle imp
Bowers, Elizabeth. The black
agate; or, Old foes with new
faces
Caldor, M. T. Conjuration *in his*
Social charades
Campbell, Bartley Theodore.
Siberia
Chase, Frank Eugene. A ready
made suit; or, A mock trial
Coale, George B. Magpie and the
maid
Cobb, Mary L. Queen Vashti *in
her* Poetical dramas for home
and school
Daly, Augustin. Leah: the
forsaken
---- The merchant of Venice
The days of the know nothings
Denison, Thomas Stewart.
A dude in a cyclone
Fitch, Clyde. Beau Brummel
Goodrich, Frank Boott. Flir-
tation, and what comes of it
Hageman, Maurice. Hector
Hiland, Frank E. Who caught
the count
Hinton, Henry L. The merchant
of Venice
Hoefler, Henry A. A day in
a doctor's office
Howe, Julia Ward. The world's
own
Hurd, St. Clair. Counsel for
the plaintiff
Jessop, George Henry. Sam'l of
Posen; or, The commercial
drummer
The Jewess
Lazarus, Emma. The dance of
death
Maguire, John. Honesty is the

best policy; or, True to
the core
Malone, Walter. Inez
Moates, William Gurney. The
changing scales
Moos, Herman M. Mortara; or,
The Pope and his inquisitors
Morrison, George Austin.
Captain Kidd; or, A peerless
peeress and a haughty pirate
Morse, Mabel. A foolish invest-
ment
Nobles, Milton. The phoenix
Norton, Morilla Maria. Gloria
Victis
The (old clothes) merchant of
Venice; or, The young judge
and old jewry
Orton, Jason Rockwood. Arnold
Pelham, Nettie H. The old
fashioned husking bee
A queer fit *in* Dramatic
leaflets
Schindler, Anthony J. Knaves
and fools
Shakespeare, William. Merchant
of Venice *in* Booth, Edwin.
The Shakespearean plays of
Edwin Booth *also in* The
modern standard drama, vol. 8
Shelland, Harry E. Fun in a
school-room
---- The great libel case
Shylock, the Jew; or, The
pound of flesh [scene from
Shakespeare's Merchant of
Venice] *in* Steele, Silas
Sexton. Collected works.
Book of plays
Stecker, Tom. The man Mohammed
Stephens, Robert Neilson. The
alderman
---- On the Bowery
The thieving magpie
Townsend, Charles. The golden
gulch
---- The iron hand
---- The jail bird
---- Perils of a great city
Tullidge, Edward Wheelock.
Ben Israel; or, From under
the curse
Williams, Henry Llewellyn.

The bells; or, The Polish
jew

MALAYSIANS IN CAST
Dumont, Frank. The scout of
the Philippines

MEXICANS IN CAST
Dillaye, Ina. Ramona
Fisher, Abraham Lincoln.
Little trump; or, A Rocky
Mountain diamond
Hamilton, George H. Sunlight;
or, The diamond king
Harte, Bret. Two men of Sandy
Bar
Herbert, Bernard. Second sight;
or, Your fortune for a dollar
McKee, W. J. Gettysburg
Miller, Chester Gore. Father
Junipero Serra
Miller, Joaquin. The Danites in
the Sierras
Nona, Francis. The fall of the
Alamo
The sea of ice; or, A thirst
for gold, and the wild flower
of Mexico
Thomas, Augustus. Arizona
Ward, Lew. My pard; or, The
fairy of the tunnel

MOORS IN CAST
Hentz, Caroline Lee Whiting.
De Lara; or, The Moorish
bride
The sisters of Alhama *in*
Silvia and other dramas
Thomas, Lewis Foulk. Cortez,
the conqueror
Williamson, Eugene F. The
sisters of Alhama

NEGROES IN CAST *see* Blacks
in cast

PENNSYLVANIA DUTCH IN CAST
Rauch, Edward H. Pennsylvania
Dutch Rip Van Winkle

PERSIANS IN CAST
Bridges, Robert. The household
of F. Marion Crawford *in his*
Overheard in Arcady

Brunswick, Herman. Amina; or,
The Shah's bride

PERUVIANS IN CAST
Cazauran, Augustus R. The
man of success
Woodward, John A. Which will
have him?

PHILIPPINES IN CAST
Dumont, Frank. The scout of
the Philippines

POLISH IN CAST
Campbell, Bartley Theodore.
Little sunshine

PORTUGUESE IN CAST
McLellan, Charles Morton
Stewart. The belle of New
York

QUAKERS IN CAST *[It is recog-*
nized that Quakers do not
represent either a racial or
ethnic group. However, because
of their importance in the
drama of nineteenth-century
America, plays with Quakers
as members of the cast have
been included here in order
to relate the attitude toward
this group as expressed in
the authors' treatment of
the characters]
Baker, George Melville. One
hundred years ago; or, Our
boys of 1776
Brooks, E. S. A dream of the
centuries in Bartlett,
George Bradford. A dream of
the centuries and other
entertainments
Caverly, Robert Boodey.
Miantonimo
---- The regicides
Congdon, James Bunker. Quaker
quiddities; or, Friends in
council
Denison, Thomas Stewart. Our
country
Fowle, William Bentley. The
fugitive slave *in his*
Parlor dramas

Hamilton, Alexander. Canonicus
Howe, C. E. B. Signing the
Declaration of Independence;
or, Scenes in Congress, July
4th, 1776
McLellan, Charles Morton Stewart. The girl from up there
Moorehead, Henry Clay. Tan-gó-
ru-a
Raymond, George Lansing. Cecil
the seer *in his* Collected
works
Shoemaker, Dora Adèle. A
fighting chance; or, For the
blue or the gray
Tan-gó-ru-a
Taylor, Frederic W. A Pennsylvania kid; or, A soldier's
sweetheart
White, Charles. Glycerine oil

RUSSIANS IN CAST
Appleton, Nathan. Centennial
movement, 1876
Balatka, Hans. Peter the great
in Saardam; or, The Czar and
the carpenter
Campbell, Bartley Theodore.
Siberia
Coale, George B. The drop of
water
Daly, Augustin. Love in tandem
---- The passing regiment
Fawcett, Edgar. Americans
abroad
Mathews, Frances Aymar. En
voyage
Matthews, Brander and Jessop,
George Henry. On probation
Steele, Silas Sexton. The
brazen drum; or, The Yankee
in Poland
Woodward, John A. Which will
have him?

SCOTTISH IN CAST
Brewster, Emma E. A bunch of
buttercups *in her* Parlor
varieties
---- The Don's stratagem *in*
her Parlor varieties
Bridges, Robert. The household
of James M. Barrie *in his*
Overheard in Arcady

---- The house of Robert
Louis Stevenson *in his*
Overheard in Arcady
Cobb, Mary L. Home *in her*
Poetical dramas for home
and school
The fortune hunters; or, Lost
and found
Herbert, Joseph W. "Thrilby"
Horne, Mary Barnard. The
other fellow
MacKaye, James Steele. Hazel
Kirke
Pastil *in* Arnold, George and
Cahill, Frank. Parlor theat-
ricals; or, Winter evening's
entertainment
Toler, Sallie F. Bird's Island

SPANIARDS IN CAST
Beaty, Thomas R. Old Glory
in Cuba
The bottle imp
Brewster, Emma E. The Don's
stratagem *in her* Parlor
varieties
---- Poor Peter *in her* Parlor
varieties
Brooks, E. S. A dream of the
centuries *in* Bartlett,
George Bradford. A dream of
the centuries and other
entertainments for parlor
and hall
Busch, William. Tell tale
eyes; or, Daisy and Don
Cannon, Charles James. The
oath of office
---- The oath of office *in*
his Collected works. Dramas
Carleton, Henry Guy. Ambition
Chase, Frank Eugene. In the
trenches
Coon, Hilton. Under the
American flag
Daly, Augustin. Love in
tandem
Darcy, Fred. The devil's mine
Dumont, Frank. The scout of
the Philippines
Fowle, William Bentley. The
tables turned *in his* Parlor
dramas

Fraser, John Arthur. Dewey,
the hero of Manila
Lapoint, William W. Loyal
hearts
Lynd, William John. Brantley
Marble, Scott. The stars
and stripes
Miles, George Henry. Señor
Valiente
---- Señor Valiente; or, The
soldier of Chapultepec
Miller, Chester Gore. Father
Junipero Serra
Moore, Bernard Francis. The
Rough Rider
Munson, A. J. A midnight
mistake
Pierra, Adolfo. The Cuban
patriots
Read, Harriette Fanning. The
new world *in her* Dramatic
poems
Smith, Harry Bache. The idol's
eye
---- The rounders
Story, William Wetmore. Nero
Thomas, Lewis Foulk. Cortez,
the conqueror
Townsend, Charles. A loyal
friend
---- Rio Grande
Winters, Elizabeth. Columbia,
the gem of the ocean
Yellott, George. Tamayo

SWEDES IN CAST
Broadhurst, George Howells.
What happened to Jones
Davis, Paul P. An amateur
triumph
Lynd, William John. Brantley
Melrose, Thorn. The commercial
drummer

SWISS IN CAST
Cobb, Mary L. Home *in her*
Poetical dramas for home
and school

TURKS IN CAST
Davis, Mary Evelyn Moore. A
dress rehearsal
Horne, Mary Barnard. The last

of the Peak sisters; or, The
great moral dime show
Requier, Augustus Julian.
Marco Bozzaris
Shields, Sarah Annie Frost.
Blue beard
Smith, Harry Bache. The
rounders
Stace, Arthur J. The upstart

This appendix groups those plays dealing with particular broad subject areas, or representing specific literary and dramatic forms, into a variety of appropriate categories. In general, plays with "History" as a subject subdivision are those in which actual historical characters are named. For example, a play dealing with Christopher Columbus may be listed under the heading "Spain--History" and "America--History." If the play deals exclusively with the American aspect of Columbus' voyage, however, the play is listed only under the heading "America--History." Although the phrase "Women's movement" obviously is one in current use, it was felt that the modern terminology was not ill-suited to many of these plays.

AMERICA--HISTORY *[see also United States--History for those plays taking place after 1776]*
Barnes, Charlotte Mary Sanford. The forest princess; or, Two centuries ago
Byers, Samuel Hawkins Marshall. Pocahontas
Caverly, Robert Boodey. Chocorua in the mountains
---- King Philip
---- The last night of a nation
---- Miantonimo
Columbus, the great discoverer of America
Freeman, Mary Eleanor Wilkins. Giles Corey, yeoman
Furman, Alfred Antoine. Philip of Pokanoket
Grimm, Edward. The king's judges
Hamilton, Alexander. Canonicus
Harrison, Gabriel. The scarlet letter
Hartnedy, M. M. A. Christopher Columbus
Hendrick, Welland. Pocahontas
Jones, R.? Wacousta; or, The curse
Leavitt, Nason W. The frogs of Windham

Longfellow, Henry Wadsworth. Christus
Lord, Alice Emma Sauerwein. A vision's quest
McCarty, William Page. The golden horseshoe
Mackenzie, James Bovell. Thayendanegea
Macomb, Alexander. Pontiac; or, The siege of Detroit
Mathews, Cornelius. Witchcraft
Moorehead, Henry Clay. Tan-gó-ru-a
Opal (pseud.) Captain John Smith *in her* The cloud of witnesses
Owen, Robert Dale. Pocahontas
Peterson, Henry. Columbus
Preston, Daniel Swann. Columbus; or, A hero of the new world
Raymond, George Lansing. Columbus *in his* Collected works
---- Columbus the discoverer
Sir Harry Vane
Sutherland, Evelyn Greenleaf Baker. The story of a famous wedding *in her* In office hours and other sketches for vaudeville or private acting
Tan-gó-ru-a
Williams, Espy William Hen-

dricks. Witchcraft; or, The
witch of Salem

BRAZIL--HISTORY
Huntington, Gurdon. The guests
of Brazil; or, The martyrdom
of Frederick

CALIFORNIA--HISTORY
Bausman, William. Early
California
Dean, Frank J. Joe Ruggles;
or, The girl miner
Delano, Alonzo. A live woman
in the mines; or, Pike
county ahead!
Hanshew, Thomas W. The 'forty-
niners
Miller, Chester Gore. Father
Junipero Serra
Miller, Joaquin. '49: Forty-
nine. An idyl drama of the
Sierras

CANADA--HISTORY
Campbell, William Wilfred.
Daulac *in his* Collected
works
Curzon, Sarah Anne. Laura
Secord, the heroine of 1812
Duvar, John Hunter. De Roberval
Hunter-Duvar, John. De Roberval
Mackenzie, James Bovell.
Thayendanegea
Macomb, Alexander. Pontiac; or,
The siege of Detroit
Mair, Charles. Tecumseh

CHARADES
Backgammon *in* Arnold, George
and Cahill, Frank. Parlor
theatricals; or, Winter
evening's entertainment
Baker, George Melville.
Conjuration
Bandage *in* Arnold, George and
Cahill, Frank. Parlor theatricals; or, Winter evening's
entertainment
Bartlett, George Bradford. Tell-
tale *in* Bartlett, George
Bradford. A dream of the
centuries and other enter-

tainments for parlor and hall
Bell, Lucia Chase. Buoyant *in*
Bartlett, George Bradford.
A dream of the centuries and
other entertainments for
parlor and hall
Blue Beard *in* Follen, Eliza Lee
Cabot. Home dramas for young
people
Brewster, Emma E. Cent-any-all:
centennial *in her* Parlor
varieties
---- Holidays *in her* Parlor
varieties
Cahill, Frank. Aunti(Aunty)-
Dote *in* Arnold, George and
Cahill, Frank. Parlor theat-
ricals; or, Winter evening's
entertainment
---- Con-Test *in* Arnold, George
and Cahill, Frank. Parlor
theatricals; or, Winter
evening's entertainment
---- Dram-At(t)ic *in* Arnold,
George and Cahill, Frank.
Parlor theatricals; or,
Winter evening's entertainment
---- Phan-Tom *in* Arnold, George
and Cahill, Frank. Parlor
theatricals; or, Winter
evening's entertainment
Caldor, M. T. Social charades
Charade in two syllables and
three scenes *in* Follen, Eliza
Lee Cabot. Home dramas for
young people
Denison, Thomas Stewart. Grateful *in his* Friday afternoon
series of dialogues
---- Intensity *in his* Friday
afternoon series of dialogues
---- Scandinavia *in his*
Friday afternoon series of
dialogues
---- Scintillate *in his* Friday
afternoon series of dialogues
---- Stockade *in his* Friday
afternoon series of dialogues
De Peyster, John Watts. A
night with Charles XII of
Sweden; or, A soldier's
wife's fidelity

Eberhart, B. F. Home rule
Follen, Eliza Lee Cabot.
Parkington *in her* Home
dramas for young people
Friendship *in* Arnold, George
and Cahill, Frank. Parlor
theatricals; or, Winter
evening's entertainment
Heywood, Delia A. Insect *in*
her Choice dialogues no. 1
---- Pseudo *in her* Choice
dialogues no. 1
Historical acting charades *in*
Follen, Eliza Lee Cabot. Home
dramas for young people
Johnson, Fannie M. Dotage *in*
Bartlett, George Bradford.
A dream of the centuries and
other entertainments for
parlor and hall
A little misunderstanding *in*
Arnold, George and Cahill,
Frank. Parlor theatricals;
or, Winter evening's enter-
tainment
Neighbor *in* Arnold, George
and Cahill, Frank. Parlor
theatricals; or, Winter
evening's entertainment
Pastil *in* Arnold, George and
Cahill, Frank. Parlor
theatricals; or, Winter
evening's entertainment
Patriot *in* Follen, Eliza Lee
Cabot. Home dramas for young
people
Pigtail *in* Arnold, George and
Cahill, Frank. Parlor theatricals; or, Winter evening's
entertainment
Shields, Sarah Annie Frost.
Parlor charades and proverbs
Steele, Silas Sexton. Christmas charades, etc. *in his*
Collected works. Book of
plays
---- The house that Jack built
in his Collected works. Book
of plays
Sweepstakes *in* Arnold, George
and Cahill, Frank. Parlor
theatricals; or, Winter
evening's entertainment

CHILDREN'S PLAYS *[see also*
School plays; Youth plays]
Alexander, Sigmund Bowman.
King winter's carnival
Baker, George Melville. Santa
Claus' frolics
---- Titania; or, The butter-
flies' carnival
Barnard, Charles. Joe, a
comedy of child life
Beach, Stanley Yale and Powell,
H. Arthur. The widow Mullin's
Christmas
Bertram, Eugene and Bassett,
Willard. The mystic midget's
Liliputian carnival of nations
Brewster, Emma E. Holidays *in*
her Parlor varieties
Carter, Alice P. The fairy
steeplecrown
Castle, Harriet Davenport.
The courting of Mother Goose
Chase, Frank Eugene. Santa
Claus the first
Cinderella--under the auspices
of the auxiliary society of
the N. O. A. A.
Crane, Eleanor Maud. The lost
New Year
Cunningham, H. The golden goose
D., F. A. Maiden Mona the
mermaid
Davidson, Belle L. A visit from
Mother Goose
Debenham, L. Grannie's picture
Denton, Clara Janetta Fort.
From tots to teens
---- When the lessons are over
Dulcken, Henry William. Dolly's
doctor *in* Venable, William
Henry. The school stage
---- Master Goat, the tailor
in Venable, William Henry.
The school stage
Fessenden, Helen May Trott.
Troublesome children; or,
The unexpected voyage of
Jack and Pen
Field, Henrietta Dexter and
Field, Roswell Martin.
Collected works
Fitch, Clyde. The children
The grand baby show

in her The luck of the golden pumpkin

---- The luck of the golden pumpkin

---- The old woman who lived in a shoe *in her* The luck of the golden pumpkin

A world's affair

Zediker, N. My day & now-a-days

CHRISTMAS PLAYS

Alexander, Louis. The reception of the months

Baker, George Melville. The merry Christmas of the old woman who lived in a shoe

---- Santa Claus' frolics

Beach, Stanley Yale and Powell, H. Arthur. The widow Mullin's Christmas

Brewster, Emma E. The Christmas box

---- The Christmas box *in her* Parlor varieties

Carter, Alice P. The fairy steeplecrown

Chase, Frank Eugene. Santa Cluaus the first

The Christmas box *in* Brewster, Emma E. Parlor varieties

Collyer, Dan. Christmas Eve in the South; or, Uncle Caleb's home

Coxe, Arthur Cleveland. Advent

Davidson, Belle L. A visit from Mother Goose

Davis, Mary Evelyn Moore. Christmas boxes

---- A Christmas masque of Saint Roch

Denton, Clara Janetta Fort. A gay Christmas ball *in her* When the lessons are over

---- New Christmas *in her* From tots to teens

---- While the joy goes on *in her* When the lessons are over

Elliott, Everett and Hardcastle, F. W. Santa Claus' daughter

Graham, Mary. Mademoiselle's

Christmas gifts *in* Bartlett, George Bradford. A dream of the centuries and other entertainments for parlor and hall

Greenough, James Bradstreet. The rose and the ring

Gutterson, John H. Charlie's Christmas dream

Hadley, Lizzie M. At the court of King Winter

Hartmann, Theodore. The Christmas fairies; or, Shakespeare's dream

Hidden treasure; or, The good St. Nicholas

Huse, Carolyn Evans. Under the greenwood tree

Keatinge, Ella. A Christmas eve adventure *in her* Short plays for children

---- The legend of the Christmas tree

Lewis, Abbie Goodwin. Caught napping

Pelham, Nettie H. The Christmas ship

Phelps, Lavinia Howe. A Christmas address *in her* Dramatic stories

---- A substantial Christmas wish *in her* Dramatic stories

---- Three ways of keeping Christmas *in her* Dramatic stories

---- What Christmas means *in her* Dramatic stories

Polding, Elizabeth. The dawn of redemption; or, The adoration of the Magi kings

Steele, Silas Sexton. Christmas charades, etc. *in his* Collected works. Book of plays

Tiffany, Esther Brown. The spirit of the pine

Warren, Nathan Boughton. Hidden treasure; or, The good St. Nicholas

Wilson, Ella Calista Handy. The bachelor's Christmas

Wilson, Olivia W. Christmas *in her* The luck of the golden pumpkin

---- The luck of the golden pumpkin
---- The old woman who lived in a shoe *in her* The luck of the golden pumpkin

COLLECTIONS

Abbott, Jacob. Orkney the peacemaker; or, Various ways of settling disputes

Alcott, Louisa May. Comic tragedies

Arnold, George and Cahill, Frank. Parlor theatricals; or, Winter evening's entertainment

Bartlett, George Bradford. A dream of the centuries and other entertainments for parlor and hall

Beadle's...dialogues no. 2

Benedict, Frank Lee. The shadow worshiper

Bird, Robert Montgomery. The cowled lover and other plays

Block, Louis James. Capriccios

Booth, Edwin. The miscellaneous plays of Edwin Booth

---- The Shakespearean plays of Edwin Booth

Boxer, James. Sacred dramas

Brewster, Emma E. Parlor varieties

Bridges, Robert. Overheard in Arcady

Bunner, Henry Cuyler. Three operettas

Caldor, M. T. Social charades

Campbell, Bartley Theodore. The white slave and other plays

Campbell, William Wilfred. Collected works. Poetical tragedies

Cannon, Charles James. Collected works. Dramas

Cobb, Mary L. Poetical dramas for home and school

A collection of temperance dialogues

Connell, George Stanislaus. The old patroon and other plays

Daly, Augustin. [Three preludes to the play]

Denison, Thomas Stewart. Friday afternoon series of dialogues

---- Wide awake dialogues

Denton, Clara Janetta Fort. From tots to teens

---- When the lessons are over

Dialogues dramatized from the works of Charles Dickens

Dramatic leaflets

Dugan, Caro Atherton. Collected works

Dumont, Frank. The amateur minstrel

Everett, Alexander Hill. The Grecian gossips

Field, Henrietta Dexter and Field, Roswell Martin. Collected works

Finn, Sister Mary Paulina. Alma mater; or, The Georgetown Centennial and other dramas

Follen, Eliza Lee Cabot. Home dramas for young people

Fowle, William Bentley. Parlor dramas

Fuller, Henry Blake. Collected works

Gildenhaus, Charles. Plays

Grant, Robert. The little tin gods-on-wheels; or, Society in our modern Athens

Greenly, William Jay. The three drunkards

Harrison, Constance Cary. Short comedies for amateur players

Herne, James A. The early plays of James A. Herne

Heywood, Delia A. Choice dialogues no. 1

Hovey, Richard. The plays of Maurice Maeterlinck. First series

---- The plays of Maurice Maeterlinck. Second series

Kavanaugh, Mrs. Russell. Original dramas, dialogues

Keatinge, Ella. Short plays for children

Kobbé, Gustav. Plays for amateurs

Longfellow, Henry Wadsworth.
Christus [1872]
---- Christus [1873]
Lucas, Daniel Bedinger. Col-
lected works. The dramatic
works...
McBride, H. Elliott. Latest
dialogues
---- New dialogues
MacKaye, James Steele. An
arrant knave & other plays
Massey, Charles. Massey's
exhibition reciter; and
drawing room entertainments
Matthews, Brander. Comedies
for amateur acting
Merriman, Effie Woodward.
Comedies for children
Meyers, Benjamin F. Collected
works
The modern standard drama
Monroe, Harriet. The passing
show
Opal (pseud.) The cloud of
witnesses
Osborn, Laughton. The last
Mandeville
---- Ugo da Este
Paulding, James Kirke and
Paulding, William Irving.
Collected works. American
comedies
Phelps, Lavinia Howe. Dramatic
stories
Piatt, Donn. Various dramatic
works
Raymond, George Lansing.
Collected works
Read, Harriette Fanning.
Dramatic poems
Robinson, Lucy Catlin Bull.
Various dramatic works
Shields, Sarah Annie Frost.
Parlor charades and proverbs
Silvia and other plays
Smith, Richard Penn. Dramatic
fragments
Steele, Silas Sexton. Collected
works. Book of plays
Sutherland, Evelyn Greenleaf
Baker. Collected works. Po'
white trash and other one-
act dramas

---- In office hours and other
sketches
Taylor, Bayard. Collected works.
The dramatic works...
The temperance school dialogues
Tillson, Jesse Paxon. Collected
works. The dramatic works
Townsend, Frederic. Spiritual
visitors
Venable, William Henry. The
school stage
Welcker, Adair. Romer, King of
Norway and other dramas
Wilson, Olivia W. The luck of
the golden pumpkin

CUBA--HISTORY
Ballou, Maturin Murray.
Miralda; or, The justice of
Tacon
Pierra, Adolfo. The Cuban
patriots

DENMARK--HISTORY
Osborn, Laughton. Matilda of
Denmark *in his* The last
Mandeville
The school for politicians; or,
Non-committal

EGYPT--HISTORY
Carleton, Henry Guy. Memnon

ENGLAND--HISTORY
Aldémah. The queens
Ascher, Anton. Scenes from
Mary Stuart
Bannister, Nathaniel Harrington.
England's iron days
---- Gaulantis
Boker, George Henry. Anne Boleyn
Brooks, Edward. Mary Stuart
Campbell, Lorne J. King Darnley
Campbell, William Wilfred. Mor-
dred *in his* Collected works.
Poetical tragedies
Caughy, Charles M. Love and
jealousy
Clarke, Hugh Archibald. Harold
Conrad, Robert Taylor. Aylmere;
or, The bondman of Kent
---- Jack Cade, the captain of
the commons

De Peyster, John Watts. Both-
well
Dix, Beulah Marie. Cicely's
cavalier
Donoho, Thomas Seaton. Oliver
Cromwell
Hamilton, Alexander. Cromwell
---- Thomas a' Becket
Hazelton, George Cochrane.
Mistress Nell
Hollister, Gideon Hiram.
Thomas à Becket
Hovey, Richard. The birth of
Galahad
---- The Holy Graal and other
fragments
---- The marriage of Guenevere
---- The quest of Merlin
---- Taliesin
Howard, George H. Tyrrel
Keteltas, Caroline M. The
last of the Plantagenets
Knox, John Armoy and Snyder,
Charles McCoy. The false
prophet
Leighton, William. At the
court of King Edwin
---- The sons of Godwin
Lookup, Thomas. Queen Eliza-
beth; or, Love and majesty
Mansfield, Richard. King
Henry V
---- King Richard, the third
Maria Stuart
Marie Stuart
Massey, Charles. Guy Fawkes;
or, A match for a king in
Massey's exhibition reciter
Mitchell, Silas Weir. Francis
Drake
Opal (pseud.) Bishop Hooper
in her The cloud of wit-
nesses
Owen, Orville Ward. Robert,
Earl of Sussex
Payne, John Howard. Charles
II; or, The merry monarch
in The modern standard
drama, vol. 3
Perine, Charles E. Henry,
the fifth
Piatt, Donn. A king's love
in his Various dramatic works

Prentiss, Elizabeth Payson.
Griselda
Puritan's daughter
Rice, George Edward. Blondel
Rishell, Dyson. Elfrida
S., N. S. Armada days
Shakespeare, William. King
Henry IV, Part I in The
modern standard drama, vol.
10
---- Henry VIII in Booth,
Edwin. The Shakespearean
plays of Edwin Booth
---- King Henry VIII in The
modern standard drama, vol.
10
---- King John in The modern
standard drama, vol. 5
---- Richard II in Booth,
Edwin. The Shakespearean
plays of Edwin Booth
---- Richard III in Booth,
Edwin. The Shakespearean
plays of Edwin Booth
---- King Richard III in
Hinton, Henry L. King Richard
III
---- King Richard III in Mans-
field, Richard. King Richard
the third
---- Richard III in The modern
standard drama, vol. 2
Sutherland, Evelyn Greenleaf
Baker. A comedie Royall in her
Collected works. Po' white
trash and other one-act dramas
Townsend, Eliza. The wife of
Seaton; or, The siege of
Berwick
Townsend, George Alfred.
President Cromwell
Troubetzkoy, Amélie Rives
Chandler. Athelwold
Tullidge, Edward Wheelock.
Ben Israel; or, From under
the curse
---- Elizabeth of England
Van Rensselaer, Henry and
Stanton, William J. King
Alfred
Venable, William Henry. Alfred
the king in his The school
stage

Wiley, Sara King. Cromwell:
an historical play
Williams, Francis Howard.
The Princess Elizabeth
Wilson, John G. Tent and
throne

FEMALES IN CAST *[this heading
is used for plays whose casts
consist entirely of female
characters]*
Allen, Lucy. Débutantes in
the culinary art; or, A
frolic in the cooking class
Armstrong, L. M. C. Gertrude
Mason, M. D.; or, The lady
doctor
Aunt Mehetible's scientific
experiment *in* Brewster,
Emma E. Parlor varieties
Baker, George Melville. The
champion of her sex
---- The greatest plague in
life
---- A Grecian bend
---- Love of a bonnet
---- Rebecca's triumph
---- The red chignon
---- The revolt of the bees
---- Using the weed
---- The war of the roses
Baker, Rachel E. The chaperon
---- A king's daughter
Bates, Ella Skinner. The
convention of the Muses
Brewster, Emma E. Aunt
Mehetible's scientific
experiment
---- Aunt Mehetible's
scientific experiment *in
her* Parlor varieties
---- A dog that will fetch
will carry
---- A dog that will fetch
will carry *in her* Parlor
varieties
---- Eliza's bona-fide offer
---- Eliza's bona-fide offer
in her Parlor varieties
Buxton, Ida M. A sewing
circle of the period
---- Why they joined the
Rebeccas

By special desire
Byington, Alice. "Cranford"
dames
Campbell, Marian D. A Chinese
dummy
---- An open secret
---- Sunbonnets
Case, Laura U. May court in
Greenwood *in* Dramatic leaf-
lets
The chronothanatoletron; or,
Old times made new
Cobb, Josephine H. and Paine,
Jennie E. The Oxford affair
Cold-water cross *in* Dramatic
leaflets
Côté, Marie. The witch of
bramble hollow
The country aunt's visit to
the city *in* Beadle's...
dialogues no. 2
Crosby, Frances Jane. The
flower queen; or, The
coronation of the rose
Cushing, Harry H. The lost
child *in* Dramatic leaflets
Daly, Augustin. A sister's
sacrifice
A dead heat
Debenham, L. Grannie's picture
Denison, Thomas Stewart.
Anniversary meeting *in his*
Friday afternoon series of
dialogues
---- Bachelor girls' club *in
his* Wide awake dialogues
---- Becky Calico *in his* Wide
awake dialogues
---- A domestic wanted *in his*
Friday afternoon series of
dialogues
---- The gossipers *in his*
Wide awake dialogues
---- Lessons in cookery *in his*
Friday afternoon series of
dialogues
---- The lost opportunities
in his Friday afternoon
series of dialogues
---- Madame Princeton's temple
of beauty
---- Pets of society
---- The pull back

---- Sitting up for husbands
to come home *in his* Wide
awake dialogues

---- The society for the
suppression of gossip *in
his* Friday afternoon series
of dialogues

---- The tea party *in his*
Friday afternoon series of
dialogues

---- Two ghosts in white

---- What bird would you be?
in his Wide awake dialogues

---- When I am a woman *in his*
Wide awake dialogues

Denton, Clara Janetta Fort.
The appointment *in her*
From tots to teens

---- Brave little Mary *in her*
From tots to teens

---- The four judges *in her*
From tots to teens

---- In the morning *in her*
From tots to teens

---- Leaflets and ladybugs
in her From tots to teens

---- Like a nettle *in her*
When the lessons are over

---- The lost opportunity *in
her* From tots to teens

---- A message to the children
in her When the lessons are
over

---- Nuts to crack--no. 2 *in
her* When the lessons are
over

---- Parasol drill *in her*
When the lessons are over

---- A peace maker *in her*
When the lessons are over

---- A rebuff *in her* From
tots to teens

---- Surprised

---- To meet Mr. Thompson

---- When I am a woman *in her*
When the lessons are over

---- Writing a book *in her*
From tots to teens

Dickens, Charles. Mrs. Gamp's
tea-party *in* Dialogues
dramatized from the works
of Charles Dickens

Dunne, Norah. Miss tom boy

---- Mrs. Plodding's nieces;
or, Domestic accomplishments

Elwyn, Lizzie May. Murder will
out

---- Switched off

Enebuske, Sarah Folsom. A
detective in petticoats

Fawcett, Edgar. An idyl of the
slums

Felter, Will D. A bunch of
roses *[cast includes one
male impersonator]*

---- The Sweet family

Field, Henrietta Dexter and
Field, Roswell Martin.
Cinderella *in their* Collected
works *[cast includes one
male impersonator]*

---- The muses up-to-date *in
their* Collected works

Finn, Sister Mary Paulina.
A Georgetown reunion and
what came of it *in her*
Alma mater; or, The Georgetown Centennial

First and last *in* The temperance school dialogues

Fitch, Clyde. The gamblers

Furniss, Grace Livingston.
The corner lot chorus

The gifts of the fairy queen
in Beadle's...dialogues no. 2

Goodfellow, Mrs. E. J. H.
Young Mr. Devine

The governess

Griffith, Benjamin Lease
Crozer. A mistake in identity

Griffith, Helen Sherman. A
borrowed luncheon

---- The burglar alarm

---- A fallen idol

Halpine, Charles Graham. Some
talk about poets

Hanssen, C. J. The queen of
Sheba

Hardman, Richard. Clarissa's
first party

Herbert, Bernard. A lesson in
elegance; or, The true art
of pleasing

Heywood, Delia A. Be truthful
but courteous *in her* Choice
dialogues no. 1

---- Grammatical difficulties
in her Choice dialogues
no. 1
---- Labor is honorable *in
her* Choice dialogues no. 1
---- A tea party *in her* Choice
dialogues no. 1
Horne, Mary Barnard. The
darktown bicycle club
scandal
---- The Peak sisters
Jane the orphan
Jaquith, Mrs. M. H. Ma Dusen-
berry and her gearls
Kavanaugh, Mrs. Russell.
Araminta Jenkins *in her*
Original dramas, dialogues
---- The aunt's legacy *in her*
Original dramas, dialogues
---- The elopement *in her*
Original dramas, dialogues
---- Health vs. riches *in her*
Original dramas, dialogues
---- The mechanic's daughter
in her Original dramas,
dialogues
---- Mrs. Vatican Smythe's
party *in her* Original
dramas, dialogues
---- The perfection of beauty
in her Original dramas,
dialogues
---- The wreath of virtue
in her Original dramas,
dialogues
Keatinge, Ella. A white lie
Knapp, Lizzie Margaret.
An afternoon rehearsal
Latour, Eugene. A meeting
of the young ladies club
The little philosophers *in*
Beadle's...dialogues no. 2
Locke, Belle Marshall. Breezy
Point
---- A heartrending affair
---- The Hiartville Shake-
speare club
---- Marie's secret
Luce, Grace A. Brass buttons
McBride, H. Elliott. A baby
show at Skilletville *in
his* Latest dialogues *[cast
includes four male imper-
sonators]*

---- A girls' debate *in his*
Latest dialogues
---- Trying to raise the price
of butter *in his* Latest
dialogues
McConaughy, Julia E. Loomis.
The drunkard's daughter *in*
A collection of temperance
dialogues
Mathews, Frances Aymar. At the
Grand Central
---- Cousin Frank
Matthews, Edith Virginia
Brander. Six cups of choco-
late
Merriman, Effie Woodward.
The mysterious guest
---- The mysterious guest *in
her* Comedies for children
---- The quarrel *in her*
Comedies for children
---- The sick doll
---- The sick doll *in her*
Comedies for children
Mrs. Gamp's tea
Morton, Marguerite W. Poison
The mystic charm; or, A
wonderful cure
Norton, Jessie. Sappho *[cast
includes one male imperso-
nator]*
Our country aunt; or, Aunt
Jerusha's visit
Packard, Winthrop. The man
in the case
Parker, Harry. Gertrude
Wheeler, M. D.
Pelham, Nettie H. The belles
of Blackville
---- "Patchwork" *in her*
The belles of Blackville
[bound with] "Patchwork"
Percival, James Gates. The
sister spirits
Phelps, Lavinia Howe. A game
of nuts *in her* Dramatic
stories
---- Sorrowing Nettie *in her*
Dramatic stories
---- What Christmas means *in
her* Dramatic stories
Poyas, Catharine Gendron.
The Huguenot daughters; or,
Reasons for adherence to
the faith...

Pratt, Sarah H. Penelope's
symposium

The queen of beauty *in*
Dramatic leaflets

Ready answers *in* The temperance school dialogues

Renauld, Charles. The wanderer
*[cast includes one male
impersonator]*

Reynartz, Dorothy. Carnival;
or, Mardi Gras in New Orleans

---- A cup of coffee

---- It is never too late to
mend

---- A mother's love; or, A
wreath for our lady

---- Two mothers

Reynolds, S. S. Nelly's rival

Rosse, Jeanie Quinton. The
Egyptian princess

---- The Japanese girl (O Hanu
San)

Sadlier, Mary Anne Madden.
The secret

---- The talisman

Sanford, Amelia. The advertising girls

---- Maids, modes, and manners;
or, Madame Grundy's dilemma

Schlesinger, Olga Steiner.
The fortune-teller

---- The ghost in the boarding
school

---- Hard of hearing

---- Miss Nonchalance

Shields, Lottie. Kate's infatuation

---- When the cat's away

Shoemaker, Dora Adèle. A
fighting chance; or, For
the blue or the gray

Silsbee, Alice M. and Horne,
Mary Barnard. Bells in the
kitchen *in their* Jolly
Joe's lady minstrels

The sisters of Alhama *in*
Silvia and other dramas

Smith, S. Jennie. Not a man
in the house

The society for doing good,
but saying bad *in* Beadle's...
dialogues no. 2

Speed, Belle Lewis. Columbia

Tammie, Carrie. The birthday
cake

Tibbetts, Martie E. Two Aunt
Emilys; or, Quits

Tiffany, Esther Brown. Anita's
trial; or, Our girls in camp

---- Bachelor maids

---- A blind attachment

Tom's arrival

Townsend, Frederic. Corinna-
Lady Grey *in his* Spiritual
visitors

Trumbull, Annie Eliot. St.
Valentine's day

---- The wheel of progress

The two crowns

Ursula of Brittany

Venable, William Henry.
Chinese damsel *in his* The
school stage

---- Contentment *in his* The
school stage

---- The sincere mourner *in
his* The school stage

The virtues *in* Beadle's...
dialogues no. 2 *also in*
A collection of temperance
dialogues

W., J. M. A brown paper parcel

Water or wine? *in* The temperance school dialogues

West, Emma Elise. Their
graduating essays

Who's to inherit?

Williams, Henry Llewellyn. A
Romeo on "the gridiron"

Williams, Marie Josephine.
A brown paper parcel

---- A nice quiet chat

Williamson, Eugene F. The
sisters of Alhama

Wilson, Louise Latham. The
Smith mystery

---- The trouble at Satterlee's

A wonderful cure

Young, Margaret. Kitty

Zediker, N. Family discipline

---- My day & now-a-days

FRANCE--HISTORY

Adams, Henry Austin. Napoleon

Calvert, George Henry. The
maid of Orleans

---- Mirabeau
The coup d'état
Crane, Elizabeth Green. Berquin
Dement, Richard Sheffield.
  Napoleon
---- Napoleon and Josephine
Donnell, Florence T. A
  revolutionary marriage
Duvar, John Hunter. De Rober-
  val
Field, A. Newton. The new
  Magdalen
Forrest, Harry. Marie Antoin-
  ette: Queen of France
Hunter-Duvar, John. De Rober-
  val
James, Charles. Joan of Arc
Joan of Arc
Jones, Joseph Stevens. The
  surgeon of Paris
---- The surgeon of Paris;
  or, The massacre of St.
  Bartholomew
La Shelle, Kirke. The princess
  Chic
Lytton, Edward George Earle
  Lytton Bulwer-Lytton.
  Richelieu; or, The conspiracy
  in Booth, Edwin. The mis-
  cellaneous plays of Edwin
  Booth
---- Richelieu; or, The
  conspiracy in The modern
  standard drama, vol. 1
MacKaye, James Steele. Paul
  Kauvar; or, Anarchy
Mayo, Frank and Wilson, John G.
  The royal guard
Mickle, Isaac. The old North
  Tower
Moore, Horatio Newton. The
  regicide
Morey, Amos C. Charlotte Corday
Nash, Joseph. Josephine
Nirdlinger, Charles Frederick
  and Meltzer, Charles Henry.
  More than queen
Opal (pseud.) Joan of Arc in
  her The cloud of witnesses
---- Madame Guyon in her The
  cloud of witnesses
Phelan, Agnes Vivien. Margaret
  of Anjou

Pray, Isaac Clarke. Marie
  Antoinette
Ritchie, Anna Cora Ogden
  Mowatt. Armand; or, The peer
  and the peasant
---- Armand; or, The peer and
  the peasant in her Plays
Schönberg, James. Narcisse the
  vagrant
---- True as steel
Schwab, Frederick A. Adrienne
  Lecouvreur
Stephens, Robert Neilson. An
  enemy to the king
The two crowns
Tullidge, Edward Wheelock.
  Napoleon

FRENCH AND ENGLISH [bilingual
texts]
Adrienne Lecouvreur
Andromache
Angelo; or, The tyrant of Padua
Bailey, G. Geneviève de Brabant
Bajazet
Baker, Theodore. Carmen
Barnett, M. J. Samson and
  Delilah
La belle Hélène
Bluebeard
Les brigands
Chilpéric
Coale, George B. Magpie and the
  maid
La dame aux camélias
F., W. F. The little red riding
  hood
Frou frou
Ginty, Elizabeth Beall. Sappho
The grand duchess of Gerolstein
Hélène de la Seiglière
Horace
Joan of Arc
Lady Tartuffe
Mademoiselle de Belle-Isle
Marie Stuart
La marjolaine (The sweet
  Marjoram)
Phaedra
Polyeuctes, the martyr
Raymond, Fanny Malone. Orpheus
Révoil, Bénèdict Henry. La
  favorite

---- The queen of Cyprus
---- The queens musketeers
Schwab, Frederick A. Adrienne
Lecouvreur
---- Frou-Frou
---- Le sphinx
The sparrow of Lesbia
Sunshine follows rain
Virginia
The white lady

GERMAN AND ENGLISH [bilingual
text]
Alceste
Barker, Theodore T. and
Baxter, Sylvester. Fatinitza
Catarina the second
The damnation of Faust
Deborah
Grau, Maurice. Faust
Jameson, Frederick. Dusk of
the gods
---- The mastersingers of
Nuremberg
---- The Rhinegold
---- Siegfried
---- The Valkyrie
Macy, James Cartwright. Der
Freyschütz
Maria Stuart
Marlow, George. Adrienne
Lecouvreur
Masaniello
Medea
Morgan, Geraldine Woods.
Tannhäuser and the minstrels
tournament on the Wartburg
Neumann, Louis. The flying
Dutchman
Paine, John Knowles. Azara
Phaedra
Rattermann, Heinrich Armin.
Gustavus III; or, The masked
ball
Sumichrast, Frederick Caesar
John Martin Samuel Rossy de.
Athaliah
Tartuffe; or, The imposter
Williams, Frederick. The rat-
charmer of Hamelin

GERMANY--HISTORY
Henry IV of Germany

Kelly, Thomas J. F.   Henry IV
of Germany
King Friedrich Wilhelm First
Lazarus, Emma. The dance of
death
Opal (pseud.) Bucer in her
The cloud of witnesses

GREECE--HISTORY
Cheney, John Vance. Queen Helen
Deering, Nathaniel. Bozzaris
Gildehaus, Charles. Aeneas
---- Aeneas in his Plays
---- Telemachus in his Plays
Grice, Louis May. A daughter
of Athens
Leahy, William Augustine.
The siege of Syracuse
Lewis, Estelle Anna Blanche
Robinson. Sappho
Ross, Joseph M. Phintias and
Damon
Woods, Virna. The Amazons

HAITI--HISTORY
Easton, William Edgar. Dessalines; a dramatic tale

IRELAND--HISTORY
Cannon, Charles James. The
oath of office
---- The oath of office in
his Collected works. Dramas
Chivers, Thomas Holley. The
sons of Usna
Clarke, Joseph Ignatius Con-
stantine. Robert Emmet, a
tragedy of Irish history
MacSwiney, Paul. Brian
Moore, Bernard Francis.
Captain Jack; or, The Irish
outlaw
---- "Erin go bragh"; or, The
mountain rebel
---- Faugh-a-Ballagh; or, The
wearing of the green
Pepper, George. Kathleen
O'Neil; or, A picture of
feudal times in Ireland
Pilgrim, James. Robert Emmet,
the martyr of Irish liberty
---- Shandy Maguire; or, The
bould boy of the mountain

Rizy, F. X. O'Neil the Great

ITALIAN AND ENGLISH [bilingual
text]
Adrienne Lecouvreur
Attinelli, Joseph. Matilda di
Shabran and Corradino
The barber of Seville
Barker, Theodore T. and Baxter,
Sylvester. Fatinitza
Byrne, Charles Alfred and
Marras, Mowbray. Gabriella
The child of the regiment
Civil death
Day, Willard Gibson. Cavalleria
rusticana
Dole, Nathan Haskell. Friend
Fritz
Don Giovanni
The elixir of love
Ernani
La favorita
The favorite
La figlia del reggimento
Il giuramento
Howells, William Dean. Samson
"Ingomar, the barbarian"
The Lombards at the first
crusade
Lowell, James Russell. Il
pesceballo
Lucretia Borgia
Lucy of Lammermoor
Macy, James Cartwright. Rustic
chivalry (Cavalleria rus-
ticana)
Othello. As performed by
Salvini
The outlaw
Parisina
Parker, George S. Moses in
Egypt
Ponte, Lorenzo da. Eliza and
Claudio; or, Love protected
by friendship
---- Moses in Egypt
---- The pirate
Pray, Isaac Clarke. Angelo
the tyrant of Padua
---- Marie Antoinette
---- Sor Teresa; or, Isabella
Suarez
Révoil, Bénèdict Henry. Gemma
of Vergy

Samson
Sappho
Semiramis
Shakespeare's...King Lear
Shakespeare's...Macbeth
Sullivan
The thieving magpie
Tretbar, Helen D. Rustic
chivalry
Zampa; or, The marble bride

ITALY--HISTORY
Anderson, Edward Lowell. Nero,
the parricide
Carleton, Henry Guy. The lion's
mouth
Codman, Henry. The Roman
martyrs
Comfort, Richard. Nero
Cunningham, Virginia Juhan.
The maid of Florence; or,
A woman's vengeance
Ellet, Elizabeth Fries Lummis.
Euphemio of Messina
---- Teresa Contarini
Elliott, William. Fiesco
Gayler, Charles. The son of
the night
The gladiator
Goodloe, Abbie Carter.
Antinoüs
Gray, Henry David. Hannibal
Gunter, Archibald Clavering.
The fighting troubadour
Hale, Louisa Jane Park. Miriam
Head, Edward Francis. Pol-
troonius
Heywood, Joseph Converse.
Sforza
Kinney, Elizabeth Clementine
Dodge. Bianca Cappello
Knowles, James Sheridan.
Virginius in The modern
standard drama, vol. 4
Lawson, James. Giordano
Lazarus, Emma. The Spagnoletto
Logan, Algernon Sydney.
Messalina
McCord, Louisa Susannah Cheves.
Caius Gracchus
McCullough, John. Virginius
McFadden, Theodore. Madalena;
or, The maid's mischief

McGee, Thomas D'Arcy. Sebastian; or, The Roman martyr
The maid of Florence; or, A woman's vengeance
Manning, Kathryn. Francesco Carrara
Medina, Louisa H. The last days of Pompeii
Osborn, Laughton. Bianca Capello
---- Ugo da Este
---- Virginia in his Cavalry-- Virginia; tragedies
Otway, Thomas. Venice preserved in The modern standard drama, vol. 3
Peterson, Henry. Caesar
Phillips, Jonas B. Camillus; or, The self-exiled patriot
Quincy, Josiah Phillips. Charicles
Robinson, Fayette. The Cardinal
Sanford, Myron Reed. Temporibus hominis Arpinatis
Shakespeare, William. Julius Caesar in Booth, Edwin. The Shakespearean plays of Edwin Booth also in The modern standard drama, vol. 11
Sheil, Richard Lalor. Evadue; or, The statue in The modern standard drama, vol. 7
Spencer, Edward. Maternus
Story, William Wetmore. Nero
---- Stephania
Walker, Alfred. Giorgione, the painter of Venice
Welcker, Adair. Flavia
---- Flavia in his Romer, King of Norway and other dramas
Willard, Edward. Julius Caesar
Williams, Henry Llewellyn. Isabella Orsini
Willis, Nathaniel Parker. Bianca Visconti; or, The heart overtasked
---- Dying to lose him; or, Bianca Visconti in his Two days of dying for a husband

KOREA--HISTORY
Isoleri, Antonio. Religion and fatherland; or, The martyrs of Corea

LATIN AND ENGLISH [bilingual text]
Sanford, Myron Reed. Temporibus hominis Arpinatis
The two captives

LIBRETTOS
Andre, R. The new moon
Attila
Attinelli, Joseph. Matilda di Shabran and Corradino; or, The triumph of beauty
Bailey, G. Geneviève de Brabant
Balatka, Hans. Peter the Great in Saardam; or, The Czar and the carpenter
The barber of Seville
Barker, Theodore T. The infanta's dolls
Barnett, M. J. Samson and Delilah
Belisarius
La belle Hélène
The black hussar
Bluebeard
Boccaccio
Les brigands
Brown, Charles Hovey. Elfins and mermaids; or, The red rock wave cruiser
---The red rock wave
Brunswick, Herman. Amina; or, The Shah's bride
Buel, David Hillhouse. Penikeese; or, Cuisine and Cupid
Burkhardt, Charles B. Der Freischütz
Byrne, Charles Alfred. Pearl of Pekin; or, The dashing tar outwitted by his wife
Calcattera, G. Lucrezia Borgia
The child of the regiment
Chilpéric
Cinderella; or, The fairy and little glass slipper
Clayton, Estelle. The Viking
Coale, George B. Magpie and the maid

Cobb, Charles E. The heroes
  of '76
Cook, Charles Emerson. The
  walking delegate
Cornell, John Henry. Romeo
  and Juliet
Crosby, Frances Jane. The
  flower queen; or, The
  coronation of the rose
Crumpton, M. Nataline.
  Theseus
The daughter of the regiment
Day, Willard Gibson. Cavalleria
  rusticana
Dinsmore, William. His chris
  cross mark. "The man of mark"
Dixon, Frederick Augustus.
  Canada's welcome
Don Giovanni
The elixir of love
Elson, Louis Charles. La
  mascotte [joint author:
  J. W. Norris]
---- Nanon
Ernani
Estabrook, Jones E. Columbia
Fatinitza
La favorita
The favorite
Felter, Will D. A bunch of
  roses
Fidelio; or, Constancy
  rewarded
La figlia del reggimento
Flora's festival
Fox, H. K. The betrothal
Fra-Diavolo; or, The Inn of
  Terracina
Der Freischütz
Fry, Joseph Reese. Norma
---- Notre-Dame of Paris
Gerardy, D. Centaurine
Ginty, Elizabeth Beall.
  Werther
Il giuramento; or, The oath
Godoy, José Francisco.
  Robinson Crusoe
Goldmark, George and Rosen-
  feld, Sydney. Amorita
Goldschmidt, William. Hadassah;
  or, The Persian queen
Goodrich, Elizabeth P. Cobwebs
Goodwin, John Cheever. Fleur-
  de-lis

---- The merry Monarch
---- Wang
The grand duchess of Gerolstein
The great rebellion
Gregg, Helen A. The little
  vagrants
Hardman, Richard. The adven-
  tures of little Red Riding
  Hood
---- Clarissa's first party
---- The pigeons; or, The
  bonnie lass of Brittany
Harrison, William. The beggar's
  opera
---- The marriage of Georgette
Hart, George G. E. C. B.
  Susan Jane; or, A sailor's
  life on the raging main
Hazelton, William B. and
  Spencer, Edward. Electric
  light
Hendrick, Welland. Pocahontas
Herbert, Joseph W. "Thrilby"
Hewitt, John Hill. Jephtha
Hidden treasure; or, The
  good St. Nicholas
Horne, Mary Barnard. The four-
  leaved clover
---- The Peak sisters
Hoyt, Charles Hale. The maid
  and the moonshiner
Huse, Carolyn Evans. Under
  the greenwood tree
Jenks, Almet F. Robinson
  Crusoe
Jervey, Mrs. Lewis. The lost
  children
Kellogg, Clara Louise. The
  Bohemian girl
---- Faust
---- The Huguenots
---- The star of the north
Knox, John Armoy and Snyder,
  Charles McCoy. The false
  prophet
Lathrop, George Parsons. The
  scarlet letter
Leavitt, Nason W. The frogs
  of Windham
Linda of Chamouni
The Lombards at the first
  crusade
The love-spell

---- The tzigane
---- The wizard of the Nile
Smith, Hubbard Taylor. A new
year's reception
The somnambulist
Spenser, Willard. The little
tycoon
Staples, H. A. Joseph in
bondage
The thieving magpie
Thompson, Caroline Eunice.
Blind Margaret
Tiffany, Esther Brown. Apollo's
oracle
The valley of Andorre
Wainwright, John Howard. Rip
Van Winkle
Ward, Thomas. The fair truant
---- Flora; or, The gipsy's
frolic
Watson, Henry C. Giovanna of
Naples
Weil, Oscar. Adina; or, The
elixir of love
---- The maid of honor
The white lady
Williams, Frederick and
Sullivan, Thomas Russell.
The little duke
Woodward, Matthew C. Rosita;
or, Boston and banditti
Woolf, Benjamin Edward. Djakh
and Djill
---- The doctor of Alcantara
---- Manola; or, The day and
the night
Zampa; or, The marble bride

MALES IN CAST *[this heading
is used for plays whose casts
consist entirely of male
characters]*
Abbott, Jacob. The lost ball
in Abbott, Jacob. Orkney
the peacemaker; or, The
various ways of settling
disputes
---- The teasing brothers *in*
Abbott, Jacob. Orkney the
peacemaker; or, The various
ways of settling disputes
A Beckett, Gilbert Abbott.
The man with the carpet bag

in Massey, Charles. Massey's
exhibition reciter
Ambition *in* A collection of
temperance dialogues
Appleton, Nathan. Centennial
movement, 1876
Art and artifice *in* Dramatic
leaflets
Atherton, George. A peaceful
assault
Back from Californy; or, Old
clothes
Bailey, George W. Diagram of a
modern law suit; or, A satire
on trial by jury
Baker, George Melville. A close
shave
---- Coals of fire
---- Freedom of the press
---- Gentleman of the jury
---- Humors of the strike
---- The hypochondriac
---- Ignorance is bliss [and]
A stitch in time
---- The man with the demijohn
---- My uncle the captain
---- New brooms sweep clean
---- A public benefactor
---- The rival poets
---- The runaways
---- Shall our mothers vote?
---- "Stand by the flag"
---- A tender attachment
---- Thief of time
---- Too late for the train
---- Wanted a male cook
Baker, Robert Melville. Black
magic
Barking up the wrong tree; a
darkey sketch
Barnes, James. The black barber;
or, Humours of Pompey Suds'
shaving saloon
---- Doctor Snowball
Bauman, E. Henry. Everybody
astonished
The black bachelor
Black mail
Bleckley, Paul. Thomas A'Becket
Bliss, Frank Chapman. Lessons
of life
Block, Louis James. On the
mountain top *in his* Capriccios

Browne, M. C. The landlord's
  revenge; or, Uncle Tom up
  to date
Browne, W. Gault. Ripples
Campbell, Thomas. The wizard's
  warning; or, The warrior's
  faith *in* Steele, Silas Sex-
  ton. Collected works. Book
  of plays
Carleton, John Louis. More
  sinned against than sinning
Carter, St. Leger Landon.
  Debate on the crow bill
Challenge dance
Chandler, A. N. Crimp's
  trip to the Centennial
Chapman, W. F. April fools
---- Over the garden fence
---- Wanted: a confidential
  clerk
Chase, Frank Eugene. The
  great umbrella case
Cherrytree, Herr (pseud.)
  More truth than poetry
---- The renegade [and] More
  truth than poetry
Childs, Nathaniel. Robinsonade
Choosing a trade *in* A collec-
  tion of temperance dialogues
Coes, George H. Badly sold
---- Everyday occurences
---- A finished education
---- Mrs. Didymus' party
---- Music vs. elocution
---- Oh, well, it's no use
---- A perplexing predicament
---- The police court
---- Scenes in a sanctum
---- Sublime and ridiculous
---- The three o'clock train;
  or, The haunted house
---- Tricks upon travellers
Colman, George (1762-1836).
  Sylvester Daggerwood *in*
  Massey, Charles. Massey's
  exhibition reciter
Congdon, James Bunker. Quaker
  quiddities; or, Friends in
  council
Connell, George Stanislaus.
  The guardian angel *in his*
  The old patroon and other
  plays

---- The mild monomaniac *in his*
  The old patroon and other
  plays
Courtright, William. The motor
  bellows
---- Zacharias' funeral
Crockett, Ingram. The Inca's
  daughter
Crosby, Frank. Teacher wanted
  in Dramatic leaflets
Cutler, F. L. Actor and servant
---- The Dutch prize fighter
---- Lodgings for two
---- The musical darkey
---- Pomp's pranks
---- Seeing Bosting
---- The sham professor
---- $2,000 reward; or, Done
  on both sides
D'Arcy, James J. Dark before
  dawn
The darkey tragedian
Deaf in a horn
Debates of conscience with a
  distiller, a wholesale
  dealer, and a retailer *in*
  A collection of temperance
  dialogues
Denison, Thomas Stewart. The
  boaster rebuked *in his*
  Friday afternoon series of
  dialogues
---- The bootblack *in his*
  Wide awake dialogues
---- The cobbler
---- A convention of papas
---- Country justice
---- The debating society *in*
  his Friday afternoon series
  of dialogues
---- A first-class hotel
---- Fred's visit to town *in*
  his Wide awake dialogues
---- The gold brick *in his*
  Wide awake dialogues
---- The great pumpkin case
  of Guff vs. Muff
---- Initiating a granger
---- New boy in school *in his*
  Wide awake dialogues
---- The patent right agent
  in his Friday afternoon
  series of dialogues

---- Sea serpent vs. mermaid
in his Wide awake dialogues
---- The secretary *in his*
Friday afternoon series of
dialogues
---- Stolen watermelons *in his*
Wide awake dialogues
---- The traveler *in his*
Friday afternoon series of
dialogues
Denton, Clara Janetta Fort.
The four photographs *in her*
From tots to teens
---- Going to the corner *in*
her When the lessons are
over
---- Hat drill *in her* When
the lessons are over
---- In nonsense land *in her*
From tots to teens
---- Joe's way of doing chores
in her When the lessons are
over
---- Lazy or not *in her* When
the lessons are over
---- The lost letter *in her*
From tots to teens
---- Making an orator *in her*
When the lessons are over
---- Nuts to crack--no. 1 *in*
her When the lessons are
over
---- The obedient servants *in*
her When the lessons are
over
---- The rebellion *in her*
From tots to teens
---- The weed and the boy *in*
her When the lessons are
over
---- What is a gentleman? *in*
her From tots to teens
---- What they will do *in her*
From tots to teens
Dickens, Charles. The circum-
locution office *in* Dialogues
dramatized from the works
of Dickens
---- The friendly move *in*
Dialogues dramatized from
the works of Charles Dickens
Dulcken, Henry William. Master
Goat, the tailor *in* Venable,

William Henry. The school
stage
Dumont, Frank. False colors
---- Helen's funny babies
---- The lunatic
---- Making a hit
---- The midnight intruder
---- The painter's apprentice
---- Queer, quaint and quizzical
questions *in his* The amateur
minstrel
---- The race track *in his*
The amateur minstrel
---- Stupid servant *in his* The
amateur minstrel
---- The sulphur bath
---- The two awfuls
---- A visit to the zoological
gardens *in his* The amateur
minstrel
---- Who's the actor?
Eberhart, B. F. Yacob's hotel
experience
The echo *in* The railroad
explosion [and] The echo
Edgcome, John. The last coat
An elephant on ice
Engle, Walter K. "Medica"
The English traveler *in*
Beadle's...dialogues no. 2
An equal chance
Farrell, John Rupert. The
haunted hat
Faust *in* Everett, Alexander
Hill. The Grecian gossips
Fawcett, Edgar. In the year
ten thousand
Field, A. Newton. School
Finn, Francis James. Echoes
from Bethlehem
First and last *in* The temper-
ance school dialogues
A frightened lodger *in* Drama-
tic leaflets
Gallus Jake
Gentlemen coon's parade
A glass of double X *in* The
temperance school dialogues
Glengall, Richard Butler, Earl
of. The Irish tutor *in*
Massey, Charles. Massey's
exhibition reciter
Gordinier, Charles A. Tim

Latour, Eugene. Tricks of
  trade; or, An obstinate
  Romeo
Lazarus, Emma. Prologue for
  the theatre
Leavitt, Andrew J. and Eagan,
  H. W. The academy of stars
---- The arrival of Dickens
---- The black Ole Bull
---- Boarding school
---- The body snatchers
---- Deaf as a post
---- The deserters
---- Jeemes the poet
---- The lucky number
---- No pay no cure
---- Ten days in the Tombs
---- That wife of mine
---- The thumping process
  [without Eagan]
---- The two Pompeys
---- Who stole the chickens?
Lester, Francis. Flirtation
  cured
---- The new squire
Lindon, Patrick C. Dr. Baxter's
  servants
Lindsley, Philip. The humor of
  the court room; or, Jones vs.
  Johnson
The lost heir; or, The abbé de
  L'Épée
The lost "spade"; or, The grave
  digger's revenge
Lover, Samuel. The white horse
  of the Peppers in Massey,
  Charles. Massey's exhibition
  reciter
Luster, James O. Dutchey vs.
  Nigger
Lyons, Joseph Aloysius. The
  miser
McBride, H. Elliott. A boy's
  rehearsal
---- Breaking up the exhibition
  in his New dialogues
---- The Cucumber Hill debating
  club in his New dialogues
---- A debate in Squigginsville
  in his Latest dialogues
---- I'll stay awhile
---- An introductory speech
  in his Latest dialogues

---- A little boy's debate in
  his New dialogues
---- The opening speech in his
  New dialogues
---- Opposing the new school-
  house in his Latest dialogues
---- Playing school in his
  New dialogues
---- The poisoned darkys
---- Scene in a jury-room in his
  Latest dialogues
---- A talk on temperance
---- Turning around in his
  New dialogues
---- Well fixed for a rainy day
McDermott, J. J. and Trumble.
  The wrong bottle
McGee, Thomas D'Arcy. Sebastian;
  or, The Roman martyr
Madden, Eva Annie. A noble spy
Magnus, Maurice. Eldyle
Maguire, John. Honesty is the
  best policy; or, True to the
  core
The masonic lodge
Massey, Charles. Guy Fawkes;
  or, A match for a king in
  Massey's exhibition reciter
---- The school for orators
  in Massey's exhibition
  reciter
Merriman, Effie Woodward.
  In Klondyke
---- In Klondyke in her
  Comedies for children
---- Three newsboys
---- Three newsboys in her
  Comedies for children
Mischievous Bob
Mitchell, Silas Weir. Barabbas
---- Francis Drake
---- François Villon
Morris, Felix James. Circum-
  stantial evidence
Mowrey, Phil H. The musical
  servant
Mumbo Jum; or, The enchanted
  clogs
Murray, Ellen. Licensed snakes
  in Dramatic leaflets
The musical bore
My mother's gold ring in A
  collection of temperance
  dialogues

Mysterious stranger

N., S. T. A. A lover's stratagem

The new and the old *in* Beadle's...dialogues no. 2

No peddlers wanted

Not as deaf as he seems

Notes and notices

Old Hunks, the miser

The old lady's will *in* Beadle's...dialogues no. 2 *also in* A collection of temperance dialogues

Oppenheim, Charles. The wigmaker and his servants

Osgood, L. W. The Union spy; or, The battle of Weldon railroad

Othello and Darsdemoney

Parker, Walter Coleman. Jimmy the newsboy

Phelps, Lavinia Howe. What makes a man? *in her* Dramatic stories

Picton, Thomas. A hard case

Pinkopki, Phillip. A colonel's mishap

A plea for the pledge *in* A collection of temperance dialogues

Political dialogues. Soldiers on their right to vote, and the men they should support

Prevention better than cure *in* The temperance school dialogues

Pullen, Elizabeth Jones. Algernon in London

A queer fit *in* Dramatic leaflets

Rawley, Bert C. A crazy lot!

---- Deacon Jones' wife's ghost

---- Stupid Cupid

Read, Thomas Buchanan. A vision of death. An extract

Ready answers *in* The temperance school dialogues

Reid, Charles S. Joe Simpson's double

Richards, Bert. Colored senators

Ross, Joseph M. Phintias and Damon

Roth, Edward. The gray tigers of Smithville; or, He would and he wouldn't

St. John, Charles Henry. The misanthrope melted

Sambo's return

Sargent, Epes. The lampoon

Saunders, Charles Henry. The North End caulker; or, The mechanic's oath

Savage, John. Dreaming by moonlight

Scenes at Gurney's

Schindler, Anthony J. Knaves and fools

The schoolmaster abroad *in* A collection of temperance dialogues

Sedgwick, Alfred B. The law allows it

A sensation at last *in* Beadle's...dialogues no. 2

Shackell, G. Chops

Shelland, Harry E. Fun in a school-room

---- The great libel case

---- Pomp Green's snakes [joint author: Wadsworth M. George]

Sheridan, Richard Brinsley Butler. The rivals (scene from) *in* Dramatic leaflets

Simms, George A. Room 44

Simms, William Gilmore. Caius Marius

16,000 years ago

Smith, Richard Penn. Dramatic fragments

Sport with a sportsman

Stace, Arthur J. The upstart

The stage-struck darkey

Stanton, F. J. The select school

Steele, Silas Sexton. The lawyer, doctor, soldier and actor; or, Many minds in a minute *in his* Collected works. Book of plays

---- The painter's studio; or, Art and artifice *in his* Collected works. Book of plays

---- The well of death; or, The brothers of Padua *in*

his Collected works. Book
of plays
Stocks up! Stocks down!
Sutherland, Evelyn Greenleaf
Baker. A bit of instruction
in her Collected works. Po'
white trash and other one-
act dramas
Tees, Levin C. Hypnotizing a
landlord
---- A red-hot massage
The three men of science *in*
Beadle's...dialogues no. 2
To the right or left? *in*
The temperance school dia-
logues
Townsend, Charles. The dark
tragedian
---- The darkey tragedian
Townsend, Frederic. Alcibiades-
Sheridan *in his* Spiritual
visitors
---- Amphion-Bellini *in his*
Spiritual visitors
---- Archimedes-Fulton *in his*
Spiritual visitors
---- Aristides-Jay *in his*
Spiritual visitors
---- Ben Jonson-Sam Johnson
in his Spiritual visitors
---- Chrysostom-Channing *in*
his Spiritual visitors
---- Diogenes-Rabelais *in his*
Spiritual visitors
---- Father Nile-Father
Mississippi *in his* Spiritual
visitors
---- Henry Dandolo-Peter Stuy-
vesant *in his* Spiritual
visitors
---- John Smith-Sydney Smith
in his Spiritual visitors
---- Julius Caesar-Zachary
Taylor *in his* Spiritual
visitors
---- Lucian-Lamb *in his*
Spiritual visitors
---- Marcus Aurelius-Howard
in his Spiritual visitors
---- Pericles-Hamilton *in his*
Spiritual visitors
---- Phidias-Raphael *in his*
Spiritual visitors

---- Pindar-Drake *in his*
Spiritual visitors
---- Roscius-Kemble *in his*
Spiritual visitors
---- Rubens-Cole *in his*
Spiritual visitors
---- Star Amaranth-Twenty-ninth
hundredth birthday of Homer
in his Spiritual visitors
---- Timon-Swift *in his* Spiritual
visitors
The trial of alcohol *in* A
collection of temperance
dialogues
De trouble begins at nine
Trusty and true *in* Dramatic
leaflets
Trying the character *in*
Beadle's...dialogues no. 2
Turkeys in season
The two captives
The two roads *in* The temperance
school dialogues
The two Romans *in* The temperance
school dialogues
Two sides--"which are you on?"
in The temperance school
dialogues
Uncle Tom
Under de kerosene
Vane, Larry. Troubled by ghosts
Van Wart, F. B. Stanley's dwarfs
Venable, William Henry. A
champion, though no fighter
in his The school stage
---- A colored witness *in his*
The school stage
---- Grit as well as manners
in his The school stage
---- Imaginary possessions
in his The school stage
---- Irish equivocation *in his*
The school stage
---- Lazy Lawrence *in his*
The school stage
---- A lighter-boy at school
in his The school stage
---- Nonsense; or, Two ways of
training boys *in his* The
school stage
---- Tarleton *in his* The school
stage

---- Tricks in a doctor's shop
    in his The school stage
Ware, Eugene Fitch. The Kansas
    bandit; or, The fall of
    Ingalls
Water or wine? *in* The temper-
    ance school dialogues
White, Charles. The African
    box; or, The magician's
    troubles
---- Ambition
---- Big mistake
---- The black chemist
---- The bogus talking machine;
    or, The puzzled Dutchman
---- Coalheaver's revenge
---- The Coopers
---- Daguerreotypes; or, The
    picture gallery
---- The draft
---- Dutch justice
---- Fisherman's luck
---- Getting square on the
    call boy
---- The ghost
---- Glycerine oil
---- Going for the cup; or,
    Old Mrs. Williams' dance
---- Good night's rest
---- Gripsack
---- Guide to the stage; or,
    Unappreciated talent
---- High Jack, the heeler
---- Hippotheatron; or,
    Burlesque circus
---- In and out
---- The lost will
---- Malicious trespass; or,
    Nine points of law
---- The mutton trial
---- A night in a strange
    hotel
---- One night in a bar room
---- The policy players
---- Pompey's patients
---- The recruiting office
---- A remittance from home
---- Rigging a purchase
---- Rival artists
---- Rival tenants
---- Scenes on the Mississippi
---- The serenade
---- Siamese twins

---- The sleep walker
---- Storming the fort
---- Streets of New York; or,
    New York by gaslight
---- Stupid servant
---- Them papers
---- De trouble begins at nine
---- Wake up, William Henry
---- Wanted, a nurse
---- Young scamp
White lies *in* A collection of
    temperance dialogues
Why don't you drink? *in* The
    temperance school dialogues
The wig makers
William Tell
Williams, Henry Llewellyn.
    Challenge dance
---- Dar's de money
---- Deaf--in a horn
---- Dem good ole times; or,
    Sixteen thousand years ago
---- Fetter Lane to Gravesend;
    or, A dark romance from the
    "Railway library"
---- Go and get tight
---- Sport with a sportsman
---- Stocks up! Stocks down!
---- Three black Smiths
Wilton, M. J. Fun in a cooper's
    shop
---- How to pay the rent
---- Mickey Free
---- Oleomargarine
---- Waiting for the train
Wright, Henry Clarke. Dick
    Crowninshield, the assassin
    and Zachary Taylor, the
    soldier
Ye quest

MALES IN CAST (ONE FEMALE
IMPERSONATOR)
Barnes, James. The darkey
    phrenologist
Barnes, Thomas. The Nigger
    night school
Dumont, Frank. Absent-minded
    in his The amateur minstrel
---- An awful plot
---- Cupid's frolics
---- Cupid's frolics *in his*
    The amateur minstrel

---- Election day
---- Gambrinus, king of lager
beer
---- Happy Uncle Rufus *in his*
The amateur minstrel
---- The lady barber
---- The midnight train *in his*
The amateur minstrel
---- My wife's visitors
---- The noble savage
---- One night in a medical
college
---- Pleasant companions
---- The polar bear
---- The rival barber shops
---- Scenes in front of a
clothing store
---- The serenade party; or,
The miser's troubles
---- Too little vagrants; or,
Beware of tramps
---- Unexpected visitors
---- Unlimited cheek; or, The
sewing machine agents
---- What shall I take?
---- Whose baby is it?
---- The wonderful telephone
---- The wonderful telephone
in his The amateur minstrel
A Dutchman in Ireland
Felter, Will D. The widow's
proposals
Fothergill, F. Race for a wife
Griffin, George W. H. Camille
---- Corsican twins
---- The Fenian spy; or, John
Bulls [sic, Bull] in America
[joint author: George Christy]
---- Hamlet the dainty
---- No cure no pay
---- Othello
---- Rooms to let without board
[joint author: Tony Denier]
---- Rose Dale
---- The ticket-taker; or, The
masquerade ball
Hiland, Frank E. A town meeting
Leavitt, Andrew J. and Eagan,
H. W. Blinks and jinks
---- Cousin Joe's visit
---- The intelligence office
---- No tator; or, Man-fish
---- Rip Van Winkle

McBride, H. Elliott. Miss Ara-
bella Clipperton's speech
in his Latest dialogues
A night with Brudder Bones
The railroad explosion
Shaw, J. S. R. How Sister
Paxey got her child baptized
Townsend, Charles. The darkey
wood dealer
Wenlandt, Oliver. A holy terror
---- Nigger boarding-house
White, Charles. Bad whiskey
---- The coming man
---- Damon and Pythias
---- Hard times
---- Jealous husband
---- The jolly millers
---- Julius the snoozer; or,
The conspirators of Thompson
Street
---- Laughing gas
---- The live injin; or, Jim
Crow
---- Mazeppa
---- The mystic spell
---- Obeying orders
---- Oh! hush!; or, The Vir-
ginny cupids!
---- 100th night of Hamlet
---- One, two, three
---- The portrait painter
---- Sam's courtship
---- A slippery day
---- Squire for a day
---- The stranger
---- Vilikens and Dinah
---- Vinegar bitters
---- The Virginny mummy
---- Who died first?
Williams, Henry Llewellyn.
The black Forrest
---- The darkey; or, Ill-
treated ill somnambulo
---- The Lime-Kiln Club in
an uproar!

MALES IN CAST (TWO FEMALE
IMPERSONATORS)
Dumont, Frank. The black
brigands
---- A desperate situation
---- A desperate situation *in
his* The amateur minstrel

---- Other people's troubles
---- The yellow kid who lived
  in Hogan's Alley
Fisher, Abraham Lincoln. A
  manager's trials
Griffin, George W. H. Feast
---- Fighting for the union
---- Jack's the lad
---- Shylock
Leavitt, Andrew J. and Eagan,
  H. W. The upper ten thousand
Sheddan, W. B. The joke on
  Squinim
Shettel, James W. and George,
  Wadsworth M. A coincidence
Tees, Levin C. Snobson's stag
  party
White, Charles. The black
  shoemaker
---- The black statue
---- A lucky job
---- Old Dad's cabin
---- The rehearsal; or, Barry's
  old man
---- The rival lovers
---- The sham doctor
---- Thieves at the mill
---- Uncle Eph's dream
---- Uncle Jeff
---- The wreck
Williams, Henry Llewellyn.
  Bobolino, the black bandit
---- Love and lockjaw

MALES IN CAST (THREE FEMALE
IMPERSONATORS)
Batchelder, Samuel Francis.
  Hamlet; or, The sport, the
  spook, and the spinster
Dumont, Frank. Dodging the
  police; or, Enforcing the
  Sunday law
---- How to get a divorce
Warden, Edward. Robert Make-
  airs; or, The two fugitives
White, Charles. The hop of
  fashion
---- Scampini
Williams, George W. Cleve-
  land's reception party

MALES IN CAST (SIX FEMALE
IMPERSONATORS)

Griffin, George W. H. The
  black crook burlesque

MALES IN CAST (SEVEN FEMALE
IMPERSONATORS)
Dumont, Frank. The cake walk

MARYLAND--HISTORY
Adams, Charles Frederick. Rob,
  the hermit; or, The black
  chapel of Maryland

MASSACHUSETTS--HISTORY
Sir Harry Vane

MEXICO--HISTORY
Brinton, Daniel Garrison. Maria
  Candelaria
Cuevas, José de Jesús. The heart
  and sword; or, The conquerors
  and conquered; or, The Spanish
  and Aztec races
Cummings, G. D. The history of
  Geronimo's summer campaign
  in 1885
Fyles, Franklin. Ayleenya the
  blameless
Hopkins, Rufus Clement. Losada
---- Malinche
Layman, Frederick O. Maximilian I
MacDonald, Malcolm. Guatemozin
Raymond, George Lansing. The
  Aztec god *in his* Collected
  works
---- The Aztecs
Roskoten, Robert. Carlotta
Royle, Edwin Milton. Mexico
Skiff, Frank D. Ouchilanca;
  or, The rancher's fate
Thomas, Lewis Foulk. Cortez,
  the conqueror
Wright, Henry Clarke. Dick
  Crowninshield, the assassin
  and Zachary Taylor, the
  soldier

MINSTREL PLAYS *[only those plays
which are identified as minstrels
in the plays themselves (i.e. by
subtitle, list of characters,
preface, etc.) or which are found
in contemporary lists of minstrel
plays, are included below]*

Bangs, John Kendrick. The
  young folk's minstrels
Challenge dance
Coes, George H. Everyday
  occurences
---- A finished education
---- The old parson
Corsican twins
Dancing mad
The darkey tragedian
Deaf in a horn
Don't get weary; or, Johnny,
  you've been a bad boy
Don't get weary; or, Johnny,
  you've been a bad boy *in*
  Gentlemen coon's parade...
  and Don't get weary; or,
  Johnny, you've been a bad
  boy
Dumont, Frank. Absent minded
---- Absent minded *in his*
  The amateur minstrel
---- Africanus Bluebeard
---- An awful plot
---- The black brigands
---- The cake walk
---- Cupid's frolics
---- Cupid's frolics *in his*
  The amateur minstrel
---- A desperate situation
---- A desperate situation
  in his The amateur minstrel
---- Election day
---- Gambrinus, king of lager
  beer
---- Happy Uncle Rufus *in his*
  The amateur minstrel
---- Helen's funny babies
---- How to get a divorce
---- Making a hit
---- The midnight intruder
---- The mid-night train *in*
  his The amateur minstrel
---- My wife's visitors
---- The noble savage
---- One night in a medical
  college
---- Other people's troubles
---- The painter's apprentice
---- Pete and the peddler *in*
  his The amateur minstrel
---- Pleasant companions

---- The polar bear
---- Queer, quaint and quizzi-
  cal questions *in his* The
  amateur minstrel
---- The race track *in his* The
  amateur minstrel
---- The rival barber shops
---- Scenes in front of a
  clothing store
---- The serenade party; or,
  The miser's troubles
---- Stupid servant *in his*
  The amateur minstrel
---- The sulphur bath
---- Too little vagrants; or,
  Beware of tramps
---- The two awfuls
---- Unexpected visitors
---- Unlimited cheek; or, The
  sewing machine agents
---- A visit to the zoological
  gardens *in his* The amateur
  minstrel
---- What shall I take?
---- Who's the actor?
---- Whose baby is it?
---- The wonderful telephone
---- The wonderful telephone
  in his The amateur minstrel
---- The yellow kid who lived
  in Hogan's Alley
The echo *in* The railroad
  explosion [and] The echo
An elephant on ice
Gallus Jake
Gentlemen coon's parade
Goode, George W. Ebony flats
  and black sharps
Griffin, George W. H. The
  actor and the singer; or,
  Gaily the troubadour
---- The black crook burlesque
---- Camille
---- Corsican twins
---- Feast
---- The Fenian spy; or, John
  Bulls [sic, Bull] in America
  [joint author: George Christy]
---- Fighting for the union
---- The great arrival
---- Hamlet the dainty
---- Jack's the lad

---- Nobody's son
---- Othello
---- Rooms to let without
    board [joint author: Tony
    Denier]
---- Rose Dale
---- Shylock
---- The ticket-taker; or, The
    masquerade ball
---- The troublesome servant
---- An unhappy pair
---- William Tell
Haunted house
Horne, Mary Barnard. The
    darktown bicycle club
    scandal
Mowrey, Phil H. The musical
    servant
Mysterious stranger
A night with Brudder Bones
Old Hunks, the miser
Othello and Darsdemoney
Pelham, Nettie H. The belles
    of Blackville
---- "Patchwork" in her The
    belles of Blackville [bound
    with] "Patchwork"
The railroad explosion
Richards, Bert. Colored
    senators
Sambo's return
Scenes at Gurney's
Shackell, G. Chops
Shaw, J. S. R. How Sister
    Paxley got her child baptized
Sheddan, W. B. The joke on
    Squinim
Silsbee, Alice M. and Horne,
    Mary Barnard. Bells in the
    kitchen in their Jolly Joe's
    lady minstrels
16,000 years ago
Stanton, F. J. The select
    school
Stocks up! Stocks down!
Townsend, Charles. The dark
    tragedian
---- The darkey tragedian
---- The darkey wood dealer
De trouble begins at nine
Warden, Edward. Robert Make-
    airs; or, The two fugitives

Wenlandt, Oliver. A holy terror
---- Nigger boarding-house
White, Charles. The African
    box; or, The magician's
    troubles
---- Ambition
---- Big mistake
---- The black chemist
---- The black shoemaker
---- The black statue
---- The bogus injun
---- The bogus talking machine;
    or, The puzzled Dutchman
---- Bone squash
---- Bruised and cured
---- The coming man
---- The Coopers
---- Cremation
---- Daguerreotypes; or, The
    picture gallery
---- Damon and Pythias
---- The darkey's stratagem
---- The draft
---- Dutch justice
---- Excise trials
---- Fisherman's luck
---- Getting square on the call
    boy
---- Glycerine oil
---- Going for the cup; or,
    Old'Mrs. Williams' dance
---- Good night's rest
---- Guide to the stage; or,
    Unappreciated talent
---- Hard times
---- High Jack, the heeler
---- Hippotheatron; or,
    Burlesque circus
---- The hop of fashion
---- In and out
---- Jealous husband
---- The jolly millers
---- Julius the snoozer; or,
    The conspirators of Thompson
    Street
---- Laughing gas
---- The live injin; or, Jim
    Crow
---- The lost will
---- A lucky job
---- The magic penny
---- Malicious trespass; or,
    Nine points of law

---- Mazeppa
---- The mutton trial
---- A night in a strange
hotel
---- Obeying orders
---- Oh! hush!; or, The
Virginny cupids!
---- Old Dad's cabin
---- 100th night of Hamlet
---- One, two, three
---- Pete and the peddler
---- The policy players
---- The recruiting office
---- A remittance from home
---- Rigging a purchase
---- Rival artists
---- Rival tenants
---- Sam's courtship
---- The sausage makers
---- Scampini
---- Scenes on the Mississippi
---- The serenade
---- The sham doctor
---- Siamese twins
---- A slippery day
---- Squire for a day
---- The stage-struck couple
---- Storming the fort
---- The stranger
---- Streets of New York; or,
New York by gaslight
---- Them papers
---- Thieves at the mill
---- Three strings to one bow
---- De trouble begins at
nine
---- Uncle Eph's dream
---- Uncle Jeff
---- Vilikens and Dinah
---- Vinegar bitters
---- Wake up, William Henry
---- Who died first?
---- The wreck
---- Young scamp
The wig maker
William Tell
Williams, George W. Cleve-
land's reception party
Williams, Henry Llewellyn.
The black chap from White-
chapel
---- The black Forrest

---- Bobolino, the black
bandit
---- Challenge dance
---- The darkey sleep-walker;
or, Ill-treated ill somnam-
bulo
---- Dar's de money
---- Deaf--in a horn
---- Dem good ole times; or,
Sixteen thousand years ago
---- Go and get tight
---- The Lime-Kiln Club in an
uproar!
---- Love and lockjaw
---- The Moko marionettes
---- Sport with a sportsman
---- Stocks up! Stocks down!
---- Three black Smiths
---- Wax works at play
Wilton, M. J. Fun in a cooper's
shop
---- Mickey Free

MUSIC *[plays containing
musical notation]*
Alceste
Alexander, Sigmund Bowman.
King winter's carnival
Allen, Lucy. Débutantes in
the culinary art; or, A
frolic in the cooking class
Atherton, George. A comedy of
error...; or, The cousin
and the maid
---- A peaceful assault
Baker, Theodore. Carmen
Barker, Theodore T. and
Baxter, Sylvester. Fatinitza
Barnet, Robert A. "1492"
---- Jack and the bean-stalk,
the strange adventures of
---- Miladi and the musketeer
---- Prince pro tem
Barnett, M. J. Samson and
Delilah
Batchelder, Samuel Francis.
Hamlet; or, The sport, the
spook, and the spinster
Bates, Ella Skinner. The con-
vention of the Muses
Bradley, Nellie H. A temperance
picnic with the old woman who
lived in a shoe

Les brigands
Bunner, Henry Cuyler. The
    seven old ladies of
    Lavender Town
---- Three operettas
Burkhardt, Charles B. Der
    Freischütz
Byrne, Charles Alfred and
    Marras, Mowbray. Gabriella
Christie, Albany. The martyr-
    dom of St. Cecily
Cobb, Charles E. The heroes of
    '76
Cobb, Mary L. Coming of spring
    in her Poetical dramas for
    home and school
Cook, Charles Emerson. The
    Koreans; or, The ancestors
    of King-Ki-Too
Crumpton, M. Nataline. Ceres
---- Pandora
---- Theseus
Cusack, Sister Mary Frances
    Clare. Tim Carty's trial;
    or, Whistling at landlords
Daly, Augustin. The great
    unknown
The damnation of Faust
Day, Willard Gibson. Cavalleria
    rusticana
---- The lovely Galatea
Dole, Nathan Haskell. Friend
    Fritz
Don't get weary; or, Johnny,
    you've been a bad boy
Don't get weary; or, Johnny,
    you've been a bad boy *in*
    Gentlemen coon's parade...
    and Don't get weary; or,
    Johnny, you've been a bad
    boy
Dugan, Caro Atherton. Collected
    works
Dumont, Frank. Africanus
    Bluebeard
---- Gambrinus, king of lager
    beer
---- Happy Uncle Rufus
---- Happy Uncle Rufus *in his*
    The amateur minstrel
Eichberg, Julius. The two
    cadis

Elson, Louis Charles. The
    merry war
---- The queen's lace handker-
    chief
Felter, Will D. A bunch of
    roses
---- Over the garden wall
---- The Sweet family
La figlia del reggimento
French, Arthur W. Gipsy queen
    (The Tyrolean queen revised)
---- Tyrolien queen
Fry, Joseph Reese. Leonora
Gabriel, Charles W. The merry
    milkmaids
Gaddess, Mary L. A dream of
    fair women and brave men
---- The Ivy Queen
Gentlemen coon's parade
Glover, Howard. Palomita; or,
    The veiled songstress
Goodrich, Elizabeth P. Cobwebs
Goodwin, John Cheever. The
    merry monarch
---- Wang
Gregg, Helen A. The little
    vagrants
Griffin, Caroline Stearns.
    Villikins and his Diniah
Hanson, Carl Fredrik.
    Fridthjof and Ingerborg
Hardman, Richard. The adventures
    of little Red Riding Hood
---- Clarissa's first party
---- The pigeons; or, The
    bonnie lass of Brittany
Hart, George G. E. C. B.
    Susan Jane; or, A sailor's
    life on the raging main
Haughwout, L. May. The princess
Hazard, Eleanor and Hazard,
    Elizabeth. An old plantation
    night
Heywood, Joseph Converse.
    Sforza
Hidden treasure; or, The good
    St. Nicholas
Horne, Mary Barnard. The four-
    leaved clover
---- The last of the Peak
    sisters; or, The great moral
    dime show

---- The Peak sisters
---- A singing school of ye
olden time
Howard, Bronson. Young Mrs.
Winthrop
Hoyt, Charles Hale. A trip to
Chinatown; or, An idyl of
San Francisco
Huse, Carolyn Evans. Under
the greenwood tree
Jameson, Frederick. Dusk of
the gods
---- The mastersingers of
Nuremberg
---- The Rhinegold
---- Siegfried
---- The Valkyrie
Jervey, Mrs. Lewis. The lost
children
Jessop, George Henry. Shamus
O'Brien
Kelley, Edgar Stillman. The
tragedy of Macbeth
La Shelle, Kirke. The Princess
Chic
Lewis, Abbie Goodwin. Caught
napping
MacDonough, Glen. The Algerian
McLellan, Charles Morton
Stewart. The belle of New
York
Macy, James Cartwright. Der
Freyschütz
---- Rustic chivalry (Caval-
leria rusticana)
Meltzer, Charles Henry. The
sunken bell
Miller, Frank Justus. Dido
Morette, Edgar. Let love but
hold the key
Morton, Marguerite W. The
blind girl of Castèl-Cuillè
Najac, Émile de and Landers,
Jean Margaret. The scarlet
letter
Neumann, Louis. The flying
Dutchman
Nona, Francis. The fall of the
Alamo
Norcross, I. W. The merry war
Norcross, J. W. Gillette; or,
Count and countess

Olivette
Pailler, William. The magic
bell
Paine, John Knowles. Azara
Parker, George S. Moses in
Egypt
Parker, Walter Coleman. Jimmy
the newsboy
The pierced eye
Pilgrim, James. The female
highwayman; or, The blighted
lily
Pratt, Silas Gamaliel. Zenobia,
Queen of Palmyra
Ranken, Frederic and La Shelle,
Kirke. "The ameer"
Raymond, Fanny Malone. Orpheus
Renauld, John B. Our heroes
Reynartz, Dorothy. A mother's
love; or, A wreath for our
lady
Rodenberg, Julius. The tower
of Babel
Rosenfeld, Sydney. Gasparone
Rosse, Jeanie Quinton. The
Egyptian princess
---- The Japanese girl (O Hanu
San)
Schell, Stanley. An old maid's
conference
Schwab, Emil. The beggar
student
Sedgwick, Alfred B. The big
banana
---- Circumstances alter cases
---- The decree of divorce
---- Estranged
---- I love your wife
---- The law allows it
---- Leap year
---- Let those laugh who win
---- A mad astronomer
---- Molly Moriarty
---- My walking photograph
---- The queerest courtship
---- A single married man
---- Sold again and got the
money
---- The spelling match
---- There's millions in it
---- Tootle, tootle, too; or,
The Frenchman and his pupil

---- The twin sisters
Shannon, J. W. Rip Van Winkle
She stoops to conquer
Skelly, Joseph P. The charge
of the hash brigade
Smith, Dexter. Boccaccio; or,
The Prince of Palermo
Smith, Harry Bache. The casino
girl
---- Cyrano de Bergerac
---- Don Quixote
---- Foxy Quiller
---- The highwayman
---- The idol's eye
---- Jupiter; or, The cobbler
and the king
---- The Knickerbockers
---- Maid Marian
---- Rob Roy
---- The rounders
---- The serenade
---- The singing girl
---- The tar and the tartar
---- The three dragoons
---- The viceroy
Smith, Hubbard Taylor. A new
year's reception
Sousa, John Philip. The bride-
elect
Stratton, George William. The
fairy grotto
---- Laila
Thompson, Caroline Eunice.
Blind Margaret
Tiffany, Esther Brown.
Apollo's oracle
Tretbar. Helen D. Rustic
chivalry
Tullidge, Edward Wheelock.
Ben Israel; or, From under
the curse
The two crowns
Vickers, George M. Two lives
in Dramatic leaflets
Ward, Elizabeth Stuart Phelps.
Within the gates
West, A. Laurie. Shades of
Shakespeare's women
Whalen, E. C. From Sumter to
Appomattox
---- Under the spell
The White lady

Williams, Frederick. The little
duke [joint author: Thomas
Russell Sullivan]
---- The rat-charmer of Hamelin
Woolf, Benjamin Edward and
Field, Roswell Martin.
Fantine
Zampa; or, The marble bride

NEW YORK--HISTORY
Baker, Benjamin Archibald.
A glance at New York
Smith, Elizabeth Oakes Prince.
Old New York; or, Democracy
in 1689

NORWAY--HISTORY
Barron, Elwyn Alfred. The
Viking
Oluph; a tragedy
Welcker, Adair. Romer, King
of Norway *in his* Romer, King
of Norway and other dramas

OREGON--HISTORY
Miller, Joaquin. An Oregon
idyl

PANTOMIMES
Brewster, Emma E. Arabella
and Lionel *in her* Parlor
varieties
Buxton, Ida M. Cousin John's
album
Corbyn, Wardle. Blanche; or,
The rival fairies
Denier, John. Humpty Dumpty
Field, Henrietta Dexter and
Field, Roswell Martin. The
wooing of Penelope *in their*
Collected works
Foster, Joseph C. The seven
dwarfs; or, Harlequin in
the world of wonders
Fox, George Washington
Lafayette. Jack and Gill
went up the hill
Griffin, Caroline Stearns.
Villikins and his Diniah
Lehmann, M. The elf-king; or,
Wealth and poverty
Ravel, Jerome. Kim-Ka; or,
The misfortune of Ventilator

Tracy, J. Perkins. Harlequin
old bogey; or, The imps of
the school and the secret
of the old oak chest
White, Charles. The mystic
spell
---- The portrait painter
---- Scampini
Wilson, Bertha M. A Chinese
wedding

PENNSYLVANIA GERMAN AND
ENGLISH [bilingual text]
Moss, Alfred Charles. H. M. S.
Pinafore; oder, Das maedle
und ihr sailor Kerl

PERSIA--HISTORY
Cobb, Mary L. Queen Vashti
in her Poetical dramas for
home and school
Ingersoll, Charles Jared.
Julian

PERU--HISTORY
Sheridan, Richard Brinsley
Butler. Pizzaro in The
modern standard drama,
vol. 3

POLAND--HISTORY
Lewis, Estelle Anna Blanche
Robinson. The king's
stratagem; or, The pearl of
Poland
Pilgrim, James. Wild Irish
girl

PORTUGAL--HISTORY
Garnier, John Hutchinson.
Prince Pedro

PROMPT-BOOKS
Adams, Justin. The rag-picker's
child
Aladdin; or, The wonderful lamp
An American wife
Around the world in eighty days
Baker, George Melville.
Capuletta; or, Romeo and
Juliet restored
Balch, William Ralston. Like
Caesar's wife

Bannister, Nathan Harrington.
Rookwood
Barker, Theodore T. and Nor-
cross, I. W. The mascot
Barnet, Robert A. "Prince pro
tem"
Barry, S. The Dutchman's ghost;
or, All right
Belasco, David. La belle Russe
---- The charity ball [joint
author: Henry Churchill De
Mille]
---- The heart of Maryland
---- The highest bidder [joint
author: Edward Hugh Sothern]
---- Madame Butterfly
---- Naughty Anthony
---- Under the polar star
[joint author: Clay Meredith
Greene]
Belknap, Edwin Star and Carnes,
Mason. The better part
Benson, William Henry. Three
scenes in the life of Lady
Flavia
Bert, Frederick W. Snowflake
and the seven gnomes
Bixby, Frank L. In the wilds
of Tennessee
Blaney, Charles E. A run on
the bank
Blumenthal, Oscar and Kadelburg,
Gustav. When I come back
Boker, George Henry. The
betrothal
---- Calaynos
Brady, William A. Lights of
London
---- The wages of sin
Burnett, James Gilbert. Blanche
of Brandywine
Cagliostro
Campbell, Bartley Theodore.
A brave man
---- Fate
---- My partner
Cantell, Lilia Mackay. Jephthah's
daughter
Carleton, Henry Guy. The butter-
flies
---- A gilded fool
---- The lion's mouth
Childs, Nathaniel. Robinsonade

Cinderella

Clarke, Joseph Ignatius Constantine and Phelps, Merridan. The first violin

Coleman, Mrs. Wilmot Bouton. Maud Stanley; or, Life scenes and life lessons

Connelly, James Henderson. A drama.

Conway, H. J. The talisman; or, The fairy's favor

Creagh, Henry. The sorrows of Satan

Cunningham, Virginia Juhan. Madelaine, the bell of Faubourg

Daly, Augustin. The belle's stratagem

---- The last word

---- Love on crutches

---- The merry wives of Windsor

---- Much ado about nothing

---- The school for scandal

---- Under the gaslight

Darcy, Fred. The devil's mine

Davenport, Fanny Lily Gypsy. La tosca

---- Olivia. Vicar of Wakefield

Dazey, Charles Turner. In old Kentucky

The defender

De Mille, Henry Churchill. John Delmer's daughters

---- Governor Rodman's daughter [joint author: David Belasco]

---- Lord Chumley [joint author: David Belasco]

---- Men and women [joint author: David Belasco]

Dr. Kearny

Fast men of olden time

Fitch, Clyde. Barbara Freitchie [sic], the Frederick girl!

---- Beau Brummel

---- The cowboy and the lady

---- Frederic Lemaitre

---- The masked ball

---- Sappho

Ford, Daniel K. My friend Isaac

Forty thieves

Fraser, John Arthur. Dewey, the hero of Manila

---- The little minister

Furniss, Grace Livingston. The flying wedge

Fyles, Franklin. Ayleenya the blameless

Gailey, Florence Louise. Ez-Zahra

Gerardy, D. Centaurine

Gillette, William Hooker. All the comforts of home

---- Held by the enemy

---- Mr. Wilkinson's widows

---- Sherlock Holmes [joint author: Arthur Conan Doyle]

The gladiator

Gorman, Richard. Half a day off

Greene, Clay Meredith and Grismer, Joseph Rhode. The new south

Gunter, Archibald Clavering. The fighting troubadour

---- Prince Karl

Hagarty, W. H. The gold bug

Hardy, Edward Trueblood. Widow Freeheart; or, The woman haters

Hearts are trumps; or, Atout... coeur!

Heermans, Forbes. An old vagabond

Henermans, Herman. The "Hope"

Herbert, Joseph W. "Thrilby"

Herne, James A. Shore Acres

Hill, Grace Livingston and Richardson, Abbey Sage. A colonial girl

Hitchcock, James Ripley Wellman and Hitchcock, Martha Wolcott Hall. David Harum

Holbrook, Amelia Weed. Jack, the commodore's grandson

House, Edward Howard. Larcher's victories

Howard, Bronson. Aristocracy

---- The Henrietta

---- Old love letters

---- Young Mrs. Winthrop

Hoyt, Charles Hale. A black
sheep
---- A brass monkey
---- A bunch of keys; or, The
hotel [joint author: Winnie
Edouin]
---- A hole in the ground
---- A midnight bell
---- A milk white flag
---- A parlor match
---- A Rag Baby
---- A temperance town
---- A Texas steer
---- Texas steer; or, Money
makes the mare go
---- A tin soldier
---- A trip to Chinatown
The hustler
Jackson, N. Hart. The bottom
of the sea
Jefferson, Joseph. The rivals
The Jewess
Johnson, Samuel D. In and out
of place
---- Our gal
Jones, Joseph Stevens. Captain
Kyd; or, The wizard of the
sea
---- The carpenter of Rouen;
or, The massacre of St.
Bartholomew
---- The people's lawyer
---- The usurper; or, Americans
in Tripoli
Jones, R.? Wacousta; or, The
curse
Joseph and his brethren, the
Hebrew son; or, The child
of Babylon
Kaler, James Otis. A devil of
a scrape; or, Who paid for
the supper
Kester, Paul. In the palace of
the king
Kidder, Kathryn. The heart of
her husband
Kimball, George M. Disinherited
King Friedrich Wilhelm First
La Bree, Lawrence. Ebenezer
Venture; or, Advertising for
a wife
The lash of the whip
The last of the Mohicans

Leahy, William Augustine. The
wedding feast
Lloyd, David Demarest and
Rosenfeld, Sydney. The
senator
Logan, Cornelius Ambrosius.
Yankee land
Ludlow, Fitz-Hugh. Cinderella
Ludlow, Noah Miller. Coriolanus;
or, The Roman matron
McCabe, J. L. Maloney's wedding
MacKaye, James Steele. Hazel
Kirke
McLellan, Charles Morton
Stewart. The girl from up
there
Marble, Scott. Down in Dixie
---- The great train robbery
---- The stars and stripes
Marie, a woman of the people
Matthews, Brander. Edged tools
Mayo, Frank. King Lear
---- Macbeth
---- Nordeck [joint author:
John G. Wilson]
---- The royal guard [joint
author: John G. Wilson]
Miles, George Henry. Señor
Valiente
---- Señor Valiente; or, The
soldier of Chapultepec
Milner, Frances S. Brothers
in name
Morris, Felix James. The old
musician
Morris, Ramsay and Bell,
Hillary. The social trust;
or, The spider's web
Morse, Woolson. Cinderella
at school
Morter, E. J. and Abarbanell,
Jacob Ralph. Under ma's
thumb
Morton, Charles H. Three years
in a man-trap
Morton, Martha. A bachelor's
romance
---- His wife's father
Murdoch, James Edward. Laugh
when you can
My aunt
My daughter-in-law
Najac, Émile de and Landers,

Jean Margaret. The scarlet letter

A night of knights

Nobles, Milton. From Sire to son; or, The hour and the man

---- Interviews; or, Bright Bohemia

The organist

Palmer, John Williamson. The queen's heart

Pickett, Haskell. The rake's lesson; or, Taming a husband

Pilgrim, James. Eveleen Wilson, the flower of Erin

---- The female highwayman; or, The blighted lily

---- Jeanie Deans; or, The heart of Mid-Lothian

---- Shandy Maguire; or, The bould boy of the mountain

---- Yankee Jack; or, The buccaneer of the Gulf

Pitman, James R. Never again

Pray, Isaac Clarke. Julietta Gordini, the miser's daughter

Prichard, Joseph Vila. The iron master

Rankin, McKee and Maeder, Frederick George. The runaway wife

Reid, James Halleck and Reid, Bertha Belle Westbrook. The prince of the world, the great Christian play

Richardson, Abbey Sage. Americans abroad

Ritchie, Anna Cora Ogden Mowatt. Armand; or, The peer and the peasant

---- Fashion; or, Life in New York

Rose, Edward Everett. Richard Carvel

Rosenfeld, Sydney. No questions asked [joint author: Alexander Charles Auguste Bisson)

---- Subtleties of jealousy

Royle, Edwin Milton. Mexico

Runnion, James B. Miss Manning

St. Clair, Clarence. Fear of a scandal

Saunders, Charles Henry. The

North End caulker; or, The mechanic's oath

---- The pirate's legacy

---- Rosina Meadows, the village maid; or, Temptations unveiled

Scoville, Nesbit Stone. A country kid

Scribble, Sam (pseud.) The king of the beavers

Shipman, Louis Evan. D'Arcy of the guards; or, The fortunes of war

---- On parole

Silver, W. A. Clouds

Smith, Edgar McPhail. "Catherine"

---- Pousse cafe [joint author: Louis De Lange]

---- Sapolio [joint author: Harry Bache Smith]

---- Trilby

---- "Waffles." A travesty upon "Raffles"

Smith, Harry Bache. The fortune teller

---- Hurly burly [joint author: Edgar McPhail Smith]

---- The wizard of the Nile

Smith, Solomon Franklin. The hypocrite

Smith, W. H. The drunkard; or, The fallen saved

Sothern, Edward Hugh. Antony and Cleopatra

---- Ingomar the barbarian [joint author: Julia Marlowe]

---- King Lear

Stafford, J. Benson. Her trump card

Stapleton, John. A bachelor's honeymoon

Steele, Silas Sexton. The lion of the sea

Stephens, Robert Neilson. The alderman

---- An enemy to the king

---- Girl wanted

---- On the Bowery

Stewart, Grant. A respectful burlesque on Peter Pan

Stoddard, Lorimer. In the palace of the king

Stuart, Clinton. Our society

Tayleure, Clifton W. Horseshoe
Robinson; or, The battle of
King's Mountain
Thomas, Augustus. Alabama
---- Don't tell her husband
---- Editha's burglar [joint
author: Edgar McPhail Smith]
Tom and Jerry; or, Life in
London
The touchstone of truth; or,
The harlequin travellers
Trumbull, Annie Eliot. St.
Valentine's day
Van Harlingen, Katherine. An
original widow's pension;
or, The fugitive fortune
Wainwright, John Howard. Rip
Van Winkle
Waldauer, Augustus. The female
cavalier
---- Little barefoot
Wallack, Lester. Rosedale
Waller, Daniel Wilmarth. Into
the world
Walsh, John. Irish inspiration
Walsh, Townsend. The boys of
Kilkenny
Webber, Harry A. Man and wife
Weston, Effie Ellsler. A wolf
in sheep's clothing
Wilkins, W. Henri. The turn of
the tide; or, Wrecked in
port
Williams, Barney. Alive and
kicking
Williams, Frederick. Romeo and
Juliet
---- The streets of New York
Wilstach, Paul. A game for two
---- An ounce of prevention
---- A partial eclipse
Winslow, Catherine Mary Reig-
nolds. Broken trust
Woodworth, Samuel. The forest
rose; or, American farmers
Wuttke, Hermann. Crown jewels

RUSSIA--HISTORY
Catharina the second

SCHOOL PLAYS *[see also*
Children's plays; Youth plays]
Beadle's...dialogues no. 2

Cobb, Mary L. Poetical dramas
for home and school
Colclough, Emma Shaw. An object
lesson in history
Côté, Marie. The witch of
bramble hollow
Crumpton, M. Nataline. Ceres
---- Pandora
---- Theseus
The schoolmaster abroad *in* A
collection of temperance
dialogues

SCOTLAND--HISTORY
Aldémah. The queens
Cannon, Charles James. Rizzio
Dugan, Caro Atherton. The
queen's coffer *in his*
Collected works
Marie Stuart
Opal (pseud.) The Bruce *in her*
The cloud of witnesses
Pilgrim, James. Jeanie Deans;
or, The heart of Mid-Lothian
Smith, Harry Bache. Rob Roy
---- Rob Roy; or, The thistle
and the rose
White, James. Feudal times;
or, The court of James the
third *in* The modern standard
drama, vol. 6
---- The king of the commons
in The modern standard drama,
vol. 4

SPAIN--HISTORY
Cannon, Charles James. Dolores
in his Collected works.
Dramas
Christopher Columbus
Columbus, the great discoverer
of America
Dorbesson, Fern. Aldemon's
daughter (Cassilda)
Harden, John J. Columbus and
Isabella
Hartnedy, M. M. A. Christopher
Columbus
Kester, Paul. In the palace of
the king
Lord, Alice Emma Sauerwein.
A vision's quest
Osborn, Laughton. The Cid of

Seville *in his* Ugo da Este
Packard, Hannah James. The choice
Pierra, Adolfo. Nobility; or, The alcalde of Zalamea
Preston, Daniel Swann. Columbus; or, A hero of the new world
Raymond, George Lansing. Columbus *in his* Collected works
---- Columbus the discoverer
Robertson, John. Riego; or, The Spanish martyr
Sargent, Epes. Velasco
Sheridan, Richard Brinsley Butler. Pizarro *in* The modern standard drama, vol. 3
The sisters of Alhama *in* Silvia and other dramas
Stoddard, Lorimer. In the palace of the king
Warren, Walter. Columbus the discoverer
Williamson, Eugene F. The sisters of Alhama

SWEDEN--HISTORY
De Peyster, John Watts. A night with Charles XII of Sweden; or, A soldier's wife's fidelity
Planché, James Robinson. Charles the twelfth *in* The modern standard drama, vol. 6
Rattermann, Heinrich Armin. Gustavus III; or, The masked ball

SWEDISH AND ENGLISH *[bilingual text]*
Hanson, Carl Fredrik. Fridthjof and Ingerborg

SWITZERLAND--HISTORY
Knowles, James Sheridan. William Tell *in* The modern standard drama, vol. 5
Schaad, John Christian. Nicholas of the Flue. The savior of the Swiss Republic

Shields, Charles Woodruff. The reformer of Geneva

SYRIA--HISTORY
Dawes, Rufus. Athenia of Damascus

TEMPERANCE PLAYS
Allen, John Henry. The fruits of the wine cup
Ames, A. D. Wrecked
Babcock, Charles W. Adrift
Baker, George Melville. "A drop too much"
---- The flowing bowl
---- The last loaf
---- Little brown jug
---- A little more cider
---- The man with the demijohn
---- Seeing the elephant
---- The tempter; or, The sailor's return
---- We're all teetotalers
Barnard, Charles. The silver dollar
The bottle imp
Bradley, Nellie H. The first glass; or, The power of woman's influence
---- Marry no man if he drinks; or, Laura's plan, and how it succeeded
---- Reclaimed; or, The danger of moderate drinking
---- The stumbling block; or, Why a deacon gave up his wine
---- A temperance picnic with the old woman who lived in a shoe
---- Wine as a medicine; or, Abbie's experience
The bridal wine cup *in* Dramatic leaflets
Burleigh, George S. The conqueror conquered *in* Dramatic leaflets
Buxton, Ida M. On to victory
Cold-water cross *in* Dramatic leaflets
A collection of temperance dialogues
Colman, Julia. No king in America

Mitchell, Thomas. The household tragedy
Morton, Charles H. Three years
  in a man-trap
Murray, Ellen. Cain, ancient
  and modern in Dramatic
  leaflets
---- Licensed snakes. Temper-
  ance dialogue in Dramatic
  leaflets
Optic, Oliver. The deamons of
  the glass in Dramatic
  leaflets
The pen and the press in
  Greenly, William Jay. The
  three drunkards
Pratt, William W. Ten nights
  in a bar-room
Prevention better than cure
  in The temperance school
  dialogues
Ready answers in The temper-
  ance school dialogues
Saved in Dramatic leaflets
Seymour, Harry. Aunt Dinah's
  pledge
---- The temperance doctor
The shipwrecked strangers; or,
  Wanted and not wanted in
  The temperance school dia-
  logues
Signing the pledge in Dramatic
  leaflets
Smith, William Henry. The
  drunkard; or, The fallen
  saved
---- The drunkard; or, The
  fallen saved in The modern
  standard drama, vol. 11
Tardy, Edwin. Saved
Taylor, C. W. The drunkard's
  warning
The temperance school dialogues
Thayer, Julia M. Fighting the
  rum-fiend in Dramatic leaf-
  lets
To the right or left? in The
  temperance school dialogues
Todd, John W. Arthur Eustace;
  or, A mother's love
The two alphabets--alcohol and ·
  water in The temperance
  school dialogues

The two roads in The temperance
  school dialogues
Two sides--"which are you on?"
  in The temperance school
  dialogues
The unexpected convert in The
  temperance school dialogues
Vautrot, George S. At last
Vickers, George M. Two lives
  in Dramatic leaflets
Water or wine? in The temper-
  ance school dialogues
Whalen, E. C. Under the spell
Which will you give up? in
  The temperance school dia-
  logues
Why don't you drink? in The
  temperance school dialogues
Wilkins, W. Henri. Three
  glasses a day; or, The
  broken home
---- The turn of the tide; or,
  Wrecked in port
The wine cup; or, Saved at last
Woodward, T. Trask. The social
  glass; or, Victims of the
  bottle

TEXAS--HISTORY
Blandin, Isabella Margaret
  Elizabeth. From Gonzales to
  San Jacinto
Nona, Francis. The fall of
  the Alamo

UNITED STATES--HISTORY [see
also America--History for
those plays taking place
before 1776]
Brooks, E. S. A dream of the
  centuries in Bartlett,
  George Bradford. A dream of
  the centuries and other
  entertainments for parlor
  and hall
Cummings, G. D. The history of
  Gerinomo's summer campaign
  in 1885
Curzon, Sarah Anne. Laura
  Secord, the heroine of 1812
Denison, Thomas Stewart. Our
  country
Dowd, Jerome. Burr and Hamilton

Fitch, Clyde. Nathan Hale
Le Grand, Dr. The genius of
liberty *in* Beadle's...
dialogues no. 2
Grover the First
Jones, George. Tecumseh and
the prophet of the west
Kiralfy, Imre. Grand historical
spectacular [sic, spectacle]
masterpiece America
Mair, Charles. Tecumseh
Piatt, Donn. Blennerhassett's
island *in his* Various
dramatic works
Pidgin, Charles Felton. Blen-
nerhassett; or, The irony
of fate
Royle, Edwin Milton. Mexico
Safford, De Forest. Watertown
in '75
Schoolcraft, Henry Rowe.
Alhalla; or, The lord of
Talladega
The Tipperary warbler; or,
The fraud of the dry goods
boxes
Trumbell, David. The death
of Capt. Nathan Hale
Wheeler, Esther Gracie
Lawrence. A cup of tea
drawn from 1773
Wright, Henry Clarke. Dick
Crowninshield, the assassin
and Zachary Taylor, the
soldier

UNITED STATES--HISTORY--
CENTENNIAL

Bartlett, George Bradford.
America's birthday party
in Bartlett, George Bradford. A dream of the
centuries and other entertainments for parlor and
hall
Brewster, Emma E. Cent-any-
all.--Centennial *in her*
Parlor varieties
Cupid's little game
Guernsey, Alice M. Five
centuries

UNITED STATES--HISTORY--CIVIL
WAR

Adams, Justin. At the picket-
line
Ames, A. D. and Bartley, C. G.
The spy of Atlanta
Andrews, Fred G. Hal Hazard;
or, The federal spy
Baker, Delphine Paris. Solon;
or, The rebellion of '61
Baker, George Melville. Enlisted
for the war; or, The home-
guard
Baker, Rachel E. After taps
Barker, Benjamin Fordyce. The
rise in Harlem
Barnes, William Horatio. The
drama of secession; or,
Scenes from American history
Belasco, David. The heart of
Maryland *also in his* The
heart of Maryland and other
plays
Blood, Henry Ames. How much I
loved thee!
Boothman, William. His last
scout
Brown, J. S. A southern rose
Brown, S. J. In the enemy's
camp; or, Stolen despatches
Buzzell, Arthur L. Captain
Dick; or, Our war corres-
pondent
Campbell, Bartley Theodore.
The Virginian *in his* The
white slave and other plays
Channing, William Ellery. John
Brown and the heroes of
Harper's Ferry
Chase, George B. Penn Hapgood;
or, The Yankee schoolmaster
Clark, William Adolphus. Gen.
Grant; or, The star of union
and liberty
Cornish, O. W. Foiled; or, A
struggle for life and liberty
Daly, Augustin. A legend of
"Norwood"; or, Village life
in New England
D'Arcy, James J. Dark before
dawn
Dawson, J. H. and Whittemore,
B. G. Lights and shadows of

the great rebellion; or,
The hospital nurse of
Tennessee
Downing, Laura Case. Defending
the flag; or, The message
boy
Duganne, Augustine Joseph
Hickey. Woman's vows and
Mason's oaths
Emerson, W. Burt. The musical
captain; or, The fall of
Vicksburg
Eshobel, Raymond. How much I
loved thee!
Fitch, Clyde. Barbara Freit-
chie [sic], the Frederick
girl!
Fraser, John Arthur. Our
starry banner
Gillette, William Hooker. An
American drama arranged in
four acts and entitled
Secret Service
---- Held by the enemy
The great rebellion
Harrigan, Edward. The blue
and the grey
Heermans, Forbes. Between two
foes
---- On both sides
Heller, Robley Eugene. Appo-
mattox
Herne, James A. The Reverend
Griffith Davenport *in*
The early plays of James
A. Herne
Heywood, Delia A. A reunion
in her Choice dialogues
no. 1
Hiland, Frank E. Broken bonds
Hildreth, David W. The volun-
teers; or, The pride of
Company G
Howard, Bronson. Shenandoah
Kilpatrick, Hugh Judson and
Moore, J. Owen. Allatoona
Lacon (pseud.) The devil in
America
The lost "Spade;" or, The
grave digger's revenge
Lucas, Daniel Bedinger.
Hildebrand *in his* Collected
works
---- Kate McDonald *in his*

Collected works
---- The maid of Northumberland
also in his Collected works
McKee, W. J. Gettysburg
Moore, Bernard Francis. Brother
against brother
---- The weeping willows
Muscroft, Samuel J. The drummer
boy; or, The battlefield of
Shiloh
Osgood, L. W. The Union spy;
or, The battle of Weldon
railroad
Piatt, Donn. Lost and won *in his*
Various dramatic works
Pickett, A. St. J. The sublime
tragedy of the lost cause
Political dialogues. Soldiers
on their right to vote, and
the men they should support
Powers, Thomas F. The Virginia
veteran
Reeves, George. The slave's
strategy
Renauld, John B. Our heroes
The rise in Harlem
Rocchietti, Joseph. Charles
Rovellini
Rodebaugh, T. Wilson. John
Winchester; or, Between
love and duty
Rogers, James Webb. Madame
Surratt
Saphar, Will D. The German
volunteer
Serrano, Thomas K. Between two
fires
Shipman, Louis Evan. On parole
Shoemaker, Dora Adèle. A
fighting chance; or, For
the blue or the gray
Snider, Denton Jaques. Clarence
Stedman, W. Elsworth. The
Confederate spy
---- The midnight charge
Swayze, Mrs. J. C. Ossawottomie
Brown; or, The insurrection
at Harper's Ferry
Taurus-Vertus (pseud.) Vendetta
Tayleure, Clifton W. Won back
Thayer, William Roscoe. Hesper;
an American drama
Thomas, Augustus. "Surrender!"

Townsend, Charles. Down in
Dixie
---- The spy of Gettysburg
---- The woven web
The tragedy of Abraham Lincoln;
or, The rise and fall of the
Confederate States
Triplet, James. A supper in
Dixie
The tyrant of New Orleans
The Union sergeant; or, The
battle of Gettysburg
Vegiard, J. T. The Dutch
recruit; or, The blue and
gray
Ward, Cyrenus Osborne. Tbe
great rebellion
Warren, Horatio N. Tilmon Joy,
the emancipator
Whalen, E. C. From Sumter to
Appomattox
Woodville, Henry. "Confede-
rates"
Woodward, T. Trask. The
veteran of 1812; or, Kesiah
and the scout
Woolf, Benjamin Edward. Off
to the war!
Woolson, Constance Fenimore.
Two women: 1862

UNITED STATES--HISTORY--
REVOLUTION
Allen, Ethan. Washington;
or, The Revolution
Arthur, Robert. The Quakers
Bacon, Delia Salter. The
bride of Fort Edward
Baker, George Melville. One
hundred years ago; or, Our
boys of 1776
Bannister, Nathaniel Harring-
ton. Putnam, the iron man
of '76
Bunce, Oliver Bell. Love in
'76
Burnett, James Gilbert.
Blanche of Brandywine
Calvert, George Henry. Arnold
and André
Cobb, Charles E. The heroes
of '76

Cronkhite, Henry McLean.
Reymond: a drama of the
American Revolution
Dailey, W. B. Saratoga: a
dramatic romance of the
revolution
Davison, E. Mora. The New
Englanders
Dawes, Rufus. The battle of
Stillwater; or, The maniac
---- [or H. J. Conway?] The
battle of Stillwater; or,
The maniac
Finn, Sister Mary Paulina.
Heart of gold, true and
tried *in her* Alma mater;
or, The Georgetown Centennial
Glover, Stephen E. The cradle
of liberty; or, Boston in
1775
Grinnell, V. B. The heroic
Dutchman of seventy-six
Haid, P. Leo. Major John
André
Herne, James A. The Minute Men
of 1774-1775 *in his* The
early plays of James A. Herne
Hill, Grace Livingston and
Richardson, Abbey Sage. A
colonial girl
Holland, Elihu Goodwin. The
highland treason
Howe, J. Burdette. The Golden
Eagle; or, The privateer
of '76
Hubbell, Horatio. Arnold; or,
The treason of West Point
Lockwood, Ingersoll. Washington
Lord, William Wilberforce.
André
Madden, Eva Annie. A noble spy
Meyers, Benjamin F. A drama of
ambition *in his* Collected
works
Norcross, Frederic. Mistress
Nan
Orton, Jason Rockwood. Arnold
Rose, Edward Everett and Ford,
Paul Leicester. Janice
Meredith
---- Richard Carvel [without
Ford]

Shipman, Louis Evan. D'Arcy
of the guards; or, The
fortunes of war
Steele, Silas Sexton. The
lion of the sea
Tayleure, Clifton W. Horseshoe
Robinson; or, The battle of
King's Mountain

UNITED STATES--HISTORY--
SPANISH-AMERICAN WAR
Beaty, Thomas R. Old Glory
in Cuba
Chase, Frank Eugene. In the
trenches
Coon, Hilton. Under the
American flag
Fraser, John Arthur. Dewey,
the hero of Manila
---- Santiago; or, For the
red, white and blue
Lapoint, William W. Loyal
hearts
Marble, Scott. The stars
and stripes
Moore, Bernard Francis.
The Rough Rider

UNITED STATES--HISTORY--
WAR OF 1812
Emmons, Richard. Tecumseh;
or, The battle of the Thames
Tayleure, Clifton W. The boy
martyrs of Sept. 12, 1814

UTAH--HISTORY
Deseret deserted; or, The
last days of Brigham Young
English, Thomas Dunn. The
Mormons; or, Life at Salt
Lake City
McKinley, Henry J. Brigham
Young; or, The prophet's
last love
Stern, H. I. Evelyn Gray; or,
The victims of our western
Turks
Taylor, Bayard. The prophet
---- The prophet *in his*
Collected works. The
dramatic works

THE WEST
Adams, Justin. T'riss; or,
Beyond the Rockies
Baker, George Melville.
Nevada; or, The lost mine
Felch, William Farrand. The
pet of Parsons' ranch
Fisher, Abraham Lincoln.
Little trump; or, A Rocky
Mountain diamond
Hamilton, George H. Sunlight;
or, The diamond king
Harte, Bret. Sue [joint author:
Thomas Edgar Pemberton]
---- Two men of Sandy Bar
Heermans, Forbes. Down the
Black Cañon; or, The silent
witness
Heywood, Delia A. Hospitality
on the frontier *in her*
Choice dialogues no. 1
Hildreth, David W. Lone Tree
mine
Marble, Scott. The great train
robbery
Miller, Joaquin. The Danites
in the Sierras
---- Tally-ho
Moore, Bernard Francis. Poverty
flats
Nobles, Milton. From Sire to
Son; or, The Hour and the Man
Smith, Edgar McPhail. Travesty
upon "Arizona"
Thomas, Augustus. Arizona
Towndsend, Charles. The golden
gulch
---- The mountain waif
Ward, Lew. Claim ninety-six
---- Gyp, the heiress; or, The
dead witness
---- My pard; or, The fairy
of the tunnel
Willard, Charles O. Little
Goldie; or, The child of
the camp

WOMEN'S MOVEMENT
Anderson, Thomas F. The trials
of a country editor
Baker, George Melville. The
champion of her sex

---- Shall our mothers vote?

Brokmeyer, Henry Conrad. A foggy night at Newport

Busch, William. Sorosis; or, The onward march to freedom

Buxton, Ida M. Matrimonial bliss

Curtis, Ariana Randolph Wormeley. The spirit of seventy-six; or, The coming woman

Curzon, Sarah Anne. The sweet girl graduate

Davis, Mary Evelyn Moore. The new system

Denison, Thomas Stewart. The new woman

Drey, Sylvan. Woman's rights

Dumont, Frank. The new woman's husband

Ele, Rona. Woman's lefts A foggy night at Newport

Fowle, William Bentley. Woman's rights in his Parlor dramas

Fraser, John Arthur. Bloomer girls; or, Courtship in the twentieth century

Goodfellow, Mrs. E. J. H. Vice versa

Hazelton, William B. and Spencer, Edward. Electric light

Lacon (pseud.) The devil in America

Lewis, Richard Henry. Robert and Cornelia

McBride, H. Elliott. When women have their rights in his New dialogues

Merriman, Effie Woodward. A pair of artists

Rugg, George. The new woman

Spring, Retlaw. Women's rights

Thayer, Ella Cheever. Lords of creation

Trumbull, Annie Eliot. A masque of culture

Varrie, Vida. The coming man; or, Fifty years hence

Whitaker, Lily C. Young American Progressive Hobby Club

YOUTH PLAYS [see also Children's plays; School plays]

Abbott, Jacob. Orkney the peacemaker; or, The various ways of settling disputes

Baker, George Melville. The revolt of the bees

---- The rival poets

---- The tournament of Idyl-court

---- The war of the roses

Bartlett, George Bradford. A dream of the centuries and other entertainments for parlor and hall

Bates, Ella Skinner. The convention of the Muses

Beach, Stanley Yale and Powell, H. Arthur. The widow Mullin's Christmas

Bien, Herman Milton. Purim

Brewster, Emma E. and Scribner, Lizzie B. Beresford benevolent society

Corner, Julia. Cinderella; or, Pride punished in Venable, William Henry. The school stage

Denison, Thomas Stewart. Friday afternoon series of dialogues

---- Wide awake dialogues

Denton, Clara Janetta Fort. From tots to teens. Some merry times for young folks

Dickinson, Eva Lyle. A Thanksgiving lesson in Schell, Stanley. A real Thanksgiving [and] A Thanksgiving lesson

Follen, Eliza Lee Cabot. Home dramas for young people

Gaddess, Mary L. A dream of fair women and brave men

---- The Ivy Queen

Goodrich, Elizabeth P. Cobwebs

Greenough, James Bradstreet. Queen of hearts

Griffin, Caroline Stearns. Villikins and his Diniah

Heywood, Delia A. Be truthful but courteous in her Choice dialogues no. 1

---- Labor is honorable in her Choice dialogues no. 1

Horne, Mary Barnard. Gulliver and the Lilliputians up to date

Huse, Carolyn Evans. Under the greenwood tree

Kavanaugh, Mrs. Russell. Original dramas, dialogues

Lewis, E. A. and Lewis, C. M. Mother earth and her vegetable daughter's [sic]; or, Crowning the queen of vegetables

McBride, H. Elliott. A baby show at Skilletsville *in his* Latest dialogues

---- A boy's rehearsal

---- A girls' debate *in his* Latest dialogues

---- New dialogues

---- Speaking extemporaneous speeches *in his* Latest dialogues

Madden, Eva Annie. A noble spy

O'Leary, James. Ellie Laura; or, The border orphan

Pelham, Nettie H. The realm of time

---- The white caps

Phelps, Lavinia Howe. Dramatic stories

Roth, Edward. The gray tigers of Smithville; or, He would and he wouldn't

Sanford, Amelia. The advertising girls

---- Maids, modes, and manners; or, Madame Grundy's dilemma

Silvia and other dramas

The two alphabets--alcohol and water *in* The temperance school dialogues

The two roads *in* The temperance school dialogues

Ursula of Brittany

Venable, William Henry. Alfred the king *in his* The school stage

---- A colored witness *in his* The school stage

---- Contentment *in his* The school stage

---- The fag's revolt *in his* The school stage

---- Good actions mend bad actions *in his* The school stage

---- Grit as well as manners *in his* The school stage

---- Imaginary possessions *in his* The school stage

---- Irish equivocation *in his* The school stage

---- The Irish valet *in his* The school stage

---- A lighter-boy at school *in his* The school stage

---- The little dependent *in his* The school stage

---- Nonsense; or, Two ways of training boys *in his* The school stage

---- Rigmarole *in his* The school stage

---- Tarleton *in his* The school stage

---- Tricks in a doctor's shop *in his* The school stage

Why don't you drink? *in* The temperance school dialogues

Winters, Elizabeth. Columbia, the gem of the ocean

REFERENCES

The American catalogue...July 1, 1876-Dec. 31, 1910. 8 vols. in 13.
New York: Peter Smith, 1941.

Binger, Norman. *A bibliography of German plays on microcards.*
Hamden, Conn.: Shoe String Press, 1970. 224p.

British Museum. Department of Printed Books. *General catalogue of
printed books.* 263 vols. London: Trustees of the British
Museum, 1959-1966.

Brown, Thomas Allston. *History of the American stage.* New York:
Burt Franklin, 1969. 421p. [reprint of the 1870 edition]

Brown University. Library. *Dictionary catalog of the Harris
Collection of American poetry and plays, Brown University
Library, Providence, Rhode Island.* 13 vols. Boston: G. K.
Hall, 1972.

Burton, C. E. *Burton's amateur actor: a complete guide to private
theatricals.* New York: Dick & Fitzgerald, 1876. 150p.

Chambers's biographical dictionary. Revised edition, edited by
J. O. Thorne. New York: St. Martin's Press, 1968. 1432p.

Coyle, William. *Ohio authors and their books...1796-1950.*
Cleveland: World Publishing Company, 1962. 741p.

*Cumulated dramatic index, 1909-1949: a cumulation of The F. W.
Faxon Company's Dramatic index.* 2 vols. Boston: G. K. Hall,
1965.

Dictionary of American biography. Published under the auspices
of the American Council of Learned Societies. 20 vols. and
Index. New York: Scribners, 1928-1937.

Dictionnaire de biographie française. Paris: Letouzey, 1933-
[in progress; 13 vols. to date]

Du Bois, William R. (comp.) *English and American stage produc-
tions: an annotated checklist of prompt books, 1800-1900,
from the Nisbet-Snyder drama collection, Northern Illinois
University Libraries.* Boston: G. K. Hall, 1973. 524p.

Hart, James David. *The Oxford companion to American literature.* Fourth edition. New York: Oxford University Press, 1965. 991p.

Harvard University. Library. Theatre Collection. *Catalogue of dramatic portraits in the Theatre Collection of the Harvard College Library, by Lillian Arvilla Hall.* 4 vols. Cambridge, Mass.: Harvard University Press, 1930-1934.

Harvey, *Sir* Paul. *The Oxford companion to English literature.* Fourth edition, revised by Dorothy Eagle. New York: Oxford University Press, 1967. 961p.

Hatch, James Vernon. *Black image on the American state: a bibliography of plays and musicals, 1770-1970.* New York: DBS Publications, 1970. 162p.

Haverly, Jack. *Negro minstrels: a complete guide.* Upper Saddle River, N. J.: Literature House/Gregg Press, 1969. 129p. [reprint of the 1902 edition]

Hill, Frank Pierce (comp.) *American plays printed, 1714-1830.* Stanford University, Calif.: Stanford University Press, 1934. 152p.

Ireland, Joseph Norton. *Records of the New York stage from 1750 to 1860.* 2 vols. New York: Benjamin Blom, 1866-1867.

Johannsen, Albert. *The House of Beadle and Adams and its dime and nickel novels.* 3 vols. Norman: University of Oklahoma Press, 1950-1962.

Kelly, James. *The American catalogue of books, (original and reprints), published in the United States from Jan., 1861 to Jan., 1871.* 2 vols. New York: P. Smith, 1938. [reprint of the 1866-1871 edition]

Litchfield, Hope P. and R. E. Stoddard. "A. D. Ames: first dramatic publisher." *Books at Brown,* 21:95-156 (1966).

Long, Eugene Hudson (comp.) *American drama from its beginnings to the present.* New York: Appleton-Century-Crofts, 1970. 78p.

National cyclopaedia of American biography. 53 vols. New York: J. T. White, 1892-1971.

National union catalog, pre-1956 imprints. London: Mansell, 1968- [in progress; 475 vols. to date]

New York (City). Public Library. *Foreign plays in English: a list of translations in the New York Public Library.* Compiled by Daniel C. Haskell. New York: New York Public Library, 1920. 86p.

New York (City). Public Library. Research Libraries. *Catalog of the theatre and drama collections.* 51 vols. Boston: G. K. Hall, 1967-1976. [pt. I (1967): *Author listing* (6 vols.) and *Listing by cultural origin* (6 vols.); pt. II (1967): *Books on the theatre* (9 vols.); pt. III (1976): *Non-book collection* (30 vols.)]

The New York Times obituaries index, 1858-1968. New York: New York Times, 1970. 1136p.

Nicoll, Allardyce. *English drama, 1900-1930: the beginnings of the modern period.* Cambridge, Eng.: Cambridge University Press, 1973. 1082p.

----- *A history of English drama, 1660-1900.* Fourth edition. 6 vols. Cambridge, Eng.: Cambridge University Press, 1952-1959.

Nolan, Paul T. *Provincial drama in America, 1870-1916: a casebook of primary materials.* Metuchen, N. J.: Scarecrow Press, 1967. 234p.

Odell, George Clinton Densmore. *Annals of the New York stage.* 15 vols. New York: Columbia University Press, 1927-1949.

Paris. Bibliothèque Nationale. *Catalogue général des livres imprimés: Auteurs.* Paris: Impr. Nationale, 1900- [in progress; 220 vols. to date]

Parrish, Morris L. *Wilkie Collins and Charles Reade.* New York: Burt Franklin, 1968. 354p. [reprint of the 1940 edition]

Quérard, Joseph Marie. *La France littéraire, ou Dictionnaire bibliographique.* 12 vols. Paris: Firmin Didot père et fils, 1827-1964.

Quinn, Arthur Hobson. *History of the American drama, from the beginning to the Civil War.* Second edition. New York: Harper and Bros., 1943. 530p.

----- *A history of the American drama, from the Civil War to the present day.* Revised edition. New York: Harper and Bros., 1936. 432p.

Rice, Edward Le Roy. *Monarchs of minstrelsy, from "Daddy" Rice to date.* New York: Kenny Publishing Company, 1911. 366p.

Rigdon, Walter (ed.) *The biographical encyclopedia & who's who of the American theatre.* New York: J. H. Heineman, 1966. 1101p. ["Necrology" section, p.995-1101]

Roden, Robert F. *Later American plays, 1831-1900.* New York: Burt Franklin, 1969. 132p. [reprint of the 1900 edition]

Roorbach, Orville Augustus. *Bibliotheca Americana; catalogue of American publications*...4 vols. in 2. New York: Peter Smith, 1939. [first published in New York, 1852-1861, 4 vols.]

Sabin, Joseph. *Bibliotheca Americana: a dictionary of books relating to America*. 29 vols. in 15. Amsterdam: N. Israel, 1961. [reprint of the 1868 New York edition]

Stieger, Franz. *Opernlexikon*. Tutzing, Ger.: Schneider, 1975- [in progress; "Titelkatalog" used (3 vols.)]

Talvart, Hector and Joseph Place. *Bibliographie des auteurs modernes de langue français*. Paris: Ed. de la Chronique des Lettres Françaises, 1928- [in progress; 20 vols. to date]

Tasch, Peter A. *The dramatic cobbler: the life and works of Isaac Bickerstaff*. Lewisburg, Penn.: Bucknell University Press, 1972. 322p.

Thompson, Lawrence Sidney. *Nineteenth and twentieth century drama: a selective bibliography of English language works, numbers 1-3029*. Boston: G. K. Hall, 1975. 456p.

Toll, Robert C. *Blacking up: the minstrel show in nineteenth century America*. New York: Oxford University Press, 1974. 310p.

Townsend, Charles. *Negro minstrels, with end men's jokes, gags, speeches, etc.* Upper Saddle River, N. J.: Literature House/ Gregg Press, 1969. 76p. [reprint of the 1891 edition]

United States. Copyright Office. *Dramatic compositions copyrighted in the United States, 1870-1916*. 2 vols. Washington: Government Printing Office, 1918.

Van Duzen, Henry Sayre. *A Thackeray library*. Port Washington, New York: Kennikat Press, 1965. 198p.

Van Tieghem, Philippe. *Dictionnaire des littératures*. 3 vols. Paris: Presses Universitaires de France, 1968.

Wallace, William Stewart. *A dictionary of North American authors deceased before 1950*. Detroit: Gale Research Co., 1968. 525p. [first published by The Ryerson Press, Toronto, 1951]

Webster's biographical dictionary. Springfield, Mass.: G. & C. Merriam, 1972. 1697p.

Wemyss, Francis Courtney. *Wemyss' chronology of the American stage, from 1752 to 1852*. New York: Benjamin Blom, 1968. 191p. [reprint of the 1852 edition]

Who was who in America. 5 vols. Chicago: Marquis, 1942- [in progress]

Who was who in America: historical volume, 1607-1896. Chicago: Marquis, 1963. 670p.

Who's who in the theatre: a biographical record of the contemporary stage. London: I. Pitman, 1912-

Wittke, Carl. *Tambo and bones: a history of the American minstrel stage.* Westport, Conn.: Greenwood Press, 1971. 269p. [reprint of the 1930 edition]

Young, William C. *Famous actors and actresses on the American stage.* 2 vols. New York: R. R. Bowker, 1975.